GREAT

SOCIETY

GREAT SOCIETY

A NEW HISTORY

AMITY SHLAES

HARPER

An Imprint of HarperCollins*Publishers*

HarperCollins books may be purchased for educational, business, or sales promotional use. For information, please email the Special Markets Department at SPsales@harpercollins.com.

FIRST EDITION

Designed by Fritz Metsch

Library of Congress Cataloging-in-Publication Data has been applied for.

ISBN 978-0-06-170642-4

19 20 21 22 23   LSC   10 9 8 7 6 5 4 3 2 1

For my father,

Jared Shlaes

Nothing is new, it is just forgotten.

—*Adage*

Contents

GREAT

SOCIETY

The Clash

Why not socialism?

That was the question on the author's mind as he headed to Washington. He had secured an invitation to lunch with a high official in the new Administration. The president had been in office three months, and he wanted new ideas to distinguish himself from his predecessor. Could the author bring up socialism at the lunch? The very word "socialism" had been toxic until recently. Socialism inspired murderous dictatorships in Russia and China. In America red baiters called people "socialist," sliming their targets and themselves in the process. The taboo was weakening, though. The author actually was a socialist, and proud of the fact. He came from a Catholic family, and the transition from old-time Catholic social service to government social service, and, yes, socialism, felt natural to him. Socialism seemed no threat to a democracy as hardy as the United States. Party leaders in Scandinavia were socialists, and democracy thrived in Scandinavia. What's more, America was certainly prosperous enough to afford a vast experiment such as socialism. American unemployment was low and heading lower. American business boomed. As Stalin was said to have joked, America was the only country in the world that could *afford* communism.[1] Socialism could work within one of the major parties. The Democratic Party could be, should be, socialist. To fail to try out socialism was to lack compassion.

Still, the author was not fresh out of college. That month he turned thirty-six, plenty old enough to see that "socialism" might sound too controversial for the White House. The writer could, however, pitch ideas that took the country *toward* socialism. In a recent book the author had itemized the kinds of reform America needed. Laws that backed up organized labor so it might represent a greater portion of the American workforce, including black Americans or immigrants from Mexico. Higher minimum wages—the current levels were a cruel joke. Minimum wages that covered more workers, even those who did not work in an office or full-time. A dramatic change in the training of bigoted policemen in the big cities. A reinvigoration of the poor so that they became a force in political life. America was a country made of classes, the author thought; it just didn't know it. The money was simply in the wrong hands. The writer wanted a tax system that captured the elusive wealth of the superrich. The moment had come to level incomes in a systematic fashion.

Poverty was the obvious lunch theme. Just days before, the president had tapped the author's host to lead a new campaign against poverty. In his State of the Union address, the president had told the country he wanted not only to alleviate suffering but to actually "cure poverty." No American leader had ever taken on poverty in this way before. There wasn't even a real poverty office yet, so the new poverty czar worked from a suite at the Peace Corps, which he already headed. The focus of the author's book was the cycle of poverty in one region, Appalachia. The man had also seen poverty in the city where he grew up, St. Louis. In St. Louis the poverty was in part caused by government plans gone wrong, as in the case of the bulldozing of streets people loved in the name of moving them into public housing slums they didn't love. America, the author thought, should invest billions to abolish poverty. It was incredible that America knew so much about poverty and had done so little. The state governments could not do this work. State governments were beholden to retrograde conservative legislatures. For systemic change, the author had come to believe, there was "no place to look except toward the federal government."

When the author and the poverty chief met, they discussed the budget for a poverty program. The president was mooting the amount of $1 billion a year. The author couldn't help himself. He was frank. Only a billion? He personally hoped that America would pull together and, in a surge of sentiment, support, if not socialism, then at least a new version of Franklin Roosevelt's New Deal. The very name "New Deal" sounded so grand to young people; you could sell anything to them by invoking it. A billion sounded like "nickels and dimes," the author told his host. "Oh really?" the official answered drily. "I don't know about you, but this is the first time I've spent a billion dollars."[2] Still, the poverty office head was impressed enough to invite the younger man to help out drafting the billion-dollar poverty law.

The chance was too good to miss. The author set aside the socialism and put on a tie. He joined a number of other new hands, many of whom were also still camped out in the Peace Corps office. The poverty team included professors, government officials, and policy people, all producing memos for the new poverty law at assembly-line speed. Their boss set a grueling pace. It was not unusual for the chief to ask for a memo at ten in the evening and suggest that it be delivered later that night. The man put Benzedrine in the air conditioning, one of the author's friends joked. The author worked on an employment proposal. Socialists and centrists could agree on one thing, that unemployment was the greatest source of poverty.

Still, as he sat in the makeshift offices, the author kept returning to what he saw as the problem behind the problem, American capitalism. He and his friend took to concluding their memos with a half-serious line: "Of course, there is no real solution to the problem of poverty until we abolish the capitalist system."[3] At one point the author stopped censoring himself and wrote a few lines of what he actually felt: "that the abolition of poverty would require a basic change in how resources are allocated." The boss actually took this bold call for redistribution to the president, who, the boss reported, proved remarkably friendly. The boss said that the president, a Roosevelt fan, told him that if serious economic redistribution was necessary to realize the long-delayed completion of the New Deal, then redistribution might be worth it.

Nothing, though, came of the author's radical memo. The writer left the poverty team before the president signed the poverty bill. When the president handed out pens to those who had contributed to the poverty legislation, another staffer went through the line twice so he could collect an extra pen for the absent author. From afar, the author could see that the Democrats on the Hill and in the White House were indeed settling for the beginning of social democracy. Well, the author could tell himself, social democracy was the start.

The story sounds like something that could happen today. But the author, a man named Michael Harrington, made his proposals to the White House in 1964. His book about poverty was a then-famous best-seller called *The Other America*. The boss who ribbed Harrington about a poverty budget was Sargent Shriver, the brother-in-law of the late president, John F. Kennedy. The president whose poverty initiative Harrington briefly served was Lyndon Johnson. The man who stood in line to collect a pen for his friend was Daniel Patrick Moynihan, both witness to and conspirator in 1960s policy, the same Moynihan who later became the legendary senator from New York.

There were not many self-described socialists in the country in the early 1960s. The Young People's Socialist League, the premier socialist youth group, was reporting a doubling across the colleges, but that increase was merely from four hundred to eight hundred members. Still, socialists such as Harrington were far from alone in their insistence on transcendent change. Many Americans ached to make American society over, whether by tinkering or rebuilding, in the name of improving life for all. In the early 1960s the groups that nursed this ambition were diverse. They were university students who hoped to fashion their own utopia— Harrington worked with a new group called Students for a Democratic Society, or SDS. There were union chiefs who sought explicitly to re-create the benefits of Northern European socialism, uppercase or lower, not just for union members, but also for the nation at large. There were government officials such as Shriver who believed the right president could indeed lead the country in epic reform. There were engineers who envisioned transformation through technology. There were businesses that thought great corporations would lead in raising the standard of living for all. Typical was General Electric, whose motto was "Progress is our most important product." There were factory workers whose lives had improved in the 1960s and who hoped to finally make it into the middle class by the 1970s. There were priests, ministers, and rabbis who sought collective spiritual renewal in aspects of life far beyond their pulpits. There were civil rights leaders like Martin Luther King, who dreamed of a time when race would no longer matter.

Most Americans shared something else with Harrington: confidence. In the 1930s, the New Deal had failed to reduce unemployment. The prolonged periods of joblessness were what had made the Depression "Great." But the memory of the New Deal failure had faded just enough that younger people liked the sound of the term. And memories of more recent success fueled Americans' current ambition. Many men were veterans. They had been among the victorious forces that rolled across Europe and occupied Japan at the end of World War II. Compared with overcoming a Great Depression, or conquering Europe and Japan, eliminating poverty or racial discrimination had to be easy. American society was already so good. To take it to great would be a mere "mopping up action," as Norman Podhoretz, who had served in Europe, would put it.[4]

Underlying the new American ambition was dissatisfaction with the pace of projects that had been launched in the 1950s: civil rights law that had not desegregated train stations or schools, the construction of the interstate highways that didn't seem to help the poor, urban renewal funding that could not meet the needs of all. Now the country wanted more, faster. In the 1960s America sensed "the fierce urgency of now," as King said. *The Magic of Thinking Big* was the title of a popular self-help book. Americans wanted to see change that blasted like a space rocket. The country had to use its power to do something superlative. This good society had to become, in the words of President Johnson, a Great Society.

The question was how to become great. The United States could look to the private sector to change the country. Or it could seek change through the public sector. In the 1960s, over and over again, America chose the public sector. The result was a string of federal campaigns conducted in the name of the betterment of society. First came a campaign, led by President John F. Kennedy, to rehabilitate troubled youth. Soon after, President Johnson led the passage of series of federal civil rights laws. Around the same time came Johnson's War on Poverty. Next were Johnson's national housing drive and his health care drive. Richard Nixon followed up with a guaranteed-income campaign and an environmental drive. One must also count a less noticed campaign by all three Administrations, the campaign to redefine Americans' legal rights. Where they could, authorities built on New Deal programs, or on postwar urban renewal undertakings. But many of the 1960s initiatives established new institutions. And all three presidents, Kennedy, Johnson, and Nixon, worked at a frenetic pace. The ability of Johnson, especially, to formulate laws and see them passed was unprecedented. Johnson, as his aide Joseph Califano put it, adopted programs the way a child ate chocolate chip cookies. Even President Nixon, together with Congress, contributed massively to the Great Society endeavor. Total annual entitlement outlays grew 20 percent faster under the Republican Nixon than under President Johnson, the Democrat.[5]

One of the thinkers of the era, a microbiologist at the University of California in Santa Barbara named Garrett Hardin, sketched a picture to try to convey the need for great public-sector interventions. Shepherds live by a rich common pasture. All want to graze their own sheep there, and all do, each driving as many of his own sheep as he can into the common area without regard to the needs of others or the grass of the commons. Soon, the grass is gone. The sheep starve. This dynamic Hardin labeled the "Tragedy of the Commons." Hardin recommended a collective solution of the sort Harrington would have praised: let governments play the shepherd, managing or rationing resources of the common.

The reforms of the 1960s nearly always made the federal government the shepherd. Because they were ambitious, and because they demanded selflessness, the reforms sounded great. And the federal shepherd worked hard to make the reforms look as great as they sounded. Ambitious reforms needed time to succeed. It would be a shame if a project aborted because early results didn't look good. So, for display purposes, presidents emphasized inputs, not outputs. Congress, too, as the Hoover Institution's John Cogan has put it, "measured success by labels and dollars attached to legislation"—not by results. The political success of a project mattered more than empirical success. Occasionally, the effort got a new name. The "New Frontier" of Kennedy became Johnson's "Great Society," which became the "Great Nation," and then the "Just and Abundant Society" of Richard Nixon. All the efforts were, however, of a piece in their effort to get to "great." One can include all three presidencies in a description of a what may be called the Great Society era. In that era, the federal government also redefined its role in the arts, on television and radio, and in public schools. Washington left no area untouched.

In its Great Society endeavor, the country relegated the private sector to the role of consultant, workhorse, and milk cow. And, at first, business went along. Soon enough, however, businesses came to find the 1960s intrusions by the federal government too much of a burden. Federal rules squelched innovation. Federal law made labor too expensive. The 1960s reforms first impinged upon, then violated, what a 1966 candidate for governor of California, the actor Ronald Reagan, called the "creative society." And soon enough states and towns also grew disturbed. Local authorities discovered that under the polite letters, official visits, and federal funds from Washington operated a competitor that threatened to weaken the states and towns permanently. The New Deal had expanded the federal government so much that for the first time, Washington had surpassed the towns and cities as a presence in the economy. The 1960s reforms seemed designed to finish the job, to squeeze the states and towns out of government altogether. This was true even when the reforms bore names that suggested towns had nothing to fear from Washington, such as the "New Federalism." Often, the business executives and the mayors noted, these great reforms did not seem to be achieving their goals. Their suspicion mounted as they observed that the incessant rebranding concealed the questionable results of a reform. When an extant index or measure delivered disappointing results, the authorities tinkered with the measure or blithely abolished it altogether. The cooperation of the early 1960s morphed quickly into a public contest. On the one hand stood the federal government and its allies, most often labor unions. On the other hand stood the rest of the nation. This book chronicles that epic clash.

Great Society also seeks to capture the figures who struggled on each side. "The Best and the Brightest" was what the author David Halberstam called the advisors tapped by Kennedy and Johnson to prosecute the Vietnam War. But Kennedy, Johnson, and Nixon also fielded domestic teams of "the Best and the Brightest," cabinet officers, staffers, and professors who planned domestic reform with the same pretense of precision that Defense Secretary Robert McNamara maintained in planning Operation Rolling Thunder. The best and brightest on the home front included Federal Reserve chairmen William McChesney Martin and Arthur Burns; Lyndon Johnson's poverty czar Sargent Shriver; Pat Moynihan; and George Romney, governor of Michigan and later secretary of Housing and Urban Development. Leaders of organized labor such as Walter Reuther of the United Auto Workers played large roles in supporting federal expansion—far greater than traditional histories suggest. Reuther was the star and visionary among union men, dazzling in debate.

Fending off incursions of the federal government and its allies, wittingly or unwittingly, were mayors such as Sam Yorty of Los Angeles and Richard J. Daley of Chicago, and governors, including Reagan in California and John Connally in Texas. Also finding themselves in battles were company executives such as Ralph Cordiner and Lemuel Boulware of General Electric; Robert Noyce and Gordon Moore of Fairchild Semiconductor, the computer chipmaker that became Intel; and the executives at the auto company Toyota, then a minor importer. In the thick of the scramble were smaller institutions such as churches or individuals, among them Martin Luther King, the theologian Nathan Wright, Father John Shocklee of St. Bridget of Erin Parish in Harrington's own St. Louis, and the prophetess of cities, Jane Jacobs. As it turned out, these small figures sometimes wrought more significant change than Shriver's giant programs. In the era of great, these institutions and people proved the power of small.

For a number of years it seemed that the federal expansion actually could serve the collective, and that the government could afford "guns and butter," the experiments that were the Vietnam War and the Great Society. This was because into the mid-1960s, at least, that now resentful beast of burden, the private sector, still could be corralled into shouldering nearly any burden, just as Harrington said. Even before the founding of the chipmaker Intel, Gordon Moore, while still at Fairchild, pointed out that the pace of the development of the computer chip was exponential, a speed far beyond that imagined by the plodding government officials. Computers made everything cheaper. Tax revenues from even mutinous companies and their workers supplied, or would supply, a flood of money to the government programs. Soon enough, the executive branch of three succeeding Administrations told itself, the Vietnam conflict would be over, and the country would no longer need to worry about the "guns" side of "guns and butter." Should anything go wrong, in any case, citizens need not worry, for government seemed maestro of the kind of planning that made all the other planning possible, the successful management of economic growth itself.

Yet by 1971, for the first time, federal spending on what we now call entitlements—benefits for the aged, the poor, and the unemployed, along with other social programs—outpaced spending on defense. Butter, it seemed, might prove costlier than guns. A key stock index, the Dow Jones Industrial Average, measured not only the economy's current performance, but also, and more important, expectations about the future. In 1966, the measure moved tantalizingly close to the 1,000 line, a landmark. Soon after, however, the index stalled, and stayed stuck below the 1,000 line, year in, year out. By the end of the decade, inflation, always present, was expanding to alarming levels. The same period brought another alarm, this time from abroad. Foreign governments started to turn more of their dollars in for gold from the United States' coffers. The U.S. papers went into denial, quoting a Yale professor, Robert Triffin, who argued that the withdrawals were the result of crossed incentives in the international monetary arrangement, a technical, rectifiable flaw. What came to be known as the Triffin dilemma provided a convenient explanation for the mysterious outflows.

The 1971 run on American gold also, however, reflected foreigners' insight. Outsiders knew a tipping point when they saw one. America had moved closer to Michael Harrington's socialism than even Harrington understood. The United States had locked itself into social spending promises that might never be outgrown. Today, interest in Bitcoin and other cryptocurrencies serves as a measure of markets' and individuals' distrust of the U.S. dollar. In those days there was no Bitcoin, but gold played a similar role. The dollar was the common stock of America, and foreigners used gold to short it.

The disastrous performance of the U.S. economy in the following years proved the foreigners' 1971 wager correct. To pay for its Great Society commitments, the U.S. government in the next decade found itself forced to set taxes so high that it further suppressed the commercialization of innovation. Products that could have been developed from patents awarded in the 1960s remained on the researchers' shelves. Today we assume all markets will rebound given a decade. But there was to be no 1970s rebound for the Dow Jones Average. The Dow flirted with the 1,000 level throughout the decade, but did not cross the line definitively until 1982, an astonishingly long period to stagnate, nearly a generation. While markets languished, unemployment for all Americans rose. High prices, high interest rates, and federal budget deficits plagued the nation. "Guns and butter" had proved too expensive, but so indeed had butter alone. The 1960s commitments required spending that, then and down the decades, would be far greater than for Vietnam or most other wars. Those on the far left who had originally pushed for aggressive public-sector expansion had achieved what they sought, to subordinate the private sector. In 1977, Harrington actually titled a new book *The Twilight of Capitalism*. Those who had counted on the private sector to sustain prosperity saw they had expected too much. The nation's confidence evaporated. Indeed, by the late 1970s, President Jimmy Carter felt the need to undertake a national campaign to restore confidence, the kind of campaign Franklin Roosevelt had launched in response to the Great Depression. From being a nation that could afford everything, America morphed into a country that could afford nothing, a place where the president warned citizens to set their living room thermostats to sixty-five in January, or face catastrophe.

In a supreme irony, many of the people who caused the economic damage found themselves mired in the dirty work of reversing what they had wrought. The task of reducing inflation through punishing interest rates fell to Paul Volcker, who as a junior official aided leaders in the 1971 decisions that triggered the 1970s inflation in the first place. Mortgage rates rose to today incredible-sounding levels, over 15 percent. In the 1980s, the same John Connally who as treasury secretary in 1971 pounded on Nixon's desk for populist measures that ensured an economic quagmire, went bankrupt, a casualty of the mess he had helped to create.

By the late 1970s and 1980s, America was ready to look back at the 1960s and evaluate not only the costs but the programs themselves. Had the reforms been worth it? Which individual reform achieved what it had promised? Kennedy's Man to the Moon space program inspired the country and put Woodstock, the Vietnam War, and even riots in cities into perspective. Kennedy's and Johnson's early civil rights reforms indeed redeemed our democracy. They enabled black Americans to enter shops, vote, find work, and conduct their lives with dignity. Medicare and Medicaid, our two giant health programs, saved or improved the lives of many seniors and poor families.

But the results of many other 1960s reforms fell short. Johnson had promised to try to "cure poverty, and above all to prevent it." No cure occurred. The government lost the War on Poverty. Though official poverty levels did decrease over the course of the 1960s, it is hard to prove that the 1960s decrease did not occur because of private-sector growth rather than government efforts. After the 1960s, official poverty stabilized at 10 to 15 percent. In fact, what the War on Poverty and the new flood of benefits *did* do was the opposite of prevent—they established a new kind of poverty, a permanent sense of downtroddenness. They washed away hope. They destroyed migrants' dream of progress in the North and gave them benefits payments instead of property. Appalachia's troubles, the same troubles showcased by Harrington, continue to abide today, as *Hillbilly Elegy*, a compelling update of Harrington's book, *The Other America*, more than confirms. Black unemployment, which had been the same as whites' in the 1950s, from the early 1960s rose above white unemployment. The gap between black and white unemployment widened. Welfare programs funded by presidents Johnson and Nixon expanded rolls to an appalling extent—appalling because welfare fostered a new sense of hopelessness and disenfranchisement among those who received it. "Boy, were we wrong about a guaranteed income!" wrote that most honest of policy makers, Moynihan, in 1978, looking back on a pilot program that had prolonged unemployment rather than met its goal, curtailing joblessness.[6] The "worker versus employer" culture promoted by the unions and tolerated by the automakers suppressed creativity on the plant floor and in executive offices. Detroit built shoddy autos—the whistle-blower Ralph Nader was correct when he charged that American cars were unsafe. Detroit failed to come up with an automobile to compete with those made by foreign automakers. Whereas in the 1930s American automakers' productivity amounted to triple that of their German competitors, by the late 1960s and the 1970s, German and Japanese automakers were catching up to it or pulling ahead.[7] In the end the worker benefits that union leaders in their social democratic aspirations extracted from companies rendered the same companies so uncompetitive that employees in our industrial centers lost not merely benefits but jobs themselves. Vibrant centers of industry became "the rust belt," something to abandon. *Fahrenheit 11/9*, the filmmaker Michael Moore's documentary that covers the Flint, Michigan, water crisis, depicts a city that the public and private sectors both have abandoned. United Auto Workers head Walter Reuther emerges as one of the most compelling characters in the story that follows. Yet it is no exaggeration to say that Reuther, in league with Henry Ford II and other automakers, committed the economic murder of Flint and Detroit. Michael Harrington never got the pure socialism he sought. But the compromise that he and others did win, social democratic expansion, moved America closer to socialism than it had ever been in a period of prosperity. What the 1960s experiment and its 1970s results suggest is that social democratic compromise comes close enough to socialism to cause economic tragedy.

––––––––

THE DAMAGE of the 1960s showed up in a subtler area: political trust. The overpromising in social programs disillusioned voters, black and white. How could it be, asked the narrator of a film on Pruitt-Igoe, a failing housing project in Harrington's St. Louis, that in the end, after all the federal government's claims in regard to public housing, "the government gave up"? The reforms of the 1960s and early 1970s created a Silent Majority, resentful and disappointed. The early civil rights laws, as important as they were, set a precedent for federal supremacy over states to an extent some of the Constitution's authors would have likened to tyranny. The later civil rights laws, with their emphasis on group rights, pitted Americans against one another. Both Johnson and Nixon conducted domestic policy as if they were domestic commanders in chief. As his advisor the economist Herb Stein noticed, Nixon's heavy-handed management of the economy came to infuriate citizens, even when Nixon was merely cleaning up after Johnson, as when the thirty-seventh president impounded money to reduce annual spending. In fact, Stein later recalled, "the impoundments were cited as an example of Nixon's grasping for power that was covered by the term 'Watergate.'" Watergate was not merely a national indictment of a single chief executive. It was an indictment of executive overreach generally, that of Lyndon Johnson as well. In the pain of the 1970s and early 1980s, many Americans came to recognize that the ultimate executive-led expert-driven social project of the 1960s, the White House application of Keynesian economic doctrine, was also the ultimate domestic failure. In retrospect, citizens finally saw Keynesianism for what it was, mere window dressing for political expedience. The popular expression of these new insights was the 1980 election of Ronald Reagan.

The decline both of social democratic economies in Western Europe and of dictators behind the Iron Curtain over the course of the 1970s also weakened socialism's credibility. The failure of the doctrine abroad and at home seemed to ensure that America would never again talk of socialism, or even social democracy. "The most important political event of the twentieth century," declared the commentator Irving Kristol in 1976, "is not the crisis of capitalism but the death of socialism." When, in 1989, the year the Berlin Wall came down, Michael Harrington happened to publish a book titled *Socialism*, he looked like yesterday's fool. In Britain, the rise of Margaret Thatcher reflected a post-socialist respect for the individual: "There is no such thing as society," Thatcher said. "There are individual men and women and there are families."[8] For a time, under presidents Reagan, George H. W. Bush, Bill Clinton, and George W. Bush, it even seemed that America had finally managed to outgrow Great Society collectivism. This was mainly due to the resurgence of the private sector and a federal policy, commenced with Reagan, of staking national hope for greatness on that private sector once more. Businesses that had survived the 1960s and 1970s whole, and not all did, eventually recovered and exploited innovations that sooner or later created far more jobs than the Peace Corps, the Job Corps, and other Great Society programs combined. Some of those businesses came in traditional form, such as the fast-food franchise. In the end, McDonald's employed more young men than the U.S. Army. But some of the new businesses came in forms and with products no wise man had predicted. In the 1990s, America came to recognize that Silicon Valley could shape the country's future. The level of the Dow soared, that "1,000" level multiplying manyfold. The Great Society's challenges seemed a thing of the past.

Today, though, the 1960s are catching up with us. Medicare and Medicaid, undertakings that sounded reasonable at a time when life expectancy was lower, now cost the country trillions it cannot afford. Younger generations can expect no pensions: the budget of Social Security, the national pension fund expanded so dramatically in the 1960s, will be exhausted before it is time for those generations to retire. Nowadays we know we must reform New Deal and Great Society programs if the country is not to go broke. Yet the interest groups bolstered or created in the 1960s render the nation's ability to promulgate obvious reforms, even those that Lyndon Johnson and Richard Nixon would themselves have rated deeply desirable, near impossible. We tend to think of the 1930s New Deal reforms as more radical than the 1960s Great Society programs. Yet as Hoover's John Cogan notes, starting in 2002, the expense of Great Society–era benefits commitments outpaced the expense of benefits established by the New Deal. The New Deal created a forgotten man. The Great Society created more.

The beleaguered participants in 1960s policy making have often pointed to an obvious cause for their failures: politics. It is true that in the Great Society era individuals saw their ideas hopelessly distorted by the political process. Figures ranging from Mayor Sam Yorty of Los Angeles to George Romney of Michigan, the housing secretary, were abused by the White House of Johnson or Nixon and then blamed for not standing up for their cause. Sargent Shriver, Daniel Patrick Moynihan, Walter Reuther, and Arthur Burns also repeatedly suffered such humiliation. In the monetary drama, Burns, the chairman of the Federal Reserve, played a complicit Cassandra, both predicting inflation well in advance and participating in decisions that made what he had predicted inevitable. The failure of policies resulting from compromises struck at Nixon's Camp David summit in 1971 proved so dramatic that a number of summit attendees were each later overcome by the need to produce an *apologia pro vita sua*, a memoir that minimized their own culpability. Today, more than half a century on, the bitter memory of being wronged by circumstances, of being underappreciated, still burns in the 1960s officials or their children. In 2012, Mitt Romney, the son of the frustrated housing secretary, ran for president. Speaking to a private group of donors, he ruefully suggested that if elected, he might abolish the Department of Housing and Urban Development altogether. Still, to write it all off as "politics" is to ignore reality. Many programs that were completed failed. There were also more profound sources of the unexpected tragedies of the Great Society endeavor. Delving into those mysterious sources is the task of this book.

MOST AMERICANS do not recall much about the Great Society. Perhaps this is an inevitability of time. Just as the 1960s forgot the failures of the 1930s, we today forget the failures of the 1960s. Part of the trouble is what schoolbooks and history books omit. Some texts and documentaries focus on advances in civil rights—inspiringly, but neglecting the rest of the story. Other histories of the 1960s devote so much content to Vietnam that they underplay other important events. A third literature, vast, portrays the period as setting in train a powerful progressive youth movement. The Youth Movement of the 1960s certainly shaped the subsequent culture, whether in the availability of marijuana, the original hippie drug; in music; the sexual revolution; or in the freewheeling dress codes at even the stuffiest bank. But when it came to establishing a new political or economic culture, the hippies failed, in part because they began, as they aged, to see the risibility of what they proposed. "In every case," as Harrington himself later concluded, Students for a Democratic

Society "identified a very real source of discontent. But in no case did they define a force, or even a coalition of forces, capable of transforming American society." In the 1960s and later, Federal Bureau of Investigation agents tracked leaders on the left aggressively, succeeding mainly in dignifying the targets they disdained. The trouble with the 1960s leftists was not that they were traitors. Few were. The trouble was that they were wrong.

A genre of its own, presidential biography, also distorts the picture. The genre elevates President Kennedy so close to beatitude that it obscures him. Presidential biography celebrates President Johnson as an action figure, glorifying his ability to see ideas into law with scant regard to the consequences of those laws. Presidential history vilifies Nixon, who in reality replayed Johnson's moves to a disconcerting extent. A final set of histories displays all these trends, but does so in nonnarrative, noneconomic kaleidoscope fashion—napalm, Martin Luther King Jr. at the Lincoln Memorial, the electric guitar at Woodstock, the riots in Watts—making the period impossible to analyze, but easy to reminisce about. The narratives of public television and public radio, both Johnsonian creations after all, emphasize similar themes and memes. So do our college texts, written by university faculty members who started out on the American left and made their way upward through institutions of higher education. The "long march through the institutions" that Antonio Gramsci sketched out and Rudi Dutschke demanded has succeeded. Reinforcing such histories are primary and high school teachers who belong to public-sector unions whose power derives from policies promulgated by presidents Kennedy and Johnson. Few dare to attempt the counterfactuals, to try to depict what the 1960s might have been like had the government and labor unions held back and Americans planned their economic future themselves. This economic question may sound dull. But the astounding reality is that the economic legacy of the Great Society era matters more than the Vietnam conflict, now stored away in a national mental file cabinet labeled "Cold War."

For today, the contest between capitalism and socialism is on again. Markets do promise strong growth; we do live in a creative society, the most creative in the world, creative enough to lift the nation to new heights. Yet new, progressive proposals bearing a strong resemblance to those of Michael Harrington's and his peers', from redistribution via taxation to student debt relief to a universal guaranteed income, are sought yet again. Once again, many Americans rate socialism as the generous philosophy. But the results of our socialism were not generous. May this book serve as a cautionary tale of lovable people who, despite themselves, hurt those they loved. Nothing is new. It is just forgotten.

NEW

FRONTIER

1

The Bonanza

1960 TO 1962

Guns: 9.0% of GDP[1]
Butter: 4.5% of GDP
Dow Jones Industrial Average: 679[2]

The current rapid trend has got to be changed, or we are
through with every good thing we cherish.
—Lemuel Boulware, vice president, General Electric

Why doesn't the Government mind its own business? What
is the Government's business, is the question.
—President John F. Kennedy, 1962

On the first Saturday night of the 1960s, NBC aired a Western that posed a question that would preoccupy the decade: how to handle America's wealth.[3] In the episode, from the series *Bonanza*, two young cowboys, Joe and Hoss Cartwright, run into trouble after their father gives them $15,000 to buy a prize bull. The theme was unusual for the 1950s Western, but not for *Bonanza*, which, though only a few months old, had already made a name as a different kind of show. Heretofore Westerns treated the single gunslinger's efforts to make his fortune, whether by staking a claim to land or at the card table. By 1960, however, the story of one loner striking it rich lacked allure. Americans nowadays routinely became prosperous. It was time, *Bonanza*'s creator, David Dortort, determined, to transcend "the myth of the lone gunfighter." *Bonanza* therefore featured not one but four main characters: a patriarch, Ben Cartwright; and his sons. "On this land we put our brand," sang Lorne Greene, who played the patriarch, in his gravelly voice. The important thing, *Bonan-*

za's first episodes suggested, was what a man, family, or community did with a bonanza. You had to protect your bonanza from bad guys. You had to spend your bonanza carefully—invest in something like a prize bull that causes your wealth to multiply. You had to tend your bonanza. Most important, you had to share your bonanza, and teach others how to earn and share. That meant a father training his sons, or a clan like the Cartwrights coaxing the vigilantes of Main Street into becoming virtuous town elders. The wealth part, that initial bonanza, was a given.

Nor were the scriptwriters for NBC alone in this assumption. There would always be moments when America stumbled. But those were exceptions like the Great Depression, now a safe two decades back in time. In 1960, America was wealthy. An economist favored by the coming politicians, John Kenneth Galbraith, described America as "the affluent society." Fortune, Americans believed, rewarded anyone who showed character, for example by heading West. Americans *did* show character, and reaped the rewards. "The land was ours before we were the land's," as Robert Frost wrote in one of his poems, "The Gift Outright."

The gift outright seemed likely to continue giving in the future. At corporate headquarters, profits rolled in, and the cleverer American companies knew how to adjust to any change. If viewers wearied of black-and-white television, networks could shift to color, as NBC did with *Bonanza*, the first color Western. In Detroit, the chief executive at American Motors, George Romney, had noticed the industry's fixation on building the same big cars over and over again—"gas-guzzling dinosaurs," as Romney labeled them. Americans wanted something smaller, and Romney delivered a splendid small car, the Rambler. Even fifteen years after World War II, American businesses faced scant competition from abroad. What did Motor City have to fear from agricultural Asia, or from the small nations of Western Europe, still struggling as they were with the threat of communist coups or invasion? What did RCA, or General Electric, have to fear? Or workers in their great unions? One of the few foreign-made products General Electric salesmen noticed was the little Sony radio from Japan. General Electric made its own small radios.

Individual U.S. businesses looked so strong that any bruises or nicks they might suffer scarcely mattered. That included bruises or nicks from the U.S. government. The economist John Maynard Keynes had once told President Franklin Roosevelt that businessmen resembled domestic animals. All you need to get profit out of cattle was to treat the animals decently and herd them. Then you would get the beef and the milk. And most Americans trusted the federal shepherd. The relationship was reciprocal: Americans needed the government, and the government needed them. It was the U.S. government, after all, that had given many men their first job as soldiers in Korea or World War II, and paid for millions to attend college and training programs afterward. Any young men seeking to make breakthroughs in science turned to the government for employment first, including Homer Hickam, the teenager from Coalwood, West Virginia, whose hobby, rocketry, launched his career. The hands of the federal government had played freely in the economy for half a century now, through Woodrow Wilson's wartime nationalization of the railroads, through Franklin Roosevelt's New Deal, through World War II, and recently, in the Cold War. That involvement had coincided, at least since World War II, with an increase in the standard of living and better jobs for Americans, white or black. What America lived in now was not pure capitalism. It was what Professor Paul Samuelson, the author of the nation's premier economics textbook, called a "mixed economy."

Living in a mixed economy meant living with the government's laws, and the obligations those imposed. The income tax was the most prominent burden. In Eisenhower's time, the top rate on the income tax was over 90 percent, a level that put a damper on individual initiative, and channeled money into sometimes near ludicrous projects just because they enjoyed certain tax advantages. There were other challenges. In 1890, just before GE was created, Congress had passed the original antitrust law, the Sherman Anti-Trust Act. From time to time the Justice Department would descend on companies to investigate possible violations of the act's statutes on company collusion. From time to time as well, Justice might even bring down a company.

In 1935, Roosevelt and Congress had set the terms of the modern corporate-labor relationship through the Wagner Act. That act had transformed "labor," lowercase, into the uppercase "Big Labor." The AFL-CIO, the unions' umbrella organization, was a power with a war chest replenished annually by tens of millions of dollars in dues. Organized labor counted as members seventeen million workers, a quarter of the American workforce. The Wagner Act gave the labor movement its own special court for adjudication, the National Labor Relations Board. In twentieth-century labor negotiations, Big Labor sat across the table from Big Business, another reciprocal relationship. Often enough, a third party convened them: the shepherding federal government, or "senior partner" as Theodore Roosevelt had called it, more politely. The White House led, but it was not all-powerful. For after the Wagner Act, what happened at the table, especially how unions fared, was key to a president's political future. Support from big corporations affected an election. Support from the unions decided it.

Wages were not the only number set by Big Labor, Big Business, and the government. When the three met, and in the early 1960s that was often, they also set prices. In fact, the great table *ran* the economy, following charts handed to it by economists. The most important chart, as respected as if it demonstrated a law of physics, was one created by the economist A. W. Phillips. The Phillips curve postulated that an economy must always choose between two poisons, unemployment or inflation. The nation might suffer from one or the other, but not both at the same time. Conversely, there was no such thing as simultaneous low unemployment and low inflation. Economists also argued that higher wages begat higher prices, and higher prices in turn triggered higher wages. A dangerous dynamic called a "wage-price spiral" ensued. Serious inflation required official countermeasures, whether "fiscal tightening" (less spending, higher taxes) or higher interest rates from the Federal Reserve. Big Labor, Big Business, and the executive branch made the trade-offs and fine-tuned the results. Paul Samuelson's guru, Keynes himself, had justified such management in his great opus, *The General Theory of Employment, Interest, and Money*. Each move by the figures at the great table had consequences for employers, workers, and shopkeepers. The country kept an eye on the actions of the mighty threesome via the evening news, before the Westerns.

But it all, even the thousands of strike days that idled factories, seemed part of an eminently bearable routine. Only the rich, it was said, paid those high taxes. The value of the private sector's relationship with the government seemed especially obvious in the Western state that Americans regarded as the land of the future, California. For many Californians, the government *was* their job. More active-duty military and civilian Defense Department employees were stationed in California than in any other state. The presence of Pentagon money in California wasn't merely large, it was overwhelming.[4] In one year, 1959, the Defense Department was awarding more than $3 billion in contracts to four aerospace firms in Los Angeles. Nor was the federal money pouring into factories alone—universities and firms conducting research and development received hundreds of millions in support as well. California's growing electronics industry lived off Defense. The California divisions of firms such as Fairchild, itself based like RCA in the East, would shortly develop computer chips for the federal government's new space program. California well understood the importance of Air Force spending and back in the early 1950s had elected a former air officer, Sam Yorty, to Congress. The question in the Golden State was not whether to flee Washington's orders. It was what California would do when those orders stopped.

The same cooperation with government existed to a less dramatic extent in the rest of the nation. Thanks to Congress and President Dwight Eisenhower's Interstate Highway program, the federal government had funded most of the Interstate system's construction, generating work for thousands. The government had paid yet more on defense procurement. In fact, annual spending by the Defense Department on equipment had more than doubled in the past decade, while the economy generally had grown more slowly. It was said that when U.S. senators from any state even sensed that competitor states were gaining in the contest for defense contracts, they "stood up on [their] hind legs and roared."[5]

You could point to the East Coast giant General Electric as a prime example of how much a firm depended on government contracts. In the year 1959, General Electric had been the nation's fourth-largest defense contractor, after Boeing, General Dynamics, and North American Aviation.

GE was receiving nearly $1 billion for military projects, including participation in the manufacture of the Sidewinder missile.[6] General Electric served other arms of the federal government, most notably the massive hydropower concern the Tennessee Valley Authority, like the Wagner Act a creature of the New Deal. Some people said government scientists were overpaid, but GE's chairman, Ralph Cordiner, actually led a committee that recommended pay raises for 360,000 Defense Department workers. Even outside crucial areas such as defense or energy, GE readily teamed up with government. For years now, for example, GE had been an advocate of Urban Renewal, a Washington program that joined states and towns in rebuilding cities. The federal government was everywhere on GE's books and GE's factory floors, whether as partner or client.

And that was just fine with most of the management at GE. The majority of GE executives shared the national consensus that American growth was unstoppable, regardless of how tax authorities, or Congress, or regulators might behave. The pragmatists believed that the intelligent thing to do was work with the "senior partner" in Washington. Their heroes were GE's heads in the 1920s and 1930s, Owen Young and Gerard Swope. Young had argued for corporate conciliation with organized labor at President Woodrow Wilson's National Industrial Conferences in 1919 and 1920, and had attached himself to Franklin Roosevelt's 1932 campaign.[7] While Young's support for Roosevelt cooled when the new president proved more progressive than expected, Swope, Young's successor, enthusiastically aided Roosevelt in implementing the New Deal, sitting on just about every government committee relating to business, including an advisory committee on the federal pension plan created in those years, Social Security.[8]

But there were a few executives at GE who did not believe that cooperation between government and corporations like GE was benign. Indeed, these executives thought that such cooperation imperiled not only GE but also capitalism and the American bonanza. One was GE's veteran vice president for labor relations, a man who ran a propaganda mill for the corporation. If the cooperation remained close, this man said, the bonanza of prosperity would disappear. "The current rapid trend has got to be changed," the executive intoned in memos and at meetings, "or we are through with every good thing we cherish." He saw scant difference between East Europeans' toleration of communist dictators, abhorrent to them all, and Americans' acquiescence in progressive reform at home. The executive was always telling colleagues that it was up to GE to shoot down creeping socialism—now. He argued that in 1960, the company should campaign especially hard. This vice president seemed no threat to newer executives. They didn't see that American capitalism was in need of saving. Ranters such as this man were a fading minority. The boss who permitted such ideological talk from a vice president, CEO Ralph Cordiner, was approaching the age of sixty, good for only another few years. The ranter himself was even older, turning sixty-five soon, past due for his retirement in Delray Beach. If this man wanted to take another shot against socialist phantoms, the others thought, let him take it. It would be his last shot.

THE NAME of the executive who wanted one last shot was Lemuel Ricketts Boulware. Boulware's presence and his extreme defense of pure capitalism weren't as out of place at GE as the younger men made them out to be. Companies have souls, and the soul of GE was riven. In recent decades it had indeed been the pragmatic GE that had ruled the plants of the industrial powerhouse. But in the early days, before Owen Young and Gerard Swope, old laissez-faire capitalists had predominated. GE's founders, Thomas Edison and Charles Albert Coffin, believed that the kind of company that sustained American capitalism was the company that stood aloof, that wore no harness, that came to no big negotiating table.

In the time of Edison and Coffin, there had been no business school, no military-industrial complex, no electrical workers' union, and no federal income taxes. Even the taxes that states levied, so modest when compared with today's, had sometimes been too much for GE leadership to take. Each inventor at such a company should likewise work on his own. In the day the journalist Ida Tarbell had summarized the attitude of the GE pioneers: "Research must be free and where it pointed the way business must have the discernment, the ingenuity and courage to follow."[9] Only free researchers allowed serendipity to take them to unexpected discoveries. In 1932 GE scientist Irving Langmuir had validated this hypothesis when he won the Nobel Prize in chemistry for research in lamp filaments that, as it turned out, made it possible to take images of blood vessels.

The few mossbacks around GE told a story about GE's first star engineer at Schenectady, Charles Proteus Steinmetz. Steinmetz *was* a socialist, had run for office as a socialist, and had even corresponded with Lenin himself. After one election, his colleagues learned that the Wizard of Schenectady had actually voted Republican. Charles Coffin had teased Steinmetz. "Steiny, I thought you were a socialist," Coffin had commented. "I was, until my salary went over $5,000," Steinmetz had answered.[10]

Back in the day, the older conservatives at GE had regarded the ascent of the progressives Young and Swope with dismay. Swope had preached something he called "New Capitalism."[11] What, exactly, was wrong with the *old* capitalism? You could argue, as the Chase Bank analyst Benjamin Anderson did, that government was the perpetrator who put the "Great" in the Great Depression, prolonging the agony with its interventions. To the conservatives the great institutions of the New Deal, the National Labor Relations Board or the GE client Tennessee Valley Authority included, imperiled not only GE's innovating spirit, but that of all enterprise. Labor unions, especially, forced an artificial class war on the country. The Wagner Act's "closed shop," a rule that anyone accepting a job at a union shop must also join the union, was undemocratic. The National Labor Relations Board that the Wagner Act created was a kangaroo court that favored one side, labor bosses. Even Congress's palliative update of the Wagner Act, the 1947 Taft-Hartley Act, dictated that companies negotiate with unions, rather than settle wage packages with individual workers. That gave the union leaders a large say in how wealth was distributed. It also gave them a chance to seize the stage and hold it, to lengthen the to-and-fro period of company-union negotiation until it was a public drama as compelling as any match between two cowboys outside a saloon in the best Western. This theatrical class warfare made employ-ers and employees into enemies—bad for communication; discussion of assembly-line improvement; and, to the GE trading analysts, seemingly wholly unnecessary.

One of the CEOs who came after Swope, Charles Wilson, had him-self served at the quintessential government office, the War Production Board, supervising industry during World War II. Surveying the economy at the war's end, Wilson judged that the great government that had been necessary in war was not necessary in peace. Wilson also came to share some of his predecessors' conviction that New Deal "pro-labor" laws truly disadvantaged business and even workers themselves. For following the New Deal and the war, the unions had sometimes negotiated packages more favorable to themselves than to their own workers.

The unions extracted wage agreements that companies could ill afford—so high that the companies later had to lay off workers. Forced to pay high wages, businesses also responded by hiring fewer people. What's more, New Deal law required union members to supply funds for the union's political work, which meant, by and large, that part of work-ers' weekly pay went to serve only one political party. And that party was not the party of Thomas Edison, a Calvin Coolidge man.

During the war Charlie Wilson and Ralph Cordiner, who also served at the War Production Board, had noted the competence of one of their colleagues, Boulware. Boulware, who had trained in accounting, seemed just right for GE. On the one hand, especially when talking to the press, Boulware knew how to play it cool. On the other, he knew how to sell. The magazine *Fortune* described Boulware as a figure who combined "the folksiness of a Kentucky farm background with the fervor of a washing machine salesman."[12] Most important to these GE executives, Boulware himself was deeply suspicious of union law. Cordiner and Wilson reck-oned that Boulware could help them keep the Edison-Coffin spirit alive at GE. They hired Boulware to think about—and act on—threats to capi-talism. Communists within GE were considered one danger, albeit small. Far greater dangers were the heavy taxes, or those thuggish unions. Boul-ware also quickly identified the fundamental challenge: public ignorance.

The public didn't understand that the freedom of markets was necessary to make companies like GE grow. America was, through its own social welfare measures, gradually heading toward socialism, and Americans didn't even know it.

This ideologue Boulware proved a good hire, handling union challenges so well that GE soon put him in charge of labor negotiations.[13] If anyone could go head-to-head with feisty union leaders, it was Boulware in his younger days. By the 1950s, he came to be known for being as wily as any union head. Boulware even developed his own tactic for shutting out union brass: GE would make a generous salary package, dangle it before the noses of the workers—and refuse to negotiate with their union heads. Among union heads this ploy of shoving unions off the stage became so infamous they gave it its own name, "Boulwarism." But the whole theater of *Plutocrat v. Worker*, Boulware argued again and again, was unnecessary. In a better world, Boulware contended, labor problems would be "thought out, not fought out."

As both Boulware and the unions knew, American law did provide an escape hatch out of unionland. Taft-Hartley, the postwar update of the original Wagner Act, permitted individual states to make the choice to allow companies to welcome workers who did not join the union. By the early 1960s, a number of states outside the industrial core had indeed opted to be what were known as "right to work" states—among them, Alabama, Texas, the Carolinas, the Dakotas, and Mississippi. Companies and professionals who struggled with debilitating strikes, GE included, sometimes joined that wagon train and built or expanded factories in those states. Naturally, the unions were fighting back, and lately, with good success. One reason Barry Goldwater, the Republican senator, was regarded as an extremist was that he represented, loudly, "right to work" Arizona. Goldwater, attacking the old unionized East, even suggested "that this country would be better off if we could just saw off the Eastern seaboard and let it float out to sea."

But to turn tail was cowardly, and this the GE of 1960 believed with all its soul. Boulware and Cordiner, who had succeeded Charlie Wilson as president, had long since determined to hold their ground. There was nowhere better than New England, the bedrock of American capitalism, to halt the leftist unions and restore the ancient pre-union relationship between employer and worker. Obviating unions, to Boulware and Cordiner, even made economic sense, like obviating a middleman and lowering a price. The company could share directly with the workers all the revenue it gained because of higher productivity, and that profit would be larger if no work days were lost to strikes. Wouldn't workers rather receive a steady stream of income, the most possible, than one last glorious strike-generated raise before the inevitable layoffs? And shouldn't higher productivity, not union clout, be what gave workers higher pay?

Cordiner funded a propaganda mill whence Boulware could instruct GE families, hundreds of thousands of people, on the beauties of pure capitalism. One of the primers Boulware favored was *The Road to Serfdom*, by an Austrian economist named Friedrich von Hayek. Hayek made what Boulware considered the most important point. Collectivist planners, gradually, even unconsciously, aggregated power, and their solutions were so poor that the frustrated populace eventually turned to autocrats. The autocrats shackled free men and women. Boulware was not alone in his admiration of Hayek—General Motors had distributed a cartoon version of *The Road to Serfdom* in its own civic education program, its "Thought Starter" series.

Boulware took seriously another volume, published like Hayek's as the country emerged from the war: *The Road Ahead to Victory and Lasting Peace*, by a communist, Earl Browder. Browder envisioned a future for socialism *within* a "democratic progressive majority." Browder's book validated Hayek's claim that even moderate politicians might, perhaps unwittingly, be tricked by the Browders into paving a road to serfdom. Boulware routinely handed the two *Roads* out to GE workers and managers. He also lectured workers on the international failings of socialism, under the communists and also in Western Europe. Britons openly elected self-declared socialists, and Britain had even implemented socialist policy, the nationalization of health care. "Let's watch our British friends to see what happens in their experiment," Boulware counseled workers. Boulware crafted arguments against the minimum wage—it reduced hiring—or on how inflation cheated the worker, giving him a paycheck worth less than he thought.

Another key teaching in Boulware's material involved the stock market. Some workers held GE shares. Tens of thousands now worked at GE. When the government was too tough on a company, it produced less, and the share price went down. If a government beat up on a company, its share price went down further. There were lower profits, and so the company had to pay the workers less. Boulware had also long distributed pamphlets aimed at dispelling myths propagated by unions or progressives. A recent GE primer of this sort was titled "Building Employee Understanding in 1960." The primer armed middle managers with twenty-eight arguments for the virtue of the free market. The headings ranged from "How Automation Makes More and Better Jobs" to "The Role of Profits in Providing Jobs" and "The Why and How of Curbing Inflationary Settlements."

Info sessions and pamphlets, Boulware and Cordiner had realized early, couldn't alone convince workers. GE also must model the merit of unfettered innovation through its own management. A few years before, Cordiner had taken steps to apply Edison's "bottom up" theory within GE. Cordiner had loosened the corporate reins on his own charges, GE's 120 departments, making them as autonomous as possible and giving assignments "not too big for one man to get his arms around."[14] Just as had been the case in Edison's day, it was now true, Cordiner thought, that men who ran their own labs had more ideas than men who were mere cogs. In the aggregate, Cordiner wagered, the finds of these small departments would add more value for the company than any single big project ordered up and scrutinized at each stage by top executives. After all, today, just as in GE's early years, sometimes valuable ideas were not planned, but discovered almost by accident, as in the case of the surprising discovery of Lexan, a GE plastic as hard as metal. Decentralization also had its disadvantages. In a decentralized giant, management could not keep track of what was going on in departments day to day.

At times even Cordiner, the decentralizer himself, couldn't resist trying to kill an innovative pilot, famously seeking to suppress GE's own computer business because a computer business would antagonize GE's customer IBM. Some of GE's engineers thought this was ridiculous. Later, they recalled that Cordiner even sent a memo: "Under no circumstances will the General Electric company go into the business machine business."[15] Here, Cordiner fitted the caricature of the golf course Republican, too chummy with other big executives to see opportunity when it was before his nose. In the mid-1950s, GE was a far richer company than IBM.[16] General Electric had the resources necessary to get into computers, the computer fans reckoned, whatever Cordiner said. A clutch of engineers did manage to land a successful contract with the Bank of America for an innovative check sorter, the first computer system for banking applications, a testimony to the gumption of GE professionals and, ironically, to Cordiner's own culture of department autonomy. California was the home of Bank of America, and also the home of the GE group that won the contract. The machines would serve the Sacramento, Fresno, Los Angeles, and San Diego areas. But California was a state where GE could endure the same troubles with organized labor as it did out East. GE internal reports noted that the company was looking to avoid the Golden State's "punitive labor legislation."[17] GE based production of the project's computer, weight 23,000 pounds, in Phoenix.

But Cordiner's prissiness over the computer business was the exception in a general entrepreneurial drive. Cordiner also pushed against external restraints, including the restraint of the government partnership. Defying surprised lawmakers, as well as the chairman of the Atomic Energy Commission, he had a few years before announced to Congress that nuclear power for civilian use could be handled by the private sector, and that by 1965 GE would lead the nation in producing commercial atomic power without government subsidy. GE's atomic power plant in Vallecito, California, would be an example of how California could wean itself off the Defense Department. The plant could sell private power and minimize government patronage. "The atom is the power of the future, and power is the business of General Electric," Cordiner ordained. *Time* magazine, impressed, put him on its cover.

One of Cordiner's and Boulware's allies in the free-market crusade

was a GE executive named Robert Paxton. Paxton was born in Edin-
burgh, Scotland, the home of the great markets philosopher Adam Smith.
William Ginn, the head of the Schenectady plant, would later character-
ize Paxton as coming "closer to being an Adam Smith than any businessman I have met in America." One day, free marketeers such as Cordiner
and Boulware hoped, there would be more Paxtons in management. Then
the old free-market culture would prevail again at GE. GE could demonstrate to the world what a free-market company looked like.

Early on in their tenure, Boulware and Cordiner found they wanted
more than to tutor GE's own employees or showcase GE's virtues. They
wanted to waken all Americans to the threat of socialism. Boulware had
his eye on younger citizens, who, especially on the campuses, betrayed
an irrational attraction to collectivism. In the early 1950s it seemed
that the moderate Dwight Eisenhower, new to the presidency at the time
Boulware and Cordiner raised their sights, might become an ally: it was
Ike who had first dropped the term "creeping socialism," the president's
description of the Tennessee Valley Authority.[18] Other companies were
falling down in the work of educating workers. Unions intimidated them.
George Romney of American Motors let it be known he thought it beneath
the dignity of Big Business to teach or get involved in politics: business
should "deplore" organized labor's political activities. Boulware took the
opposite view: Big Business, by abdicating, was allowing politicians to
get away with speaking "economic baby talk" to voters, deceiving them
about the cost that organized labor imposed. Someone had to lead a national citizen education drive to end such ignorance. Who better than the
model company GE?

Staying clean required work. No big company could stay clear of all
legal trouble. In the mid-1950s the Justice Department had filed suit
charging that GE had conspired with Westinghouse and a Dutch firm,
N.V. Philips's Gloeilampenfabrieken, to prevent the sale of American radios and televisions by others in Canada. President Eisenhower's attorney
general launched a review of top electric companies, including GE, on
the suspicion that the companies were colluding on prices, an illegal activity, so that their clients would not be able to "buy cheap" from any of

them. On the floor of the Senate, Senator Joseph O'Mahoney of Wyoming charged that U.S. courts weren't doing enough to deter colluders: "How many executives have been sent to jail up to this time for violation of the Sherman Act? Practically none."[19] If GE was to lead in the 1950s or 1960s, the executives knew, the company could not get into trouble again. GE must always be, as one of Boulware's colleagues, Earl Dunckel, later remembered, "ultra careful that no taint of anything negative would attach to any of its people."[20] GE's top management therefore codified in its ethics statement a clear prohibition of antitrust violations. That prohibition was these days known as Policy 20.5. Cordiner's nickname was "Razor Ralph." Conscious of all the scrutiny companies like his were getting, Razor Ralph made a big point of Policy 20.5 compliance. When GE hired a new manager, Razor Ralph called him into the GE headquarters on Lexington Avenue and personally reminded him that GE salesmen must never collude.

Time and again, GE reviewed such policies and, time and again, determined itself clean enough to lead. And so, with the support of management and GE's advertising agency, Batten, Barton, Durstine and Osborn, Boulware maintained his perpetual national propaganda campaign. GE placed ads pointing out that its goods exemplified capitalist achievement, from great engines for rockets to washing machines and televisions, as well as its little radio, as small as a couple of packs of Old Gold cigarettes. These pictures appeared beside the GE motto: "Progress is our most important product."[21] In 1959, Vice President Richard Nixon and the Soviet leader, Nikita Khrushchev, had debated before an exhibit of model kitchens in Moscow. The appliances in the kitchens had dazzled the Russians, many of whom shared cooking space and had no refrigerator at all. The American kitchens were an in-your-face example of the superiority of the American standard of living. Naturally, one of the kitchens—lemon yellow—had been, as the Soviet news agency TASS duly reported, "completely outfitted by General Electric."

For both internal and external work, Boulware, Cordiner, and their advertising company eventually concluded, GE needed a spokesman— someone people would come to hear just because they already knew his voice and face. It wouldn't do to pick a harsh antiunion voice, or a European philosopher with an accent and a difficult name. GE wanted to lure, not force. GE's spokesman himself had to model virtue. Casting its eyes over the celebrity landscape, GE considered a Western star who was the president of an actual AFL-CIO affiliate, the Screen Actors Guild. The star was also a Democrat, someone who deeply respected Franklin Roosevelt. So much the better—that conveyed nonpartisanship. The actor's only flaw was that he was divorced. But since he had recently remarried, you could play down the divorce, the GE men told one another. GE indeed offered the job to Ronald Reagan.

Fortunately for GE, Reagan needed the job, and in 1954 had started out on GE's mashed potato circuit, appearing at suppers for workers and the communities in which they lived. At first the actor focused on talking up GE and its products, and defending his own trade, acting. Hollywood was less of a den of sin and communism, Reagan told the crowds, than people supposed. Reagan's GE handler, Earl Dunckel, called this the "Defense of Hollywood Speech." Reagan also spoke, but at first just generally, on GE itself, and its model of progress. For a fading actor—Reagan, who had played action roles, was over forty—the GE setup was its own bonanza. GE bent over backward to make Reagan comfortable, accommodating his aversion to flying with tickets for the Super Chief, the train from Los Angeles to Chicago. GE even built the Reagan family a model house, the GE Home of the Future, featuring every electric appliance it could come up with. Looking out of the house's eighteen-foot glass windows, you could see Mandeville Canyon and get a glimpse of the Pacific Ocean. The house was so wired that the electrical switch box weighed three thousand pounds. "Everything in the house will be electric," joked Reagan, "except the chairs." The GE motto was "Live Better Electrically," and the emphasis was as much on the "Live Better" as on "Electrically."

The largesse turned out to be worth it. Reagan proved as clever a hire as Boulware himself. As Dunckel later recalled, when Reagan arrived on a factory floor, the GE women crowded around. The men would at first stand back, dubious, even calling the actor a "fag." By the end of the meeting, however, the men were slapping Reagan on the back. Before town audiences, Reagan operated equally professionally. Reagan's eyesight was poor, and when he put on his contact lenses, the cigarette smoke at the plants or the dinners bothered his eyes. Still, he would not descend to wearing eyeglasses. Reagan chose rather to memorize whatever he had to say. When it came to ad hoc patter, Reagan was a master. All GE products became Reagan's as he sold them, and he joked about that, too—"I didn't really want a submarine, but I've got one now."

As part of the plan General Electric also gave Reagan a television show to host, *GE Theater*, standard black-and-white, airing on CBS Sundays at 9 p.m. Eastern time. *GE Theater* episodes usually recast a novel or short story into a twenty-five-minute script, leaving room for GE to air its current generation of commercials. *GE Theater* proved a marvelous platform for Reagan, allowing him to both introduce and, when he felt like it, star in a show. As important, perhaps more so, the show permitted Reagan to invite friends from Jack Benny to Zsa Zsa Gabor to star, or even direct. *GE Theater*, unlike *The Twilight Zone*, was realistic, without the alluring supernatural element. But its plots, like those of *The Twilight Zone*, did conclude with an earnest moral. *GE Theater* made *Bonanza*, the new show, look happy-go-lucky. A half decade after the Russian regime crushed the Hungarian uprising in 1956, the actress Ida Lupino directed an episode about it for Reagan, titled "The Iron Silence." Reagan himself played a Soviet officer. "The Iron Silence" would air just weeks after East Germany erected the Berlin Wall.

In their actor, Cordiner and Boulware had gradually come to see, they were winning a free-market convert. Moving past General Electric's consumer goods, or lectures on the character of Hollywood actors, Reagan began to include material about markets and government excesses in his speeches as well. GE raised Reagan's salary to $150,000 from $125,000. But Reagan noticed how little difference that made when the government took 75 cents of the last dollar he earned. Though his agent, MCA, was well known for its ability to defray tax bills, the confiscation by the taxman irked Reagan. Eisenhower and Congress dropped the top tax rate from 92 percent to 91 percent, a minuscule concession. Reagan found he enjoyed lecturing his audiences on the need for greater cuts. Reagan also spoke, like Boulware, on the merits of competitive capitalism. At some point Reagan even gave his teenage son, Michael, ninety shares of General Electric stock, a legacy of Reagan's newfound enthusiasm.

In the spring of 1960, the influence of Reagan's GE training in capitalism showed up in a labor strike led by Reagan's own Screen Actors Guild. After a grueling 140 days—grueling for studios—Reagan, still heading the union, cut a deal with the actors' employers. Actors heretofore hadn't earned royalties, known as residuals, when their cinema shows aired in the new medium of television. Under Reagan's deal, movie actors would get residuals from TV. The contract Reagan extracted applied only to movies made from 1960 going forward, so it cut out the possibility of new revenue from old films by older actors such as Reagan himself or Mickey Rooney. Rooney complained. But the precedent was important. Actors had their own property, not the Ponderosa ranch of the Cartwrights, but intellectual property. Reagan's score would be a life changer for younger actors. Reagan told SAG members in April that "the benefits down through the years to performers will be greater than all the previous contracts we have negotiated, put together." The union president would prove correct. What Razor Ralph and Lem Boulware, who made their names opposing strikes, thought of the GE spokesman's decision to stage a dramatic strike of his own they did not make public. What mattered more to them in any case was that in that election year, Reagan chose to lead a group called "Democrats for Nixon," for Razor Ralph himself backed the Republican vice president for the presidency. Republicans were the party more likely to weaken laws protecting unions.

Others at GE, some conservatives along with pragmatists, reckoned Richard Nixon's opponent, Senator John F. Kennedy of Massachusetts, would not be so bad for business either. Tougher anticommunists than either the red-baiting Nixon or Kennedy would be hard to find. When it came to budgeting, both candidates started with a commitment to preserving the single greatest outlay for the government, defense, and work backward from there. Both Nixon and Kennedy paid lip service to the free market—especially the way the market kept America strong. Nixon had done a stint during World War II at the Office of Price Administration, where as a young attorney he had been involved in a tire rationing program. Nixon had seen how his fellow bureaucrats "seemed to delight in turning down some poor guy at a service station" who needed tires. That experience had given Nixon, as he explained to others later, "a very good feeling about why government should be limited to what is necessary." Nixon's memory of the perversity of rationing meant he would understand when companies struggled with government rules. Kennedy for his part picked a Western theme, "The New Frontier," as his 1960 slogan. The senator from Massachusetts told voters that the New Frontier was "not a set of promises, it is a set of challenges."[22] That sounded auspicious. With such candidates, who needed the preachy Reagan?

Overall, the year 1960 placed a big question mark over any claim that a multimillion-dollar education campaign for free markets was of any use. The electorate was younger now, with memories of World War II beginning to fade, and more voters were put off by the Cold War debate. In Cuba the new Castro regime was snatching up more than $1 billion in U.S. property, including operations of Sears Roebuck, F.W. Woolworth, Coca-Cola, and General Electric itself. Yet young people didn't seem to even want to care. The *Chicago Daily News* reported the astounding results of a study of teachers college students' knowledge of capitalism. Most of the students—they were teachers in training—expressed confusion over capitalism: "Capitalism is the extreme measures that are taken by a group, country or even a single person. . . . It can be dangerous," wrote one trainee. "I am sure there are many places where capitalism is going on at the present time," said another student, "and if this practice should ever become nationwide, the country is in for a lot of trouble." A third student claimed capitalism was "on the order of communism." Could you change such a person's mind? Did doing so even matter? Couldn't capitalism afford ignorance?

The doctrinaire Boulware and Cordiner thought ignorance still mattered. Nixon and Kennedy could still do damage. It was not clear enough that the two presidential candidates were solid on Boulware's or Professor Hayek's definitions of the challenges to *American* capitalism. Nixon was a lawyer, a prosecutor type, not a businessman. Kennedy, the son of a cunning, successful empire builder, Joseph Kennedy, lauded economic growth, but didn't seem to know exactly where growth came from. On the touchy question of labor, Jack Kennedy was clearly no Boulwarite. As a U.S. senator, Kennedy served on a committee that investigated racketeering by unions, and his brother Robert had been one of the committee lawyers. But neither Kennedy brother appeared to see anything wrong in the system of collective bargaining itself. Indeed, as the *Newsweek* columnist Henry Hazlitt, one of Boulware's go-tos, noted, anticorruption legislation that Kennedy proposed "placed more burdens and restrictions on management." In 1960, the brothers were siding with Reuther's United Auto Workers in a long-drawn-out strike against Kohler, the maker of plumbing fixtures. John Kennedy also appeared likely to give a progressive whom the old free marketeers regarded as dangerous, the economist John Kenneth Galbraith, a key position in a Kennedy Administration. Kennedy, schooled by Galbraith, divided America into haves and have-nots—"Private opulence and public squalor."[23] In London, a market in private gold served as a metric of distrust in the value of the dollar. When countries or private investors downgraded their expectations of the United States, they traded dollars in for gold. Noting that Kennedy wasn't speaking much about what the plans in the Democratic platform would cost, traders in London that election fall sold dollars. All an observer at home could conclude about Kennedy was that his soul, like GE's, was riven. Some big test—a strike, for example—would force Kennedy to come down on one side or the other. Until that test, it was anyone's guess how he would perform as president.

AS IT turned out, the year 1960 found GE leadership too busy to pursue further study of John Kennedy's soul. For, to the horror of GE executives, the Justice Department was again scrutinizing General Electric for violations of antitrust law. A grand jury convened in Philadelphia and indicted several GE executives on charges of colluding with Westinghouse and others in sales of turbine generators to the Tennessee Valley Authority.

The evidence that some executives had indeed met with competitors was too copious to ignore, and Cordiner suffered the embarrassment of reviewing abuse of Policy 20.5 with executives. Boulware and Cordiner composed Calvinist speeches assuring middle management that just "a few" General Electric execs had violated the law. The speeches reminded employees that "over and beyond all consideration of what the *outward* consequences of any particular act may be"—whatever the Justice Department charged—"we simply must keep before us always that being a General Electric leader presents each of us constantly with a top priority *moral* challenge deep inside our *inner* selves."

At this most sensitive of moments in relations between General Electric and the TVA, the normally politic Reagan put his foot in it. In an Ohio speech, Reagan listed forms of "socialism" already in place—the type of extra spending for health care for seniors that the political candidates spoke of, federal aid to education, the income tax—and included the TVA. Reagan underscored that the TVA "pays no taxes." This last line misled: the TVA did not pay official taxes, but it did make payments in lieu of taxes.

Reagan's jab got the TVA's attention, and then some. "We are a very good customer of General Electric. In our opinion it is wrong for anyone to attack his customer," said the chairman of the board of directors of the TVA, Herbert Vogel. Vogel had planned a trip to inspect William Ginn's plant at Schenectady. Now, said Vogel, there "would be about as much sense in our board making this trip to Schenectady as there was for President Eisenhower to go to Paris"—a reference to an unsuccessful presidential parley with Khrushchev in May.

The flap gave Reagan's opponents within GE the opening they'd sought. The moderates asked why GE did not institute a policy of reviewing the actor's speeches before delivery. These critics were just like *New York Times* readers, and the paper was notoriously liberal, Dunckel thought. "I am not ever going to have GE censor anything you say," Cordiner told Reagan. But Cordiner did tell the complaining executives that Reagan wasn't truly GE's spokesman. Reagan was a spokesman for himself, hired by GE. This fine distinction stretched the truth and was lost on Reagan's critics.

The fall of 1960 brought another distraction. GE's largest union, the International Union of Electrical Workers, led a walkout of tens of thousands of workers. This was the first major strike since 1955 against GE or its competitors in the appliance business. As in the past, Boulware engaged, not only in historic Schenectady but in another key plant, Pittsfield, Massachusetts. And as in the past, Boulware and GE colleagues did not hesitate to score Jim Carey, the IUE leader, or mayors and local officials who displayed sympathy to union workers. The reaction of the plant towns to Boulware's belligerence was mixed. Raymond Haughey, the mayor of Pittsfield, hosted an emergency meeting of mayors of seven GE cities to discuss not only the usual strike topics—picket lines, the occasional violence—but also how town governments could defend themselves against political attack whatever position they took. George B. Shaw, a native of Pittsfield, wrote to the *Berkshire Eagle* to warn that it was wrong to "let the likes of James Carey try to bankrupt our economy." Were not the *Eagle*'s editors aware that GE's motors indeed confronted keen competition from Japanese factories? Mayor Haughey for his part tried to soften the pain of the strike for workers, allowing that town welfare money might help them over the duration of the strike. In the archives of Boulware's personal papers there is a publicity pamphlet prepared at this time, warning that companies like GE would leave Pittsfield if Haughey didn't get friendlier. "YOUR MAYOR IS MURDERING PITTSFIELD," read GE's title. Underneath, the text was just as dramatic. "Your cowed mayor and his cowed police are stupidly driving out not only General Electric," the mimeographed page read, "but any other employers of this town." The pamphlet became even more vehement: "Grass will and should grow in Pittsfield streets if your mayor does not stop instantly his dishonorable abandoning of his sacred oath to enforce the law." Whether the pamphlet was actually handed out is hard to know; what is clear is that it was typical Boulware.[24]

Carey's IUE did not represent all GE workers. Employees split over Carey's strike, just as Boulware had hoped. In St. Louis union members did picket a GE service division. But other GE workers at the same division were not unionized, and hesitated to picket. They included many

Schenectady workers. In mid-October, defying Carey, the 8,700 Schenectady workers who were members of Carey's IUE Local 301 ended their walkout and accepted the GE plan. Other locals, including Pittsfield's, followed. In the end, Boulware prevailed. Carey won some raises and hospital coverage for his workers. But the union chief failed to get some items he'd counted on, including a 3.5 percent wage increase each year and a cost-of-living adjustment, into the final contract. Boulware and the workers might call the deal generous, but Carey and his IUE couldn't agree. One irony of the deal was that workers would have to bear the risk of the inflation Boulware himself so often warned them about. Summing up recent national wage settlements, Carey complained that unions' gains were so slim that "we certainly didn't need an armored truck to take home the gains we won in the big negotiations this year. We could have used a kiddie car." Boulware's side cheered. "It appears to me that the failure of the strike is one of the noteworthy events of 1960," wrote a labor attorney from Detroit, Raymond Dykema, to Boulware. "I think America owes you a debt of gratitude."

A debt of anger would be more like it, Carey thought. Among union men, Carey was himself considered a moderate. The very reason Schenectady was vulnerable to Boulware was that Carey and others, doing GE's bidding, had helped to supplant the old Union of Electrical Workers, whose members had included communists, with the communist-free IUE. Walter Reuther of the UAW had helped with that. GE's washing machine salesman was playing dirty. Carey told the press the combat was not over: Local 301's action was "a direct violation of the IUE constitution," Carey said, and he would pursue the matter at the National Labor Relations Board. Still, in the moment the Boulware victory suggested unions weren't quite the terror the Boulwares of the world depicted. And soon after the strike, just before his January 1 retirement, Boulware came down with pneumonia, scarcely a good omen.[25]

Boulware may have been down because his own time did seem to be passing. The very demeanor of the president America elected, John Kennedy, continued to undermine Boulware's dire warnings. The capitalist side of the Kennedy soul appeared to be prevailing. Kennedy set a target for economic growth—4.5 percent or even 5 percent—so ambitious it promised either tax cuts, more defense jobs, loose money, or all three. In their profiles the newspapers, scrutinizing the president-elect, reported that Kennedy was reflexively conservative and opposed to high taxes, telling others, "I'm a taxpayer myself." The recent run on U.S. gold appropriately—appropriately, at least, to minds in the field of finance—spooked Kennedy, whose staff noticed his habit of saying the dollar must be "good as gold." Kennedy recognized what economists counseled, that gold outflows could be a technicality, a result of the mechanics of the international gold exchange standard, not a lack of American virtue. Indeed, America's purchases abroad actually caused the outflows, by giving foreigners dollars they wanted to redeem in gold. But Kennedy also believed something else: that indeed the dollar was like the common stock of the country, and when foreigners withdrew gold in great quantity, they were shorting the United States. Those around the president-elect noted that Kennedy behaved almost like a Victorian banker, repeatedly, almost obsessively, checking the amount of American gold reserves. At $35 an ounce, the gold in U.S. coffers at the time of the election was worth about $18 billion, but heading downward, and Kennedy asked about levels of gold in U.S. vaults so often that his staff joked about it.[26] In the Kennedy view the gold challenge was eminently fixable. All America had to do was produce more and buy more of its own goods, and the world would regain confidence in the dollar. American growth might be secure, after all, thought the critics; and younger people liked Kennedy. The poem that Robert Frost repeated at Kennedy's inauguration was "The Gift Outright."

With his old ally Boulware departing, Cordiner was already weakening, and the year 1961 turned Cordiner's small struggles into serious conflicts. The International Union of Electrical Workers might have lost when it walked out of GE plants in 1960, but the union was confident it could get the National Labor Relations Board to rule that Boulwarism, GE's longstanding "take it or leave it" style of negotiating, was outright illegal. The Justice Department's antitrust suit was proving a quagmire that threatened to pull down not only the culprits but all of GE. The Justice

Department's indictments were broad and charged millions of dollars of price fixing. In December 1960, the General Electric executives charged with price fixing pleaded nolo contendere, "I do not contest," a plea that did not acknowledge guilt, but did preclude appeal.[27] The incoming attorney general, Robert Kennedy, sent the federal judge handling the case, J. Cullen Ganey, a stiff letter saying that having reviewed the cases, he considered the abuses "so willful and flagrant that even more severe sentences would have been appropriate." On a cold day in February 1961, the GE men presented themselves to Ganey for sentencing. One of the defendants was William Ginn, the very official to whom the TVA's chairman had complained about Reagan mouthing off. In an effort to win a light sentence for his client, Ginn's attorney jettisoned what remained of GE's tattered case and told the judge that the decision to attend meetings with competitors had not seemed wrong to Ginn, because "what he did was something that he inherited as a way of life that had been established within the General Electric Company even before he came to the General Electric Company." Perhaps by singing, the defendants could get Judge Ganey to display leniency.

But Ganey displayed no leniency. The judge castigated the defendants, including eleven from GE, for violating the Sherman Act. The force of Ganey's opinion took the GE men aback. Ganey told the company that its Policy 20.5 had been "honored in its breach rather than its observance." The judge called the GE action "a shocking indictment of a vast section of our economy." The acting chief of the Justice Department's antitrust division read Robert Kennedy's statement aloud in the courtroom. In a disconcerting echo of the attorney general, the judge commented that GE had "flagrantly mocked the image of that economic system of free enterprise which we profess to the country and destroyed the model which we offer today as a free world alternative to state control and eventual dictatorship." On Capitol Hill, Senator O'Mahoney had admonished judges for failing to sentence antitrust violators to prison. Now Ganey did order jail time for GE executives. Though some of these sentences were suspended, others were not.[28]

For a company like GE, this outcome represented a reputational catastrophe. The country could see that GE, which had complained so long and loud about the government fixing prices, was fixing prices itself. Now GE's soul did not look riven. GE's soul looked hypocritical. The company's old internal division between pragmatists and ideologues was showcased before the nation as pure corporate cynicism. Nationally, GE's free-market campaigns might not always have penetrated, but America did place faith in GE products. A wave of disillusionment spread across the land. Some even compared the discovery that GE fixed prices to the mood at the discovery that the White Sox had rigged the World Series of 1919. GE's president, Robert Paxton, the "Adam Smith man," took early retirement.[29] Ginn entered prison in Montgomery County, Pennsylvania. Jim Carey, the head of the IUE, sent a jailhouse gift to Ginn: the board game Monopoly.[30]

The sentences and jail time were only the start. The customers who bought heavy electrical equipment from GE now launched thousands of civil suits against it, some eligible for treble damages. The Dow Jones Industrial Average rose that spring of 1961, but GE shares did not recover. A blackout in June in New York reminded customers how much they relied on GE and other power companies. The GE men who served their sentences were haled down to Washington for hearings after their release. To add insult to injury, the commerce secretary, Luther H. Hodges, leapt in with a contention that large companies—read, GE—suffered from problems of communication between top management and subordinates. Management, Hodges said, "must assume the responsibility for acquainting its own people with its policies." In other words, the GE system of decentralized autonomous units, Cordiner's baby, warranted scrutiny as well. Decentralization's true purpose was not innovation, you could contend. Decentralization was just a screen that gave GE's top management, men such as Cordiner, plausible deniability.

Reeling at these blows, GE's stock jerked down so wildly that even Carey, the union leader, expressed alarm, saying, "We do not want to see these corporations injured or damaged economically any more than their officers have already damaged them." Reagan, suddenly anxious about his own job, continued to deliver his civics lessons, no longer about the TVA, of course, but about other threats to a free economy, including President Kennedy's plan to extend health benefits to the elderly, an action Reagan skewered as "socialized medicine." The stepfather of Reagan's wife Nancy, a neurosurgeon named Loyal Davis, had contributed to Reagan's political education as well, and Davis and other members of the American Medical Association detested government intrusions into medicine.

People now knew what the attorney general made of GE, but the mystery of President Kennedy's economic soul abided. A number of the policies the president introduced suggested he truly was what the moderates at GE believed, a friend of enterprise. The White House proposed dropping the top rate on the income tax to 65 percent from 91 percent, dramatic compared with Eisenhower's tiny cut. Kennedy also proposed a giant cut on the key tax for markets and enterprise, the capital gains tax, to an effective 19.5 percent from 25 percent. Nothing could be more capitalist than allowing those who added value to the economy to keep their rewards. Congress balked on the tax bill, but Kennedy did manage to get past lawmakers and into law another kind of tax cut, a reduction in tariffs. GE might not like the competition, but lowering tariffs was admired in Boulware's primers. The fact that to fill the job of defense secretary Kennedy had turned to a chief executive from industry, Robert McNamara of Ford, also suggested Kennedy liked business. Kennedy turned *away* from his progressive advisor, John Kenneth Galbraith, dispatching the professor to serve as ambassador in India, where, at least from the point of view of GE, Galbraith could do little damage. Kennedy was also dangling before defense contractors a new bonanza all its own: a space program to dwarf Eisenhower's with the goal of landing a man on the moon.

But, as Boulware's economists always counseled, pro-business was not always pro-innovation. And Kennedy seemed to favor organized labor's vision of a broader social welfare state. The free marketeers at GE and outside it watched with rising concern when Kennedy created the White House Council on Labor-Management Relations, yet another planning office, and as far as people like Cordiner were concerned just one more bureaucracy in the union-government-industry complex. Kennedy didn't see anything wrong with government playing the mediator in union-management disputes. "Government can help by encouraging labor and management to smooth the adjustment to technological change," Kennedy said.

One figure whom Kennedy had tapped for his cabinet gave business leaders special pause: Arthur Goldberg, the new labor secretary. Goldberg had served as general counsel for the United Steelworkers of America, a union that had besieged steelmakers for 116 days in 1959. The union had persisted notwithstanding the complaints of U.S. Steel's head, Roger Blough, who warned that American steelmakers were not so productive that they could afford to lose that many days. Goldberg was seeking to expand the union movement's power by trying to find a way to permit the federal government to recognize unions of government workers. Goldberg tapped a young social scientist in his employ, a man named Daniel Patrick Moynihan, for the task. Moynihan's chief experience with labor had been writing a dissertation on the International Labour Organization, a study that had left him with a profound distaste for the bureaucracy of organized labor. Still, Moynihan sprang to it, reviewing public-sector associations and unions and determining to "go around pretty fast and learn what I could." In January 1962, Moynihan and Goldberg presented for presidential signature an executive order that permitted unions of federal workers to organize and negotiate on behalf of their colleagues. To Moynihan's mind and probably Kennedy's, this was a modest document, unlikely to have many consequences. The most important feature of Executive Order 10988 was, Moynihan noted to himself proudly, what it didn't include: the right to strike. Denying federal employees the right to strike seemed like a victory for moderation. How much could collective bargaining affect the government, Moynihan wondered, if its unions could not walk out? Moynihan did not expect what came next, or at least did not expect it to come so quickly. Even without a formal right to strike, federal workers used their new power and, unified, demanded and received higher raises than they might have in the past. The sheer number of federal employees—520,000 at the Post Office alone—meant that the raises made a significant dent in the federal budget. That in turn made balancing the budget tougher. Public-sector workers in states and towns, watching, determined to gain the same kinds of raises. The obscure executive order penned by a junior staff member increased political clout for organized labor. An electricians' union and a postal workers' union seemed different, but when they voted identically in a polling booth, they elected yet more pro-union lawmakers.

What else might Kennedy do? Observers looked for clues to his personality in everything he did. The president didn't favor Westerns generally, but reportedly Kennedy would watch James Garner in *Maverick*, a show about a cardsharp, a mischievous rogue who did the right thing at the end, just before riding off on his horse. The first episode of *Maverick* was "War of the Silver Kings," which happened to treat the topics of metal and money. But the favorite show in the Kennedy White House was a Broadway musical, *Camelot*, about a heavenly place where nothing could go wrong.

The year 1962 brought the test of the divided president for which markets and GE had waited. Steel unions threatened yet another strike. Kennedy jumped in to prevent a replay of the 1959 strike. The president recognized that company-union deals were highly political, and felt he could play the referee. He publicly warned that a deal including high wages and high prices for steel could foster inflation. In 1961, the Federal Reserve had gone on a bond buying spree, injecting money into the economy. Critics charged that the Fed, which was supposed to be independent, was instead in Kennedy's thrall. "Fed's Chastity in Peril," read a headline. If Kennedy managed to talk down wages and prices, inflation would be lower—or so his counselors taught. Then he would not have to tangle with the Fed.

At around the same time, following the lead of the Justice Department in the TVA case, the Federal Trade Commission was hinting at charging the steel companies with price fixing. At least one party, the *Wall Street Journal*, noted that this time, the hypocrisy was the U.S. government's. An interest rate was a price. A wage was a price. Price fixing, or a form of it, was what the president himself was doing when he locked companies

and unions in the Oval Office to cut a deal. What was the difference
between such deals and the deals GE salesmen had struck in their illegal meetings? "The Washington planners are making it abundantly clear
that they don't like prices that are too high, too low, or identical," the
Journal commented wryly. Perhaps, the paper suggested, as Eisenhower
had, all the big players in the economy had become too close. But few
voters thought much about the *Journal*'s point or the concerns of a former
president.

In January 1962, President Kennedy summoned the union and the
steelmakers to the table.[31] A low-wage, low-price agreement would mean,
in the economics Kennedy's advisors followed, less inflation. It would
also mean lower prices for a government whose Defense Department
purchased so much that was made of steel. Kennedy and Goldberg did
manage to get the union, the United Steelworkers, to agree to fewer or
smaller raises. The president took away the impression that Big Steel
would go along and hold the line on steel prices. But Roger Blough, chair
and chief executive at U.S. Steel, didn't want merely to preach about the
ratio of wages to productivity; he wanted to act on it. Past wage gains had
outpaced increases in productivity. Blough, whose name was pronounced
to rhyme with "now," needed higher prices to pay wages, and he needed
cash to buy equipment.[32] Unlike many other corporate leaders, Blough
sensed a threat in competition from abroad, and was not too shy to mention his concern. European productivity in his sector had been rising at
a rapid rate. To match that, U.S. Steel needed new machines. "You've got
to have a facility which can compete, cost-wise," said Blough. Cool as a
cucumber, Blough announced a hefty price increase in steel, $6 a ton.
Other big steelmakers followed U.S. Steel. Then Blough flew to Washington to inform the president of this fait accompli.

Kennedy went incandescent. "My father always told me that all businessmen were sons of bitches, but I never believed it until now," the
president told others. He had been double-crossed. Blough couldn't
agree. "If he was double-crossed, he must have double-crossed himself," Blough later said of Kennedy.[33] The White House men got on the
phone and berated the steel men. Kennedy blasted the industry's move

as "unjustifiable," and reminded the press that recently he had asked Americans to consider what they could do for their country. "I asked the steel companies," Kennedy said. "In the last twenty-four hours, we had their answer." Blough's name became a pejorative, like "Boulware." Kennedy sicced his brother on Big Steel. The attorney general set about investigating whether the steel companies were colluding on prices as GE had been. Via the Federal Bureau of Investigation, Kennedy even roused a reporter at 3 a.m. to collect details about the steel industry, on the suspicion that Bethlehem Steel and U.S. Steel were colluding.[34] The Pentagon announced it would reassign a big defense contract for armor plate to a group of smaller steel firms that had not gone along with the Blough increase. Suddenly fearful that they had pushed the president too far—what if Kennedy tried to nationalize steel, as Harry Truman had?— Blough and the other steelmakers gave in.

But the presidential rage at profit-takers was not quenched. Kennedy moved determinedly to address the very core of the dispute: whether big companies were responsible citizens on the New Frontier or mavericks, Lone Rangers. On May 20, 1962, Kennedy explicitly took up the theme of the American West to explain his outrage. This idea of pure capitalist Western independence, Kennedy argued at Madison Square Garden, was mostly myth, for the administration of Abe Lincoln himself gave home-steads to people who went West, and he used government property to establish land grant colleges. The president said he was weary of hearing from rich company heads or the American Medical Association what he should do. Kennedy didn't like being informed that introducing social benefits "saps our pioneer stock." Kennedy had only contempt for that ar-gument, and for the grandees who made it. Sounding much like Franklin Roosevelt, who had taken on the wealthy at the Garden in 1936, Kennedy sketched out his contempt for senescent capitalists who flew into Wash-ington on their own planes to lobby.

I remember one day being asked to step out into the hall, and up the corridor came four distinguished-looking men, with straw hats on and canes. They told me that they had just flown in from a

State in their private plane, and they wanted me to know that if we passed a bill providing for time and a half for service station attendants, who were then working about 55 to 60 hours of straight time, it would sap their self-reliance.[35]

Franklin Roosevelt's New Deal work, giant programs like Social Security, had seemed radical at the time. But now, Kennedy noted, such programs were accepted. The fact of the matter, Kennedy said, was that the United States was now rich enough for a round of new benefits. Kennedy, unlike the now isolated Ronald Reagan, appreciated the health care plans of British social democracy. The president told the others that by expanding federal funding of health care, the United States would only be doing what "most of the countries of Europe did years ago." Kennedy laid out the details for coverage of hospitalization costs for the elderly. Such coverage, Kennedy imagined, would be tough to get through Congress at the moment, but passage might be easier in the future. Who could speak against such a plan?

One quarter did speak against it: the stock market. The market was already down from its highs of the autumn before. Now share prices supplied evidence for Boulware's old theory that government intervention chilled markets. After the May 20 speech, the Dow Jones Industrial Average dropped in one week from 649 to 612, well below where it had stood at the beginning of 1960, when Kennedy had been preparing to run for office. The following Monday, a week after the speech, brought a plunge that was out of the experience of many of the market men: the Dow didn't drop; it tumbled, from 612 to 577. In all, the market on that day had lost about $21 billion in value, or about half of what President Kennedy had proposed to spend on his moon landing project.[36] Trading volume in this crash was so intense that the ticker, the wire reporting transactions, could not keep up, and by the end of the day was a full historic hour behind in its reporting. When the arithmetic was done the brokers and shareholders, and in fact the whole country, were confronted with the daunting fact: they had seen the greatest one-day drop since October 1929, when a crash had signaled the commencement of the Great Depression.

For a moment this "flash crash," as it came to be known, indeed brought back 1929. Tens of thousands of shareholders did not have enough collateral in their accounts to cover their losses. Brokerage houses therefore sent out tens of thousands of margin calls by telegram or phone, letting investors know they had to put more money in their accounts unless they wanted to see all their assets liquidated within hours. The margin call provoked further selling. Suddenly the Depression did seem closer, even in the era of the New Frontier. "The Night of Blue Monday 1962 was the grimmest evening of the New Frontier since the failure of the Bay of Pigs invasion," concluded the editors of *Time* magazine, referring to the failed invasion of Cuba in 1961. Kennedy ordered an emergency meeting of Treasury Secretary C. Douglas Dillon, the Federal Reserve chair William McChesney Martin, Council of Economic Advisers chair Walter Heller, and budget director David Bell. Perhaps the problem, some speculated, had been the margin rules for selling and buying stock. If shareholders were not allowed to buy "on margin," they wouldn't speculate without cash and there would be no margin calls.

Market players, however, preferred the conservative explanation: Kennedy's rich-baiting. "Eisenhower had to have a heart attack to throw the country into recession, but Kennedy just had to open his mouth to wipe out $70 billion in values of stocks in two months. As a small businessman, I resent being called an S.O.B. and resent the multimillionaire Kennedy family's seeming aversion to anyone else's making a few bucks," said a *Time* magazine reader from Los Angeles. "Businessmen regard Mr. Kennedy as being primarily responsible for the stock market slump," commented a writer in the *New York Times*.

Kennedy nonetheless prepared to take another swipe, this time aiming at the uncooperative market traders. His venue was the commencement at Yale University, the rival of his own college. Yale, and America, had a venerable past, the president conceded, a Harvard man's way of teasing. President William Howard Taft and Vice President John C. Calhoun were Yale alumni. Kennedy himself had praised Calhoun's statesmanship in his 1957 book, *Profiles in Courage*. But men like Taft and Calhoun weren't relevant now. "Every past generation has had to disenthrall itself from an inheritance of truisms and stereotypes." Today one myth to overcome, Kennedy said, was that "unfavorable turns of the speculative wheel"—stock market gyrations—reflected "a lack of confidence in the national administration." That was not entirely true, Kennedy said. What was key was to sustain the "necessary partnership of government with all the sectors of our society," not Lone Ranger behavior. Provoked, the Dow dropped again, from 595 to 581. Kennedy's worry now focused not merely on markets but also on gold: reserves, while holding steady, were still low, $16.4 billion at the end of June 1962, down from the $18 billion at the time of Kennedy's election. Seeking to find utility for the troublesome Roger Blough, Kennedy assigned the steel executive to a new commission to study the gold outflow. The gold problem was proving harder to manage than Kennedy had once imagined. And after the first meeting of this new group Treasury Secretary Dillon reported that no solution could be found.

IF THE crash of 1962 vindicated capitalism's purists, that vindication did not last long. For the markets did recover. The Dow Jones Industrial Average climbed, especially after the Cuban Missile Crisis that autumn, when Kennedy prevailed against real communists, the ones in Moscow. Within a year, the Dow would be bobbling around 720, back where it had been before Kennedy lambasted the plutocrats. Boulwarism was coming to seem even more beyond the point. Some of the big companies were swimming in cash. In the case of General Motors, for example, the amounts ran into the billions. Labor union officials and reporters joked that they'd heard a rumor on Wall Street that General Motors was saving up to buy the U.S. government.[37] Surely such wealthy companies could afford to do a president's bidding.

In 1962, life was even looking up at the besmirched General Electric. As executives noted with relief, GE was still getting fat government contracts after all. GE's managers were in the final stages of work on two Air Force deals worth more than $40 million, as well as a Navy contract for classified equipment. Sales for 1962 proved even higher than they had been in 1961 or 1960, a record $4.8 billion, with increases in all four categories of GE's business: consumer goods, industrial equipment, and defense and aerospace.

Even as it booked such numbers, GE absorbed the lesson: in times as good as these, it was treacherous for a company to wage ideological war. Capitalism, apparently, indeed needed no saving, not even at GE. Cordiner, under a shadow, was marching toward his retirement. The National Labor Relations Board was still looking into GE and Boulwarism, and seemed likely to outlaw Boulware's legacy strategy altogether. Sniffing blood now, Attorney General Kennedy pursued an investigation of the last Boulwarite standing: the actor Reagan. The Justice Department subpoenaed Reagan's tax returns, asking whether he, too, had illegally colluded, in his case the issue being negotiations between the Screen Actors Guild and MCA, the agent.[38]

Late spring 1962 brought the final blow to the Boulware crowd. GE fired Reagan and killed *GE Theater*. Reagan went home and told his son Michael, aged seventeen, that GE had cut him off because of those anti-Administration barbs. It was true that Reagan had put GE in a difficult spot with his attacks on the TVA and assaults on socialized medicine. But other factors also drove GE to cancel its sponsorship. There was something that was simply too outdated about *GE Theater* and its black-and-white Cold War moralizing. Fans in the new decade liked color. Fans liked action. *GE Theater* was slipping in the ratings. Sunday evening viewers were switching away from *GE Theater* to watch another series that now aired at the same time. That show was *Bonanza*.

2

Port Huron

JUNE 1962

Guns: 8.9% of GDP
Butter: 5% of GDP
Dow Jones Industrial Average: 581

We are people of this generation, bred in at least modest comfort, housed now in universities, looking uncomfortably to the world we inherit.
　　　　　—Port Huron Statement, 1962

The test of democratic trade unionism in a democratic society is its willingness to lead the fight for the welfare of the whole community.
　　　　　—Walter Reuther[1]

The same month when Ronald Reagan learned that his television show was history, a University of Michigan student named Sharon Jeffrey arranged a meeting to plan the future. The meeting of students and activists would take place at some lakeside cabins outside the town of Port Huron, Michigan. Alan Haber, the son of an Ann Arbor economics professor, would lead. Michigan undergraduates and recent alumni, as well as students from other campuses, would attend. So would Michael Harrington, the progressive writer who had published the bestseller on poverty, *The Other America.* Harrington was thirty-four, "the oldest young socialist" around, as he described himself.

Some of the students traveled from the South, where they had volunteered to help the disenfranchised blacks of Mississippi in voter registration drives. Tom Hayden, a former editor of the Michigan student newspaper, came. Hayden had spent his twenty-second birthday in a jail in Albany, Georgia, after trying to integrate the train station there. Casey Hayden, a graduate student from Austin, Texas, who had recently married Tom, had joined sit-ins to desegregate restaurants and worked with Ella Baker, already a famous civil rights leader. Casey had helped blacks build up a new group to halt discrimination, the Student Nonviolent Coordinating Committee. A few academics came to Port Huron, including a former president of Sarah Lawrence College, Harold Taylor. Taylor was known for mounting a bold petition to expel the red baiter Joseph McCarthy from the U.S. Senate.

Years later, many in the Port Huron crowd would write down what they remembered. The concerns the attendees took up varied from the particular to the universal. The students resented infantilizing university deans who enforced visiting hours in female-only dorms, for example. They could not understand how men aged nineteen could serve the military in places as far away as Thailand, yet could not vote. The students worried about the effect of automation upon the American soul. They were tired of the siege mentality of the Cold War that they had grown up with. And they wanted to see an end to segregation in the South. America, the students told one another as they gathered, was stuck in a kind of national stalemate. The country wasn't truly a democracy any longer.

Before departing office, President Eisenhower had worried about the great clique at the national economic table. The danger was that America would become a nation led by a "military-industrial complex." The students shared Ike's concern. A few interest groups ran the country: the automakers of Detroit; the Defense Department; and Big Labor, which they considered complicit, "too quiescent." Like Ike, or Lem Boulware, the students suspected the military-industrial complex as sinister. Monoliths shut individuals out, forcing them into "powerlessness." How could a new movement be started? Some thought the best starting point, as notes written in preparation for the meeting argued, was the university: "the only mainstream institution that is open to participation by individuals of nearly any viewpoint." But what drew them all to Port Huron was the same question that *Bonanza*, or GE, had asked: what to do with American prosperity? The students acknowledged that they themselves had been "bred in at least modest comfort," and were "housed now in universities." What could they do for those who didn't enjoy the same comfort? They were not yet sure.

As the students settled in at the cabins, they told one another they were the New Left, with the emphasis on "new." Most of the students did not stop to wonder why they were near the town of Port Huron, which happened to be the boyhood home of Thomas Edison, the place where the young genius had conducted his earliest experiments inside an old railroad car.[2] Most did not know who had built the cabins. The camp's name was Four Freedoms, after the four freedoms for Americans that Franklin Roosevelt had outlined late in his presidency. Even that did not matter to some of the attendees. To them the setting was a kind of accident. Any new "agenda for a generation," as they called what they hoped to write together, had to spring from youth itself, not from some relic of Franklin Roosevelt's time. Some of the students believed that meaningful change could come only through what they called participatory democracy, or what was now an alternative term for the same concept, community action. The way to ensure a democracy was to ensure "that the individual share in those social decisions determining the quality and direction of his life." There would be an end to the America where the promise of equality "rang hollow before the facts of Negro life in the South and the big cities of the North."[3] The group knew that to realize their dreams they had to be serious: "We seek to be public, responsible, and influential—not housed in garrets, lunatic, and ineffectual," read the language of a draft Alan Haber brought. To pursue their dreams some of the attendees had already created a new organization, which they called Students for a Democratic Society.

In 1956, the poet Allen Ginsberg had revolutionized his medium with a meterless, rambling poem called "Howl." Now, Tom Hayden hoped the group could compose something that would galvanize politics in the same way. "I craved for a political 'Howl'," he later recalled. Hayden, whose friendly, puckish face contrasted with his strong rhetoric, tried to build up the drama as they all worked on the agenda's language, still general. A New Left "must start controversy across the land," as a draft of the statement read. The New Left "must include liberals and socialists," the draft said, the socialists "for their sense of thoroughgoing reforms in the system." The meeting at the cabins outside Port Huron would itself be a trial run of participatory democracy, so any agenda had to be the result of independent, spontaneous work. Taking their places in the meeting area and talking, the young activists and students could almost feel the friendly emanations, inklings of the statement they would agree upon. The meeting felt spiritual. "Are there any prophets," Hayden asked the others in letters inviting them to the meeting, "who can make luminous the inner self that burns for understanding?"[4] At Port Huron, words and ideas flowed. As Hayden would later describe the mood by the lake: "it was like God was sending us a message."[5]

God—and Walter Reuther. For while the Port Huron retreat felt independent and spontaneous, it was not. The camp itself belonged to the United Auto Workers and its parent, the Congress of Industrial Organizations. Sharon Jeffrey's mother, Mildred, worked at the UAW, where she served in various jobs, including as director of the women's bureau at the union and Walter Reuther's political lieutenant.[6] The reason the students could use the camp at all was that Millie Jeffrey had called the executive director of the Michigan office of the CIO and arranged permission.[7] Sharon Jeffrey herself had spent time at Four Freedoms labor retreats as a child, teaching other children union songs like "Solidarity Forever." There was little spontaneity about the agenda, either. Months before, the UAW on the one hand and Haber, Hayden, and Harrington on the other had been planning a convention like this, and had also discussed the content of any report or manifesto that came out of such a meeting.[8] Hayden, the newspaper editor, had in fact arrived at the cabins with not just scribbled notes but a lengthy draft he and Haber had already circulated to some of the attendees. The United Auto Workers had long funded a group on the left called the League for Industrial Democracy. LID had a small student branch, the Student League for Industrial Democracy, or SLID. SDS was an update of SLID. Irving Bluestone, another of Reuther's advisors, thought Haber and his friends were just right for the work of political education—they were "our kind of youngsters," as Bluestone put it.[9] Victor Reuther, Walter's brother and also his aide, worked on outreach for Reuther as well. Victor liked the idea of a rebranded student group and arranged $10,000 in funding for Haber to take Students for a Democratic Society national. The students didn't merely hope for support for SDS;[10] they counted on it. "Whenever we were in trouble, and needed money or help from the elders," Hayden recalled much later, "the call would go out to Sharon's mother, who was invariably on the road with Walter Reuther."[11]

Nor was getting a student movement off the ground the only area where the mighty union leader was at work. In his day job Reuther could idle a mighty company with a snap of his fingers, as he did that month, when forty-two thousand men at sixteen assembly plants of the Ford Motor Company had walked off their jobs on United Auto Workers' orders. General Electric executives might appear to joust with James Carey alone, but they were really jousting with Reuther as well, for Reuther backed up Carey and had helped to create Carey's union. So tenacious was Reuther in tangling with companies that George Romney, the auto executive, referred to him as "the most dangerous man in Detroit." Senator Goldwater of Arizona, the "right to work" militant, went a step further, calling Reuther a "more dangerous menace than the Sputnik or anything Soviet Russia might do to America." All the union powerhouses, like George Meany of the AFL-CIO and Jimmy Hoffa of the Teamsters, enjoyed tremendous clout. American labor unions by the 1960s had grown mighty, and were, taken together, worth $3 billion, on a scale with General Electric and General Motors. Meany and Reuther, along with other union leaders, regularly attended Washington meetings with Labor Secretary Arthur Goldberg and Henry Ford II. Just recently JFK himself had dropped into one of those meetings.

But Reuther was livelier and earthier than the officious Meany, who actually claimed, with pride, that he had never walked a picket line. Reuther was also squarer than Hoffa, who was always under investigation. And Reuther enjoyed better access to the Kennedys, both the president and the attorney general. Indeed, Reuther would spend fifty minutes without

the other union men at the White House on Friday, June 15, the very day
the conference at Port Huron finished up its manifesto. Reuther's power
could also be felt everywhere in the new civil rights movement. He stood
side by side with Martin Luther King, who had written to him the year
before that "more than anyone else in America, you stand out as the shining symbol of democratic trade unionism."[12] It would be Reuther to whom
Attorney General Kennedy would turn in 1963 when Alabama courts set
an exorbitant bail for the release of King and fellow protesters from a Birmingham jail. Reuther and others would raise $160,000 and dispatch two
UAW staffers—Irving Bluestone and William Oliver—to Birmingham,
their midsections bulging with cash in money belts.[13] Reuther's support
for Martin Luther King was admired by whites and blacks alike. Reuther
was one of the few whites who would speak at a march on Washington
for civil rights the following year. The largely black crowd on the Mall
would applaud, though not everyone in the crowd recognized him. "Who
is that?" one member of the crowd asked another. "Don't you know him?"
came an answer. "That is the white Martin Luther King." It seemed that
in every new movement—or what promised to be a movement—Reuther
or his people were present financially and physically, obviously or behind the scenes. The Port Huron meeting was no exception. Millie Jeffrey
drove over to the FDR camp to check up on her daughter and the others.
Millie later recalled that she was "intimidated by all those brilliant university students."

Students did not intimidate Reuther. Unlike the tentative attendees
at Port Huron, Reuther knew what to do with prosperity. The thing to do
with American prosperity was to share it. Reuther did not believe you
could count on private individuals or private companies "to do the right
thing voluntarily," as the Boulware pamphlets exhorted them to. Reuther,
like President Kennedy, had scant time for Westerns on television. But
he did see prosperity as a vein of gold or silver in rock, or something to
be mined, and carefully, so that all Americans, even the poorest, could
work their way up to a living room with a television—hopefully, a color
set. Reuther believed in the U.S. political process. He believed America
could end inequality through socialism, or social democracy, if it was

safer to call it that. But what Reuther had long sought he did not yet have. That was an American president to lead his redistribution revolution.

————

EXACTLY HOW to bring socialism to America had been the question that drove the Reuther family even before Walter Reuther was born. The Reuthers came from Edigheim, a small town on the Rhine, and Valentine Reuther, Reuther's father, was still a boy when the family departed for the United States, refugees from the bayonets and bureaucracy of the Prussian empire. Grandfather Jacob always rose at 4:00 a.m. to read the Bible, but he rejected much of the church, and he was said to have commented that churches did "too much for God and not enough for men." Valentine himself settled in Wheeling, West Virginia, delivering beer by cart by day and organizing with the Ohio Valley Trades and Labor Assembly by night. When one of the founders of Roger Blough's U.S. Steel, Andrew Carnegie, sought to give the town of Wheeling a library, Valentine had been among those who had strenuously argued against accepting the gift, on the premise that acceptance would whitewash Carnegie's brutal treatment of steelworkers in the Homestead Strike in Pennsylvania. There ought to be, said an anti-Carnegie ally of Valentine's, "one place on this great green planet where Andrew Carnegie can't get a monument to his money." Valentine and the others prevailed over Carnegie, and the nation noted it: "Wheeling alone stands aloof and will have nothing of the great steelmaker's millions," commented an Ohio paper. Wheeling built its own library.

The family Americanized the pronunciation of the name to "ROO-ther." But whether in German or English, Father Valentine called himself a socialist, and preached against inequality and for worker power to his sons, Theodore, Walter, Victor, and Roy. Valentine even took young Walter to visit an earlier labor legend, Eugene Debs, while Debs sat in prison, accused of sedition during World War I. Walter himself dropped out of high school to work, and learned his first lesson about safety in the workplace when a four-hundred-pound die crushed his big toe.[14]

From their teens on, the Reuther brothers played union activism the way other men play a contact sport: physically, statistically, and as a team. They gravitated toward the new center of industrial might, Detroit. As a young man, Reuther worked the night shift, learning the details of a precise trade, tool and die work, so that during the day he could work his way through Dearborn High School and then Detroit City College. Reuther so impressed his boss at the Ford River Rouge Plant that the executive spoke to him, telling him one day he'd make it to company vice president. But Reuther had already determined he was on the worker side, the socialist side. Val Reuther was proud, writing to his son, "to me socialism is the star of hope that lights the way."[15] While still young, Walter was fired for organizing a rally for Norman Thomas of the Socialist Party. When, in 1931, Henry Ford sold the production equipment of the Model T to the Soviet Union, Walter and Victor went over to teach Russian workers how to run assembly lines. The two Reuthers worked on the Ford-built assembly line in Gorki, spending eighteen months in Russia but also inspecting Nazi Germany, Turkey, Iran, and China, and even making a bike tour of Japan.[16] Once back in the States, Reuther joined the United Auto Workers, working closely with socialists and, occasionally, communists.

The young man had, however, taken away something from Russia and Europe: it would be dangerous, heinous, for American socialists to replicate Soviet communism. Upon his return Reuther plunged into an effort to bring American unionism into the mainstream. His great heroes became Franklin and Eleanor Roosevelt, especially after President Roosevelt shepherded through and signed the Wagner Act, whose power Reuther knew even better than Lem Boulware. Roosevelt had also led others in establishing Social Security, the public American pension system. In fact, the father of one of the young men at Port Huron that June, Alan Haber, was William Haber, who had helped draft supplemental language for Social Security legislation at the end of the New Deal. With his allies Roosevelt had managed what later presidents hadn't, to shove the country toward socialism while sustaining democracy. The Four Freedoms in the camp name were ideals Roosevelt had enumerated: freedom of speech, freedom of worship, freedom from want, and freedom from fear.

The union crowd woke to young Walter Reuther's potential when in 1936, just after passage of the Wagner Act, Reuther scored his first big victory with automakers at the Kelsey-Hayes plant, winning 75 cents an hour for both men and women. Though at that point he was busy consolidating Local 174 in Detroit, Reuther also played a role in the unionization of General Motors in 1937, helping his brothers lead a GM sit-down strike in Flint. After the Reuther men had locked up GM and Chrysler, they turned to the big holdout, Ford. During one strike, as Walter Reuther waited on a public overpass for a group of women to bring pamphlets, a clutch of men in Ford's private army had beaten him and others to the ground and thrown him down a flight of stairs. The moment was still recalled as the Battle of the Overpass. Several years later, Reuther finally managed to force Ford to give in to unionization, too. His brothers joined him in his work, at the UAW and outside it. Back during the early struggles to unionize, Reuther had also won the attention of a Michigan undergraduate. "He was a pale and reflective man with red hair and a simple, direct quality of respectful attention to me," the playwright Arthur Miller later wrote. "I realized that he did not think of himself as controlling this incredible event but as best guiding and shaping an emotion that boiled up from below."

By the time World War II ended, the determined Reuther had become a figure on the national stage, leading at the growing United Auto Workers and at times, at the umbrella group, the Congress of Industrial Organizations. The U.S. Senate and House overrode President Truman's veto with a new labor law that required union leaders to sign a document confirming they were not communists. Reuther, realistic, saw that for the UAW to play a major role on the U.S. stage it must force out its communists. Reuther purged them—personally, at times. It was Reuther who severed the UAW's relationship with a left-wing publishing house, the Federated Press, where Betty Friedan, then a young radical, wrote.[17] After consolidating the UAW, Reuther had then proceeded to convert his hopeful worker alliance into national powerhouse. In 1948 a would-be assassin had shot through the window of the Reuther family bungalow in Detroit, hitting Walter in the back, stomach, and hand, where dozens of bones were broken. Soon afterward, Victor was shot, also through a window, and lost an eye and partial use of an arm. The hit men were never caught, but the Reuthers' courageous recovery only drew them more admiration. "Take my eye, or my arm or leg, but please fix up my tongue. I've got a living to make," Victor told the surgeons.

Discipline elevated Reuther above his peers. It took great patience to seal a union negotiation with a big company. Reuther was as focused in a session with a company rep as he was theatrical before a camera. One company executive told another that there were two kinds of Walter Reuther, the radical on the battlefront and the logical one in the negotiation room. Colleagues noted that Reuther carried a toothbrush to parleys with corporate executives. When the others took breaks to smoke, or even take a sip, Reuther refreshed by brushing his teeth.

Building a union that could beat the automakers at the negotiation table sounded like enough work, but Reuther also, early on, decided he wanted more. Reuther was falling in love with Northern Europe's social democracies, countries where democratic government supplied health care and good schools, and even, Reuther noticed, funded time at worker spas for workers to recover from strenuous labor. It seemed to Reuther there was no reason America could not replicate the Scandinavian model. In the 1940s, Lem Boulware spoke at a graduation at Harvard University, making an early case for Boulwarism. During the same years Reuther gave the commencement address at Howard University, the historically black college in Washington. At Howard, Reuther said that U.S. unions needed to deliver better housing and medical aid to all Americans, not just union members. Otherwise, unions weren't worth much. "The test of democratic trade unionism in a democratic society," Reuther said, "is its willingness to lead the fight for the welfare of the whole community."[18]

An American version of socialism was a big dream, but by the 1950s, there had seemed no reason Reuther could not dream it. Politicians liked the earnest redhead. Camping on a trip to Washington, Reuther had even slept on the couch in the apartment of Lyndon Johnson, then still a congressman on Capitol Hill. Reuther had wooed Harry Truman relentlessly, and the president returned the affection, even serenading Reuther on the piano. Reuther's brother Victor was so comfortable with Truman that he referred to him as "Harry." With every jump in the economy—and the 1950s economy did jump—Reuther gained more for his workers. After unionizing the Big Three, Reuther had pressured the automakers into granting factory men and women pensions, thereby, again almost personally, hauling the American worker into the middle class. Reuther admired the new, modern architecture of the social democracies. He hired the modernist architect Oscar Stonorov to design UAW headquarters, and Solidarity House was one of the first great modern buildings in Detroit when it was completed in 1951. Reuther believed in Detroit, and believed that copying European developments there would help to ensure that Motor City remained great. Reuther also worked on the plans for Lafayette Park, a modern development in downtown Detroit designed by the fashionable International School architect Ludwig Mies van der Rohe. Creating Lafayette Park had meant razing Paradise Valley, an area that was home to poorer blacks. But Lafayette Park, at least theoretically, also increased the supply of middle-class homes and thereby helped sustain the city's dwindling tax base. The FDR camp at Port Huron stood on a beautiful site. But they were just a halfway point. Reuther imagined larger retreat centers, not just for union leaders or international powwows, but also for American progressives and workers. The union retreats would not reek of wealth, as did Bal Harbour in Florida, where the AFL-CIO held its convention. They would be plain but elegant, good for families, not for fooling around. At his retreats, Americans could, as Reuther said, begin "putting the world together."

In the 1950s the Reuthers and their union were an obvious target for Senator Joseph McCarthy, who could have delved into the Reuthers' prewar time in Russia. But rather than hide from McCarthy, Walter chose to bluff and tangle with the bully, contending that McCarthy, too, had a communist connection—he had been supported by UAW communists. Whether this was true or not, McCarthy, intimidated, backed off. Another potential antagonist was Robert Kennedy, who was making a name for himself targeting unions for corruption. Kennedy made a crusade of his investigation of Jimmy Hoffa of the Teamsters, saying publicly that he would jump off the Capitol dome if Hoffa was not convicted. The same committee investigated the UAW, but far less strenuously. At one point Kennedy went out to Sheboygan, Wisconsin, to investigate the UAW's strike at Kohler, the plumbing supply company. He later described his impression of the union men at Kohler, so different from the Teamster men. "It was a striking contrast, one I noted again and again as I came in contact with the other UAW officials. These men wore simple clothes, not silk suits and hand-painted ties; sported no great globs of jewelry on their fingers or their shirts; there was no smell of the heavy perfume frequently wafted by the men around Hoffa."[19]

To keep the McCarthys and Kennedys off his case—and to live up to his father and his family—Reuther did make a point of leading a clean, alcohol-free, almost ascetic life. One year Reuther rejected, for example, a luxurious set of digs at an AFL-CIO convention. James Carey of the Electrical Workers promptly took the suite, joking that he would tell newsmen hunting for Reuther that Reuther was down the hall in the linen closet, "squeezing his own orange juice."[20] The Teamsters, who drove trucks, were natural partners of the United Auto Workers, who built the trucks. Yet the AFL-CIO had ejected the Teamsters recently for corruption, and Reuther took care to distinguish himself from the Teamsters. In the case of the Kennedy brothers, however, there was another reason Reuther escaped targeting. The Kennedy clan recognized in the Reuthers a mirror of themselves, another clan of brothers who together had achieved more than any one of them could have alone. The Kennedys' favor made another of Reuther's dreams seem feasible: he wanted to supplant the aging George Meany as head of the AFL-CIO.

While waiting, Reuther pursued yet better union packages and more health care for workers. Since the passage of the Taft-Hartley Act, Reuther and George Meany had been running a race against time: companies were indeed moving South and West. The union men saw, just as the executives at GE had seen, that one factor driving the moves was the Taft-Hartley provision that allowed state governments to make working with unions optional for employers. The provision was so controversial that Americans could not even agree on what to call it: the Republicans, proudly, called it "right to work," but union leaders simply referred to the provision as 14(b), after its location in the Taft-Hartley Act. The passage of the act had come over Truman's veto, and all union men regarded repeal of section 14(b), the "right to work" section, as the ne plus ultra of legislative goals. But in the meantime, Reuther and Meany had to prove to workers that unionland offered a better life. Reuther came up with his own reform: profit sharing with workers by corporations, an idea for which neither America's great companies nor his fellow union men could marshal enthusiasm. In 1961, George Romney of Detroit's fourth carmaker, the American Motors Corporation, gave Reuther his chance on profit sharing. Romney secretly invited Reuther to negotiations. Romney, after all a bishop of the Church of Jesus Christ of Latter-day Saints, felt he could deal only with a man with a moral basis. Romney had commenced the meeting sanctimoniously, by asking Reuther if he believed in God. Well, Reuther said, he was a Methodist. Romney had thereupon launched the talks, and the pair concluded a deal that included a pilot profit-sharing component, something unusual in the world of labor. Ten percent of AMC's pretax profit would be contributed to a "progress-sharing fund." The fund would increase benefits to hourly workers. But another 5 percent of pretax profit would go to the purchase of AMC stock in workers' names, though the voting rights would remain with the company trustees. Reuther's colleagues remained skeptical. Sharing profits was fine in good years, and the prospects for the next years did look good, but what would happen in bad years? The payout from profit sharing would be less, and to workers that would feel like a simple clawback by the company. To many company lawyers, as well, profit sharing looked like a lose-lose proposition. To keep it up, a company might have to cut wages. "Do you think George Romney will enforce that? When the time comes to cut into wages, will he do it?" asked a columnist in the *Washington Post*.[21] Nonetheless, Reuther could be proud. Now, at least, he had something to hold Romney to, if Romney did not honor the deal.

Throughout the 1950s and 1960s, Reuther often traveled overseas. His trips abroad served a business purpose: narrowing a pay differential between American and European industrial workers. Americans' pay was higher, and ate up a greater share of company budgets. When Arthur Goldberg, while still a lawyer for the steel union, described the wage packages American steelworkers got, the German steelworkers were "shocked and stunned," commented another U.S. official. A European plant resembled an American steel plant: "the plants look alike, they smell alike." But the Europeans got less pay.[22] Eventually, the Americans knew, foreign steelmakers could take advantage of those low labor costs to cut prices, and challenge American steel. The American union men went over to Europe, or Japan, to try to convince local workers to demand higher pay. Goldberg was pleased when Harry Douglass of Britain's steelworkers' unions came over to him at a conference and said, "By God, we've got to stiffen our demands."

In the case of Reuther, the trips also represented a chance to draw strength from his European models. If pay in Europe was less generous than American pay, government benefits there were greater. Reuther saw, to his satisfaction, that the heavy presence of government in European countries did not seem to slow growth—the German economy had more than doubled in size in the 1950s. Reuther nursed friendships with the leaders of the social democracies he admired. He always took care, as Meany did, to make it clear in America that while social democratic, or socialist, he, too, abhorred East Bloc communism. To paint socialism as communism was a tragedy. The mayor of West Berlin, a man of Reutheresque charisma himself, Willy Brandt, invited Reuther to speak at a May Day rally in 1959. Reuther's German was rusty, but he wanted to speak in the language of his listeners. To prepare, he brought home a tape player and a German grammar book, and practiced as assiduously as Ronald Reagan before the filming of *GE Theater*. For weeks, Reuther's daughter Elisabeth later recalled, Reuther recited grammar phrases to build up his confidence. "Lisa, if I speak in German, then thousands of people behind the Iron Curtain will hear an affirmation of their hope for freedom," Reuther told her. Some half a million Berliners, East and West, showed up to hear Reuther speak and call for reunification. Reuther and Brandt also traveled outside Berlin to speak to East Germans—this was before the 1961 construction of the Berlin Wall. Twenty thousand showed up there, too.[23] The Berlin event got international attention.[24]

John Kennedy was not the UAW's first choice for a presidential candidate in 1960. In fact, "all hell" had broken loose among the union men when Kennedy announced that his running mate was Lyndon Johnson.[25] Johnson was one of the men who had voted to override Harry Truman's veto of Taft-Hartley.[26] The labor fury was so palpable that John Connally, Johnson's protégé, and Robert Kennedy had even discussed whether organized labor would riot and break up the entire convention over the Johnson surprise. Reuther nonetheless in the fall of 1960 put enough force behind the Democratic campaign that he could claim he'd pulled Kennedy and Johnson over the line. After the election, Reuther planted one of his aides, Jack Conway, at the Housing and Home Finance Agency. There Conway was assigned the brief of realizing one of Reuther's goals, the elevation of the housing agencies into a formal cabinet-level federal housing department. Reuther was ready to move to John Kennedy's side in both the good and the bad. After the Bay of Pigs fiasco in 1961, Reuther's brother Victor tried to cheer Kennedy on by seeking the president's endorsement of a plan that traded American tractors to Castro in exchange for the prisoners Castro had taken. Reuther along with other unions joined Kennedy in a push for tax cuts. The worker, Reuther said, was "shortchanged."

Kennedy, however, suspected that Reuther could also be treacherous, doubtless in part because Reuther's rival, George Meany of the AFL-CIO, told the president so. Kennedy, astutely, divined that the union corruption battle was a sideshow. He had been awake during the fight over Taft-Hartley. The real issues were the laws that gave the unions their power. A clean union was more of a threat to corporations and the Boulwares than a corrupt one. Barry Goldwater took the same view, saying, "I would rather have Jimmy Hoffa stealing my money than have Walter Reuther stealing my freedom." Reuther was a powermonger, a rival for presidents. On meeting Kennedy, Nikita Khrushchev told him that "we hanged the likes of Reuther in Russia in 1917."

As 1962 arrived, Reuther, now fifty-four years old, found he was not any closer to making the United States the social democracy he sought, or even winning presidential support for key union crusades. Try as he might, Reuther would never be able to convince the wary Kennedys to make their number one issue repeal of Taft-Hartley, even though companies were gradually moving West to "right to work" states. Even William Haber, the old New Dealer, father of the Port Huron leader and still a progressive, acknowledged that the labor-heavy Michigan business climate was too hostile to attract business.[27] Thinking ahead of John Kennedy, the UAW chief built friendships with future potential leaders. In 1963, Reuther would take Senator Hubert Humphrey of Minnesota to attend a retreat of the prime ministers of Britain, Sweden, Denmark, and Norway—all labor party men or social democrats—at Harpsund, the country home of the Swedish premier, Tage Erlander. The idea of labor coming together somewhere green and quiet appealed deeply to Reuther. The UAW leader found that the commute from his home in rural Paint Creek outside Detroit to Solidarity House on Jefferson Avenue was well worth the effort. He could think about unions' future at Paint Creek. A disturbing sign for both Reuther and Meany was that union membership was not keeping up with population, a point that someone made sure was duly inserted into at least one draft of the Port Huron Statement. To get any 1960s president to back a social democratic platform, Reuther needed a larger coalition, which was one reason he hosted Martin Luther King in Detroit and helped fund the civil rights revolution, or handed out small checks to the idealistic students at Port Huron.

For the students to succeed, Reuther saw, they had to believe they were operating independently, not as tools of the old guard. New generations needed their own slogans and their own missions. "You can't keep talking to a guy about what happened in the Depression when he wasn't even born then," as they said. "This is the trouble with the American Labor Movement," Reuther would explain just a few years later. "It is becoming part of the Establishment." The elders behind the Port Huron meeting felt comfortable with figures like Michael Harrington, whom they recognized as both reliable and thoughtful. Harrington could be counted on to deplore communism. For reading, Harrington assigned students in the Young People's Socialist League *The God That Failed*, a collection of first-person essays by European and American writers who had personally worshipped communism until they witnessed the Communist Party, here or in Europe, in operation.[28] Harrington had followed the Soviet repression of the Hungarian uprising in 1956 closely, drawing about the same conclusions as Ronald Reagan. Norman Thomas, the head of America's Socialist Party, might reject the corrupt regime of South Vietnam, but he did not advocate teaming up with the Stalinist Ho Chi Minh in North Vietnam.

Harrington took a frank position on the shame of urban renewal, in which unions had been complicit. After World War II, the unions had joined the federal government in a great plan to rebuild the cities. The bulldozers obliterated the slums, but also evicted entire black communities like Paradise Valley. This was not "urban renewal," it was "Negro removal," as the writer James Baldwin said. Two-thirds of the families displaced by urban renewal were black.[29] Harrington argued that when the heavy equipment, whether Dwight Eisenhower's in the past or new presidents' in the 1960s, arrived at so-called slum neighborhoods, it crushed untold value. Old slums hadn't merely been slums; they had been starting points: "there was community, there was aspiration."[30] New communities did not come to life in the new projects. The projects were cages that became graveyards. Harrington noted that the new housing that supplanted old tenements created "a new type of slum," which isolated black families in ghettos. Harrington had seen the new type of slum firsthand in his hometown, St. Louis, where black families had been moved out of the Mill Creek areas to one of the largest of the urban renewal public housing projects in the country, Pruitt-Igoe.

Reuther welcomed such arguments. Maybe he could learn something from Harrington. Reuther always thought in terms of interest groups and social classes. *The Other America* portrayed poverty as a kind of festering wound that threatened the American organism, a new concept for the United States, if not for Europe or in biblical times. By focusing a spotlight on this poverty, Harrington had handed Reuther another potential constituency, the poor. "You know, we didn't know we were poor until we read your book," Martin Luther King once told Harrington later, only half joking.[31] What Reuther's crowd saw was that the outrage Harrington generated might even be converted into legislation. It wouldn't hurt if Big Labor got the credit. Some of the other young people heading to Port Huron also looked promising. Tom Hayden was aware of the danger of staking a position too far to the left. In a memo he wrote to the others before the meeting about the statement, Hayden pointed out that their group could render itself politically irrelevant. "We will be 'out' if we are explicitly socialists, or if we espouse any minority political views honestly," he noted. Like Reuther, Hayden understood that "we can be further 'in' if we are willing to call socialism liberalism."[32]

Other young people the UAW supported posed more of a risk to the union, and to Reuther's strategy. Activists could criticize the UAW or unionism among themselves, as in a family discussion. But they had to understand that in public you represented a larger group and picked your battles, sustaining solidarity on less important issues. Reuther's and Harrington's entire effort to move America toward socialism could be sabotaged by activists within days if the activists antagonized or divided the Democratic Party.

FROM THE moment the Port Huron conference kicked off, the split between those willing to work within the great American political machine and those who wanted to work outside that machine made itself felt. When Harrington and another labor movement socialist, Donald Slaiman, arrived at the conference, they could see that the SDS parvenus failed to appreciate the key distinction between communists on the one hand and socialists, or social democrats, on the other. One of the faces at Port Huron was that of a high schooler, Jim Hawley. Hawley was there to represent a communist-affiliated youth group, the Progressive Youth Organizing Committee. What was Hawley doing there? Harrington wanted to know. The presence of any possible communist affiliate, even a high schooler, at this conference represented a serious risk to the credibility of the SDS. Modern union law required that union members swear they were not communists. Harrington issued warnings—more like orders, the Michigan students thought. By the time the conference finally compromised and conceded Hawley might hold lowly "observer status," the attendees discovered their problem was academic. The young man was embarrassed into silence and departed early.[33]

More serious tensions emerged over the drafts of the Port Huron Statement, as they were starting to call it. The group allowed that placing "manifesto" in the title would be too provocative, evoking Karl Marx's *Communist Manifesto*. But they did not agree to expunge all hostile references to organized labor or to the anticommunist movement. Unwilling to pin the others down, Hayden played referee, emphasizing that both in the drafting and in its initial publication, the statement would be a "living document," one that could be rewritten, and might never be final the way a book was. To Harrington and the others, this living document idea seemed a dodge. At least one version of Hayden's draft contained some lines arguing that Russia "was becoming a conservative status quo nation state." Since "conservative" and "status quo" were terms radicals used to criticize the United States, the effect was to sound as though the students equated the Soviet Union with the United States, and that would be untenable. Another section of the material claimed that "unreasoning anticommunism has become a major social problem for those who want to construct a more democratic America." The "unreasoning anticommunism" line represented a slap at American union leaders, Harrington thought. Slaiman went berserk. "The American labor movement has won more for its members than any labor movement in the world," another attendee remembered Slaiman reminding the students. "You people have some nerve attacking the labor movement."[34] The students were good with "any left-wing Stalinoid kind of thing," Slaiman continued, but had no problem criticizing American unions. That was a fatal double standard. The attendee who later recalled the scene best, Hayden, remembered Slaiman yelling in rage in defense of the AFL-CIO head: "George Meany, don't you attack George Meany."

The others were shocked. Of course they wanted something different from old party lines. "We were very aware we were taking a position different from the LID's," Sharon Jeffrey remembered later, "and we were *very* willing to do it." The storm passed with promises of further edits, and Harrington departing early. The SDS group dutifully included anti-communist boilerplate: "as democrats we are in basic opposition to the communist system." In the end that language seemed a relatively small compromise to make for the moment, a compromise after all that in a "living document" could be changed. The great emphasis of the meeting, as it turned out, was on establishing a formal doctrine for what many Port Huron attendees were already doing in the South, helping poor people overcome disenfranchisement. The name of the doctrine was "participatory democracy." Staughton Lynd, a professor at Spelman, later reminded Casey Hayden of the moment when she had told him about that missing piece. "I shall never forget your coming back from Port Huron and telling us about the new words, 'participatory democracy,' very slowly and pronouncing each syllable separately as if you were eating a chocolate éclair."[35] Hayden and the others created little individual teams to craft different sections of the statement. The teams covered capitalism, automation, and statistics on wealth, which revealed a "have" and "have-not" gap at home. America should "abolish squalor," one draft said, and undertake a "full scale initiative for civil rights." What did not make it into the draft, in any iteration, was a thorough review of the role of religion, or the opportunity that the public-sector unions presented for union expansion, an omission that attendee Kim Moody later found significant. There was no section on progress for women. When the teams finished their formulations and agreed on the statement's language they went down to a dock at the lake and watched kids swimming. "We were elated," Sharon Jeffrey later recalled. "We were sure we had done something visionary and had done it collectively."

After the meeting, Hayden and Haber got into a car and drove to Washington in the hope of meeting the president. Talk about audacity of audacity, Hayden thought. Meetings with anyone important in Washington were the next best thing and demanded concessions, including sartorial concessions. Hayden dressed up, donning not only a shirt but a tie and a suit. The pair met with Senator Joseph Clark, an ally of the UAW and an advocate of the Nuclear Test Ban Treaty. As for the White House, it was "because of Mildred," Tom later recalled, that they got as far as Arthur Schlesinger Jr., and Hayden presented Schlesinger with their copy of the Port Huron Statement.[36] Schlesinger already had Michael Harrington's book. The pair talked their heads off, laying out the plan for Schlesinger, and left the statement on Schlesinger's desk. Tom and his wife, Casey, were now ready to work at a small office in New York, laboring at their Gestetner mimeographing copies of the Port Huron Statement. Casey would type the mailing list onto Addressograph stencils.[37] Each envelope they mailed would include a membership form for the SDS.[38] Kim Moody, from Baltimore, was going back to Johns Hopkins dead set on building up an SDS chapter there.

Harrington, however, was in no mood to let the others settle down to work. Shortly after Port Huron, the author went to SDS's formal parent group, LID. Without reviewing the changes to the document made at Port Huron, Harrington, officious now, lodged a formal complaint about the Port Huron Statement with LID's executive committee. The LID executive director then told her board that SDS had adopted "a policy statement which placed the blame for the cold war largely upon the U.S." A LID committee, a kind of Alice in Wonderland tribunal, haled Hayden and Haber in for a tough interrogation. Considering themselves the grownups in the room, the LID authorities then fired Haber and refused to put another activist, Steve Max, on the payroll, despite the fact that Max had been elected to the SDS staff at Port Huron. The trouble with Max was that he was a "red diaper baby," the son of the editor of the communist *Daily Worker*. At the time, SDS was still tiny, with only 750 or so members. LID was trying to strangle the baby in its cradle out of spite, Hayden thought. Harrington, himself a congenital rebel, had forgotten what a spur a display of authority can be to rebels. Haber did not retreat in humiliation. He returned to the SDS offices in New York and gleefully picked the locks. To the SDS crowd, their LID minders were not really parents, after all, but midwives, at best, to this new, independent movement. And what was LID? A group of older people whose own political impact had peaked in 1937. The LID leaders backed off.

Nonetheless, for Tom and Casey Hayden, the sting of Harrington's betrayal did not fade. After all, Harrington was just an older version of Hayden. Harrington and Hayden were similar—Catholic activists, Midwesterners with disarming smiles. Harrington had attended the Haydens' wedding. The men were drinking buddies. In September, Casey Hayden went to a meeting at the University of Ohio where Norman Thomas, the granddaddy of the Socialist Party, appeared.[39] Harrington was there. Casey acidly told Harrington that in its procedure LID had acted just like the communist officials it so abhorred. "Well I know now what it must have been like to be attacked by the Stalinists."[40] To Casey, Harrington was now just another member of the Establishment—the old left establishment. The fight would simmer on. Later, published, versions of the Port Huron Statement still contained the "unreasoning anticommunism" line, and claimed that to the average American, "'big labor' is a growing cancer." His friends' naïveté, the distraught Harrington told himself, merely had to do with their age. "The Christopher Columbus vision of themselves as the first to discover the truths of radicalism was," Harrington concluded, "alas, a most logical deduction from their own experience and our failures." They could not see the evil way Maoists or Stalinists took over idealistic organizations. Harrington knew enough to see a danger in the SDS group's arrogance—and not just danger for the unions. By defining its leftism "emotionally," he later wrote, and turning away from mainstream labor and liberalism, the SDS might indeed deprive itself of any meaningful impact. Economic redistribution took discipline. The SDS would surely then also undermine the causes of all traditional liberals—and traditional American socialists. Depressed at what he had wrought, Harrington left to spend 1963 in Europe.

There is little evidence that Reuther or others at the top of the UAW seriously scrutinized drafts of the Port Huron Statement. What the UAW cared about was the scale of the potential constituency that students represented. At the beginning of the 1960s, there had been more than 3.6 million Americans enrolled in institutions of higher education, up from 2.4 million at the beginning of the decade before.[41] That figure was set to double in the coming decade. Students would join workers in a great future UAW. And the UAW could also find much to like in the principles that had come out of Port Huron. The first advantage was the name, "Port Huron Statement," rather than "Manifesto," which felt too close to Karl Marx for political comfort. Many of the points actually read as though they had come out of Reuther's UAW propaganda mills, as they may have. In addition to emphasizing income inequality, the statement noted that "the wealthiest 1 percent of Americans own more than 80 percent of all personal shares of stock," a concentration of wealth that Reuther also railed against. The students noted the domination of the military in the economy—Reuther was concerned about that, too. The statement quoted Charles Erwin Wilson, who had headed GM, as noting that the country could be characterized as living in a "permanent war economy." Well, in a way, the country was.

Other goals listed in the statement aligned reassuringly with the UAW's and Reuther's own goals. Making the Declaration of Independence line "all men are created equal" true for black Americans everywhere—Reuther was pouring UAW money into that cause, despite some resistance from his more conservative membership. Giving the underrepresented Americans outlets "for the expression of personal grievance" and a voice in decisions about their lives—that was what social democrats sought. Making work "involve incentives worthier than money or survival"—Tage Erlander or Willy Brandt could have written that. On economics, the students also concluded that "the economy itself is of such social importance that its major resources and means of production should be open to democratic participation and subject to democratic social regulation." The automakers might read that last as a demand for nationalization. But "democratic participation" could also be construed as a version of the profit sharing that Reuther had elicited from Romney. The Port Huron Statement advanced the progress of American social democracy, in a fashion its history-averse conferees might not have intended. Working day and night the students had, whether consciously or not, covered three of Roosevelt's Four Freedoms: freedom of speech, freedom from want, freedom from fear. The only freedom they had missed was freedom of worship, and that, Hayden said, had happened because the man running the religion draft section, James Monsonis, had fallen asleep in the last moments of Port Huron, exhausted.

As Reuther, his brother, and Mildred Jeffrey watched, SDS students and their colleagues moved forward. Those students who had gone to the South to help out in voting drives found meaningful and even dangerous work. Casey Hayden joined the leader of the Student Nonviolent Coordinating Committee, whose acronym, SNCC, they all pronounced "snick." Together with Robert Parris Moses, a black teacher who had left the classroom to come down, Casey moved precincts of angry Southern sheriffs. Hayden, following it all, heard that in Greenwood, Mississippi, Bob Moses had been shot at in a car. Another activist took a bullet in the spine. A SNCC office burned to the ground. The UAW itself cast an occasional parental eye on Tom Hayden, who was settling in at Ann Arbor to make the University of Michigan SDS a model for other campuses, and saw to it that he received his funds. Hayden was brash, claiming to have thought up the Peace Corps himself and pitched it to Kennedy when Kennedy visited Michigan in the fall of 1960, but the reality was that Reuther himself had mooted such an idea with the presidential candidate while visiting him that summer at Hyannis Port. Still, they told one another again, brashness was sometimes necessary. Someone like Hayden could serve as the UAW's national messenger.

By fall Reuther and Mildred Jeffrey were giving much of their attention to other topics, for 1962 was a midterm year. In California, Richard Nixon, the former vice president, was losing support in a humiliating contest for governor with the popular incumbent, Democrat Pat Brown. Benefiting the Democrats was an ugly little fight within the Republican Party. Nixon, perhaps seeking to win the support of Californians put out by Joseph McCarthy, was calling for a ban of the controversial John Birch Society. Other Republicans were supporting the society's right to Roosevelt's first freedom, the freedom of speech. Another divide involved Ronald Reagan, the Republican statewide campaign chairman. California Republican Howard Jarvis assailed colleagues for allowing Reagan to get such a post, as Reagan had so recently been a Democrat. The more right-wing the candidate, however, the better for Reuther: a John

Birch–type Republican was an optimal opponent for a broad Democratic Party. In 1963, scanning the horizon for national candidates in the next presidential race, Reuther disingenuously would tell the press he liked Goldwater of Arizona, unions' great enemy. "I would be pleased if the point of view of Goldwater became the guiding policy of the Republican Party," Reuther said. Goldwater would be far easier than some others for Reuther's new coalition to beat.

Reuther's efforts to gain advances for labor from either Lansing or Washington, however, were not succeeding as well as he would like. His leverage with Romney of American Motors on profit sharing was now in doubt, for Romney had decided to leave AMC and run for governor of Michigan—as a Republican. That meant Romney was running against the Democratic allies of the UAW. To emphasize solidarity, Reuther joined the Democratic governor, John Swainson, on the stage at the annual Labor Day rally. Romney was not permitted to speak. Nonetheless, Romney persevered, bragging about his past dealings with Reuther. Romney even turned the AMC-UAW agreement Reuther and he had concluded the previous year—the one with the profit sharing—into evidence that he could out-union the Democrats. Irritatingly, Romney quoted Reuther, who had called the profit-sharing agreement "perhaps the most significant and the most historic collective bargaining agreement that has ever been written in the United States." Romney won.

Early in 1963, Reuther tangled again with Romney. Reuther struggled to block the governor from signing a bill that would limit the pool of strikers who received jobless pay in a given strike. On the national scene, Kennedy was moving Goldberg over to the Supreme Court and replacing him as labor secretary with Willard Wirtz, who, Reuther politely assured Kennedy, was "a good choice." Wirtz, however, was not as interested in labor-management disputes as Goldberg, who lived that fight. As 1963 progressed, Reuther found that President Kennedy kept more distance than he had in the Goldberg days. Kennedy sometimes seemed to favor George Meany. The president just wasn't enthusiastic enough about Reuther's programs. Reuther was coming to realize that the New Frontier would never dramatically deepen the achievements of the New Deal. "I met with Walter Reuther and Hubert Humphrey," Arthur Schlesinger at the White House wrote in his diary that spring. Humphrey and Reuther spoke like New Dealers. But, Schlesinger went on, the truth was that "the New Frontier has a deep mistrust of what it regards as the pat liberal sentimentalities and clichés of the Thirties." The difference was one of commitment. The New Dealers wanted "to do something because it is just and right," whereas New Frontier men were "technocrats who want to do something because it is rational and necessary. The New Frontier lacks the evangelic impulse," Schlesinger noted, "in part no doubt because there is no audience for it."[42] Even UAW members did not care about Reuther's big picture. The old belligerent union men who would once have insisted that their congressman force repeal of Taft-Hartley were now more concerned with pay packages.

Some of the UAW's students were meantime stalling. Hayden initially set up in Ann Arbor, the goal being to take SDS national. But he found Ann Arbor depressing, for he could not seem to move SDS from talk to action—in part because the goals in Michigan were far less compelling than those in the South. Hayden just couldn't figure out what the new institution he led was supposed to do. "SDS remained mostly an intense subculture of discussion," Hayden later recalled. The others grew frustrated with Hayden. "He didn't understand economics," Sharon Jeffrey later observed.[43] His wife, Casey, had taken secretarial jobs in Ann Arbor to help fund her household. Accustomed to the genuine work and actual danger of the South, she grew impatient with SDS seminars. Like Harrington, she began to see folly in the SDS effort to write philosophy from scratch. One night Casey Hayden walked out of another of those freewheeling seminars, saying to the assembled group (men), "I seriously believe y'all are discussing bullshit." Casey left Ann Arbor and went South. The SDS discussions were nothing like the action being taken by courageous blacks in Alabama or Mississippi.

Once again, the UAW rode to the rescue. If SDS itself was not sure what SDS should do, Reuther and his allies in the labor movement were. SDS should organize a poor people's movement in the cities, perhaps a union to represent the unemployed, a SNCC of the North for whites and blacks. Organized, that movement could demand jobs, schools, and homes. Reuther and other unions, including the Packinghouse Workers, the Shoemakers, and the union of Operating Engineers, would fund staff for more than a dozen on-the-ground offices in different locations. Irving Bluestone of the UAW and Ralph Helstein of the Packinghouse Workers would write letters to friends and colleagues in the communities to make the initial contact with locals for SDS. Though the economy was booming, there were always poor corners, in the countryside or the towns. The point men and point women for this new network would move in and take their place in time to be ready when the real trouble of a recession hit. This project of unionizing the poor represented more than pro forma outreach for Reuther and the others—it was where their hearts lay, and where they placed their children. Toni Helstein, the daughter of Ralph Helstein; and Leslie Woodcock, the daughter of Reuther's deputy Leonard Woodcock at the UAW, were dispatched to man one pilot, in the Uptown neighborhood of Chicago.[44] Sharon Jeffrey would head to Cleveland to organize welfare mothers to demand school lunches and higher welfare benefits. Tom Hayden would try to build an interracial movement of the poor in Newark. The inspiration for many of the young people was Saul Alinsky of Chicago, who believed in awakening poor people in the cities not only to the franchise but to their own rage. This Northern participatory democracy program was now given a formal name: the Economic Research and Action Project, ERAP, which the workers pronounced "ee-RAP."[45] Maybe the North was more like the South than Americans knew.

Or maybe not. In April 1963, Martin Luther King reminded them all of the North-South contrast when he was jailed in Birmingham, then released, then jailed again. If Jack Kennedy was keeping his distance, his brother the attorney general was not. It was Robert Kennedy who contacted Reuther about putting up bail. "Why do you call me?" Reuther asked. "Because we don't know anyone else that we can call," Kennedy replied.[46] Civil rights now seemed the obvious way to lure the president himself closer, and Reuther began advertising a new coalition, which he and others were now calling the Coalition of Conscience. To catch Kennedy's eye, Reuther and the others worked with King to build up plans

for a genuine showstopper, an August march on Washington. The entire march, "For Freedom and Jobs," would be organized by a man who
worked for the AFL-CIO. That was Bayard Rustin, whom Tom Hayden
and others knew from their chats at Al Haber's apartment. Rustin had
just left Martin Luther King's group, the Southern Christian Leadership
Conference, and in the case of the march, proved a marvelous organizer.
One of Rustin's aides was Eleanor Holmes, a Yale graduate student who
would later become a congresswoman. "There had been ten years of
movement in the South, but there were no remedies in the South," she
later recalled. "The only remedy was in Washington." An old Reuther
ally would speak: A. Philip Randolph, the man who had organized the
first great black union, the Brotherhood of Sleeping Car Porters. So would
Martin Luther King. It was because of Randolph and Reuther, the union
men, that the march would be subtitled "For Jobs and Freedom," and not
merely "For Freedom."

The president, the men learned, didn't particularly like the idea of the
event—why not march after the presidential election? He himself argued
that new civil rights legislation was an absolute necessity. But men from
Kennedy's own party, Southern Democrats in the Senate, were filibustering his civil rights bill already, and a disruptive march on Washington
would only strengthen their argument that the new law would give black
Americans license to protest yet more. More useful and inclusive at this
point, Kennedy told others, might be general statements from America's
leaders about freedom. In late June, Kennedy flew into divided Berlin
without Reuther, giving a ride on Air Force One to Reuther's competitor, George Meany. Kennedy appeared before hundreds of thousands at
Berlin's Rathaus Schöneberg, the provisional town hall since the Berlin
Wall went up in 1961. Kennedy did not try to pull a Reuther and speak
paragraphs in German, but he did drop what became a famous line: "Ich
bin ein Berliner"—"I am a Berliner." The president also included a line
that referred to the American civil rights struggle, along with Soviet communism: "When one man is enslaved, all are not free."

Reuther and King determined that Kennedy's reluctance would not
stop them from bidding for presidential attention, and they planned

rallies building up the excitement for the great August march on Washington. Days before Kennedy spoke in Berlin the pair upstaged him with a march for civil rights in Detroit. City leaders and Reuther called this march the Walk to Freedom, a chance for Detroit to speak out about racial segregation in the South and discrimination in the urban North. The date was significant because it marked the anniversary of a Detroit race riot during World War II in which more than two dozen had been killed. Working with local black leaders, Mayor Jerome Cavanagh, Reuther, and King were together able to turn out a crowd of 125,000. King delivered an impassioned speech that prefigured his speech in Washington. "I have a dream this afternoon that one day my four little children . . . will be judged on the basis of the content of their character, not the color of their skin." The Gordy label, a division of Motown, recorded King's speech for a single.

Well prepared after its Detroit dress rehearsal, members of Reuther's coalition spent the summer readying themselves for the Washington march. Some Port Huron alumni were helping.[47] In Baltimore, Kim Moody's new SDS organized buses. Moody's group's special initiative was to ensure that buses were also provided for the unemployed. At Washington more than 200,000 people materialized—some observers later claimed 300,000. On the agenda Reuther enjoyed pride of place, coming after John Lewis, the new head of the Student Nonviolent Coordinating Committee; and before James Farmer, the national director of the Congress on Racial Equality. Reuther made his most expansive bid: "I am here today with you because with you I share the view that the struggle for civil rights and for equal opportunity is not the struggle of Negro Americans but the struggle for every American." Demand freedom now, Reuther told the crowd. Demand "fair employment within the framework of full employment." You couldn't have freedom in Berlin if you didn't have freedom in Birmingham—Reuther was echoing over the crowd what Kennedy had said in Berlin. Aside from Rabbi Uri Miller, a Jewish leader, Reuther was the only white man on the schedule.

Reuther's ultimate prey that summer day in 1963 was the still elusive President Kennedy, and Reuther and other march leaders headed over to the White House after the march. Reuther and King were pleased because the day had run so smoothly. They and Bayard Rustin and the hundreds of thousands of people who had come to Washington had exercised the self-discipline of worthy citizens. "Everything was perfect, just perfect," Reuther praised Martin Luther King as they trailed in, for Reuther, after all, still had more experience with big rallies than King. But the guests, once again, did not find the New Frontier president especially receptive to instant change. The White House in fact expressed its alarm at a SNCC notice charging that the Kennedy Administration was moving too slowly on civil rights. Kennedy complimented King on his speech, and King politely asked if Kennedy had heard Reuther. "Plenty of times," the president said, a comment that had to be recognized as further evidence that Kennedy was tiring of Reuther.[48]

That fall of 1963, Reuther continued to make little headway in Washington. He had long nursed the idea of creating a federal department of housing, and while Kennedy assented, the president never managed to get Congress to go along. Robert Weaver, a black housing official expected to be the head of the new agency, was twiddling his thumbs. The tax cut Kennedy and Reuther had pushed hard for remained mired in committee on Capitol Hill, and Reuther complained loudly, arguing that the longest strike in America now was not a worker strike but a "congressional strike." The big initiative on poverty that Harrington sought wasn't going anywhere, though the Kennedy Administration did talk about poverty problems piecemeal. Eunice Kennedy Shriver, a personality every bit as powerful as her brothers, had pushed for an initiative to study juvenile delinquency and poverty, and that research was going strong. An informal task force with economic advisors from various departments in Washington was meeting to discuss a "Widening Participation in Prosperity" plan, but these were only meetings. In November, Walter Heller, the president's economic advisor, spoke with the president about some kind of anti-poverty program. The president allowed that it would probably happen in 1964, and in tones that scarcely suggested a revolution. Reuther meanwhile suffered setbacks close to home. There was bitter news from American Motors, where Reuther's old opponents, the profit-sharing skeptics, found vindication. With Romney in the governor's mansion, Romney's successors at AMC reduced the contributions to the profit-sharing kitty, even though AMC profits were up and the directors boosted the quarterly dividend to shareholders. The economic pie at AMC was growing, but, the union men thought, the growth was not being shared. Reuther had long hoped to supplant George Meany as head of the AFL-CIO. On November 20, though, the AFL-CIO reelected the sixty-eight-year-old Meany to a fifth term. Reuther began to prepare for his next chance to widen his influence, the 1964 presidential election. He called for a law that would doubtless be popular, a $2 minimum wage. What else could he do?

Two days later, Harrington and his wife, Stephanie, were dining in a restaurant in Milan. One of their recent stops, Poland, had reinforced Michael's convictions about the evils of Eastern communism. Harrington had also attended the Eighth Congress of the Socialist International in Amsterdam and met with Reuther's friends Harold Wilson of Britain and Willy Brandt of Germany.[49] But that night, a waiter paused by their table to tell them some shocking news: "It's just terrible, they have just killed Kennedy." Disbelieving, the Harringtons raced to a telex to read the wires. It was November 22, and Kennedy was gone. The Texas governor, John Connally, had been shot as well. Harrington reflected on Kennedy and his interest in the progressives. Vice President Johnson was sworn in as U.S. president. Walking by a Communist Party office the following day, the Harringtons saw a large poster the Italian communists had hung, mourning Kennedy's death. Despite his deficiencies, Harrington saw, "Kennedy had opened many windows." Perhaps Johnson would close them.

The New York Stock Exchange closed. Not only Reuther, but leaders from all across the world, including the Social Democrat Olof Palme of Sweden and Harold Wilson of the Labor Party in Britain, raced to Washington to attend services for the assassinated statesman. The small group of social democrats hoped against hope that the suspicious Johnson, the new leader of the free world, would pick up where Kennedy had stopped. Walter's immediate reaction was to draft a statement of policy, his brother

Victor later recalled.[50] Would Johnson even read such a statement? Or even heed progressives, except insofar as to collect their support for the Democratic Party? The men in the room at the Statler Hilton on Sixteenth Street where the UAW met had little clue.

Years later scholars would find the first evidence of the political agenda of the new president in a single document: the White House appointment book. On Saturday, November 23, the day after Kennedy's death, the new president held meetings and telephoned all day. The incoming calls were largely ones of condolence. At 3:22 p.m., for example, Romney of Michigan called the White House to convey his sympathy.[51] But for a man who had been vice president just a day before, a man whose president had been shot down, Johnson also paid great attention to policy and coalition building. At 3:42 p.m. Johnson met with Sargent Shriver, the director of the Peace Corps and the president's mourning brother-in-law; and Bill Moyers, Shriver's associate director of public affairs at the Peace Corps. After that, at 3:52, Johnson met with Arthur Goldberg, now a Supreme Court justice. At 4:15 Johnson placed a call to Pittsburgh, to David McDonald of the United Steelworkers, Roger Blough's old antagonist.[52] Johnson asked McDonald to stand by, as he might be asked for help.

At 4:20 p.m. Johnson called Reuther. "I'll need your friendship more than I ever did in my life," Johnson said.[53] Reuther promised "every possible help I can offer." A lawyer named Joseph Rauh was in Reuther's suite at the Statler Hilton at the time. Rauh remembered the moment. "Everybody was pretty set up about the fact that the new president wanted advice from Walter and wanted his help. We all thought that was great." Even on that somber weekend, Rauh and the crowd in the suite had to smile. For soon enough, it became clear that Johnson wanted more than one call to Reuther's crowd. At some point a bodyguard came in and said, as Rauh remembered it, "Joe, the White House operator wants to know if you can get the phone numbers of David Dubinsky, I. W. Abel, Dave McDonald"—all union leaders, and some on the more belligerent end of the spectrum.[54] Rauh later recalled their surprise. The new president was supposed to be a conservative. Yet "Johnson was contacting liberal labor people all over the place."

There was more. Though Reuther didn't know it yet, at 7:41 p.m. the inexhaustible Johnson greeted Walter Heller, the economic advisor who had looked into the idea of an anti-poverty plan. It turned out that Johnson was far more interested in poverty than Kennedy had been. "That's my kind of program," Johnson told Heller. "Move full speed ahead." What Johnson was thinking, even in those early hours, was that he could at this moment, in part because of the tragic circumstances, pursue larger aims than Kennedy did. "Labor's White House Stock Rises" read a headline just a few days after Kennedy's assassination.[55] On the following Monday, November 25, Johnson spoke with Martin Luther King by phone, and told King that he would try to show "how worthy I'm going to be of all our hopes." King elegantly laid out a plan and promised to pay tribute to the late president by supporting Kennedy's "great progressive polices." "Well I'm going to support them all, and you can count on that," LBJ said. In the following days, Johnson began to make good on his word, one by one telling constituents, cabinet members, and lawmakers that he would deliver. In early December, for example, Kermit Gordon, the director of Johnson's bureau of the budget, informed the president that big programs for housing were expiring. Would there be a new law? Johnson said others thought they ought to get "some urban renewal and some public housing."[56] Johnson didn't fail to get to Republicans, especially the Senate minority leader, Everett Dirksen. Dirksen represented Illinois, the Land of Lincoln, and would help him prevail over Southern Democrats and push through unfinished civil rights legislation. At 9:00 p.m. on January 1, 1964—Johnson placed many such calls at night—the president phoned Dirksen to wish him a happy New Year. Within a quarter hour, Johnson was on the phone to another key player, the Senate majority leader, Mike Mansfield of Montana, telling Mansfield that he was "mighty proud of your friendship."

When Harrington returned to the United States that winter, he discovered his own ideas for a drive to halt poverty—the abstract noun, "poverty," was a meme now—were also moving full speed ahead. Word was that Johnson would announce a major federal program for the poor shortly. All the evidence suggested that Johnson might even do more than a poverty initiative, and that he was even willing to understand and support Reuther's and the students' idea for a banner of great social change. In January, Johnson did more than any of them had imagined. The president declared an "unconditional war on poverty" in his State of the Union address. He promised he would fight not merely to address the symptoms of poverty, but to "to cure it." Johnson recommended more federal support for education, health, and retraining than any president had in American history, plans so expansive they rang European to listeners' ears.

The price of such friendship to Reuther's causes, Reuther knew all too well, would be electoral support. Later that January, Johnson called Reuther, who was in Michigan. The president was of course already thinking about November. "Now listen Walter . . . I don't want you to raise any hell until after I get elected . . . I don't mind how many times you march after November but don't do it in September." Reuther was silent on that point, but did assure Johnson that in a recent speech he'd "agreed completely with your economic policy on wages." As they chatted, the two agreed on one point: car prices. If the Big Three cut car prices, there would be less competition from Europe. Or maybe it was time to shrink autos some more. Johnson offered the government might buy a smaller car. The call between the president and the union leader concluded with Johnson asking Reuther to vet a man for him, someone who had been recommended for a high position at the newly unionized Post Office.

In the same period Johnson also asked Richard Goodwin, a progressive who had been working for Robert Kennedy, to move over to the West Wing as a presidential aide for domestic affairs. "Those Harvards think that a politician from Texas doesn't care about Negroes," Johnson said to Goodwin, accurately enough.[57] Johnson would show them. Goodwin sensed Johnson's strong will: not only intellectually, but also viscerally, Johnson wouldn't be content with extending Kennedy's agenda.

At his ranch in Texas, the president astounded the young Goodwin by inviting him and Bill Moyers of the Peace Corps into his pool for a skinny dip. The Skinny Dip Session, despite its disconcerting circumstances, marked another turning point in history. For it was here, paddling around the kidney-shaped pool in Johnson City with the chief executive, that

Goodwin and Moyers heard Johnson say that he wanted not merely to carry on the Kennedy mission, but to "create a Johnson program, different in tone, fighting and aggressive."

How aggressive Reuther and the others could not know at the time. On February 1 the president was ready to name Sargent Shriver to coordinate his new program on poverty, even if that office didn't exist yet or have a strategic plan. LBJ phoned Shriver to let him know he would announce Shriver's new job in a press conference. Shriver hemmed and hawed— "You announce somebody . . . and they don't know what the hell they are doing . . . then you're in a hell of a hole." Well, "you've got to do it," Johnson retorted, in effect ordering Kennedy's brother-in-law to take an undefined job.

Except when he was angry, as in 1962, with the steel men, Kennedy led by indirection. Johnson, they all were learning, operated in your face. Johnson pointed out to Shriver that he had already made it clear he was going to devote resources to what everyone was now calling the War on Poverty. So why was Shriver hesitating? "You've got the authority, you've got the power, you've got the money," Johnson warned. "Now, you may not have the glands." Shriver was incredulous at hearing a phrase like that from his chief executive. "The *glands*?" LBJ: "Yeah."[58] By mid-February, Sargent Shriver, now willy-nilly Mr. Poverty, was inviting Harrington to Washington to help him consider how the new administration might put muscle into its poverty war.

The meeting was Harrington's moment. Socialism, his ideal, might be too grand and controversial for even what was emerging as an administration more progressive than Kennedy's. The writer spoke about Appalachia, the basis for his book; about poverty in the South; about poverty in New York; about health care; about the civil rights movement. Harrington had great authority on civil rights; he had worked with Bayard Rustin, who organized the March on Washington the prior summer. Mayor Robert Wagner of New York was piling on with his own plan for a municipal war on poverty, but Wagner's program had to be aggressive. Harrington offered advice that related to his hometown, St. Louis, and the big housing project there, Pruitt-Igoe. That old failure, urban renewal, Harrington said, could work if you trained the slum dwellers to clear the properties themselves and build integrated, classless housing projects. In discussion with Harrington and Paul Jacobs, a fellow labor activist with whom Harrington had coedited a book, Shriver mentioned the amount Johnson was thinking about spending on poverty: somewhere between a quarter of a billion dollars and a billion. Shriver, after all, had some experience in Washington, and had labored mightily in the past two years to build up a small endeavor, the Peace Corps. Just weeks before, in another lifetime, he had fought like a lion to get Congress to vote to approve a budget of $102 million for the Peace Corps. Now poverty spending could be ten times that. Harrington countered that even a billion dollars was "nickels and dimes." A billion was in fact just a bit higher than the $800 million President John Kennedy and Congress had allocated to Americans of all social classes when they extended benefits for Social Security in 1961.[59] Shriver would have none of it. "I don't know about you, but this is the first time I've spent a billion dollars."

Observers could wonder if Harrington, not Shriver, was the better reader of the political mood. In Michigan that winter, joblessness stood at 3.5 percent, the lowest rate since 1955. Experts had long said that two good automobile years could not occur in a row, yet they did, a Motor City bonanza. In Michigan, relatively few seemed to mind that George Romney, who had campaigned on the theme of restraint and the success of his downsized Rambler, had as governor put through the largest budget in the history of the state of Michigan.[60] Detroit, too, had deep pockets, deep enough to model dramatic social change for the rest of the country.

The Detroit mood spilled over into the rest of the country, where the enthusiasm for expansion of new programs kept growing. Onto the table came other plans for helping the poor. Shriver's Peace Corps had been a great success, "wonderful," as Arthur Schlesinger put it, and especially good at transforming Venezuelans' vision of America.[61] Now the success would be replicated with a domestic social service plan whereby young people would spread across the country into cities to help enable local communities to act for themselves. There would be what was soon known as Head Start, school for three- and four-year-olds to prepare for kindergarten. Adam Yarmolinsky, one of Shriver's aides, was drawing up a plan to open one-stop social service centers for the poor in cities. Those centers would offer a new service: legal advice and representation funded by Washington for the poor.

Through the spring, Johnson kept increasing his own obligations. The president promised Shriver he would stick to Shriver and the poverty project forever, "Death do us part." Johnson told lawmakers he would deliver a major tax cut, legislation Kennedy had sought but failed to steer through. The tax cut would stimulate the economy. The Dow Jones Industrial Average had already nosed past 800, up by 35 percent since June 1962. How much faster could an economic heart beat? Yet Johnson pressed on: "It would be self-defeating," the president told others, working the logic he'd heard so often, "to cancel the stimulus of tax reduction by tightening money." From ignoring Harrington, the *New York Times* went to quoting him as a prophet. The paper respectfully quoted Harrington's suggestion that the nation needed "a great national upsurge" in public opinion for the new war against poverty to take place.[62]

On the Hill, some lawmakers were alarmed at the alacrity with which Johnson wanted to drive so many other laws through Congress. To do all Johnson wanted, Senate minority leader Dirksen bleated to the press, "it would take fiscal legerdemain." Someone at the White House "made a mistake in arithmetic," said Senator Hugh Scott, a Republican from Pennsylvania. "We suffered through the New Deal and the Fair Deal," commented Senator Thruston B. Morton of Kentucky, "and now we've got the Fast Deal." But these men were all Republicans, and Democrats held both houses of Congress.

Many of the students who had been at Port Huron hesitated to support Johnson, whose fellow Democrats guarded the polling booths to keep blacks out in the South. But for men like Reuther or Harrington, "fast" couldn't come fast enough. During the halting Eisenhower and Kennedy years, they had longed for a president who dared to try himself to "put the world together," in Reuther's phrase, a president who would take America to social democracy, who would complete Franklin Roosevelt's revolution. Now they had one.

GREAT

SOCIETY

3

Great Society

MAY 1964

Guns: 8.3% of GDP
Butter: 4.7% of GDP
Dow Jones Industrial Average: 820

In May 1964, administrators in Ann Arbor laid out academic regalia for a commencement speaker. The hat size for the mortarboard was a standard man's: seven and three-eighths. The breadth of the gown was to suit a man whose chest spanned forty-one inches, average again. But the gown was unusually long, for the speaker stood six foot three and a half. Lyndon Johnson was coming to the University of Michigan.[1]

When Air Force One took off from Andrews Air Force Base at 9:10 a.m. on Friday, May 22, the plane bore not only Michigan's 1964 commencement speaker, the president, but both Michigan senators and members of the state's congressional delegation. An equally impressive crowd of dignitaries awaited the presidential party at the Detroit airport: Henry Ford II; Governor George Romney; Detroit mayor Jerome Cavanagh; Detroit newspaper editors; the Reverend James Wadsworth of the local chapter of the NAACP; the Michigan leader of the AFL-CIO, Gus Scholle; and, of course, the UAW's Walter Reuther and Mildred Jeffrey.[2] A crowd of thousands waited beyond the greeters. The year 1964 was an election year, after all. The president paused to give a message to the citizens of Motor City.[3] It was Detroit in particular that was, Johnson said, "the herald of hope in America. Prosperity in America must begin here in Detroit." Wages nationwide were up, and the economy was growing. More good would come. Johnson paid special attention to the labor leaders in these airport remarks. If labor and industry would stick by his side, the president said, "the sky is the limit, and the sky is bright today."

The sky *was* bright. At the stadium in Ann Arbor, the waiting crowd roared its greeting. Both the crowd and the nation were certain that Johnson would offer more than Kennedy did on his visit to the same university in 1960. Everything about the Johnson trip was bigger—Texas scale. Whereas Kennedy had arrived exhausted from a debate with Richard Nixon and dropped remarks after midnight, Johnson spoke in warm daylight. Whereas Kennedy had stood before his audience at the Michigan Union, a campus building, now Johnson enjoyed the wide grandeur of the stadium. Back in 1960, Kennedy had been merely a candidate in a race he could still lose, throwing students a Reuther-prepared bone, the idea of the Peace Corps. Johnson was an incumbent with a majority in Congress who was already changing their world. The very fact that Johnson had accepted the invitation was a coup for Michigan. Everyone tried to count the attendance. The crowd numbered eighty thousand, the press guessed.[4] But the university's alumni magazine counted eighty-five thousand. The crowd was enough, in any case, for Michigan to claim "the world's largest commencement."

Reaching the dais, the president prepared to speak before a teleprompter. This address, unlike past graduation speeches, would be aired on television. When the cameras panned they showed what looked like a football game, with the crowd on the field, and without the hot dogs. In camera view with Johnson as he moved to the microphone was not only the university president but also Governor Romney. Dotted around were "peace officers," the kind of guard that had accompanied the president since Kennedy's assassination. The music, typical for Michigan, was perfect: "taps excellent, singing loud and clear," as the recipient of an honorary degree noted. Finally, at 10:55, Johnson started speaking. He ended at 11:15, a full ten minutes more than officially allotted. Fourteen times, the crowd interrupted Johnson with applause.

And no wonder. For what Johnson offered went beyond mere agenda. Johnson offered a vision as fantastic as the vision of Port Huron, as transformative as that of Reuther. Johnson started with students: "I have come from the turmoil of your capital to the tranquillity of your campus to speak about the future of your country." In the past, presidents had striven for abundance, Johnson noted. Now the country had abundance. The challenge of the next half century was proving "whether we have the wisdom to use that wealth to enrich and elevate our national life." Some corners of the country were still poor. The Great Society, therefore, required, as Johnson had said before, an "end to poverty."

Johnson spoke on civil rights. In the South a recent check had found that only 6.7 percent of eligible black citizens in Mississippi were registered to vote, while 70 percent of whites were registered.[5] Indeed, a few of the Port Huron alumni were in Mississippi right now, preparing a massive vote drive they had given the name "Freedom Summer." The time had come for the Great Society to put an end to racial injustice, Johnson said. America would strive for its goals on three stages: "in our cities, our countryside, and in our classrooms." Once such goals were reached, there would be yet more to do. For the Great Society was no safe harbor; it was a constantly renewing challenge, Johnson said. Wealth and power were not enough. America needed to move "upward to the Great Society."

"Great Society." The name had been in the planning for months. Scholars had advised the Johnson entourage that the term had a past. Long ago an English socialist named Graham Wallas had written of a "Great Society," by which Wallas had meant a new society in which isolated citizens of villages were now linked in a great network, connected by rails, roads, newspapers, and jurisdictions. The American commentator Walter Lippmann had written a book, *The Good Society.*[6] Johnson's entourage that spring had chosen "Great Society," without regard for provenance. They liked the grandeur of "Great Society." Horace Busby, on Johnson's staff, had written a draft of a speech defining a Great Society as one that addressed technological challenges and opportunities for the country. But Johnson and the men sought to make the phrase something broader that could capture the aims of all constituents. "You could fit a lot of what we were trying to do within the curve of this phrase," one of LBJ's closest advisors, Jack Valenti, said later. The staff planned to unveil the Great Society in a big speech, which turned out to be the Michigan commencement address. That was appropriate, since Richard Goodwin, assigned to pull together various drafts for Michigan, would later conclude that it was Tom Hayden with his aspirations, hazy but great, who had inspired them all, "without even knowing it." In the writing of the speech, Goodwin wanted to avoid "screaming and invective," and sought rather language that reflected a discontent he sensed across society. Goodwin had looked at the letter Martin Luther King wrote from jail in Birmingham. Goodwin had perused the Port Huron Statement, too. Three abstract nouns in the statement jumped out at the speechwriter: "loneliness, estrangement, isolation." In the meantime, the Johnson entourage socialized their president to "Great Society," and he fell for the phrase. The White House didn't want its new brand dribbled out. Yet even before the trip to Michigan, when others were present, Johnson hadn't been able to help repeating "Great Society," "fondling and caressing this new phrase," Valenti noted.[7]

Even as he stepped off the stage at Michigan, Johnson could feel the truth: the speech wasn't just a local triumph, it was a national triumph. On his way out the president stopped at a trailer to change out of his regalia, and found Walter Reuther, waiting to thank him. Back in Washington after Michigan, Johnson summoned Goodwin to the small study that served as the president's second office, to thank him. "Come on in, Dick," he said. "Sit down. Try some of this scotch." Even the editor of *Time*, which had given its 1963 Man of the Year cover to Martin Luther King, not the new president, now contacted Johnson. "Henry Luce called me this morning," Johnson told Goodwin. "Old Man Henry himself. He said he'd support me on the basis of the Great Society speech alone." On June 8, Johnson, emboldened, delivered an encore at the commencement at Swarthmore College in Pennsylvania. At Swarthmore, Johnson spoke more bluntly than at Ann Arbor. He not only advanced his Great Society agenda, but made clear who would deliver on it. The country should suspend its "phantom fears." A scaled-up government, the president told the students, was the answer to the problems of the 1960s. "The truth is, far from crushing the individual, government at its best liberates him from the enslaving forces of his environment."

—————

THE IDEA that the federal government could lift the country to new heights was relatively new. Until the 1930s, Washington had confined grand-scale domestic interventions to wartime. Woodrow Wilson, for example, had nationalized the railroads during World War I. Yet, as Johnson, in the early 1930s a congressional aide, had personally observed, that had changed with Franklin Roosevelt's election to the presidency in 1932. The country was mired in the Great Depression. In 1933, Roosevelt led lawmakers in the passage of the New Deal, a vast peacetime program of legislation premised on the idea that the government could manage and cheer the economy back to recovery. Within his first hundred days as president, Roosevelt and Congress had put through great changes in banking law but also laws creating multiple other programs crafted to shore up the domestic economy. For the unemployed, Roosevelt had created a kind of domestic Peace Corps, the Civilian Conservation Corps, as well as the Public Works Administration, to put men and women to work constructing schools and municipal buildings. For the parts of the South where electricity had not yet arrived, FDR established the Tennessee Valley Authority, which had landed GE in so much trouble, and the Rural Electrification Administration. Roosevelt and his advisors crafted the National Recovery Administration to bring recovery in the industrial sector, and the Agricultural Adjustment Act to restore America's farmers, then struggling.

The New Deal with which the young Johnson himself came into contact first was the agricultural New Deal. Crop prices had dropped violently, and farmers, unable to pay mortgages, were losing their farms. To Johnson, Roosevelt seemed like a savior. Other young men got the same impression. "There's only one thing to do here, that's fade away and go broke," a man in rural Doland, South Dakota, told his son, Johnson's future ally, Hubert Humphrey.[8] Roosevelt's new bank loans helped farmers keep their farms. This Agricultural Adjustment Administration sought to help them by raising commodity prices. The method Roosevelt, Congress, and the AAA settled on was curtailing supply, literally. Farmers received payment to plow over crops—in the end, millions of acres.[9] It was Johnson who in South Texas cajoled the dubious farmers into signing the contracts, leading resistant mules to plow over rows of cotton.[10] And it was Johnson who saw to it that the Texas farmers got their pay, their loans, or, eventually, electrification. Johnson would be especially proud of his own role in the electric New Deal, bringing electricity to the Hill Country of Texas.[11] What Johnson also observed was that when one program delivered subpar results, Roosevelt didn't give up. The president simply added another program on top of it. In 1935, Roosevelt signed a public pension plan for seniors, Social Security, along with the Wagner Act for the unions.

Johnson's job was to sell and get the benefits to the people. The tall young man had proved a whiz at this work. Later, statistics would show that as New Deal programs commenced, the Fourteenth District in Texas, where Johnson worked first, received more than its share of New Deal aid.[12] Commodity prices eventually rose, and Johnson attributed the successes to the New Deal. On the Hill, the aides maintained their own mock congress, the "Little Congress," where they debated the same issues as the lawmakers. When Johnson won the election as head of the Little Congress in 1933, he promised his victory would "mark a New Deal for all the Little Congresses." When Roosevelt signed another new program for employment into law, the National Youth Administration, Johnson was tapped to head the Texas office. Through the NYA post, Johnson had the power to create employment: "727 jobs have been made available to youths in this section," commented the Marshall, Texas, *News Messenger* with satisfaction. When Johnson ran for Congress himself in 1936, Roosevelt endorsed him, and Johnson rode in on the longest coattails in history, for Roosevelt took forty-six of forty-eight states. "Roosevelt and Progress," read a Johnson campaign advertisement. By the time Johnson ran for his third election, he was well known as a powerful Roosevelt lieutenant. The columnists Drew Pearson and Robert Allen reported in 1940 that when the president asked for advice on who could get something "done quick," House Speaker Sam Rayburn suggested Johnson. "Sold," Roosevelt replied. "That was my idea, too."[13]

As the New Deal progressed, unemployment failed to retreat to normal levels. In January 1937, when unemployment was 12 percent, Roosevelt, rather than concede defeat, moved again to escalate and shift goals, turning, in fact, to poverty.[14] Roosevelt, like Johnson in Michigan so much later, defined three areas for attention: the president warned that one-third of the nation was "ill-housed, ill-clad, and ill-nourished." The New Deal reforms must continue in America until the country reached "our happy valley." The Depression endured nearly to the end of Roosevelt's second term, and unemployment rose in 1938. Many of the original actors in the New Deal saw the perversities—plowing cotton under—and rated Roosevelt's great reforms more bureaucracy than progress. Some of Roosevelt's old allies spoke up. One was the columnist Walter Lippmann, the one who gave his book the careful title *The Good Society*. Lippmann rated "great" as too ambitious.[15] He argued that "no new social order can be designed."

But the young lawmaker Lyndon Johnson did not mistrust the New Deal, as John Kennedy's crowd later would. Johnson believed in the New Deal, without caring too much about its shortcomings. In any case the sheer political feat of the New Deal, not its economic performance, seemed the important thing to the striving Texas politician. Johnson carefully noted the chain of factors that made the Roosevelt tenure of the 1930s, two terms' worth, even possible. The basis was political predominance. Unlike his successor, Harry Truman, who struggled against Republican majorities in Congress for part of his time in office, Roosevelt held secure Democratic majorities in both houses throughout his presidency. Roosevelt demonstrated that it was also key to have top advisors: Roosevelt had brought in what he called a Brain Trust, experts who heightened the reputation of New Deal programs. A sense of emergency was critical to the undertaking: many of the powers ceded to the New Dealers were rated permissible by the public or the courts only because of the emergency of the Great Depression. Another factor was timing: it was no accident that Roosevelt had dropped a veritable blitz of laws in those first hundred days, so many that the period later came to be written as a proper noun: "the Hundred Days." An ambitious president had to move with alacrity right at the start, as FDR did, or he was lost. Time was the enemy. In 1936, Roosevelt had been reelected with "a mandate as clear as any that has ever been written," including victory in forty-six of the forty-eight states, as Johnson later noted. But even with such a mandate, the second term was tougher. Finally, Johnson saw that the only way Roosevelt managed to take his revolution as far as he did was by locking in political constituencies. Early on, Roosevelt had given farmers the payments from the AAA, given senior citizens Social Security, given labor men like Reuther and Meany the Wagner Act. How the economy had performed before the 1936 election mattered less to that election because Roosevelt could turn out such blocs of voters.

From the moment he had been sworn into office, even in grief, Johnson had seen that he might elude the humiliations suffered by Harry Truman when Truman had sought to expand the New Deal. For Johnson in 1964 enjoyed some of Roosevelt's advantages, including Democratic majorities in both houses of Congress. And Johnson also could count some advantages of his own. First, there was his long record in the Senate, which gave him unparalleled experience as the shepherd of legislation. Roosevelt, a mere governor with a famous name, had had nothing like that. There was also the aching advantage of tragedy: Kennedy's death would make Congress eager to pass Kennedy's tax law and Kennedy's languishing civil rights bill. There was also a disadvantage: no national economic crisis on a scale of the Great Depression loomed in Johnson's day. In fact, unemployment was heading down below 5 percent. The sense of urgency would have to be generated—by Johnson.

He made his wager. Johnson would indeed make his own New Deal a "fast deal," as Thruston Morton had called it, giving Roosevelt a run for his money. If Johnson did move fast enough, he'd win a solid victory in November 1964 and then finish the job. Johnson's Great Society would be law within two or three years, well before the nation tired of it, or him. Of course there would be collateral damage. When Johnson's aides had expressed their trepidation, he intoxicated them with his bold reply. "Well," the new president said, "what the hell's the presidency for?"

———————

EVEN IN the sunny June of 1964, outsiders could identify a few obstacles to Johnson's do-or-die fast deal. The Federal Reserve chairman, William McChesney Martin, was warning Johnson that the Fed needed to raise the interest rate, currently 3.5 percent.[16] A hike to more than 4 percent could impede grand plans. The Freedom Summer in Mississippi could become so violent that lawmakers would turn against Johnson's plan to pass Kennedy's legacy civil rights bill. Weeks before he was killed himself, Kennedy had learned that the South Vietnamese leader, Ngo Dinh Diem, had been assassinated. Now South Vietnam was in chaos, making it vulnerable to a belligerent North Vietnam. A few days after he gave his Michigan address, Johnson told one of the "wise men" he had inherited from Kennedy, McGeorge Bundy, that he wanted out of Vietnam, because "it looks like we're getting into another Korea." Johnson just didn't see *how* to get out. Every politician, left, right, or mushy middle, was urging Johnson to do something on the situation in Vietnam. The only variation was in what the politicians demanded.

That February, Johnson had already put through Kennedy's tax legislation, an act that lowered rates for everyone and buoyed the economy. Whatever William McChesney Martin said, the bump up would help in an election year. Another Kennedy legacy, civil rights legislation, was proving tougher to deliver. Johnson's own colleagues in the Southern delegation were again filibustering, and ready to continue filibustering until the first Tuesday in November. Competitors were snapping at Johnson's heels. Governor George Wallace of Alabama was not running for president but was still making speeches that rallied segregationists against Johnson. Wallace, a Democrat, was throwing his support behind the Republican Barry Goldwater, who might also turn out to be a threat later in the year. So for that matter was Strom Thurmond, one of the filibuster men in the Senate. To Johnson, these men were just ankle biters.

The California primaries were coming in early June. Johnson's chances looked strong. His name was not on the primary ballot in California, but a slate of unpledged Democrats led by Governor Pat Brown, his ally, won 68 percent of the vote. A Harris poll of the Golden State suggested that Johnson would carry the state by 65 to 35 delegates over Nelson Rockefeller or Barry Goldwater.[17] Los Angeles had recently elected the former congressman Sam Yorty mayor. Yorty had always been a maverick. He had even backed Richard Nixon in 1960. But now Yorty, too, was signaling he would line up his own separate group of delegates for Johnson.[18] For that, much could be forgiven. Johnson would head to the West Coast in June to lock up the pledges.

Johnson stood a strong chance of locking up contests elsewhere as well. Americans found Nelson Rockefeller unexciting. Wallace might fade, but only, Johnson thought, if the summer in the South was quiet. And Goldwater was so wild in his rhetoric that not only Democrats but also the media and moderate Republicans mocked him as irresponsible. No one, however, could say that the race was over that summer. A dynamic reminiscent of both Huey Long, the Louisiana populist of the 1920s and 1930s, and Wallace was developing in Goldwater's favor. The more the media or Democrats derided Goldwater, the more popular the feisty senator from Arizona became. The more others called Republicans "irresponsible" for favoring Goldwater, the more loyal Republicans became to him. Goldwater had already beaten out other Republican candidates in Johnson's own Texas, as well as Illinois and Indiana, and needed only California to get the majority of convention delegates. Former GE men Ronald Reagan and Ralph Cordiner, both of whom were now campaigning for Goldwater, knew how to make the most of this. They mocked the mockery and lovingly repeated the insults. Opening a Republican rally in late May, days before the California primary, Reagan merrily commenced: "And a good morning to all you irresponsible Republicans." The former actor brought down the house. Goldwater won California.

Johnson plunged ahead with his agenda. When it came to the civil rights legislation, the key was the man Johnson had telephoned so soon after Kennedy's death, Senate minority leader Everett Dirksen. And the press could see that Dirksen was moving toward Johnson. Did not every man have the right to opportunity? Dirksen asked. Dirksen once explained his lack of hesitation when it came to backing civil rights. "I am just like little Johnny," Dirksen said, when a teacher asked him to spell "straight." "He said, 's-t-r-a-i-g-h-t.' She said, 'and what does it mean?' and he said, 'without ginger ale.' And that's the way I take my freedom."[19]

When it came to writing his own legislation, Johnson took comfort in the sense that like Roosevelt and Kennedy he had brilliant minds about him: Robert McNamara at Defense, McGeorge Bundy at the National Security Council, Sargent Shriver, Ted Sorensen, and Richard Goodwin. "We are assembling the best thought and the broadest knowledge to find those answers for America," Johnson told the Michigan crowd when he delivered his speech. Johnson did not merely showcase these men, "Harvards," as he called them: he placed faith in them and was sure that they could, through study, come up with more and better ideas than had ever preceded them. His old friend Sam Rayburn had uttered a warning when he heard Johnson's praise of such men in the Kennedy years: "Maybe, Lyndon, but I'd feel a hell of a lot better if even one of them had ever run for sheriff."[20] Johnson ignored Rayburn. The poverty experts, new and old, were especially impressive. The press was beginning to call them "poverticians." To back the experts up, Johnson that year would establish fifteen task forces, including many academic names, and challenge the standard hierarchy of civil servants in the executive branch.[21] Already it was clear that even Johnson's favored "Harvards" within the traditional chains of command were exerting unusual power: McNamara, for example, drove the Defense Department as he drove one of his Ford automobiles. McNamara actually defined his job as "active management at the top."

The men around Johnson felt the weight of his faith in them, and strove hard. Vietnam would be sorted out. There would be a Great Society. Poverty would be cured. Blacks of the South would win full citizenship. The Great Society would succeed. But they also could not help asking themselves a second question: by what measures? Daniel Patrick Moynihan, still at the Labor Department, was nursing a paper that would appear in a new journal, *Public Interest*. Moynihan sketched out the validity of what Johnson promised at Swarthmore, benign large-scale planning for all governments, whether led by Democrats or Republicans. The reason large-scale planning would function well Moynihan offered in a phrase that became his paper's title: "The Professionalization of Reform." No longer, said Moynihan, could planners be dismissed as vague professors, the garret people whom the draft of the Port Huron Statement had also dismissed. Planners were scientists, social scientists who used not ideology but statistics to arrive at serious conclusions. Moynihan quoted a star economist, the late Wesley Mitchell, who had written that social scientists "rely, and with success, upon quantitative analysis to point the way." If planning had failed in the past, that was because it had not been perfected yet. Social scientists advanced, Mitchell had written, "because we are constantly approving and applying such analysis."[22] The funds for projects were now available, Moynihan pointed out. Nations could be counted on, because they were managed by economists, "to operate their economies on a high and steadily expanding level of production and employment." This reliable prosperity, Moynihan noted with accuracy, was "the central fact of world politics today."

But how to measure the progress of the plans of the Great Society? On the surface, it looked as if the vote drive to permit blacks to achieve equality in the election booth would be the easiest to measure. The Mississippi numbers were perhaps the worst. But the disparities prevailed across the South, with only four in ten black adults registered, compared with six in ten white citizens.[23] If blacks got the vote in the South, the legislation could be said to have "worked." That would be a first victory.

In other areas the federal government lacked baselines against which to measure the progress of its campaigns. "Progress begins on social problems when it becomes possible to measure them," as Moynihan would say.[24] Would cleaning up along the highways constitute improving the countryside, and if so by how much? When it came to the classroom, one of Johnson's targets, benchmarks were also scarce. Johnson believed strongly in college, as his choice of the University of Michigan—and not the Ford factory floor—for his Great Society speech had reminded the public. From Southwest Texas State Teachers College, he had moved right into teaching at a tiny school whose pupils were poor Hispanics. Perhaps you could measure progress by the level of Americans' preparation for college? The College Board had for decades studied students' performance through standardized tests, especially the Scholastic Aptitude Test. The test was designed to ignore the benefits of private school and highlight analytic skills. During the 1940s, 1950s, and early 1960s, American students' scores on the SAT had improved. In 1963, the average SAT verbal score was 478. The average math score was 502.[25] Perhaps a great initiative to teach reading and arithmetic would push those numbers up. Robert Parris Moses, now planning the bold, dangerous Freedom Summer in Mississippi, focused on reducing illiteracy, at first to help more blacks register to vote, but also to help all the poor advance. Perhaps you allowed more blacks to become teachers. Even qualifying to teach public school was tough, because of the obstacles unions and state regulators threw up. Moses complained that it was easier for him to teach at a "fancy prep school," Horace Mann, than at a Harlem school. Or perhaps another national number to measure American education should be developed. The SAT was designed for the college bound, and therefore could be slammed as elitist.

The most important enemy to define, however, was poverty, the principal target in Johnson's great war. Earlier in the century, joblessness and poverty had been considered synonymous. When Roosevelt made the claim in January 1937 that one-third of the nation was "ill-housed, ill-clad and ill-nourished," the relationship had seemed obvious. Now, with unemployment so low, it was hard to build the case for action around jobs, as even Reuther conceded. You had to focus on poverty, with or without jobs. You could launch a war on poverty now, but as Martin Luther King had said, there was no clarity about who, precisely, was poor. Native Americans were poor, dirt poor, but it was hard to compare their poverty with the poverty of someone in downtown St. Louis. Defining poverty was the first work of the Great Society.

Johnson's advisors wanted to do something fresh. They cast about. At the Social Security Administration an economist named Mollie Orshansky was researching definitions of poverty. The share of a family's income that went for food seemed like a legitimate metric. If a family paid a third, or half, of its cash income for the bare essentials, it could certainly be classed as poor. Orshansky's first calculations, based on groceries and basic needs, suggested that the poverty threshold for a family of four in 1963 should be set at an income of $3,128.[26] The White House drew its own poverty threshold, $3,000. By this arithmetic about a fifth of Americans—an improvement from FDR's third, but not enough of one to obviate a poverty campaign—were poor, some thirty-five million citizens. Now the White House had a baseline. Poverty, 20 percent. John Kennedy might have read Harrington's *The Other America*, and Kennedy and Congress had indeed dramatically extended Social Security, adding $800 million to social insurance spending in the twelve months following the extension's passage. But in the 1963 edition of the Economic Report of the President, an annual volume that supplied the formal White House take on American prosperity, the word "poverty" had not appeared. In the 1964 edition of the Economic Report, Johnson's advisors by contrast inserted no fewer than 196 references to poverty, as well as a special chapter on poverty.[27] If poverty was to count as a crisis, poverty had to be official.

Johnson's advantage in his poverty war started with one name: Sargent Shriver. The president liked the fact that Shriver was a Kennedy by marriage, and one originally brought into the clan by the patriarch himself, Joseph Kennedy. In fact, Joe Kennedy had actually hired Shriver years before to manage his Merchandise Mart, the giant Chicago building. Johnson could wrap himself in the mantle of the Kennedy name and enjoy all the authority of the lost president's heir when he made his case. More important, though, Shriver was not Robert Kennedy, the grief-stricken, ambitious, unpredictable competitor to Johnson. Shriver did not labor under the burden of a complicated private life as other Kennedy males did. Shriver was a straight arrow, a better Kennedy than the Kennedys.

REGARDLESS OF his Kennedy family status, Americans found, Shriver was worth watching because he embodied an old American principle: service.

In a way Shriver's whole life explained where the Great Society impulse had come from. Shriver's parents, devout Catholics, had raised the young man not only to honor service but to serve. Starting as an altar boy, Shriver had served at nearly every point of his career, whether at the Canterbury School, where he met a young John Kennedy in passing, or at Protestant Yale, where he led a recruitment drive that doubled the membership of the Thomas More Society. For Shriver, religion was not an aside, a box to check. As editor of the *Yale Daily News*, Shriver had had the assignment of writing the opening editorial of the year. After promising the reader that his editorials would contain opinion and morality, Shriver laid out his principles: "First, therefore, we are Christians."[28]

At Yale Law School Shriver had done his very first legal work pro bono, in a volunteer program in New Haven. Before World War II, while still at law school, he had been one of the cofounders of America First. Some of the other early supporters of the isolationist group had eluded military service, telling themselves they were staying out on principle. Not Shriver. Whatever his objections to the war, in fact because of his objections, Sarge had gone over to the Navy office and enlisted. He gave not one or two but five years to the Navy, winning a Purple Heart for wounds received in the harrowing Battle of Guadalcanal. In the years after the war, in addition to working for Joseph Kennedy, Shriver had served together with his future wife, Eunice Kennedy, at the Justice Department, trying to build a program to reduce juvenile delinquency. There Eunice and Shriver planned a program that emphasized community service and cooperation among social workers, teachers, parents, and churches. Sarge's most recent service, as founding director of the Peace Corps, was his proudest and most successful. He had recently made the cover of *Time*. Though Shriver had waffled about taking the job of Mr. Poverty, and hesitated at Johnson's crude language, he'd relented when Johnson told him he could serve as head of both the Peace Corps and a new poverty agency. Shriver believed he was ready for such a great task. "More. More work, more sacrifice, more men to serve the greater glory of God," as he said in one of his own commencement speeches, at Georgetown University.[29]

All the Kennedys were Catholics. Among them, though, it was Shriver who most pointedly drew the connection between Christian service in charity and deepening the service of the U.S. government. If service was a traditional idea, Shriver put the new twist on it: local work or church work couldn't suffice. What was good government but a continuation and expansion of charity? If Shriver was taking the job of Mr. Poverty, he was doing that, too, for God. For God, the humiliation of being President Johnson's vote collector, of being caught in the crossfire between a sulking Bobby and a demanding Lyndon, was worth it. The government had more resources than any individual; therefore it *could* do more.

More was certainly what Shriver set out to do at his office as he haled advisors to his Peace Corps office at 806 Connecticut Avenue, or even to his home, Timberlawn, in Maryland.[30] As the men began planning, the pages of programs proliferated. Everywhere he went Shriver took with him five briefcases: two for the Peace Corps; two for his poverty work; and one for the Kennedy Foundation, which he headed and which had been established by his father-in-law. Before Johnson, Shriver—like a knight before a king—laid out his riches, ideas of his own to end poverty or expansions of projects originally mooted under Kennedy. First, there could be a domestic version of his Peace Corps, Volunteers in Service to America, or VISTA. Shriver's new poverty office would also build a Job Corps, to give opportunities for training for those who needed to find their way into the workforce. In addition there would be a Youth Corps, which would pull the teenagers, long Eunice Shriver and Robert Kennedy's focus, into legitimate employment. After all, as Robert Parris Moses pointed out when he spoke on college campuses, large percentages of black youth were unemployed. A new program for children below school age, Head Start, would ensure toddlers were ready for regular school. There would be loans for small businesses.

The new poverty office would fund the kind of community action the youth had spoken of at Port Huron, the goal being "to provide stimulation and incentive for urban and rural communities to mobilize their resources to combat poverty."[31] In other words, the government would now support the same sort of participatory democracy drives that the UAW was funding via the SDS activists. The thought was that federal representatives, or people who had contracts with Shriver's office, would work with, or around, local officials to empower the poor, getting "maximum feasible participation" of locals. Shriver also had his eye on special projects, including some for Native Americans. One of his early programs would be Rough Rock Demonstration School in Apache County, Arizona. His new office would supply teachers' aides and cash for the school's administration. A final program inspired Shriver, for it recalled his law school pro bono work. That was legal services. No longer would the lowly public defender in towns and counties be alone. Old-fashioned pro bono lawyers working after hours to help individual cases would gain allies, too. Shriver's agencies would fund them. And Shriver's lawyers would go into towns, too, furnishing talented attorneys who might appeal, and even take a case to the U.S. Supreme Court. Shriver had support for this new idea of providing federally funded lawyers across the nation from the attorney general himself, Robert Kennedy. In a speech Kennedy gave that May of 1964, a few days before Johnson's Michigan speech, at the University of Chicago, he had challenged law grads to take up serious work for the public.[32] The attorney general told graduates that to sustain the rule of law was one of the obligations of the legal profession—a given. But, echoing his late brother's "ask not" line, Kennedy also challenged the young lawyers at Chicago to think of their obligations. "Here at this university they are peculiarly yours. That is so because, whether you welcome it or not, graduating from a great school puts an obligation squarely upon you." That obligation included serving in public interest law.

Even as Shriver planned and sold, he recruited. The same Michael Harrington who had spent 1963 abroad, quasi-exiled, now found himself encamped at the center of policy power: sitting in the Peace Corps Office, with Shriver, Labor Secretary Willard Wirtz, Walter Heller from the Council of Economic Advisers, and others, writing memos for the president and his Poverty Task Force. Paul Jacobs, Harrington's friend, even helped out as an administrative coordinator for a while. It was gratifying for Harrington to find that one of the emphases of the War on Poverty was Appalachia, whose stubborn impoverishment he had first highlighted in

The Other America. Wirtz seconded his assistant secretary, Daniel Patrick Moynihan, to work on the poverty project. The meetings at Timberlawn, the Shrivers' home, were now supplemented by evening meetings at the Moynihan house over spaghetti dinners prepared by Moynihan's wife, Liz. The energy of Shriver's team impressed observers in other departments—even the most important observer, Johnson, who saw that Shriver, like himself, made Roosevelt's New Deal his template. "They went at it with a fervor," Johnson would note in his memoirs, "and created a ferment unknown since the New Deal, when lights burned through the night as men worked to restructure society."[33]

Still, not all the new hires at the poverty office were reassured that the whirlwind that was Shriver in action could be counted on to do this restructuring. Even the man who provided the cogent justification for the work, Moynihan himself, had some tweaks. Moynihan thought urban poverty should get more attention. The welfare rolls in his hometown, New York City, had grown by 12.4 percent in the past year. But Moynihan was even more concerned with the way Shriver, like Johnson, seemed to confuse enthusiasm, or faith, with results. Benchmarks such as Mollie Orshansky's poverty figure had to be not only created but also used. "Unless you are in a position to measure your results you will never be able to bring the program to a high level of efficiency, much less to prove it to Congress," Moynihan wrote in a letter to Shriver. Even Paul Jacobs, one of the farthest to the left and dreamiest of the people in Shriver's employ, found himself wondering at the Shriver optimism. The entire project, Jacobs would write later, was born in "an almost mystical belief in the infinite potentials of American society. Poverty, like polio, will be defeated when the right vaccine is found." The War on Poverty was plainly a political project, Johnson's choice of Shriver reflecting that. Shriver was, to Jacobs's mind, "an attractive figure against whom very little personal antagonism had developed anywhere in the country"—but *not an expert*, and one who knew "nothing of poverty."[34]

Harrington by contrast found Shriver's fief too businesslike. This kind of poverty work was more Washington, more *capitalist* than what Harrington was used to. He noticed that others spent serious energy making the War on Poverty look moderate, not Marxist. For example, Adam Yar-molinsky, a staffer lent from the Defense Department, suggested that "pockets of poverty" might be called "targets of opportunity" ("pockets of poverty," whatever the moderating impulse, stuck). Shriver, sounding like the preacher Billy Graham or Barry Goldwater, promised to offer "a real American chance to escape from poverty." As the plans were written, Harrington and Jacobs could not contain their own mischievous streak, and repeatedly ended memos with a phrase from their stock of socialist dicta: "Of course, there is no real solution to the problem of poverty until we abolish the capitalist system." That, and the pair's general light tone, alarmed the government people, the secretaries and assistant secretaries, some of whom recalled a time in the coldest years of the Cold War when a federal employee could be fired or worse for a joke milder than that.

Harrington, isolated, nonetheless did find a friend, the interesting, eclectic Moynihan. During his time under Kennedy, Moynihan had worked on the executive order that allowed government employees to unionize. But he had also made the shabby, disappointing architecture of the District of Columbia his project, even penning a small guidebook on federal architecture for the White House. Harrington and Moynihan—like Shriver—were part of the Catholic streak in the Great Society, all raised as Catholics, all out of a culture deeply committed to social reform long before LBJ. But Moynihan, unlike Harrington or Shriver, had actu-ally grown up genuinely poor. Moynihan's alcoholic father, John Henry Moynihan, had abandoned the family. Two facts of that period of hardship stuck with Moynihan: that he had always found work, even if it was rough work as a stevedore on the New York piers, and that state and federal government had always lifted him up through education. Moynihan had passed through City College of New York and Middlebury, as well as graduate school at Tufts, without ever seeing a tuition bill.

Now Moynihan wanted to be sure that at least the jobs were available to those who came after him. Harrington and Moynihan pulled together a memo that sought to shift the spotlight from poverty back to where it belonged: "if there is any single dominant problem of poverty in the U.S. it is that of unemployment," they wrote. Moynihan believed in the government, and saw it as a moral imperative that the government serve as employer of last resort. He believed, too, in reform—that talented professionals could improve on the law that had been written in the past. Maybe the government ought to get up a $3 billion to $5 billion building program that could employ workers. But the jobs program went nowhere. The most logical way to pay for it was a cigarette tax, and Johnson, the experts were told, thought such a tax would kill him politically. As for Shriver, he was proving hyperaware of the price tags, for Johnson had tasked the Kennedy brother-in-law with convincing lawmakers to vote for any poverty legislation the Administration proposed. Johnson ordered "his" Kennedy, via Bill Moyers, "to live in the House until the poverty bill passed."[35]

Sometimes, but not always, the poverty team turned to what seemed to be cheaper projects. Jack Conway, Reuther's old ally at the UAW, became involved, and Conway, true to his union background, emphasized rallying the poor, "to structure community action programs so that they would have an immediate and irreversible impact on the communities." There must be "mobilization"—in other words, the poor should be encouraged to shake things up; this was the community action Johnson mentioned. Hiring a few neighborhood organizers was far cheaper than a massive countrywide employment program. The target group for Conway's community action was the same group that was now the focus of the SDS and the Economic Research and Action Project ERAP: citizens in cities.

Outside Shriver's shop, officials were developing other, separate poverty projects. Johnson built up the Appalachian Regional Commission, a lite version of Roosevelt's Tennessee Valley Authority. It included plans for roads. Farmers, the idea was, would no longer languish isolated; the Great Society would give them hundreds of miles of highway to connect them with the world. Moynihan noticed an irony. Whether a program's beneficiaries were black or white, its planners were white. Blacks were scarcely present in all the work undertaken for the disadvantaged. Indeed, Moynihan later wrote, "at no time did any Negro have any role of any consequence in the drafting of the poverty program."[36]

Most of the projects rolled forward so quickly that there was scant time for irony. Office of Economic Opportunity work required constant communication with the president, and getting that communication was not easy, even for Shriver, whom the president had recently courted so breathlessly. The president, who loved communication, was always busy communicating with someone else. Those around Johnson found themselves by turns amused and alarmed at his energy. The new president, noted one staffer, Doris Kearns, "embraced the possibilities offered by his presidential communications network with the unqualified excitement of an eleven-year-old who'd been given the world's biggest walkie-talkie." Phones with both dials and rows of push buttons, the latter then a novelty, were installed not only in the Oval Office, but also in Johnson's bedrooms and bathrooms, and on his motorboats and planes. There was even a floating phone in the swimming pool at the president's ranch. Through these gadgets, Johnson could manage the nation minute to minute, like a pilot in the cockpit of a new Boeing 727. Through June, the White House continued to be the busiest anyone could remember. Bill Moyers, Pierre Salinger, Jack Valenti, Sargent Shriver when he got in—all the men crowded around the president, walked in from his outer halls to the Oval Office, walked out, typed, telephoned, and crowded back. Behind the telephones, the televisions, and the teletype machine, Johnson hung a portrait of another energetic man of the frontier, Andrew Jackson, that he borrowed from the National Portrait Gallery. The Johnson day started at 6:00, sometimes before, with a call from the chief executive, and didn't end until midnight.

Through the month, Johnson's fellow Democrats from the South used the Senate floor as a stage to lay out all the arguments made since Reconstruction against enforcing integration. A "public accommodation" section of the civil rights bill required businesses to serve whoever came in. That in theory, at least, allowed blacks to shop and eat where they pleased and use the facilities. But if you gave one group this freedom, you took freedom away from the businesses to sell to whomever they chose. Was that really wise? Indeed, said Senator George Smathers of Florida, "inherent in our Constitution is the right for every free American to do that which he wishes with his own property. If he wishes to do it erroneously, if he wishes even to discriminate in many respects that is his own privilege." Insisting on open stores and restaurants might be "morally right," Smathers allowed. "But legally under our Constitution [a business owner] can do with his own property and with his own money that which he wishes to do." Smathers was trying to get at something: the civil rights bill was establishing a precedent. A law that defined new rights at the national level was taking away from individuals the authority of their own conscience, and substituting a federal, national conscience to overrule them. And who knew whether the federal government's conscience would always be better? The Civil Rights Act filibuster was now in its second month, and that included Saturdays. But Johnson could see that Hubert Humphrey and the Republican minority leader, Everett Dirksen, his point men, would soon count the sixty-seven votes needed to end the filibuster.

Johnson's success in Congress gave even those civil rights activists reluctant to acknowledge Johnson a tremendous boost. Robert Parris Moses, a Northerner and what Johnson would call a "Harvard"—he'd earned a master's degree in Cambridge—now led the umbrella group of all civil rights groups organizing the voting rights drive in Mississippi. So many students trailed down from the North that Moses, Casey Hayden, and their network did not know what to do with them. Others joining Moses would come from the Congress on Racial Equality, including two young men from New York: Andrew Goodman, a student at Queens College; and Michael Schwerner, a graduate student at Columbia. These two were going to join a third volunteer, a local named James Chaney, to get blacks the vote in Mississippi's Neshoba County.

The sheer danger and the stakes in Mississippi—more than one thousand people would be arrested that summer—made Casey Hayden know she truly was doing important work, pushing change through participatory democracy. There without Tom, who was now in Newark, Casey was finding friends and allies in the South, among them Mary King, a minister's daughter, with whom she lived for a time. Casey especially liked the no-nonsense Ella Baker, who worked behind the scenes and had mentored Stokely Carmichael, Rosa Parks, and Bob Moses. All their hearts lived with Fannie Lou Hamer, who had been beaten so hard in prison that she suffered permanent damage to her eyes and kidneys. Moses had gotten a grant to help adults learn to read. He even planned to go to Harlem soon to field-test his methodology. Moses was black. He, like Moynihan, had noticed that nearly all the activists who came from the North to work with him, as he had come, were white. That had to change. Moses believed in a "crucial point": "the movement also demanded that black people challenge themselves," without social workers supervising or civil rights interns slowing them down.

All the activists wondered what kind of representation Southern blacks would get at the convention of Lyndon Johnson's Democratic Party, to take place in Atlantic City come that August. The Mississippi Democratic Party "regulars" were sure to deny blacks seats at the convention, regardless of how many new registered voters the Freedom Summer yielded. Casey Hayden and the others wanted to stress test not only reading but democracy itself: would the Democratic Party of Mississippi allow black delegates, chosen by the people in orderly fashion, to take their seats? That would be an important moment for Lyndon Johnson, along with democracy. While Shriver was still at his drawing board—and while Tom Hayden was still trading postulates in philosophic conversations with Haber—Casey, Ella Baker, and Bob Moses were seeking certification for a new party, the Mississippi Freedom Democratic Party. Moses couldn't believe it. Before his eyes, locals had "learned how to stand up and speak." Joseph Rauh, the general counsel of the UAW, helped them with the legal work.

Walter Reuther found the emergence of groups like the Mississippi Freedom Democratic Party difficult. Here was the old insider-outsider challenge. On the one hand, Reuther had to please Johnson. Johnson would be likely to insist he had to side with the official Mississippi delegates, who smeared the little Freedom Party as "known communists." On the other, Reuther wanted to build up his Coalition of Conscience, so that it, and he, would have power to turn future elections. A UAW convention earlier that spring in Atlantic City had provided an opportunity to recruit. Reuther's team invited a few attendees from Students for a Democratic Society. Among them was Rennie Davis, an Oberlin graduate whose father had served on Harry Truman's Council of Economic

Advisers. During a break, Reuther spoke with some of these New Left reps. A man named Frank Joyce was surprised by Reuther's dramatic demands. "We just sat there stunned because we thought we were the radicals, we were the tough kids, the street fighters. And this guy comes in and blows everybody away." Another way Reuther gained credibility with the left was in showcasing his disagreements with Johnson, to demonstrate that he himself was outside the establishment, whatever others said. The same Atlantic City UAW convention gave Reuther that chance. He had waited for the kind of profit sharing he and Romney had imagined to spread and become typical in industry. Profit sharing wasn't spreading. So now Reuther was moving to "seek our equity," as he put it, another way, by demanding the highest possible wages for the UAW membership, a 4.9 percent raise. Reuther knew full well that Johnson feared high wages would convince Walter Heller and William McChesney Martin that the Fed had to raise interest rates now. At Atlantic City for the union powwow and the cameras, the president played to his own audience, and his economic advisors, in a speech that was the equivalent of the Walter Heller Riot Act: stability, i.e., smaller wage increases, was imperative. If Reuther demanded higher wages, he would contribute to inflation, forcing automakers to raise prices, in a dangerous "price-wage spiral." Reuther amused reporters by noting he considered it "significant" that the president said "price-wage spiral," not "wage-price spiral," the more common language for the phenomenon studied by the high priests of economics. Johnson was acknowledging, Reuther was suggesting, that it was the automakers who started it all. Workers were hostages to inflation, not instigators of it. Reuther even took aim at Johnson's Brain Trust, suggesting that Johnson heeded the experts too often: "Nothing Walter Heller says will change our position at the bargaining table."[37]

There was a public figure who shared and even explained Reuther's visceral skepticism at the notion that actions by employees could drive inflation. That was a professor of economics at the University of Chicago, Milton Friedman. Friedman believed that the money supply was what mattered, and therefore those who controlled money—the Federal Reserve, banking regulators, and banks—determined inflation or deflation.

Prices and wages merely reflected what authorities and banks did. But such ideas were far enough from Heller, John Kenneth Galbraith, John Maynard Keynes, or even William McChesney Martin that they couldn't be taken seriously. Friedman, a *New York Times* reporter noted incredulously, took no offense at suggestions that he was heading back to the old world of prewar economics, and even of the classical liberal Adam Smith. Friedman sounded like the old GE. In any case a serious discussion between Reuther and Friedman was impossible, since Friedman advised Goldwater and Goldwater and Reuther were mortal enemies. Reuther had once, back in 1958, told the press that Goldwater was a good subject for a psychiatrist's study.

On June 10, Senator Robert Byrd of West Virginia delivered a final speech in the "extended conversation," fourteen hours and thirteen minutes, and with that the filibuster ended. The Senate voted 71 to 29 for the civil rights bill. Earlier legislation, the Civil Rights Act of 1957, had established a Civil Rights Division in the Justice Department, and had given federal officials the authority to prosecute those who tried to block black Americans from voting. The new civil rights act banned discrimination in the workplace and in public places. It was a historic moment, the first time the Senate had been able to assemble the votes to cut off a filibuster of a civil rights bill. Everett Dirksen quoted the great French eminence Victor Hugo: "Stronger than all armies is an idea whose time has come." Martin Luther King, however, was not satisfied. Days later, King demanded service at a whites-only restaurant in St. Augustine, Florida, and was promptly arrested. George Smathers, the senator from Florida, offered to pay the bail if King would never come back to Florida again. King refused. Segregation wasn't over until it was over.

Within weeks came tragic news that underscored King's point. The Mississippi voting drive volunteers, Chaney, Schwerner, and Goodman, disappeared while driving to a voter registration center at Mount Zion Methodist Church. As the hours passed, the public began to suspect the Ku Klux Klan had murdered them. That fear grew stronger when the group's station wagon was found burned by the side of the road on Mississippi State Highway 21. On June 23, J. Edgar Hoover of the Federal

Bureau of Investigation told Johnson that this discovery meant the young men were likely dead. The men were not found. In early July the president directed the Navy to assign four hundred sailors, assisted by helicopters, to search through Neshoba and neighboring Newton County in Mississippi.

The day Johnson signed the civil rights law, July 2, Chaney, Schwerner, and Goodman were still missing. Johnson made clear the law would establish "the rule of justice" in the United States. The president also worked in an expression of appreciation for all those who fought for freedom, even and especially those in Vietnam. The country placed trust in those who fought for justice. "From the minutemen at Concord to the soldiers in Vietnam, each generation has been equal to that trust." The war hawks noted that Johnson had said "soldiers"—not "advisors," the term used heretofore. Perhaps the president did shift this lexicon consciously, to socialize the idea of greater intervention in Vietnam. The reaction to the signature of the civil rights law was muted, but in some cases muted relief. Perhaps now the country could move on from the topic of civil rights. Thomas Sowell, a young black professor at Howard University, thought that "to expect civil rights to solve our economic and social problems was barking up the wrong tree." Sowell hoped that once such a law was signed, the black community could turn inward, and "toward our own self-development as a people."

But the political power of the law's passage seemed obvious and immediate. The civil rights law divided the splintering Republican Party into two truly separate factions: moderates, who supported the new law and, perhaps, further civil rights legislation; and states' rights conservatives. The front-runner for the moderate spot was Governor Nelson Rockefeller of New York. Governor Romney was playing assist, and even put forward an amendment to the Republican platform that would exclude from the party "extremists of the right." Goldwater led the other group. By the time of the Republican convention in San Francisco in mid-July, the divide had expanded to a chasm—and an abyss. Rockefeller rose, triumphant, to announce it was essential that the party "reject extremism from either the left or the right," including supporters of the hard-right John Birch

Society and the Ku Klux Klan. But instead of applauding, the delegates booed.

"We want Barry," they chanted, interrupting the patrician Rockefeller twenty-two times. To the horror of party strategists, a fight among party leadership played out right there on the dais. The crowd's noise kept Rockefeller from being heard. "It's not my fault if you don't control the audience," a furious Rockefeller muttered to the convention marshal. "I've got five minutes' worth. You control the audience and I'll make my five minutes," Rockefeller said. Rockefeller's words were picked up by the microphone for all to hear. The party voted down an endorsement of the civil rights law. The delegates nominated Goldwater.

Goldwater rose to criticize Johnson's Great Society spending as "bread and circuses" and uttered a line that would be quoted for the rest of the 1964 campaign: "extremism in the defense of liberty is no vice." Reporters crowded up to Goldwater, noting that not just a majority, but more than two-thirds of the Republican convention delegates had voted against the civil rights endorsement. Couldn't the Republicans now officially be labeled retrograde? Wasn't Johnson the man who led in these times? "Well," snapped Goldwater, referring to Johnson, "he himself opposed civil rights until this year. Let them make an issue of it. He's the phoniest individual who ever came around." In the convention hall at the Cow Palace, Goldwater tried to pivot to the topics of foreign policy and the economy, warning that the nation must "not cringe before the bullying of communism," that the nation had "lost the brisk pace of diversity and the genius of individual creativity." He also said the country must overcome a habit of "bureaucratic make-work"—a clear swipe at all the job training programs being prepared by Shriver's team in the poverty legislation.

Johnson now had the Grand Old Party leaders exactly where he wanted them. With the nation locked into anticipatory mourning for the civil rights workers, the Republicans' chaos looked irresponsible, and its rejection of his civil rights emphasis sounded callous. The GOP's economic focus simply seemed beside the point: unemployment was heading down below the 5 percent mark. Government might be growing, as Goldwater said, but damage was not in evidence. All summer he worked on his campaign image, filling in details like an artist at an easel. The great gap remaining in Johnson's campaign profile that summer regarded Southeast Asia. If Goldwater seemed too hawkish, Johnson seemed too soft. McNamara at the Defense Department was egging the president on to deepen U.S. involvement, and Johnson had developed great respect for McNamara. George Reedy, another aide, recalled later that McNamara "could rattle off statistics like a Hotchkiss machine gun." Johnson, Reedy also saw, "regarded Bob McNamara as the Messiah." To win support for escalation that McNamara told him was necessary, Johnson needed a moment to demonstrate the commander in chief was not soft on communism.

Early August gave Johnson that chance. In the night of August 4, two Navy destroyers in the Gulf of Tonkin, the *Maddox* and the *Turner Joy*, thought they had spotted torpedoes from North Vietnamese torpedo boats. The U.S. destroyers fired back, hundreds of rounds. The attack by the North Vietnamese was so egregious that Defense Secretary McNamara asked President Johnson to escalate to air strikes against North Vietnam. Johnson declared America had suffered an "unprovoked" attack—the adjective "unprovoked" was code that presidents in the past had used to signal they were moving toward war. Within a few days, both House and Senate voted the president authority to expand the military combat without further authorizations. The air strikes proceeded. This was a declaration of war in all but name, and Goldwater had supplied the cover. The language of the authorization was so broad that Johnson joked: "It's like grandma's nightshirt, it covers everything." The Tonkin Gulf resolution meant Johnson could send "soldiers," not mere "advisors," to Vietnam.

Johnson's authority only solidified when in the same hours as the Gulf of Tonkin crisis came word that three bodies, most likely those of the civil rights workers, had been found underneath an earthen dam near Philadelphia, Mississippi. The president handled this, too, insisting that the families be called even before preliminary word of the discovery was announced. Johnson was almighty, both commander in chief and clergyman at once.

Johnson's campaign portrait was nearly finished now. But in the time before his own August 24 convention, he needed one last piece: his poverty law. The legislation called for the creation of an office to coordinate and lead the anti-poverty effort. The office was given the name that seemed least threatening to conservatives or centrists, Office of Economic Opportunity, not "Office of Poverty." Shriver, Humphrey, and Dirksen managed to seal the Senate, with Shriver contributing significantly to the courtship of the Republicans. As a key "povertician," Wisconsin economist Robert Lampman, noted, Shriver's success could be explained in part by the still clubbish nature of the Senate: Shriver "had been at Yale Law School with half of them, I guess."

The senators respected a Democratic member of the House, Howard Smith. Smith initially rated the bill "the worst piece of legislation that's ever been introduced." But the senators saw that Shriver was working magic on Smith. The poverty bill passed the Senate 46 to 44.

But as late as August 1, Johnson found himself scrambling to claim the House. One evening on a 7:00 p.m. call with Reuther, Johnson stressed the urgency of the legislation. Johnson mentioned that this very night he was hosting Robert Wagner, the mayor of New York (Mayor Wagner was staying in the Lincoln Bedroom), so the two of them could powwow about recent unrest in Harlem. Reuther swore that he already had his own people on the ground in New York, that with his own UAW poverty initiative, "we're going to have an army to back your poverty program." As for the poverty bill that both men believed would help Harlem, Johnson warned Reuther that "they're going to defeat it next week." Johnson needed 210 votes in the House and he had only 195. The beleaguered Shriver needed backup. Johnson asked Reuther to get him some help from the autoworkers and the Michigan delegation; Reuther promised he would, beginning that very night, try to scare up at least two more votes for the bill.

The Republican objections to the poverty bill were twofold. The first was that the legislation was just an election-year gimmick. The second was the same problem Republicans and Southern Democrats had seen in the civil rights legislation: that the bill stepped on states' rights. People elected governors, not presidents, to be in charge of their states. The bill's opponents sought a gubernatorial veto on projects that the poverty office brought into their states. They got the governors' veto, and Shriver spent the early part of August talking himself hoarse. It seemed likely that the Republicans might nonetheless try to kill the legislation, on the argument that it was too socialist. Johnson, well aware of this, took every additional step he could to make not only his bill but his entire team look moderate. Hubert Humphrey of Minnesota was at the top of the lists among candidates for the vice-presidential slot. Humphrey had enjoyed his visit the summer before to Sweden with Harold Wilson and other West European socialists. He wanted to attend again this summer. But at word that the man who might join him on the Democratic ticket wanted to attend a socialist summit, Johnson turned hot. "My God, no." Humphrey did not go.

To secure the poverty legislation, there were other sacrifices, even among Shriver's staff. Congressman Harold Cooley, a Democrat from North Carolina, withheld his vote for the poverty bill, and finally gave Shriver his reason: Adam Yarmolinsky, who had put forward the language on "opportunity" instead of "poverty," was a "dangerous radical." Porter Hardy, a Republican colleague of Cooley's from Virginia, told Shriver that he, too, had heard concern about "some wild-eyed radical with a Russian sounding name." Shriver took a breath and explained: Yarmolinsky did indeed have a Russian background. Yarmolinsky's father translated works of Tolstoy for the Modern Library. Yarmolinsky was not a radical, he was a bureaucrat, deputy director of the poverty task force. And there was no evidence he was anything but loyal. As a student, Yarmolinsky had in fact led a fight at Harvard to stop a clutch of Soviet sympathizers. The Southerners countered: they would not support the bill if Yarmolinsky was allowed to work at any of the offices created by the law. Shriver consulted Johnson. Yarmolinsky was duly sacrificed. The poverty bill passed the House, 226 to 184.

At the August 20 signing ceremony, Johnson took further pains. The president told the public that the Economic Opportunity Act did not represent a "a handout or a dole." He continued: "We know—we learned long ago—that answer is no answer. The measure before me this morning for signature offers the answer that its title implies. The answer is opportunity." Spending now would bring savings later. Johnson promised the voters that this law would reduce the costs of "crime, welfare, of health and of police protection." The act would yield a new era, and "the days of the dole in our country are numbered." America would remember the 20 percent in poverty, the "forgotten fifth."

The president signed the poverty bill slowly, using seventy-two pens, in order to have one to give as a souvenir to each of those who had participated in the poverty project. Adam Yarmolinsky collected his pen with what speechwriter Eric Goldman later called "a tight smile." Michael Harrington was not present, so Pat Moynihan went through the line twice and picked up a second pen for him. The *Wall Street Journal* characterized the law as "an opportunity to eradicate poverty, not opiate it." Some observers speculated that Johnson might pick Shriver as his vice-presidential running mate.

The political artist Johnson had now completed his self-portrait; the president turned to place final touches on the convention image. The president's hope was that this convention, in Atlantic City, would provide a peaceful contrast to the ugly, heckling, Grand Old Party event at the Cow Palace in San Francisco. The president counted on at least some of the Southern Democrats to forgive him for the recent bill and strengthen his convention victory. Johnson and his team therefore managed many of the details of the convention, right down to picking where his staff would stay—the new Pageant Motor Inn, across the street from the convention—and the music to be played: "Hello, Lyndon" to the tune of "Hello, Dolly." In some of this work, Johnson relied on his old friend and mentee John Connally of Texas. Connally had recovered from his wound in Dallas. And Johnson had recovered from a recent disappointment, that Connally had not supported his civil rights bill. Now what mattered was that Connally continue helping Johnson on the presidential campaign, that the governor take care of the details. Johnson's advance men felt their concern rise when their eyes fell on a large billboard in Atlantic City picturing the Republican candidate over the words "In your heart, you know he's right." Johnson operatives fixed even that: at 6:00 on the morning of Johnson's arrival, the billboard firm added a postscript in a banner below: "Yes—Extreme Right." When it came to the agenda of the convention itself, Johnson also joined in the management. Johnson feared that any disruption would enable Robert Kennedy to make trouble for him, and perhaps even pull a shocker and win the nomination. The convention scheduled Robert Kennedy's speech, a eulogy for his brother, after the nomination, toward the end. Humphrey was now considered the favorite for the vice-presidential slot, but still waited for confirmation.

The most hopeful group heading to Atlantic City was the Mississippi Freedom Democratic Party delegation. Bob Moses, Casey Hayden, Fannie Lou Hamer, and the others counted on the UAW and counted on Johnson's Democratic Party to support it in its bid to claim its seats at the convention. The little party had gone through all the paper motions of qualifying for spots on the floor. The Mississippi group followed the rules. And its members had great moral authority. That summer, after all, not only had there been perpetual arrests, but thirty people had been beaten, and some churches burned, to claim the right of representation in American democracy. Chaney, Goodman, and Schwerner had been murdered. The seating of the Mississippi Freedom Democratic Party would show that all the laws, including the newest one, did actually mean something. Bob Moses, who liked to link all the dots in a problem, thought not only of Mississippi but also about the recent riots in New York. Yet, as he later remembered, "No one saw the connection between [Atlantic City] and the urban situation."[38] No one in politics, that is. Moses, Michael Harrington, and indeed Pat Moynihan often warned that blacks' troubles were not confined to the South: youth unemployment in America, much of it in the North, much of it black, had in part to do with blacks' sense of discouragement. Many young blacks had so little education that they were a "new lost generation," Harrington said. A quarter of teenagers reviewed by the Selective Service could not read at the seventh-grade level. Moses was a thoughtful man, but his friends remembered that when he climbed into the bus to head to Atlantic City, he "was seen to smile." His hope was that the Mississippi Freedom delegation's victory could lift the spirits of every black person in the North as well as the South.

When the little group arrived in Atlantic City, its members' own spirits lifted. Supporters from outside Mississippi met them there: Tom Hayden drove down from Newark. Their first job was to make their case before the credentials committee of the party. Aaron Henry, with Moses one of the founders of Mississippi Freedom Democratic Party, spoke of the care with which they had followed the rules to form the party. Fannie Lou Hamer described how she was beaten in Winona. "Is this America, the land of the free and the home of the brave, where we have to sleep with our telephones off the hooks because our lives be threatened daily because we want to live as decent human beings?"[39]

Even as the Mississippi Freedom Democratic Party traveled north to make its case, LBJ was making a decision that would force a mutiny at his own convention as ugly as any at the Cow Palace. The decision was that he would not fight for the little Freedom delegation. The president haled black leaders—James Farmer, director of the Congress on Racial Equality; Bayard Rustin; and A. Philip Randolph—to the White House and warned them of the perils of retaliation by Southern whites. Johnson spoke with Walter Reuther multiple times, telling him he guaranteed the Freedom delegation seats in 1968 if they all could work out a way to get through this convention. Johnson warned Reuther that if the Freedom Party delegates offended the regular Mississippi delegation, or played games with the credentials committee at the convention, there would be trouble.[40] There had to be a compromise some way—the Mississippi Freedom delegation couldn't just take its seats—and Reuther had to figure out what that compromise was.

Reuther in turn told Rauh that if they all—the Mississippi Freedom Democratic Party—didn't behave, Humphrey, their favorite, would not get the vice-presidential spot. Rauh exploded. He had worked hard to support the Mississippi Freedom delegation. "Look, Walter, I am acting not as your general counsel but as a citizen. I've got a private law practice. If you want to fire me, for Christ's sake, be my guest." Then it was Reuther's turn to get mad, "so fucking mad," Rauh said later, "you could fry an egg on his heart." If Humphrey didn't get the number two slot, Rauh would have to remember that the rest of his life, Rauh later recalled Reuther saying. Reuther and Johnson spoke again, and agreed to meet. Johnson asked Reuther to come quietly to the White House, "through the Southwest gate" where people wouldn't see him, because at that gate, "they come in and out all day long." Johnson told Reuther that if the Freedom Party delegates were seated, and the regular Mississippi delegates were offended, then Goldwater would win in November. The Freedom Party had to stay out for their own good, Johnson said. Johnson reminded Reuther that he, Johnson, was the best president the civil rights cause had ever had, but each time there was violence, or a big sit-in, he lost some of his ability to fight for blacks. Johnson told Reuther, "The Negroes are really just murdering themselves," busting up his, and Reuther's, Great Society coalition. Johnson had lost ten points in New York polls already for his civil rights work. Reuther then swore to Johnson that he had already laid the line down with Rauh, telling Rauh, "I'm in the president's corner on this, all the way."

At Atlantic City, Bob Moses, Casey Hayden, and the others from Mississippi found themselves therefore not in the great hall but parked at the Gem Hotel, one of the few hotels in New Jersey that welcomed black travelers. At the Gem, hour after hour, they waited for the convention leaders to seat them. Hayden, who did not even have a bed, slept on the floor and organized demonstrations on the boardwalk outside the convention. "These good people, patient and exhausted," she wrote later, "sat three and four in a row on the bed they shared, in their Sunday clothes, eating cheese and crackers from a paper bag, watching TV to see if they were getting permission to take their legal and righteous place." Perhaps Rauh would, somehow, work out a deal.

The deal did not come. The Mississippi Democratic regulars and the credentials committee wouldn't budge. Johnson, who had asked Reuther to compromise if possible, was himself furious that the old Southern delegation would not. On the telephone, the president complained to Governor Carl Sanders of Georgia about the old Democrats from Mississippi and their unwillingness to seat blacks. What was wrong with these retrograde bigots? Why did they treat blacks that way? "You and I just can't survive our political modern life," Johnson told Sanders, "with these goddamn fellows that are eating 'em for breakfast every morning. They got to quit that." And here his own party was finding itself telling the Southern regulars, "We're going to seat you, every damn one of you, you lily-white babies, we're going to salute you." This would split the Democratic Party "much worse than Goldwater and Rockefeller" had split the Republicans, Johnson told Connally. Johnson also asked John Connally to try working on the problem. Connally was the sort of man a president could count on in a tight moment.

The week of the convention, Reuther found himself in the middle of another standoff that matched the one in Atlantic City in tension: selecting a strike target for his high-stakes battle with the automakers. The entire negotiation mattered because whatever agreement Reuther made with his target—it would be Chrysler—would set the pattern for the industry. But Johnson, irate at being caught in this bind, ordered Reuther to Atlantic City to negotiate between the convention leaders and the group from Mississippi. Reuther chartered a plane and arrived with a heavy mission: talking people into giving up something he had helped them build. At risk, or so Reuther could argue, was not only Humphrey but Democratic Party solidarity, the basis for Reuther's great movement, not to mention his wage increases. On White House instructions, Reuther planned to offer at-large delegate spots for two cofounders of the Mississippi Freedom Democratic Party. The first was Ed King, a white Methodist minister who had suffered a beating when he supported a sit-in at the Woolworth's lunch counter in Jackson. The second was Aaron Henry of the NAACP. Both Ed King and Aaron Henry, a veteran, were more moderate than some of the other MFDP delegates. Fannie Lou Hamer, who herself had endured such severe beatings when she tried to register to vote, did not get one of the slots. Reuther met with Martin Luther King, asking him to support the deal and reminding him of the funds and friendship the UAW had provided in the past. As for Rauh, Reuther told him over the phone, "I am telling you to take this deal." Reuther, Humphrey, Martin Luther King, and Bayard Rustin, the man who had organized the great march on Washington, came together. Then they summoned the Mississippi Freedom group to a suite at the Pageant Motel.

In the room, Reuther and Humphrey threw out consolation prizes. The Mississippi Freedom delegation would be seated at the next convention, a lifetime away as far as the attendees were concerned.[41] Humphrey assured everyone that if Johnson was elected, all that was sought when it came to civil rights would come to pass. At some point Fannie Lou Hamer spoke back to him: "Senator Humphrey, I been praying about you, and I have been thinking about you, and you're a good man. The trouble is, you're afraid to do what you know is right." That was clearly true. Even as the Freedom delegates were taking the compromise offer in, they learned that Walter Mondale, Minnesota's attorney general, was already announcing the compromise of two at-large delegates on television, as if the Mississippi Freedom delegation had already signed off. That was insult added to injury. Robert Moses slammed the door in Humphrey's face and stomped out, as he later recalled, also "furious." Fannie Lou Hamer expressed what the group felt: "We did not come all this way for no two seats." Still in a daze, Moses borrowed convention passes, so that he and others from the Freedom Party could at least make a small demonstration, a sit-in, on the convention floor.

"Finks" was how Casey Hayden later labeled these former friends like Reuther, according to Tom Hayden. One of the youngest of the civil rights leaders from the South, John Lewis, chairman of the Student Non-violent Coordinating Committee, had traveled up to Atlantic City and also remembered the blow of exclusion his entire life. "We had played by the rules, done everything we were supposed to do, had played the game exactly as required, had arrived at the doorstep, and found the door slammed in our face." The irony was heavy. The civil rights law and the poverty law were just weeks old. They guaranteed voters the right to participate in democracy. Yet here Johnson and Reuther were denying the disadvantaged the chance to participate in the ultimate democratic event, their own party's convention. Heading back to Newark after the convention, in a daze, Tom Hayden hit two deer, killing them both.

That the country was not as angry as they were dawned only slowly on the members of the rejected delegation. "The first piece of mail to tumble over the transom," Mary King later remembered, was an $11,000 invoice for copies of the legal brief that had been written by Rauh.[42] The Mississippi Freedom Democratic Party had taken it for granted that the UAW would fund the printing costs. They called Rauh. "Well," Mary King later recalled Rauh saying, "you're independent." The party would have to pay its own bills from now on.

After Atlantic City, it did indeed prove harder for George Wallace to threaten Johnson. For a while, Johnson, who had in the end indeed selected Humphrey as his running mate, continued to worry about Goldwater. If Johnson's majorities in the House and Senate were not large enough, the rest of the Great Society would abort. Johnson's spinmeisters decided to take advantage of Goldwater's defense of extremism. They produced a commercial called "Confessions of a Republican" featuring a conservative young man expressing concern about Goldwater's well-known inconsistency: "a president ought to mean what he says," said the character in the commercial. Goldwater's convention "extremism" quote left him open to the argument that he would launch a nuclear war. Goldwater suffered, it was said, from "an itchy-finger image." The advertising firm Doyle Dane Bernbach was hired to pull together an attack commercial to scare out the vote against Goldwater. The commercial, which aired with the NBC Monday Movie (*David and Bathsheba*), depicted a girl of about four, playing with a daisy, who looks up to see a mushroom cloud exploding in the heavens. The message was clear: select Johnson, or apocalypse. "Vote for President Johnson November 3. The stakes are too high for you to stay home."

These jabs seemed gratuitous, for the public was beginning to sense that Goldwater had already lost. By late October, the Johnson-Humphrey ticket maintained a 2-to-1 lead in the Midwest.[43] The Republican Party had outspent the Democrats. Ralph Cordiner, the former GE head, gave $10,000 himself. But the Republicans were still trailing. The campaign staffers wondered not whether Goldwater was wrong, but whether Goldwater was the wrong messenger. Perhaps the party might rescue the election by letting the country hear a spokesman who could shift the topic from civil rights for blacks to civil rights for all, who was serious, and above all, who was not Goldwater.

That spokesman was Ronald Reagan. In late October in Los Angeles, Reagan recorded twenty-nine minutes for a long Republican television advertisement. Reagan had prepared some comments on recent news.

He criticized the government expansion behind "terms like the Great Society." He poked at the Tom Haydens for their mincing distinction between communism and "not undemocratic socialism." And Reagan targeted the Office of Economic Opportunity. "Now do they honestly expect us to believe that if we add $1 billion to the $45 billion we're spending . . . do they believe that poverty is suddenly going to disappear by magic?" Reagan also assailed the new camps being built for young workers. Room and board for each young person cost $4,700. Harvard tuition at $2,700 was less than that. Reagan took his jab at the college, and at Johnson's misty affection for a humanities education: "I'm not suggesting Harvard is the answer to juvenile delinquency." Reagan also turned to economics, mentioning the gold reserves that the United States held, now down to $15 billion from the $20 billion or $18 billion that had preoccupied Kennedy so. And Reagan argued that Johnson's "we never had it so good" theme belied fragility in the economy: we couldn't count on prosperity forever. The speech had required little preparation. Most of it came from the very same speech Reagan had been giving for years, the speech he'd developed for General Electric. America, Reagan said, was at a key moment—the country must choose whether it was a collectivist nation or a free one. The title of Reagan's speech was "A Time for Choosing."

In early November the nation chose. It elected Johnson with an overwhelming majority. Johnson had certainly out-Kennedyed Jack Kennedy. Kennedy had just barely beaten out Richard Nixon in 1960. Johnson pulled 61 percent of the vote to Goldwater's 38 percent, a stronger outcome, as Harry Truman noted in a congratulatory call, than anyone could remember. That memory for both presidents included Franklin Roosevelt, who had won a hair less than 61 percent of the popular vote in his 1936 landslide. Just after the election, Martin Luther King, who had just won the Nobel Peace Prize, spoke with Johnson, too, and the two men congratulated each other. Johnson promised that in the new term he would "spend a lot of time with Shriver on the poverty thing." The billion-dollar Economic Opportunity Act, Johnson suggested, was just the beginning, for getting going, "and next year we can do it a lot bigger." The election,

King said, was "a great victory for the forces of progress, and a defeat for the forces of retrogress." King affirmed Johnson's original pronouncement on that bright day in Michigan. What's more, King told Johnson, there were more "bright days ahead."

Reuther also looked forward. The union head was heading out for a meeting with Britain's Harold Wilson—after an election, meetings with socialists were again acceptable. But before that when Johnson and Reuther spoke, each sought to please the other. Johnson, his victory only hours back, focused first on consoling Reuther for the fact that Governor Romney, not the Democratic candidate, had won reelection in Michigan. Reuther praised Johnson, mentioning that vigorous campaigning, much of it by the UAW, had won Johnson at least two new congressmen from Michigan. He noted that Johnson had prevailed over Goldwater by hundreds of thousands of votes. Reuther had delivered 80 percent of the vote for Johnson in his stronghold, Detroit. Reuther and Johnson would be able to continue the Great Society revolution. Jack Conway, the AFL-CIO official, would be taking leave to become deputy director of Shriver's antipoverty program. Reuther reminded Johnson that "this time we shouldn't wait til the last minute" on black voting rights, a warning that they could not and should not report their errors of the convention in Atlantic City.

The cities were already counting the ways the Office of Economic Opportunity would deepen their resources to help the poor. Mayor Raymond Tucker of St. Louis, for example, had heretofore been able to provide about two hundred children with free lunches daily, using school board funds amounting to about $11,000 for the underprivileged. Now the city was looking forward to receiving a $603,000 grant to fund thousands of such lunches, serving up to 3,500 lunches for the children of the housing project Pruitt-Igoe alone. With the election safely behind them, the poverticians felt free to take strong positions again. At the Chase Plaza Hotel in St. Louis, Harrington, this time more politic than he had been alone with Shriver at the year's heady beginning, allowed that the $800 million allocated for the Office of Economic Opportunity "represented a starting point in the right direction." But voluntary organizations had to take the lead, Harrington continued, because in each metropolis Shriver's program would become "a city hall operation." This billion would abolish "very little poverty." For that, $100 billion was needed.

Toward the end of November 1964, safely after the election, William McChesney Martin led the Federal Reserve Board in raising the interest rate, then called Johnson with a lengthy explanation. This had come about, as Martin carefully told Johnson on the phone, only because of an event outside the country. The victor in the election in Britain had been Reuther's friend Harold Wilson of the Labour Party. Whereas Johnson talked about planning but left that planning to his wise men, Wilson was scientific about planning, establishing a new Department of Economic Affairs to practice what the UK Labourites called "indicative economic planning." After World War II, Clement Attlee's Labour government had nationalized steel. With great effort the Tory Party had led the nation in denationalizing most of steel in the 1950s. Now it was clear the new Wilson government would do its best to nationalize again. The uncertainty exhausted investors. The prospect of so much government intrusion, planned or no, socialist or social democratic, in the United Kingdom caused gold to flow out of England. The Bank of England had therefore raised interest rates to lure the gold back. The United States now had to follow with its own interest rate hike, to move up toward 4 percent from 3.5 percent, or it would lose yet more of the remaining $15 billion in its own gold. None of Martin's actions, the Fed chairman assured the president, even the postelection timing of them, had anything to do with American politics. But it was convenient that the UK prime minister was giving the Fed chair some cover for an action the Fed chair wanted to take anyhow.

To the general public, what the Fed did now did not seem to matter. The Administration and its Great Society allies congratulated one another. It was winter and the cities were quiet. The Dow Jones Industrial Average was approaching 880, up from 820 when Johnson had given his Michigan speech. Big companies were crowing. General Motors had suffered a strike that year, but this hadn't prevented its profits from hitting the highest level in history. General Electric's financial numbers were not as good as they could be, but that was only because the cost of the antitrust damage suits, hundreds of millions, was hurting GE's bottom line. The good results weren't confined to the giants. RCA was promoting "more reliable" computers made with electronic components known as "fully integrated circuits." A reporter who tried to describe the circuits came up with "tiny crystal specks packed with components." The makers of the specks included Fairchild Camera and Instrument, a heretofore little-known company. The stock of Fairchild Camera and Instrument, an innovator in the computer field, stood at 27⅞ but was poised for strong growth in 1965. Small firms in electronics were generally faring well, including another small computer company, Scientific Data Systems, whose orders of $18 million were up from $7 million a year earlier. The company, known as SDS, like the student group, had started with only 1 percent of an industry where monsters like GE and Honeywell roamed. But Max Palevsky, the company president, told the press that even so, his company's future was "wonderful." Employment at the West Los Angeles computer maker was at 1,400, up from 480 the year before. If the jobs did not go to the poor, well, then Shriver's funds were there to help them prepare. Eventually, the new "lost generation" that Harrington had described would find its way. The president's "forgotten fifth" would be remembered. In January, Sargent Shriver had announced twenty-two Job Corps camps were under construction, and some would open soon. Shriver would have trouble spending his appropriations fast enough.

Before the inauguration, Johnson called Reuther again, this time to urge him and his wife, May, to attend. In another call Johnson discussed "my medical care" (what would become Medicare), "my health benefits," "my education," and "my immigration" (an immigration act). The president swore he would meet his campaign promises, old and new, to put through repeal of Section 14(b) of the Taft-Hartley Act, the part of the law that allowed individual states to become harbors for nonunion businesses. Everything took time, Johnson warned. Reuther's colleague George Meany was heartless and impatient, Johnson told Reuther. Meany was relentless in his fixation on repeal of 14(b), arguing that the only way American organized labor could be rescued was by closing the "right to work" escape hatch. Listening to Meany demand repeal urgently, Johnson told Reuther, "I just wanted to cry." Meany didn't understand the timing of a difficult action like repeal of 14(b).[44] Meany wasn't grateful for all Johnson did. If Johnson waited to attempt repeal of "right to work" until after he completed a few other "touchdowns," then winning congressional support for repeal of the heinous statute would be likelier. "Timing is very important," Reuther agreed.

In Ford Hospital that winter to remove a growth on his lung, Reuther wondered at the comforts of a newfangled mechanical bed, and made a joke of such beds: "to build the great society, we must insist that they become standard equipment in every home."[45] The point was indeed that nothing was impossible. In 1965, Reuther had Johnson's ear. And this year, it was Johnson whom *Time* magazine placed on the cover as its "Man of the Year." The president had won his wager. Johnson was delivering his own New Deal. The Johnson coalition would make the Great Society real, just as Hubert Humphrey had promised the frustrated Mississippi Freedom delegate at the convention. All was well.

4

Revolt of the Mayors

JANUARY 1965

Guns: 7.1% of GDP
Butter: 4.9% of GDP
Dow Jones Industrial Average: 870

We are a great city.
—Mayor Sam Yorty of Los Angeles[1]

If you were a mayor in the United States in early 1965, your mind was on the coming summer. The U.S. economy was moving toward its fiftieth month of expansion, a postwar record. Unemployment was below 5 percent and heading down. But in the poorer corners of the Northern or Western cities, especially the corners where black Americans lived, the bonanza hadn't materialized. The engineering jobs that filled the want-ad section of the newspapers demanded a level of education that untrained blacks, especially those who had recently arrived from the South, believed they would never attain. Some of the factory floor jobs, which the migrants *could* fill, were departing Northern cities. What jobs were open and near to blacks in cities did not lead to promotion: blacks represented one-quarter of the workforce in the auto industry, for example, but only about 4 percent of those who held a skilled job.[2] People this disappointed could riot, the mayors feared—especially in June, July, or August, when underemployed young men took to the streets.

A factor the mayors had not reckoned with before, television, made protests more likely. When Reagan had started at GE, only half of American households had televisions. Now more than eight in ten families, including many poor families, had a TV. *Bonanza* was a top popular series.

Also popular was *The Beverly Hillbillies*, a show about members of a backwoods clan from the Ozarks, the Clampetts, who, after selling their land for millions to an oil company, lived like kings in the wealthiest area of Los Angeles. People watched more than prime-time entertainment. They watched news. When mobs with clubs attacked Freedom Riders and burned Greyhound buses, viewers in Newark, Los Angeles, or St. Louis saw the charred bus. When Bull Connor, Birmingham's public safety commissioner, turned water hoses and police dogs on demonstrators, the nation saw that, too. The images especially impressed recent migrants. The migrants knew all too well the kind of back roads of Mississippi where Chaney, Goodman, and Schwerner had disappeared.

The possibility of a riot was especially evident to a mayor who was running for reelection that spring, Sam Yorty of Los Angeles. Back on Memorial Day in 1961, as Yorty's first campaign for mayor ended, a rumble at the Griffith Park Zoo surprised the city. A black teenager had insisted on riding the merry-go-round without paying for a ticket. The seventy-five-year-old operator of the carousel tried to eject the boy. The zoo staff and police blocked the merry-go-round. More teenagers came, and soon two hundred people were caught up in a brawl that injured four police officers. Black families had made much progress in Los Angeles after the war. With great effort, and demonstrating considerable courage, families had moved to formerly all-white neighborhoods, staying despite catcalling and even firebombing. Blacks in Los Angeles were becoming homeowners, and in one neighborhood, West Adams, landlords. But each gain seemed to be offset by a loss. In the 1950s control rules had frustrated the humble business plans of black families who had hoped for an income from a rental. Planners had mapped out the new Santa Monica freeway so that it cut right through what the papers called the "most prosperous, best kept and most beautiful Negro owned property in the country," West Adams.[3] In 1965, Yorty worried especially about a neighborhood known as Watts. Watts, with its rows of houses and front yards, did not look like a slum. But the unemployment rate for men in that part of the city was over 13 percent, more than triple the national average.[4] According to the federal "poverty level" marker—the papers still printed the term in quotation marks because it was so new—Watts was definitely poor. Four in ten people there were members of families whose income was below Mollie Orshansky's line. Many of the jobless young men in Watts could not read well, and as in other cities, didn't find work. A youth who did go through one of the city's job training programs—there were already several such programs—often found that no job specific to his training waited at the end. "Train for what?" one youth asked a researcher later that year. These people lived just miles from Beverly Hills, but a universe away from the Clampetts' double staircase and its mansion. Walter Reuther was planning to dedicate two new United Auto Workers halls in the area, but both lay outside Los Angeles, southward, in Anaheim and Lakewood. Not only jobs but working people were leaving Los Angeles. In South Los Angeles, the total population was down 9.7 percent since 1960. Yet those with the lowest incomes could not find someone to rent to them outside the rough neighborhoods. In fact, just the year before, the state's voters had overturned a fair-housing law that would have required landlords in the suburbs to rent or sell to all comers. A riot could start in Watts and spread. In 1965, that was Yorty's nightmare.

Other mayors shared Yorty's concern about Los Angeles. Across the country, the Los Angeles Police Department had a reputation of being particularly tough. Many Americans nowadays also watched reruns of an old show about the Los Angeles police, *Dragnet*, in which policemen were relentlessly portrayed as the good guys, and the law as supreme and fair. In fact William Parker, LA's legendary police chief, had supplied technical advice to *Dragnet*'s producers. Off the stage set, the Los Angeles police could be overly insensitive, and occasionally brutal. People still recalled the story of Dr. Joseph Hayes, an African-American physician, who, just after World War II, was pulled over because he "looked suspicious." Police had beaten Hayes unconscious. The mayor who preceded Yorty, Norris Poulson, had seemed cavalier about the frustration of poor Los Angelenos, especially blacks.

Yorty had won the office of mayor in the first place back in 1961 in part because he had promised to improve life for all citizens so there would be no more police violence, no riots at the zoo. In that first campaign, Yorty had told blacks they would gain a voice if he was elected. The mayor had made good on those promises; under Yorty, Los Angeles had elected three new black members to the city council, which prior to Yorty's arrival had had no black members.[5] Yorty had vowed to "school" Chief Parker into better behavior.[6] Most residents of poor neighborhoods were victims of riots, not perpetrators. Yorty had committed to increasing police presence in the city, to protect all citizens. Yorty and Chief Parker had discussed exactly how the police would manage a riot. The Los Angeles budget for 1963 to 1964 included $50,930 for the purchase of three thousand riot helmets for the police. People tended to like Yorty, whether they were comfortable, Beverly Hills rich, or poor. Yorty had also delivered on other goals. The mayor had, for example, fulfilled a promise to reverse a rule requiring citizens to separate cans from the rest of the garbage. By the 1960s, Californians felt, they had reached a level of prosperity where they were entitled to be spared the chore of sorting their rubbish.[7]

This record convinced Yorty that he had a fair shot both at winning his second mayoral election, set for April 6, and at preventing the nightmare. Yorty also nursed hope for a second reason, one that buoyed other mayors as well: the new poverty money from Washington. "Community Action" had initially sounded small to mayoral ears. But Casey Hayden's little philosophical concept, participatory democracy, was now enshrined as federal doctrine. The mayors were waking up to the reality that Shriver's office wasn't merely a kind of domestic copycat Peace Corps, but rather an agency so well endowed and vigorous it might indeed have the potential to enable cities to solve their problems year-round. The new Office of Economic Opportunity was planning to approve and fund not dozens but over a thousand Community Action agencies in cities across America. Some individual grants ran into the millions. Within forty-five days of the congressional appropriation, Los Angeles, for example, had received $2.7 million as a first big starter grant, and talks with Washington suggested it might receive as much as $20 million. When the mayors' offices totted up the numbers, they found that 125,000 jobs were set to be created nationwide by the Community Action agencies alone. This level was higher than the number of servicemen who were in Vietnam that spring. It was also high enough to affect the problematic urban joblessness.

Johnson's evocations of Franklin Roosevelt signalled ambition. "In the first 101 days of this unique national war effort," Johnson said of the War on Poverty in January, in that instance making his hundred-day count from back in the fall, when the Office of Economic Opportunity had started to gun its engines, "we have brought nearly 400 transfusions of new opportunity to disadvantaged Americans in every part of this land." Johnson was falling in love with this project. And in 1965, the mayors could see, Johnson's passion was just beginning to blossom.

The mayors talked the poverty funding over among themselves. Their cities' own resources were "strained," as Johnson put it. To prevent riots, mayors needed more money—from somewhere. Given a choice between raising taxes and accepting help from outside, the mayors were willing, at least as a stopgap, to take money from outside. After all, the mayors could assign much of the blame for their restless neighborhoods to outside forces: to companies that moved away, or to unions, or to automation, or to television, or even to Martin Luther King himself. King had encouraged protest in Yorty's city by telling a crowd of thirty thousand at Wrigley Field in 1963, "Birmingham or Los Angeles, the cry is always the same. We want to be free." Around the same period, the mayor of Baltimore, Theodore McKeldin, had asked the Administration to be ready with federal aid for Baltimore—and McKeldin was a Republican.

The mayors thought over Shriver's conditions. The Poverty Office in Washington required what it called "maximum feasible participation" by locals on the ground. Well, the mayors could arrange participation. Johnson asked for "cooperation." The mayors could cooperate. Some of them had cooperated pretty well in the campaign to get Johnson elected. The mayors conferred some more. OEO, the acronym for Shriver's office, had already, in a few short months, established itself in the mayors' vocabulary. In each town, OEO-funded agencies could team up with, or, better yet, report to, a mayor's office, churches, the fire department, the Urban League. The new agencies could also work with a new program the UAW had created, the Citizens' Crusade Against Poverty. The new agencies could lend a hand at the Economic Research and Action Project, or ERAP, which had already stationed Tom Hayden at Newark's Clinton Hill. The older institutions could guide Johnson's new ones. Big nonprofits such as the Ford Foundation had been working in the cities for years, and might pitch in as well.

The mayors saw that some of their constituents were enthusiastic about community action, sometimes compellingly so. When Cyril Tyson, a civil rights leader in Newark, spoke about Shriver's work at a public meeting, he inspired the room. "Tyson's definition of maximum feasible participation made me feel that the War on Poverty might differ from the other social agencies," thought Bessie Smith, another resident. "Some people began to feel that the 'War on Poverty' was a program that would be able to help them."[8] Any new qualms the mayors had, they silenced again. After all, the Economic Opportunity Act itself contained a crucial check on Shriver's poverty shop. The act provided governors with veto authority over OEO programs. If a mayor wanted to kill a plan, he could turn to his governor.

The trick, the mayors decided, was to respond with alacrity, to take the lead. And, if the mayor was a Democrat, to remind the povertician in Washington of all that the bidding mayor's city had done for the Democratic Party. Mayor Hugh Addonizio of Newark, a Democrat, had been quick off the mark. On November 4, 1964, the very day after the presidential election, the city of Newark had passed an emergency resolution appropriating $15,000 in seed money to create its own vessel for federal funds. Dallas, which had bucked its own Republican tradition to vote for Johnson, figured a few cosmetic changes to its extant programs were all it needed to be ready for OEO. And to the shock of old segregationists, the Dallas Citizens Council, similar to a chamber of commerce, was now inviting local leaders to join in programs aimed at the poor. "Why they're even inviting Negroes and union leaders to sit in on some of the mayor's special committees now," commented a Dallas citizen nastily. John Connally, the Texas governor, remained a key Johnson supporter in the South, especially as other governors from the region turned their backs on Johnson. Connally would have extra say in crafting programs for Texas, starting with a Job Corps center at Camp Gary outside San Marcos. Johnson himself had gone to college in San Marcos, and the Job Corps reminded him of his heady days in the Texas office of the New Deal's National Youth Administration. From New Haven, Mayor Richard C. Lee had contributed significant support to both the Kennedys in 1960 and Johnson in 1964. Lee had long since established an entire alternate city government, parallel to the first, which could function as a vessel to receive public moneys for city redevelopment.[9] Now all he needed to do to qualify for the new War on Poverty money, Lee figured, was to add representatives from the poorer neighborhoods to his committees. Jerome Cavanagh of Detroit was also a Democrat and enormously popular—Cavanagh had first won his office by garnering the early backing of the city's African-American community, and had marched in downtown Detroit together with Walter Reuther and Martin Luther King just the year before. Cavanagh had Reuther's endorsement, and Reuther delivered votes. The mayors reckoned Detroit would have no trouble with Shriver's office, either.

The city that seemed likely to benefit most was mighty Chicago. Shriver had worked and lived in Chicago for years, and it was clear that Illinois was the place where he hoped one day to run for office. Chicago's mayor, Richard J. Daley, had played a key role in Johnson's victory in 1964, and—indeed, to a questionable level—in Kennedy's narrow victory in 1960. Besides, Johnson and Daley thought alike, in terms of constituencies, not political philosophy. Daley suspected rightly that given a choice, Johnson would find him a more trustworthy recipient for cash than any community group or any liberal club. The year before, the president had told his aide Bill Moyers of community action, "I'd a whole lot rather Dick Daley do it than the Urban League"—a national civil rights group led by blacks. Daley was so sure of Johnson that now he simply created a community action agency and made himself head of it. The mayor wrote up a budget request for Chicago community action that amounted to about half of the program's entire budget, Daley's measure of what Chicago was worth to Johnson. Then Daley pulled together all the poverty remediation proposals from his own departments and shipped them to Shriver's office in a two-foot box.

The non-favorites among the mayors, however, couldn't just ship their ideas to Washington in a box. These mayors had to approach Shriver carefully. Mayor William Francis Walsh of Syracuse was a Republican, and had already irritated Washington by exhibiting publicly his skepticism about community action. Saint Louis was losing population and businesses, and its Pruitt-Igoe public housing project represented the ultimate "poverty pocket." Yet St. Louis's new mayor, Alfonso Cervantes, though a Democrat, was not a Johnson man—that had been Raymond Tucker, whom Cervantes upset in the primary that year. Cervantes therefore had to prove his bona fides to Johnson and Johnson's men.

Another mayor in the uncertain crowd was Yorty. Yorty had served in Congress in the 1950s, when he'd been an ally of Lyndon Johnson, who at the time was a senator. Yorty had liked Johnson so much that at the Democratic National Convention in 1960, he had advised Johnson not to settle for the second spot on the presidential ticket. Yorty suspected the Kennedys, however, and in the end had not only endorsed his fellow Californian Richard Nixon but published an inflammatory pamphlet titled *I Cannot Take Kennedy* to boot. One concern that had moved Yorty was protection of local authority for towns and states. "I feel certain," Yorty had said, that "Nixon believes less in the transfer of power to Washington than Kennedy."[10]

Exactly how that history would affect his applications to the brother-in-law of the late president, Yorty could not know. Still, Johnson himself, Yorty saw, was acting out of conviction. "I think the man recognized poverty and wanted to do something about it, more than any president before him that I can think of," Yorty recalled later.[11] And Yorty already had his starter grant. The mayor could count on several key allies to help him run and dispense funds from the federal government. They included two new black members in the state legislature: an African-American minister and state assemblyman named F. Douglas Ferrell, a Republican; and Mervyn Dymally, a West Indian Democrat, who also represented Los Angeles in Sacramento. These men were moderates, but both agreed on one plan: to "change the nature of discrimination through legislation." Governor Pat Brown could also be useful in Yorty's bid for poverty money.

Brown's personal trajectory ran from right to left. Long ago, during the New Deal, Brown had switched from the Republican Party to the Democratic Party. Yorty's own trajectory was from left to right. Though still a Democrat in name, Yorty was finding himself increasingly conservative. Maybe Brown and Yorty could meet up in the middle. In fact, Yorty told himself, he could spin the whole situation positively. If Johnson was leading a War on Poverty, this was Yorty's chance to redeem his relationship with the party in power by proving himself a loyal colonel. To Yorty the War on Poverty could be a godsend twice over, a chance to help his city and to win back the Democratic Party all in one.

Yorty and his staff therefore studied the Economic Opportunity Act thoroughly, noting specific programs that could help their city, such as education for preschoolers and new social service staff. The mayor read Shriver's press releases. He thought about which of his own agencies would take custody of the funds. Los Angeles, an intensely decentralized city, was already difficult to govern. Yorty might "school" the police chief, William Parker, but he did not boss Parker, who reported to an independent body, the Board of Police Commissioners. Yorty did not manage the schools, for schools had their own independent board as well. Even plans for a new zoo were mired in a jurisdictional squabble: it wasn't clear whether the city or the Greater Los Angeles Zoo Association would tend the zoo's baby Indian elephant. Still, Yorty thought, cooperation was worth it. Together, he and others had established a special vessel to receive funds, which they called the Youth Opportunities Board. With summer concerns foremost, the mayor fastened on finding money for jobs for high school dropouts first. Yorty and his staff wrote up a meticulous bid for their high school jobs plan. With about $1 million from Washington, some two thousand high school age youth could be given jobs working for the City of Los Angeles. Yorty would lodge the workers in various city departments. A full thousand would serve in Recreation and Parks, 500 more in Public Works, 268 at the water and power plants and offices, 150 in city libraries, and 98 at the Housing Authority. The mayor's office offered examples to strengthen the bid: one task for trainees would be removing paper cardholders from the back of four million library books and replacing them with plastic holders that were part of the city's new automated lending equipment. Yorty's team carefully calibrated the pay for teenagers, setting it at $1.27 an hour, three cents below the state minimum wage for adults, but still above the federal minimum of $1.25.[12] With the poverty money, Yorty might achieve what he had long said he would do: reach the people over the heads of what he called "a hostile metropolitan press." What mattered most, perhaps, was that the OEO teenage jobs could start just in time, at the beginning of summer.

To give the Los Angeles Youth Opportunities Board the edge it needed, Yorty and his colleagues selected as its head Joseph Maldonado, a Mexican-American nonprofit leader in the state of California with a proven record as a grantsman. As executive director of Alameda County's Council of Social Planning, Maldonado had managed to corral the Ford Foundation, elected officials, and charity groups into cooperating on a program, winning a $100,000 subsidy. So determined was Yorty to secure Maldonado that the Youth Opportunities Board offered a salary of $25,000, the same amount the mayor himself earned, and more than the average pay in those years for a major league baseball player. The Youth Opportunities Board and Maldonado were Los Angeles' signal to Washington: Los Angeles is ready. Over the winter, Yorty and the other mayors had learned more as they watched more of the OEO money flow. Richard Daley of Chicago at first seemed to be faring best. The sums his city-sponsored community action program received were so generous that he was able to hire one thousand Chicagoans, an almost absurdly high number, as "community representatives" at a pay of $4,070 each. Yorty told the papers that he expected cash for summer jobs in Los Angeles somewhere between April 1 and June 30—but, naturally, he was hoping for a check on the nearer side of Tuesday, April 6.

Early on in 1965, however, Yorty and the other mayors began to discern clouds on the horizon. Staffers at Shriver's OEO seemed erratic, unheeding, even when you discounted for political loyalties. Sometimes the OEO staffers seemed to satisfy themselves with the mere appearance of getting things done. As Adam Yarmolinsky would observe: "It was less expensive to prepare people for jobs than to create jobs for people."[13]

Sometimes the OEO moved too fast, sometimes far too slowly. Most troublingly, the poverticians did not want to hear from the cities or the churches. The men under Shriver had their own agendas, following a cerebral and planning-oriented trend set in the days when Robert Kennedy, Shriver, and Eunice Shriver had sought to address the problem of juvenile delinquency. Like their counterparts in the Defense Department, the men at OEO seemed temperamentally to prefer grants for studying feasibility over grants for real-time "action." In fact, the new poverty law incentivized pilots and theoretical studies, because onetime trials were not subject to the already much-discussed gubernatorial veto. The year before, Americans had crowded into movie theaters to see Stanley Kubrick's film *Dr. Strangelove*, a parody of Cold War military zeal. One OEO officer, Sanford Kravitz, made odd and dictatorial choices when it came to funding projects. The policy crowd nicknamed Kravitz "Dr. Strangegrant." But the reviewing and the papers cost the mayors their precious time.

The mayors' second discovery was that the OEO didn't always like mayors' and governors' new poverty proposals, however curated. The OEO sometimes even rejected plans of favored Democrats. After signaling it was happy with Daley, the OEO was now telling others it was taking a second look at Chicago, and would offer money to non-Daley groups. Shriver's office turned away one of Cleveland's plans, as well as plans from New York, Los Angeles, and San Francisco. The OEO wanted more of a lead in selecting which agencies would receive the money, and wanted more of a hand in picking who led those agencies. The main issue, the OEO told the mendicant mayors, was that the mayors were not meeting the OEO's requirement of "maximum feasible participation" of the disadvantaged in community action projects. Go back to your cities, the OEO executives told the mayors. Find more poor people. Find different poor people.

Other demands from Shriver's office came as an outright shock to mayors, and governors as well. The prekindergarten program, Head Start, sounded benign enough. Who could not want to help four-year-olds? The program provided lunches, breakfasts, and transportation for small children. But Head Start was proving unexpectedly large, and growing larger, with many tens of thousands to enroll by summer. The OEO was occasionally demanding "maximum feasible participation" when it came to employment at the Head Start project centers, and those in a position to hire often chose civil rights activists as teachers. A number of the demoralized Freedom Summer activists were now turning their energies to Head Start, especially in Mississippi, where it would serve twenty-one thousand children. The shift was so great that it bothered SNCC veterans. Mississippi "suddenly in 1965 had a government anti-poverty program called Head Start with lots of federal money," Mary King, the activist, later recalled. The Head Start program "in some ways rendered redundant the role that SNCC and COFO (Council of Federal Organizations) had played."[14] OEO, an institution designed to foster a movement to enfranchisement, was crowding out a real movement.

Others, particularly in state legislatures and county offices, were suspicious of Head Start for a second reason. Curricula for these preschools would emphasize African heritage in a way that public schools in the South heretofore did not.[15] That seemed to some a backdoor way of taking over curriculum, traditionally and legally the states' and towns' territory. To say the Southern curricula needed change was an understatement. Some elementary school texts still treated the Civil War as "the war for Southern independence."[16] But even Southerners who wanted just text-books resented the sneakiness. The trouble was not so much what Head Start did, but what it portended for schools. What if Head Start for tod-dlers morphed into Head Start grammar school? The state of Mississippi hadn't thanked the old party leadership for keeping the little Freedom Party off the convention floor. Instead the state showed its conservatism by giving Barry Goldwater 87 percent of its vote in the 1964 presidential election, the first time Mississippi had chosen a Republican in a presidential race since Ulysses S. Grant. Now voters were quick to complain about Head Start. Texans for their part found that not only Head Start but two other programs—the Job Corps and the Youth Corps—disturbed them. The War on Poverty seemed as much gravy train as service; in areas of Texas designated "poverty pockets," for example, all children could attend Head Start, even children who weren't poor.

"GREAT" BEFORE GREAT. After World War II, the federal government launched a giant program subsidizing home purchases, largely in the suburbs, for working- and middle-class Americans. For the poor, Washington created urban renewal, a costly undertaking that included vast housing projects of rental apartments. Small businesses and families in the bulldozers' path protested. "Urban renewal . . . means negro removal, and the federal government is accomplice to this fact," concluded the writer James Baldwin. The Supreme Court backed the bulldozers, and complexes such as Pruitt-Igoe of St. Louis (below) replaced much-loved neighborhoods. As the 1960s dawned, federal planners confidently predicted that a growing economy and even more ambitious spending would ensure unqualified success for projects like Pruitt-Igoe and their inhabitants.

Walter P. Reuther Library, Wayne State University

Getty Images/Bettmann/Contributor

PLANNERS AND THEIR BONANZA. Most politicians and experts believed that when three groups—the government, big business, and unions—sat at one table, optimal growth for the country resulted. Economists counseled that a "mixed economy"—part public, part private, and heavily coordinated—suited the nation best. Above, President John F. Kennedy hosts Henry Ford II, Joseph Block of Inland Steel, Thomas Watson of IBM, George Meany of the AFL-CIO, Walter Reuther of the United Auto Workers, and future Federal Reserve chairman Arthur Burns, among others. What Americans should do with wealth once they had it was the topic of a TV Western that debuted as the 1960s commenced, *Bonanza*.

Getty Images/Corbis Historical

Associated Press/Getty Images/University of Southern California/Contributor

THE THREAT TO THE BONANZA. One man believed that top-down coordination actually threatened growth, and that America could slide into populism or dictatorship. Lemuel Boulware (above, left), an executive at GE, argued that seemingly benign social institutions, such as labor unions, put America on the wrong path. Boulware hired an aging actor, Ronald Reagan, to make the case for purer capitalism. (Above right, Reagan plays a Soviet colonel on *GE Theater.*) A philosopher who also warned of the dangers of the "mixed economy," Friedrich von Hayek (below), suggested America risked stepping onto the "road to serfdom." For many, such fearmongering seemed outdated and extreme.

Getty Images/Paul Popper/Popperfoto/Contributor

Getty Images, Michael Ochs

Getty Images/Robert Elfstrom/Villion Films/ Contributor

IT STARTED AT PORT HURON. In June 1962, a number of young Americans gathered at cabins outside Port Huron, Michigan, to forge their own plans to transform society and to build up new institutions, including the Students for a Democratic Society. Michael Harrington (above left), a socialist, argued for partnership with the established Democratic Party. Robert Parris Moses (above right), a math instructor who became a civil rights leader, led dangerous voter registration drives in the segregated South. Tom and Casey Hayden (below) pushed for new protests and community action to win jobs and dignity for workers.

Getty Images/Frew W. McDarrah/Contributor

Courtesy of Casey Hayden

Getty Images/William C. Shrout/Contributor   *Walter P. Reuther Library, Wayne State University*

THE UNIONS IN THE BACKGROUND. Though the student activism of the early 1960s appeared spontaneous, it was not entirely so. Union groups, including Walter Reuther's (above left) United Auto Workers and the AFL-CIO, funded the Port Huron activists. Reuther's UAW aide, Mildred Jeffrey (above right, with Lady Bird Johnson), actually arranged the stay at the Port Huron cabins for the students. Reuther believed that engaging a youth wing would help unions lead the entire country away from bigotry and toward his ideal, Western European social democracy. Reuther was also an early supporter of Martin Luther King Jr. When King and other demonstrators landed in a Birmingham jail, Reuther sent UAW executives with $160,000 in cash strapped to their belts to bail them out.

Associated Press

THE BEST AND THE BRIGHTEST. The automakers who employed Reuther's workers operated from the top down. George Romney of American Motors (left) was among several successful executives, including Robert McNamara of Ford, who believed their mastery of business would translate to mastery in government. Throughout the 1960s, Detroit's mayors, automakers, and union leaders (below from left, Detroit mayor Louis Miriani, Henry Ford II, and Reuther) did follow the lead of European social democrats, agreeing on unprecedented wages and benefits for workers. Few asked whether the generous pay packets would render Detroit uncompetitive.

Getty Images/Grey Villet/Contributor

Walter P. Reuther Library, Wayne State University

Courtesy of NASA

MANKIND—OR MAN? In the early 1960s, government offered one model of how to "get to great"—collective projects. The most inspiring of such projects was Kennedy's "Man to the Moon" space program, which distracted the country from its own troubles: errors in Vietnam and riots in the cities. In the same period, however, business startups were beginning to demonstrate the potential of the individual to move the country forward. Below, the "Traitorous Eight": Robert Noyce, Gordon Moore, and six others who left Shockley Semiconductor in 1957 to found Fairchild Semiconductor. Fairchild in turn begat Intel—and an entire new culture of enterprise.

Wayne Miller/Magnum Photo

THE GREAT SOCIETY BECOMES OFFICIAL. As a U.S. congressman and senator, Lyndon Johnson had lionized both New Deal father Franklin Roosevelt and Harry Truman. On becoming president, Johnson sought to implement a program that expanded on his predecessors' progressive legacy. At the University of Michigan in 1964, Johnson made the Great Society official, declaring he would cure poverty. "Our aim is not only to relieve the symptom of poverty, but to cure it, and above all to prevent it," the president said. With the Michigan speech, Johnson made the portentous choice for the entire nation: America would attempt advancement through the public sector. To the private sector, Johnson assigned the job of funding the undertaking.

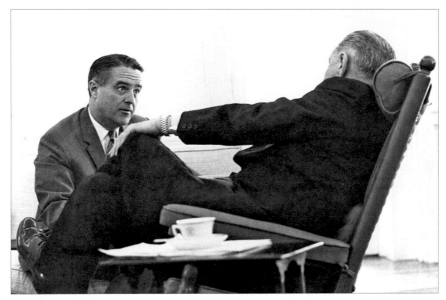

BENZEDRINE IN THE AIR-CONDITIONING. Sargent Shriver, President Kennedy's brother-in-law, directed the Peace Corps. Johnson tapped the energetic Shriver to lead the War on Poverty as well. If church charity helped the poor, Shriver reasoned, so should government spending. Shriver's Office of Economic Opportunity commenced multiple controversial programs.

STUDENTS TRY TO CHANGE THE CITIES. Inspired by the unions and the federal government's War on Poverty, many young activists headed to northern cities, where they hoped to help the poor find a voice. Tom Hayden created the National Community Union Project for Newark, but NCUP had trouble finding a constituency.

Getty Images/Fred W. McDarrah/Contributor

THE IDEA MAN. Daniel Patrick "Pat" Moynihan helped craft John F. Kennedy's Executive Order 10988, which gave federal workers' unions the authority to bargain collectively on workers' behalf. Few thought the change meant much, but 10988 set the stage for a new kind of labor powerhouse—public sector unions.

Getty Images/New York Daily News Archive/ Contributor

Associated Press

PLANNING SOME MORE. President Johnson placed faith in young experts. As Kennedy had turned to whiz kids to manage foreign policy, so Johnson assigned them to the Great Society as well. Here poverty czar Shriver hands out cigars to celebrate the birth of his fourth child; Secretary McNamara sits to Shriver's left.

Associated Press

THE MAYORS STRIKE BACK. In a landmark 1965 speech at Howard University, President Johnson shifted the Great Society's emphasis from equality of opportunity to equality of result. "Freedom is not enough," Johnson said. The nation's mayors first welcomed the flow of help and cash that the Great Society represented, assuming that the funds available would go into their own poverty or community programs. Soon enough, however, the mayors started to resent the intrusion of the federal government, especially when Washington funded social activists to challenge the mayors politically. Two of Johnson's fellow Democrats resisted the federal usurper: Sam Yorty of Los Angeles (left) and Richard J. Daley of Chicago (below), an old ally of President Johnson's.

Associated Press

Associated Press

TENSION FROM THE BEGINNING. "Guns and butter" was how Johnson's dual commitment to spending on Vietnam and the Great Society was described. The "butter" part included two expansive health care programs—Medicare for seniors and Medicaid for the poor. But could the country actually afford both guns and butter? Federal Reserve chairman William McChesney Martin (above, with Johnson) feared not, believing overspending would challenge not only budgets but the U.S. currency. Governments of other nations shared the Fed chair's concern about the future of the dollar. French leader Charles de Gaulle (below) was among them. "The world needs an indisputable monetary base that bears the mark of no country in particular," de Gaulle said.

Getty Images/Bettmann/Contributor

A METAL THAT REFLECTED DISTRUST, AND A COUNTRY THAT NO LONGER TRUSTED ITS PEOPLE. Like Bitcoin today, gold in its day was the measure of the world's distrust of the U.S. dollar. The infatuation with the commodity spread to the popular culture. Pictured above is the Paris opening of *Goldfinger*, about a plot to take over the world's gold supply by irradiating Fort Knox. At home, federal, state, and city authorities felt increasingly estranged from their constituents. Below is an elaborate riot repsonse crisis protocol readied by Detroit police.

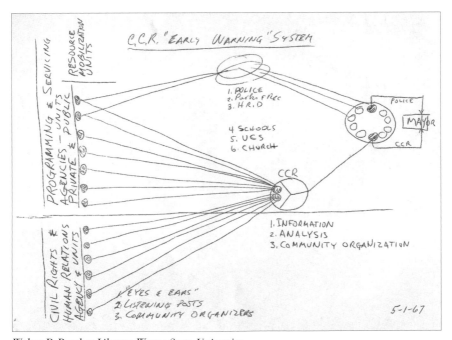

THE FIRE THIS TIME. The experts notwithstanding, 1960s reforms made as little progress as earlier federal efforts. Still isolated, poor and working-class families found too little of the bonanza was reaching them. The wonder world they viewed in the shows on their new television sets only deepened their disillusionment. Detroit's elaborate riot prevention plan was never implemented—riots erupted too quickly. The August 1965 Watts riot in Sam Yorty's Los Angeles (above) left thirty-four dead, a thousand injured, and millions of dollars in property damage across days of violence.

US National Archive/HUD Staff

GREAT SOCIETY II. Frustrated that civil rights laws and new entitlements were not reducing American discontent, President Johnson turned to housing. The massive scale of the new Department of Housing and Urban Development's headquarters (above), designed by brutalist architect Marcel Breuer, reflected the federal government's desperation to get "great" right this time. Part of Johnson's housing drive was new construction, including further attempts to fix up past errors at public housing projects such as Pruitt-Igoe (below). But federal dollars could not offset another emerging problem. Industry was migrating out of cities—and even out of the country.

Missouri Historical Society/Mac Mizuki Photography Studio Collection

STOP THE SLUMLORDS. Landlord exploitation of black families was the focus of Martin Luther King Jr.'s 1966 housing drive in Chicago. King's emphasis on class—poor versus landlord—was one Reuther shared. King also pushed for "open housing," integration of heretofore white neighborhoods. Here are the Kings at 1550 South Hamlin Avenue, a house they occupied to publicize landlord neglect.

Chicago Tribune

Associated Press

Getty Images/John Harding/Contributor

BUILD IT YOURSELF. Other black Americans thought the black community should turn inward to solve its problems. Among them were Nathan Wright, an Episcopalian minister in Newark (left), and a young economist named Thomas Sowell (right).

When the local school boards in the South scrutinized the Head Start programs further, their skepticism grew. The Head Start program did not take all children for two or three hours in the morning, as traditional nursery school did. A pupil might stay all day, and receive medical and dental treatment, as well as the attention of a social worker.[17] "It's a federal kindergarten, that's what it is," a McAllen, Texas, school board member, Othal Brand, complained, "more cradle to grave." Head Start was also a kind of mini-utopia, the sort of which Walter Reuther dreamed. In Texas, Connally, one of Johnson's closest allies, had personally supported a preschool program for Mexican-Americans when he became governor in 1963. But it seemed to Connally as he observed Johnson's new program enroll an astounding seventy-one thousand children in Head Start, that the federal government didn't want cooperation, as Johnson had promised. It wanted to control.

As the mayors and the governors watched, OEO justified these unprecedented interventions. "Maximum feasible participation" was better than preceding plans, the OEO staff said, and would therefore prove more successful than prior federal efforts. The new community actions avoided the transactional taint of city hall. The men at OEO, the mayors could see, were not ashamed of their slow process, they were proud of it. The way OEO worked represented, as Daniel Patrick Moynihan put it, the professionalization of reform. In the future, OEO was certain, lower poverty numbers and a more democratic society would vindicate it. The mayors struggled to accommodate this arrogance. In New York, Mayor Wagner had created the Mayor's Council Against Poverty. Now he dropped "Mayor's" from the title.

Shriver himself was a good speaker, a combination of Boy Scout and superhero. You wanted to approve of Shriver's projects because Shriver wanted you to. And those mayors who did manage to win over Shriver's team told themselves they were making progress. Mayor Cervantes of St. Louis was one of those who found favor, and he advertised the fact. "Saint Louis is highly regarded by Sargent Shriver," the *St. Louis Post-Dispatch* lectured that spring, "because of the forthright nonpolitical character of the Human Development Corporation," St. Louis's equivalent of the Youth

Opportunities Board in Los Angeles or the United Community Corporation of Newark. The *Post-Dispatch* concluded smugly that "Congress has heard enough testimony about such chicanery elsewhere . . . such abuses would be intolerable in St. Louis." Saint Louis suffered from high infant mortality, and the Human Development Corporation was applying for $705,000 for a new pre- and postnatal care center near Pruitt-Igoe.

Yorty was having more trouble than Cervantes. To disburse part or all of its $20 million for the Los Angeles area, the OEO was imposing a condition: Los Angeles must introduce twelve underprivileged private citizens to the Youth Opportunities Board by merging it with another foundation, and some of those private citizens would be representatives of "Mexican American and Negro minority groups." Yorty opposed that, and not, he argued, on racial grounds. Such a plan would be giving control of the strings of a potentially heavy purse to the very groups that would receive the money. That was old-fashioned moral hazard, like making a bank borrower a bank officer as well. Couldn't Johnson, so far away, hear the warning of his colonel? Mayor John Shelley, to Yorty's north in San Francisco, put his concerns about community boards and agencies bluntly: "What if they elect a communist or a criminal?" Others noted that the trouble, often enough, was that the new community agency boards were not elected at all.

Mayor Theodore McKeldin of Baltimore, the same mayor who had asked about possible aid from Washington the year before, now dared to warn Johnson first. After a January meeting of the Board of Advisers of the U.S. Conference of Mayors, McKeldin wrote to Johnson that it was the "almost unanimous feeling" of the mayors that the federal programs were being run by new people "who do not understand the problems and operations of local governments." No one knew whether Johnson even knew what his community action program was doing. As far as observers could tell, the president envisioned community action as a kind of New Deal redo with jobs for teenagers. Bill Moyers, Johnson's aide, forwarded the McKeldin letter to Vice President Humphrey. The president didn't want to involve himself. As Moyers wrote to Humphrey, "he asked that you and Sarge get together and work out the problem."

That February, union work was preoccupying Reuther. The UAW leader was busy trying out the idea of a union between the UAW and James Carey's Electrical Workers, Boulware's old antagonists. A merger could give the Electrical Workers "great leverage in their long feud with the management of General Electric," said Reuther. It would also take the size of the UAW up to 1.3 million members, within shouting distance of the biggest union, the Teamsters. Nonetheless, the loyal Reuther took time to show he was still in Johnson's corner, just as he had been during those terrible moments at the August convention. On February 10, Reuther hosted a UAW conference of civic groups in Washington, with Vice President Humphrey representing the Administration. For his own speech, Reuther knew, tales of West European holidays or Scandinavian health benefits would not suit. They sounded too socialist for the Johnson Administration. Instead, Reuther turned to an American image, that of the Puritan John Winthrop on the *Arbella*. Reuther quoted Winthrop: "We must consider that we shall be as a city set upon a hill and the eyes of the people will be upon us." That city on a hill must also serve black Americans. There was no going back on the poverty war—Johnson and the UAW, Reuther told the crowd, sought "the eradication of poverty in all its forms."[18] Black Americans could not live without greater protection for their civil rights and greater opportunity for jobs. Otherwise, there would be, as the black leader Whitney Young said, "a mouthful of civil rights and an empty dinner table." What happened in the War on Poverty must happen in a "complementary and constructive manner," Reuther said, but it had to happen.

That same February, the OEO codified in formal rulebooks the vague and random statements that it had made to grant seekers. Agencies funded by the Community Action program, the mayors now learned, should always include members from three groups: public and private nonprofits, existent community groups (churches, unions, minority groups), and the poor themselves. In Washington, OEO staffers were also preparing another document, the Community Action Program Workbook—262 pages on how to apply for and run a federally funded program.[19] The goal of community action, the workbook said, was "not merely improvement of the standard of living of the poor," but also a "move into the mainstream of American life." Old ideas—the kind mayors had—"have not and will not be enough." Community action programs, the authors wrote, should provide the "stimulation of change." One marker of a successful community action group was that it "increased competence in protest activities." The OEO also allowed that it welcomed experiments, including those where community action organizers paid by Washington were "facilitating the opportunities for the poor to participate in protest actions."

That kind of language was enough to send mayors like Dick Daley through the roof. Daley telephoned Johnson's aide Bill Moyers, who, as he later remembered, scarcely had time to breathe "Hello" before the Boss started in. The Administration was giving grants to radical groups, not just churches or elected officials, Daley said. On the South Side of his own city there was a relatively new coalition of radicals and activists known variously as the Temporary Woodlawn Organization, the Woodlawn Organization, or TWO. It was Saul Alinsky himself who had inspired the creation of TWO, and now the government was treating TWO as a serious institution. The Woodlawn Organization worked with gangs like the Blackstone Rangers, a South Side rabble. Would a man who hoped to have a political future in Daley's city, Shriver, really send money to gangs there? "What in hell are you people doing?" asked Daley. The mayor spelled it out. "Does the president know he's putting M-O-N-E-Y in the hands of subversives?[20] The Reverend Lynward Stevenson, who headed the Woodlawn Organization, was aware of Daley's complaints. Stevenson blasted back. The groups Daley created were just an expansion of the notorious Daley machine. "We want the law on maximum feasible participation enforced in Chicago," Stevenson said. What Chicago didn't want, Stevenson said, was the Daley crowd, "men who drive Cadillacs, eat three-inch steaks, and sip champagne at luncheon meetings." Saul Alinsky called Mayor Daley's initial allocation of poverty funds to his own machine as "a prize piece of political pornography." The public enjoyed the crossfire.

Daley, however, wasn't alone in ringing an alarm. Syracuse University had received a grant of $314,000 to train community activists in Saul Alinsky–style tactics, which meant protest and shaking things up. The grant paid Alinsky himself to consult. The Syracuse University Bulletin described the candidates sought: trainees "should have a controlled but intense anger about continued injustice and should be committed to hard work for people who are grappling with apparently overwhelming problems." The program had "no academic prerequisites." The organizers were forming tenant unions, bailing out protesters, and registering voters who were more than likely to vote against Mayor Walsh in the next election. "These people would go into a housing project and talk about setting up a 'democratic' organization—small 'd'—that sounds just the same as Democratic—big 'D,'" the mayor told the press.[21] Walsh told OEO he was "not going to take this lying down." As one of Walsh's colleagues said, "we are experiencing a class struggle in the traditional Karl Marx style in Syracuse, and I don't like it."

WHAT SET the mayors off that spring of 1965 was not merely their outrage at a power grab in their territory. It was commitment to a principle: local authority. Back at the time of America's founding, the Constitution's framers had explicitly defined rights of the states. In the Bill of Rights, the Tenth Amendment ensured that any powers not delegated to the federal government were "reserved to the States respectively, or to the people." The new capital in Washington should be, and was, a pygmy next to the states. States and their differences, America believed, kept democracy alive. This attitude held even after the Civil War, even into the 1920s. At the dedication of the Arizona state stone at the Washington Monument in 1924, President Calvin Coolidge had made a point of insisting that "the nation can be inviolate only as it insists that Arizona be inviolate."[22]

But where, a mayor might ask, was the line in the Constitution that protected the town? From their own earliest days, towns that found themselves in battle against a state government or Washington often lost. Traveling across the young nation in the 1830s, the Frenchman Alexis de Tocqueville likened the vulnerable towns and villages to vulnerable patients on a sick ward: "no immunities are so ill protected from the encroachments of the supreme power as those of municipal bodies in general."[23] Nonetheless, Tocqueville saw what Americans saw, which was that towns provided the base for American democracy: "Town meetings are to liberty what primary schools are to science," he concluded. "They bring it within people's reach." Tocqueville had also reassured himself and his readers, noting of the town that "its sphere is indeed small and limited, but within that sphere its action is unrestrained." Schooling was unquestionably a local responsibility, and towns had a vehicle to pay for the schools, the local property tax. Maintenance of the streets and of public areas was a town or county matter. Rubbish management, the issue in Yorty's 1961 campaign, fell within a mayor's purview. The maintenance of law and order lay within the sphere of town and county. Aiding the towns in all this work were other groups: clubs, fraternal societies, associations, charities, and churches. If a poor man went to a hospital, it was likely to be a town hospital or a church hospital, or even a company hospital—Reuther had been treated at Ford Hospital—not one funded by Washington. "Public assistance" meant money from town or community coffers. The power of associations had especially struck Tocqueville. Church groups or fraternal organizations supplied much to families, from burial to disaster relief. The dominant religious denomination in each town or state shaped philanthropic work. In the St. Louis of Michael Harrington, for example, or in Baltimore, the town fathers and the Catholic Church built the churches, the hospitals, and many schools. Both Harrington and Father Shocklee had attended St. Louis University High School, a Catholic institution that trained young men not only to tend the church, but also in the precious work of tending the community. The pride of America was the mighty community chest.

American citizens paid keen attention to any encroachments on local authority, whether from Washington, the state government, or even the town. Sometimes even the idea of a strong town government unnerved citizens, and, as in the case of Los Angeles, they structured local law so that America's famous system of checks and balances operated at the local level. Up to the end of the 1920s, Tocqueville's town lived. One of the merits of the towns had been their differences. Cook County, Chicago's county, was as powerful as the city mayor and aldermen; both needed the governor to get things done. Los Angeles happened to represent that extreme model of decentralization.

The New Deal had tested both state and municipal independence, as so much else. Under Roosevelt, federal spending had grown repeatedly, so that in 1936, the balance tipped: suddenly, the federal government was a larger presence in the economy than states and towns combined. The New Deal programs came like a railroad, laying tracks over old roads and rendering old local markings, once all-meaning, irrelevant. In the 1950s, the bulldozers of Harry Truman and Dwight Eisenhower had further erased local landmarks. In fact, the postwar federal government had offered such big bounties for participation in urban renewal or highway construction that they had seduced the mayors. After each new project, the mayors told one another: this, but no more. Fighting back, if only symbolically, Mayor Daley had seen to it that one of the big new highways that was part of the construction was named after a local, the president of the Cook County Board of Commissioners, Dan Ryan. Ryan had raised the funds from the federal government for the highway, but he'd done it *for Chicago.* The conflict between the federal government on the one hand and the states and towns on the other settled into an uneasy truce. The towns and states accepted dependence on federal funds, but that didn't mean they liked this dependence.

By the time Johnson made his speech at Michigan, the issue was no longer reestablishing balance; it was whether the new Great Society endeavor would, by its sheer weight, squash states and towns altogether. The critics of the Head Start program might be histrionic, but they were correct in suspecting the Administration did want Washington to get into the school business, and might one day, even, create a federal Department of Education. That spring President Johnson was overseeing passage of two bills, one to supply unprecedented federal funding for colleges and financial aid, the other to fund kindergarten through twelfth grade. The amounts that would flow from Washington would truly give Washington a say in each classroom.

How had it happened? One of the reasons was the South. In, say, Mississippi, Alabama, or Georgia, the state government had abused its power since Reconstruction. Why should states whose governments had failed to stop lynching have any rights? Why should governments of states where fewer than one in ten blacks voted—such as Mississippi—be considered responsible? But the question the governors and mayors asked themselves in 1965 was whether what remained of state and local authority warranted scuttling because of great abuses in the South that were already being rectified by new federal civil rights law. Northerners were especially indignant. To be sure, Northern or Western mayors could be corrupt. They often were. But were they necessarily more corrupt than officials in Washington? What could Washington, DC, itself still struggling to desegregate, teach a New England selectmen's meeting about community participation? Why should that town meeting whose portrait Norman Rockwell had so lovingly painted fall casualty to the abuses of bigoted Bull Connor? Was Los Angeles racist, or was it merely failing in its efforts to help blacks?

The problems of Northern towns were, the mayors told one another, more economic than social. What towns wanted was not a federal opportunity program but genuine economic opportunity, the kind provided by the jobs at General Electric, or by unions that welcomed and trained black teenagers. The mayors saw their own work as partly salesmanship: Yorty traveled the world, seeking friends in new companies he could bring to Los Angeles to employ both whites and blacks. The sideshow of the OEO made it harder for mayors to concentrate on such work. Insofar as the intruding federal institutions took away from mayors, they were de-democratizing cities. The mayors or the selectmen were truly democratic representatives, for the people voted them in or out. Mayors and even governors were close enough to their constituents' problems to be able to deliver something approximating what people needed. The chance that the federal government would manage that was smaller. The trouble with the War on Poverty wasn't merely waiting for OEO officers or their funds. It was that those officers and their money, when they finally did arrive, so often proved counterproductive. When Washington again exponentially increased what it offered, as now, the mayors of other towns might again find themselves forced to accept a bonanza, but again, that didn't mean they liked doing so.

From the mayors' point of view, the very demeanor of the Johnson Administration and the lawmakers on the Hill betrayed a disconcerting arrogance in regard to cities. The Washington of the Great Society seemed to wish for a single, obedient interlocutor in its dealings with towns. The following year Senators Robert Kennedy and Abraham Ribicoff would haul Yorty before a committee to berate him about his behavior in the War on Poverty. All Washington wanted, Kennedy explained, was that Yorty lead as he was supposed to. Kennedy expressed exasperation at Los Angeles' quirky decentralization. "In other words, basically you lack jurisdiction, authority, responsibility for what makes a city move?" Kennedy asked. That was exactly it, Yorty said. "We need some leadership," Kennedy said. Yorty hit back: Los Angeles did not need a new senator, especially a Kennedy transplant in New York, to tell Los Angeles how to run itself. Los Angeles was imperfect, but it was undoubtedly succeeding: the population was growing so fast that new school buildings rose every month. *Time* magazine wondered at Los Angeles, calling it a "magnet in the West." New York, Senator Kennedy's state; and Connecticut, Ribicoff's, were not growing like that. Yorty was making the point for all the mayors: decentralization didn't always spell disenfranchisement or incompetence. "We are a great city," Yorty said.[24]

AS THE spring of 1965 arrived, the mayors posed more questions. It bothered them that OEO was now defining the culture of all community groups, and that that culture seemed more about protest than the betterment of the life of the poor. In Newark, Mayor Addonizio experienced a usurpation more farcical than anything else. At the encouragement of the Newark Community Union Project, a group Tom Hayden had helped create, tenants were launching strikes against landlords. "The real cause of poverty," as Hayden put it, "is that the landlord fleeces the tenant so much that the tenant doesn't have enough money to get out of poverty." Several tenants protested against a landlady named Mamie Hayes. In an altercation, the landlady was hit, and she contended Hayden had hit her, perhaps with her own pocketbook. Prosecutors charged Hayden, and the trial was held in Newark, in the same building as the mayor's office. Another man came to court to testify that he, and not Hayden, had hit Hayes. Once the second man was arrested, Newark Community Union Project members moved to the part of the building where the mayor had his office and demanded a meeting. Mayor Addonizio suggested the group make an appointment in what a reporter for the *Jersey Journal* called "normal fashion." The mayor also offered them a chance to sit in the hall, where they wouldn't disrupt the city's work. The NCUP group consulted, and the *Jersey Journal* reported that "the young men and women remained sitting on the floor while they took a vote and decided against following the mayor's suggestion." Policemen carried out about half of the group, and the mayor got back to business. Addonizio and his staff found such pressure distracting, to say the least, but they could do little about it since occupying a mayor's office was now a federally sanctioned activity. "The War on Poverty became a government for those of us in opposition," Junius Williams, an organizer, concluded.

Early March brought a round of OEO disbursements—the money was going to Cleveland, Huntsville (Alabama), Stamford (Connecticut), Tucson, and Washington, DC, but not to Los Angeles. The same month SNCC and other civil rights groups organized a great march in Alabama. The television networks covered the march extensively. For Sunday, March 7, ABC was mounting a challenge to *Bonanza*: the first television airing of Stanley Kramer's much-praised film depicting the postwar trials of the Nazis, *Judgment at Nuremberg*. An astounding forty-eight million viewers tuned in. In the middle of the film or after, ABC newsmen broke in to show footage of state troopers attacking protest marchers with clubs and tear gas at the Edmund Pettus Bridge in Alabama. The images of the Nazis on the one hand and the Alabama troopers on the other were too close for comfort. Martin Luther King afterward commented on the power of the new medium: "We are here to say to the white men we no longer will let them use clubs on us in the dark corners. We're going to make them do it in the glaring light of television."

Yorty that month did not have much time to follow events in Alabama, for April would bring the mayoral election. The mayor was still mired in battles with Shriver's office over exactly how the poverty money would be managed. Shriver's team continued to take issue with the leadership at Yorty's Youth Opportunities Board. Yorty's April election was now weeks away. With each passing day as he waited for his millions, the mayor's temper grew shorter. Yorty tried to entertain his citizenry by campaigning on other topics, reminding voters for example that the city tax rate had dropped in the preceding year. At the end of March, Yorty cut the ribbon to open one part of his new zoo project, a children's zoo, personally taking Boy Scouts, the Boys Club, and Girls Scouts to visit the ocelots, the gorillas, and the new baby male elephant. Perhaps Yorty's problem was the Kennedys. In case anyone forgot that Yorty had published *I Cannot Take Kennedy* in 1960, Yorty's opponents now distributed the four-year-old pamphlet. He always had better luck with Johnson and the people from Texas than with JFK's old staff and family. Yorty went to the president to ask about Shriver. Shriver, the ultimate Kennedy, might be taking the war on poverty in a direction Johnson didn't want to go. Did the president trust Shriver? Should he? Johnson asked back. Yorty offered the president his own conclusion about the poverty czar: "I don't think he's helping you any."[25]

Under the Los Angeles election system, two Democrats might both run in the general election. This year Yorty did have a Democratic opponent: James Roosevelt, a member of the United States House of Representatives and a son of President Franklin Roosevelt. The Roosevelt name, Yorty knew, meant much to Johnson, always so susceptible to New Deal nostalgia, and Roosevelt had won the backing of the United Auto Workers. Perhaps Roosevelt could beat Yorty. Yorty earned the endorsement of three key black public officials: state assemblymen Dymally and F. Douglas Ferrell, and city councilman Billy Mills. The three men told a news conference that reelecting Yorty would "best serve the interest of the citizens of Los Angeles in general and of the Negro community in particular." Sixty black ministers, however, endorsed James Roosevelt. Roosevelt attacked Yorty over a building project in the city's Bunker Hill area that moved low-income workers out to put skyscrapers in their place. Roosevelt was suggesting that Yorty was erecting another Pruitt-Igoe. He was creating "pockets of poverty."

Yorty slammed Roosevelt: skyscrapers were business, job creators. Yorty called Roosevelt "a carpetbagger with a carpetbag full of promises." This was a bit of a stretch since Roosevelt, though originally from the East, had represented California's Twenty-Sixth Congressional District for a decade. Roosevelt suggested Yorty was failing Los Angeles by failing to get federal money. The success of federal programs locally depended, as Roosevelt put it, "on the ability of local communities to give leadership in such programs." Roosevelt outspent Yorty. But when April 6 arrived, Yorty outpolled Roosevelt 392,775 to 247,313. Yorty came out punching. And he was not punching James Roosevelt, who quickly flew back to Washington. Rather, Yorty denounced the efforts to expand the Youth Opportunities Board to include leaders of additional groups selected by foundations or by Sargent Shriver and his poverticians.

Yorty was feeling feisty for reasons beyond the ballot box. He could sense that public opinion nationwide was turning against the Office of Economic Opportunity. In Newark, the sentiment of Tom Hayden's ally Junius Williams was not shared by those black or poor citizens who were not inclined to spend an afternoon mounting a sit-in. The black citizens of Newark, said the Reverend Nathan Wright, executive director for urban work in the Episcopal Diocese of Newark, were in need of education, or lower taxes, not housing rights. Education was "the Negro's debt to himself." Even the old activists who had advanced community action in the first place had their doubts now. In Newark, Bessie Smith, who had hoped for community action at the beginning, said that "these officials want a few of us to sit and listen so they can say they have poor people in the program." Hayden criticized the city's United Community Corporation, or UCC, which, he said, offered merely "a range of paternalistic remedies." Hayden, however, also saw the absurdity of his own protests. The rent strikes didn't yield the improved apartments for which Hayden had hoped. Perhaps he should build a new political group to support the poor, so that the poor would have a voice *within* government. Hayden determined to give Newark one more try.

Since the 1964 Democratic Convention, the old SDS and SNCC communities had been slowly coming apart. Robert Moses had begun to turn away from friends like Casey or Tom Hayden, and even, it was said, ceased speaking to white people altogether. John Lewis, the current SNCC leader, was proving too moderate for many of its black members. The SDS crowd continued to hold meetings and conventions. But women were finding themselves shut out of leadership there. What was Students for a Democratic Society for if it did not respect the power of women? Why had there been no section on women in the Port Huron Statement? Casey Hayden was divorced now, and angry. She and Mary King, her roommate and fellow get-out-the-vote activist, were not eager to break with the men. But they were finding that equality in love was not carrying over into equality at work. An article in *The Nation* that year would catch the women's eye: the author had written that "the work plans for husbands and wives cannot be given equal weight." A woman was supposed to be a supporter, like a lab technician to the scientist. It was time, Hayden and King thought, to advance women's authority, so that women, too, might put their lives into solving problems of "war, poverty, and race." Hayden and King would write up their own Port Huron Statement, a women's memo with a partially tentative subtitle: "A Kind of Memo." But in the text King and Hayden turned accusatory. The protest movement, King and Hayden observed, was divided by "Sex and Caste."

Washington's hundreds of millions were supposed to inspire activists, but instead many felt co-opted, bought out. Michael Harrington was traveling on the West Coast in the spring of 1965, giving a string of speeches about poverty, a topic he now knew by heart. Some of Harrington's speeches brought in handsome money, $1,000 or $1,500 each. That was half of Mollie Orshansky's annual wage. The amounts started to bother Harrington, who still believed in socialism. Robert Hutchins, an old advisor to Harrington, put his finger on the contradiction when he introduced Harrington as "the only man ever to get rich off poverty." The joke didn't sit well. In San Diego, speaking at a Unitarian church, Harrington suffered a panic attack. Returning to his hotel, he found the panic continuing: it was as if, he later wrote, "my unconscious had seized me by the scruff of the neck in a surge of destructive pent-up fury." Harrington headed home to New York and entered psychotherapy. One of the causes of Harrington's breakdown was his own sense of betraying the old socialists by participating in the federal government's Great Society. Now Harrington was just another povertician serving mammon and the poverty czar. Harrington began to look for any sign of disapproval from his old heroes. Friends had given Norman Thomas, the granddaddy of all American socialists and a mentor of Harrington's, a birthday check to use as he pleased. Thomas then handed out checks to all his favorite organizations. But LID, Michael's organization, received only a small amount. Was Thomas snubbing LID because Harrington had been co-opted by Johnson? Harrington sent Thomas a petulant note: "Upset you did not discuss your low evaluation of me. Perhaps you think we should end the organization."

May arrived, and Yorty was still waiting for his summer money. As the rest of the nation watched, Yorty brawled with James Roosevelt and another California congressman, Augustus D. Hawkins, the topic again being seats on the Youth Opportunities Board. Hawkins, Yorty said, was too stubborn. The Washington crowd were "either determined to get control of the end-poverty program, or wreck it." The Los Angeles chairman of the Congress on Racial Equality, Don Smith, staged a sit-in at Yorty's office and, not content with that intrusion, personally picketed Yorty's home in the evening, bearing a provocative sign that said, "Mayor Yorty Can Help End Poverty." Yorty for his part began to rally mayors, saying that his colleagues all over were being "harassed by agitation promoted by Sargent Shriver's speeches."

The mayors' discontent both puzzled and irked staffers at Shriver's OEO, and they began to have their own second thoughts about community action. What if OEO's costly campaigns did not yield a peaceful summer? The White House was beginning to take on the mood of a fortress, with staffers beginning to ready proposals for alternatives to community action. On May 4, Labor Secretary Willard Wirtz forwarded to Johnson a memo summarizing a report by Pat Moynihan. The title of the report was "The Negro Family: The Case for National Action." The memo quantified what the mayors had been finding anecdotally: that black unemployment was no longer marching in tandem with white unemployment, as it had in the 1950s. Black unemployment stayed higher longer. And even when black unemployment dropped, applications for welfare payments did not. Moynihan suggested this change was due to something more than the departure of jobs from cities and from union-dominated states. Black children suffered because of the breakup of the black family. When they became teenagers, they failed to find the education or focus necessary for employment. This story line made intuitive sense to Moynihan, whose own childhood had featured more than one father. Boys like the young Moynihan struggled when they encountered the discipline of the workplace. Moynihan traced the roots of the black problem back to slavery, and noted that black families' troubles had been exacerbated from the New Deal on by welfare programs and the isolation of what Moynihan termed "urbanization"—exemplified through the Pruitt-Igoes.[26] Blacks in the 1960s overall were faring, Moynihan said, "worse, not better." Moynihan's report concluded that the United States somehow had to help the black family, and that only by helping that family would America see the black American get "full and equal sharing in the responsibilities and rewards of citizenship." In other words, families, not community rights, not housing, were where the federal government should do its work.

In the same period, Johnson took a blow. The president expected that at some time Governor George Wallace would attempt to exercise the gubernatorial veto on an OEO program. Instead Johnson's own Texas and its governor, Johnson's own John Connally, were rebelling. Connally exercised the gubernatorial veto to kill an OEO program, an eleven-county Neighborhood Youth Corps project.[27] The governor disliked the salaries in the program, $15,000 for the director and $5,400 for the deputy director. That was too high. Connally also disapproved of the $1.25 wage for the youth workers in the program.[28] That was above what youth got in Texas, or even than what the parents of a youth in the program earned. Others mocked Connally with satire, as a governor who thought a wage of "a dollar and twenty-five cents would ruin the economy of Texas."[29] But Connally was making a point: Johnson, through his OEO program, was eroding the competitive advantage of Texas, its lower wages. In the end there would be fewer jobs, and youth would be "unfortunate losers."

Connally, no shrinking violet, headed to Washington, calling first on Johnson, next on Shriver. Connally told Shriver that the best thing was for governors to run poverty programs. In one program the OEO had installed "a former convict, an actual felon." Was this the intent of Johnson's executive branch? asked Connally. Shriver told Connally that he had examined the case of the ex-con, and what Shriver cared about was the man's recent years of good behavior, when the ex-con had proved himself a model citizen.

Johnson and Shriver, furious, plotted their revenge. Johnson encouraged Senator Ralph Yarborough of Texas, with whom Connally had already been feuding, to campaign for legislation that would abolish the gubernatorial veto. A bill containing the repeal of the veto was rammed through the state's house, moving all the faster because George Wallace of Alabama had in the interim also used his veto to kill a program proposing to integrate in Birmingham. It would be only a matter of time before there was a new OEO law that enabled Shriver to override the veto of a governor. Yarborough bragged: "It was the crippling actions of a few governors who caused this veto power to be taken away from the governors of all fifty states."

At home in Texas, Connally simply escalated. If Shriver and Johnson were going to be tough on governors, he, a governor, would be tougher. Connally would close the symbolic Camp Gary, part of the Job Corps. "You've got to remember that most people down here dislike the poverty program," Connally told Johnson's staffer Marvin Watson, likewise a Texan and former head of the Democratic Party in Texas. Texans, Connally said, thought the poverty program was "a big boondog."

Still, Shriver, sensing a turning tide, picked up his pace. Nationally, unemployment stood at 4.7 percent. The poverty czar began ratcheting up expectations, suggesting that a national unemployment rate of as low as 3.5 percent was possible, if OEO-type spending could be expanded. Sounding like Harrington, whom he had mocked just a year earlier, Shriver told senators that doubling poverty spending to $2 billion was too modest a goal. He stuck by his Job Corps. Young men entered the program where they prepared for the job market, even attending special camps away from home or city boarding schools. Did this not address the kind of family problems that Moynihan was now highlighting? In January, Shriver had boasted that the Job Corps would enroll ten thousand students. When by April only two thousand materialized, Shriver moved to act, creating "Operation 10,000," an OEO drive to fill the rest of the spots. By the end of June, the ten-thousandth person would be registered at the Job Corps.

Such a rapid ramp-up meant the OEO-funded agencies could be none too picky about whom they enrolled. At Job Corps sites, the predictable scuffles, arson, even rape, ensued. After a Job Corps recruit shot at a policeman in a bar in his home state, Montana, Senate Majority Leader Mike Mansfield wrote to Johnson: "I do not like admonishing the Jobs Corps," Mansfield said, "but it seems to me there is something wrong." James Rowe, an old New Dealer and Johnson loyalist, also piped up. Echoing Daley, Rowe told Johnson that "innocents" at OEO were unwisely disbursing money to militant radicals. "The political implications of using public funds to instruct people how to protest are quite obvious," Rowe wrote. Johnson sent Rowe's letter to his aide, Bill Moyers, marked with an order: "Bill, for God's sake, get on top of this and just put a stop to it at once."

The governors, state legislators, and mayors finally had Johnson's attention. Daley's loud objections were beginning, Moyers later recalled, "to form a dark cloud in Johnson's mind." The cloud only grew when men Johnson respected, like Mansfield, wrote in. Shriver would continue his work, and Johnson would continue, for now, to back him. But Johnson, like the men around him, began to look beyond the OEO and "maximum feasible participation." Johnson was proud of a bill on voting rights he was shepherding through Congress. The bill allowed the federal government to oversee elections in areas where it believed blacks were being denied the vote. The bill's language on discrimination was strong enough that it ought to preclude debacles like the convention the year before at Atlantic City. The Democratic National Committee would have to change its rules. Here, Johnson was indeed honoring a promise to blacks. But the president now felt he had to do yet more. Johnson summoned the same writer who had produced both a voting rights speech and the Great Society speech, Richard Goodwin. When Goodwin entered the president's office, Johnson was standing at the teletype machine, reading the words of his critics in the press as they sputtered out. Johnson complimented Goodwin on the voting rights speech, but then told him that voting rights were "only the tail of the pig."[30] The president went on: "What good are civil rights if you don't have a decent home or someone to take care of you when you're sick?"

Johnson, who had never been a governor or a mayor, wanted Goodwin to write a speech in which the federal government made a new promise that would further change life in every state and town. The president told Goodwin, "We've got to find a way to let Negroes get what most white folks already have." Goodwin set to work on a speech, to be delivered at Howard University, the flagship of the historically black colleges. This speech, the White House hoped, would establish Johnson, who had claimed almost all the black vote the year before, as the "Great Emancipator" of the twentieth century. Goodwin thought about Moynihan at the Labor Department, and about the increasing disparity between black and white unemployment. Voter registration drives, the kind Bob Moses or John Lewis led, could not suffice. Blacks didn't just need rights, they needed the rewards that rights brought. It was easy to see why Johnson might do this. The black civil rights movement was getting angrier by the day. The number of American servicemen in Vietnam had been rising all year, and many of those men were black. The White House had to get ahead, to "leapfrog the movement," as one White House observer put it.

In his introduction to the speech, Howard president James Nabrit thanked Johnson, "for what you have done for our country . . . and for what you propose to do." Nabrit reminded his audience that the Great Society was not a gift, it was a "challenge" to the nation that included a challenge to American character. Johnson himself picked up on Harrington's theme of "the Other America," telling the audience that blacks had been living in "another nation." "Freedom is not enough," Goodwin had written into the address. "You do not take a person who had been hobbled by chains and put him at the starting line of a race and say, 'You

are free to compete with all the others.'" By the time Johnson delivered
the remarks at Howard on June 4, the thought was crystallizing. The
nation needed "equality as a fact and equality as a result." The president also announced a conference titled "To Fulfill These Rights," set for
October. Martin Luther King telegraphed his approval. The *Washington
Post* said Johnson was lighting "a candle of understanding."

Lighting dynamite might have been the better metaphor, from the
mayors' point of view. Just the year before, at Michigan, Johnson had
emphasized the government's responsibility to provide opportunity, not
results. Now the president was institutionalizing a right to results. Johnson had already "aroused a lot of hopes," Yorty thought. After the speech
at Howard, the hopes would be even more numerous. Mayors' own constituents would surely feel themselves to be owed something that mayors,
county commissioners, and state lawmakers could not provide. Moynihan's report had actually left open what might allow black citizens to
regain power and confidence. Perhaps the goal should be black property
ownership. Perhaps money should flow to individuals along with benefits.
In 1963 the Urban League's Whitney M. Young had proposed a Marshall
Plan for black Americans, including direct payments to poor families
to lift them over the poverty line. Thomas Sowell, a graduate student,
was concentrating on his PhD, an essay on the pre-Keynesian economist
Jean-Baptiste Say. But Young's idea irked Sowell so much that he'd written a letter to the *New York Times*. The reaction to such a Marshall Plan,
Sowell wrote, or to any other offer, would be the same from black Americans as it was from whites. "People who have been trying for years to tell
others that Negroes are basically no different from anybody else," Sowell
said, "should not themselves lose sight of the fact that Negroes are just
like everybody else in wanting something for nothing." Perhaps what was
owed should be education, as both Sowell and Nathan Wright suggested.
Perhaps blacks had to take matters into their own hands. Wright, a man
of the cloth, would shortly publish a book with the provocative title *Ready
to Riot*.

The Johnson Administration attempted to still such questions with
an early summer goodwill campaign. Vice President Humphrey assured

the dubious mayors that the coming establishment of an official Department of Housing and Urban Development, with a cabinet-level secretary, would overcome any damage from the excesses of the recent community action period. The commitment only partially placated the mayors: did not Humphrey see the gratuitous damage of fostering class warfare? Reuther, who had funded people like Tom Hayden to promote community action in the first place, was also turning to housing now, and a new project dubbed Demonstration Cities. Reuther promised that whatever urban ills remained would be fixed by housing—he was developing a pamphlet titled *Detroit: Demonstration City.*

Sensing a diminishment in Johnson's interest, Shriver felt betrayed. What had happened to Johnson's promise that he would stick with Shriver, "Death do us part"? Johnson had so recently ordered Shriver, and the nation, to cure poverty, but now Johnson was telling Shriver to hold off on giant requests, at least until the congressional midterms passed. Perhaps the jig was up, Shriver told himself.[31] It didn't help the poverty czar's mood that he continued to sense skepticism within the ranks of his own experts. The OEO's deputy director of community action, John Wofford, was tracing a pattern. When mayors first tried to establish the community action groups for OEO, the OEO phone lines would ring with calls from moderate, established civil rights groups claiming they had been wrongfully cut out of the initial process. At the OEO's bidding, the mayors would try to adjust, including some, or more, parties from the established civil rights groups. Then, more militant groups would emerge from the woodwork to oppose the "establishment-oriented" mayors' committees. Then the mayors, encouraged by Shriver, would negotiate with the militants, and after a while, offer one of them a top staff job at a city-created poverty office, "frequently the staff directorship." Then yet another committee would appear, claiming that *it* represented the people, and that the "militant" who took the job had "sold out to the establishment."[32] Instead of praising Shriver, many of these figures were taking aim at him.

Trapped in his thicket, Shriver became desperate. Maybe the OEO's trouble was simply marketing, Shriver told himself. Shriver thought of hiring the cartoonist Al Capp to make a Job Corps comic book. Television divided people in cities. Television could unite them. If Shriver could use TV to win the loyalty of young people in the cities, then community action would be considered a success, whatever the jurisdictional squabbles. Shriver's inspector general at OEO, William C. Haddad, had been working on TV ideas for a while, and had even gone to New York to meet with a popular radio host, known as Murray the K. Murray, whose full name was Murray Kaufman, fancied himself a civil rights activist, and had led a campaign to help high schoolers in the Bedford-Stuyvesant neighborhood in Brooklyn. Haddad told Kaufman that at OEO, "we are greatly concerned about the coming 'long hot summer.'"[33] The solution, Kaufman counseled Haddad, was not to talk at but to work with young people. The radio host knew this from his own experience, having organized gang leaders to round up young people for a one-off show at a school. Kaufman thought Shriver should think big. What was needed was a fifty-city campaign, in which disc jockeys would work with local poverty directors to organize events, including both dancing and "think-ins" for young people to engage with one another and see their community was on their side. Of course, Kaufman allowed, there had to be a catalyst event. He suggested to Haddad that a network television special might provide that catalyst.

The plan for the TV special fell together delightfully fast. Jack Schneider, the new president of CBS, assented to the idea—and even offered help from CBS to cover production costs. Dauntingly famous artists volunteered their time. Not only the Righteous Brothers, but Ray Charles, Smokey Robinson, and the Temptations would appear on the special. Kaufman estimated he was getting the government $150,000 in free talent. Proud, he traveled to Washington to meet with Shriver to finalize plans for the production. Shriver liked the plan so much that he put out a feeler to Kaufman, suggesting that the OEO might supply him with funds for other projects in the future. "Now Murray, suppose you were given a few million dollars? What would be the first problem you would tackle?" Caught off guard, Kaufman found himself joking that he would use the money to pay his taxes.

The moment passed. Shriver underscored his point, that for the OEO money was not an issue. "We have plenty of money. What we need are more ideas for new programs to be initiated!" Haddad and Kaufman had only one more question. What on earth would a rock and roll show sponsored by a government agency led by a Kennedy in-law be called? An embarrassed Haddad admitted to Shriver, who was American nobility after all, that he and CBS wanted to select a name that would appeal to teenagers on the streets. "We want to call it: *It's What's Happening, Baby!*" Shriver, father of four with another baby on the way, bearer of the Purple Heart for service at Guadalcanal, told the others that the title was just fine.

Excited, Kaufman finalized his lineup. Along with the Supremes, the Four Tops, Bill Cosby, and the Righteous Brothers, Shriver himself could make an appearance. The special would make an appeal to dropouts and explain all the benefits—jobs, job programs, civics education—that OEO-funded community action offered them. Pouring his heart into the project, Kaufman developed a new feature: footage of stars singing their hits in fictional scenes, with a whisper of plot. Ford had an opportunity to showcase its star vehicle, the Mustang, with a clip of Martha and the Vandellas performing "Nowhere to Run" for the cameras as they danced on a Mustang assembly line. The Supremes belted "Stop! In the Name of Love" in a conspicuously biracial park scene, reminiscent of Los Angeles' Griffith Park. Such footage was an early anticipation of the MTV video. Bill Cosby contributed a melancholy monologue, later singled out for praise, on the importance of education.

Nevertheless, the production of *It's What's Happening, Baby!* did not close out smoothly. Kaufman sought a "soft-sell explanation of the show, putting it into a definite frame of reference for everyone who might be watching." He didn't win that argument: Shriver didn't care about much but employing angry youth in new summer jobs. Kaufman's distraught taskmasters kept asking him to tape messages for the show backing an individual OEO program, then killing his tape and picking another program for him to advertise. Kaufman taped separate messages about the Job Corps, the Community Action Plan, and other parts of the War on Poverty. There were even wrangles about the goal that, at least to Kaufman's mind, was the purpose of the show: the case for action in fifty cities. Kaufman called Haddad to ask if there was something about his segments that dissatisfied OEO. Was Kaufman presenting it all wrong? No, said Haddad. "It isn't that, Murray." It was just that the OEO wanted Murray to say something general: "hammer home that we want the audience to participate." One night during production, Kaufman became so frustrated at the back-and-forth that he marched out of his studios in Hollywood and walked around until 3 a.m. The newspapers, getting wind of the special, wondered how it would work. The *St. Louis Post-Dispatch* politely called Shriver's planned special "the most improbable TV show of the year."

On June 28, Shriver spent a few rock and roll–free hours making his pitch on the Hill for more funding for the War on Poverty. The $1.5 billion he was asking in this go-round might be 50 percent higher than the original billion he had discussed that day in Washington with Harrington, but $1.5 billion was still, Shriver warned, a conservative number. George Murphy of California, a freshman senator, reported Yorty's statement that "mayors all over the country were being harassed" by Shriver's insistence that "the poor run the poverty program in their cities." Shriver, as always nowadays on the defensive, carefully explained that "maximum feasible participation" was not the same as maximum feasible domination.

It's What's Happening, Baby!—ninety minutes long—finally aired the evening after Shriver's testimony, complete with Martha and the Vandellas. In the ratings game, *It's What's Happening* proved a win, attracting, by some claims, at least sixteen million viewers, fewer than *Judgment at Nuremberg*, but still an enormous share. The reaction to the show was mixed. Teens themselves mocked the effort of the adults on the show to talk the language of youth: "What do you think teenagers are, a babbling bunch of idiots?" asked a high schooler from Arlington, Virginia. Some Republicans expressed concern that the special might incite rioters, not channel them into peaceable temporary assignments. Others proclaimed their disgust. Senator Gordon Allott of Colorado called the president of the network and said, simply, "I am about to throw up." On the floor of the Senate, Allott launched a flaming attack on the profligacy of the community action exercise, saying the message of the show's master of ceremonies added up to "Tell us how to spend our money," or "We have so much money we don't know what to do with it." A group of Republican senators prodded their leader, Everett Dirksen, to ask publicly "who inspired it, who put it together." Dirksen, Johnson's coalition builder on civil rights, didn't consider Shriver's publicity something the Great Society's fathers must sanction. Republicans "were almost incandescent in their fulminations," Dirksen said, telling the minority leader the show was "lousy, double lousy." The truth was Shriver *had* met his goals, creatings tens of thousands of summer or temp jobs for teens. But for whatever reason, Shriver did not follow up the special with action in fifty cities. "The OEO 'chickened out' because of political pressure and criticism, unwarranted as it was," Murray Kaufman concluded. How, Kaufman asked himself, could the government allocate money to an agency that vacillated so much, it couldn't make specific plans? In his own head, the disc jockey wrote a line of advice for the OEO: "Next time have something to shout about before starting to shout!"

July found Yorty's anti-poverty millions still in Washington, with the OEO demanding that Yorty accept a new screening agency more to its liking. On July 8, some of the sponsors of the Los Angeles program wired Sargent Shriver directly to complain that two thousand young people who could be working were not. In Sacramento, Assemblyman Mervyn Dymally focused on education, seeing two bills through to address the problems of poorer citizens: a bill to fund child care center construction, and one to apply state money for technical education for the poor. While Yorty waited for *his* money, the mayor occupied himself with building goodwill. Yorty met with the mayor of Los Angeles' sister city in Mexico, Puerto Vallarta, and received a gift: a mother-of-pearl tray in the shape of a lobster. Perhaps some business for Los Angeles would be forthcoming as well. One neighborhood in Los Angeles—Pacoima, not Watts—finally qualified as adequately poor for one of Shriver's "pockets of poverty" programs. Early in August, Pacoima leaders would meet to establish an anti-poverty committee to determine how to spend federal dollars from the OEO.

Aware that he had to get to Labor Day, Johnson pushed hard on all his legislation: a health care bill and the voting rights legislation. The former Senate majority leader was still so good at getting legislation passed that other politicians could only admire Johnson's modus operandi. When you traced the arc of the Johnson presidency, you could see that Johnson translated everything into legislation, a new aide, Joseph Califano, noticed. At one point, Califano's young son swallowed a bottle of aspirin and was sent to the hospital to have his stomach pumped. When Johnson learned of the accident, he promised legislation to make medicine bottles child-resistant.[34]

Califano, whom Johnson had recently commandeered from McNamara at the Defense Department, was a fresh pair of eyes. But with them, Califano saw the same Johnson as his predecessors. Califano endured the same swimming pool hazing as his predecessors, and the same demand for impossible hours. And he saw the intensity of the Johnson competitiveness. Johnson so impressed upon Califano the need for instant communication and instant updates that Califano began to hunt around for "the best pocket-size radio." He eventually chose the Sony—not an American radio—and bought twenty-four, along with seventy-two batteries, three per radio, for distribution to the White House staff. With their Sonys in their breast pockets, members of Johnson's entourage could always be ready to deliver the latest news to the president. When Johnson sought speechwriter Goodwin on an urgent matter later that summer, and learned that Goodwin was sailing off Martha's Vineyard, he told Califano that "we ought to blow up that Goddamned island." The president, Califano noticed, systematically sought to suppress or even eliminate those he thought of as competitors. Martin at the Fed was complaining too much about spending for Johnson's taste, and Johnson even asked the new attorney general, Nicholas Katzenbach, to ascertain whether a president could remove a Fed board chairman. There wasn't much precedent for doing that, Katzenbach replied.[35]

But Katzenbach, Califano, and the older White House staff also observed fleeting expressions of satisfaction on Johnson's face, rare seconds of calm. They were evident especially on the day Johnson made a special trip to Independence, Missouri, the home of former president Harry

Truman, to sign his health care provisions, Medicare and Medicaid, into law. Congress had blocked Truman's great expansions of public health care, but Johnson had succeeded where Truman failed. Medicare would serve senior citizens and Medicaid, the poor. Ceremoniously, Johnson enrolled Truman in Medicare, making him the first recipient of a Medicare card. The eighty-one-year-old Truman looked at the fifty-six-year-old Johnson and found himself at a loss for words, saying only, "I am glad to have lived this long, and to witness the signing of the Medicare bill." The two presidents had given their lives to fulfilling and furthering Roosevelt's New Deal, and here they had done so. The only question that remained was whether the angry cities would recognize all that Johnson had done before September. To buy himself that time, to show the country that he meant what he was doing, Johnson readied his pen for the final move: putting his signature on the Voting Rights Act. Johnson asked Califano to get a special table, "so people can say, 'This is the table on which LBJ signed the Voting Rights Bill.'"

On August 6, the hour for signing the Voting Rights Bill arrived. Johnson decided to revive an old custom: he would sign the bill at the Capitol, not at the White House, to show his gratitude to Congress and the nation for their support. Martin Luther King; James Farmer, the founder of the Congress on Racial Equality; and John Lewis, president of SNCC, all arrived to join their president. Since his signing of the Economic Opportunity Act, Johnson had handed out pens at these ceremonies. By now, because it had to give out pens so often, the White House had switched from fountain pens to felt tips. The next day, the Justice Department officially certified—named for oversight—states and counties that in one way or another might be denying citizens their right to vote.

The ebullient Johnson was already looking even further ahead, planning the conference on civil rights that he had announced at the time of the Howard University speech. The president summoned the civil rights attorney Morris Abram, who would cochair the preliminary conference session that autumn; and Berl Bernhard, the former staff director of the Civil Rights Commission. What mood did the president want for his conference? the pair asked. For his captive audience—Califano was there as well—the president began to develop one of his excruciating risqué metaphors. The country was like his cows in the spring, the president said, waiting for more civil rights legislation the way cows waited in anticipation of the bull. "These cows just get so goddamn excited, they get more and more moist to receive him, and their asses just start quivering and then they start quivering all over, every one of them is quivering, as the bull struts into their pasture." Abram's and Bernhard's jaws went ajar, Califano later recalled, "just as the president wanted." Well, Johnson told the men, he wanted a "quivering conference."

Johnson still had not finished, the mayors saw. On Tuesday, August 10, a day when the thermometers at the Los Angeles Civic Center recorded a temperature of ninety-five degrees, the president added another layer of government above the mayors. He signed the Housing and Urban Development Act, which set the stage for Congress to create another cabinet-level antagonist for the beleaguered mayors, the HUD secretary. "We have the resources in this country, we have the ingenuity, we have the courage and the compassion," Johnson said, "and we must in this decade bring all these strengths to bear effectively so that we can lift off the conscience of our affluent nation the shame of slums and squalor and the blight of deterioration and decay." Housing was clearly to be the next endeavor of the Great Society. One reason Johnson was so eager to look ahead was that Shriver and Yorty were continuing to embarrass him with their now entirely public squabble. Labor Day was still weeks away, and Yorty still hadn't received his money. "Nowhere," the *Los Angeles Times* wrote, "has the turn in the war from fighting the enemy to fighting over who is going to run the war been more evident than in the Los Angeles area."[36] There were conflicts between Yorty's Youth Opportunities Board and Shriver's OEO, but there were also tussles between the Youth Opportunities Board and the United Civil Rights Committee, yet another new institution, whose office was provided for a dollar a year by the United Auto Workers. City councilman Billy Mills was claiming that whatever resources the United Civil Rights Committee received would end up going to politics and those political candidates who aimed to unseat him or Yorty. Dr. H. Hartford Brookins, who chaired the United Civil Rights

Committee board, claimed that Yorty in his zeal to exclude activists was shutting out Brookins's group entirely. Important meetings were taking place, said Brookins, but "we have not been invited to appear."

Los Angeles, Yorty was aware by now, was becoming a kind of joke. Yorty determined that he had to take the lead and use his own mayoral coffers to hire teenagers himself. On that same ninety-five-degree day, August 10, Yorty welcomed fifteen young people at city hall, "the first of 1,500 boys and girls who will go to work for the City," the *Los Angeles Times* reported.

The next day, the president signed another bill, on saline water, again handing out pens to a crowd of supporters, this time including Senator Robert Kennedy. Johnson communed with Katzenbach, and he made remarks at a water emergency conference. In the afternoon, Johnson met with A. Philip Randolph, Whitney Young, and others to work on plans for his conference on civil rights. The president released a report from Sargent Shriver on the career status of returned Peace Corps volunteers. He telephoned with Walter Reuther. Late in the evening, the president dined with Mrs. Johnson. She was planning to head to Newark the following day to join Shriver in inspecting the outcome of the dozens of Head Start projects operating there. Before retiring, Johnson spoke by phone with Buford Ellington, the former governor of Tennessee.

That night, the night of August 11, Percy Green of ACTION in St. Louis, another young community group, hosted an outdoor rally at Pruitt-Igoe. The ostensible purpose of the event was to teach adults and children how to combat police violence. Green called for volunteer "freedom patrols" of blacks to police the police. Before seventy-five attendees, many of them children, Green and James Peake of another organization, the DuBois Club, also staged a mock arrest to dramatize police brutality. Manacling one volunteer with toy handcuffs, the civil rights leaders carried him a few yards and placed him, facedown, on some folding chairs. Next, they covered his head with ketchup, to symbolize the wounds of a head beaten with a policeman's nightstick.

The same evening in Los Angeles, officers from the California Highway Patrol stopped in the Avalon neighborhood of Los Angeles to pull over a twenty-one-year-old named Marquette Frye on suspicion of drunken driving. The police stopped Frye in front of his mother's home. Frye's mother emerged from the house to dress him down. The confrontation took place on Avalon Boulevard, where protesters had marched in the past. This time, a crowd also gathered, and the patrolmen called for backup. Observers and hecklers arrived. Frye resisted arrest, and his mother jumped on the back of the arresting officer. A yet larger crowd gathered and first hundreds, then thousands, began to throw bricks and rocks. The police arrived with sirens and began beating members of the crowds. State assemblyman F. Douglas Ferrell, whose own Tabernacle of Faith Baptist Church was in the neighborhood, commented of the rioters that "a lot are newcomers to California. They bring their hatred and their pent-up emotions with them." What if the riot spread to other neighborhoods? Watts was a likely candidate.

The next morning, the morning of Thursday, August 12, Yorty raced back to Los Angeles from a trip to San Diego, checked in with his police chief, and then raced up to San Francisco to give a long-scheduled speech at the Commonwealth Club. It would not do, Yorty thought, to look "like we were panicking." What else could the police do? Half the country was on vacation. Tom Bradley, a key black city councilman, was in Spain. Governor and Mrs. Brown had just departed for Greece, where they would be the guests of the American Hellenic Educational Progressive Association.[37] As the fighting continued, those community leaders who *were* in Los Angeles quickly stepped forward. Mervyn Dymally went to the center of the unrest to try to stop the rioters from throwing rocks. Why, Dymally asked, did the rioters hate "the Man"—the white man, the police? "Who you with?" asked a youth. "I'm with you, man," Dymally answered. The youth gave Dymally a rock. "Then here's a rock, baby. Throw it." Dymally would not. The rioter answered, "Hell! You're with the Man." Murray Kaufman had been correct. People needed something to shout. But they had not chosen to shout praise for Shriver's Community Action. Instead they were shouting for community action on their own terms. The same day, Police Chief William Parker, already fending off a barrage of criticism, took a swat at Shriver's community action principles. "When you keep telling people they are unfairly treated and teach them disrespect for the law," Parker said, "you must expect this kind of thing sooner or later." In the hours and days that followed, Joe Califano tried to reach the president. But for once, a Johnson point man could not get through the operators to his chief executive. Califano rang, and rang again. This time, he really needed to find the president.[38] The nightmare had become reality. Watts was burning.

5

Creative Society

AUGUST 1965 TO JANUARY 1966

Guns: 7.1% of GDP
Butter: 4.9% of GDP
Dow Jones Industrial Average: 891

---

*Americans admire a people who can scratch a desert and
produce a garden.*
—Richard Nixon

Try to get the East Coast out!
—Note to himself, Robert Noyce of Fairchild Semiconductor[1]

"SPACEMEN SCORE," read the headline in giant type filling the top of
the *Los Angeles Times* on August 25, 1965. The astronauts aboard *Gemini V* had stayed in space eight days, twice as long as preceding manned
flights. The men had even managed to snap, from above, a photograph
of a Minuteman Missile bursting through the clouds from Vandenberg
Air Force Base in California. The demonstration of American ingenuity,
like a circus act adding a bonus trick, tickled the nation's fancy. There
were other pictures, for the astronauts had photographed all they could,
including an angled blue, milky view of California's own Imperial Valley taken on Orbit 17 by Gordon Cooper. There were a thousand ways
Gemini V could have failed and become tragedy. Yet *Gemini V* was a
glorious success.

The *Gemini V* flight was something many Americans enjoyed personally, as if they themselves had donned the white space suits and boarded
a capsule. If NASA could play in the heavens, Americans thought, well
then so could they. Radio hobbyists, some of whom had day jobs in

aerospace or at NASA, had several years back launched a baby fourteen-pound satellite of their own by packing it as a stowaway on the *Discoverer*, part of an Air Force satellite program. Earlier in 1965, 300,000 licensed ham radio operators around the world had tracked the slightly heavier OSCAR III, a successor. Hobbyists of the TRW Radio Club of Redondo Beach, California, were readying OSCAR IV. Perhaps science wasn't merely making space habitable by man. Maybe science was also showing America the way out of its quandaries.

A way out was something Americans certainly longed for. In Vietnam the past week, even as Los Angeles took stock of Watts, fifty Americans had died in action. Marines were making their first landing south of Da Nang, and clearly the war had much further to go. The Great Society had been up and running for a year, yet the cities felt angrier than before. Up until the *Gemini V* triumph, images of smoking buildings or looters heaving appliances out of broken store windows in Los Angeles had dominated the front pages. Watts hadn't merely caught fire, it had exploded into a genuine urban battle, complete with Molotov cocktails and beatings, the worst most observers could remember. The battle had inflicted $40 million in damage, much of it to small businesses. Some one thousand people had been injured. Thirty-four, or perhaps even thirty-eight, people had died. The first victim had been a black bystander who was caught between police and rioters sometime around 6:00 and 7:00 p.m. on the Friday, and was hit in an exchange of gunfire.[2] Another early casualty was a white deputy sheriff, the father of two. The rioters had targeted whites specifically. "We'll kill whites!" they shouted. The story of Mervyn Dymally, the black lawmaker who had refused to throw a rock, was just one of many. Police asked Dick Gregory, a much-loved stand-up comic, to take a bullhorn and encourage people to return to their houses. "Go home!" Gregory told the crowd. But before Gregory could say more, he was shot in the leg by a random gunman.

Mayor Yorty and OEO director Shriver were already deep into a mud fight over what had caused the riots in Los Angeles, with Yorty blaming Shriver for the late delivery of OEO funds and Shriver blaming Yorty as mayor of "the only major city in the United States that had failed" to agree with the OEO on a plan. Governor Pat Brown tapped John McCone, a former director of the Central Intelligence Agency, to lead a commission to figure out what caused the riots. But Americans already knew one thing. Watts demonstrated the opposite of *Gemini V.* A thousand things could have failed in Watts, and they had. Watts appeared to be the living demonstration of Murphy's Law, the rule that if something can go wrong, it will. Especially, the White House now saw, the implementation of Sargent Shriver's community action. Post-Watts, Shriver and budget director Charles L. Schultze sent a memo to the president warning that OEO had "got off on the wrong foot by organizing the poor politically." Schultze recommended that OEO be told to "soft pedal its conflicts with local officials over heavy representation of the poor on poverty boards." Johnson responded. "OK. I agree."[3]

Many Americans were still confident that the war in Vietnam and the Great Society would not fall casualty to Murphy's Law. Someday soon, the communists would be out of Vietnam, and someday soon, the poorest Americans would no longer be poor. But in the interim the country needed a rich economy to pay for space capsules, guns, and butter. Private companies were especially important. Nothing demonstrated the contribution of companies more than the Gemini program itself. *Gemini V* had been able to stay in orbit as long as it did because the spacecraft was powered by fuel cells that had been produced by General Electric in West Lynn, Massachusetts. The photos had been possible because of a special wide-angle lens made by Fairchild Camera and Instrument. The Minuteman missile flew because it was powered by Texas Instruments microchips.[4] Douglas, Lockheed, McDonnell—all had played a role in the *Gemini V* show.

But what kind of company advanced science faster? And what kind of company advanced America faster? Most Americans' assumptions about companies had not changed much since the days when Ronald Reagan hosted *GE Theater.* The best kind of company was the kind that sat at the legendary table with the federal government and unions and worked out all the problems. The old rule that only big companies had the deep pockets for research labs also appeared to hold. A hopeful scientist with a big idea needed a big company. Company loyalty was a matter of survival, because only big companies had access to government and capital. Only big companies knew how to handle unions. The optimal career for a scientist therefore started at university, went to government, and then, perhaps, moved to a big company where government was a client.

The career path of the boy who aspired to build rockets, Homer Hickam of Coalwood, West Virginia, was following that pattern. As a high schooler, Hickam had watched the Soviet launch of the satellite *Sputnik* with a combination of awe and ire. Hickam's own success with hobby rockets had been good enough to win him local attention and a science prize. That prize launched Hickam himself. After Big Creek High School, Hickam had gone to Virginia Polytechnic Institute. After that, he had joined the Army. If Hickam wanted to build rockets once he got out, he would have to join a big company like Lockheed or go to NASA. Among many Californians the old assumption, that California needed government to survive, was even stronger than it had been at the start of the decade. The year before, Kennedy's press man, Pierre Salinger, had lost a Senate election to the former actor George Murphy in part because Salinger was perceived as an insufficiently vigorous booster of defense contracts for California enterprises. "Silent Salinger cannot sit out an issue which involves one out of every ten industrial jobs in California," Murphy had charged.

The McCone Commission would not issue findings on the Watts riot for months. But everyone in the world of policy or government now felt free to fly into Yorty's city and speculate on the causes of the riot. Watts so shook Americans that some were beginning to look at the traditional cozy arrangement of the federal government, companies, and unions with new eyes. Over the summer Northrop, Bank of America, Douglas Aircraft, General Electric, and other companies had held a seminar to look at why blacks were unemployed. The finding was that the answers were bigoted employers and lack of the right kind of job training. That might be true. Why weren't companies doing more in cities? Why didn't they train more? If people in Watts could not read at high school level, maybe the companies should teach them. The critics also focused on unions in a way they hadn't before. Walter Reuther might bail out Martin Luther King in Alabama, but within his UAW Reuther's own locals, including those in California, often shut out blacks. The high wages that the UAW or the AFL-CIO won from employers also hurt minorities. Companies for whom labor was expensive tended to hire the most qualified applicants— they couldn't afford to give a new, unskilled worker from Watts a try. In order to obtain for the rest of society what they got for their own workers, Reuther and Meany had also pushed for, and repeatedly won, increases in the national minimum wage. But the rest of society had not always benefited. The minimum wage increases shut blacks out, too, in this instance from nonunion companies, again by making it too expensive to hire untrained young men.

There were numbers to back up contentions that labor costs were too high, the very same numbers Lyndon Johnson relied on. Just as the president had noted at Howard University. Black and white youth unemployment had run about the same until the middle of the 1950s, 8 to 11 percent. But when Congress raised the federal minimum wage by a third in 1956, unemployment rose far higher among black teenagers than among whites, to 25 percent. At the University of Chicago, situated in an area rougher than Watts, Chicago's South Side, the economist Milton Friedman was reaching a conclusion: those who were supposed to benefit from a minimum wage were nearly always actually hurt, as "the intended beneficiaries are not employed at all." Friedman the following year would slam the minimum wage as "the most anti-Negro law on our statute books." Beyond the minimum wage laws, there was another federal law, the Davis-Bacon Act. Davis-Bacon held that any government contractor—often a defense firm—had to pay the prevailing wage in any area where the contractor worked. Prevailing wage often meant union wages, again, prohibitively high. Looking back at postwar history, you could be confident in saying that the trio of government, companies, and unions had launched the *Gemini* rocket. Perhaps the trio had also helped to launch the rocks in Watts.

For reasons that appeared at the time to have to do with helping the inner city, some young scientists and engineers were already testing the old rule that a scientist had to serve an old company at the old negotiating table. The first rule the engineers questioned was the importance of being a lifer, loyal to one company to the end. Perhaps a scientist was better as a lone wolf. Americans were often lone wolves. Even though they'd sent their satellite as a stowaway, individual hobby scientists had managed to launch and track OSCAR. The year before, *The New Yorker* had carried the story of an engineer in the spacesuit department of B.F. Goodrich who had dared to accept a job with a competitor in the same field, International Latex. What had struck readers was not the security risk—the danger that space suit technology might reach the Soviet space program—but rather the audacity of the young man who dared to leave his company.[5] That was a new kind of behavior for Eisenhower's military-industrial complex. General Electric was a fine employer, the young scientists and engineers said to one another. Bell Labs, which had a record of innovation, would also do. But what if the young men wanted to run their labs as though they were Thomas Edison, not Ralph Cordiner or Lemuel Boulware? The independence Cordiner had sought to give by allowing individual GE departments to run themselves was only a leash that could be jerked back at any time.

These bold thoughts were expressed more often by scientists in the West than back East. Partly this was because California was the land of the iconoclast. The year before, on the University of California's Berkeley campus, a free speech group had tangled with the administration. A student leader, Mario Savio, gave a heartfelt plea. Students, Savio said, didn't want to "end up being bought by some clients of the University, be they the government, be they industry, be they organized labor, be they anyone. We're human beings." At Berkeley students sang a parody version of Beethoven's Ninth with its own antiestablishment lyrics: "Keep the students safe for knowledge / Keep them loyal, keep them clean / That is why we have a college / Hail to the IBM machine!" Despite its dependence on defense work, the West still felt like the frontier to young scientists. Andrew Grove, an immigrant from Hungary, had not stopped long in New York before he headed West, considering the West the more American America. The other reason young scientists felt bold was that theirs was a seller's market. The Cold War and now defense spending meant companies were begging for engineers. In addition, the very makeup of companies was changing: more brains, less brawn. At Lockheed in 1955, for example, 8 percent of the workforce had been engineers or scientists. Now that share was closing in on 25 percent: "This is the era of the white-coated technician and the electronic brain," concluded the *Los Angeles Times*. Since engineers and scientists could return to the large companies virtually anytime, the risks of joining or starting a new company were low.

When young engineers did set up companies, they set them up differently. They rejected IBM hierarchy for a workshop atmosphere. They established offices in the West, where sunny days were more frequent and land was cheaper. California was not a "right to work" state. When a group of workers in California decided to unionize, employers had to accept the union, and workers who were not in the union had to pay dues. In part to solidify their territory here, Reuther and the United Auto Workers had recently extended the name of their union to the United Automobile, Aeronautics and Agricultural Implement Workers of America. The AFL-CIO and the UAW were spending hundreds of thousands to unionize defense workers. Reuther had even targeted young engineers, "white collar, technical and professional." But the young engineers saw that nearby Arizona, Utah, and Nevada did have "right to work" laws. Wyoming had just voted in "right to work." Why not open the plants there? General Electric's renegade computer department was in Phoenix. The companies knew that opening in a "right to work" state incurred the wrath of the union men. "Right to shirk" is what Reuther called states' "right to work" laws. Therefore companies, old or new, were quiet about the labor factor in their location decision. Instead they cited a reason less controversial— air-conditioning, for example, a new feature that made Arizona livable. Most reporters displayed bewilderment at sophisticated engineers who chose to head labs in a desert. "Arizona seems to be a sort of Mecca for all kinds of job hunters, including electronic engineers and technicians," commented a reporter in the *New York Times*, noting that each year fifty thousand people moved to Arizona in search of new jobs, many of them trained or would-be technicians. None of the companies, old style or new, felt the need to enlighten the reporters.

———————

NO PAIR of young men more typified the rebellious attitude than two engineers named Robert Noyce and Gordon Moore. Moore was a California local, having received his doctorate at the California Institute of Technology, but Noyce was from Iowa and had earned his PhD at the Massachusetts Institute of Technology. Moore, who had originally planned for an academic career, received an offer from General Electric to work on research and development in atomic energy, Cordiner's pride. His biographers, Arnold Thackray, David Brock, and Rachel Jones, wrote that "the Cold War focus on nuclear bombs and atomic power stations did not excite him."[6] Both men had been lured to work in Mountain View, California, by another rebellious mind, that of William Shockley, a physicist who had won the Nobel Prize in 1956. Shockley in his day had broken off and out from Bell Labs, which had come out of the tinkering of yet another rebel, Alexander Graham Bell. After a brief productive, bumptious period at Shockley Semiconductor Laboratory in Mountain View, seven scientists had dared to do their own breaking off, and sought capital to found their own firm to build transistors. As they left, they convinced an eighth, Robert Noyce, to join them. The "Traitorous Eight," as the men who walked out on Shockley were known, found their money via a figure then unfamiliar in the world of engineers, an investment banker. The banker, Arthur Rock, pitched the idea of a semiconductor company to dozens of firms before finally interesting Sherman Fairchild, the founder of Fairchild Camera and Instrument. Fairchild Camera and Instrument did not want to invest in a new company, but it did offer the Traitorous Eight a good deal if they formed a new company that Fairchild would control, Fairchild Semiconductor. Under the deal, each of the Traitorous Eight put in $500 and received shares in Fairchild Camera and Instrument. (Noyce borrowed the money from his grandmother.)[7] Fairchild lent $1.38 million to Fairchild Semiconductor. Fairchild retained the option to buy out Noyce, Moore, and the others. But for now, the engineers had equity. They were no longer mere employees. They owned at least part of their work. The men found that the equity energized them. By 1959, Noyce's own work at Fairchild had yielded seven patents, including U.S. Patent 2,981,877, Semiconductor Device-and-Lead Structure, a model for the integrated circuit.[8] Fairchild Semiconductor and all the other new activity in California so inspired Arthur Rock himself that he moved to the West Coast and invested in other science start-ups: Scientific Data Systems and a company called Teledyne.

The rule that nothing could proceed without a government client seemed immutable to the maverick engineers, even once they had settled in at Fairchild Camera and Instrument. Moore and Noyce told each other they would never have had the confidence to turn traitor and decamp to Fairchild in the first place without the government market for military products containing transistors. The early client that helped Fairchild Semiconductor in its own liftoff was IBM's Federal Systems Division, yet another government contractor. IBM sought a transistor that could function at high temperatures, for a long-range strategic bomber. The company wanted it so badly that it paid $150 for a transistor that cost Fairchild Semiconductor around $5 to produce. Early on at Fairchild, the young Fairchild Semiconductor also cut a deal worth nearly $8 million with Autonetics, a division of North American Aviation, which in turn served as prime contractor for the Air Force's Minuteman. Fairchild would contribute technology to the Apollo program, which followed Gemini.

Nonetheless Noyce found he was not comfortable with a heavy government presence in his shop. "Government funding of R&D," Noyce said, "has a deadening effect upon the incentives of the people." The review processes and quality control at Autonetics irritated Noyce, as they were so lengthy. Government contracts ordered scientists to hunt for one thing, what the government sought, thereby forcing the scientists to ignore what Noyce called "interesting slop"—the unexpected by-products of lab work.[9] Moore also bridled. Government might buy Fairchild products, but the pair kept the share of government's contribution to Fairchild Semiconductor research at 10 percent. "And we like it that way," Noyce said.

A second premise, that only big old-fashioned corporations had the culture or money to innovate, Fairchild Semiconductor tested unrelentingly. At Fairchild the hierarchy was loose. Noyce, unlike many of the men who managed engineers or scientists at old companies, took the lead as head of Research and Development. The others noticed that Noyce understood that managing bright minds was more like herding cats than leading a platoon. "At Fairchild we had a lot of creative people, and he knew how to direct them in general terms, not specific terms," Jean Hoerni, another scientist with a key patent, later recalled. "He was casual about it and didn't interfere. And as a result of this freedom came original thinking."[10] Serendipity mattered. Here, the scientists at Fairchild were echoing the playful founders of GE. The rules were looser here than at the old companies as well. Noyce insisted those at the top and those at the bottom, the women who made the chips, share a lunch space. The engineers drank too much: a new hire noted that when Fairchild partied, it served a frat house pairing of brownies and scotch. Fairchild Semiconductor hired immigrants whose confidence in America was unbounded: one was the Hungarian Andy Grove. Fairchild Semiconductor also hired rule breakers. One job applicant, Marshall Cox, for example, turned up for an interview with manager Don Valentine half an hour late, and without a résumé. Cox therefore expected no consideration from Fairchild Semiconductor. He had blown the interview. "If you want to end it right now, I don't give a shit," he told Valentine. Valentine hired Cox.

To advance at Fairchild Semiconductor, Noyce and Moore told the new hires, you had to spend time in sales, calling on accounts, which gave even the most cerebral scientist a chance to know his market.[11] Mountain View reported to the Fairchild headquarters in Syosset, New York, but at first was free to make most of its own decisions. In 1959, Fairchild Camera and Instrument exercised its option to buy out the men at Fairchild Semiconductor, and each man received shares of the parent, Fairchild Camera and Instrument, in exchange for his Fairchild Semiconductor shares, now worth about $300,000, enough to buy twenty houses at the median price of California homes.[12] Chagrin was mixed with elation when the eight received their cash. With their direct stake in their department gone, their leverage at headquarters diminished as well. Now there was little difference between the men at Fairchild Semiconductor and the men at General Electric's computer division in Phoenix. The men at Fairchild Semiconductor started to drop the new word: "equity." Four of them invested some of the cash they received from selling shares of Fairchild Camera and Instrument in a fund to buy other companies started by Arthur Rock. Noyce also asked Fairchild Camera to introduce a general policy of giving stock options to those employees management wanted to keep. That would be a number far greater than eight. But Sherman Fairchild considered his scientists' desire to create a stock option democracy weird. Sherman Fairchild's view was the same as that of Lemuel Boulware in his day. Spreading stock options all around to everyone like that, Sherman Fairchild said, was "creeping socialism."

This epiphany of equity was shocking engineers at other new firms around the same time. It was a giant shift for a field where credentials and innovations had always mattered more. Floyd Kvamme, a scientist who had trained in Syracuse, landed a job at a small company in Los Angeles, but, as he later recalled, he "didn't even know who owned the company." The situation had been similar at GE, where Kvamme had worked before that. But when, upon joining Fairchild, he was offered stock options, he felt free and almost weightless, like a man in a shifting space capsule. Kvamme's equity, he said, "caused me to be sensitive about where the company's shares were."[13] Once you started thinking about equity, you couldn't stop.

For a while, Noyce and Moore enjoyed enough freedom to satisfy them. They understood they had to respect the past: when Fairchild Semiconductor opened a factory in South Portland, Maine, an old-fashioned state, the advertisements for female assembly workers promised "stability of employment" and "free insurance coverage (dependents included)." The Fairchild Semiconductor want ads in the Western papers took a freer tone: "If you prefer a young dynamic organization, you are invited to either forward your résumé to John P. Walsh or visit our Employment Office at 545 Whitman Road in Mountain View between the hours of 9:00–11:00 a.m. and 1:30–4:00 p.m." ran one ad in a San Francisco paper.

Noyce made bold decisions, including a price cut for silicon transistors so dramatic that they sold for less than it cost to make them. The price cut was aimed at capturing new markets for nonmilitary products, such as televisions. Noyce won his bet: at lower prices, the orders flowed in and Fairchild challenged its competitors. Even more exciting was that Fairchild Semiconductor was indeed winning nongovernment contracts as well, along with the old government ones. A 1964 federal rule requiring that all televisions be equipped with UHF tuners guaranteed transistor business to companies like Fairchild Semiconductor.

Fairchild Semiconductor grew fast, adding hundreds, and then thousands, of employees. And even though it was based in California, a state where Reuther had vowed to unionize white-collar workers and professionals, Fairchild Semiconductor proved tough to unionize. The company often located the unionizable part of a project abroad: integrated electronic circuits were made in Mountain View but were shipped to Hong Kong, far from Walter Reuther's reach, for packaging and testing. The founders at Fairchild Semiconductor didn't think professionals like themselves should be unionized, and they sought to make those around them, including the workers who crafted the chips, feel the same way. Fairchild Semiconductor succeeded. In the week when *Gemini V* splashed down, workers at Fairchild Semiconductor's San Rafael factory had rejected by a 422-to-122 vote representation by Local 238 of the International Association of Machinists. This came on top of an earlier "no" vote in 1962 elsewhere in the division.

Frustrated at their inability to penetrate some of these new companies, union leaders turned elsewhere. In Walter Reuther's case, another target was Cesar Chavez, who had mounted a prolonged strike against grape growers. In Delano, California, the Agricultural Workers Organizing Committee, a prime candidate to be brought under the UAW umbrella, was pressing for a $1.40 minimum wage, and Reuther offered help. The UAW's Paul Schrade lobbied for state-funded programs for the poor. At the end of 1965, with funds from Sargent Shriver, a young attorney named James Lorenz would establish a law firm, California Rural Legal Assistance, to awaken farmworkers to their right to unionize.

But the whole agricultural drama seemed far away from Noyce and his scientists, who continued to stay away from unions when they could. At Philco on the East Coast, where Noyce had worked earlier, a debilitating strike had cost the company so much in earnings that it had given up plans to fund its own original research. Noyce had noticed that. Philco had also raised prices on televisions after the strike, explaining that the boost was due to a cost increase "including a substantial wage increase." Those price rises contrasted with cuts in television prices by other manufacturers. At Fairchild, Noyce tried to act preemptively, rewarding employees so much that they would not want to strike. As his biographer, Leslie Berlin, would later note, Noyce "thought that collective bargaining by definition undermined individual striving." Noyce's managers tried when they could to work with those on the assembly line, so that they could produce "something that worked smoothly and that the people who were subject to it helped to create." Not all the workers at Fairchild would get equity, but enough did, or hoped to, or hoped to work for scientists who had equity, that they did not want to strike. Science and share price, not union fraternity, dominated the culture.

The more independent Fairchild Semiconductor grew, the more Noyce, Moore, and the others found themselves resisting headquarters in Syosset. When John Carter, the president of Fairchild Camera and Instrument, arrived at the headquarters of Fairchild Semiconductor for a full day's work, what the Fairchild men noticed was the car. "Nobody had ever seen a limousine and a chauffeur out there before," as the writer Tom Wolfe later said, paraphrasing the engineers' reaction. What put off the scientists, though, was that "the driver stayed out there for almost eight hours, doing nothing. . . . Here was a serf who did nothing all day but wait outside a door to be at the service of the haunches of his master instantly." It gave the men in California a peek at New York corporate life, and to the Fairchild Semiconductor men that life seemed "terribly wrong."

Yet the executives back East kept milking the semiconductor unit as their cash cow. In the annual report, the Fairchild parent referred to Fairchild Semiconductor as "the division," a title that understated its contribution.[14] Tithing to headquarters was no different than paying taxes. Fairchild Camera and Instrument did try to reward Noyce and his men just as another company, or the military, traditionally rewarded talent: by promotion into new areas, with greater responsibility. Noyce was duly promoted to Fairchild group vice president. But promotion in an established corporation was not really what Noyce, Grove, and the other scientists found they wanted. Promotion meant more flights East, and more meetings, and Noyce didn't like meetings, writing, during one of them, a note to himself: "Try to get East Coast out."

What the men in Mountain View wanted was to stay exactly where they were and get equity, so they could run their own company. The frustration became so powerful that some of Noyce's recruits decided to leave. Filling out an exit questionnaire before his departure, engineer Bob Widlar wrote one line explaining his departure. "I . . . want . . . to . . . be . . . RICH." The company asked Widlar what compensation could keep him: "one million tax-free by whatever way you chose," Widlar said.[15] This the midlevel executives at a publicly traded company could not grant. Widlar went to a company called Molectro, which would become National Semiconductor, where he later received options for twenty thousand shares at $5 a share. The value was a zero short of Widlar's ultimatum demand at Fairchild, but National Semiconductor had potential to grow.

Upstarts like Fairchild Semiconductor were already winning the attention of scholars. One of the early students of such companies was a Princeton professor, Fritz Machlup. Machlup reckoned that traditional indicators such as gross national product didn't really capture what was going on in the United States. Machlup posited that scholars ought to try to quantify what he called the "knowledge economy." That included traditional knowledge-gathering activity—schools and universities—and also government science: the space program. But Machlup's math also sought to capture new companies like Fairchild, which fell, in his paradigm, into the category "information services." By his own measure knowledge had been a significant share of growth even back in the 1950s: for the year 1958, for example, Machlup reckoned that the knowledge economy amounted to 29 percent of GNP. Machlup did not know what to make of his information economy. He believed that one should try to arrive at an economy that was "socially good." And how to do that? In any case, the commentators observed, a knowledge economy had to be expensive. A review of Machlup's book that had appeared in the *Washington Post* was headed "The High Cost of Knowledge in America."

But to Noyce and Moore, knowledge did not seem overpriced. Compared with what it could produce, knowledge was a bargain. Earlier in 1965, Gordon Moore had published in the magazine *Electronics* a paper with a seemingly workaday title: "Cramming More Components onto Integrated Circuits." The paper depicted a future as dazzling as any view from the window of a space capsule. In the paper, Moore posited that for the same "minimum component costs" the number of components on a chip could double every two years. At present, fifty components fitted on each circuit, but Moore had no trouble envisioning one thousand components per circuit in 1970, or sixty-five thousand in 1975, all on a single wafer. The projection of exponential growth, a revolution in miniature, soon became known across the industry as "Moore's Law."[16]

The article became legendary, but the cartoon published with it also mattered. Drawn by Grant Compton, the cartoon depicted a retailers' fair for the average consumer. There was a stand for notions—sewing items. There was a stand for cosmetics. But the crowd in the room turned its back on these goods to gather around a vendor under a sign reading "Handy Home Computers." Moore's Law might interest NASA or radar scientists. But the law also made the breakaway from defense for which Noyce and Moore had wished so long a true possibility. If a company could use its chips to make small appliances, along with transistor radios, or such small computers, or chip-driven cars, that company need no longer rely solely on the Defense Department. The company would no longer need to pander to government, either, and could express its pro-market sentiments out loud. The company would be able to drop the heavy load of hypocrisy that had brought Boulware and General Electric to their knees. The innovation of the chip might even do what Americans had not been able to manage through the courts or laws. It might topple Ike's military-industrial complex and replace it with a more reliable civic prosperity, prosperity in the style of Thomas Edison or Henry Ford.

Geeks such as Robert Noyce, Gordon Moore, and their colleagues were considered by the union men as the ultimate in selfishness. But the companies were still so new that such a judgment was harsh. Nobody yet knew what the culture of these newbies would become. Already it was clear that one thing was not selfish about Noyce and Moore, or Fairchild Semiconductor: the thousands of jobs they were creating in California and around the world. In addition to working in California and Maine, Fairchild had opened those factories in Hong Kong, which the following year would employ five thousand.

The executives thought hard about their bottom line, but they also thought hard about where they could create jobs in poorer areas within the United States, even jobs for people who had limited education, like those in Watts. Doing something like that, they decided, was worth even the sacrifice of partnering with the U.S. government in a state that did not have "right to work": New Mexico. Fairchild decided to build a chip factory and employ Native Americans there. The Bureau of Indian Affairs located the site, in Shiprock, about one hundred miles, at least as the crow flew, from a War on Poverty project, Shriver's Rough Rock Demonstration School. The Fairchild Semiconductor manufacturing site opened in a gymnasium. It started out by employing hundreds on a budget of $1 million, but would soon employ a thousand. The workers, mostly female, produced circuits that were used in calculators and missile guidance systems. In a few years, Fairchild would also build a real plant. A brochure produced at that point argued that Navajo women naturally gravitated toward the meticulous work involving chips: "Weaving, like all Navajo arts, is done with unique imagination and craftsmanship . . . building electronic devices, transistors and integrated circuits, also requires the same personal commitment to perfection."[17] The plant manager that winter of 1965 would start to look for qualified men who "would like to discuss a career with us in the management field." The expansion at Shiprock eventually would make Fairchild the largest private employer of Native Americans in the United States. The potential for jobs followed Moore's Law as well. What Fairchild and its successors offered was a number of jobs exponentially greater than the summer gigs Shriver hawked with his Murray the K TV special. More important, the jobs Fairchild created, and the training it offered, came closer to integrating workers into the real economy than near any post a government official in Shriver's office might contrive.

————————

WHILE JOHNSON, Governor Brown, and Mayor Yorty waited for the findings of the McCone Commission, intellectuals from everywhere continued to weigh in on Watts—and on everything else. A new thinker on the scene was Charles Reich, a young law professor at Yale and former clerk to Supreme Court justice Hugo Black. To help the poor, Reich turned an old property rights argument on its head. Executives and private-sector people had property, Reich noted. Patents like that of Noyce were considered precious property, to be protected at all cost. Employees, whether at GE, Fairchild, or the Defense Department, where they numbered about 3.5 million, or about twice those in the auto industry, kept their salaries as property. That was their right. But those who received dollars from the federal government in another form, not as salary but, say, as welfare payments or even Social Security payments, had no right to the payments. That money was dispensed at the whim of social workers. In a recent case, the Supreme Court had even affirmed the idea that Social Security was not a right by backing up the Social Security Administration when it chose to cut off payments to a retiree because he had been deported as a communist.[18] It was time, Reich argued, to consider whatever government benefits already went to poor people as their property. The question was intensely relevant, for as the government grew, it distributed more and more of those assets, in the form of welfare checks, Social Security payments, or housing subsidies. America maintained an "unacknowledged double standard." Payments were a right, not a privilege. Reich called what the poor or old received "new property." He argued that Americans needed a "Homestead Act for rootless Twentieth Century man."

Others took the opposite view. To call welfare "property," and pretend that doing so was strengthening property rights, was retrogress, not progress. In fact, you were placing a greater claim on the property of everyone else, through the increased taxes necessary to make welfare property, and thereby weakening the property rights principle. California was a good example: the unemployed blacks in Los Angeles were few in number relative to the rest of the people in a prosperous state, and an exception. Most blacks, the argument went, wanted to rise. Soon enough they would have the kind of property enjoyed by the rich. That would eventually obviate their need for government largesse. The government should get out of the way in the meantime. Black people were doing better in the 1960s than before, finding employment in places where they had once not been permitted. They were also getting education. In 1960, only 20 percent of black people over age twenty-five had completed four years of high school, compared with 40 percent of whites. By 1965, the figure for blacks was 27 percent, compared with 50 percent for whites. By 1970, 31 percent of blacks would be high school grads. The share of blacks who had completed four years of college was tiny, but rising fast as well. Wouldn't it be better if all underemployed Americans viewed salaries, and not government payments, as the desirable "property"?

The main exponent of this optimistic view was the publisher of *Jet*, *Ebony*, and *Negro Digest*, John Johnson. The Johnson periodicals covered black civil rights causes and black militants extensively and aggressively. They had introduced many of their readers to Malcolm X, the black leader who argued for black separatism before his death that February. One of the edgiest items Johnson published—just that August—was a fiction piece about a young black man who killed a white man who refused to slide over to yield space at the front of a bus. But Johnson also made the point in his pages that "the masses," as leftists liked to call the angry poor, were not actually massive in number. For the press to cover them too much missed the story. To Johnson, the big story of the 1960s was the rise of the majority of blacks. Johnson saw himself as an example. He'd started from nothing and built up a company that *was* massive, in an area no one had ever imagined existed: black middle-class magazines. This was a biography for which Johnson would never apologize to black-power advocates. In the fall of 1965, the twentieth-anniversary year of *Ebony*, the magazine was selling 900,000 copies a month. For his readers, John-son would define success in a few rules: "Winning a civil rights battle was success. Raising a family was success. Sending children to college was success. Earning an MBA or making an outstanding professional contribution was success."[19] Johnson's fellow Chicagoan, Milton Friedman, was now mooting a related idea: a negative income tax, payments to low earners to offset whatever cash they gave up to Social Security taxes—more money of their own. In Newark, Reverend Nathan Wright spoke of "equity." By equity Wright didn't mean stock shares in Fairchild. But he did mean something not so far off from Wall Street equity either—an equal share in opportunity and a chance to play in the game of life.

THAT FALL of 1965, as it happened, Congress was turning to the single piece of legislation most important in the contest between old-world companies on the one hand and new upstarts on the other. That was the bill Johnson had promised Meany and Reuther he would get to after Medicare and Medicaid, one that ended the "right to work" exception for states nationwide. If the "right to work" rule was thus repealed, then all states would be far easier to unionize, and employers would have no choice but to accept unions. All of America would be unionland. The House had already passed repeal. Only the Senate vote remained. And Johnson thought he had the votes, including the key support of Everett Dirksen, the Senate minority leader. Dirksen, though in the opposing party, had made so many things easy for Johnson, especially civil rights legislation. Yet to Johnson's chagrin, his "touchdowns," the success of past legislation, didn't seem to make repealing "right to work" easier. In the Senate, opposition emerged, led by none other than Dirksen. He had broken the civil rights filibuster for Johnson. Now the senator planned to use the same tool, the filibuster, to defy the president. The political explanation for Dirksen's theatrics was obvious: after accommodating Johnson so often, the senator wanted to prove he was still a Republican. Dirksen gave other explanations, all of them, in his filibuster, which he commenced on October 4. Dirksen had perused constituents' letters, and they were opposed to repeal. In states that did not have "right to work," workers were forced to join the union and pay dues, a good share of which served his opponents, the Democratic Party. That wasn't freedom, Dirksen said. "This is a fight for a civil right—the right of people to work without paying tribute to an organization or a despotic leader."

There was little Johnson could do about Dirksen's filibuster. The president needed Dirksen on so many other fronts, including support for Robert McNamara and McNamara's bombing campaign in North Vietnam, Rolling Thunder.[20] George Meany of the AFL-CIO, who, unlike Reuther, recognized this as an existential struggle, called on Dirksen to make a plea for repeal. The state Dirksen represented, Illinois, was not a "right to work" state. Didn't Illinois want to end the disadvantage that "right to work" Indiana exploited? Dirksen commenced the conversation in a friendly, Lyndon Johnson style. "How's Mrs. Meany?" Meany went straight to the point. "Everett, you know why I'm here." The senator did not budge. Dirksen told newsmen he was ready to talk repeal of "right to work" to death.

Advocates of repeal now turned on Dirksen, contending that those who defended "right to work" were motivated by racial bigotry. "The Southerners feel that if the unions become stronger in the South they will be furnishing bases for stronger civil rights activity," one union source told the papers. With this argument, repeal's advocates trapped a senator from the Land of Lincoln on the wrong side of an issue they assumed he cared more about than personnel policy at big corporations, namely, civil rights. Being grouped with backward, bigoted Southerners, the unions reckoned, would make Dirksen cave in.

Dirksen's opponents guessed wrong. The senator was as good as his word. Dirksen swore his readiness to read aloud thousands of editorials supporting "right to work." Civil rights, Dirksen had said in 1964, were an idea whose time had come. Now the idea whose time had come was "right to work." As he continued his filibuster, Dirksen elaborated on his thoughts. The Administration called itself liberal. But progressive support for unions was not the same as classical liberalism, the school Dirksen liked best. "No true liberal," Dirksen said, "modern or otherwise, can fail to stand up for the right of the individual to make his own choice in the matter." Johnson might give his loyalty to Meany or Reuther. But Dirksen would give "mine to the people."[21]

In his filibuster theater, Dirksen enjoyed the autumn advantage: law-makers were tired, and had appropriations they desperately wanted to get through this session. Another advantage for opponents of repeal was that the most powerful proponent of repeal was distracted by a health problem. On October 5, the second day of the filibuster, Johnson announced he was having surgery to remove his gallbladder. Johnson called important leaders, as was standard, to alert them to his absence. The presidential call to the Senate minority leader proved especially awkward. Dirksen said that Johnson had "all his prayers," but didn't say much else. On October 7, the president underwent the operation, which in those days required a week, or weeks, in the hospital.[22] On October 12, Mike Mansfield, the Senate majority leader, dropped the drive to repeal states' rights to decide whether workers had to be compelled to accept union membership. Johnson promised George Meany he would continue the fight: "Just as we had to come back last year to finish the unfinished battle for Medicare," he told Meany, "we will come back in the next session to remove this divisive provision." But Dirksen, less-unionized America, and the new, playful companies had prevailed.

Johnson had always told others time was his enemy, and now, indeed it was. To buy himself more congressional sessions, to lessen the likelihood of more riots, to make his next effort on "right to work," the president needed to ensure that his now legendary boom would continue. Yet once again, William McChesney Martin was warning Johnson that he was about to raise interest rates. Johnson had been nervous about it all fall: he had even said to Martin at the time of the gallbladder surgery: "You wouldn't raise the discount rate while I'm in the hospital, would you?"[23] The consumer price index seemed to validate Martin's concern. The index had increased by an annualized 2.6 percent in the second quarter of the year, double the rate of the preceding twelve months. Total gold reserves, which Martin watched with a keen eye, in early December stood at $13.8 billion, down several hundred million from the summer. Foreigners were removing their gold.

Johnson and Treasury Secretary Henry Fowler told themselves, and then Martin, that if the Fed had to raise rates, it could do so in 1966, not

1965. Martin was just too independent, Fowler said to Johnson. "It makes the country feel we're divided, and it makes the country feel there are two quarterbacks down here, one fellow's playing one game and one fellow's playing another." Fowler believed in work at the great table, and believed that the Fed chairman should come to it. Fowler told Johnson that the country was entitled to have the assurance that "economic and financial policies are being determined by a sensible group of reasonable men sitting around together."[24]

But Martin's interest rate increase was yet another idea whose time had come. Martin believed that if the United States was going to sustain its status as world financial capital, and fund future wars—never mind this one in Vietnam—the Fed would have to act. The central bank would have to set an interest rate that inspired confidence in America's ability to control the value of the dollar, and draw money from abroad. On December 3, 1965, Fowler learned from Martin that that day the Fed chair intended, if he got the votes, to lead the Open Market Committee in voting to raise the interest rate by half a percentage point, to 4.5 percent.[25] Martin cast the deciding vote for the increase. Fowler communicated this betrayal by Martin to Johnson, who grew so warm he was moved to mention Andrew Jackson, the president who had abolished America's central bank in his day. "I would hope that he wouldn't call his board together and have a Biddle-Jackson fight—I'm prepared to be Jackson if he wants to be Biddle—have a fight like that." Biddle was Nicholas Biddle, the head of the central bank that Jackson had forced to disappear in 1836. Now it was December 1965, and Johnson had had it with Martin, and told Fowler that he ought to start thinking about how the White House could get "a real articulate, able, tough guy to take this Federal Reserve place." An interest rate increase meant that any borrowing the government did—and it was doing plenty—would cost more, and permit fewer outlays, whether for Vietnam; Gemini's successor, Apollo; or the War on Poverty.

On December 4, Johnson watched the launch of *Gemini VII*, and thought over how he would handle his rogue central banker. The president summoned William McChesney Martin to his ranch. Johnson actually picked the Fed chairman up at the airport, along with Fowler; Bureau of the Budget chief Charles Schultze; and Gardner Ackley, the chairman of Johnson's Council of Economic Advisers. Johnson suspected that a central banker like Martin did not harbor any large sympathy for the poverty program. But Martin had to be a patriot. The necessary dialogue followed. Martin, who had served at the Fed since the time of Truman, told the president that he, too, liked to see interest rates low. There was one way, "the only way," Martin said, you could have low interest rates. That was "budgetary responsibility, both in respect to government spending and taxing."[26] Guns and butter cost too much. By all accounts, Johnson replied forcefully. By some, the president even shoved the smaller Martin up against a wall and picked him up by the lapels of his suit jacket. "Martin, my boys are dying in Vietnam," Johnson said, "and you won't print the money I need."

In December 1965 the McCone Commission on the Watts Riot was finally, after 64 meetings and 530 witness interviews, ready to make its report. The document did not turn out to be the damning accusation of the police that the activists hoped for. It did not tie community action groups, whether the UAW's or the government's, to the riots in the way Chief of Police Parker had suggested might be done. Instead McCone and the others provided a tale of wrongs, wrong turns, misunderstandings, and unexpected failures. Watts really was Murphy's Law, in all its glory. But the report did offer a number of conclusions. The first was what the White House already knew. There were parts of the War on Poverty that caused the opposite of Johnson's or Shriver's intent. Unemployed men rioted. But the newly generous War on Poverty welfare benefits actually encouraged men not to work, adding to the ranks of unemployed. With the average family welfare check between $177 and $238 a month, and wages at $220, the commission concluded that "the financial incentive to find work may be either negative or non-existent."[27] The report didn't make community action look good, either. Another reality, the commissioners wrote, was that Californians' vote against a fair-housing law had affronted blacks stuck in Los Angeles. The final conclusion, and the most important, was that the missing jobs in Watts had indeed driven men to riot.[28]

Here the McCone Commission blamed old-style companies and unions. The companies should be forced to supply a head count of minorities they employed to the California Fair Employment Practices Commission, the report said. The report also affirmed as valid the suspicions of union discrimination against blacks. In the unions, bigotry, especially in the building trades and apprenticeships, had caused hiring "discrimination against the Negroes." That had to stop. The unions should be required to report to California's Fair Employment Practices Commission, too.

Another round of speculation about where the missing jobs might come from ensued. The Urban League interpreted the job shortage to mean that hiring required further regulation: that "all firms holding government contracts be required to contribute toward financing and staffing" a black-organized job training center. Paul Schrade, the regional director for the UAW, argued that the federal government needed to expand its jobs programs, so numerous already, to employ fifty thousand more people. Michael Harrington had joined others in advocating birth control as a solution to poverty, a real insult to the Catholic Church that had reared him. At a conference in New York, Harrington charged that families were poor "because they were effectively denied access to family planning." Harrington had just published a book that argued that technology, Noyce's and Moore's magic, was yielding a "slave civilization," with machines as master of workers. Harrington suggested that modern ills would be reduced if America achieved true socialism, which he defined as "the freedom of individual man." Harrington never missed a chance to remind his wayward SDS friends, indeed the entire American left, that American socialists should deplore communism. In December, Harrington joined other authors, including Edward Albee, Hannah Arendt, and Philip Roth, in signing a public petition demanding that Moscow release two writers the regime had recently arrested.

But as 1966 commenced, the Watts riot and the thoughtful discussions fell out of the news without resolution. Accounts of space rockets and electronics replaced urban troubles in the papers. Perhaps companies not yet born would hire workers in the city in the future. Perhaps new inventions would provide food and shelter for all. Perhaps Moore's Law, not Murphy's Law, would triumph, even in an area like South Los Angeles. Ronald Reagan decided to run for the governorship of California. As soon as word got out, the actor received news that Lemuel Boulware would support his campaign. Reagan wrote back to his friend Lem that the prospect of big-time politics still felt strange, "like stepping off the high dive and realizing you were on the way to the water and it might be cold." Still, Reagan wrote, even if he didn't get many votes, "I think I'll be proud for the rest of my life of the support and efforts that have been shown by people like yourself."[29] Reagan thought about what he might say in his campaign. Reagan could slam Shriver, obvious and easy. He could criticize the amount spent per youngster in the federal poverty programs as too high—he had done so in the past. He could call for law and order. After the riots, many Californians, including many in Los Angeles, didn't want anything to do with Watts. These voters were taking a good look at Reagan, who, they were certain, wouldn't conciliate with radicals.[30] Yorty was taking a strong law-and-order stand, and voters liked it. The progressive magazines and papers were mocking that. "Yes, out of the rubble of the Southeast section of his city, Mayor Samuel W. Yorty, within that strange Southern California syndrome of parochial paranoia, has apparently risen phoenix-like with an ever broader base of power," commented *New Republic*.

Yet, as he prepared to run, Reagan focused on another phoenix. It was the California that might arise from the genius of the Hollywood studios he knew so well, from the geeky universities, from small companies, from the ranchers, from simple individual minds. Managing scarcity, or insisting public police promote birth control, wasn't the right approach. The state should consider products yet uninvented, and standing back to let them be invented. Those inventions would yield a future of plenty. The state had to remember what it would be enforcing law and order *for*. A Glendale evangelist named W. S. McBirnie offered Reagan a term to capture the potential in the golden West. The phrase stuck in Reagan's ear. He decided to use McBirnie's phrase in the official announcement of his candidacy, the moment when the new candidate hoped to evoke all the Golden State might be. Reagan called California the "creative society." As political slogans went, "creative society" was on the soft end. But it made clear that California planned to do all Edison and Steinmetz had done in their day, and far more. Boulware would understand.

6

Interlude: Looking for Socialism

SEPTEMBER 1965 TO JANUARY 1966

Here we began to understand the possibilities for a social-
ism of the heart.
                        —Description of North Vietnam,
                        Tom Hayden and Staughton Lynd[1]

Tom Hayden spent the fall of 1965 losing elections. They were New Jersey state and county races. Recently the state had reapportioned seats in the New Jersey senate, giving Essex County, Newark's county, more seats. Hayden's hope was to grab some of these new state senate seats by fielding a coalition called the United Freedom Ticket, the "freedom" in the name being a tip of the hat to the forlorn Mississippi Freedom Democratic Party. Hayden's Newark Community Union Project teamed up with two other local groups, mostly black and Hispanic, to create United Freedom. The truth was that Newark was badly in need of a change: the Addonizio crowd and their friends ran the city as their own business. At the outset of the campaign season, therefore, Hayden and others were optimistic enough to invite a documentary filmmaker, Hayden's friend Norman Fruchter, to trail the campaign and capture its success.[2] Fruchter's camera was instead capturing a rout. Come November, there was a dramatic result, but not for the United Freedom ticket. Voters across New Jersey traded one traditional party for another, electing Democrats to the state assembly and state senate after half a century of Republican legislative majorities. Where one Republican had held the single senate seat for Essex County, now four establishment Democrats sat.[3]

The 1965 election frustration was coming on top of other frustrations for Hayden in Newark. The activist had spent time with his old ally Junius Williams on the most humdrum of projects: getting the city of Newark to install a stoplight at a treacherous intersection. Even that effort had failed, notwithstanding biracial demonstrations and the singing of spirituals.[4] By funding Hayden in Newark, the UAW and other unions had helped to create his community action group, NCUP. By supporting President Johnson in his Great Society work, the unions had, albeit indirectly, also caused Addonizio's United Community Corporation to be funded. Yet the UCC turned its nose up rather than hire NCUP workers. Hayden, who was divorced now, always found girlfriends. But he did not always find friends. He had grown close to one of the mothers in the neighborhood, Bessie Smith, and involved Bessie and her husband, Thurman, in community action. There were few other Bessies. Though Hayden wanted to organize black Newark, black Newark did not necessarily want to be organized by him.

The frustration in Newark was a microcosm of the national challenges confronting Hayden's crowd. In other cities, the War on Poverty was crowding out ERAP projects as well. Hayden's old Michigan ally in the founding of SDS, Al Haber, was now condemning Hayden's vision of multiracial community action to end poverty in Northern cities as "romantic [and] almost apolitical."[5] After Watts, Haber's criticism of community action could not be called wrong. Paul Booth, the current national secretary of SDS, was calling for a "real movement." That suggested the old SDS was a fake. In the South, SNCC was also dividing, partly a casualty of its own success. The Civil Rights Act of 1964 and the Voting Rights Act of 1965 made public official discrimination, on trains or in elections, less likely to occur. That was an indisputable victory for civil rights, the greatest in memory.

But many in SNCC wanted another campaign. And President Johnson had given them one, in June at Howard University, with his insistence that the nation go beyond equality of opportunity and pursue equality of result. Nonviolence was in SNCC's very name—the Student Nonviolent Coordinating Committee. The current SNCC leader, John Lewis, was a seminarian who believed in nonviolence and had the scars to prove it. Yet the organization was changing, disavowing, as Casey Hayden reported, its "nonviolent, interracial culture." One of the figures on the periphery at SNCC was Stokely Carmichael, a recent Howard graduate who took seriously the demand of equal results that Johnson made at his own college. Carmichael had heretofore played minor roles at SNCC—at Atlantic City, he had operated the walkie-talkies. But others at SNCC liked Carmichael's bluntness: "To ask Negroes to get in the Democratic Party," Carmichael said at one point, "is like asking Jews to join the Nazi Party." It appeared that Carmichael was supplanting Lewis. In the past, Casey Hayden had always felt, as she put it, "powerful and at home" in SNCC.[6] Now leadership at SNCC was making it clear that white protesters were indeed no longer welcome. Casey was devastated. "We lost our community," she later recalled. Everywhere Tom and Casey looked there was tension between radicals and liberals, activists and seminar leaders, blacks and whites.

The greatest divide in the protest movement was a new one: the astounding U.S. military ramp-up in Vietnam. Week by week, Johnson sent out thousands more troops. Week by week, the frustration among younger Americans grew, and not only within the old protest movement. With their bombing campaign in North Vietnam, Operation Rolling Thunder, Johnson and McNamara promised both to achieve a quick victory and to limit destruction to military targets. The president and the defense secretary were delivering neither. Instead of awing the world with American strength, the bombers' sorties were revealing American weakness. Gordon Cooper and Pete Conrad might spend record time on *Gemini V* in space. But the North Vietnamese, like David with a slingshot, were managing to knock Robert McNamara's planes out of the sky with humiliating regularity. Rolling Thunder did not bomb Hanoi, but the bombing elsewhere was so intense that even a regular American civilian could surmise that damage to nonmilitary targets, villages, must be occurring.

Earlier that year Hayden's own University of Michigan had inaugurated a kind of protest that was now catching fire across the country: the "teach-in," during which professors suspended classes or permitted students to drop homework while the teachers led discussions on the American escalation. On August 6, 1965, the twentieth anniversary of Hiroshima and just before Watts, a pacifist acquaintance of Hayden's, the activist and professor Staughton Lynd, had joined others in mounting a Washington demonstration, much smaller than the March on Washington, but still newsworthy, on the sidewalk beside the White House fence. A snapshot taken that day became famous: Lynd and Robert Parris Moses of SNCC, arm in arm and covered with red paint splashed upon them seconds before by hecklers. "Don't Be Misled by a Red"—one heckler's poster had read. Lynd had been raised a Quaker, and believed Quakers had a moral obligation to halt the war. A few months later, in November, another Quaker, Norman Morrison, staged a tragic protest. Arriving at the Pentagon with his baby daughter, Emily, in his arms, Morrison planted himself near Secretary McNamara's office window and doused himself with gasoline. Only at the last moment had Emily been placed away—or taken away—from Morrison. Then Morrison struck a match.

The war moved closer to Hayden himself when the Selective Service summoned him over the river to the Army induction center at 39 Whitehall Street in Manhattan. The Army rated Hayden "1-Y," qualified for service in a time of war, but deferred for now. Hayden, however, watched with some discomfort as the others, "very young and nervous men standing in naked embarrassment," were absorbed into the great U.S. military apparatus. Some of his fellow SDS members in Michigan, including the state SDS chairman, a student from Hayden's own hometown, Royal Oak, had been reclassified 1-A, top of the list, after they staged sit-ins at the Ann Arbor Selective Service office. This final fissure, between those in SDS or SNCC who wanted to stick to domestic policy and those who wanted to build an entirely new movement to fight the war, was widening to a chasm.

Following Morrison, a former seminarian, Roger Allen LaPorte, went to the United Nations and, on November 9, just after the Newark defeat, also set himself ablaze. Hayden at first publicly opposed extreme protests such as Morrison's. Standing atop a rented truck in New York City several weeks later, toward the end of November, Hayden warned that those who protested Vietnam, especially flamboyantly and tragically, as with self-immolation, should instead stick to now humdrum sit-ins or marches. "Otherwise," he told the crowd, "we will go on in a dangerous path, acting in more and more thrilling ways and getting more and more articles about ourselves . . . which have nothing to do with ending the war."

But Hayden no longer believed even himself. He was actually beginning to wonder if he should also protest the war in some "thrilling way." So when Lynd, a junior professor at Yale, called to invite him along on a mission to North Vietnam, Hayden assented. To Hayden, the idea was simultaneously unreal and intensely exciting. The pair discussed the trip, Lynd later remembered, on top of a snowy hill in New Haven as they watched the Lynd children sled.[7] Lynd told Hayden that he was committed at any cost to speaking with the North Vietnamese government. Lyndon Johnson himself had, months ago, claimed his willingness to open "unconditional discussions." What was so different about Lynd's opening such discussions? Lynd was furious at the Ivy League establishment for participating in the war. He scored figures like National Security Advisor Walt Rostow or McGeorge Bundy, both Yale men themselves. "Annihilation in a Brooks Brothers suit is still murder," Lynd said.[8] Since the State Department made a special point of banning U.S. citizens from even entering North Vietnam—let alone negotiating with the regime of Ho Chi Minh—heading into Hanoi would certainly be dramatic. It would be satisfying for both Lynd and Hayden to unearth evidence of Pentagon cover-ups in Operation Rolling Thunder. A mission such as this would provide Hayden with what he lacked in Newark: a real, breathing enemy, his own government.

Still, the trip drew Hayden for another reason, which also had to do with the future of his movement. It had been three and a half years since he had tangled with Michael Harrington at Port Huron over the treatment of communist nations in the statement drafts. Back then, as always, Harrington had insisted that socialism was the real goal, and that the Soviet Union and Mao's China were not socialist nations, just communist dictatorships. Hayden had always disagreed with Harrington's categorical distinction between socialism and communism. You couldn't pretend that the Czechs, or the Russians, or the Chinese, or the North Vietnamese weren't socialist at all, Hayden thought. Hayden didn't call himself a socialist. But now he thought maybe socialism might offer something new to believe in. At the very least, socialism *interested* him. Lynd told others he believed the 1960s protest movement could never yield real change unless it began to utter the "forbidden word," socialism. Maybe Lynd was correct. Even Hayden, the ultimate meetings man, was now tiring of meetings. If he was going to learn about socialism, Hayden wouldn't do it through mere talk. He wanted to see the thing for himself.

Before arriving in Hanoi, the Vietnam trip would take Lynd and Hayden through Prague, then Moscow and Beijing. That itinerary would give Hayden ample chance to sample not just socialism but socialisms, the "varieties of revolutionary experience." Hayden's traveling companions would make ideal company for such a tour. Staughton's father, Robert Lynd, the famous sociologist, had described history as a "vast wandering enterprise."[9] Staughton thought history required directing. As a professor and a pacifist, the younger Lynd had long preached and taught, especially about Marxism, transcendentalism, and socialism. That Herbert Aptheker, a respected scholar of Marx and theoretician of the American Communist Party, would lead the tour would be another bonus. With Aptheker and Lynd by his side, Hayden would surely see and understand what collective experiments were all about.

Hayden applied for a passport. As he made other preparations for the trip he thought again about the risks. They started with his parents, who already did not know what to make of their son. Hayden's mother, Gene, divorced, would forgive and defend anything. But her friends would not, and Tom's activities caused her, he later allowed with chagrin, "boundless embarrassment." Tom in Hanoi was something that Tom's father, a marine who had once scanned the skies over San Diego for Japanese fighter planes, would never understand. Tom's father had a new family. It was clear now that Tom might never get to know his half sister, a new baby girl.

Word of the trip to North Vietnam began to get around. Hayden waited for the reproach: the higher-ups, the ones who contributed financially to ERAP or the War on Poverty, would not like the trip. Neither Walter Reuther nor George Meany was ready to turn against Johnson, or soften on communism. At an AFL-CIO convention in mid-December, antiwar students had demonstrated, and Meany ordered his sergeants at arms to "throw the kookies out." Meany rejected any analogy between the role of the United States in Vietnam and that of France: "I resent very much our country being compared to French exploiters who were there as a colonial power." Reuther's deputy, Emil Mazey, called Jay Lovestone, director of the AFL-CIO's international affairs department, a "war hawk." Reuther and Meany agreed to an AFL-CIO resolution pledging "unstinting support of all measures the administration might deem necessary to halt Communist aggression." Bayard Rustin, the black organizer for the great Civil Rights March on Washington, pointedly refrained from criticizing the war. Lynd accused Rustin of being in "coalition with the marines." James Farmer of the Congress on Racial Equality that summer had led a group in reversing a CORE convention resolution calling for U.S. withdrawal from Vietnam.[10] Others active in the civil rights movement, such as Hayden's successor as leader at SDS, Carl Oglesby, argued that it was important to demonstrate that the movement represented traditional American values. That case became tougher to make, Oglesby pointed out, when two heroes of the movement "picked this moment to go to Communist North Vietnam in the company of one of the [CPUSA's] principal theoreticians."[11] Michael Harrington did oppose the war. But he had recently warned about the appearance of chumminess a Vietnam trip generated. A legitimate peace movement must always, Harrington said, avoid "any hint of being an apologist for the Viet Cong."

Offending Harrington, his old friend, was the toughest for Hayden. Hayden's traveling to Vietnam would mean more than a quarrel. It would mean a betrayal. Harrington raised the same question of morality he had raised at the Port Huron cabins. The protest movement's members were all supposed to be democrats. The name of Tom's institution, his greatest creation, also told something: Students for a *Democratic* Society. But the "democratic" in North Vietnam's formal name, the Democratic Republic of Vietnam, made a mockery of the principle. North Vietnam was the opposite of democracy. As in the case of SNCC, when you diverged from the cause named in your organization's title, you were taking a grave step. Moscow Stalinists and French totalitarians had schooled the

North Vietnamese leader, Ho Chi Minh. Ho had conducted purges and ordered the murder of opponents just as the men in Moscow had done in the 1930s. Hundreds, perhaps thousands had starved or been killed in Ho's land reforms, expropriations reminiscent of Soviet land theft in the Ukraine.[12] To provide photo ops for such a dictator was to prettify tyranny. "I do not think that one can be in favor of defending the outcasts and victims of Mississippi and Harlem," Harrington wrote that fall in a *Village Voice* article that read like a personal letter to Hayden, "but be indifferent about those in Hanoi and Peking."[13]

But Hayden found he was now spoiling for a fight. Drawing a distinction between social democrats on the one hand and the socialist authoritarians on the other might be precious to Harrington. To Hayden, that distinction was becoming pretention. How was North Vietnam so much worse than the corrupt, authoritarian regime in South Vietnam that the United States favored? How was shooting down American planes worse than napalm? Aptheker, Lynd, and Hayden all wondered how communism in the countries they were to visit might differ. Did each nation feature its own homegrown socialism? They also wanted to know whether and how the communists in each country would work across borders. In the case of America, both Lynd and Hayden wanted to "redefine communism" and drop old Cold War taboos. Hayden and Lynd openly mocked anticommunism. They called themselves "anti-anticommunists." In the second half of December, as he made his last preparations, Hayden weighed the trip over and over again. Each time he decided it was worthwhile. The chance of "turning a corner of history," as he put it, felt irresistible. What did Hayden really have to lose? At home, as his ex-wife said, they had lost their community.

A TRIP abroad when they were frustrated at home was nothing new for American activists. In the early talks over this 1965 Vietnam trip, Staughton Lynd had thought of another Quaker, a man who lived at the time of America's founding, George Logan. His own government's prosecution of the Quasi-War with France frustrated Logan, but he had few allies and little influence. In the end Logan, a private citizen, had traveled on his own to France in 1798 to conduct unauthorized negotiations with the French government. The negotiations indeed helped bring an end to the war. But Congress, furious at the usurpation, had promptly passed a law criminalizing such actions by nondiplomats. Legal scholars considered the Logan Act, as it was known, too vague to enforce. Nonetheless, the fact that Hayden, Lynd, and Aptheker would be skirting, even violating, the act with this trip made the trip that much more enticing.

More recently, activists on the American left had headed for illicit, dangerous, or even forbidden destinations in hopes of finding a foreign model they might one day replicate at home. Most Americans had heard about Lincoln Steffens, who traveled to Russia at the time of the revolution there and reported, "I have been over into the future, and it works." But others traveled as well—the educator John Dewey, and John Reed, who wrote *Ten Days That Shook the World*. In the 1920s, progressivism appeared to be a dead letter, and the United States a Republican stronghold. Leftist progressives sought consolation in romantic trips. The U.S. government did not recognize the Soviet Union. The leading American trade unions of the day rejected communists' authority outright. Still, in 1927 an unofficial labor delegation that included professors, writers, and James Hudson Maurer, president of the Pennsylvania Federation of Labor, traveled to Russia and was entertained by Stalin and Trotsky themselves. The scale of Soviet economic planning struck the visitors. The U.S. leadership might negotiate at one table, but even together President Coolidge, Samuel Gompers of the American Federation of Labor, and Thomas Edison of GE wielded nothing like the authority of the Gosplan, the committee that was writing the first Soviet five-year plan. "These sixteen men in Moscow salt down the whole economic life of 146 million people for a year in advance as calmly as a Gloucester man salts down his fish," one of the 1927 travelers, an economist named Stuart Chase, observed.[14] The Soviets carefully protected their guests from the reality of Russia, and it came as a surprise to the guests, when, shortly thereafter, Stalin exiled a hero of the American left, Trotsky.

These voyagers returned to the United States in great excitement.

Chase published a book titled *A New Deal*, in which he asked frankly, "Why should Russians have all the fun in the world?" Franklin Roosevelt, whether intentionally or by coincidence—for the phrase was in the air—made "the New Deal" the slogan for his reforms. Two professors on the 1927 trip, Rexford Tugwell and Paul Douglas, influenced the New Deal. Though neither man became a communist, what they had seen in Russia informed their work crafting key reforms: farm and housing policy for Tugwell and planning for Social Security in the case of Douglas. Tugwell proved too progressive for even the Roosevelt Administration, but when Roosevelt named him governor of Puerto Rico, Tugwell applied socialist theory to the island's economy, creating a vast planning bureaucracy and tangling with the sugar planters.

A few others who traveled to the Soviet Union, whether at the time of the revolution or in the 1920s or 1930s, came away with a more cautious view. The anarchist Emma Goldman, deported to Russia during the Red Scare after World War I, expected to find a new utopia. Despite reassurances from Lenin himself, Goldman was appalled at the lack of free speech and at the oppression, and returned to the West to write a book she titled *My Disillusionment in Russia*. It was a few years later that Walter Reuther tried out Russian communism for himself when, with his brother Victor, he worked in Russian factories. Upon his return, he joined the American union movement and made clear his contempt for the Soviet regime. Much later, Reuther personally chased communists out of the UAW. Goldman and Reuther, however, were exceptions.

Cuba also was a destination for the American left. In 1960, in the middle of Castro's takeover, one of Hayden's heroes, the philosopher C. Wright Mills, had traveled there, and concluded that Cuba was going socialist without loss of human life.[15] Watching Castro nationalize, Mills decided that the revolution in Cuba was "a moment of economic truth."[16]

Such trips enabled American dissidents, most of them intellectuals after all, to draw analogies that satisfied them: blacks in the American South were like serfs before the Russian Revolution. The trips boosted the American dissidents' pride. If they were pariahs at home, they were statesmen abroad. The junkets by American dissidents were likewise precious to their hosts, revolutionary governments. In 1927, Stalin had blared the news of his meeting with the unofficial delegation, evidence that not every American opposed Russia. Cuban papers advertised Mills, and elevated him. When Mills passed away in March 1962, the Cuban newspapers declared that the United States had lost "a mentor and a distinguished representative."[17]

TO PREPARE for his own expedition, Hayden read *Man's Fate*, by the French statesman André Malraux. It was a novel about a communist insurrection in Shanghai in 1927. That insurrection had failed, but two decades later, China indeed fell to communists. Malraux counseled patience and determination for revolutionaries: "There are not 50 ways of fighting, there is only one, and that is to win." Perhaps, Hayden thought, he had failed so far simply because he had not sacrificed enough. "Neither revolution nor war consists in doing what one pleases," Malraux also said. Hayden later underlined one passage of *Man's Fate*, about personal sacrifice: a policeman who put a revolutionary to death asked him, "What do you call dignity?" The martyr responded, "The opposite of humiliation."

On December 19, in a mix of caution, elation, and rain, Lynd, Aptheker, and Hayden finally touched down in Prague. The three men noticed that the farmland was plowed right up to the landing strips. The Bohemian landscape offered both the medieval and the modern. Everything seemed to the travelers to be on a smaller scale than in the United States, even the streetcars. A representative of the Czech Communist Party delivered them to their hotel, where a suite with a shortwave radio and a vast, ornate bathtub awaited them. The first communist city of the trip itself struck them all as dull—a place where you would rather work than live. As part of the Soviet bloc, Czechoslovakia maintained relations with North Vietnam, and the first night the jet-lagged Hayden and the others attended a celebration of the fifth anniversary of the National Liberation Front, the Viet Cong. Five hundred people listened to chamber music from the two lands; the host was Nguyen Van Hieu, who led the National Liberation Front in Prague. These were people Hayden thought he might ask about the distinctions between Czech communism and Vietnamese communism. Though Hayden could not know it yet, he was getting first-class treatment. Hieu was widely regarded as a shadow foreign minister to the North Vietnamese government. The following year when the French leader Charles de Gaulle would visit Cambodia, it was Hieu who would meet him. Hieu flattered Hayden by repeating the name of Hayden's Students for a Democratic Society—"SDS, SDS."

But those three letters, "S-D-S" were about all that Hieu, or any of the other Vietnamese in Prague, could say to the Americans. The language barrier was high and impenetrable. "All of the Vietnamese political people spoke French, but I did not speak French and neither did Herbert and neither did Tom," Lynd later recalled. Instead of taking in what the Vietnamese were saying, the Americans had to guess through the screen of jet lag and interpreters. Aptheker, a veteran, had participated in Operation Overlord, the invasion of Northern France. Lynd had been overseas before. To them, this was one of many trips. But Hayden was overseas for the first time.[18] All was fresh. How to gauge what he was being told?

It emerged that the handlers and interpreters who led the three in the communist capitals had a talent for finding relevance. Sometimes they used images rather than the awkward translations to remind Hayden of the scope of U.S. oppression of its people, now, and as far back as Southern slavery, or World War II. The Czech guides took Hayden and the others to Lidice, the town that the Nazis had destroyed in retaliation for the assassination of Reinhard Heydrich, the Nazi officer who ruled occupied Czechoslovakia. Engraved words at the memorial site offered the official East Bloc context for the destruction: "Lidice, Coventry, Hiroshima, Nagasaki." The destruction of Lidice and Coventry, the latter leveled in Wehrmacht bombing raids, was morally equivalent to the destruction of Hiroshima and Nagasaki, destroyed by America's murderous nuclear bombs. Lynd, Hayden, and Aptheker thought not only of how U.S. atom bombs had leveled Japanese cities, but also about villages in Vietnam. The bits of news they picked up only reinforced the impression of the United States' abuses in Operation Rolling Thunder. To Aptheker, Lynd, and Hayden, Lidice and the Vietnamese targeting seemed identical displays of military vengeance.

As new travelers often do, Hayden found his best conversation partner in the interpreter. Hayden tried explaining anti-communism such as Harrington's in the American peace movement. The whole idea baffled the man, a student. There was plenty not to like about the communist regime in Czechoslovakia, the interpreter allowed. The pro-worker state maintained a "workers' mystique." The Marxist culture unrelentingly denigrated university students—in the past, the guide told Hayden, Czech students had even been called "immature parasites." Hayden took this complaint as evidence of freedom of speech in Czechoslovakia. Students wore their hair longish, Beatles style, which seemed to Hayden another sign of freedom. The theater and books in Prague leaned left, but didn't feel Stalinist. An American play, Arthur Miller's *After the Fall*, was showing in Prague. Late in their Prague stop, the three lunched with a Czech professor. The professor reminded them of a classic Marxist point: socialism was not a state. It was a process. Even a country that called itself communist considered communism an unreached goal. If the Soviet foreign policy had reflected many misjudgments—"mistakes due to applying the Marxian analysis to situations where we have limited experience"—this did not mean that Soviet policy was flawed. It sounded like Hayden's hero, the late C. Wright Mills, who had said that "revolution is construction."[19] As socialism evolved, it had to be allowed a "margin for error."

When the newness overwhelmed him, Hayden reverted to his original trade: journalism. He undertook the laborious work of interviewing through interpreters. Lynd, however, took his self-assigned role of citizen diplomat seriously. He wanted to broker some deal, however small, between the United States and North Vietnam. The first step was to learn the North Vietnamese mind. In Prague, Lynd arrived at his first conclusion: the Czechs and the Vietnamese "could be allies." In Moscow, Lynd asked Dang Quang Minh, the Viet Cong's lead representative in Russia, if there was a way the United States could both withdraw from Vietnam and save face. "They should cease aggression, then their face will be saved," was the reply. The Viet Cong official, for his part, used the encounter to assert that communism in Southeast Asia had expanded and deepened: "concretely the people are stronger than in 1954 at Dien Bien Phu"—the moment at which Vietnamese revolution- aries had trounced the French and driven them from Vietnam.[20] Now the communists of North Vietnam would certainly defend themselves, and defeat the mighty United States as the Viet Minh, their predeces- sor, had defeated France. This argument sounded more legitimate than it would have the previous February, before forces as yet to be entirely identified—North Vietnamese with Soviet missiles? North Vietnam- ese with Soviet teachers? North Vietnamese with their own makeshift weapons?—had downed eighty-five Air Force and ninety-four Navy planes deployed for Operation Rolling Thunder.[21]

Beijing struck Hayden and the others as different from both Moscow and Prague, but also compelling. Here was a society where everybody, whether a soldier jogging or a teamster carting cabbages, was busy. Ap- theker was an old Stalinist. His contacts among European or Russian communists had assured their party of an official welcome. The group suspected the Chinese regime might not be so welcoming. Gratifyingly, their Chinese hosts nonetheless proved friendly enough. At home, the disciples of participatory democracy had lived under a vow of poverty. Hayden had at one point lived without heat in a Newark apartment. In Beijing, Hayden, Lynd, and Aptheker were royalty, chauffeured around in a black limo. For an interpreter, the three were assigned not just a staffer but a high-ranking diplomat, Tang Ming-Chao, an American-educated man who had once edited a daily in New York's Chinatown. Tang had translated for the first American journalist to tell the story of the Chinese revolution, Edgar Parks Snow. Tang, like the interpreters in Prague, Mos- cow, and Beijing, also knew how to find common points with his guests. The interpreter sent his greetings to Aptheker's daughter Bettina, with whom he had studied in Berkeley. Their Chinese hosts spoke to the group about John Foster Dulles and John Steinbeck, playing to academic van- ity Like so many travelers before him, Hayden found that what he also wanted to know was whether the Chinese could like Americans, could like *him*. "Yes, we distinguish between the aggressive policy and the American people," a girl reassured them.

Their Beijing hosts briefed the trio on the progress of communism in China. Mao had risen to power less than two decades before. But the party representatives told the travelers the party feared that Chinese communism, which the Chinese prized as purer than that of Yugoslavia or Moscow, was softening. People were turning individualist. "We could become capitalist," one of their handlers said, a sentence whose meaning the travelers did not quite know how to place. To suppress the sense of privilege among young adults, literate and born with a silver spoon in the mouth, the guides told them the party was launching a "socialist education campaign." The guide laid out the details: retraining the "bourgeois" element via "new systems of education and labor in which the workers and peasants attend school part-time, and professional or bourgeois people spend part of their careers performing manual labor." Tang made it all seem normal. Even his own wife, he said, was now away in the countryside for six months, performing such labor. The travelers could not sense the scale or violence of it. But what Tang was describing was the regime campaign that would later be called the Cultural Revolution.

By December 27, the three travelers were in Wuhan, preparing for their flight to Hanoi. The next morning, after a Russian-prepared breakfast, they stepped into a two-engine Soviet Ilyushin and flew over the Vietnamese border into North Vietnam.[22] Alighting from their plane, the men were met by girls with flowers and a group introduced as the Vietnam Peace Committee.

Rolling Thunder did not target Hanoi, so there would be little bombing there. As it happened, President Johnson had called a Christmas bombing cease-fire generally, and the trip felt calm. As Hayden toured Hanoi and factories in the first days, his impression—and, as he reminded himself, he valued first impressions—was of a people on alert. Weapons lay by the workers' stations at the factories, and bomb shelters ringed a lake at the center of Hanoi. But workers themselves were preternaturally calm, and Hanoi seemed to be enjoying, as Lynd and Hayden wrote later, "the fruits of peace." Hayden and the others wondered if this was because of the cease-fire, but the fact was that even before the Christmas pause, Americans had not yet commenced heavy shelling of the capital city. If America was betraying its great promises, it was not doing so in Hanoi.

Another chastening moment came when they were given a formal interview with an American prisoner, one of a number of pilots whose planes the Vietnamese had shot down since the commencement of Rolling Thunder. Two North Vietnamese soldiers briefed them before their meeting. They asked the Americans to "explain the war to the prisoner." Doubt seized Lynd and Hayden as the moment for the meeting arrived: "in general," they later wrote, "we identify with anyone behind bars rather than the captors." For the interview itself, the three were led into a room with three tables, covered with cups, saucers, candy, and cigarettes. They found that one table was lower, with a stool rather than a chair, the place for the prisoner, and protested. Americans sat level with Americans. While the Vietnamese replaced the stool with a chair, they left the lower table, because, as they told their guests, the prisoner was a "criminal." When the prisoner arrived, clad in green fatigues and a sweater, the travelers were again confronted with what the Vietnamese had done: taken a fellow American.

This fellow was, Aptheker thought, "a good Joe"—"a good father, no doubt good at his job"—like himself in World War II. Aptheker told himself that such pilots were themselves true victims. "These are not the officers of the German army whom I met as prisoners—cocky, arrogant, sneering, venomous, and most of all, brutal."[23] The feeling of standing with the Vietnamese in such a room, the travelers wrote later, was "nearly insufferable." As Aptheker, Lynd, and Hayden discovered, the prisoner knew who they were. Lynd was at Yale, a historian. Hayden had done work "with some student committees," the man said. The prisoner did not look to them as if he had been tortured. How could they tell?

The pilot told the three that he had been brought down on his first mission. They learned that he had been allowed to write one letter to his family, and that his treatment could have been worse, but that, as he said, captivity was "no bed of roses." On the day of a protest march in Washington that December, the North Vietnamese had released two U.S.

prisoners, their way of talking past Johnson and McNamara to the American people, as Stalin had tried to talk past the Coolidge Administration to the American people. One told the press at his release that he was going home "so Americans can see the light about the war in Vietnam." Now the two ex-prisoners were being held by the United States at Okinawa. Upon hearing of the detention, this prisoner "seemed upset."[24] Tom tried to explain to the prisoner the travelers' position—that the United States was on the wrong side of Vietnam's social revolution. When the moment came for his minders to return him to his cell, the prisoner stuffed candy and fruit up his sleeves. The travelers left the meeting reeling at their own helplessness. What were they doing there? The prisoner needed to be rescued. They could not rescue him. The prisoner had asked the travelers to let his family know he was all right. They could do that.

This visit with a prisoner would stay with the travelers throughout their trip, and after their return home. Back in the United States, Aptheker, Lynd, and Hayden would take comfort in a Defense Department statement that when it came to captured American pilots, there had thus far been "no brainwashing—apparently no torture."[25] Difficult in another way was the group's meeting with the North Vietnamese prime minister, Pham Van Dong. The meeting was gratingly formal: the Americans were asked to submit questions in advance. Pham told them that there were no North Vietnamese troops in the South, a contention they knew to be false.

The rest of the trip was sobering, but less soul-wrenching, for the travelers. Hayden and the others inspected bombing damage outside Hanoi. They rode to the city of Nam Dinh, which U.S. bombers, they were told, had attacked eleven times. Bombs had fallen on a kindergarten—more like an overnight day care—and killed six children. The travelers inspected the collapsed roof and the rubble of the first floor. The largest pagoda in the town was damaged as well. This was the kind of evidence of bombs falling on civilians that had prompted their fact-finding mission in the first place. It enabled the three, or at least so they told themselves, to make their own case for moral equivalence: the democratization of the North Vietnamese resembled the struggles for democratization at America's founding, or in the American South now. "We suspect that colonial American town meetings and current Vietnamese village meetings, Asian peasants' leagues and Black Belt sharecroppers' unions have much in common, especially the concept of a 'grass-roots' or 'rice-roots' democracy," they concluded.[26] Like the North Vietnamese leader Pham, "President Johnson simply was not telling the truth," Aptheker wrote. The Nam Dinh militia had shot down twenty-eight American aircraft. American bombing was technocratic. McNamara bombed as he built autos, from numbers. North Vietnamese resistance felt soulful, and therefore stronger. There was an indisputable reality to this imbalance, and the imbalance increased the travelers' sympathy for the North Vietnamese.

As reports published later show, the travelers missed much of what was going on in North Vietnam. The prowess of North Vietnam's youthful sharpshooters was not the only reason the North Vietnamese Army was downing so many American bombers. Soviets were aiding Ho militarily, bringing hundreds of North Vietnamese to the Soviet Union to learn to operate Soviet surface-to-air missiles.[27] The Russians were also sending the North Vietnamese the missile launchers, and the missiles. Hanoi was at this time no easy place to live. The North Vietnamese currency was the dong. A handbook to North Vietnam published later noted that the average income in 1965 was 21 to 40 dong per month. Rice cost 0.40 to 0.50 dong a kilo. A sweater was 100 to 110 dong.[28] John Colvin, a British diplomat who served in Hanoi in 1966, also took stock. Colvin's Vietnamese staff earned 100 dong a month, a princely amount.[29] A colonel earned 60 dong a month and an ordinary soldier, 2 dong. Sugar was 2.3 dong per kilo, and even that might not be available, because of rationing. A chicken cost 6 dong, if you could get it. Rice a year later still cost 0.45 dong per kilo, but was rationed. American prisoners were paraded around in carts. The crowds on the streets, which sometimes included the random Cuban diplomat or visitor, spat on the prisoners and threw stones. The Soviet definition of communism, as the diplomat noted to himself, *was* electrification, yet in Vietnam electricity was scarce or unavailable. The normal rule in Vietnam, as elsewhere, was that diplomats lived better than locals. Yet Colvin was not permitted to have a bicycle. When he needed a tooth pulled, there was no anesthetic; he simply drank a bottle of Haig Gold Label Whisky and then had himself dragged, suitably stupefied, to a car for the ride to the dentist. Children were allocated extra rations, at least in theory, but did not always get them.

This level of detail, however, was not available to Lynd, Hayden, and Aptheker, who were being chauffeured about in black Russian-built Volgas, luxury cars, yet again. The men saw much of Vietnam outside the car windows: people guiding buffalo in the fields; adults walking shoeless or in sandals made of scrap rubber. "If the buildings were drab," noticed Hayden, "the people's faces were not." To Hayden and the others, the Vietnamese seemed engaged, willing to persevere until their slingshots felled the American Goliath. A museum director who had fought at Dien Bien Phu gave Hayden a little bronze arrow that was said to be a thousand years old. The director cried when they departed. So much, Hayden thought, for the stereotype of the "stoic Oriental."

The Americans met with groups of young people, who always asked why America bombed North Vietnam. The North Vietnamese Army, the Americans learned, taught citizens how to shoot down an American plane with a rifle, and the travelers later found a formal description elaborating on what they heard: "When an enemy plane comes diving toward you, there is a split second moment when the plane's rudder and stabilizer became invisible and the whole plane looks like a big round dot. . . . Don't shut your eyes. Pull the trigger." The Americans asked about North Vietnam, and were told that life was better than it had been before the rise of "Uncle Ho," as Ho Chi Minh was called, a play on the nickname for Stalin, "Uncle Joe." Hayden's inner journalist gave him moments of skepticism: sometimes the pro-communist declarations by the young people sounded "wooden," Hayden allowed. He could also see the Stalinism in the place—"Decent men have been purged," he wrote. But these moments were only moments. Hayden had no idea of the reality, and would not learn for many years, that more than few "decent men" were gone: ten thousand had died in North Vietnam's purges. The intellectuals the three met were not the top minds in Vietnam—those men had been sidelined, too, or worse. For Hayden's tape recorder, the young North Vietnamese listed improvements that socialism had made in their lives: literacy, education, a better standard of living, electrification, tractors instead of buffalo for the plow. Again, Hayden found himself enchanted with a handler, this time a member of North Vietnam's peace committee who spoke BBC English. How could you not like someone who had translated *The Adventures of Huckleberry Finn* into Vietnamese?

The name of Norman Morrison, the Quaker who had burned himself to death before McNamara's window, was not known to many Americans. But at his death Morrison had become a hero overnight in North Vietnam. A Vietnamese poet had written a poem about Morrison's orphaned baby daughter, Emily: "Johnson, dollar devil of our world, / How dare you borrow the mantle of Christ, or the saffron robe of Buddha! . . ." The lines were written from the point of view of the martyr to his child: "I cannot take you home tonight, / When the fire is over, mother will come to fetch you. . . . / My blazing body becomes the torch of truth!" For the moment it was *the* poem in North Vietnam. "Everyone seems to know it by heart," Aptheker noticed.

The other martyr of the North Vietnamese was Nguyen Van Troi, an apprentice electrician who had attempted to assassinate U.S. Defense Secretary McNamara in 1964 by laying a bomb under Cong Ly bridge, where it was expected McNamara's motorcade would pass. The plot was foiled, and the South Vietnamese had executed Troi by firing squad. Troi had become a household name in Hanoi. Here were two parallel stories: an American martyr and a Vietnamese one. Their own efforts to come close to the poor in America had not always succeeded. Here, the Americans told themselves, they *were* connecting with the common man. That was in part because the Vietnamese were a community—even more so, Tom told them, perhaps thinking of his alienation in Newark, or Casey's in Mississippi, than any he had seen in the United States. The three men taught a group of Vietnamese how to form a human circle and sing "We Shall Overcome." Lynd and Hayden later wrote up their conclusions in a book they titled *The Other Side*. The North Vietnamese Workers Party, the communists, Lynd and Hayden wrote, would continue to lead revolution. The North Vietnamese were natural socialists. They were a "rice-roots democracy," and exhibited a "socialism of the heart."

Hayden and the others were not the only ones impressed by the North Vietnamese commitment to communism. "The communists have loosed a revolutionary idea in Vietnam," Major General Edward Lansdale, one of McNamara's critics, said, "and it will not die by being ignored, bombed, or smothered by us." Even Nguyen Cao Ky, the prime minister of South Vietnam, had recently told the *New York Times* that the communists were closer than the South Vietnamese government to what the people of Vietnam sought. Knowledge of these other convictions, held by people from the American Establishment, hardened Hayden's own.

At night in the Vietnamese hotel, Hayden pondered it all. He felt like a character in Joseph Conrad's *Heart of Darkness*, ignorant and humble. A Vietnamese writer had given Hayden a narrative poem to read, *The Tale of Kieu*. Centuries old, the poem recounted the abiding troubles of a young woman on the hunt for her beloved. The young woman refused to abandon her quest. Vietnam was like that, Hayden thought, searching for its other half. "Riches dissipate like passing clouds," the poem said. Only the soulful and serious endured. The final night, Lynd stayed in his room to write up notes. Hayden, overwhelmed by it all, went to the bar and found himself watching a waitress. Her name was Minh Tinh. She was the ultimate revolutionary, a songstress who also led the hotel's anti-aircraft militia. With two glasses of rice wine, Hayden was in love—with the girl, and with North Vietnam.

As they made their way home, Hayden and the others wondered what punishment awaited them for the outrage of a trip into enemy territory. Lynd did manage to get a meeting at the State Department, so he could at least debrief his government. The travelers won a few headlines: "Three Leftists Hold Hope for Vietnam Peace," the *Los Angeles Times* reported. The State Department, however, revoked all three of their passports.[30] Though defended at first by Yale's president, Kingman Brewster, Lynd eventually would have to leave the college. Hayden's parents endured more shame. After telling the Associated Press that her son's trip had been a "fact-finding mission," Gene Hayden, a librarian, had endured so much trouble that she moved into a hotel. Tom later read the letters his mother received from those neighbors who chose not to turn against the

Hayden family. "Dear Gene, we called to no avail, and I can't blame you for not answering your phone . . . Hank and I wanted to offer you a 'refuge' from the mob. . . . My prayers and Masses have been with you and Tommy all week . . . Katie." Interviewed as to why a young man of draft age would undermine the United States in the midst of warfare, Hayden's father said simply, "I think he picked all that up in college."

The writer William F. Buckley published a column summing up the conservative view of this trip: "in point of law, they are not traitors"— legal sanctions were difficult, or inadmissible. But moral sanctions were not. Such assaults merely invigorated Hayden. After the obscurity of Newark, Hayden was a national figure again, a figure, as he would later learn through Freedom of Information requests, now dignified by more intense scrutiny from the Federal Bureau of Investigation. The elation they felt on this trip would move Hayden and Lynd to repeat the tour in 1967, traveling to Eastern Europe and finishing in North Vietnam. From his trips Hayden brought home talismans, one an aluminum comb made from the fuselage of the hundredth U.S. plane the Vietnamese downed.[31] Later yet, Hayden would marry the actress Jane Fonda. Fonda would make her own excursions to Vietnam, achieving fame—and infamy—a magnitude greater than Hayden's. Hayden and Fonda would even name their son Troy, after the Vietnamese martyr who had plotted to kill McNamara.

Protesting American engagement in Vietnam would be Hayden's focus over the next few years. But he would also try to build up, where he could, a broader movement of the American left. After the first Vietnam trip, Hayden was still not sure if he would ever believe in socialism. But now he saw that his own belief didn't matter. What mattered to Hayden, a professional protester, was the utility of socialism as a tool for extending the longevity of even flagging protest movements. In his absence at the end of December, the National Council of SDS had adopted a statement saying that "radicals have more important priorities than working simply to end the war"—SDS wanted to revolutionize America.[32] Now, or another day, socialism might inspire SDS or another organization to achieve radical feats at home. Socialism was a goal, Hayden saw, that attracted many people, even—especially—when they knew little about it. Those people would sometimes continue to be inspired even after confronting evidence of socialism's failures. It did not matter if villages in socialist lands were poor, and appearing to get poorer. The villages, or those who studied them, could always tell themselves that true socialism had yet to be tried. Socialism was so broad, vague, and romantic that it was harder to discredit than a Shriver- or Reuther-funded community action programs, or a campaign to elect a ticket to the New Jersey state assembly. And just as Marx and the Vietnamese communists said, socialism was a process, something you built toward, a utopia you aimed for. The idea justified any protest, and any shift in target. As long as socialism was never complete, as long as socialists were still protesting and building, no one could dismiss socialism. That was the beauty of it.

7

Housing Society

JANUARY 1966 TO JULY 1967

Guns: 7.4% of GDP
Butter: 4.6% of GDP
Dow Jones Industrial Average: 969

The choice before the people of every major urban center is simple and clear. It is build or burn.
—Walter Reuther[1]

Cities have the capability of providing something for everybody, only because, and only when, they are created by everybody.
—Jane Jacobs

Around the time Tom Hayden returned from Vietnam, engineers from the General Services Administration began showing up at a large vacant lot at 451 Seventh Street in the Southwest section of the District of Columbia. The engineers were checking up on the excavation for a $28 million building already known as GSA Project No. 49924.[2] GSA 49924 would be not just big, it would be massive, ten stories in concrete over the whole block, creating 700,000 square feet of office space. Even the parking area below the structure was large, on multiple levels.[3] Number 49924 would not resemble the office buildings that had risen in Washington in the 1950s, projects such as the colonial revival headquarters of the Equitable Life Insurance Company on Wisconsin Avenue, a building that was all bricks, weather vane, and cupola. That Equitable building aped Colonial Williamsburg. GSA 49924 and the spare plaza would not ape the past. Aping was beneath their architect, the modernist Marcel Breuer. Breuer liked to be first, and this new building was the first modular deployment of precast concrete, an engineering marvel. Breuer also liked to create his own symbols. He had erected a Y-shaped giant with a distinct flying-carpet-style entrance for UNESCO in Paris. For GSA Project No. 49924, Breuer was laying down another configuration of letters. GSA 49924 would form *two* Y shapes, twins lying head to foot. To some, the shape looked more like an X. But whether two Y's or an X, the letters would be discernible only from a long distance or from high above, from, say, the window of a government helicopter. What people would see from the street was a concrete behemoth, and the name of what the behemoth would house in sans-serif type affixed to a stark concrete column: DEPARTMENT OF HOUSING AND URBAN DEVELOPMENT.

The new building and its department were known simply by their acronym, HUD. HUD sounded tough, like the unscrupulous rancher in the 1963 Paul Newman Western, *Hud*. The style of the building also sounded tough: brutalism. HUD was one of a number of brutalist edifices rising in Washington. J. Edgar Hoover had outgrown his old offices, and soon the concrete would be poured for the fortress that would be the new Federal Bureau of Investigation brute on Pennsylvania Avenue.[4] The Watergate Hotel, two-thirds of an oval designed by Luigi Moretti of Rome, was also heavy concrete. The impetus for official Washington's turn to brutalism actually came from a pamphlet titled *Guiding Principles of Federal Architecture*, another of those innocuous-sounding documents crafted by Daniel Patrick Moynihan while he was still serving as jack-of-all-trades at the Labor Department.[5]

Moynihan, recovering from a bumpy Washington experience, was now in exile on the traditional brick-and-stone campus of Connecticut's Wesleyan University. But in the same years when Moynihan had fallen from grace, *Guiding Principles* had come to carry the force of scripture. Architecture, *Guiding Principles* said, should provide "efficient and economical facilities for the use of government agencies." Such buildings should also provide "visual testimony to the dignity, enterprise, vigor and stability of the American Government." To 1960s planners, brutalism seemed to provide that testimony. The word "brutalism" actually came from the French term for new or unadulterated, as in *brut* champagne. But most

Americans persisted in taking from the word "brutalist" the other con-
notation. No matter what experts said, "brutalist" had to mean what it
sounded and looked like, possessing brute power.

The emphasis on power suited the mood in America's capital. It suited
Johnson, years now into the presidency and aware of the shortcomings
of his early projects. The war wasn't going well. Operation Birmingham,
a May military operation in Vietnam, had chased the Viet Cong off the
road heading north from Saigon, but they had withdrawn behind Cambodia's border. What the Johnson Administration lacked in conviction,
therefore, it determined to make up in scale. That was true for Vietnam,
where bombing had now resumed. This very year the United States was
doubling its already substantial number of troops, 185,000. The rapid
deployment was in part possible, in turn, because of a giant cargo plane,
the Lockheed C-141. The Starlifter, as the plane was known, cut the
round-trip flight time from California to Saigon from ninety-five hours to
thirty-four. But the scaling and the speedups were also evident at home,
in the new HUD building, and a nationwide building program. For housing, Johnson promised $7.5 billion, more than nine times the poverty pro-
gram's annual budget that first year. The American people were, Johnson
said, "strong enough to pursue our goals in the rest of the world while
still building a Great Society here at home." In 1966, everything could
be, had to be, big.

Even before Watts, Washington had made up its collective mind to put
its formidable shoulder into a second Great Society drive, housing. Since
Watts, that commitment had only hardened. The Administration would
supplement, and sometimes steamroller, its flawed program, community
action, with construction. Nobody could disapprove of infrastructure improvement, politicians told one another. This new drive would emphasize
affordable housing in cities, another attempt by Johnson to deliver on
the "cities" in his now famous agenda from that day at the University of
Michigan, "cities, the countryside, and the classroom." When the HUD
building was finished, the workers would place in its lobby a bust of Catherine Bauer, an expert on urban planning who emphasized building over
social work or welfare payments.[6] Bauer had served as author or advisor

on earlier housing drives. In Bauer's view, what the government should do for people was house them.

————————

JOHNSON LAID out his second Great Society in his State of the Union address in January. The president would support construction everywhere. More than $2 billion of the funds would go to rebuilding cities. The president would also follow the Reuther plan for Demonstration Cities, "and rebuild completely, on a scale never before attempted, entire central and slum areas." Working together with private enterprise—this time, Johnson did not emphasize municipal governments—the federal government would rebuild areas of up to 100,000 people. Johnson would add shops, parks, and hospitals around the new housing. In the same speech, the president asked Congress to pass legislation funding rent assistance. Taken together, the results, the president hoped, would be something similar to what his old community action drive had sought: "a flourishing community where our people can come to live the good life." This whole second project would resemble something like what the United States had done in rebuilding Europe under the Marshall Plan.

Eager to make Detroit the star of the new campaign, Reuther rounded up support in Michigan. Reuther wrote to Mayor Cavanagh to encourage him: "Detroit can become an exciting and shining model of a 20th century city in the Great Society." Reuther promised Cavanagh that they could work together in a new institution, the Detroit Citizens Development Authority.

On the surface, Detroit didn't appear to need a Marshall Plan. A *New York Times* reporter who looked the city over later would claim that he found "no slums to match New York's Harlem or Bedford-Stuyvesant, Chicago's South Side or Cleveland's Hough section." Reuther was proud of Detroit's first great rebuilding project, Lafayette Park, two large blocks of federal housing, and an extension, all designed by another star of modern architecture, Ludwig Mies van der Rohe.[7] Detroit's police commissioner, Ray Girardin, lived there. But nonwhite unemployment in Detroit was treble white unemployment, a ratio that recalled Watts too clearly.[8]

It meant Detroit had to be ready. Girardin had already formed a plan to squelch riots: surround an area and escort rioters into police trucks. The Detroit policemen had orders to herd and cut off, not shoot. One trouble now, a contrast to the old days, was that streets were often deserted. A number of factories now lay outside Detroit, and many autoworkers had also moved out. The Big Three were beginning to notice that foreign automakers were gaining on them again: in 1966, 660,000 foreign cars were sold in the United States, and by 1967, research analysts were predicting, the figure might hit 700,000 or 750,000. If the auto industry, preoccupied with getting its own numbers up, wouldn't pay for Detroit's revival, Reuther thought, then the federal money was all the more welcome. The reality, as he would put it much later, was "build or burn."[9]

The United States' new nationwide housing drive would do more than merely build new homes or offer rent support. It would also address the deterioration of older housing stock in the cities, whether those homes were owned by private landlords or public authorities. Detroit offered plenty of examples of such old stock. A famous project known as the Brewster-Douglass homes, where Diana Ross, Mary Wilson, and Florence Ballard had grown up, needed updating. There was so much crime at Brewster-Douglass that the residents felt trapped there and were petitioning for more police. "Gangs of unruly men," as one resident put it, loitered in the only shopping area of the neighborhood. Brewster-Douglass was an island, surrounded by empty streets and highways. Whatever Reuther's Demonstration Detroit did, it would have to provide housing less susceptible to crime than Brewster-Douglass.

The reasons men such as Johnson and Reuther turned to building with such enthusiasm went beyond the political to the personal. Someone like Martin Luther King, who was not yet forty, was still young, and was likely to succeed in an even broader mission than his heroic campaign in the South; Johnson and Reuther, however, would both shortly turn sixty. Johnson expected the Democratic nomination, but this time, unlike 1964, the threat of figures like Robert Kennedy felt serious. That year the New York senator would say of the War on Poverty, "It's too little, it's nothing, we have to do twenty times as much." And even if Johnson squelched

Kennedy, Nelson Rockefeller of New York and George Romney of Michigan were likely to challenge the president in the general election of 1968. Reuther had his own challenges. Many of his workers actively disliked his civil rights campaign, eroding his UAW base. George Meany, whom Reuther had counted on succeeding years ago, was more firmly in the saddle of the AFL-CIO than before. A logical next step for Reuther would be to move into the new colossus and lead HUD, but Johnson had given the honor of the post of America's first housing secretary to a top housing official, Robert Weaver.

Johnson and Reuther therefore found their minds moving to legacy. And there was no better legacy than buildings, which could remind future generations of what the Great Society, or the UAW, had been. Both men also thought of their personal legacies. The president and Mrs. Johnson were planning Johnson's presidential library at the University of Texas in Austin, and sought to make a striking architectural statement with the structure. Lady Bird Johnson conducted a national tour of modern architecture. The First Lady inspected the Gateway Arch in St. Louis— there is no report that she saw Pruitt-Igoe—and the hard-edged marble Beinecke Library of Yale.[10] She was taken aback by the "cold, austere" outside of the Beinecke, but liked the glass stacks for the rare books inside. The Johnsons even toyed around with hiring Minoru Yamasaki, the Japanese-American architect who had designed not only Pruitt-Igoe but the World Trade Center in New York and the Woodrow Wilson School at Princeton. But William Heath, chair of the board of regents of the University of Texas, killed the Yamasaki thought by mentioning to the Johnson crowd that Yamasaki's work was "sort of effeminate."[11] I. M. Pei, who designed parts of L'Enfant Plaza, the area of the HUD building, was another possibility for the presidential library, but Pei was designing the Kennedy Library. Commissioning the architect of the late president's memorial to shape the giant Johnson Library *would* be aping. So the Johnsons selected another eminent modernist, one of the opponents of curlicues, the architect of Yale's stark Beinecke Library, Gordon Bunshaft.

Reuther, too, thought modern. His personal legacy would be a UAW retreat center. The UAW leader sold the idea to his board and directed the union staff to buy up one thousand wooded acres on the shores of Black Lake, in Northern Michigan. Black Lake would be far lovelier and more comfortable than the lakeside cabins at Port Huron. Reuther envisioned the kind of rest house he had often seen in the social democracies of Northern Europe, where friends and colleagues strolled and sat in small groups, perhaps on a patio or in a park. To design this mini-utopia, Reuther hired his favorite architect, Oscar Stonorov, the sculptor of the bust of Catherine Bauer at HUD. Stonorov had also designed both a Reuther family retreat at Paint Creek and Solidarity House, the UAW headquarters in Detroit. Together with Stonorov, Reuther lovingly studied models of Scandinavian and Japanese architecture, searching for designs for their Black Lake halls. Wearing a Tyrolean hat that reminded him of his time in Europe, the union leader also patrolled the woods, acre by acre, on a hunt for trees so beautiful they must be built around. Reuther's center would be large enough to host five hundred people. It would be equipped with classrooms and a permanent staff to hold seminars and educate workers in the tenets and history of trade unionism years after the Reuther brothers had passed from the scene.[12] Reuther's brother Victor noticed that Walter loved Black Lake; it was indeed Reuther's own "community within a park." Reuther could not always control what happened to workers or union leaders. But Black Lake, Reuther could control. His retreat could give workers a break, after which they might go forth refreshed and ready for new battles with the Big Three. Those walkways would be covered, so that two union men might stop and chat in comfort, even if snow lay on the ground. At a place like Black Lake, Reuther's successors would continue the progressive march. They would plan great projects of the 1990s, or even the next millennium—including, of course, housing projects.

THAT A beneficent authority, local, municipal, or federal, should house people was in fact an old progressive notion. Half a century earlier, long before Michael Harrington wrote *The Other America*, the social worker

Jacob Riis had published his own *Other*, a book about the ferocious poverty of tenement life, *How the Other Half Lives*. In an era of inadequate plumbing, an era when tuberculosis and rats were rampant, first charities, then city fathers, then states had stepped in to repair and build homes in urban centers. Blight had to be erased. At the time, the fashion was to remove the poor not only from their tenements but from their cities. Some urban reformers didn't even like cities. At a White House Conference on Housing back at the start of the Depression, President Herbert Hoover had opened with a lecture on the moral inferiority of urban living. Rexford Tugwell, the same professor who had returned from Russia in 1927 with ideas for American socialism, laid out with disarming frankness an attitude common among planners: "My idea is to go just outside centers of population, pick up cheap land, build a whole community and entice people into it. Then go back into the cities and tear down whole slums and make parks of them."[13]

When the Depression showcased homelessness as a national tragedy, the federal government created the Federal Housing Administration, a precursor of HUD. Just as Sargent Shriver bade cities to create agencies to receive his funds, the Federal Housing Administration invited the cities and regions to establish local housing authorities. And just as in the past, the dutiful authorities then received and dispensed funds. The St. Louis Housing Authority or the Chicago Housing Authority next teamed up with its city to build. After the war, President Truman advanced the moral imperative of broader federal investment in housing, warning that five million families were still living "in slums and firetraps." Catherine Bauer's greatest project, a 1949 housing law, had expanded further the federal government's role in shaping the American home. On the one hand, the law supported private ownership, subsidizing mortgage insurance for new buyers. On the other, the 1949 law supplied funds for the building of hundreds of thousands of public housing units. Most officials at HUD emphasized the latter job, and called themselves what Bauer and her peers called themselves: "housers." The vision was simple: once a housing project was built, it would be managed by the new city housing authority, with the mayors as kibitzers, occasional partners, and mendicants. Housing law also required that rents in public housing be lower than comparable rents for privately funded units. Another postwar requirement was demolition of the slums: a public housing authority had to knock down or renovate a "slum dwelling" for each public unit it built. Along with the housing would come new highways to bring people to the cities.

In cities, the only way to make grand-scale building possible was for the authorities to condemn and claim large swaths of private land. Governments had a right to do that because of an old doctrine, recognized since the days of America's founding, eminent domain. Under the Fifth Amendment of the Constitution, this was the taking of private property for "public use." Washington, or a state, could condemn a building to put a road, an army base, or a schoolhouse in its spot. But in the postwar period, municipal governments, states, and the federal government began to invoke eminent domain when they took much more than plots for garrisons, playgrounds, or the town hall. They began to bulldoze whole sections of cities, and then hand the land with its rubble to private developers. In Detroit, the violence to old neighborhoods was especially great. Black Detroit in the 1940s and 1950s lived packed in areas known as Paradise Valley and Black Bottom. The main retail thoroughfare, Hastings Street, was legendary, known the nation over because it was frequented by the singers and agents who later gave the country Motown music. Stores, churches, and homes stood tightly together, sometimes tightly enough to be called "slums," but often containing a vibrant life, much loved by the inhabitants. Still, to the eyes of government, Black Bottom looked like blight. To the eyes of the auto unions and the Big Three automakers, pedestrian zones were a threat: highways that replaced sidewalks represented not only modernity but job security and high company share prices. With the support of the automakers and unions, the bulldozers had leveled it all, making room for public housing towers, for Reuther's Lafayette Park, and for freeways. The Chrysler Freeway, still being built, covered the ground where Hastings Street had been. Families had been herded into tall, anonymous apartment buildings, or had simply disappeared.

In the name of urban renewal, as the process was called, hundreds of thousands of Americans, many poor or black, were evicted in this way. The James Baldwin line that urban renewal "means Negro removal" rang so true it was often repeated.[14] Eminent domain had been invoked in the 1940s and 1950s to claim space for the nation's largest urban renewal project at the time, the plan to create a whole neighborhood in Southwest Washington.[15] The residents had been a "vibrant and close-knit community" and were told they could return to Southwest when construction finished.

Not everyone had accepted such broad takings as necessary. Why would the government "condemn" something that did not need condemning? One of the property owners who resisted was a man named Max Morris, proprietor of a department store at 712 Fourth Street SW in Washington, the same area where HUD was now rising.[16] Another was Goldie Schneider, the owner of a hardware store that had been in her family for decades. Morris and Schneider talked back. His store was not blighted, Morris told the officials who came from the Redevelopment Agency with their notices of condemnation It was a going concern. The officials conceded that. The agency claimed Morris's land was necessary to "replan." Morris's parcel might be used for commercial development— that was not what America's founders had meant by "public use." Why should a private developer with a federal contract have the right to take Morris's shop? This violated the Fifth Amendment. And who was to say, Morris asked, that the business or federal building that replaced it represented improvement? Morris and Schneider went to court to fight for their property. Schneider's son, Joseph, was one of the lawyers who represented them.[17] As the suit progressed, Morris passed away. His son-in-law Samuel Berman took up Morris's challenge to the bulldozers. A decision of the U.S. Court of Appeals for the District of Columbia Circuit provided encouraging words for such homeowners. "Is a modern apartment house a better breeder of men than is the detached or row house?" asked Judge E. Barrett Prettyman. "Is the local corner grocer a less desirable neighborhood asset than the absentee stockholder in the national chain or the wage-paid manager?" That could not be proved, wrote the court. The district court dismissed the property owners' claims on procedural grounds, but also concluded with a plea for property rights: "The poor are entitled to own what they can afford. The slow, the old, the small in ambition, the devotee of the outmoded have no less right to property than have the quick, the young, the aggressive and the modernistic or futuristic."[18]

Both sides appealed to the Supreme Court, which found unanimously for the bulldozers. In *Berman v. Parker*, Justice William O. Douglas stretched the old concept of eminent domain like a rubber band. "Public welfare," Douglas wrote, equating "public welfare" with public use, should be "broad and inclusive." Authorized agencies could make their decisions about what to take freely. "It is not for us to reappraise them," Douglas said. Douglas concluded by handing over his rubber band to government authorities. "If those who govern the District of Columbia decide that the nation's capital shall be beautiful as well as sanitary, there is nothing in the Fifth Amendment that stands in the way."[19] The court's view was applied not only to the District of Columbia, but soon enough to the whole nation. At the time many observers thought of the new police power of governments as an opportunity for national beautification: "The words of the court seem to mean that laws setting aesthetic standards for building are as valid as laws setting safety standards," commented the editors of the *Chicago Tribune*, wondering at the expanse of the ruling the Supreme Court had handed down.[20] Henceforward, when a federal official or a developer chose brutalism over a cupola, his choice did carry the force of scripture.

Eminent domain takings only widened when, in 1956, Congress passed President Eisenhower's highway act, whose new roads would require the seizure of thousands of miles of property. Under the succeeding housing acts and *Berman*, Washington and its partners moved with impunity. More than six hundred thousand Americans were displaced in the process.[21] As in the case of community action, federal funds for urban renewal projects flowed so copiously that whatever authority received and dispensed the funds, be it a housing office or a parks commission, became a power unto itself. In some cities, the men who controlled the federal tap were so mighty they became known as "housing czars." As in the case of community action, the mayors found the sums so great that they had to take the money. What mayor would not prefer a federal subsidy to the ugly work of levying an extra tax on his constituents? The results *looked* grand. Eisenhower took Nikita Khrushchev on a tour of the new neighborhood in Washington Southwest when the Soviet leader visited.[22] Yet often, the small businesses and families displaced were forgotten. An employee at a nonprofit social services center later testified that housing was not made available for many of those evicted from Southwest.[23] Despite the official promises, many of the old tenants of Washington's Southwest never could move back there.[24]

No urban renewal construction, however, captured more of the ambition and failings of government intervention in housing than that in St. Louis. To start, the city obliterated entire neighborhoods of downtown. In one neighborhood, Mill Creek Valley, demolition crews razed five thousand buildings including forty-three historic churches. In the DeSoto-Carr area, a few miles from the site where the Gateway Arch would rise, there was similar demolition, though the bulldozers left standing two churches: St. Stanislaus, on North Twentieth Street; and St. Bridget of Erin, on the corner of North Jefferson Avenue and Carr Street.

Like city fathers everywhere, those who led St. Louis in the 1950s nursed qualms about taking federal money. Still, watching the towers rise on the plot they called "M-4," St. Louis's brass did feel pride. The St. Louis project, like the HUD building so much later, was enormous: thirty-three towers of eleven stories each on their blueprints. The city named the two complexes after two heroes of St. Louis: a Tuskegee Airman who died at the end of World War II, Wendell O. Pruitt; and a congressman, William Igoe, who knew St. Louis's needs especially well because he had, in the Depression era, served on the St. Louis Board of Police Commissioners. The care carried over to the architecture. To design Pruitt-Igoe, the authorities selected a modern architect who in his day was thought to be as promising as Marcel Breuer, Minoru Yamasaki, the same architect the Johnsons would later consider for the presidential library. Yamasaki took pains to distinguish what he did from Breuer brutalism: "I cannot envision buildings which are too heavy and brutal just for sensational effect," he said once. Still, Yamasaki's buildings, like Breuer's, were stark and large.

The inspiration for Yamasaki's Pruitt-Igoe plan had been not Breuer, his peer, but a great favorite of progressives, the father of modern architecture, Le Corbusier. In the 1930s Le Corbusier had sketched out a futuristic dream: the "Radiant City." Radiant City plans laid out rows of high-rises, surrounded by green space. One thesis of the Radiant City concept was economy of scale: the more people you could house in a building, the more rent you could collect, and the lower the rent could be. Yamasaki had added some low-rises among his towers, but the St. Louis Housing Authority and Washington had rejected them: the Housing Authority, following Le Corbusier, expected Pruitt-Igoe to be dense enough to fund itself. To save space, Yamasaki tried an innovation: the "skip-stop elevator," which stopped only every few floors, saving footage for extra apartments on the floors it passed by. Obliging residents to use the stairways was another experiment: the planners wanted to see if the arrangement would foster a sense of neighborhood. Since St. Louis would grow, the planners assumed, the towers needed room for all the new working families in the future. At the time Pruitt-Igoe was contemplated, Missouri was a segregating state, and the planners had created Pruitt for blacks and Igoe for whites. But in the 1950s, after *Brown v. Board of Education*, the courts had scotched the division.

Yamasaki's towers were scarcely standing before trouble arose at Pruitt-Igoe. The whites who did live there made the court's decision moot by moving out to the suburbs, many of them benefiting from the federal mortgage subsidies made available by the same laws that had created the institutions that funded Pruitt-Igoe. Instead of the working poor whom planners had envisioned living at Pruitt-Igoe, truly poor families, many unemployed, took the apartments. Joyce Ladner, a young sociologist, noted that the people in Pruitt-Igoe were not so different from those she had grown up with in Mississippi: "except for one thing: the strong, tightly knit community in which I'd grown up had begun to shatter around the people who were displaced in a northern city with few supports."[25]

In some cases, only welfare families were entitled to the lowest rents at Pruitt-Igoe. And to receive welfare under Missouri's rules, a family could have only one parent—the mother. So families considering life in the towers had to make a terrible choice: stay together or take the apartment. Families who moved into Pruitt-Igoe often lost a father. "The stipulation was that my father could not be with us," recalled a former tenant, Jacquelyn Williams. "They would put us into the housing projects only if he left the state."[26] The social workers even policed apartments at night, checking to see if fathers had secretly returned, grounds for eviction. Families whose fathers did come for a secret visit told children that if anyone ever asked about their fathers, they should lie.

The sanctimony of the officials who intervened in private life was so great that Williams remembered it all her life. "We're giving you money, so we have the right to make stipulations as to how you use it."[27] In Pruitt-Igoe, Daniel Patrick Moynihan's theories about families were borne out. The fathers departed to hunt for jobs they could not always find, for the economic growth inside St. Louis's city limits upon which Pruitt-Igoe was premised was staying away. Some of the old mainstays of St. Louis weren't merely looking West. They were moving West, or at the very least establishing Western addresses, as in the case of the merger between two aviation giants, McDonnell of St. Louis and Douglas of California. The fathers often did not come back. Pruitt-Igoe became known for housing large, single-parent families. The children ran wild, and the staff had trouble keeping up with maintenance. Occupancy dropped, reducing the rent roll and making maintenance even tougher for the beleaguered officials at the St. Louis Housing Authority. Everyone who saw Pruitt-Igoe developed a concern about the towers. Michael Harrington, the author, decided he admired Charles Farris, the St. Louis housing official who argued that buildings should be limited to eight families or so, that low-cost and middle-income homes ought to be mixed together, and that it all should occur in "existing and vital neighborhoods"—not razed lots.

By the time Johnson gave his speech at Michigan, Pruitt-Igoe wasn't merely troubled, it was failing: the vacancy rate at Pruitt was 23.9 percent; at Igoe, the rate was 29.3 percent. Both levels were far higher than vacancies at smaller public projects. Pruitt-Igoe elevators, which stopped only every few floors, were muggers' traps. Poor maintenance meant the elevators often jammed, leaving gangs' victims in with them for long extra minutes. The gangs lurked in the halls and made tenants "run the gant-let" to get to their doors. Young men threw bricks and rocks at windows and streetlamps; the activity was a regular sport. There were no good playgrounds. Because there were no toilets on the ground floor, children had accidents there and in the elevators, and the elevators gradually became public toilets. The community area was a sorry joke; its only function ultimately was as a place for collecting Housing Authority rents. No one seemed able to stop the decay. Social scientists were descending on the complex to conduct multiyear investigations, and that irritated the tenants further. "Negro people are having their privacy invaded by Washington University sociology students who are there to study them," a disgusted supervisor at Pruitt-Igoe told the papers once. Minoru Yamasaki was busy designing the World Trade Center's Twin Towers, which would also have a unique elevator function. Yet Yamasaki now apologized publicly for Pruitt-Igoe. In a 1965 issue of his trade's top journal, *Architectural Forum*, Yamasaki told readers, "It's a job I wish I hadn't done."[28]

JOHNSON'S FRESH housing plans made a show of rectifying some of the bitter errors of past housing drives. The St. Louis Housing Authority set a budget of $7 million for the Pruitt-Igoe fix-up and, under the watchful eye of the Federal Housing Administration, commenced its cleanup. The authority installed toilets on the ground floor and painted heretofore unpainted cement block walls. "Why is it so important to paint them?" asked Farris, the St. Louis Housing Authority official who had caught Harrington's attention. "Well if you don't paint them, the people who move in may have a tendency to treat you with the same respect you treat them." The Housing Authority reconditioned the disastrous elevators. It built new indoor play areas and contemplated the sale of land to a private developer for the building of the missing shopping center. It placed protective screens on the outside of the windows to deflect rocks and save the glass. Brighter mercury vapor lights went up on the streets around Pruitt-Igoe. The danger was that vandals would destroy the renovation, so the authority even paid design firms to invent unbreakable products for Pruitt-Igoe. One company,

Soundolier Manufacturing, developed an inside hall light fixture made of a high-tensile aluminum alloy that was also used in the *Gemini* spacecraft.[29] Once you covered the fixture with a strong stainless-steel screen, you could not break it. The supervisors knew that, because they tested it with a five-pound mallet. The Housing Authority found an epoxy paint that withstood graffiti. It developed a special steam pipe cover that no teenager could pull off or smash. "The standard things on the market just didn't meet our problems," Robert Gunter of the authority told the press.

One of the observers of the decline of Pruitt-Igoe was a priest at one of the remaining churches, St. Bridget's. His name was John Shocklee. The church on the corner that had escaped the Pruitt-Igoe wrecking ball now held outsize influence in the neighborhood. Shocklee did plenty of community work at Pruitt-Igoe, but he had begun to see that it might be impossible for outsiders to build a true community in the concrete towers. It might even be impossible to help the locals build the community within the complex. Why not find a means to let the people make their own way out and pick their own homes, make their own communities in the shadow of Pruitt-Igoe? Even the most dilapidated houses seemed better to some than the slum that was the complex. In Shocklee's neighborhood an independent organization was forming, calling itself Jeff-Vander-Lou, after three avenues that shaped the neighborhood, Jefferson, Vandeventer, and St. Louis. Collecting dues, the group, black citizens, made their own plan for rehabbing remaining houses or other buildings nearby. They built a model, using Styrofoam blocks and corrugated boxes to represent the buildings. Without federal support, even from the OEO, Jeff-Vander-Lou began renovating a building; crowds showed up to see the work when Jeff-Vander-Lou scheduled an open house. Eventually, a wealthy family that lived in the area helped Jeff-Vander-Lou create a charity to fund its rehab projects.

Father Shocklee had his own vehicle, the Bicentennial Civic Improvement Corp., to help residents of Pruitt-Igoe or other public housing try out life as homeowners.[30] A local bank, Pulaski Savings and Loan, provided families with mortgages. Shocklee and others helped the families purchase houses in the shadow of Pruitt-Igoe; many of these houses, though run-down, were solid brick—St. Louis had always prided itself on its craftsmanship. Getting the necessary inspectors to approve occupancy proved tough. But the families working on the houses proved patient, even if an inspector had to come multiple times before giving the okay on a heating system. Getting into the real estate business felt strange to the priests. Father Joseph Kohler, Shocklee's colleague, told a reporter that before this program he "never bought anything in my life." Everyone liked the project, including visitors from outside St. Louis. "This success was indeed happening in the shadow of Pruitt-Igoe," John McClaughry, a policy advisor to Senator Charles Percy of Illinois, later recalled.

Another new fan of home buying was Congresswoman Leonor Sullivan, who had represented St. Louis in Washington since 1953. Sullivan liked the emphasis on the individual household. Her late husband, John Sullivan, had himself served as a member of Congress from 1941 to 1953, meaning Sullivan had accumulated a quarter century's worth of wisdom about urban renewal. People needed their own homes, the congresswoman also decided. In 1966, the same year that President Johnson powered through with housing, Sullivan acted. She slipped her own plan to make homeownership possible for poor families into an amendment, and the amendment became law. Under Section 221(h) of the new National Housing Act—"Mrs. Sullivan's law," as the papers called the section—nonprofits, including churches, could buy houses, rehabilitate them, and then sell them to families. The Federal Housing Administration insured the mortgage. Mrs. Sullivan's law was just a pilot program, tiny even compared with the "pilots" that Walter Reuther created for his "model cities" (the new name for demonstration cities). But Sullivan also thought homeownership for Pruitt-Igoe tenants was worth a try.

Sullivan told reporters that federal programs ought to give poor people a "stake in middle-class living and a feeling of middle-class identification." She was seeking or expanding big government involvement in housing. Her program created new homes by new architects, houses which stuck out more in the neighborhood.[31] Her emphasis differed from Shocklee's, which was nearly all local. But if nonprofits could help people out of the government's care for good, such experiments might be worth it.

One family that Father Shocklee and the others managed to help was the Straughters, Pruitt-Igoe tenants with seven children. At Pruitt-Igoe, rents were scaled to income. Every time the Straughters' wages went up, their rent went up, a tax on striving. The Straughters didn't think their apartment was worth the rent, for they found living in Pruitt-Igoe "a madhouse."[32] Now the Straughters had become homeowners, one of eighty families whom the church had helped move out. The priests wanted to enlarge the program and buy up three hundred houses, but for that they still lacked funds. In 1968, a sanitation truck driver named Theodore Forte described the features he hoped for in a home. He wanted a barbecue pit and a landscaped patio and his own basement. But only now, with the interest-rate subsidy and the support of the church, could he reasonably expect to buy a house. As Forte would tell a reporter in 1968, "I'm living for something now."

Others in St. Louis noted that the home-buying pilot project was typical of Father Shocklee. "He is looking for a series of small successes in small areas," commented Irvin Dagen, the executive director of the St. Louis Housing Authority. But Father Shocklee didn't mind working small. Each of his successes built on another. Shocklee was fond of repeating an old axiom, "Give a man a fish, he'll eat for one day. Teach him to fish, and he'll feed himself for a lifetime." Coming from Shocklee, the tired adage sounded new. A few years later, Father Kohler, Father Shocklee's ally in the homeownership drive, would take up the question overhanging all government action, from the work at the Federal Reserve to the work at HUD: would building in cities prevent riots? People who owned property, especially, were the ones less likely to riot. "Homeowners are not home burners," Kohler said. And homeownership in the United States was still rising: by the end of the decade 63 percent of families would own their own home, up from 55 percent, when urban renewal had first gotten under way.[33] Why should America have a policy that slowed black homeownership? Sometimes, perversely, authorities even took away black homes. In Newark, Nathan Wright noted bitterly that heavy property taxes were driving those families that managed to buy a house toward foreclosure.

In Chicago, those who worked in housing, whether for HUD, the

Chicago Housing Authority, or nonprofits, also reconsidered the big questions. One of the premises for building giant public housing in the first place was class oriented, even socialist: the premise that however indifferent the government landlord of a public housing project was, that government landlord was better than a private landlord, the classic exploiter. What if the private landlords were more like their tenants than anyone knew, buffeted by external factors such as prices and government rules? Perhaps the socialist emphasis on the abusive landlord was misplaced. You could blame a landlord all you wanted, but landlords only operated in economic reality—they were not all demons. Even the radical community activists noted the perversity of the situation. A few years back one of Saul Alinsky's colleagues, Nicholas von Hoffman, had worked organizing tenants for rent strikes in Chicago. In one case, von Hoffman had begun a rent strike against a white landlord, and after much effort, von Hoffman finally scored a coup. He induced the landlord to come to the building to hear the tenant grievances. When the landlord arrived with his lawyer, he stood in the lobby of the building. Then, something unexpected happened. The landlord turned to his lawyer and said, "Well, tell them." The lawyer pulled a paper from his briefcase. The paper was the deed to the building. The lawyer told the crowd that if any of them could give him a dollar for the deed, the building was theirs. "There was much whooping," von Hoffman recalled. But von Hoffman was worried, reasoning, logically enough, that "if the landlords are giving buildings away, that means they can't figure out how to keep them up." That night, von Hoffman telephoned Alinsky "with a terrible feeling in the pit of my stomach that this was just insoluble."[34] Class war against landlords might be a kind of cartoon, exciting to college students but useless for the poor the warfare pretended to serve.

Perhaps, some of the community organizers began to consider, Malcolm X had been on to something with his talk about blacks especially needing to build their own community. The Black Power leader had died in 1965, but others continued to speak about self-sufficiency. "The Negro poor most often are the objects, rather than the subjects, of civic action," said Reverend Lynward Stevenson of the Woodlawn Organization, one of the recipients of Shriver's grants. "Here and now in 1966 America, it's far more important that things be done by Negroes than that they be done for them—even if, for a while, they're not done as well."

Chicago caught the eye of both Martin Luther King Jr. and the United Auto Workers. Perhaps Chicago was the stage where King could make his own "demonstration city." He launched his own campaign to end what he called "involuntary enslavement" of blacks in rental slums. King commenced with the traditional progressive view, that landlords were the devil. He told the public that he planned "to bring about the unconditional surrender of forces dedicated to the creation and maintenance of slums." Around the time the president delivered the 1966 State of the Union address, King and his wife, Coretta, took the dramatic step of actually moving up to Chicago. To spotlight the poor quality of homes for black citizens in the Windy City, the couple took a third-floor walk-up flat in the neighborhood of Lawndale—a neighborhood so shabby that some called it "Slumdale."[35] When the landlord realized who his tenants were, he quickly sent a team to fix up the apartment.[36] King kept after other landlords who failed to maintain the homes of black tenants in decent condition. King at first also spotlighted the biggest landlord of the poor in Chicago: the Chicago Housing Authority. Taking on this public office enabled him to remind Americans that someone needed to help not only the 145,000 Chicagoans in public housing but also the two million or so Americans living in public housing in the rest of the country.[37] King asked the Chicago Housing Authority to increase the number of guards at two of Chicago's Pruitt-Igoes: the Robert Taylor Homes and Stateway Gardens. The Chicago Housing Authority complied.

Yet as the spring and summer of 1966 approached, King, too, wearied of waging cartoon war on landlords. And he, like Father Shocklee, began to think about houses instead of rent rolls. Working with local groups, including community action groups fostered by the UAW and Reuther, King began to protest against discriminatory bank lending practices, and against neighborhood covenants that kept blacks out of certain parts of Chicago, or out of suburbs such as Cicero and Skokie. Mayor Daley, too shrewd to be lured into hand-to-hand combat with the nation's greatest civil rights hero, kept his distance. The newspapers perceived King's work as an extension of his Southern campaigns against discrimination. But King's later work in Chicago also reflected the insight of the priests in St. Louis, or Nicholas von Hoffman, Saul Alinsky's activist. When it came to getting people hot water, electricity, and heat in winter, rentals might not be the answer. Teenagers didn't mind ripping up a rental. After all, it was not *their* house. With a rental, too many factors were out of everyone's control: the St. Louis Housing Authority could not order big companies to stay and provide jobs for Pruitt-Igoe tenants.

In newspapers and the planning journals, more critics were beginning to pose skeptical questions about federal housing programs, older or newer. Black or white, people did indeed need a stake in their own place, wrote the housing scholar Oscar Newman. To Newman, a stake was physical territory. Newman talked about how people, even tenants, would be satisfied if they had "defensible space," a patio or a sidewalk leading to a door that the community considered theirs. Even a simple stoop gave people some territory on a common street. Newman would later compare Pruitt-Igoe, where no one owned Yamasaki's innovative breezeways, with North Beach Place, a development in San Francisco. North Beach Place homes stood low, they stood right on the sidewalk, and they did feature small stoops. People liked "their" stoops. But in St. Louis, trapped in Pruitt-Igoe, with nothing of their own, the tenants felt as though they were in a prison.[38] "It is the apartment tower," Newman said, "that is the real and final villain." The trouble, another scholar argued, was indeed governments' emphasis on size and the big picture. Surveying the world from the ground up, or out the busted window of the ground floor of Pruitt-Igoe, might yield more information than staring down at the panorama from Capitol Hill, from a helicopter over Breuer's brute, or even from the point of view of the St. Louis Housing Authority. Maybe, the critic wrote, it was indeed better to think small.

A second critic, whose name was Jane Jacobs, had come to her views by observing the street where she lived: Hudson Street, in New York's Greenwich Village. Hudson Street at the time was a scruffy thoroughfare, something like what Hastings Street in Detroit had been before the bulldozers arrived, the kind authorities might well hand over to a developer for rebuilding. New York's housing czar was a man named Robert Moses. But this Moses couldn't be more different from the civil rights activist Robert Parris Moses, who eschewed displays of power. New York's Moses had leveled neighborhoods in the Bronx and Upper Manhattan. Now Robert Moses claimed that Hudson Street was "blighted" and vowed to replace it as well. But the view from her Hudson Street window did not look like blight to Jacobs. Indeed, Hudson Street enchanted her. From the first stirrings of a garbage truck to the last rowdies emerging from the White Horse Tavern at night, the street was always busy. Locals emerged from their doorways, shopped in the dime stores, and, most important, looked after one another. The "eyes on the street," as Jacobs called them, were always there. In its mixture of pedestrians, trucks, and public transport, Hudson Street was something like a European street, the sort the Beatles would capture in their ode to a street in their hometown, Liverpool, "Penny Lane."

The streets thrived precisely because they felt so local, Jacobs wrote. The best kind of control in the United States, she had written in her youth, was "control from below." If there was dirt, or odors, that was all right—this was not 1910, it was the age of penicillin and Jonas Salk's vaccine. That dirty, friendly life was what was missing in the housing projects, or even in mixed-income developments like Lafayette Park. Jacobs dismissed Detroit's favorite development, and another, similar one in Chicago, Lake Meadows, as "blind-eyed purlieus." Jacobs's own opinions sharpened as she watched, and sometimes did public battle with, the housing czar Moses. Moses, like the federal offices that sent him funds, believed that cities were not something to live in; cities were something to be traversed. Snatching time in a small office her husband had rented for her in an all-male rooming house, Jacobs had recently penned a whole volume on the flaws of the development culture, titling the book *The Death and Life of Great American Cities*. In *Death and Life*, Jacobs offered a powerful critique of federal housing policy, arguing that the original hostility to cities was simply wrongheaded and outdated.

When it came to design, Jacobs said, the planners were deluding themselves, especially when they told each other that, as Robert Moses said, placing a park around a murderously dull high-rise mitigated its evil. A park was nothing unless it was surrounded by a complex set of businesses and homes, a place where families, schoolchildren, shoppers, and office people appeared all day long. Small was indeed often better than big. Jacobs rejected the very lexicon and premises from which architects or urban planners worked. Blight was not always blight. Redevelopment was not redevelopment, "it was the sacking of cities." Dumping capital into a poor neighborhood stunned that neighborhood, rather than helped it. What Jacobs called "cataclysmic money," the kind that poured from Washington in a great rush following legislation such as the 1949 Housing Act, or Johnson's 1965 law, was less helpful than gradual, local money. Slums were not inevitable. Slums did not have to be permanent. Slums truly could "unslum."[39] Jacobs titled her book not *Life and Death*, but *Death and Life*.

THE MURMURINGS of intellectuals, housing bureaucrats, and lonely tenants were however not audible to Johnson and Reuther, set as they were on their housing projects. And so the pair pressed ahead, their own minds now on hot summers, and on building quickly enough to prevent another Watts. Through the first half of 1966 Johnson labored on federal efforts to update America's housing. Johnson and Reuther, neither of whom had time for architectural journals, still regarded the slum as the source of evil. In June 1967, Johnson appointed an eighteen-man commission that included Reuther, George Meany, and Whitney Young of the Urban League: the commission's goal, the *New York Times* reported, was to lead America in an "attack on slums." Again, the goal was to preempt riots.

The ring of a telephone at 5:20 in the morning on July 23, 1967, made it clear that again, the great preempters were moving too late.[40] It was the red emergency phone that belonged to Detroit's police commissioner, Ray Girardin, and he picked up on the first ring. Motor City's police had raided several "blind pigs"—unlicensed establishments that illegally sold liquor—and arrested eighty people. Two of those detained turned out to be returning Vietnam veterans. Now the police were finding them-selves brawling with angry citizens of the area. Girardin had his riot plan, but with no time to implement it, the riot spread that fast. The violence moved especially quickly in the hot spot of Twelfth Street, the area to which families who had been displaced by urban renewal had moved. The entire neighborhood, almost all black, rose in anger.

Unlike Governor Pat Brown of California two summers earlier, George Romney was on the job in Michigan when the riots broke out. But as with the efforts to prevent unrest in Los Angeles in 1965, the 1967 efforts in Detroit quickly fell casualty to jurisdictional squabbles. Romney, a Re-publican, told the mayor of Detroit, the Democrat Jerome Cavanagh, that the state police would help and that 1,200 National Guard troops were available. By 2:00 p.m. on July 23 the state police were on their way, and later in the afternoon the National Guard was as well.[41] As Detroit burned, leaders in Michigan from both parties decided they needed a force that had not been present in Watts: federal troops. About 2:00 in the morning on July 24, Mayor Cavanaugh called Vice President Hum-phrey. Humphrey asked Cavanagh and Romney to call Attorney General Ramsey Clark. Clark initially seemed prepared to send in federal troops, and called Johnson. Then Clark called back to say that a spoken re-quest would not suffice; the attorney general needed a document from the Michigan governor. At 10:46 a.m., Romney sent another request, a formal document requesting federal troops. Clark kept changing the terms on Romney; now Clark wanted a document addressed to Johnson. Back and forth the chatter went, costing precious time. At 10:48 p.m., after confer-ring with the Army, Johnson called Reuther.[42]

At midnight, as July 24 became July 25, Johnson finally went on the air to assure the nation that he had not lagged; troops had been on flights heading for Selfridge Air Force Base outside Detroit hours ago. Johnson spoke defensively, to ward off charges, especially from Romney, that he was playing politics. Johnson announced that law and order had broken down in Detroit, and that he'd learned that "the situation was totally be-yond the control of the local authorities"—a jab at Romney. Romney felt Johnson was misrepresenting the time line, and had delayed on purpose, to hurt him. Because of Johnson's delay, in Romney's view, Michigan had lost an entire day. Romney could feel himself starting to despise the president, who, he sensed, was making hay of a possible 1968 election opponent at the expense of a major city. The *Wall Street Journal*, too, noted the Administration's delay: "President Johnson scored no points by delaying dispatch of federal troops." Romney determined to prove he was master of the situation.

But Detroit would have no master, whether federal troops or Governor Romney. For days the rioting raged. On July 25, Detroit Edison repairmen were able to restore electric service to the five thousand people in the Brewster-Douglass complex, the childhood home of the Supremes, before being driven off by snipers. That night, a combination of local police, state troopers, and the National Guard occupied the Algiers Motel in search of a sniper, and in the worst tragedy of the whole riot, killed three unarmed teenagers. The Detroit Fire Department was fighting 1,682 fires. More than one hundred city blocks were seriously damaged. The death count eventually rose to forty-three. Romney, who had moved into the police headquarters for the duration, called the destruction "the most unbelievable I have seen without a full bombing raid."

After tens of millions and decades of urban renewal spending, Detroit did not look renewed. Detroit looked, Mayor Cavanagh said, like a city that now did need a Marshall Plan, like "Berlin in 1945." Almost three thousand businesses had been sacked, with damage many times greater than in Watts just two years before. Slavery had expropriated blacks. The tractor and bigoted landowners had driven them to the North, where the bulldozers had driven them out again. After officials destroyed their homes in Paradise Valley to build Lafayette Park, many blacks had simply dropped from the city's tax rolls. It felt now as if those citizens had come back to collect revenge. "They weren't found until Sunday morning, July 23, 1967—on Twelfth Street," one local told a *New York Times* reporter.

The country drew its collective breath and again reconsidered assumptions. The first was the idea that construction prevented riots. The reality might not be "build, or burn." It might even be "build, and burn."

The second assumption worth questioning was that modern architecture set the standard for beauty. Some citizens did not love cinder blocks, however innovative, or glass office buildings, or aluminum louvers. They liked quarry stone, red brick, and wood. They liked Hudson Street in New York, or the storefronts that went down when Detroit's Paradise Valley was razed, or the careful masonry of the old German craftsmen in St. Louis. Many a family, poor or rich, did not mind, or even chose, fixer-uppers, especially when the families could form their own community as they hammered or painted. The entire housing drive could prove a mismatch, just as the make-work jobs in Shriver's programs had proven a mismatch. The very name of the department moving into the colossus in Washington, Housing and Urban Development, could be wrong. To be housed, it turned out, was not what people wanted. They wanted to house themselves.

8

Guns, Butter, and Gold

THANKSGIVING 1967 TO MARCH 1968

Guns: 8.5% of GDP
Butter: 5.1% of GDP
Dow Jones Industrial Average: 874

Fall of 1967 found producers at NBC preparing a Christmas episode of *Bonanza*. In this episode, *Bonanza*'s 283rd, gold fever seizes Hoss Cartwright, the slowest of the Cartwright brothers. Hoss orders a gold-detection machine by mail in the hope that it will help him find gold in an old mine. But the rancher cannot make the contraption work. For days, Hoss fiddles at dials and tubes without success. In the end, the machine, improbably, does seem to locate at least one vein of the metal, but on a property that Hoss does not own. Someone else gets rich. The implication of the episode is that Hoss should stick to his chores, as the patriarch, Ben, advises. Prospecting for gold is the pursuit of fools.

Yet in 1967, one of those fools was the U.S. government itself. The Johnson Administration had begun its gold hunt several years before, with a quiet program to see if recent or new technology could identify undiscovered gold in North America and make it possible to mine that gold more efficiently. The research process was indeed yielding some finds: "aqueous chemical treatment," a new process being developed by the Bureau of Mines to pull gold from certain forms of ore. And U.S. authorities were testing whether they could clear the path to underground gold through nuclear detonations. The United States Geological Survey had teamed up with the University of Oregon to launch a research craft to dredge the West Coast, though the boat, the *Yaquina*, had as yet found only traces of the metal.[1]

Both the fictional *Bonanza* episode and the genuine federal prospecting raised a question. The Cartwrights were supposed to be some of the richest men in the West. The United States was the richest country in the world. Why would anyone who was that rich be that desperate for gold? The answer the Johnson Administration gave itself, was that the nation was in a temporary jam.

The reasons for such a jam were ones that William McChesney Martin of the Fed laid out in a kind of monetary bedtime story, told not only to Johnson but to Kennedy and Eisenhower before him. The story began two decades earlier, at an international conference at a grand hotel among the White Mountains at Bretton Woods, New Hampshire. There America's supremacy, like the White Mountains, had hung over its allies, undeniable. In acknowledgment of America's status, the Allies assigned the United States the role of gold bank to the world. Under the Bretton Woods system, foreign governments could go to what was called the gold window at the U.S. Treasury and turn their dollars in for gold at $35 an ounce. At the time, the U.S. Treasury had had its own mountains, mountains of gold, and never imagined that the gold would be drawn down.

On the grand porches at Bretton Woods in 1944, the Allies had agreed that America's gold was the symbol of one thing: America's international responsibility to noncommunist nations. After the war, Germany and Japan were more rubble than country. In the 1940s, it had seemed more than possible that Japan would never become a stable democracy or that West Germany would opt to join East Germany under the Soviet umbrella. America had to prevent that by enabling Germany and Japan to recover. At the start, or so most Americans envisioned, America would benefit defeated countries by selling them consumer goods and providing advice and funding. But soon enough, within a decade or so, it became clear that another way for Japan or Germany to recover was to build up exports. When a country's currency was cheap, other countries bought more of its goods. After the war, therefore, the Bretton Woods system maintained a set of fixed exchange rates that sometimes undervalued the Deutsche mark or the Japanese yen. By the 1950s, and certainly the 1960s, it was clear that the system was working. Foreign nations trusted the American banker. Germany and Japan were now building their own cars, Volkswagens and Toyotas, selling them to their own people. Germany, and eventually Japan, began amassing dollars they could exchange at the gold window. Of course the United States also had to defend the world against communism militarily as well. Even two decades on, therefore, it was important for America to sustain the Bretton Woods system. The fight against communism was still live, as Vietnam demonstrated all too well. Any domestic sacrifices due to the strong dollar were minor in the conflict to save democracy and capitalism. A simple citizen might not comprehend the need for sacrifice, true grown-ups—even unions and automakers—understood. If Americans one day consistently bought more abroad than foreigners bought from the United States, and that could happen, it would be because America was growing *faster* than the others, not more slowly. A tricky but temporary consequence of our foreign purchases was that European coffers were overflowing with dollars. The trouble now, in 1967, was that shortfalls, trade or budget, were being interpreted by uncaring currency markets as a sign of weakness. Disloyal foreign governments, well aware they were taking advantage of America's magnanimity, were showing up at the gold window and collecting gold so quickly that the $20 billion with which the nation so cheerfully commenced this decade was now down to the $13 billion or so currently in U.S. coffers would be gone in a decade or two.

Under domestic law, the United States was still officially on a dilute form of the gold standard: American law held that 25 percent of the currency outstanding must be "covered"—backed—by real gold in American banks or the Treasury. The ratio right now stood at around 30 percent, compliant, but too close to 25 percent for comfort.[2] But here again, Martin or Johnson's other advisors reassured the president. Sometimes the outflow trend reversed, and gold flowed into the United States. And the United States would not always need to buy both guns and butter. America would end the Vietnam War soon, Secretary McNamara had always told Johnson, at least until recently. When that happened, guns would be less necessary, and the gold outflows would halt. America would be able to afford butter. But until the war ended, every extra grain of gold the United States could add to its stores bought time.

Even the quirky alchemy venture was therefore worth taking seriously. The Treasury wrote a memo reporting that the government scientists might actually find, through their own gold detectors, up to $10 billion worth of gold.[3] That would put U.S. gold holdings over $20 billion, back to the generous, easy levels of the Truman and Eisenhower years.

In every crisis, Johnson picked favorites to advise him. The top favorite in 1967, however much Johnson had railed at his ranch after the 1965 interest rate increase, was the storyteller Martin of the Fed. Johnson's recent lenience may have had something to do with the fact that Martin had, earlier that year, relented and led the Fed in lowering the interest rate back to 4 percent from the 4.5 percent that had triggered the Texas confrontation. But Johnson found himself warming to Martin for other reasons. Martin was a kind of older version of the character George Bailey in a movie about a small-town banker, *It's a Wonderful Life*. Bailey had been so eager to preserve his family savings and loan that he had even been willing to hand out his own honeymoon fund to restore confidence in the tiny business. Martin, Johnson's George Bailey, displayed the same unrelenting sincerity, though in Martin's case the bank was the U.S. Federal Reserve, or even the entire Bretton Woods system. When Johnson veered, Martin convinced him of what he believed: that it was wrong to change the price of gold at the gold window, that it was wrong to fool with exchange rates, and that Johnson must find a way to restore America to fiscal probity. Johnson liked discreet advisors, and Martin was discreet. In foreign policy, "there are limitations on what the secretary can say publicly," McNamara said, and Johnson heartily concurred with that for all policy. You didn't want the public to know you weren't winning yet. Johnson put it more frankly when he disciplined experts who sought more disclosure: "You mean that if your mother-in-law, your very own mother-in-law, has only one eye, and it happens to be in the middle of her forehead, then the best place for her is in the living room with all the company?" The president, his Treasury, and the Fed followed a corollary rule when it came to gold flows. You didn't advertise it when gold flowed out of the United States, just as you didn't advertise a military retreat. If you did, a vicious circle took over. Advertising gold losses would rile markets, and make stanching gold flows even tougher. In the end, Martin counseled, if they didn't lose their nerve, it would all work out, and for the same reason the problems arose in the first place: America was exceptional. Johnson was exceptional. The United States just didn't run out of gold.

Still, as 1968 approached, Martin found that the bedtime story wasn't lulling his president. The reality, Johnson saw, was that the technical-sounding gold problem would look awful in the daylight of an election year. If U.S. gold ran out before the election, he himself would become a laughingstock. Just as the Westerns suggested: to voters, gold still signified American wealth. The foreign governments were less likely to withdraw gold if Johnson balanced the federal budget. But the tax increases necessary to balance the budget could also cost him reelection. So could interest rate increases, the kind Martin sometimes insisted on. Most days, Johnson wanted that second full term, his second chance to make the "Great" in Great Society real and permanent, his second chance to end the war. In a second term, Johnson would prove America was indeed still as exceptional, as special, as it had always been.

As much for reassurance as anything else, Johnson sought ways to distinguish himself, and the United States, from the non-exceptionals. The figure Johnson most wanted *not* to resemble was Harold Wilson, the leader of a nation that had suffered several gold crises since Johnson took office, the United Kingdom. Johnson's advisors told him, and Johnson told himself, that Harold Wilson was untrustworthy, nothing like Johnson. The leader of the United Kingdom was a man who called himself not just a social democrat but an actual socialist. Wilson's dreams of architecture made Johnson's look modest: Wilson actually wanted to tear down most of Whitehall, the historic district of government in London, and replace it with concrete ziggurats. Wilson, the Johnson Administration told itself, was suspiciously interested in delivering peace feelers to our enemy in the Cold War. Some reports deep in the American records even suggested Wilson was a Soviet asset, and Johnson tended not to ignore such rumors.

Like Charles de Gaulle of France, Wilson was someone on whom an ally could not count, a man "widely accused of opportunistic insincerity," as Johnson's advisors wrote in a memo. When it came to the military arena, the United States and Britain were supposed to act as one. Yet after the Gulf of Tonkin, when Johnson had made the Vietnam War official, Prime Minister Wilson failed to join him with even a token dispatch of "a platoon of bagpipers" or Gurkhas to Vietnam. Wilson had negotiated separately with the Russians over Vietnam, with Johnson's irritated acquiescence. Johnson shouldn't worry about Wilson, the president's men told him. It was said in the United Kingdom that Wilson made Lyndon Johnson look like Abe Lincoln.[4] Wilson was always begging for visits to the White House, but Johnson liked to put him off.

The differences between Britain and the United States might be highlighted as well. The United States was an economic miracle, while Britain was an economic basket case. Britain featured, as one State Department analysis put it, "a history of repeated crises; organized labor's reluctance, if not unwillingness, to accept wage restraint; archaic labor and management practices."[5] Britain had long since nationalized an important sector of its economy, health care. The Wilson government had added economic insult to injury by nationalizing steel—even Harry Truman, though he had tried, had not managed that. Britain misled its own people about money, Johnson's experts reported. Britain was not loyal. The United Kingdom turned often to the United States, but only for reasons of political expedience. "We can't kick our creditors in the balls," Wilson told a fellow Laborite. Wilson's tax regime was so punitive—he had introduced a 95 percent supertax on the rich—that the Beatles mocked him in a song, "Taxman." The Beatles even referenced the top marginal rate: "here's one for you, nineteen for me," sang their Taxman. Johnson had long since internalized his advisors' arguments about Britain and made them his own. Great Britain, he once told Martin, was like "a reckless boy that goes off and gets drunk and writes checks on his father, and he can honor two or three or four of them." But finally the father would have to call the boy in "and tell him, 'Now, we've got to work this out.'"

This narrative of impervious greatness, however, was interrupted by the news that the Bank of England was suffering another run on its own money. Wilson devalued the pound by 14 percent, and, denting the Wilson reputation for credibility further, he went on the BBC to tell citizens that "the pound here in Britain, in your pocket or your purse or in your bank" had not lost value, an obvious untruth for an island country that relied on imports. Soon enough the run at the Bank of England began to spread to the United States. Week by week through that fall, the public barometer of gold levels, the *Wall Street Journal*'s Federal Reserve Report, showed the Treasury gold reserves dropping. The Treasury and Federal Reserve discussed the matter, and decided to try to stop the run in England, so that they might keep the contagion from the United States. Martin again led the Fed in an interest rate hike, this time to 4.5 percent from 4 percent. At higher U.S. interest rates, countries would prefer dollars to an inert metal. But an interest rate increase might not be enough to stop the outflow. Johnson's finance men came up with a measure that suited America's grand role in the world. Just after Thanksgiving Day 1967, several Air Force pilots climbed into giant jets and took off on a secret mission. Their planes were C-141s, the same Starlifters that rushed the troops over to Vietnam and bore back the wounded, strapped in their litters. The destination this time was not Southeast Asia but an airstrip in Mildenhall, England. Their cargo was $100 million in gold, and more would follow. The gold would be just enough, or so the Fed and Treasury hoped, to help England make its payments in a crisis.

In December 1967, his gold problem presumably tended to, Johnson turned to other matters. Early in the month the White House hosted the wedding of his daughter Lynda Bird to a Marine Corps captain, Charles Robb. Thinking of the coming year, Johnson hunted for a chance to display national unity on Vietnam. The president received word that Australia's prime minister, Harold Holt, had died suddenly while scuba diving. Holt, unlike Wilson, *had* sent troops. Johnson flew to Australia to attend the funeral, but also used the occasion to visit U.S. troops in Vietnam. He told troops at Cam Ranh Bay that the enemy "knows that he has met his master."

Johnson also busied himself with the crucial personnel moves that must be made before an election. The first order of business was to complete the sidelining any allies of the most dangerous of the possible opponents, Senator Robert Kennedy. The sidelining started with Sargent Shriver, whom Johnson wanted to ship off to Paris as ambassador to France. Johnson's first move was to make Shriver as uncomfortable as possible at the OEO, an effort that Republicans in Congress had already enthusiastically commenced. That fall, the House of Representatives had agreed to reauthorize the OEO budget, a seeming victory for Shriver. But the House had excluded the 2,700 OEO employees from the general raise it voted for government employees, totaling $2.6 billion. The trick to set off Shriver worked. "The poor have always gotten the dirty end of the stick," Shriver fumed in the press. "They have been discriminated against. Now even those working hardest to help the poor have gotten the same treatment."[6] Congress had dropped another insult. If governors could no longer veto OEO work, members of Congress wanted to provide another check on the poverty czar. Congress wrote into the legislation an amendment channeling OEO money directly to state or local governments, handing back a power of the purse to mayors and state governments. Congresswoman Edith Green of Oregon successfully led other members in making the amendment law. Johnson, the old master of the Senate, did not stop them.

The Shriver offensive was working. More and more, Shriver considered escape. If the OEO became a complete torture, he could shift into politics, represent Illinois in the Senate, or perhaps even serve as its governor. Illinois had elected the heretofore little-known Charles Percy senator in 1966. It stood to reason (Shriver's) that if an executive from Bell and Howell could serve the Land of Lincoln in the Senate, so might the poverty czar and the founder of the Peace Corps. Shriver's Illinois fate however depended on the stocky former ward committeeman from Bridgeport, Mayor Daley. Daley moved Democratic candidates for Illinois offices around like pieces on his own personal chessboard, and Adlai Stevenson III, from another "royal" Democratic family, was also asking about the Senate or the governor's office. On the Daley chessboard, the courtly Shriver was a knight, but not necessarily *Daley's* knight. The

Daley maneuvering was likely to be a relief to Johnson, who didn't relish the thought of Shriver representing a Democratic stronghold like Illinois. Johnson built out the idea of the job in Paris for Shriver. Let Shriver handle Charles de Gaulle, who drew down gold and who had the temerity to charge that the United States spent too much. Shriver began to warm to Paris. Rose Kennedy, his wife's mother, took him for a walk and told him that embassy life in London had been a wonderful break for her, Joe Kennedy, and their children. Rose thought embassy life in Paris would suit Sarge, Eunice, and their large family just fine.

Johnson was also after Defense Secretary McNamara, whom the president was coming to regard as practically another Kennedy. The Robert Kennedys and the McNamaras had been friends since the days of the Cuban Missile Crisis. Kathleen McNamara, the McNamaras' daughter, had even worked for Robert Kennedy in the summer of 1966. In November, McNamara had sent the president an almost schizophrenic memo, nine pages, single-spaced. The memo simultaneously suggested pessimism—the United States should, needed to, halt bombing by the end of the year—and complacence, recommending "stabilizing" the war at its current levels.[7] That split, Johnson rightly guessed, came out of McNamara's own split loyalties, to the president and to Robert Kennedy. By day, McNamara reported to the president. In the evening, the defense secretary was the Kennedy crowd's. McNamara might join the increasingly dovish Georgetown set for dinner—he spent time at Georgetown get-togethers with Kay Graham, the publisher of the *Washington Post*. Or, more ominously, McNamara might head over to the Robert Kennedy house in Virginia, Hickory Hill.[8] Johnson therefore had recently nominated the defense secretary to a suitably dignified alternative post: head of the World Bank, another institution created at Bretton Woods. The bank's grand nickname, "World Bank" belied the more humdrum work of infrastructure finance, roads, and power plants at the International Bank for Reconstruction and Development. At the World Bank, as Johnson would put it in one of his encomiums, McNamara might take the lead and "win the most important war of all"—converting poor nations to rich ones by helping them turn the lights on, or giving them highways.

McNamara could advance freedom around the world through development. Johnson was also in the process of seeing to it that his old brethren in the Senate confirmed McNamara's successor as defense secretary, the presumably more reliable Clark Clifford, a Washington attorney. With McNamara parked safely at the World Bank's H Street headquarters, it wouldn't matter how frequently McNamara headed over to Hickory Hill to confer.[9] After all, how many of Richard Daley's or Martin Luther King's constituents had even heard of the World Bank?

The third Kennedy threat spooking Johnson was Walter Reuther. In Reuther's case, Johnson didn't sideline; he worked to pull Reuther closer. Some nineteen million Americans belonged to unions, and the loyal George Meany of the largest umbrella group, the AFL-CIO, was backing Johnson.[10] But Reuther and his one-and-a-half-million-odd UAW members were a different story. As Johnson knew, Reuther was hesitating, in good part because he felt drawn to Robert Kennedy. The Kennedy tragedy had only strengthened the affinity between the Kennedy and the Reuther clans. Reuther and the UAW had been close to Robert Kennedy especially for more than a decade, since the days when Reuther did battle with the Wisconsin manufacturer Kohler. This election round had already seen an ominous signal. Reuther was not putting the muscle of his UAW behind the Democratic Party and its preelection-year preparation as the union usually did. The president, like Kennedy before him, had always told his aides that he had never entirely trusted Reuther. Occasionally Johnson flipped into hostility when the name Reuther came up. Johnson even mocked Reuther's lame hand, injured in that assassination attempt so many years before. "You know the difference between Hubert and me?" Johnson once asked his aide Joe Califano. "When Hubert sits across from Reuther and Reuther's got that limp hand stuck in his pocket and starts talking about burning down the cities if billions of federal dollars aren't poured into them, Hubert will sit there smiling away and thinking all the time, 'How can I get his hand out of his pocket so I can shake it?' Well, when Reuther is sitting in the Oval Office telling me that," Johnson continued, "I'm sitting in my rocker, smiling and thinking all the time, 'How can I get that hand out of his pocket—so I can cut his balls off!'" Reuther, however, was not as easy to bully as Shriver or McNamara. The Reuthers, like the Kennedys, grew tighter when tragedy struck. That November, in the middle of Johnson's crisis management, Valentine Reuther, Reuther's father and the inspiration for his social democracy dreams, had passed away. In January, Roy Reuther, Reuther's brother, would die suddenly of a heart attack. Johnson would telegraph his condolences—trying, as usual, to pull Reuther close.[11] But Bobby Kennedy would jump in between, attending the funeral and sitting beside Walter and his daughter Lisa.

By the end of December, around the time when *Bonanza*'s gold detector episode aired, the Fed and the Treasury were reporting the news: the UK stoppage action had not worked. A billion dollars in gold had left the United States recently, and some of that was *after* the Starlifter flights. The loss of gold, the *New York Times* reported, was taking the country dangerously close to the $10.6 billion required by the statutory gold cover rule of 25 percent. Some lawmakers were already plotting legislation to "disappear" the gold cover for good, symbol of shame that it was becoming. On December 30, Johnson and his money advisors met at Cedar House, the guesthouse on the Johnson property, and tried, yet again, to figure out what to tell the public next about the gold.

The president presented the group's analyses to the public in a press conference in Johnson City early in the New Year. The government reckoned that American travelers spent about $2 billion abroad a year. Reduce spending abroad, and you minimized the trade shortfalls. American businesses must invest less, but travelers also had to change their behavior. The president wanted a two-year moratorium on tourism outside the Western Hemisphere. Business and labor, Johnson said, must try for their part to keep prices and wages down at home. "No challenge before business and labor is more important than this," Johnson intoned. If America could curtail spending abroad in this way, the Administration thought, there would be less cash for foreigners to redeem for gold. A halt to travel would do more for America's trade balances than any weird gold finds. Still, what Johnson suggested was so improbable that many Americans couldn't quite take it in. No trips to Europe? The idea was almost amusing. A new television talk-and-entertainment show, *The Smothers Brothers Comedy Hour*, was airing at the same time as *Bonanza*—Sunday at 9:00 p.m. Accepting the slot opposite the popular Western was considered suicidal—nine preceding shows had died after failing to match *Bonanza*. But the *Smothers Brothers* was itself a new kind of show: snarky, quietly suspicious of government, and full of irony. And it had recently, at least in one show, beaten *Bonanza* in the ratings, in good measure, commentators said, because Americans were tiring of escapist, sentimental shows. They wanted the truth. The *Smothers Brothers* now produced a skit seeking to characterize what went through the American mind when it learned it could not travel. A war wasn't worth a travel ban, the point was. The boys in Asia should all just come on home.

Desperate to win back faith in the dollar, Johnson spent time on the phone with Europeans, trying anything, everything, to calm the gold markets. The Administration even advertised successes of its gold prospecting, a break with heretofore quiet efforts on that front. The same week when Johnson demanded that Americans halt their travel to Paris and the Trevi Fountain in Rome, scientists at the Bureau of Mines reported they had discovered the most improbable source of gold yet: rubbish. The powdered waste that remained after trash was burned in the District of Columbia contained traces of gold worth $14 a ton of ash. Perhaps if you extracted gold from the fly ash of garbage nationwide, it wouldn't matter how many dollars foreign governments cashed in at the gold window.[12]

GOLD—NOT INTERNATIONAL gold, but *their* gold—had played a part in the American imagination since the nation's founding. The metal was part of the original bonanza, the one that drew Americans west. During the Great Depression, also citing technical reasons and an economic crisis, the federal government had banned the sale and purchase of gold for private citizens. The crisis of the Great Depression had passed. Another crisis, that of World War II, had also passed. Yet the gold buying ban had never been rescinded. When the government tried to mine gold in the 1960s, it was doing so mostly for itself. Americans who wanted gold had to confine their purchases to collectors' coins or to gold for industry, dentistry, and jewelry.

That they could not purchase gold and stash it in a drawer bothered citizens. Americans should be able to buy anything they felt like buying, just as they should travel to Europe when the mood seized them. The gold ban bugged them especially because they felt the hypocrisy. The federal government told them that the dollar was backed by gold. The gold was the theoretical evidence of the government's good faith: that it would not play tricks with people's money. Gold was, or could be, the safest check on inflation—but only if that backing was real, only if people could collect gold when they felt their dollars would lose value. And unlike Harold Wilson or William Martin, they could not. Like shotguns or taxes, gold was an irritant of a topic, guaranteed to trigger a reaction. *Bonanza*'s episode was far from the only show about gold produced in the 1960s. Movie producers had taken advantage of the irritation over gold a few years earlier when they made *Goldfinger*, the third James Bond film. At the start of the film, Bond knows nothing about gold. Then a murder gets his attention: a girl suffocates gruesomely after she is covered in gold paint. Soon Bond is pulled into an investigation of Auric Goldfinger, a sleazy foreign businessman who bears a marketable resemblance to a Nazi. Goldfinger is suspected of facilitating "unauthorized leakages" from the Bank of England into the gold market. Someone like Goldfinger, a non-American, can buy gold and then melt and smuggle it, selling it in Pakistan, at $100 an ounce, and tripling his money. Goldfinger plots to corner the world gold market, which means controlling, somehow or other, the millions of ounces at Fort Knox. Goldfinger's plan is to contaminate the Fort Knox gold with a dirty bomb so that his own personal gold hoard will be all the more valuable. Only Bond can make Fort Knox's cache safe. The movie was the first Bond film to become an international blockbuster. *Life* carried the image of the woman in gold on the cover of its November 2, 1964, issue, published just before Johnson's landslide. *Goldfinger* had become part of the American consciousness. Officials involved in the quiet federal gold hunt called it "Operation Goldfinger."

In the 1960s, President Johnson had already fiddled with money in a way that deepened citizens' suspicions. Dimes and quarters had been 90 percent silver. Half-dollars contained silver, too. With inflation, the silver in coins became more valuable than the face value of those coins. People melted the money down for the silver. Silver dollar coins became rare. The Administration countered by introducing new coins: silver-free dimes and quarters made of copper and nickel, and half-dollars with a reduced share of silver, only 40 percent.[13] People held on to the half-dollars. The Administration told the public that the earlier shortage of dimes was due to the proliferation of vending machines, which took dimes and quarters. The authorities also tried to explain away the popularity of the new half-dollar: John Kennedy was the president on its face. The reason for hoarding half-dollars was nostalgia for an assassinated president. Citizens took a different view: the coin changes by the government suggested that the government had less money for guns and butter than it pretended. Perhaps the government wasn't telling the entire truth about its resources. Perhaps it would drop its commitments to $35 an ounce, or close the gold window even to foreign governments. Perhaps it would stop insisting, as it did with the gold cover, that the dollar was still based in gold. Those who saved gold or silver preferred to be safe rather than sorry. If you were beginning to wonder about the future, and people were, then you did want something to stick under the mattress.

Two new philosophers on the scene were making the case for outright pessimism. The first was Garrett Hardin, the microbiologist who spoke of a "Tragedy of the Commons." Hardin sketched his picture again and again: Men grazed their own cattle without concern for the rest. The grass—or food, or energy, or clean air, or gold—disappeared. A government shepherd was therefore necessary. In offering his solution, collective cooperation, Hardin emphasized the imperative of rationing. Population control, he believed, was key. In fact, Hardin was known in California for preaching the right to abortion. In 1967, the California legislature had passed a law permitting abortion, though with heavy restrictions. An ambivalent Governor Reagan had signed the legislation. But Hardin sought further liberalization. "Abortion should be on demand, with no restrictions whatever," he said. America, and the world, could not afford to keep adding people.

The second scientist, a biologist at Stanford named Paul Ehrlich, went further than Hardin. Ehrlich's original passion had been entomology. His dissertation had dealt with the classification of butterflies ("Lepidoptera: Papilionoidea"). From entomology Ehrlich had moved to the study of oceans and a new field, ecology, developing a profound concern about the world's resources. Ehrlich took a position opposite to that of Jane Jacobs. People themselves were the problem. A trip to India had sealed his conviction that overpopulation, most vivid in the cities, was the world's greatest doom: "The street seemed alive with people. People eating, people watching, people sleeping. People visiting, arguing and screaming. People thrusting their hands through the taxi window, begging. People defecating and urinating."[14] Now, from his post in Palo Alto, Ehrlich was ringing a global alarm: the fight against famine was "already lost." India was the image of the world's future. As soon as the 1970s, hundreds of millions of people across the globe would starve to death, no matter what crash programs the United States or any other Western power might undertake. The only thing the United States might do now was set a new model for the smaller world. Ehrlich favored the creation of a federal population commission in the United States with a hefty fund for propaganda. He demanded a reworking of the United States tax code to eliminate "American tax laws so that they discourage rather than encourage reproduction." He proposed an increase in graduated rates for each additional child in a family. To discourage people from reproducing, Ehrlich even proposed a diaper tax. The United States was already ramping up its support for birth control programs abroad. Just five years before, birth control had been a minor part of the world of AID, the government's aid arm. More recently AID had set aside large amounts, $25 million for birth control and $2.5 million for Planned Parenthood, and even made foreign aid conditional on governments' institution of birth control programs.

Most Americans did not believe all the food in the world would run out—yet. But an alarm that had only recently begun to ring told them something was wrong and getting wronger by the day. The Consumer Price Index was rising 3 percent annually, significantly when compared with the old rate, which had hung somewhere between 1 and 1.5 percent. The recent economic boom, as Senator Russell Long of Louisiana pointed out, was not always a boom for the "little fellow." Inflation offset the gains of growth. The purchasing power of weekly wages for nonsupervisory workers had actually gone down in 1966 and 1967.[15] Perhaps the money trouble signified not a general shortage but simply that the government had grown too large for itself.

And by 1968, Johnson found, Congress was ready to challenge the Administration on money. There was, said Senator Alan Bible of one of the old gold states, Nevada, a "growing mistrust of currencies, and when such mistrust exists, people of the world will turn to minerals of value, namely gold and silver." From France, Charles de Gaulle kept up the mockery. In the United States, those away from government work were also frank. One economist in the private sector, a Wall Street forecaster named Alan Greenspan, revived the old, pre-Roosevelt point: a true gold standard was the only thing that could keep a government fiscally honest. Greenspan was a fan and friend of the libertarian philosopher Ayn Rand. In *The Objectivist*, Rand's periodical, Greenspan wrote that American overspending wasn't strength or a wartime phenomenon; it was predictable. A welfare state, which was what the United States had become, always overcommitted. "The welfare statists," Greenspan said, were always "quick to recognize that if they wished to retain power, the amount of taxation had to be limited and they had to resort to programs of massive deficit spending, i.e. they had to borrow money, by issuing government bonds. . . . Gold stands in the way of this insidious process. It stands as a protector of property rights. If one grasps this, one has no difficulty in understanding the statists' antagonism toward the gold standard."[16] Another expert safely out of reach of Johnson, at the National Bureau of Economic Research, was Arthur Burns. Greenspan was just one economist; Burns, who headed the NBER, was the voice of the entire economics profession, independent and proud. Back in the 1950s, he had warned that "the problems of inflation will return to haunt us." It had been Burns who back in 1960 had warned the presidential candidate Richard Nixon—correctly, as it turned out—that tight monetary policy at the Fed was slowing growth and could cost Nixon the election. Lately, Burns had been charging that Lyndon Johnson's brand of prosperity featured serious "perils of inflation." Burns, like Greenspan, pointed to the costs of the butter, not the guns. To attribute the recent large increases in the budget, and certainly future increases, to the costs of war, Burns said, frankly, was "a misconception." The anti-poverty programs were the problem—a good share of them, as Burns told the *New York Times*, were "pure waste."[17] Precisely because they were outsiders, Greenspan and Burns could speak truth to power. Johnson was trading in the Great Dollar for the Great Society, and it was a lousy trade.

Stripped of their silver trick, Americans looked around for other metals to hoard. South Africa, a country outside the Bretton Woods system, was producing a new gold coin. The Krugerrand, weight one ounce, would clearly retail above the official $35. Since it was a coin, it might, some Americans thought, qualify as a legal purchase under the numismatics exception. News reports that the rest of the world was snatching up gold more quickly than ever made the Krugerrand seem tempting. First City National Bank, an American bank that did enjoy an exceptional permission from the Treasury to deal in gold, estimated that $2.5 billion in gold had gone into private hands in 1967 worldwide, up $1 billion from the year earlier. Were all the gold hounds abroad and at home fools like Hoss Cartwright, small-time Goldfingers, or simply wise investors?

———

HIS MONEY troubles notwithstanding, January 1968 started out well for President Johnson. The recession he had feared would arrive this election year was staying away. Vietnam simmered, but so many good things were happening at home that it appeared American growth might indeed prevent a money crisis in an election year. That spring new industries, such as electronics, were doing better than before, in part thanks to the McNamara-scale orders placed by the Defense Department. Though Johnson could not take it all in, the wild growth in electronics that Gordon

Moore had predicted was already well in train. Failures in the electronics industries were dropping to a new low, and Noyce, Moore, and Andrew Grove, a third key player, would finally leave Fairchild, replicating their departure from William Shockley the decade before. Noyce founded a new company, which the men first called NM Electronics for Noyce and Moore. In contrast to their first fund-raising effort, this round proved a breeze. Every industry used computers now: a new advertisement campaign by Volkswagen, a competitor of Reuther's Big Three, announced that its Squareback station wagon now contained its own computer, which, as the ads said, "looks like a box, about a foot wide, and is connected to the engine in nine places." In a sad way, the electronics firms even profited from public concern about more riots. The U.S. Army would shortly establish an "emergency action headquarters" to coordinate riot management in up to twenty-five domestic hot spots simultaneously; the headquarters would use integrated circuit technology."[18] Computers were everywhere now. One headline described the moment as "the Age of Electro-Aquarius."

This mysterious, buzzing America was what Johnson proposed to highlight in his State of the Union address in mid-January. This time, the speech would also showcase the work of his first term and set the stage for a second. The speech would be seen or read abroad, and Johnson also wanted to address foreign nations, especially those where anti-U.S. sentiment was growing. That month in Ethiopia, for example, students in Addis Ababa hanged him in effigy. Hubert Humphrey, there for a speech, had to cancel it. Johnson determined to rise above the jabs, even when they came from his family. His daughter Lynda Bird, newly married, was engaging in a home front anti-Vietnam action of her own. On the day Johnson was to deliver his address, Lynda brought to the White House letters from servicemen's wives, including one from a young Texas woman whose husband died thirteen days before his tour was up. Johnson would have none of it. The president said what he wanted his ladies to do was get ready for the speech. They ought "to wear bright colors and have professional makeup jobs for tonight so they would look good."[19]

In the speech Johnson indeed proved energetic, thoughtful, and, true to his record, politically masterful. Those who listened for it could hear that each line or paragraph in the speech addressed the concerns of one interest group or another. One could almost visualize names of lobbies or key administration players penciled in parentheses at the end of a sentence. First, the president assured the country that in Vietnam "the enemy has been defeated in battle after battle" (General Westmoreland, soldiers, and veterans). America must understand, Johnson said, that the South Vietnamese had elected leaders who wanted to fight the fight against the North Vietnamese. Three elections had actually been held there in the past year, suggesting that not all the South Vietnamese were deserters (National Security Advisor Walt Rostow). Turning to domestic matters, Johnson pushed a new effort, the War on Crime (stray Republicans and conservative Democrats such as John Connally of Texas, who might abandon Johnson's crowd and turn to Alabama's George Wallace). Johnson asked for $1 billion again for model cities (Walter Reuther).

Johnson had recommended a 10 percent Vietnam surtax the year before and had gotten nowhere. Now he tried again, arguing for a 6 percent surcharge on both corporations and individuals, a concession to his bedside storyteller, William McChesney Martin.

Not willing to scale down, the president in the State of the Union called for an even larger building goal: six million new housing units in ten years (the new HUD director, Robert Weaver, and all the staff who would be going to the rising HUD building, plus mayors). Johnson also, in a warm gesture of bipartisanship, recognized Senator Charles Percy of Illinois, for picking up on the importance of home ownership. "We must make it possible for thousands of families to become homeowners, not rent payers" (a nod to home finance fans like Leonor Sullivan of Missouri, Percy, and Republican reformers, as well as perhaps some of the Black Power leaders, such as Nathan Wright of Newark).

The president took time to call for a highway beautification act (a hat tip to Lady Bird, who had indeed dressed in orange for the speech). He demanded new consumer protections, showing respect to fans of the corporate gadfly Ralph Nader and to his own hardworking aide, Joe Califano. Johnson asked for a multiyear program of new job creation, the one that would be outside Shriver's portfolio. Finally Johnson paid lip service to budget cuts (William McChesney Martin, Ways and Means chair Wilbur Mills). The president reminded the country that the war cost $25 billion a year. If Congress backed the tax increase, the economy would not overheat (Gardner Ackley, his economics advisor). The deficit might also narrow. Then the president could at least make a straight-faced claim that both the Great Society and the war in Vietnam could be paid for. "Guns and butter" was still possible.

On January 18, 1968, the day after the State of the Union, Mrs. Johnson received a reminder that many Americans could not agree. The First Lady hosted a "Women Do-ers" lunch at the White House, with fifty guests. Among them was the black star Eartha Kitt, whom Americans knew as an actress, singer, activist, and star on *Batman*, where Kitt played Catwoman. Johnson himself entered mid-lunch to address the group. The president spoke about expanding Social Security. Kitt spoke up, too, speaking not about entitlements, but noting that "because taxes are so heavy, both parents have to work." Johnson was taken aback, and announced he had just seen through the passage of a Social Security bill that allotted millions for day care. A "non sequitur" was how Kitt characterized Johnson's reply. Kitt so intimidated the president that he fled the room, saying such questions were "something for women to discuss here." By some accounts, Kitt went further, complaining that the best of the country rebelled, or smoked marijuana, or refused to go to school "because they're going to be snatched off from their mothers to be shot in Vietnam." To Kitt, the meeting felt staged and hypocritical. Lady Bird Johnson, stung, defended the Great Society: the war didn't "give us a free ticket not to try for better things such as against crime in the streets, better education, better health for our people." By the end of the luncheon, Lady Bird was near tears.[20]

As January moved to a close, Johnson and his team kept up the public front. Johnson introduced yet more ideas to improve America's trade balance: he would increase European tourism in the United States by waiving visa requirements. To do so was only fair—"35 other nations require no visas from American tourists," the president noted politely.

The more the Administration spoke of the postwar period, the more real it could become. Walt Rostow, the national security advisor, talked confidently about postwar agriculture in Vietnam, briefing a *New York Times* reporter about a new kind of farming "which would double the rice yields in Vietnam and would win the peace now that Americans had won the war." It certainly wasn't clear that Americans believed every optimistic detail anymore, but plenty still wanted to believe. In any case, Americans liked the upbeat tone. January polls showed Johnson gaining over Gene McCarthy of Minnesota, a surprise candidate, with a four-to-one lead. Johnson occasionally dropped hints that he would not run for a second term, but few in his entourage took the prospect seriously.

What was obvious, though, was that Johnson was enjoying the idea that his work would soon be history, memorialized at the Presidential Library in Austin. So was Mrs. Johnson, who on January 27 hosted Mrs. J. J. Pickle, the wife of a Texas congressman, in a private White House theater viewing of the old Kennedy favorite, *Camelot*.[21] The next morning, after sitting through Ted Kennedy on *Face the Nation* and Dr. Benjamin Spock, a fierce antidraft activist, on *Meet the Press*, the president and Mrs. Johnson took a late afternoon break to welcome the president of the University of Texas, Harry Ransom, and the architects of the Presidential Library.[22] It was time to decide what the museum might display in its exhibits, the architect, Gordon Bunshaft, said. In two or three weeks, after all, the builders would start in on the electrical work. Johnson told his guests he thought that the library could "perhaps" use a Treaty Room such as the one they happened to be sitting in. The president mentioned that he had signed twenty treaties in the past year: that kind of presidential work was never sufficiently honored. And what, in any case, those assembled wondered, should the ratio of domestic display to international be? Horace Busby, a former aide whom Johnson had pulled back to work with him that year, recommended that 80 percent of space be used to depict international achievements, "the President and the World." Johnson might prefer the Great Society to Southeast Asia, but Southeast Asia was part of the president's legacy.

The sooner South Vietnam could move to peaceful, legacy status, therefore, the better. In this election year, why not just declare victory and start building? In the third week of January, some two thousand Angelenos responded to a U.S. Agency for International Development advertisement recruiting civilians to work in Vietnam. Engineers, construction workers, teachers, and agricultural advisors would be paid in a range from $5,000 to $19,000, plus housing, health care, and a 25 percent hardship bonus. Once in Vietnam the workers would construct housing and roads, or improve public works. HUD Secretary Weaver had already suggested making Saigon one of Reuther's model cities. The South Vietnamese were involved in the AID project: "the effort has tremendous support among the local people," William Platt, AID's public affairs chief, explained. "We're looking for people who want to share in history," Platt said. The hiring was possible, the suggestion was, only because of progress in the war. Workers, the officials said, would "fill in areas not secure before, places where they might be able to build a schoolhouse now that won't be blown up."

But there was no place in Vietnam where you could build a schoolhouse and be sure it wouldn't be blown up. That became clear just a few days later, on January 30. A truce had been called in Vietnam, where citizens were preparing for the Lunar New Year, or as the Vietnamese called it, Tet. Johnson was sitting in a meeting with Walt Rostow and others when someone slipped Rostow a note. Rostow exited, and came back with a dramatic report: in Saigon, the presidential palace, military installations, and even the American embassy were under attack.[23] Mortar and rocket fire were waking South Vietnamese all over their country. The North Vietnamese were firing at not only Khe Sanh, but also the crucial Tan Son Nhut Air Base. Within hours what had happened was clear. Under cover of the truce for maximum surprise, the North Vietnamese were launching their largest ever incursion into South Vietnam, a countrywide series of attacks on more than one hundred towns and cities. The Viet Cong had blown a hole in the wall at the U.S. embassy and entered the grounds before being driven out, many hours later, at 9:00 a.m. Dead marines and Viet Cong lay about the embassy grounds. Instead of gradually powering down in Asia, the United States was finding itself in a fight for its life.

The offensive horrified Johnson. From his days on the Hill, the president recalled the French fiasco in Indochina, Dien Bien Phu. The humiliation had yielded the ultimate political consequence in France, the collapse of the government and the ouster of Prime Minister Joseph Laniel. At the time, Johnson the senator had also assigned blame to the United States, saying, "It is apparent that American foreign policy has never in all its years suffered such a stunning reversal."[24] This time, it was the United States, not France, that the press would blame first. And the air base at Khe Sanh was already being compared to the French catastrophe. As Johnson had told the chairman of the Joint Chiefs of Staff, General Earle Wheeler: "I don't want any damn Dinbinphoo."[25] Now his critics, including Richard Nixon, leapt all over Johnson. And the truth could not be denied; a Dien Bien Phu would certainly force a change in the foreign policy exhibit at the Johnson Presidential Library.

On January 31, as attacks in Vietnam continued, Johnson spoke with McNamara, who first briefed him on a submarine that had in recent hours barely escaped a nuclear accident. As a result of his preoccupation with that incident, McNamara said, disconcertingly, that on this day, he was "really not up to date on Southeast Asia." The new attacks, McNamara did allow, showed that the North Vietnamese Army and Vietnam had "more power than some credit them with." But the attacks also represented "a maximum effort" for the Northerners—this was all they could do. McNamara predicted that the United States would inflict heavy losses. Others noted that the Tet cloud had a silver lining. For so long Johnson and his generals had wanted to smoke out the North Vietnamese guerrilla, engage him in battle. Now that he was out, the United States, must, as General Westmoreland would put it, "seize the opportunity to crush him."

By and large, editors at major papers had heretofore supported Johnson in the war. But they did not know what to make of what was instantly known as the Tet Offensive. Often, the reporters on the field were greater opponents of the war than their editors at home. In those same first days of fighting, the head of South Vietnam's National Police, General Nguyen Ngoc Loan, executed a Viet Cong soldier gang-style with a pistol. The scene was damning: a South Vietnamese, in fatigues, firing a Smith and

Wesson revolver at a handcuffed man in a civilian's plaid shirt on a Saigon street. Eddie Adams of the AP caught the execution on film in a series of shots. The *New York Times* received the photos around 4:00 p.m. on February 1. The editors would obviously use the execution photo on page one.[26] What kind of thugs were these South Vietnamese, anyhow? One photo—the very moment when Loan shot—seemed to demonstrate all that was wrong with the U.S. decision to ally with South Vietnam. An editor at the *Times*, Theodore Bernstein, thought that it was also the paper's duty to supply perspective. The Viet Cong man was alleged to have himself killed the wife and six children of a South Vietnamese officer. Bernstein decided his paper should publish the Loan execution photo together with another photo: that of a South Vietnamese officer carrying the body of one of his children, slain by North Vietnamese. Nonetheless, it was the former photo that other papers made famous: an icon of North Vietnamese martyrdom. The tide of opinion was turning.

In the days after the attacks the question arose: should the United States continue to send more troops? McNamara was set against that— General Westmoreland already had more than 500,000, ten times the number just a few years before. McNamara was indeed on the way out, and Johnson no longer trusted him, but for now he was the one Johnson had to talk to. Johnson, the commander in chief, had to handle the military challenge but also the political one: the same day the *New York Times* ran the photo of the execution, it carried news that Richard Nixon, the former vice president, had announced his candidacy for president. George Romney of Michigan was running, too, under an irritating copycat motto: "Great for '68." Alabama governor George Wallace was running on a segregationist platform and on behalf of a new party, the American Independent Party. With the Tet Offensive in train, McCarthy, more antiwar than Johnson, Humphrey, or even RFK, was sure to gain in popularity, whatever the earliest 1968 polls had said.

If Vietnam had been in the news during the winter, now, with Tet, Vietnam *owned* the news. Walter Cronkite, the television anchor, turned against Johnson. So did others in the news media. On February 7, the Associated Press correspondent Peter Arnett quoted a United States major on the attack on Ben Tre, the capital city in Ben Tre province. The major, Arnett reported, said that "it became necessary to destroy the town in order to save it." The sheer absurdity of the line captured the U.S. effort in Vietnam; Arnett's quote was repeated throughout the United States. Several days later Americans for Democratic Action, a liberal group, showily endorsed McCarthy. This was another slap from the Kennedy crowd—Arthur Schlesinger, a Kennedy speechwriter, was active in the ADA. Walter Reuther was one of the ADA's founders. Reuther criticized the ADA for picking a candidate but did not throw his weight behind Johnson. Nine days into the Tet Offensive, Robert Kennedy spoke up. The senator attacked United States Vietnam policy personally. It was time for the truth, Kennedy said: "a military victory is not within sight or around the corner." Military victory might never come.

Johnson for his part had to worry about not only the traitorous press, the candidates' comments, or his troops' progress, but also his budget and his currency. He was now seeing or speaking to the treasury secretary, the Treasury staff, or Martin of the Fed nearly every day. That week the Federal Reserve reported gold reserves valued at well below $12 billion, after a $100 million loss from the week before. The ratio of gold reserves to federal reserve notes was down to 27.5 percent, indeed close to the legal requirement of 25 percent.[27] Wilson of Britain had finally won the favor he sought, a state visit, and arrived February 8. True to form, Johnson worked hard to find common ground with a guest, even one whom his staff knew the president didn't like. Johnson respected the English commentator Barbara Ward. So, the president knew, did Wilson. Johnson shared with Wilson a deeply pessimistic memo on the future of the world that Ward had sent him. Ward warned that the world economic picture reflected "dangerous overtones of the 1929/1931 disaster." She said that dislocation of world trade—an event that could follow the breakup of the gold exchange system—could trigger a depression and mass unemployment. In addition, suggested Ward, "the Russians might scent the long-hoped-for failure of capitalism and revert to hard-line adventurism and hostility." Somewhere between a visit for the prime minister and Johnson with the Boy Scouts (scouting had gotten its start in Britain), lunch, and a state dinner, the president received two other visitors: Henry Fowler of the Treasury and the chairman of the House Ways and Means Committee, Wilbur Mills.[28] They spoke off the record.

Mills was now key. By this point the Administration and the Fed didn't have many weapons left in their gold kit. Johnson needed to see a tax hike through now, a signal of fiscal probity that might stem the gold outflow. For this cause Mills, Johnson's fellow Southerner, was the necessary ally. Mills, like Johnson and William Martin, had been around a long time. The newspapers and TV announcers so routinely referred to him as "the powerful chairman of the Ways and Means Committee, Wilbur Mills" that "powerful" had become part of his name. Mills's power was genuine, not only because of the post but because of of his peers' respect: "If Wilbur insisted that the tax moon is made of green cheese, most folks in the House would nod their heads dutifully," one colleague said. Mills had initially opposed Medicare and blocked proposals within his committee. But the 1964 election had loaded his committee with so many Medicare advocates that they could outvote him. Then, rather than face humiliation, Mills had turned around and let Medicare through.[29]

But as had been the case with Dirksen and "right to work," Johnson was now finding that an old ally would not automatically back him in a new project. Because all tax legislation originated in Mills's committee, the Vietnam surcharge also had to be Mills's baby. Mills must not only bless, but also write and steward, Johnson's tax increase bill if the increase was to become law. Mills had already been showing resistance to the tax hike, even though Johnson had put the familiar squeeze on him. In Mills's case Johnson sent both Secretary of State Dean Rusk and Treasury Secretary Fowler all the way to Arkansas to meet Mills at the Coachman's Inn in Little Rock to try to sway him into support for a tax increase. Mills hadn't budged.[30]

Johnson understood Mills's hesitation.[31] The costs of the previous legislation Johnson had pushed Mills into had already far outrun the projections. Budget officials had predicted that Medicaid, for example, would cost less than $400 million in fiscal 1967. Instead it had cost $1.1 billion. To a man like Mills, whatever happened in London seemed distant. Mills wanted Johnson to show he could cut the budget. It was guns or butter. Mills told *U.S. News & World Report*, "I just do not believe our economy can tolerate expansion of nonessential expenditure programs." Recently Mills had berated the Administration for demonstrating "no change in attitude toward government spending." Where was William McChesney Martin? The Ways and Means chairman's attitude mirrored the Fed chair's: let some other guy take care of your gold problem.

Johnson's aide Joe Califano could see the president was wearying, and tried to protect him. In late February a long-awaited report on civil disorders, from a commission led by the former governor of Illinois, Otto Kerner, was ready. Califano peeked at the pages and saw that Kerner declared that America was "moving toward two societies, one black, one white—separate and unequal." This effectively damned Johnson's civil rights laws and War on Poverty as failures. The report could devastate the president. Califano, who in the old days would have run to the president with the report, held back for a few hours. Johnson was so busy. On the last day of the month, February 29, sterling sank to its lowest level in two months, practically guaranteeing that Martin and Johnson would have to do something more to protect the United States.

The same day, a mishap captured the sense that Murphy's Law had spread from Los Angeles across the land and taken over every corner of Washington. It was McNamara's retirement day. Johnson went over to the Pentagon for the ceremony for the long-serving defense secretary. McNamara and Johnson and their entourage entered an elevator to ride up to McNamara's office. But the elevator halted between the third and fourth floors. A sergeant in the car called maintenance on the elevator phone. "Do you have a full load?" maintenance asked. "We sure do," the sergeant responded.[32] But there was no movement. The elevator, the men realized, was Number 13, and it was carrying 13 passengers. Could something so barbaric as luck play a role at the Pentagon? The capacity limit on the cab read: 15.

The president made a joke: "This is an indication of how much the Defense Department thinks of you," he told McNamara. "They're trying to keep you until the last possible moment." Then, the men waited.

Inside the closed elevator, the president and McNamara could hear the footsteps of officers in the hall who were randomly shouting the news of the snafu. Twelve minutes elapsed. One of the men outside finally used the president's speech book and notes to pry the doors open. Then the men managed to widen the opening some more. Someone handed a chair down to Johnson, and the leader of the free world stepped on it and was pulled out of the elevator.

In early March, the dollar joined Vietnam in the headlines. A gold rush was sweeping Europe. In London demand for gold in the private market increased by ten times, to $200 million a week. Foreign governments were cashing in their dollars for gold at America's gold window at a rate of more than $300 million a week. But Mills, stalwart, continued to resist the tax increase. The congressman was telling others that he just didn't believe anyone was clever enough "to fine tune the economy."[33]

Johnson sensed Mills might not yield. Mills was taking advice from Arthur Burns, normally a Republican guru. Later, Mills told a story about an encounter at the White House during these tax battles. Mills obeyed a summons to the White House, arriving to discover other House committee chairmen already present. Johnson had decided to put the pressure on for his Vietnam surcharge. As Mills told it, Johnson went around the room, starting with the Appropriations chairman, George Mahon of Texas. "George, you are with me on my tax proposal?" Mahon: "Yes, Mr. President." Then one by one, Johnson asked the other chairmen, including Wright Patman of Banking and Currency and William Poage of Agriculture, if they were with him. Each man told the president he was with his chief executive on the tax surcharge. When Johnson got to Mills, the president put the squeeze on: "Now you see where you are, you are alone." Mills did not lose his nerve. "Yes, I see where I am. I am in the wrong place!"[34]

And Mills was not Johnson's only problem when it came to the budget. Just as the press had turned against him on Vietnam, now it was turning against him on gold, making Martin's hold-tight position of $35 an ounce harder to support. Even influential bankers—not mere fringe Westerners—were beginning to utter heresy, proposing that the United

States consider devaluing its most important symbol, the dollar, by raising the price of gold. The *Wall Street Journal* suggested the Administration was being "rigid." The *Journal* quoted economists from two New York banks, Chemical and First National City. Martin did his part by relenting and leading the Fed in raising the interest rate yet again. But the gold exit did not stop. On March 7, Martin canceled his appointments and got on a plane to Switzerland. At a meeting of central bankers there, he won support for sustaining coordination among the central banks to keep the gold price at $35 an ounce. Martin himself believed the cooperation among gold nations was nearly dead, absent an extraordinary event such as Congress passing the Vietnam surtax. Only confidence for confidence's sake could sustain them. As the English central banker Sir Leslie O'Brien said to Martin's colleague Charles Coombs, the art of central banking was to figure out "how to exude confidence without positively lying."[35] The Federal Reserve report that the *Journal* published on March 8 showed the key gold–dollar ratio still hanging disconcertingly close to the 25 percent line.

March 12 brought the New Hampshire primary, the first test of all the polls Johnson had been prepping for. Romney, "Great for '68," had dropped out for now. Robert Kennedy was not on the ballot. But Richard Nixon and Nelson Rockefeller of New York were competing hard on the Republican side, foreshadowing what Johnson would have to confront in the general election. Johnson chose not to place his name in the running, a move that emerged as a mistake when it became clear McCarthy was pouring resources into the Granite State. For McCarthy the number one issue was Vietnam, but he wrapped the dollar and inflation into his pitch. "There is uneasiness about the economy, there is uneasiness about the dollar, and there is uneasiness about what is happening to a whole generation of Americans," McCarthy told a crowd in Claremont, New Hampshire.

McCarthy, Johnson could see, got out the youth vote. Young men even shaved their beards and cut their hair, so that they were "Clean for Gene" and could make a good impression in stolid New Hampshire. Entering the primary at all was optional, and Johnson had not campaigned, counting on the party to put him forward late in the game should he run, and afterward at the convention. Johnson's supporters printed up pledge cards, asking voters to give their names and indicate whether they were Democrats. The cards included this line: "As an expression of your support this card will be forwarded to President Johnson and the White House in Washington, D.C."

On the evening of primary day, March 12, Johnson busied himself looking for support in another area—a vote on the gold cover, the requirement that the government maintain the equivalent of 25 percent of currency outstanding in gold. Again, he turned to Everett Dirksen. LBJ, for the moment still captured by William Martin, told Dirksen that the United States had to stick with $35 an ounce, but had to quit "just being the tools and the stooges of a bunch of goddamn speculators." The least damaging move for the moment was to abolish the gold cover and the legislature proposed that. If there was no gold cover rule, then America could not break it. After all, Johnson told Dirksen, "we just can't make 'em make boobs of us."[36] Johnson concluded with a plea to Dirksen to hurry on the gold cover bill. When it came to the dollar, Americans were living on borrowed time, Johnson said, "Please get that gold [bill] quick as you can."

The next day, as Johnson hunted for other votes to end the gold cover, he learned how much his incumbent's arrogance had cost him in New Hampshire. Righteous New Englanders, who prized their independence above all, felt Johnson took them for granted with those cards. Gene McCarthy called the Johnson pledge cards "an intrusion into a free Democratic process." McCarthy also noted, correctly enough, that the effort for the president concentrated on "the implication that the opposition to the president's policies is somehow disloyal." Johnson did garner a plurality of the votes, 49.6 percent. But McCarthy took 41.9 percent, a stunning tally for a newcomer. In addition, McCarthy claimed twenty out of twenty-four delegates.

Even as Johnson digested the primary reports, the gold cover debate proved treacherous for him. Senator Jacob Javits of New York, a moderate Republican who actually supported the abolition of the gold cover, couldn't resist taunting Johnson about the illogic of Martin's $35-or-die position. The gold in federal coffers was down to 340 million ounces, or $11.88 billion at the $35 exchange rate. William McChesney Martin might resemble George Bailey in *It's a Wonderful Life*, handing out ingots instead of Bailey's dollars through a teller window to save his bank. But the gaggle of foreign treasury secretaries, arbitraging investors in Dubai or India, and anonymous parties who were cashing dollars in for gold bore no resemblance to the responsive, lovable community in Bailey's Bedford Falls. The *Wall Street Journal* had reported just recently that "hoarders" in India would pay up to $85 an ounce.[37] If there was more gold available, the foreign governments and the investors behind them would just present more dollars to redeem that cheap gold. "At some point," Javits warned, "the United States will either have no more gold with which to buy dollars presented by foreign central banks or will decide that the remaining gold stock will have to be husbanded as a strategic reserve." If you abolished the gold cover rule, you abolished a meter that signaled your failure. If you closed the gold window, you abolished the most important meter.

Members of both parties used the gold emergency to mock the president over a war they now opposed. George McGovern of South Dakota piled on, listing the profits of big corporations on the war—Colt Industries made a 1,400 percent profit on M16 rifles in just one deal. McGovern announced he opposed not only the 10 percent surtax, but also the taxation of tourists abroad. To suggest that a tax on regular people when they traveled would help the situation was like "trying to repair a leaky dam with a Band-Aid," McGovern said. Lifting the gold cover, McGovern said, would not build confidence in America, as Martin claimed. It would "further open up our dwindling reserves to foreign claimants."

The credibility gap on gold widened along with the gap over Vietnam. By March 14 the trading in London was so wild, and depleting the UK coffers so seriously, that Sir Leslie O'Brien of the Bank of England gave up pretenses. O'Brien called his U.S. counterparts to talk about closing London's financial markets. The United States agreed it was a necessary step. In London, officials would shortly rouse the queen out of her bed to declare the markets closed. Martin and Fowler returned to the White

House to confront Johnson: America and Britain were losing *all* their gold. Johnson agreed this was an emergency. Removing the gold cover was not enough by itself. It was time to show the country that Johnson, too, could stand for austerity. The queen declared the markets closed for what would turn out to be a number of days.

What brought the story home to Johnson was not bankers' hysteria but anecdotes from those American tourists who were risking his disapproval and venturing abroad. European banks were now swimming in dollars and could absorb no more. The banks and the hotels were turning away Americans who wanted to exchange their dollars for local currencies. Even at the George V, one of Paris's premier hotels, management refused to accept traveler's checks in dollars and convert them to francs for anyone but hotel guests. At London's Heathrow airport, banks limited the amount visitors could exchange for sterling to $60. The picture jarred Johnson. It was one thing for the mighty U.S. government to counsel, or even order, citizens to curtail travel spending; it was another for foreign hotelkeepers or governments to do so. "He was scared almost out of his body," Wilbur Mills later remembered.[38]

By March 15, the political news Johnson had feared arrived. Robert Kennedy was indeed running for president. The president took in the fact but had little time for reflection: in the afternoon he conducted a two-hour review of the Vietnam situation with his defense team, including the new defense secretary, Clark Clifford. Next he spoke with Secretary Fowler twice and Bill Martin once. The following day, Kennedy made his formal announcement. Johnson worked at completing the new dollar rescue plan. Congress passed, and Johnson signed, the legislation removing the gold cover, that shameful evidence of the government's inability to show that its money was worth gold. On March 15, the *Wall Street Journal*'s "Federal Reserve Report" carried, as it had every week, a line reporting the ratio of gold reserves to Federal Reserve notes. On that date the ratio stood at 26.4 percent, close to the statutorily required 25 percent and down from the 27.5 percent of just a week earlier. In the next week's "Federal Reserve Report," however, the "ratio" line carried no numbers, just a series of ellipses. That looked like editors were trying to figure out what to do. The *Journal* of March 29 dropped the ratio line from the "Federal Reserve Report" altogether. It was as if the ratio had never existed.

Yet the gold crisis still refused to end. Martin and the others worked on a new plan to prevent further runs triggered by private investors, or even by mischievous governments. They would seal off the gold that governments held, so that the governments in the gold-exchange system could trade only among themselves, and at $35 an ounce. Goldfingers or rogue governments could never touch that central bank gold. Therefore, the Goldfingers would never get America's final $10 billion. Under Martin's plan, the private markets would continue to trade the metal, however its price fluctuated, but entirely separately. This two-tier system was, like the silvery coins without the silver, or the gold cover abolition, a form of denial. If no one but reliable partners who depended on you for their military defense could buy or sell your gold, then you could pretend forever, or so the hope was, that $35 really could buy an ounce of gold. Johnson was Martin's fifth, his last, president. This was not how the storyteller hoped to go out.

The next Democratic primary, in Wisconsin, would take place on April 2. One of the shocks the president had to address by then was how well Gene McCarthy's line about "uneasiness" had resonated, and how much it reflected not only the war but pessimism over America's domestic prospects. Martin's two-tier pretense wasn't holding up. The disparity in the price of "free gold" on the private market on the one hand and Martin's official $35-or-die price on the other was a quantification of international distrust of the Administration's rosy claims about the American budget and growth prospects. In the monetary turmoil, that private market gold price had risen on March 18 to $44 an ounce, $9 above the official $35 price. The $9 gap was the equivalent of the Vietnam body count. You couldn't deny it. The U.S. currency and its economy were worth less than the Administration said.

Seen through the unforgiving eye of international markets, the resemblances between the United States and Johnson's nemesis, Britain, were also becoming undeniable. Britain had nationalized health care, and now, between Medicare and Medicaid, the United States was moving in the same direction. Britain was loading heavy taxes on its voters; the United States was doing so, too. Britain's unions were pricing British products out of world markets; Walter Reuther and Henry Ford II were pricing the American auto out of markets, too. Financial data provided further evidence for this conclusion, with bond yields up and the Dow Jones Industrial Average even lower than at the moment of the British crisis. Markets, like Tom Hayden and the SDS students, were beginning to grow impatient with the careful line Cold Warriors drew between social democracy on the one hand—necessary to keep Western Europe stable, possible as a goal for the Land of the Free—and true socialism: the kind that enabled tyranny from Moscow. One set of countries might be democracies, the other dictatorships. But the price of the compromise, social democracy, was not low.

Even Johnson, Great Society father, was coming to see that. In the days before the Wisconsin primary, he busied himself stumping for the dollar. The president traveled to Minnesota, McCarthy's home territory, and made his frankest pitch yet. Johnson used a term that sounded odd coming from him: "austerity." "I ask you," he said in Minneapolis, "to join in a program of national austerity to ensure that our economy will prosper and our fiscal position will be sound." When Johnson left the venue of his speech, the Leamington Hotel, he was jeered by protesters carrying McCarthy signs. ("Beards, etc.," Johnson's stenographer noted drily in the daily presidential diary.) After boarding Air Force One, the president immediately phoned the treasury secretary. Taking the pulse of the international economy had become as obsessively necessary as checking the progress in Vietnam.

Martin for his part also traveled for the Fed into enemy territory, in his case Reuther's Michigan. The Federal Reserve chairman told the Detroit Economic Club that the dollar was stronger than gold, and the dollar rested "on the resources and productivity of the U.S. per se." But while nowhere near the histrionic Paul Ehrlich and his talk of a population bomb, the professional optimist Martin now also spoke in sober tones. He told the crowd he shared the president's desire for a Great Society. But he also offered a few lines of wrenching doubt. "I have no idea whether the president is going to escalate or de-escalate in Vietnam . . . but from past experience I know every time they've told us defense expenditures are leveling off, they've leveled off for a little while and then they've gone up. The point I'm making here is in a period when we've had four years of remarkably good business, the deficit has been getting progressively worse." Martin offered a stunning conclusion about the American national character: "We don't have the self-discipline," he told his audience, "we don't have the capacity to govern ourselves in such a way that we can be great."[39]

As the month of March ended, Johnson worked the phones, using any opportunity to gather political information—or to assign political work. On March 23 he spoke with Labor Secretary Willard Wirtz about the problem with "these liberals," the dissidents within the Democratic Party who were lining up with Kennedy or McCarthy. "We're worried about Walter Reuther," Johnson said.[40] Reuther's endorsement for Johnson still had not come. It might never come. The UAW head had told Johnson he would do "what's right." But of course, Johnson said, "what he thinks 'what's right' and what I think 'what's right' is a different thing." Reuther's ally Jack Conway was already advising Bobby Kennedy. Should Reuther get a phone call from the Johnson team? Wirtz asked. That had already been tried, Johnson said. "The vice president called him and pled with him, I called him and pled with him." Johnson told Wirtz he'd been plenty solicitous, wiring Reuther when his brother and father passed away recently. Reuther owed him another term, Johnson said. "We're entitled to this. We're entitled to a second term." Even Bobby Kennedy acknowledged what Johnson had done for Reuther's causes. Reuther made excuses by hiding behind his board of directors. "I have done every damn thing he ever asked me, without any question," said Johnson. Reuther should call his board of directors and fix this up. If Reuther didn't cooperate, they'd all, Johnson said, have "Dick Nixon president just as sure as you're sitting here." Johnson told Wirtz that Reuther should know "we're trying to avoid cutting these human programs." There was not another thing in the world that Bobby Kennedy could do for Reuther, Johnson said, "that we're not already doing." Why should Reuther change horses in mid-race? At one point Johnson turned menacing, telling Wirtz that Reuther "must not murder us and if he does murder us by God he can expect an eye for an eye." Though he had always suspected Reuther, now that betrayal was undeniable, the president could scarcely believe it.

At the end of March, Johnson received a dark report from his advisors on Vietnam. The president scheduled a TV speech for the evening of Sunday, March 31. For a Texan, even a Texan president, to preempt *Bonanza* was a bold move: this had to be an important speech. On March 27, he took Califano and another aide, Harry McPherson, aback by asking what would happen if he didn't run. Robert Kennedy would get the nomination, Califano said—not Humphrey. "What's wrong with Bobby?" Johnson queried. It was common knowledge that Johnson detested Bobby Kennedy. But now Johnson told Califano that Bobby might perpetuate his legacy best: "Bobby would keep fighting for the Great Society programs." And Kennedy might see the war differently if he sat in the Oval Office. On Sunday, as the president worked on drafts of his speech, the Johnsons' daughter Lynda arrived to visit them. She had just dropped her husband, Chuck Robb, off at Camp Pendleton for a tour of duty in Vietnam. The Johnsons were shocked at Lynda's appearance: tired, thin. Now it was Lynda's turn to jab at her father. "Why do we have to go to Vietnam?" she asked.[41] Johnson replied with a fixed stare. Lady Bird later recalled that she had not seen that stare since the days when Johnson was mourning the passing of his mother.[42]

In the speech, Johnson reiterated an earlier offer to stop the bombardment of North Vietnam. This time, Johnson also ordered a halt to attacks on both North and South Vietnam, except in areas where the military buildup threatened American and South Vietnamese populations. All in all, Johnson was stopping attacks in a large area, covering about 90 percent of the population. To many people, the news came as its own bombshell. Next, the president spoke of his frustration with Congress—the deficit was widening, and the gold was draining away because Congress would not raise taxes. Yet Congress—again, the unspoken name in parenthesis was there, and this time it was Wilbur Mills—ignored presidential requests. The result of Congress's failure to suppress demand with tax hikes was clear to all: "prices and interest rates have risen." Toward the speech's end, Johnson reminded the country that he had served thirty-seven years in Washington. He wanted to be a nonpartisan leader in this difficult time, even though 1968 was an election year. And then Johnson dropped his real bombshell: he would not seek reelection.

Johnson was scarcely alone for the rest of that evening. The president's appointment diary records that he was curious about the reaction to his bombshells. His family trailing behind him, Johnson went "into his little room to watch all three networks." The president donned a blue turtle-neck to relax. He ate, talked on the phone, and asked the staff about his chocolate dessert—was it dietetic? Lynda Bird made a joke relating to the New Year's travel proscriptions: "Can I go to England now?" Lynda told her mother it might be time to visit the Greek isles. Johnson held a press conference, and then had guests over to the White House, including his friend Arthur Krim, the Democratic National Committee chairman.

Johnson's staff, in shock at his news, recorded in the presidential diary that the president spoke to Krim about Vietnam and the U.S. troop presence in Asia. "I have 525,000 men whose very lives depend on what I do, and I can't worry about the primaries." The calls continued nonstop. Sargent Shriver telephoned the president that night but did not get through. Wirtz did get through, at 10:26. Wirtz asked Johnson whether he might reverse, and run after all. Johnson told Wirtz the announcement was "not reversible." There had been many factors driving Johnson's announcement, Vietnam prominent among them. But just as important was the narrowing of the prospects for the federal government's mighty domestic undertaking. Johnson, a lifelong politician, thought in the government framework. Government had to be great to make the Great Society. What if, in the long run, government could not be great? The president would let the others sort out the details. When it came to his own participation, Johnson had made his decision. If not great, then not at all.

9

Reuther and the Intruder

AUGUST 1968 TO DECEMBER 1968

Guns: 9.1% of GDP
Butter: 5.6% of GDP
Dow Jones Industrial Average: 894

*We need not be concerned. We need only continue as al-
ways, making our improvements.*
                    —Kiichiro Toyoda

On August 27, 1968, executives from the Japanese auto company Toyota
took space at the New York Hilton to present to the American market a
new car: the Corolla.[1] Until recently Toyota had ranked only twenty-first
among importers, and was known best in the States for a four-wheel-drive
jeep derivative called the Land Cruiser. In 1965, the company had introduced a small car, the Corona, and now it was offering the even smaller
Corolla. Toyota hoped to sell eighty thousand cars in the United States
that year, or about one-fourth of what General Motors sold in a month.[2]
Improbably, the two-door Corolla sedan was only 153 inches long, more
than two feet shorter than autos in the compact class, the Big Three's
smallest. The Corolla featured a four-cylinder engine that could hit 75
miles an hour, which meant Americans would find it possible. Most important, though, was the price: the Corolla retailed for $1,666, slightly
below a comparable model, the Volkswagen Beetle. What mattered even
more was that the Corolla's $1,666 price stood well below that for the
Rambler American (the update of George Romney's old project), which
sold for $1,946; or the Ford Falcon, priced at $2,252.

All news about the auto industry mattered to Walter Reuther. But in late August 1968, Reuther did not have time to give the arrival of one small car on the scene his attention. The week found the union leader at the Democratic National Convention, ensconced in a twenty-fifth-floor suite at the Sheraton Chicago on North Michigan Avenue.

What mattered for the moment was not the gap in price between an American auto and an auto from a minor importer. The gap that mattered was the sudden gap in the polls between Richard Nixon's Republicans and Reuther's own Democrats. The same day that the papers carried the news of the little Corolla, they reported that Nixon led Hubert Humphrey and Gene McCarthy in the polls by six points. That gap might only widen during the Democratic convention, especially as the party debated the Vietnam War.

It was a different convention from the one Reuther had imagined. Six months ago he might have pictured spending time with Robert Kennedy, helping Kennedy himself run for election—that was what Mildred Jeffrey, his colleague, would have liked. At the very least he might be helping Kennedy scout for 1972, or making phone calls from his suite to Martin Luther King. One year ago he would have imagined chatting about strategy with his brother Roy. Two years ago Reuther might have dreamed that the convention would be congratulating the trade union movement for its early recognition that successful democratic revolution was possible even behind the Iron Curtain. Three years ago Reuther would have hoped for a dignified convention, a salubrious shift resulting from the passage of Johnson's, and Reuther's, Voting Rights Act. Four years ago, he would have expected to be working with the AFL-CIO. Five years ago Reuther would have imagined his SDS students working the convention for the UAW's candidate, placing telephone calls and knocking on hotel doors.

None of that was possible now. Reuther's two great allies were gone. In April, King had gone to Memphis to encourage striking sanitation workers, and a gunman had assassinated the great leader at his motel. In June, the same night he won the California and South Dakota primaries, Senator Kennedy had walked with Reuther's colleague Paul Schrade into the kitchen of the Ambassador Hotel in Los Angeles, and an assassin had shot both men in the head. Schrade was recovering, but Kennedy had not made it. Valentine and Roy Reuther were also gone. In Europe, the Soviets had marched in and stamped down the Czech revolution, making a mockery of Victor Reuther's assurances that, this time, Moscow would not crack down. There would be no great AFL-CIO-UAW teamwork— Reuther had led the UAW out of the AFL-CIO and joined forces with his old rivals, the Teamsters. Blacks representing Mississippi were indeed seated at the convention—they included Aaron Henry, Charles Evers, and Julian Bond just as Johnson and Reuther had promised each other in 1964 and 1965. But few reporters seemed to care, or want to praise the progressive Democratic Party for its hard-won governance changes.[3] And the "SDS kids," as Reuther referred to Tom Hayden, Rennie Davis, and the others, weren't inside the hotel lobbying politely. The UAW's former protégés were twenty-four floors down on the street taunting the Chicago police and, for all Reuther knew, throwing the election to Richard Nixon.

Still, unlike Lyndon Johnson, Reuther did not intend to give up. Reuther still wanted to "put the world together," as he said. And Reuther believed that if he, the UAW, and the Democrats could just get through the convention, they could edge Nixon out in November. Reuther had always told his membership that they had to remember the ballot along with the breadbox. Whatever a union won at the negotiating table could be taken away at an election. So Reuther stayed at the convention, strategizing victory for his union and his party. The obvious step would be to throw his weight behind Hubert Humphrey, a natural for the UAW. After all, this was the same Humphrey who had fought for repeal of the "right to work" loophole, the same Humphrey who had traveled to Sweden with Reuther to spend time with Sweden's Tage Erlander at the socialist summit.[4] George Meany of the AFL-CIO was already campaigning for Humphrey, publicly rating Humphrey "not 90 percent perfect, not 98 percent perfect, but 100 percent perfect." But Reuther believed that for the Democrats to have a chance in the general election, they would have to call for peace in a unified fashion. Reuther was therefore withholding official UAW endorsement of Humphrey for the moment, insisting that Humphrey approve a "peace plank" that the UAW and its allies put to a vote on the convention floor. Reuther even publicly needled the vice president on Vietnam, "pushing him hard" as Reuther told a reporter. Reuther looked ahead to future election cycles. From his tower at the Sheraton Chicago, a columnist wrote, Reuther "could see 1972." Reuther himself wasn't talking about it, but UAW's staff and allies were quietly using this convention to try out the idea of the next Kennedy, the Massachusetts senator Ted Kennedy, as a candidate.

In addition, even while still at the convention, Reuther was maneuvering to unify his own UAW, an institution more troubled than it had been in decades. Many of the younger members no longer wanted to belong to a union that supported the Administration on the war. Some even sympathized with the rabble in Grant Park. Many of the Teamsters, by contrast, found Reuther fatally dovish. Some of the UAW membership had had enough of Reuther's civil rights drive, and were turning, in disconcerting numbers, to a third-party candidate, the segregationist governor of Alabama, George Wallace. Generally membership in unions, Reuther's included, was not keeping pace with the population. Young people, in or out, generally didn't seem to *get* the union. When they discovered the deductions for union dues on their first pay stubs, youth of all backgrounds asked, "What for?" Union institutions and the union lexicon—"Shop steward," "checkoff," "14(b)," "NLRB," "wildcat"—did not always interest workers born after Reuther had fought off Ford's thugs at the Battle of the Overpass in 1937. They did not respond to attempts at updating, or marketing, such as Sarge Shriver's hapless TV special. That indifference disturbed Reuther more than any individual slight. But Reuther chose to see the youth problem as one of marketing and education, not substance.[5]

For many decades now the union leader had made the point that effective protesters did not use violence. Even in the radical days of the sitdown strike at Flint, as Reuther sometimes noted, his autoworkers never destroyed one piece of machinery.[6] "We knew what we were fighting for," his daughter Lisa remembered him telling SDS members, "and you only know what you are fighting against. You have no moral right to destroy something unless you have something better in its place." Younger people, whether in the SDS or outside it, just weren't acquainted with what Reuther termed the "economic discipline" of adult life. To Reuther's mind, young people who didn't join unions when they could were free riders. Reuther, as the columnist Max Lerner noted, cared "as much for a democratic society as any of the student activists gathered at East Lansing for the SDS convention, and has experienced struggle more than any of them."[7] Yet neither youth generally nor the screamers outside the hotel in Chicago were following Reuther's lead.

Indeed, the bitter truth Reuther had to concede was that Chicago was in part Reuther's own fault. Some of the protesters were in Chicago in the first place because Reuther's own offices had stationed them there. Others whom the UAW had supported elsewhere, in ERAP programs in the cities, had also converged. The SDS members had teamed up with a new and noisier group, the pro-violence Youth International Party, or Yippies. The Yippies were a kind of combo of performance artists and political guerrillas. They threatened to put the drug LSD in Chicago's water supply, and embarrassed the heretofore largely dignified antiwar movement. The demonstrators hosted intellectuals and foreigners, few of whom had ever worked on a shop floor. Allen Ginsberg, the author of the poem "Howl," read a poem-speech about the "egotistical poets in the City Hall." The comedian Dick Gregory, radicalized to unrecognizability since his early days, told the crowd the number of police present suggested that they must be doing something right.[8] In Chicago's parks, the Yippies succeeded in driving the truculent Chicago police to lift their nightsticks and launch their tear gas. Yippies baited the officers to give waiting cameramen a snapshot of violence. Tom Hayden, one of the children of Port Huron, someone whom Reuther had funded, whose very travel to Detroit he'd reimbursed, was egging on the maniacs, saying at one point, "let us make sure if our blood flows, it flows all over the city."[9] The scene was the ultimate evidence of the failure of Reuther's youth strategy, and the other union leaders wouldn't let him forget it. George Meany was calling the protesters "a dirty-necked and dirty-mouthed group of kooks." Union reps in the building trades said such protesters were like strikebreakers, breaking the solidarity of the labor movement.

The Democratic Party, Reuther's party, was struggling with the same problem. The protesters mattered to the party because some of the delegates on the floor were backing them. On the convention floor Senator Abe Ribicoff, while nominating George McGovern of South Dakota, legitimized the protesters' antipolice campaign when he said, "And with George McGovern as president of the United States, we wouldn't have to have Gestapo tactics in the streets of Chicago." Mayor Richard J. Daley, who had managed to keep his calm during Martin Luther King's Chicago drive, this time reddened and hurled back epithets at Ribicoff. On the third night of the convention, as police moved in on them, the demonstrators chanted, "The whole world is watching."

Mayor Daley and his supporters were furious. The hippies, as the police termed the protesters on their radio calls, were trashing the reputation of the Second City. Even Chicagoans who might otherwise have expressed shock at the rough Daley tactics took Daley's side. The protesters' smear name for the police was "pigs." The Yippies anointed a genuine pig as mascot and named it "Pigasus." The swine theme was an insult of the highest order to Daley and his blue-collar city. Chicago was home to more Poles than any other other city outside Warsaw. "Pigs" was what bigots called Poles. "Pigs" was what college elitists—people like David Dellinger, one of the protest leaders, who came from a well-known Republican family and had studied at Yale and Oxford—called members of the working class, Daley's, Reuther's, the Teamsters', and Meany's constituents.

What made the drama worse for Reuther was that, each in its way, not only the UAW or the Democratic Party but also the federal government's own OEO had contributed to the culture that fostered the protests. And Reuther could not deny that in his earlier efforts to engage youth, he had urged the Johnson Administration to support the culture of protest. The old lines in Shriver's OEO handbooks condoning public protests were coming back to haunt the Democratic Party. Sargent Shriver, who was at the convention hoping for a vice-presidential nomination, had just the year before given a grant of $957,000 to the Woodlawn Organization of Chicago's South Side, to create job training and motivation programs. As it turned out, some of the funds became the treasury of a South Side gang, the Blackstone Rangers.[10] Whether the Blackstone Rangers were keeping the peace at the convention or joining in the clamor (they seemed to be doing both), it was clear that it was a threat to peaceful life in Chicago generally; young black men that felt that they had no choice but to join the gang.

For the moment, Daley's crowd, television naïfs, told themselves that they had prevailed.[11] President Johnson assured Daley of the same thing, phoning one night to congratulate the mayor for controlling the protesters. "You are the one great, courageous, decent thing that I know in this country," Johnson told the mayor. And after all, the number of demonstrators, thousands, not hundreds of thousands, was not so great. More people attended the White Sox games that week than the convention demonstrations.[12] A poll taken that year found that 75 percent of Americans did not believe Daley's police had used excessive force. During the convention, Eric Sevareid of the *CBS Evening News* suggested on the air that Chicago's law enforcement style resembled that of the Warsaw Pact, whose armies had just invaded Czechoslovakia. "The city of Chicago runs the city of Prague a close second right now as the world's least attractive tourist destination," Sevareid said acidly. Many Chicagoans shared the reaction of Daley's director of special events, Colonel Jack Riley: "Who's Eric Sevareid?"[13] But the reality was that the protesters were winning the long-term public relations contest in Chicago. The nightstick-swinging Chicago police were what the rest of the country would see in their schoolbooks' 1968 convention. A federal commission headed by a local lawyer, Dan Walker, would later rate the 1968 convention a "police riot" and even draw a Nazi analogy, calling the police "storm troopers in blue." Future media legends such as Dan Rather would later trade on their experiences at the Chicago convention.

Still, unlike Daley, Reuther contained his anger this time. For once the Chicago show ended, and Humphrey was nominated, Reuther did endorse him, even though Humphrey had not disavowed U.S. engagement in Vietnam at the convention. It was time to move on to the general election. And there, Reuther was confident, his union was in good enough shape to deliver victory. Whatever their views on hippies or Vietnam, his membership ought to be feeling loyal, for Reuther had recently delivered

a true UAW bonanza. That fall, he and his shop stewards would enumer-
ate UAW contract victories for skeptical voters. The GM workers' package
was an example of the bounty. Thanks to the most recent big agreement,
from 1967, workers got a new benefit, a prescription drug plan, as well
as extra days off and pension increases worth almost half again as much
as the old pensions. An income guarantee, a new idea, gave those who
were laid off more than 90 percent of their after-tax weekly pay, and for
a full year. The UAW had squeezed yet more from automakers, including key rules to protect workers' union status and pay on the shop floor,
double-time pay for Sunday work, and even measures to protect other
unions. The packages were classic Reuther, but not only generously but
also to reinforce the formal wall between employer and employee. When
the breakdown of a piece of equipment halted the assembly line, the supervisor couldn't fix it himself, even if he knew how. The supervisor had
to fill out forms or call someone from another department, maybe even
another union. To the mind of UAW management respect for procedure or
guild were more than worth an assembly-line slowdown. Tribute to rules,
especially union rules, ensured movement solidarity.[14] If the children of
the middle class did not see the value in such a contract now, Reuther
thought, they would later.

To achieve his goals, long or short term, Reuther had seen to it that
his union packed plenty of financial muscle. Earlier in the year, the UAW
increased union dues to the equivalent of two hours of wages a month, an
average of $7 a worker instead of the old $5 per month rule. One reason
the increase was necessary now was the UAW's disappointing growth
numbers. But another was inflation: without unions, workers would not
have a prayer of forcing companies to offset high prices with higher wages.
Many believed it was time for unions to be more radical, not less. The
International Union of Electrical Workers was still trying to demolish Lemuel Boulware's legacy, the company tactic of making an all-or-nothing
offer to a union. In its next round with GE, the union would make not only
pay or benefits but the practice of Boulwarism a bargaining point. George
Meany and Walter Reuther, though no longer a team, agreed 100 percent
on the need to end Boulwarism, and would each throw millions in the

electricians' strike kitty. Fortunately for themselves, the automakers were still swimming in their own cash. Evidence of automakers' wealth was everywhere, including in a glistening new fifty-story building General Motors was just opening on Fifth Avenue in New York. The little Toyotas meant nothing. Many Americans found the new small cars from abroad endearing, but doubted that a "regular" foreign car could beat a U.S. car. American cars were too good. That was what *Bonanza*'s Lorne Greene told viewers in the commercials that featured Chevy models right on the *Bonanza* set.

After the convention, Reuther wagered, his workers would begin to consider what was at stake in the election. Unless the nation elected a Democratic president in 1968, there was no chance for the heinous "right to work" provision to be reversed. Unless the nation elected a Democratic president, the Social Security benefits and expansions of Medicare and Medicaid that progressives sought were unlikely to become law. Unless the House and Senate stayed Democratic, Congress would indeed be likely to undo many of Reuther's precious legislative gains. Nixon was, as Meany put it, "a black cloud."

But as August 1968 moved into September, the smooth ride Reuther expected did not come. One challenge was George Wallace. For many years the Alabama governor had seen his territory intruded upon by what one of his advisors described as the "communist-trained Walter P. Ruther"—away from the Midwest they spelled "Reuther" wrong— "And a rag-tag of red front groups and opportunistic Negro leaders."[15] Now Wallace took his revenge and moved deep into Reuther's territory, speaking in Detroit to the Veterans of Foreign Wars. A UAW local in Flint, the old Reuther stronghold, defied Reuther and chose Wallace as its candidate. Reuther, undaunted, traveled to St. Louis to speak to UAW members in late September, and confronted Wallace fans. Whom did the workers have to thank for their pay packages? The union, and the state of Missouri, which had passed no "right to work" law. Alabama was a "right to work" state, where compensation packages were lower. "Why don't you go down to Alabama?" Reuther asked the crowd. "Because you've got it better where you are," in unionized Missouri. "Wallace," Reuther told his audience, "ought to get his own state in order before he talks of leading America." Wallace supporters walked out on Reuther. One reason the Wallace boom hurt was that, as Reuther sensed, the Wallace fans' enthusiasm might be more about insulting Reuther than helping the governor of Alabama. But Wallace was not the only challenge; Nixon's agent, George Romney, was finding plenty of union members who thought they might support "law and order" Nixon.

Fat contracts and high stakes notwithstanding, it turned out that many UAW members did not feel loyal. The UAW was especially proud of its record on discrimination, far better than that of, say, construction workers' unions. It was the UAW, for example, that had pressured both the local union members and the company to end discrimination at Dodge Main, a factory in Hamtramck, Michigan, that had historically employed Eastern Europeans. Now African-Americans made up 60 percent of the workforce at Dodge Main. Yet after King's death, black members at Hamtramck had created their own union group, the Dodge Revolutionary Union Movement, or DRUM. DRUM members pounded on an undeniable truth: blacks were not adequately present in top jobs at either Chrysler or the UAW. DRUM claimed that officials remained "stomp down racists," and that those who led at Dodge Main were "demoralizing the integrity of the Black individual."[16] One three-day disruption by DRUM had cost Chrysler production of 1,900 cars. DRUM workers, like the Yippies, provoked East Europeans, calling supervisors "Polish pigs." DRUM defended theft from two women employed by a Chrysler concessionaire as "a question of someone receiving back pay." DRUM assailed the UAW brass directly: "The UAW bigots," one DRUM document said, went across Detroit, "scraping the back streets and searching the cracks in the walls for old retired Polish pigs." A similar group, FRUM, arose at a Ford plant. Sometimes, DRUM and FRUM made Reuther himself a target: "Behead the Red Head," a pamphlet read.[17]

Still, Reuther persevered, endorsing and stumping for Humphrey, soothing constituencies, and indeed narrowing the Nixon-Humphrey gap. Reuther deputized Doug Fraser, UAW head at Chrysler, to manage the campaign and woo restive union members to Humphrey and away from

Wallace. Together with Ford executives and Congressman John Dingell, Reuther hosted a visit for Humphrey that included a walk down the assembly line at Ford's River Rouge plant, and a chance to meet retired UAW workers in the Masonic Auditorium. At a Tigers-Cardinals baseball game, Reuther and Humphrey braved rain and sat together in a box, consulting on Vietnam. As Federal Reserve chair William Martin had before him, Humphrey addressed the Detroit Economic Club, asking members to compare economic conditions under Eisenhower, Johnson, and Kennedy—and then decide how to vote.

Hubert Humphrey's casual invitation to compare the 1960s economy with the economy of the 1950s was ill thought out. Unemployment might be low now. But Eisenhower's era had been better for the American auto industry. Then, the Big Three had had no competition. Postwar West Germany, a half nation, struggled in the 1950s. Postwar Japan exported mainly textiles at first; and U.S. leaders, automakers and unions included, had been grateful to see Japan concentrating on trade instead of guns. Reuther and the automakers had viewed the town of Toyota, Japan, where the cars were built, as the headquarters of a kind of midget brother: quaint. The unions, the automakers, and the government itself had felt little need to look up from their work at the great negotiating table. By 1968, however, the Japanese companies were growing fast. Foreign imports might not seem important to Reuther at the moment, but in fact foreign automakers mattered as much to Detroit's future as any individual event of that momentous year. Especially Toyota.

———

THE STORY of Toyota resembled that of Fairchild Semiconductor, both improbable and inevitable. As Robert Noyce and Gordon Moore would be to the microchip much later, Sakichi Toyoda, Toyota's founder, was to the loom. Starting with a primitive wooden machine, Toyoda had rigged improvements so that the loom required only one hand to operate, instead of two. Next Toyoda had added steel to the structure, allowing the machine to operate faster. Finally Toyoda, also a perpetual tinkerer, had invented automatic looms, including an innovative circular loom that increased productivity by multiples.[18] The Toyoda family added automobiles to their business in the 1930s. After World War II, the auto business nearly failed, but then found a new career, as in the case of Shockley and Fairchild, serving the U.S. military-industrial complex. General Douglas MacArthur needed trucks. Toyota, Isuzu, and Nissan made them. At the time, few anywhere, even in Japan, expected more of the Japanese automakers than truck production for an occupying army. Developing an independent automobile industry did not make much sense, Hisato Ichimada, governor of the Bank of Japan, Japan's central bank, declared carry on in 1950, a time when Japan produced only 1,594 passenger cars, to the 6.6 million produced in the United States.[19] As late as 1954, Suehiro Nishio, who would later chair Japan's Socialist Party, claimed that "the right policy is to go ahead and give up on making passenger cars and just depend on imports."[20] Even after Toyoda updated, becoming Toyota, the Japanese workers were nowhere near as productive as U.S. workers. They simply made fewer cars per hour.[21]

That, however, began to change in the 1950s. One reason was Japan's own industrial policy, which MacArthur had helped to establish. The Japanese government, moving past Ichimada's comment, made promotion of auto exports official policy, and worked hard to see that Japanese companies had the chance to craft not only trucks but also cars that Americans would like. The world's benevolent leaders smiled: Japan was stabilizing economically, just as hoped. A second reason for Japanese productivity gains was the lure of the American open market, whose tariffs were nothing like those Japan imposed on incoming autos. If making more cars faster would enable Japan to get a share of that market, companies like Toyota would make more cars faster. A third reason for the Japanese ramp-up was indeed the value of the currency, the yen. One of the gifts of the Bretton Woods gold exchange standard to nations recovering from World War II had been, and remained, a strong dollar. To build strong alliances with Western Europe and Japan, the United States was most of the time intentionally subsidizing Japanese exports.

Japan had unions, but especially at Toyota, those unions were mere pussycats compared with the UAW tiger.[22] The union federations of

Japan, the equivalents of George Meany's AFL-CIO, also wielded no great power. At Toyota, which was based in the countryside, workers came to the company from the farm. Most men in postwar Japan were too grateful for their jobs to be willing to offend management. It all meant that the contracts Toyota wrote were more modest. There hadn't been a major strike in the Japanese auto industry since 1953.

Labor was far cheaper in Japan than in the United States, especially outside Tokyo, and Toyota was in the country, sometimes too cheap for even America's cooperative unions. In 1962, labor had been so cheap that Reuther, while in Japan, had complained that Japanese workers were underpaid, and advised them to strengthen free trade unions rather than sign up with Japanese communists.[23] If Japan's unions were strengthened, they would demand higher wages, and the wage differential between Japan and the U.S. auto industries would narrow.

Toyota's gains also had to do with the company's inventive management style. One aspect of this was Toyota's habit of outsourcing; the Big Three made more of their cars than Toyota made of its. The decentralization made supply-chain management difficult. But since every company making a Toyota part specialized in that part, the parts were better— David Ricardo's theory of comparative advantage in operation. Inside Toyota factories workers' ideas were important. Like Robert Noyce, Toyota management knew it didn't know where the next idea would come from. Therefore, Toyota listened to workers. It listened to unions. The Toyota factory floor man could simply shut down the assembly line if something went wrong or could work better. Sometimes the men on the line fixed something themselves. Sometimes they put forward ideas that improved production.

This was a contrast to the United States, where companies and unions operated in a kind of ritualistic class war. U.S. unions insisted on following the rules they made, which meant that when, say, electricity malfunctioned, they called the electricians' union, and waited until a union electrician arrived to fix the glitch. The employers contributed to the formality. Frederick Taylor, Henry Ford's efficiency guru, had emphasized speed in production. Ford himself had also emphasized speed, and believed that perpetual increases in the speed of the assembly line were what sustained profits. Ford had distained variety, and even customers themselves, saying, famously, that buyers could have any color car, as long as it was black. The principles of Ford and Taylor, scientific management, had over the years hardened like concrete, incapable of adjustment. In the postwar period, a layer of managers had replaced engineers in the control of plants. Those managers tended to ignore both workers and designers. Workers in the American auto industry felt permanently shut out. What the worker got in return for his numbing hours on the line was that handsome pay package, with Reuther's extra time off. Frustration at this patronizing attitude, as much as racism real or perceived, drove the rebellion of younger UAW members. The Japanese example suggested that another way was possible, that the worker could participate in innovation, even in a traditional industry such as autos. Though most Americans would recognize it only much later, the Toyota achievement was kicking the legs from under America's Big Business–Big Labor–Big Government table.

The proximate result of the high American pay packages was that labor costs per car in the United States were by now up to three times those at European factories, and four or five times those in Japan. The trend continued with each contract round. That would not have mattered if U.S. workers made more cars. But the number of hours it took one Toyota worker to make a car was diminishing rapidly. In fact, by 1965, Toyota produced more vehicles per worker than the average for General Motors, Ford, and Chrysler.[24] By the next contract negotiations, Ford and GM would grow bold in their complaints: "The cost of the settlement," as GM's top bargainer would put it, "is substantially more than the anticipated increase in productivity."

All along, Toyota and the other Japanese automakers had studied the United States assiduously. They had therefore picked up that a smaller car might sell in the United States of the 1960s. The U.S. automakers had paid less attention. Detroit from time to time made smaller cars, like Romney's Rambler. But the effort had not been sustained. Instead, the Big Three sought to get around their labor costs by opening factories abroad. Ford, for example, was expanding the sale of Cortinas built in the United Kingdom, installing left-side steering wheels to accommodate American roads. In 1967 in Britain Ford prototyped a tiny electric slow-poke, the Comuta, only eighty inches long. But electric cars that could meet American standards, the industry estimated, were five or ten years away. Rumor had it that Chrysler was trying to buy up 20 percent of a Japanese automaker, the greatest share the Japanese government allowed. But selling "captive" imports, as the cars the Big Three brought to the United States were called, did not help employment in the automakers' troubled hometown, Detroit—especially when automakers were simultaneously moving factories to other parts of Michigan or to "right to work" states.[25]

In their way the UAW leaders recognized the problem. Reuther at one point urged Johnson to encourage U.S. automakers to make a small car. Perhaps the White House could talk the Big Three into together using a Studebaker factory to build what Reuther called an "all-American small car."[26] Johnson liked the idea and tried to get McNamara to agree to place an order for Reuther's autos. Johnson—and Reuther—contacted Attorney General Robert Kennedy, but Johnson and Kennedy agreed they had to look into whether a Big Three vehicle would violate American antitrust law.[27] One thought was to use an old Studebaker factory. The all-American small car had gone nowhere. Henry Ford II—heir, not founder—invested in a sporty car, the Mustang, but never picked up the imperative of a domestically made Toyota-size car. Sometimes, indeed, he seemed to treat Ford more like a hobby than a company. In recent years Ford had devoted much time to negotiation with Enzo Ferrari to buy Ferrari, and building his own vehicle to compete in the Le Mans.[28] Even in 1968, Henry Ford II told shareholders that "it doesn't seem to us that it would be a wise investment for us to build a new small car." Big cars were a point of pride for America. To downsize a car was to downsize the American dream. The Fords did not want that responsibility.

But the truth was that the Fords, along with the UAW, were already downsizing the dream. The share of black males of working age who were no longer in the workforce at all was expanding dramatically from the

1950s, moving toward a third.[29] In Detroit, the Big Three and the UAW had, especially since the riots, sought to address those jobless with temporary programs for what they called "the hard-core unemployed." All the programs in the world, whether from the federal government, the unions, or the Big Three, could not make up for the simple truth. The same trio—the government, the automakers, and the unions—made labor expensive. High labor costs nearly always shut out vulnerable groups and minorities first, because they lacked skills to compete with better-trained workers for what had become fewer spots. The idling of vulnerable workers was something Richard Nixon was getting at in his speeches. Government could do a lot for a worker, Nixon said, but it couldn't "provide him dignity." It was tempting to consider what life in Detroit might be like if Detroit produced ten out of the ten cars sold in the United States, instead of nine out of ten. It was tempting to imagine high tariff walls blocking all Japanese intruders. But though Walter Reuther could try to "put the world together," he could not seal out the world.

———

HUBERT HUMPHREY proved a mediocre presidential candidate; stentorian, overly earnest, and poor at making the case for his more controversial positions, especially his support for Johnson on Vietnam.[30] By the end of September, Humphrey decided to abandon Johnson. Minutes before NBC would air his betrayal, Humphrey called the president from Salt Lake City to let him know that his speech included language about halting the bombing in Vietnam.[31] Johnson, calm as an undertaker, allowed that "before we give up our whole card," Humphrey should remember the half-million U.S. servicemen in Vietnam and the South Vietnamese, easy targets for a North Vietnam emboldened by a United States turned dovish. Humphrey's statement was already on tape, and there was nothing else for Johnson to say.

From Reuther's point of view, however, the Humphrey shift was not a betrayal but a godsend. It made Reuther's case to the antiwar crowd easier. The protesters' cries of "Dump the Hump" became fainter. All October, Reuther's UAW, the Teamsters, and the AFL-CIO pounded for Humphrey and the Democratic Party. Spending hours with workers in meeting halls and on the phone, they managed to win over many voters. By late October, Gene McCarthy endorsed Humphrey, pulling to Humphrey some holdouts from the progressive left. The Wallace campaign slipped after replicating Barry Goldwater's error: Wallace's vice-presidential candidate, General Curtis LeMay, said, "I don't believe the world will end if we explode a nuclear weapon," an assertion that came off as worse than cavalier in a period when napalm was becoming an everyday term. On October 20 one of the key UAW Flint locals that had endorsed Wallace reversed itself and backed Humphrey. At the end of October, Johnson himself, party loyal, boosted Democratic prospects again when he preempted Humphrey and ordered a halt to all bombing of North Vietnam on his own terms. By November, Humphrey appeared to be closing the gap between himself and Nixon. More Democrats lined up behind Humphrey, though some waited to the last minute. Sargent Shriver mailed his ballot from Paris at the end of October, but the ballot arrived one day too late to be counted. Come election night, the Humphrey revival proved to be like Shriver's ballot: slightly and fatally late.

For Reuther, there were small consolations. The Nixon victory was narrow, and voters returned Democratic majorities to the House and Senate. The UAW had taken Michigan for Humphrey, and six of seven Democrats in the Michigan delegation won reelection. Reuther had delivered for the party, if not for the president. Mayor Daley of Chicago was not as lucky as Reuther. When he learned Nixon had prevailed in Illinois, Daley instantly called for an investigation into voter fraud. Reuther penned a dutiful note of congratulations to Nixon, pledging his union's "fullest cooperation" with the new administration.[32] But the more the UAW men thought about it, the more they realized that Nixon's victory was a disappointment to unions and to old-style, union-friendly politicians. The union dream of repealing "right to work" had been so close just a year or two before that it looked like a mere matter of coordinating presidential and congressional calendars. Now repeal of "right to work" was impossible. There was no way to stop companies from building out their second America, one unhampered by union constraints. As Reuther's brother Victor later wrote, "There was virtually nothing constructive Walter could do under the presidency of Richard M. Nixon." Reuther, the statesman of labor, understood that it is not always given to men with distinguished careers to finish strong. Still, the future looked bitter. A Democratic president could be elected in 1972—perhaps Ted Kennedy. By then, though, Reuther might be packing up his office at Solidarity House to return with his wife, May, to his retreat at Paint Creek.

It was a larger retreat than Paint Creek that consoled Reuther now: Black Lake. All who visited the site found Black Lake stunning, with its hundreds of acres to walk through. The lake itself featured clean yellow sand and, for fresh water, a wonderfully large fish, the sturgeon. The symbolism was there: one could envision regular American workers at their union retreat dining like kings on their own caviar. Black Lake would feature not only the covered walkways but also an indoor swimming pool. Elevated lounges with two-story glass windows gave guests a magisterial view of treetops. Reuther had giant beams of Douglas fir shipped from Oregon and ordered fifteen thousand tons of stone for construction. The stone came from Wisconsin, Victor Reuther remembered later, because it was both more beautiful and less expensive than what was available in Michigan.

Reuther attended to each detail. He did not want to rile the local citizens who lived around his retreat. He invited the town of Onaway to the site to inspect Oscar Stonorov's models personally.[33] Months before construction actually began, the walls of Reuther's office in Detroit were covered with pictures and blueprints for Black Lake. The retreat would cost millions. Still, Reuther believed, more than ever, that Black Lake was the "what for" of the union dues. If he could not put the world together, at Black Lake, his successors would.

After the 1968 election, Reuther, as often before, also sought inspiration overseas. As before, his visited his models, social democracies. Israel was a destination in the fall of 1968, and Reuther brought his wife, May, and daughter Lisa on the trip. Reuther's UAW and the Histadrut, the big Israeli labor federation, had long worked together. The UAW had recently helped to raise funds for a study of the peaceful use of atomic energy at the Weizmann Institute of Science in Jerusalem. Now the institute honored Reuther by naming a chair after him. Reuther also stopped in Turkey. And he headed to Belgrade to spend a week with labor leaders. While the protesters in Chicago had not impressed the old union guard, Cold Warriors to the core, the workers in Yugoslavia seemed to them genuinely brave, Reuther- and Meany-style brave. The Yugoslavians had mounted a public protest of the invasion of Czechoslovakia even as the Russians were tightening their chokehold on Prague.

So it happened that Reuther was not even in the United States when, on December 6, *Toyota Maru* Number 1, bearing 1,240 Coronas and Corollas, slid into a berth at the Port of Los Angeles. Number 1 was only the first ship in a fleet of five that Toyota planned to operate by the end of 1969, with more to follow. The foreign automakers that year reached a landmark, selling a million cars in the United States. Reuther was working so hard to save his party and his union. But one day, soon enough, it would be his industry that needed saving.

ABUNDANT

SOCIETY

10

Moynihan Agonistes

1969 TO 1970

Guns: 8.1% of GDP
Butter: 5.6% of GDP
Dow Jones Industrial Average: 948

---

*What America needs now is not more welfare but more
workfare.*
　　　　　　—President Richard Nixon, August 1969

The nation had begun the War on Poverty. Why not win it?
　　　　　　—Daniel Patrick Moynihan

In November 1968, a writer named Godfrey Hodgson went to lunch at Daniel Patrick Moynihan's house on Francis Avenue in Cambridge, Massachusetts. Of course the pair discussed the election results, and the economy. Unemployment was moving toward historic lows. In Washington experts were, however, warning about inflation: though the average for the year 1968 was in the 4 percent range, economists were betting that inflation would soon rise past 5 percent. Officials were now talking about introducing wage and price controls to tamp down prices, or raising interest rates to check the price rises, even if a recession came. But in an October radio address, Nixon had warned that he didn't approve of wage and price controls, which, he said, represented "a recession of our liberty."[1] Nixon had also signaled that he wasn't willing to sacrifice jobs in a recession. The speech, Hodgson knew, would resonate with Moynihan, who concentrated his work on unemployment. Still, when Moynihan told Hodgson that he planned to join the Administration and move to Washington, Hodgson was shocked. "I almost fell out of my chair," Hodgson later recalled.[2]

Classy academics didn't go to work for politicians like Richard Nixon. Especially not classy academics like Pat Moynihan. "Baptized a Catholic and born a Democrat" was how Moynihan had always described himself. Moynihan had campaigned for his fellow Irish-American Robert Kennedy in California right up to the senator's assassination. Like the rest, Moynihan had then moved over to Humphrey, putting in an appearance for the Democrat as recently as Halloween. During the campaign period, a rumor had circulated that Moynihan might consider joining a Nixon team. The assumption of most was that this rumor was circulated by Nixon, who was seeking to win favor by hiring advisors associated with both parties. Moynihan had vigorously denied the possibility. Why should any man walk away from the calm of academic life for the White House cauldron? Moynihan had only recently landed a spot at the pinnacle, Harvard, and felt lucky to get it. "I have life tenure at Harvard University and make twice as much money as a cabinet officer with no particular effort," Moynihan had explained to Johnson's special counsel at the White House, Harry McPherson, back in October, "and have four-month vacations besides!"[3]

Now, as word of Moynihan's defection got around Cambridge, his colleagues converged in alarm. Blair Clark, Eugene McCarthy's campaign manager and a college friend of John F. Kennedy's, spent a night drinking with Moynihan to try to talk him out of the move. Cambridge was a Gene McCarthy stronghold. The crowd at Harvard had held even Hubert Humphrey, and at times Robert Kennedy, in contempt. Any interest in Nixon Harvard rated worse than reprehensible. Nixon might talk about great reforms, but he was a schemer, not a dreamer. That Nixon was even willing to continue Johnson's war at all was heinous to Cambridge.

Moynihan, like almost everyone in Cambridge, indeed felt concern about U.S. prospects in the war in Vietnam. But like some other veterans, he looked at war differently from the protesters. All wars were awful. Some were necessary. Sometimes you had to serve even when you didn't endorse the war. Besides, this war was so unpopular already that Moynihan reckoned Nixon might indeed manage to wind the conflict down. From the Harvard point of view, anyone who seemed highly unlikely to join forces with

Nixon, such as a genuine dreamer like Walter Reuther, was to be praised and rewarded: that spring Harvard would in fact bestow on Reuther an honorary degree.[4] The schoolmates of Moynihan's children stopped talking to them. Alan Rabinowitz, a fellow academic, wrote a satirical poem chiding Moynihan for his betrayal, "The Knight Before Nixon."

Friends found Moynihan resolute. Moynihan reminded his colleagues he wasn't just going to work for Nixon. He was going to work for the government. And what was wrong with working for the government? The government had, as Moynihan had always said, made his life as a professor possible in the first place. Without the Navy, he probably wouldn't have seen Europe. Without government-funded college and graduate school, he would still be a stevedore on the piers of New York. Moynihan *believed* in government.[5] If government was imperfect, or perhaps led by someone one didn't agree with, then it was the job of policy leaders to step up and improve it. It was important, as Moynihan would later put it, to "embrace great causes, and do great things."[6] If you wanted to be like Martin Luther King Jr., with whose widow Moynihan was now corresponding, or like Walter Reuther, you couldn't be prissy about political party. Democrats shouldn't have a monopoly on dreaming big. There was a kind of nobility to taking a public service job, joining in an endeavor. This kind of nobility, he reminded the others, was what a university like Harvard had created a two-year leave program *for*. It was prissy to imagine the choice being serving only one crowd—the Kennedys—or keeping out altogether. If one's children getting the cold shoulder at school was the price for stepping up, Moynihan would pay it.

After Christmas, Moynihan replied to Rabinowitz with a verse of his own:

Eschewing his past of striving and greed,
Rabinowitz calls for an elitist creed
Of mystic abstractions subtle and dense
As to claim exemption from making much sense.
But Moynihan, seasoned in battles of yore,
Rides forth once again to the blood & the gore.

Firm of demeanor yet gentled, inclined,
He simply asks that you be so kind,
To accept his best wishes,
For the Life of the Mind.

Moynihan's final point was clear: the Life of the Mind wasn't enough. Policy, as he had long maintained, meant nothing if it did not take the test of reality. And Moynihan had policies that wanted testing. He was a strong advocate of improving auto safety. More than fifty thousand people died in auto accidents every year, more than three times as many who had died in Vietnam in 1968, the worst year yet. It was Moynihan who had brought the auto safety gadfly Ralph Nader to serve as a consultant in Washington during the Johnson Administration. Nader, whose data were so damning, illuminated what was wrong with self-satisfied Detroit. Moynihan wanted to see more of what he called "the politics of stability"—bipartisan practice—in Washington. Another Moynihan goal was rebuilding and restoring Pennsylvania Avenue, an existing project ignored by Lyndon Johnson and Lady Bird. And, most important, Moynihan wanted to take on the cause of those jobless Americans who were mired in ill-thought-out welfare programs.

Personal reasons, less often mentioned, also drove Moynihan to return to Washington. His 1965 argument that family troubles played a role in black poverty had proved so divisive, so controversial, that the Johnson Administration had shut Moynihan out. At the beginning of a civil rights conference in the fall of 1965, one Johnson official had, tongue in cheek, blithely announced "I have been reliably informed that no such person as Daniel Patrick Moynihan exists."[7] That had hurt. The taint never seemed to fade. Just the year before, none other than Ralph Ellison, one of the premier black writers of the period, had assailed Moynihan, a white man, for presuming to "interpret Negro life."[8] Launching a triumphant federal program that enabled poor families, black or white, to stay together, to leave poverty, and to find jobs would vindicate Moynihan in the public eye. For better poverty policy and public vindication, joining Nixon was a risk worth taking.

From his work at Harvard and in Washington, Moynihan thought he had learned what was wrong with American welfare. The first trouble was that poverty funding tended to flow to bureaucrats—social workers, not poor people. "Feeding the horses to feed the sparrows," Moynihan called it.[9] In many states, those social workers spent their time in perverse endeavors: inspecting apartments at Pruitt-Igoe to make sure no fathers were present, for example. Taxes hit people when they entered the workforce, reducing the appeal of working just as Eartha Kitt said. As workers made more and moved above poverty levels, welfare benefits ended, another disincentive to earning more. States all ran their own programs, the differences yielding a multiplicity of perversities. In some states, for example, a welfare mother working at the same job as a family father not on welfare took in 50 percent more than the man, because she was entitled to keep a portion of her welfare. Why not bypass the bureaucrats and send the money to families, regardless of whether fathers were present? You could offset the taxes workers paid to make working harder more inviting. Work dignified, just as Nixon insisted, and people prized dignity. It was time to replace the current welfare system, which was, as Moynihan put it, "more protective of weakness than of strength." Instead you could structure federal benefits around getting people to work, as France had via family allowances and public health care insurance. To Moynihan, the central fact about Great Britain was not Harold Wilson's sterling crises, which he did regard, as Lyndon Johnson did at first, as monetary technicality; it was that through a national policy of "continued full employment," postwar Britain had managed an unemployment average lower than that of the United States. American people, too, wanted to work. If you altered welfare programs correctly, you reduced poverty, and you reduced joblessness. Eventually, welfare, too, disappeared. The good results came together. The sparrows would take flight.

The more Moynihan thought about his welfare reform, the more propitious the moment felt. Both the House and the Senate were Democratic this year. The president was Republican. A first-term president hadn't had to face a challenge like this since Andrew Johnson and Zachary Taylor. Welfare reform could be a way for Nixon to unite parties. In 1968, the campaigning Nixon had referred to a Silent Majority of Americans, regular working-class people who believed in common sense, not lefty programs. A new family program that included them, even gave them benefits at times, would remember those forgotten voters. The unions would get behind the payments, Moynihan figured—Reuther had already campaigned not only for a guaranteed income for his workers but also for a corollary, a national health program. Lyndon Johnson himself had signed into law an incentive program to help welfare mothers find work, an early, small version of what Moynihan was considering. Conservatives also were trying to figure out what made people want to work. Milton Friedman, the star economist at the University of Chicago, had come up with the negative income tax, cash payments to those at the bottom of the tax schedule to sweeten what already came in their pay packets. The thought of winning praise from Friedman, a pure free marketeer, tickled the progressive Moynihan. Something had to be done. Despite the historically low unemployment rate, federal welfare payments were exploding. In one of the first of a number of long, careful memos that Moynihan penned to his future boss, he offered New York City as an example. New York's welfare payments alone amounted to $2 billion, double the once huge-sounding initial budget for the War on Poverty. Nationally, spending for the old welfare system had risen by half in just two years, and spending for the disabled was up by 26 percent in the same period.[10]

Of course, making such a grand compromise required a different kind of president. Was Nixon different enough? As he walked around Cambridge, Moynihan compared Johnson and Nixon in his mind. Johnson was a man of Capitol Hill. Johnson didn't really like the mechanics of laws, which was why he hadn't seen the mischief possible in community action. Nixon by contrast liked to craft policy, whichever party it came from, and hoped to be remembered for it. Nixon, Moynihan saw, took a bipartisan approach to policy and history. When the time came to prepare for his inaugural address, Nixon combed through past speeches looking for presidents who had made compelling pleas for unity at other difficult points in the nation's history. Nixon had the intellectual confidence Johnson had lacked. The inaugural address of James Buchanan, who became

president just before the Civil War, especially caught Nixon's eye. Like
Buchanan, Nixon saw something ominous in the divisions of the country,
but had faith that the nation could reach a place "where all was calm."[11]
Nixon liked Woodrow Wilson, a Democratic icon, so much that he placed
Wilson's portrait in the cabinet room. A Wilsonian cabinet room evoked
treaties among nations, signed in great halls, as in the Europe of old.

Moynihan took comfort in other differences. Johnson lived domestic
policy and merely endured foreign policy. Nixon did the reverse. Foreign
policy was Nixon's strength, his core expertise. Nixon had been deal-
ing with communist regimes since before his standoff with Nikita Khrushchev in the 1959 Kitchen Debate. Nixon loved *all* foreign trips. At the
least suggestion, RN would zoom off to Europe for a meeting with Charles
de Gaulle.[12] Such preferences matched the moment. The foreign challenge of Vietnam was arguably the greatest facing the nation, with more
than half a million troops in Southeast Asia now. Because foreign policy
was Nixon's area, he indeed stood a better chance than Johnson of wind-
ing the war down. When it came to domestic policy, however, Nixon was
at sea. In the past, he had had trouble convincing people that domestic
policy even interested him. In 1962, the year of his annihilating loss in
California's gubernatorial race, Nixon had seen a silver lining: "At least
I'll never have to talk about crap like dope addiction again," he had said.
This distance could advantage a White House advisor. A president distracted by war might allow domestic planners like Moynihan to make the
big calls on domestic reform.

What Nixon did have in common with Johnson was a keen nose for public opinion. In a divided Washington, Nixon's strategy, already becoming
obvious, was to rise above the fray and promote policies so unexpected they
shocked the country into following him. Nixon was, however, also willing to
give the other party what it wanted in the name of comity. President Johnson and Congress had recently vastly increased federal spending on food
stamps, so much so that the outlays this year were likely to be $325 mil-
lion, rather than the $280 million Congress had appropriated earlier in
1968. The number of Americans on food stamps was also rising fast: the
Agriculture Department reckoned that 3.6 million Americans would be

receiving food stamps by June 1969, up from 2.7 million just the previous November. Yet the newly elected Nixon was not sending strong signs he would halt the flow. Perhaps the country could afford them. Moynihan had watched with horror as protesters wore down Johnson, separating him from his own people, literally. When Johnson attended the funeral of Cardinal Francis Spellman, he had had to slip in a back door at St. Patrick's Cathedral, Moynihan noted, "like a medieval felon seeking sanctuary." Nixon, Moynihan judged, was tougher. He would pander to no mob. "And they are hell bent for a good time," Moynihan advised Nixon, commenting, "President Johnson took all this personally, but I have the impression that you will make no such mistake!"

For his vice president, Nixon had selected a figure most policy types considered a yahoo, Spiro Agnew of Maryland. But vice-presidential choices were politics, and had to be forgiven. To lead his staff, Nixon brought in two campaign hands, the straight arrows Bob Haldeman and John Ehrlichman. That, too, was typical: presidents required traffic cops. But other names on Nixon's list were great thinkers or experienced legislators, worthy colleagues for Moynihan. For the key post of national security advisor, the new president hired one of Moynihan's Harvard colleagues, Henry Kissinger, an expert on treaties and a professor already known for his study of Klemens von Metternich's *Realpolitik*. For defense secretary, Nixon lured Melvin Laird, who had served nine terms in Congress and was greatly admired on the Hill. With Laird, Nixon demonstrated he'd learned from Kennedy's and Johnson's errors in hiring businessmen. Laird's virtue was that he was *not* a businessman, as the president-elect wrote in his notes: "A businessman in the defense department, like McNamara or Wilson [Charles Erwin Wilson, Eisenhower's defense secretary], would employ many fine management techniques but not be able to provide insight."[13] The list went on like that. As his treasury secretary—and point man on taxes—Nixon chose David Kennedy, a former Federal Reserve hand who chaired Johnson's influential Commission on Budgetary Concepts. Kennedy had been a protégé of Marriner Eccles, Franklin's Roosevelt's Federal Reserve chairman, and brought with him a heavy quotient of institutional memory.

Nixon's coup was Arthur Burns, a conservative and arguably the best economist in the land. With his gray hair parted in the middle and his curved pipe, Burns posed a contrast to the youth cult characters around John Kennedy or the Texas cronies of Lyndon Johnson. Burns spoke so slowly that people discerned he was accustomed to being heeded. Most important, Burns went his own way. Newspapers had noticed that independence long ago: "Eisenhower's Top Economist Prefers to Speak for Himself," as one 1950s headline had read. Nixon liked Burns, the man who had, so presciently, warned him that monetary policy would cost him the 1960 election. Having Burns on board would raise the administration's prestige. Burns, like Moynihan, placed confidence in Nixon, a good sign for Moynihan. Burns's public respect for Nixon meant that Burns was likely to back Nixon if Nixon himself backed Moynihan's guaranteed income plan. Or so you could reason.

It might be possible that Burns would also be useful for killing poverty projects that competed with Moynihan's. A CBS documentary of the prior year had depicted a national hunger emergency. The film had significantly exaggerated the number of Americans who were short of calories: most poor Americans were not starving, they were getting the wrong things to eat. Nonetheless there was now a move afoot to make eradicating hunger the centerpiece of Nixon's social policy. The agricultural lobby liked this because addressing "hunger" meant the expansion of food subsidy or food stamps. Though Moynihan could not know it, Burns indeed believed Nixon had the guts to see through any hunger propaganda. Nixon, Burns wrote in his diary, "believed defiantly that there was no hunger problem in America, that the problem was being fabricated by journalists and politicians."[14] Nixon wanted to make Burns the Fed chairman in 1970, after William McChesney Martin's term ended. Meantime, Nixon parked Burns at the White House, calling him "economic counselor" and giving him cabinet rank.

Other choices on the domestic side looked as shrewd as that of Burns. For the department of Housing and Urban Development, Nixon magnanimously pulled in his recent opponent George Romney, who had made housing a focus while governor of Michigan. To the post of labor secretary, normally a slot for union leaders or corporate lawyers, Nixon drew the dean of the business school at the Midwest's Harvard, the University of Chicago, George Shultz. Shultz, like Nixon, harbored great suspicion of the popular concept that wage and price controls could halt inflation. The men were both old enough to recall, as the executives at General Electric did, the perverse outcomes when the authorities during World War II had imposed price controls. Nixon, as a young government bureaucrat, a P-3, had actually observed the absurdity of rationing firsthand at the wartime Office of Price Administration, when car owners were denied gasoline if their tires did not have the right certificates. If rations remained in place after a national emergency, they simply generated lawlessness, Nixon thought, "just like the bootleggers during the days of Prohibition." The man Nixon tapped to be OEO director, the attorney Leonard Garment, was so liberal that he flunked his first job interview by praising one of the OEO programs conservatives detested most: legal services. Nixon forgave Garment, too, and brought him to the White House.[15] It was heartening to see that many in the press approved of Nixon's choices, especially his shift away from business whippersnappers. "Like much else in the Nixon presidency, there is something of another place and time about these men," wrote a *Washington Post* columnist approvingly.

Before the inauguration, Moynihan traveled to New York to meet with Nixon and the new staff. What he, and indeed all the others, picked up from Nixon was a sense of ebullience. Nixon had dropped Johnson's famous adjective, "great," but did speak of "a just and abundant society." The abundant part of that was indubitably correct. America seemed not merely abundant, but endlessly so. At an early meeting of the future cabinet called at the Sapphire Room of the Pierre Hotel in New York, one member of the Nixon crowd, Kissinger, sounded a note of caution. The Nixon team might want to recall that the swordsmen of Kennedy's Camelot had rated their own talents too highly. Kissinger remembered the preinauguration mood in 1961. "At that time," Kissinger said, "the people on the White House staff wondered what they would do in the last two years of the president's term, when all the problems had been solved."[16] Still, the rest of the advisors felt noble, up to challenges, as in

Moynihan's rhyme. They were the knights of the new president's court, and Nixon was building his own Camelot.

For Moynihan, however, there was a final factor, the clincher in the decision to return to Washington. Nixon gave Moynihan the best gift a boss can give an intellectual: Nixon listened to him. When Moynihan met Nixon in New York, he found that Nixon had already read his articles, and rated his thinking "refreshing and stimulating." When it came to the details of Moynihan's job, Nixon also took suggestions, even allowing that Moynihan might write his own ticket. Moynihan suggested he serve as "special assistant to the president," a post that required, as he made clear, "automatic access to the president." Nixon assented, editing the title only slightly, to "assistant to the president for domestic policy." That was flatteringly close to what Nixon called the eminence Burns, counselor to the president. Even on the little things, things that had nothing to do with a key brief like poverty, Nixon seemed ready to give Moynihan license. In one of his first notes to Nixon, Moynihan suggested that President Johnson had made an error when, in a rare fit of parsimony, he had shut off the floodlights around the White House. People liked to see the White House bathed in light. An illuminated White House might inspire Americans to forget their differences, Moynihan told the new president. Maybe Nixon should turn the lights on again? Nixon turned on the lights.

At inauguration time Nixon received a warm reception from all kinds of unexpected quarters, a heartening sight for Moynihan and the others. Nixon had plenty of black supporters, in part because of the genuine questions blacks right and left were posing about the Great Society after Martin Luther King's death. "Is brotherhood enough?" Nathan Wright, one of the stars of the Black Power conferences, asked. Blacks needed to recognize "the limits of altruism," said Wright. Wright, himself a Republican, even went so far as to suggest that with some changes in attitude, "a man of Mr. Nixon's integrity, experience, and seriousness might be among the most capable leaders that our nation could expect to find in the days ahead."[17] Wright's earlier book had been titled *Ready to Riot*; his new one he called *Let's Work Together*. Even the most improbable of personalities seemed eager to find their way into the Nixon scene. Mickey Cogwell, a member of the Blackstone Rangers gang in Chicago, donned tails and attended one of the inaugural balls. Someone asked Cogwell why. After all, Nixon, the law-and-order candidate, fought for values precisely the opposite of those of the Blackstone Rangers. "*We* elected Nixon," Cogwell said, tongue in cheek for his gang. "*We* are the ones who put crime in the streets."[18] The Senate confirmed Nixon's nominees quickly. The friendly greeting Nixon received suggested that whatever the divisions in Congress, the country might actually move "forward together," another Nixon slogan.

Moynihan's early days at the White House proceeded auspiciously. When time came for the crucial assignment of offices at the White House, Moynihan's brief experience in prior administrations stood him in good stead. There were offices for staffers like Moynihan in the Old Executive Office Building, next door to the White House, but Moynihan already knew how much better it would be to sit at a desk nearer the center of power. With good humor, therefore, Moynihan accepted an office in the West Wing ground floor. He stayed with Averell Harriman, his old boss, and hired young men who were to stay up all night on projects, as he himself had done for Sarge. One of them, Christopher DeMuth, had made Moynihan's acquaintance while serving as a busboy for faculty luncheons that Moynihan had hosted at Harvard.[19] Moynihan, who cared so much for cities and architecture, was appalled to discover that the charred remains of the riots following Martin Luther King Jr.'s assassination had not been fixed up or replaced. It would clearly be months, even years, before the government got around to them. DeMuth and Moynihan visited city officials and came up with a quick fix, as happy as turning the White House lights on. They would raze a small portion of the burned-out Fourteenth Street corridor and build basketball courts. Nixon was suspicious of the housing secretary, George Romney. The job needed to be done without delay. The solution was for Moynihan staffer Richard Blumenthal to direct it all, going around Romney, a modus operandi that would become habitual with the new president.[20]

Moynihan's wife, Liz, stayed home in Cambridge, and that was just as well, for to build an entirely new public assistance program took a mountain of work. Moynihan ran the numbers and calibrated charts, seeking to replace the Kennedy-Johnson welfare services with payments.

Nixon, just as Moynihan had predicted, liked the idea of sidelining the welfare bureaucracy, for Nixon, too, "abhorred snoopy, patronizing surveillance by social workers." Swapping out the Kennedy-Johnson nanny culture for payments was the first part of the plan. The second part, more technical, was to ensure that the worker didn't pay hidden costs for entering the workforce: heavy taxes should not hit the lowest earners. Phaseouts of benefits should not set them back, either: if workers lost a dollar in benefits for every additional dollar earned, they would not want to work. The technicians called the troubling bumps of disincentive on the income scale "notches." The notches discouraged those workers from working harder. Moynihan pounded away at these notches, reporting back to Nixon when he could. Moynihan also added in money to compensate the working poor for the Social Security payments that ate away at their paychecks. The cost of Moynihan's reform would be not one billion but billions. The plan would make an additional thirteen million people eligible for benefits.[21] That risk was worth it if you actually rewarded and honored the American working class. Nixon would be able to claim he was resetting American culture, undoing errors of Johnson, Kennedy, and Truman.

The main trick, in Moynihan's view, was to contain Vietnam, and antiwar protests, for the period it took his welfare reform to become law. Outside Moynihan's White House office stood Lafayette Park, where protests had taken place daily in Johnson's time. When the new Administration moved in, however, the park was closed, surrounded by plywood for a renovation. Workers were adding a fountain and planting around the statues of two Revolutionary War heroes, von Steuben and Rochambeau. The closing was awfully convenient, the speechwriter William Safire noted while the park was barricaded, no one could demonstrate there. The park couldn't stay closed forever, but such advantages bought the new Administration time.

As Moynihan worked through the spring of 1969, his mood stayed high. For Nixon was giving him the access he'd hoped for, continuing to allow Moynihan to counsel him in all areas, from welfare details to the history of classical liberalism in Britain. Moynihan reminded Nixon that conservative leaders who adopted liberal policies sometimes enjoyed great political success. "Tory men with Whig principles" had achieved the most in Britain, Moynihan argued, and suggested that Nixon read a new biography of Benjamin Disraeli, one of the progressive Tories. Nixon's old allies perceived Moynihan's historical lectures as destructive manipulation. Moynihan had deprived Republicans of their chance to do what they had been elected to do: kill the Great Society. Nixon, the speechwriter Pat Buchanan wrote, was being "seduced by his vision that he, Nixon, could astound critics as the American Disraeli." But most in the cabinet and around Nixon cheerfully tolerated Moynihan. They saw that Moynihan was becoming the Nixon Whisperer in the White House. "Pat is great because he provides the upbeat shot in the arm that the rest of the staff lacks."[22] The writers at *Time* magazine described Moynihan almost affectionately, as padding "around his basement office in stocking feet like a kind of White House super elf." "The boss is in love," Safire concluded.

The loved one was even confident enough about his access to boast to a *New Republic* writer, John Osborne. "The poor fellow is seldom more than three hours away way from a meeting with me," the professor told the magazine. Every time Nixon got distracted, Moynihan directed him back to "their" welfare reform. If the president was giving a speech on inflation, Moynihan pushed "the case for sending up a truly momentous domestic proposal shortly thereafter." The press was already picking up on the details of the welfare plan, Moynihan warned Nixon. Nixon must present his program soon to preempt criticism. The country, Moynihan told Nixon, was sliding left faster than either of them knew. ROTC on campus had long been a symbol of star students' commitment to military service. Yet now "the detestation of the ROTC" was a fact at major universities. President Nathan Pusey of Harvard, Moynihan's other president, was being mocked by students for permitting ROTC's presence.

Nomenclature, Moynihan pointed out at another of the presidential dialogues, mattered, too. If the president's relations with black leaders were to last beyond a honeymoon period, Nixon might consider changing the terms he used in the area of race as well: "you may want as a general policy to use the term 'black' rather than Negro." "Welfare" had become tainted, but out of intellectual honesty Moynihan refused to discard it; he would still say "welfare" in discussions. The point was that the term "welfare" could fade, and newer, more hopeful terms such as "workfare" would be there to take its place. With careful consideration, Moynihan initially dubbed his new program the Family Security System, the "Security" suggesting a lineage back to the granddaddy of all income transfers, the much-respected Social Security of Franklin Roosevelt. Family Security would be as important a change for the 1970s as Social Security had been in the 1930s, Moynihan reckoned. Via Family Security, America would see the return of the traditional appreciation of work. That in turn would beget optimism, sorely missing now across the country. That spring, Moynihan gave a speech at Notre Dame University deploring violence on campus.[23] But his speech was nowhere near as dark as the lecture delivered by Robert McNamara from the World Bank. McNamara was apparently so down that he felt the need to insult an audience at Notre Dame, after all one of the nation's premier Catholic schools, by laying out his opinion that unless the world practiced birth control on a "humane but massive scale," the globe would suffer "catastrophic consequences."[24]

No new plan, however badly needed, ever got through an Administration review without some internal opposition. This time the opposition materialized in the form of Arthur Burns. The Great Society had already left heavy burdens on the taxpayers, as Burns had warned so publicly while still at the National Bureau of Economic Research. Burns, Moynihan discovered, saw the guaranteed program as just another burden, like food stamps. Even as Moynihan, HEW Secretary Robert Finch, and Moynihan's young aides readied Family Security for political battle in Congress, Burns cobbled together alternatives to Moynihan's juggernaut. Like Moynihan, Burns commenced any project by playing to Nixon's preferences. Nixon had let advisors, and the country, know that he favored financial independence as the best hope for poor black Americans. You didn't have to pass a massive social welfare program to encourage financial independence, Burns told the others.

Burns's solution was to give black business owners direct business loans—that could enable them to fund their own housing. If the Johnson experience taught anything it was that creating wealth mattered more than treating poverty as a disease. Burns, like Nixon and Moynihan, possessed powerful political antennae. The economic counselor sincerely doubted whether conservative Republicans—at least the ones who had voted for Nixon-Agnew—would support an expansion of payments up the income scale. After an early meeting on the controversial Office of Economic Opportunity, Burns wrote in his diary: "Met with Shultz, Kennedy, Moynihan to discuss President's ideas about moving Job Corps and Head Start [out of OEO]. Moynihan seems to think that whatever displeases liberals is a disaster. He is blind to the importance of the President's retaining of his political power base."[25] George Shultz also hesitated over Moynihan's plan, and suggested creating public-sector jobs for workers. Nixon established a program that coerced federal contractors into hiring more black Americans. Burns tried to persuade the new housing secretary, George Romney, to back business loans in cities. Romney focused on housing loans, his territory, instead. "Apparently the prosperity of HUD is the stronger passion," Burns commented in his diary.

The president allowed the back-and-forth to go on so long that it distressed not only Burns and Moynihan but the cabinet, which resented the airtime the squabble stole. The White House staff discovered what all White House staffs discover: sometimes presidents actually liked to watch their men joust more than they liked getting an outcome. There was a streak of cruelty in it. Haldeman wondered about the dynamic. "Burns and Moynihan both feel strongly that P not putting enough time or attention on this and that nothing will be settled until he does. I think they're right."[26] Burns did not relent; he actually disliked Moynihan, who he suspected was a preener, not a loyal political servant. Moynihan was the type who would write a tell-all memoir. Paul McCracken, the chairman of the Council of Economic Advisers, even wrote a memo about the Burns-Moynihan tiff, "Possible Resolution of the Welfare Reform Controversy."

Still, Moynihan plugged away, seeking to connect every possible policy effort to the necessity for his welfare reform. In a March 1969 cabinet meeting, Henry Kissinger allowed that a new Anti-Ballistic Missile program might cost $1 billion, nearly a billion less than what was planned under President Johnson. Burns argued that the windfall could enable the Administration to narrow the deficit; the Johnson profligacy must diminish under RN. Presidents might enjoy cockfights, but there was always a risk when one of the cocks, in this case Moynihan, escalated by putting objections to opponents in writing. Moynihan seized the chance to complain to Nixon. Burns could argue for saving any windfall, but "I would argue just the opposite," Moynihan wrote in a presidential memo. Now, spring 1969, Moynihan said, was "the moment to spend money for education, health, poverty or whatever, and to hell with the details."

In April 1969, external events pulled Nixon's attention away from family assistance. Troops in Vietnam reached a high point, 543,000. The number of U.S. combat deaths approached thirty-four thousand, a landmark level because it exceeded the number of men killed in the Korean War. May brought the Battle of Hamburger Hill, in which seventy Americans and six hundred North Vietnamese were killed. Kissinger, the other Nixon favorite, was calling for secret bombing in Cambodia to hit the retreating North Vietnamese Army in their redoubts, and Nixon, hoping to uproot the enemy, was acceding. "K's Operation Breakfast, a great success, finally came off at 2:00 our time. K really excited, as is P," noted Haldeman. Moynihan did not know about Operation Breakfast. But he could see that each time Nixon expanded his war, the president felt the need to give voters at home a concession. Congress was already forcing Nixon to demonstrate the strength of his convictions, and Nixon wasn't always doing so. Senator George McGovern of South Dakota, one of the Vietnam War's fiercest opponents, chaired the Senate Select Committee on Nutrition and Human Needs. If Nixon gave McGovern a victory on hunger, maybe McGovern would let up on the war. Nixon did give the hunger problem airtime, calling hunger and malnutrition "intolerable." Such language nearly automatically converted a problem into a federal program, the kind you wrote with capital letters, "Hunger Program." "Intolerable" meant that serious money would be spent on Hunger. The new director of the Bureau of the Budget, Robert Mayo, began scrounging to find cash he could reallocate to hunger funding. Mayo cut so many State Department jobs that Secretary of State William Rogers emitted a *cri de coeur*: "Dear Bob . . . How can you do this to me?" Mayo also announced that $250 million in defense spending could be shifted over to domestic spending, the basis for the Hunger Program. Laird had to live with that.

Burns, a numbers man to the core, was suspicious. "Something inside" told Burns, as he wrote in his diary, that that $250 million to be shifted to Hunger covered only part of a year of the new hunger program. Sure enough, when Burns dug up the program and the numbers, he saw that the full annual cost would be more than a billion, with much of the money going to U.S. farmers. Nixon and the agriculture secretary had sensed the annual figures would be inconvenient, and had not looked at them. Moynihan could see that for Nixon the balancing act was a tough one. To win allies in Congress in 1970, and to win reelection, Nixon had to get to the lower middle class, whose sons were the ones serving in Vietnam. Nixon had to restore his legitimacy in the eyes of the university students and professors. "I don't have to say again that the one indispensable step to doing that is to get us out of Vietnam," Moynihan wrote to the president. When Dwight Eisenhower died, Nixon, who had so admired Ike, broke down in tears. "He was such a strong man," others heard Nixon say. Nixon had to be just as strong to complete projects like welfare reform.

Aware that budget problems were as great a threat to his program as the war, Moynihan refined his case. Moynihan's formulas suggested that Family Security would not be unaffordable once families stayed together and men wanted to work. The long run might take care of itself. If Nixon managed to end the war, the short run looked fine, too. A commission appointed by President Johnson had already concluded that a reduction of the United States presence in Vietnam would supply a "peace dividend" of $15 billion over an eighteen-month period. That was more than Moynihan needed.

All new presidents hit a moment in their first term, two or three months in, when the pressure of the White House begins to make them long for privacy. Nixon was already beginning to resist the onslaught of people.

"Volpe wants regular monthly appointment," wrote Haldeman in his diary of the secretary of transportation, John Volpe, "and Agnew wants regular weekly appointment." Observing the hours that went to Moynihan and Kissinger, the cabinet was growing anxious. Deprived of the private meetings they sought, cabinet members hogged the stage at the meetings they were allowed, cabinet meetings. As a junior presidential advisor, Stephen Hess, later recalled, the three former governors in the cabinet—George Romney, the HUD secretary; John Volpe; and Walter Hickel, the secretary of the interior—"never shut up." Once, Volpe wondered aloud if a cabinet member could simply say, "No comment" when his turn came in a cabinet meeting, whereupon the president replied, "It's about time." The worst jabberer was Romney. Nixon's own men were "getting on his nerves," Hess saw. Three months in, Nixon simply asked Haldeman to "keep them away from him." As Haldeman wrote in his diary: "P said he can see why all presidents want to be left alone. . . . Decided Burns should explain to Agnew how the vice presidency works."[27] Any week now, Moynihan knew, Nixon could shut out Moynihan, too.

But Nixon did not shut Moynihan out. And by summer Moynihan seemed to be prevailing over the penny-pinching Burns, the others, and perhaps even the ticking clock that was the Vietnam War. The president's calendar told the tale. In the first eight months of 1969, Moynihan logged 4,573 minutes with the president, not as much as Kissinger's 6,955, but still an astounding figure. In August, Moynihan and Nixon spent days readying the Family Security System. The base provision the government would supply for a family with no income was $1,600, only 40 percent of the official poverty level, but still significant.[28] Once a family did begin to earn, its money from the government would decrease, slowly. Rather than isolate poor or black citizens, the new plan indeed grouped the poor together with the working class, recalibrating at each early stage of the tax schedule. The plan actually met the old demand of Michael Harrington for a coalition of the working people, the poor, and a new middle class. The Family Security System, once up and running, would have twice as many people to supervise as welfare did.[29] The labor secretary, George Shultz, recognized the inevitability of a successful project's momentum, and loaded on to Moynihan's plan expansions for child care and training. Nixon, a Republican president, would be backing a child care program as big as Johnson's Head Start. "P really rolling on the new domestic plan with E [John Ehrlichman] in command," wrote Haldeman on July 14, 1969. Ehrlichman even went to Bucharest to work on the Moynihan plan with the chief executive. Just a few days later television once again reminded the country of humanity's possibilities, carrying the images of Buzz Aldrin and Neil Armstrong alighting on the moon. "One small step for man, one giant leap for mankind." If Americans could go to the moon, they could reform welfare.

Nixon, thrilled at pulling a maneuver that would leave Democrats speechless, brought his cabinet together at the presidential retreat at Camp David to iron out the final details of Moynihan's plan. Burns, as one could have predicted, posed multiple questions, all getting at the weaknesses and costs of the program. It was clear to the entire cabinet that the program was moving forward, for Nixon blithely allowed the conversation to proceed to marketing. Moynihan had favored an association with Franklin Roosevelt, but the rest at Catoctin Mountain did balk at that. The name "Family Security System" was "too New Dealish." A better name, colleagues thought, might be "Family Assistance System" or "Family Assistance Program." The day after these parleys on Moynihan's extravaganza, the president called Moynihan in to congratulate him. Nixon also let Moynihan know he had been reading that biography of Disraeli, the Tory who had led Britain in promulgating liberal policy. The papers reported that Nixon even played back Moynihan's line to him: "that sometimes Tory men with liberal principles are the ones who have enhanced democracy."

On August 8, a Friday, Nixon appeared on television and launched Moynihan's rocket, the guaranteed income proposal. The president channeled his professor and intoned robustly that "the present welfare system has to be judged a colossal failure." Nixon noted that the existing system encouraged fathers to leave homes: this was wrong. Moynihan saw that Nixon spelled the technical notch problems out with gratifying clarity: the present system made it possible, the president said, to "receive more money on welfare than in a job." Those who worked would get Family Assistance payments to make working more attractive. The government had "no less an obligation to the working poor as to the nonworking poor." Nixon went on: "I therefore propose that we abolish the present welfare system." In its place the Administration offered Moynihan's Family Assistance system. Nixon made clear he still objected to a basic "guaranteed income" per se because that established a right without responsibility. Those who worked would get Family Assistance payments to make working more attractive. Day care would be provided for families who worked. Those who would not work—here Nixon addressed only men and mothers of children over the age of six—would cease to get payments. Nixon hoped Congress would make Family Assistance law by next summer. The response to Nixon's announcement was the best Moynihan could hope for. Centrists praised the speech. The *New York Times* even called the undertaking "by far the most original and constructive initiative of his Administration." Now Moynihan was more than just a favorite; he was a successful favorite, the catalyst of the launch. In the *Washington Post*, a columnist wondered at Moynihan's personal trajectory. "Before inauguration it was freely predicted he wouldn't last six months as Urban Affairs Adviser to a Republican president whose base of political support and chief concerns are not notably urban-oriented."

Moynihan presented himself to the papers for interviews, joining a magazine writer, Bernard Asbell, for lunch on a Saturday at a restaurant near the White House. After a scotch old-fashioned, a sirloin, and a Budweiser "to wash it down," Moynihan charmed his interlocutor. He explained his move to Washington: "I decided to be disabused of their image of Nixon. I had already sufficiently learned what upper middle class liberals can do to someone they don't like." As for the welfare plan, it once and for all shut out the social workers who banned the fathers, a feat for which Moynihan had campaigned for years now. Family Assistance actually "enlarged democracy"—as Disraeli would have wanted. "Isn't that a nice phrase?" asked Moynihan before he pulled out an illicit Cuban cigar—"enlarged democracy"? The official poverty numbers were down since Johnson had spoken that day in Michigan, but one in ten

Americans was still poor. The nation had launched the War on Poverty, Moynihan thought. Why not win it?

————————

THE IDEA that a prosperous commercial nation could eradicate poverty and joblessness had its roots in England, where Moynihan had once studied. The United Kingdom's relief for the poor had mostly started in counties, towns, and churches, backed from above by Queen Elizabeth I, who signed a "Poor Law" that required individual parishes to care for orphans and paupers. At times, especially in the nineteenth century, but also before, some voices in Britain called for more radical programs. Random redistribution by various heroes, princelings, or a band of outlaws could occur: Robin Hood. Or revolution might level incomes for good. The young Friedrich Engels had been so struck by the shameless oppression of workers in Manchester and Liverpool that in 1845 he predicted socialism would come to England.[30]

But even before Engels's time, Britain had made up its collective mind that the wealthy or the middle class might share with the poor without endangering their own assets. At the height of the Napoleonic Wars, when grain prices were high, local magistrates in Berkshire had established for their region a means-tested scale of wage supplements that topped up whatever farmers earned. This arrangement was known as the Speenhamland system, after the location of the inn where it had been devised.[31] The argument in the Britain of the nineteenth century, as in the 1960s, was pragmatic and preemptive: when you helped the poor you prevented unrest and ensured a safe haven for commerce and property rights. Speenhamland had "worked" for a while—until England had realized that the tax on the parishes to pay for the income assistance was too heavy. More important, over the decades, the workers who received assistance ceased to want to work. A royal commission concluded that Speenhamland had, rather than eradicating poverty, institutionalized it, creating a "system of pauperism."[32]

Victorian England had taken a different tack to limiting the costs of the poor, making poverty a synonym for humiliation. The strictness of

Victorian England terrified the generally more lenient United States. American states, towns, and counties and churches slowly set about providing a contrast to brutal Britain, humanizing their treatment of poor citizens. Surveying the drinkers and homeless who lined New York City's Bowery, the writer Ray Stannard Baker asked why there should be a Bowery at all, "in an age which calls itself civilized?"[33] In 1909, Dickens readers at the *Washington Post* characterized the English attitude: "When the word went down the line that Oliver Twist has asked for 'more,' the entire parochial system, from the head beadle to the last ragged recipient of official charity, shuddered at the audacity of his request."

But at the turn of the century, astounding America, the British government made an about-face, embracing a national program of redistribution to end poverty. Even the highest instance of government, the royalty, shifted: "We are all socialists nowadays," Edward, Prince of Wales, commented cheerfully in 1895—a line it was impossible to imagine Grover Cleveland, Benjamin Harrison, or William McKinley ever dropping.[34] In 1909, David Lloyd George, chancellor of the exchequer, anticipated LBJ's War on Poverty when he proclaimed of domestic spending: "This is a war budget for raising money to wage implacable war against poverty and squalidness." In 1911, Parliament passed the National Insurance Act, a combination of workers' compensation, health insurance, and social security. From then on, Britain created or mandated various forms of payments, whether called "unemployment insurance" or public assistance, to the unemployed. Even in the early days, there had been skeptics. The socialist Beatrice Webb warned of the Speenhamland danger: "automatically distributed money" was likely "to encourage malingering and a disinclination to work." Helping today's unemployed guaranteed there would be more unemployed in the future.

Webb proved prophetic. At points England's relief payments, known as the dole, became so generous that the jobless did not always see the merit in returning speedily to work. There was a second negative effect: the cost. Passed on premises that seemed reasonable in the sunny economy of 1920, for example, a new unemployment law turned out to require many more pounds than predicted once recession hit. Suddenly British capitalism itself had to struggle. The sight of Britain's transformation horrified Americans again. During the New Deal, President Roosevelt rejected one of his labor secretary's drafts of the 1935 Social Security Act. "Ah," the president exclaimed with distaste, "but this is the old dole under another name. It is almost dishonest to build up an accumulated deficit for the Congress of the United States to meet in 1980."[35]

Roosevelt had therefore carefully cast Social Security as an insurance contract between the worker and the federal government, and as a pension, not a dole. Roosevelt's New Deal had also featured a modest pilot, rather than a permanent law, for federal food stamps. As for monetary support for nonpensioners, Roosevelt approved only modest federal assistance, grants from Washington to supply one-third of the funding for states' own mothers' aid laws. In Britain, meanwhile, multiple policy makers and lawmakers critiqued and revised the dole. One of the lead reformers and a protégé of the Webbs, William Beveridge, in 1937 hired the future prime minister Harold Wilson to research the causes of underemployment. Maybe Britain had it all wrong? Beveridge dispatched Wilson to employment exchanges, job centers, to find answers to questions such as, "Why are there so many thousands of unemployed in all the prosperous parts of the country?"[36]

At the end of World War II Britain astounded Americans yet a third time. While Americans were still lauding Winston Churchill for his wartime feats, Britons booted the prime minister from office. His replacement was Clement Attlee, who led the country in making itself "New Jerusalem," a social welfare state that nationalized health care and created a fresh program for the jobless, the British version of welfare, National Assistance for the Unemployed. It was this New Jerusalem that Moynihan had encountered as a graduate student. By the late 1950s, when Moynihan was already safely back in the United States with his mind on other matters, Britain found that inflation was so weakening purchasing power that it drove new crowds into the National Assistance program. While there had been 1.1 million Britons on National Assistance in 1948, the figure reached 1.8 million by 1962, when Moynihan had been in Washington on his first tour. British joblessness might look admirably low, but in Britain, official poverty cost more every year.

The back-and-forth over terminology to describe Moynihan's guaranteed income program was enduring was nothing new. All along in the history of aid to the poor, the results of programs had given Britons and Americans alike some discomfort, and they had expressed that discomfort by cycling through names. In England, the Poor Law became "the dole," until the term became as distasteful to foreigners and locals alike. Hence National Assistance. In the United States, "aid to children," or "relief" had become Aid to Families with Dependent Children, and then the comfortingly opaque acronym, AFDC. In the 1960s AFDC was usually called "welfare," but to many of the recipients, the very name felt like a bad joke. "Welfare means health, comfort, and happiness," as Johnnie Tillmon, a mother who received welfare payments, put it in 1969, "and we on welfare don't have none of that." Policy makers on both sides of the Atlantic felt the hypocrisy of the name shifts, and sometimes insisted, purely for honesty's sake, on applying the old labels. One such policy maker was Moynihan, who spoke of "welfare" sometimes. Another was a young member of Parliament across the Atlantic named Margaret Thatcher. In the midst of a debate in Parliament, Thatcher said plainly, "I personally do not mind whether it is called National Assistance, whether it is called a basic standard of living, whether it is called a basic income, or what."[37] From time to time, weary of encountering unexpected outcomes, and exhausted at defending the quirks of their unemployment or public assistance payments, the politicians of Britain had turned to the simplest justification for transfers of funds from haves to have-nots, the moral imperative. Michael Foot, a member of Parliament on the Labour Party's left wing, pointed out that it was absurd to talk in euphemisms about the millions of pounds Britain was now spending on National Assistance. It was disingenuous to claim that this carefully structured money was turning workers into capitalists. The same sums, however, were certainly warranted if they were considered a necessary redistribution of British wealth. The question Foot was posing was the same as Michael Harrington's: Why all the fuss to preserve the appearance of "mixed capitalism"? Perhaps social democracy was a sham and a contradiction. Perhaps a capitalist nation could never win a war on poverty. Why not call for honest socialism?

———————

THE CAMPAIGN to make Family Assistance law by 1970 started out well. Moynihan, and Nixon, imagined a coalition of centrist Republicans and conservative Democrats. Moynihan, Nixon, and Ehrlichman wooed the Democrats, conducting strategy sessions before each new approach. As often as not, Nixon brought a gift to the committee chairs. McGovern's Select Committee on Nutrition and Human Needs was still key, and McGovern's opposition to Vietnam unrelenting. On December 2, at a conference George McGovern hosted, Nixon publicly put forward two proposals: one expanding the food stamps program even more widely than Johnson had done; and the other on birth control, controversial among conservatives. Nixon sought "adequate family planning services" for five million low-income women. With these concessions in the mix, Nixon hoped, senators like McGovern would accept Family Assistance.

Though 1969 was an off year, a few key elections were taking place, and Nixon, and therefore Moynihan, watched them closely. A Democrat was expected to win the race for the slot of governor of Maryland that Agnew had opened, and one did. In Virginia, though, Linwood Holton, who had advertised his friendship with Richard Nixon in his campaign, was elected governor, the first Republican in ninety-six years. William T. Cahill triumphed in New Jersey, the first Republican in ages. Nixon might not control Congress, but the GOP's Silent Majority controlled thirty-two state governments. The positive news energized the White House, and boded well for Family Assistance.

But the same distraction that had blinded Johnson now glared at Nixon: Vietnam. Nixon had been withdrawing troops since April, even as he fought in Vietnam. The results in these fights had not been decisive. That summer, the South Vietnamese Army had begun a drive to recapture a province now dominated by the North Vietnamese forces, Binh Dinh. When the battles ended, the North Vietnamese Army still controlled part of the province. The president spent hours on peace talks in Paris between the North Vietnamese and the Americans, and mulled the idea of renewing air strikes. That also left him less time to tend to Moynihan's legislation. The news from Southeast Asia also weighed on Moynihan, who was under constant fire now from his friends for serving an Administration that was still prosecuting the war.

In November, around the time Moynihan would have expected Family Assistance to move forward on the Hill, there came a report from Vietnam so horrific that it made domestic goodwill reforms like Family Assistance feel near irrelevant. The year before, during the transition between McNamara and Clark Clifford, a unit had descended on a Vietnamese village, My Lai. The unit had been told that only Viet Cong—the enemy—remained in the village. Over a period of hours, the U.S. soldiers had tortured the villagers, raped the women, and then killed hundreds. *Life* carried the pictures. Not thousands but hundreds of thousands of Americans now converged on the Washington Monument to protest. They even raised the Viet Cong flag. Everyone in the government departments watched out the windows. Martha Mitchell, the wife of the attorney general, gave voice to what they all thought: "It looked like the Russian Revolution." "The abhorrent thing happened," wrote Moynihan to the president. "I would doubt the war effort can ever be the same." The domestic efforts would not be the same, either, even though My Lai had occurred under Johnson. The problem now wasn't the nation's mistrust of the president, the problem was mistrust of the presidency.

And despite Nixon's politic compromises, the Hill would not be easily wooed. The first opponents were Republicans, who could not see how expanding welfare would be eradicating it. Even Congressman James Utt, who represented Nixon's own Orange County, turned against the Moynihan proposal, telling the press he objected to the costs. Welfare now cost $7 billion a year, double what it had cost in 1965. Some twelve million Americans now received some form of public assistance, four million more than in 1965. And more would come under Family Assistance. Who was to say that the new crowds on the welfare rolls of the Moynihan system wouldn't stay there as well? Family Assistance was to be a permanent expenditure, like Social Security, Medicare, and Medicaid. That was enough to label it a "megadole."

Democrats, whom Moynihan expected to like the plan, revolted for a variety of reasons. The Ways and Means chairman Wilbur Mills, weary after Johnson, had abandoned fiscal restraint for horse-trading. Mills would release Nixon's new spending program from the purgatory of Ways and Means, but only if Nixon agreed to a 5 percent increase in Social Security payments that the Administration had heretofore opposed.

Democrats more progressive than Mills also proved hostile. Rather than going along with Nixon, McGovern, perhaps already thinking of the presidential race in 1972, was readying his own plan, payments of $600 per child for all families below the middle class, a program that would cost multiples of the Nixon scheme. Hubert Humphrey, momentarily shocked, noted that the McGovern plan would place close to half of the United States on welfare. A new lobby, social workers, also made its objections known. President Kennedy's and Moynihan's Executive Order 10988 long ago had transformed once weak public-sector unions into titans. The American Federation of State, County and Municipal Employees, one of those newly powerful unions, counted thirty thousand social workers among its members. Now social workers rose up in blunt defense: "This legislation threatens to eliminate the jobs of our people," said the union spokesman. Another new force on the scene was the National Welfare Rights Organization, housed, at least for a period, in the legal services division of the Office of Economic Opportunity. The name of the institution told much: welfare was to be considered a right, and Moynihan's plan took away welfare from those who did not work. And what was wrong about people claiming rights rather than taking unspeakably poor jobs they might not even be able to perform? "Only the stupidest person would put emphasis on work when the overwhelming number of persons on welfare are the aged, the blind, the disabled, children and mothers of children,"[38] George Wiley of the NWRO said. The "dignity of work" argument that Nixon was making did not resonate.

To Moynihan's chagrin even the traditional unions, which existed to protect workers, refused to support his Family Assistance. The AFL-CIO

Getty Images/PhotoQuest/Contributor

PLANNING FAILS ON TWO FRONTS. Just as his fellow cabinet members planned the Great Society with precision, so defense secretary Robert McNamara (above) planned the U.S. assault in Vietnam to the last detail. By April 1966, the death toll averaged a hundred a week, and total U.S. fatalities in the conflict numbered more than three thousand. The planning failures abroad mirrored those at home. In the same period, an architecture writer in Greenwich Village named Jane Jacobs (below) offered up another approach: Don't plan from above. Let the people below make their own plans. Don't think big, think small. Urban planners too often ignored the "marvelous and intricate order of freedom," said Jacobs. Given autonomy, a slum could "unslum."

Getty Images/Fred W. McDarrah/Contributor

Associated Press

LOOKING FOR SOCIALISM. Frustrated with civil rights and community work at home, Tom Hayden, like so many other activists, started to ask big philosophical questions. When in 1965 the chance materialized for a trip to Vietnam, Hayden took the offer, not only to protest the Vietnam War but also to evaluate socialism firsthand. Along with the pacifist Staughton Lynd and Communist Party intellectual Herbert Aptheker, Hayden made a tour of socialist and communist capitals, traveling to Prague, Moscow, and Beijing before stopping in Hanoi. Here Hayden (tallest), Lynd (rear), and Aptheker (eyeglasses) stand with a Buddhist priest. Lynd and Hayden admired North Vietnamese solidarity and concluded that North Vietnam featured a "socialism of the heart." Below, members of a North Vietnamese air defense unit in Quang Binh province. The trip proved only the first of such for Hayden, who also traveled to Cuba.

Getty Images/Sovfoto/Contributor

Getty Images/Bettmann/Contributor

WOULD AMERICA BE NEXT? Britain's prime minister, the socialist Harold Wilson (above), introduced new government departments and nationalization plans. In the fall of 1967, a run on the pound ensued, forcing Her Majesty's government to shut down the London Stock Exchange and devalue the pound sterling. With America also adopting social democratic measures, markets wondered if the dollar would be next. Tension between Fed chairman William McChesney Martin and the president grew. The Fed chair warned America was failing in her mission. Johnson bullied Martin and ignored his data. Frustrations with Vietnam drove Johnson to forgo a second term, but another impetus was Johnson's aversion to presiding over an inevitability: government austerity. "We don't have the self-discipline . . . to be great," Martin concluded.

Getty Images/Bettmann/Contributor

Associated Press

VIOLENT SOCIETY. By 1968 the SDS of Hayden's student days had imploded and given rise to groups such as the violent Weathermen or the Youth International Party (the Yippies). Ironically, Hayden, who had so hoped socialism would be benign, saw his own organization taken over by Maoists late in the decade. Above, Yippie leader Abbie Hoffmann after an arrest on a charge of unlawful weapons possession. Below, a Greenwich Village town house used by the Weathermen exploded when bombs held there detonated.

Associated Press

Associated Press

ENTER THE COMPETITOR. Unlike American workers, Toyota workers could halt the assembly line and suggest an improvement. The result: better cars for the money—like the early model Corona above. The Corona and the German Volkswagen retailed for well below the Big Three automakers' economy models.

Courtesy of UAW

AWAY FROM THE WORLD. Sensing future defeats, Walter Reuther struggled in his last years as UAW head. In his final days, Reuther focused on a world he could control, overseeing construction of a grand union retreat at Black Lake, Michigan. Far grander than the Port Huron cabins, Black Lake resembled the rest homes of the Scandinavian social democracies that Reuther so admired.

Getty Images/Bettmann/Contributor

ANOTHER TRY AT "GREAT"—AND SOME SKEPTICISM. In the 1968 presidential election, many of the candidates retooled Johnson's old "Great Society" logo. "Great for '68" was candidate George Romney's (above) slogan. Richard Nixon, the victor, promised not a great but a "just and abundant society." Many observers found that increasingly liberal courts and government planners were going too far, especially in demanding busing of children long distances in the name of school integration. "Busing is not relevant to high-quality education," challenged James Farmer (below), cofounder of the impactful Committee on Racial Equality and an assistant secretary at the Department of Health, Education, and Welfare in the Nixon administration.

Associated Press

Associated Press

WAITING IN THE WINGS. Ronald Reagan found a new post-Hollywood life when he was elected governor of California in 1966. While in office, Reagan came to tangle personally with the federal government over many Great Society programs, especially Sargent Shriver's Legal Services. Here Reagan is sworn in as governor in 1967.

Images/Bettmann/Contributor

GREAT SOCIETY III. Though the electorate expected Richard Nixon to lead
Congress in curtailing the Great Society, the thirty-seventh president ended up
expanding it. Advisor Pat Moynihan (above) encouraged Nixon to push through
legislation committing to guaranteed income for the poor and working class.
The theory was that a simple payment dignifying work would lift the spirits of
Americans disheartened by welfare bureaucrats. The legislation failed to pass.
By 1971 a new challenge, inflation, disoriented the country. The rise in prices
caused a crisis at America's big unions—no matter how large was the wage that
union leaders demanded, inflation meant workers needed more. After confronting
the humiliation of a strike by union employees against his own UAW, Reuther's
successor, Leonard Woodcock (below center, in glasses), headed to England,
where Toyota was also making itself felt.

Getty Images/Bettmann/Contributor

THE FED VERSUS THE WHITE HOUSE, AGAIN. If Johnson leaned on Federal Reserve chairman William Martin, President Nixon leaned harder on Martin's successor at the Fed, Arthur Burns (above, at Nixon's left). Nixon, like Johnson, demanded lower interest rates. Burns, the ultimate professional, resisted. But after Nixon gave Burns the cold shoulder, Burns compromised, laying the groundwork for modern America's greatest inflation. When the nation's gold reserves dropped to $10 billion and inflation hit new highs, Nixon tapped new treasury secretary John Connally (below) to fashion a shock package to astound the nation out of its malaise.

Getty Images/Grey Villet/Contributor

ROMNEY ON THE OUTS. Housing secretary George Romney was another figure spurned by Nixon. Romney's humiliation at HUD made a deep impression on his son Mitt (both pictured here). In an unguarded moment during his own 2012 election campaign, a still-bitter Mitt recommended abolishing HUD altogether.

Polaris Images

MANAGED AND CHRONIC. As the country moved into the 1970s, it became clear that new federal programs—whether Kennedy's, Johnson's, or Nixon's—did not cure poverty, as President Johnson had promised. New entitlements merely managed poverty. Above, Pruitt-Igoe's exterior after water pipes burst. Bad economic news panicked Nixon. So he called a retreat at Camp David and won backing for Connally's populist shock package. The U.S. imposed tariffs and price controls, lowered taxes for consumers, and closed the "gold window." Like most populists, Nixon benefited enough from his stimulus to win the next election, but a decade of economic pain ensued. The reluctant Camp David team (in front, from left): Paul Volcker, Pete Peterson, Arthur Burns, Herbert Stein, Paul McCracken, Treasury Secretary John Connally, and George Shultz.

Getty Images/White House/Contributor

MORE FIX-ITS THAT FAILED. In the name of halting inflation, President Gerald Ford in 1974 would form a program to "Whip Inflation Now." WIN operated under the absurd assumption that the public, through sheer willpower, could slow inflation. WIN also included a tax increase—a challenge to the weak economy.

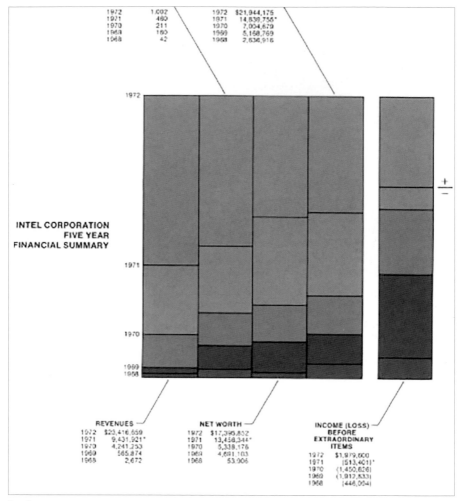

INTEL CORPORATION
FIVE YEAR
FINANCIAL SUMMARY

1972

1971

1970

1969
1968

REVENUES		NET WORTH		INCOME (LOSS) BEFORE EXTRAORDINARY ITEMS
1972	$23,416,659	1972	$17,395,852	
1971	9,431,921*	1971	13,458,344*	
1970	4,241,253	1970	5,338,176	
1969	565,874	1969	4,691,103	
1968	2,672	1968	53,906	

INCOME (LOSS) BEFORE EXTRAORDINARY ITEMS	
1972	$1,979,000
1971	(513,401)*
1970	(1,450,626)
1969	(1,912,533)
1968	(446,004)

Intel

AN UNMANAGED CAPITALISM. Even as older industries floundered and consumers struggled, some sectors flourished. In 1971 Intel, a newly publicly traded company, had to navigate the rough waters caused by Richard Nixon's Camp David program. Still, as its annual report proudly noted, 1971 was the year the young microchip company moved into the black. Intel's early profits were a portent of the new bonanza that freewheeling high-tech, removed from the old military-industrial complex, would eventually bring.

Associated Press

BOULWARE'S PROPHECY COMES TRUE. In the early 1960s, General Electric's ideologues predicted that grass would grow in Pittsfield, Massachusetts, if unions drove the price of labor there too high. Over the decades, General Electric indeed pulled thousands of jobs from Pittsfield and other unionized towns and expanded elsewhere. The consequences of the Great Society included "stagflation," the combination of slow growth and inflation. Blame was placed everywhere, even on foreigners. By the 1980s, U.S. autoworkers would take turns with a sledgehammer on a Japanese car.

Associated Press

Missouri Historical Society/Richard Moore

"THE GOVERNMENT GAVE UP." A St. Louis city official called the early 1972 demolitions at Pruitt-Igoe "the best show in town." But to those who had lived there, such demolition represented the final act of a tragedy. Following multiple efforts, federal officials and the St. Louis Housing Authority concluded that they could do nothing more and called the demolition men. "The government gave up," Chad Freidrichs, a one-time resident, later said.

Getty Images/Bettmann/Contributor

supported an income floor but "at no less than the poverty level," as George Meany put it, which meant more than double Moynihan's $1,600 family allowance. Walter Reuther of the UAW, the very Reuther who had sought and won something close to a guaranteed income for laid-off auto-workers, proved AWOL in the Family Assistance debate. Reuther plugged for a hike in Social Security payments rather than helping Moynihan. Reuther was still preoccupied with housing. His union and the Team-sters, together 3.5 million strong, were piloting a program to help poor families build and own their own homes.

The Democrats' rejection of a program crafted to please them startled Nixon less than Moynihan. The reason for the Democratic resistance was obvious. The Democrats and the unions did not want to move "forward to-gether" with the Republican. They wanted to beat the Republican. Nixon was in the act of stealing the Democrats' franchise, the War on Poverty, and neither the party nor the unions were about to aid and abet. "This was a real war on poverty but the liberals could not accept it," Nixon later wrote. ". . . They could not tolerate the notion that a conservative Republi-can president had done what his liberal Democratic predecessors had not been bold enough to do." Family Assistance might get through the House, but Senate passage would be really tough.

Moynihan enjoyed a good debate, but was not prepared for some of the substantive arguments lawmakers lodged against the bill. They started out by charging that the numbers in the Family Assistance plan didn't really work. Moynihan was after all not a tax hand, as Shultz was, or a data guru like Burns. Moynihan had thought he had ironed out the old "notches," the places on the income scale where the progressive tax structure cut the share of the last dollar a worker earned. But he had missed a few. The Senate Finance Committee chairman, Russell Long, posed the deadly question "What is the point of requiring the man to go to work if he's going to end up with less money?"[39] What mattered as well was the "effective" top rate, which included the cost of losing a benefit when one earned "too much." A mother who managed to earn the mini-mum wage for enough hours found herself priced out of Medicaid support with a value, in dollars, of four months' worth of wages.[40] Moynihan saw he had insufficiently accounted for the disincentive that the phaseout of non-cash benefits such as Medicaid, food stamps, and public housing represented. The interaction between state and federal programs meant that at least at one point on the income scale, poor workers would lose 67 percent of the next dollar they earned in the form of taxes and lost benefits. A 67 percent tax rate wasn't supposed to hit Americans until they were rich, earning well over $100,000. Moynihan had caused Nixon to propose a plan where the poor would be taxed like the rich. Worse yet, the loss of Medicaid and food stamps could at points impose an effective marginal tax rate of more than 100 percent.

A blow came from Moynihan's fellow professor Milton Friedman, whom Moynihan claimed as one of the fathers of the Family Assistance concept. Friedman, unlike Moynihan, had chosen to stay in the academy. He remained a professor at the University of Chicago, albeit one with a column in *Newsweek*. From these platforms, Friedman pointedly disowned the bill as a politician's mishmash. This was not the negative income tax Friedman had mooted. This legislation was, said Friedman, "a striking example of how to spoil a good idea."

The truth was that the trouble with the numbers was not entirely Moynihan's fault. Friedman had sought a negative income tax, the intellectual cousin of Moynihan's family assistance, under the assumption that other welfare programs would be abolished. Moynihan and Friedman saw their plans, whether called Family Assistance or negative income tax, as replacements, not additions. But the reality was that neither Nixon nor Congress was ready to abolish those older programs—the president was keeping or even extending them. So you had to include them in your arithmetic when you evaluated Family Assistance. And if you promised to keep old programs while introducing Family Assistance, you ended up with an outrageous budget, one likely to trigger a currency crisis worse than the one that had so disoriented President Johnson back in 1968.

Indeed, America might confront such a crisis even without any welfare reform. Whereas a year ago, in 1968, the country could tell itself it could control inflation, now, watching the rate pass 5 percent, Americans were throwing up their hands. One reason union leaders were not giving Moynihan's proposal much time was that the economy was taking all their energy. In its most recent round of negotiations with automakers, the United Auto Workers had allowed them to replace a provision requiring automatic adjustment of wages for inflation, whatever the rate of inflation, with a provision that capped the amount of inflation adjustment a worker received at eight cents an hour. Now workers were discovering that the eight cents did not cover the increases in costs caused by inflation. Instead of growing, wages were shrinking. "Instead of a whole ham, you have to buy half a ham," one autoworker told the *New York Times*. Moynihan saw this. "I accept my share of the blame," he would tell a labor convention early in the following year. "You can put all the blame on me if it will make somebody feel better." Reuther and his deputy, Leonard Woodcock, were planning to make restoration of an uncapped cost-of-living adjustment a demand in their 1970s rounds. Martin, the departing chairman at the Fed, was likewise shocked at the level of inflation. At his retirement party in January, Martin would tell a surprised crowd that America was "in the wildest inflation since the Civil War."[41] Martin again was chagrined: this was a poor way to close out. It was not the way Burns, who won confirmation as the next Fedderal Reserve chairman, hoped to enter the Fed, either.

Shrewd as he was, Nixon sensed the depth of the inflation trap, and found himself no longer in the mood for proposals that left him open to being labeled a big spender, progressive, or "Disraeli." Nixon still hated wage and price controls, and sensed that as inflation rose, the arguments for such controls would grow louder. At a cabinet meeting, Romney, seeing the tension, pitched a specific wage-control policy and mentioned that Britain had tried it. Perhaps Romney thought of England because of Moynihan, who so often had used Britain in those cozy tutorials with the president. This time it was Nixon the policy maker, rather than Nixon the politician, who reacted. Like Johnson, Nixon saw no use in ideas from a nation that had moved so close to socialism. After listening politely to Romney, Nixon exploded. Haldeman detailed the moment in his diary: "P finally whapped him by saying wage-price-policy never worked; Romney said it had in England; P laid him low saying 'Don't talk to me about England.'"[42] Nixon's advisors were finding that all budget numbers were running higher than the forecasts of even a year back. The peace dividend wasn't extra money to spend; it was money already committed to funding laws already on the books. Nixon could not dream after all.

But the final and most serious blow to Moynihan's arguments involved human nature. Moynihan and the other experts had assumed with Family Assistance that people were logical and optimistic, that if they could see their way out of welfare, they would go. That was not necessarily the case. Recent smaller experiments involving increases in payments had taken place. Arthur Burns, short on charm but long on data, had asked a talented member of his staff, Martin Anderson, to look at those experiments. It turned out the early results were not promising. As in old England, people did not necessarily want to work when they found they had more money at home. At Brandeis, another scholar of payments had found that more often, mothers on welfare who could get money without working preferred the money. The president's promise to cut payments off when recipients, men or women, refused to work, lacked verisimilitude as well. Even in Speenhamland in the cold nineteenth century, town fathers had found it personally difficult to cut off payments to those recipients who were only pretending to work, or not showing up. Would Nixon, a president who was allowing many increases in subsidy to lower earners, or any other president, be willing to cut off Family Assistance when recipients chose not to work? The program as Moynihan had structured it seemed likely to grow with few checks. Burns himself made an important point: it didn't help matters that to strengthen Family Assistance, Nixon and Moynihan had inserted language making assistance payments seem "a matter of right."[43] Fighting welfare mothers would only help the class warriors in their campaign to turn America into a country of class war rather than opportunity. The reality, one columnist in the Los Angeles Times wrote, was that Moynihan's plan truly was "socialistic." Republicans who supported it were hypocrites. These men were going along with Family Assistance, "yet if Truman had launched it, or FDR, or Kennedy, or Johnson, the sonic boom of rage would have blown the petals off the cherry trees." The headline of the article was "Look at the Socialist—Why, It's Richard Nixon!"

Despite Lafayette Park's reconstruction, the White House of spring 1970 was beginning to take on the air it had featured in Johnson's last year, that of a bunker. Moynihan lobbied for those evasive Senate votes. Moynihan wrote to Senator George McGovern to thank him for a relatively positive statement on Family Assistance, concluding, more wishfully than accurately, that "the subject has not become partisan." Moynihan also did battle with progressives, who rated his $1,600 floor as ungenerous. Black groups tried to cast Family Assistance as a race issue, even though the majority of Americans on welfare were white. Moynihan resented prominent whites who encouraged this attitude. The pandering of wealthy whites to black militants was, in Moynihan's view, becoming risible: Mrs. Leonard Bernstein had recently given a cocktail party with Black Panthers as guests. Where there were challenges to his work, Moynihan felt he could handle them, and wittily: a citizen of Georgia sent Moynihan $5 for a haircut and wrote that Nixon was "destroying the white people of the South." Moynihan wrote back that he would give the money to the NAACP. A black Silent Majority existed, too. Perhaps black Americans now could make their own way. The whole issue of race might be due, Moynihan wrote in a fresh memo to Nixon, for a period of "benign neglect."

The "benign neglect" memo was meant for Nixon alone, but Nixon distributed it to his cabinet secretaries, whence it was leaked to the *New York Times*. Moynihan was on his way to a conference in Antigua when the *Times* reporter called. "Oh God, this is it," he thought to himself when he heard his private letter had gone public. At the White House, a halfhearted hunt was conducted to find the leaker, who was thought to be the director of the Office of Civil Rights in the department of Health, Education and Welfare, a young man named Leon Panetta. But Panetta called the accusation "completely false." Moynihan was crushed. Once again, he had penned a memo that blew up in his face. To many Americans, "benign neglect" did not sound benign; it sounded cruel. Across the nation people mocked Moynihan and Nixon as callous. The term showed they did not care about the remaining challenges to black citizens. Few addressed the point that Moynihan had made in his memo: that outside the South, black families who stayed together had just about the same incomes as white families. Moynihan saw that the warnings of his old Cambridge friends about the perils of associating with Nixon might have some validity after all. Instead of cleaning up his reputation, Moynihan was trashing it. And after the news about My Lai, Nixon was not always available to help.

In February 1970, Moynihan mounted a ploy to rekindle Nixon's enthusiasm. The professor offered the weary president a break for ideas, assembling a group of professors from Harvard, Berkeley, and Columbia to chat at a cabinet meeting. Such a diversion would please Haldeman, the president's personal tender. The trick worked, as far as it went. Haldeman was impressed, and so was Nixon: "P in good listening form as well as participating," Haldeman noted. "Group all felt P should shift policy to helping and backing the strong instead of putting all effort into raising the weak." But the hour proved just a diversion, for as the weather warmed, so did the student protests, especially the protests in Moynihan's old sandbox, the college campus.

The demonstrations against the war were by now so intense and so numerous, on hundreds of campuses, that, again like Johnson, Nixon saw his family involved. Julie Nixon was due to graduate from Smith College that spring; her husband, David, from Amherst. The Nixon family decided that neither would attend commencement. Instead, the pair would even leave school a few weeks early. University presidents and professors, Moynihan's own peers, were writing to the White House in great numbers to attack the war. And those few academics who didn't support the peace movement, Moynihan saw, paid a heavy price. At Moynihan's own Harvard, where President Nathan Pusey had fought for the ROTC, the result had been "the destruction of Nathan Pusey." Pusey, Moynihan wrote, "was an honest and courageous man. Yet he was being destroyed by the students and faculty of Harvard, the one institution that was thought invulnerable to such attacks." Moynihan was beginning to wonder what would happen to *him* at Harvard when he returned.

There was no way to blame Nixon for My Lai. But, Moynihan argued, Nixon would be blamed for everything if he defended armies, governors, or mayors who handled protesters roughly. Prosecutors in Chicago had indicted Tom Hayden, the Yippie leader Abbie Hoffman, and the Black Panther cofounder Bobby Seale, along with five others. The charge was inciting riots at the Chicago convention. After Seale spoke out repeatedly, the judge had ordered him gagged and bound—and eventually severed Seale's trial, sentencing him to years in prison for contempt of court. At lunch, Moynihan told Ehrlichman he had been "desperately depressed" over their treatment in the courtroom. The Administration had not adequately distanced itself from such controversial behavior. The war gave protesters a moral authority they had lacked before. The White House, Moynihan told Haldeman, should make clear that such instances were "a political disaster which the president is not responsible for."[44]

Yet Haldeman and others insisted on defending the war, and, therefore, making clear that the Nixon White House, Moynihan's White House, now owned it. Even university presidents were turning against the White House. Indeed, the presidents were turning against their own professors—and the towns where their universities were situated. Typical was Kingman Brewster of Yale in New Haven, where Seale was also on trial. In New Haven the charge against Seale was complicity in the Black Panthers' murder of a fellow Panther. Activists and students planned large protests and a halt to classes. While some Yale professors objected, they were not heard in the melee. Brewster gave his sympathy to the protesters. He would say that he was "skeptical of the ability of black revolutionaries to achieve a fair trial anywhere in the United States." Brewster's administration was pursuing a campaign of conciliation, and would even allow protesters to sleep in campus courtyards, serving them lettuce, granola, rice, and water. Moynihan found himself appalled.

April brought a spark of light for Moynihan. The House passed, 243 to 155, HR16311, the Family Assistance Act of 1970, "guaranteed pay for the poor who agree to register for work or accept work training."

At the end of the month the president delivered a key speech on the situation in Southeast Asia. In that speech, Nixon reported that North Vietnam was increasing its activity in neighboring Cambodia. Nixon did not plan to "Cambodiaize" the defense of Cambodia, as he had promised to Vietnamize the conflict in Vietnam. Instead, he was going to bomb Cambodia, "cleaning out major North Vietnamese and Vietcong occupied territories." In other words, Nixon was indeed further expanding the war—despite the fact that even in this speech, Nixon mentioned his promise to end the war and vowed, "I shall keep that promise."

The Cambodia speech triggered a fresh round of protests at universities. At a school in Ohio's public university system, Kent State, the Ohio National Guard shot at students, killing four and wounding nine others. The mood of violence, which Nixon had sought office to prevent, permeated the land. The result was chaos at the colleges. At Robert Noyce's alma mater, Grinnell, the disruption was so intense that the president canceled classes for days.[45] In Washington, students gathered again to protest. Moynihan could see that Nixon was trying to absorb this domestic escalation. On the night of May 8, Nixon held a press conference. A reporter asked about the state of American society generally, where the country was heading. Nixon snapped back: "Briefly, this country is not headed for revolution." From the heights of the Abundant Society, the Administration's expectations had dropped to the hope of a society that merely survived. Unable to sleep, early in the morning Nixon ordered a shocked staffer to drive him to the Lincoln Memorial so that he might speak with the students. "The weirdest day so far," Haldeman wrote in his diary.[46] The students were likewise shocked to see the president. "I know probably most of you think I'm an SOB. But I want you to know that I understand just how you feel," Nixon told the students. The exhausted Nixon's dawn visit was a kind of last-ditch, irrational bid for approval. It had taken four years for Johnson to suffer "personally," as Moynihan had put it, from protests. Nixon had been in office less than a year and a half, and was already as desperate and lonely as his predecessor.

In the rough environment, not only the White House but the country felt paralyzed. The police were tough, but the student protesters and the protesters at the factories were too violent. Those who had heretofore considered themselves rebels found themselves siding with the conservatives. Robert Noyce spent days at Grinnell trying to calm the students and faculty, which had revoked nearly all graduation requirements in favor of "a pioneering adventure into free and open curricular territory." Privately, Noyce, too, thought the administration was pandering to the students. As Gordon Moore, his colleague, would say later, "We are really the revolutionaries in the world today—not the kids with the long hair and beards who were wrecking the schools."

That spring Reuther finally delivered the attack on his revolutionary children that he had held back for so long. "The ultra-left extremists with their revolutionary slogans and their reckless behavior," Reuther said, could "sow the seeds of a unique form of American fascism." Reuther, who knew his Lenin better than most, recalled that Lenin had castigated "infantile leftism."[47] The American left was giving a display of such infantile leftism. Rather than being for something, the protesters knew only what they were against. Like Moynihan, Reuther was disgusted at the protesters' unwillingness to support serious efforts by old union leaders or government officers. "When you are in favor of destroying the system," Reuther noted, "the worst enemy is anyone who is trying to make the system work and make it responsive to human needs."

Early May found Moynihan, still head down, trying to concentrate on his work, a rewrite of his welfare reform legislation. He had to make Medicaid or food stamps support rather than undermine the incentive to work. Not even a legislative genius could manage such a change overnight. It would take "half a decade or more," Moynihan warned reporters, to integrate America's various social programs so that they functioned as one. The Treasury had originally scored the cost of his bill at $4.4 billion per annum, and now Moynihan found himself lamely promising reporters that the updates to the law would not cost "very much" more. From California, Governor Ronald Reagan was now warning that Nixon's program "would put one in every seven of our citizens on welfare." But Moynihan also took time to tend to the clearly distraught Nixon. Writing to advise the president on colleges a few days after Kent State, Moynihan warned that Nixon must make clear that he opposed violence, which in the end actually destroyed the freedom of the university. Both sides, Moynihan allowed, were guilty of violence—dissent had to be peaceful. Moynihan also noted that the national guardsmen who had failed at Kent State had done so because "they were untrained and panicky." This was no excuse. But it was a simple reality that anyone who had served in the military could understand. Few of the protesters had served in the military.

In the same days Moynihan himself turned panicky. Word had come that the Harvard chapter of Students for a Democratic Society planned to "burn" or "trash" Moynihan's home on Francis Avenue.[48] Moynihan's wife, Liz, armed herself with a baseball bat. Six divinity students stood guard before the Moynihans' house. This level of threat was a long way from the cattiness of children of liberals snubbing one's own children at school. The barricading of the Moynihans on Francis Avenue made a mockery of Moynihan's decision to enter government. The White House the professor had joined two years ago was no longer the same place: "The Old Executive Office Building was full of soldiers," Moynihan noticed. The price of staying with Nixon was too high. In May, Moynihan let the president know he would be leaving, and received from Nixon a gracious assurance that he would continue the fight for Family Assistance. The door to Harvard still stood open. While it would have him, Moynihan was returning to the Life of the Mind.

The same May found Reuther busy preparing for the autumn union negotiations and the UAW's fight for inflation protection for its workers. It looked to be a year of strikes, with many other unions also struggling to make pay rise automatically with inflation. Some 150,000 General Electric workers were already striking, hoping not only for an inflation clause, but also, this time, finally, to force General Electric to drop its old tactic of putting take-it-or-leave-it offers on the table. Though Reuther had parted ways with the AFL-CIO, he could not resist teaming up with George Meany to support the GE workers, pledging $5 million of UAW money in strike aid. Putting an end to Boulwarism would be a real legacy, worth at least $5 million. More important to Reuther even than vanquishing Boulwarism, however, was his union haven at Black Lake. Construction was near enough to completion that the UAW was planning to cohost a United Nations conference on pollution there that June. On a Saturday, Reuther and his wife, May, joined their architect, Oscar Stonorov, and climbed into a chartered Learjet 23 to inspect Black Lake. The plane lifted off from Detroit at 8:44 p.m., after darkness had fallen, and flew into mist and fog. In their attempt to land, the pilots took the plane too low, too early. The little jet clipped the treetops and caught fire, crashing in an inferno. The passengers were gone in minutes. The great dreams were dying, and now the great dreamer had died, too.

11

The Governor of California

1970

Guns: 7.8% of GDP
Butter: 6.3% of GDP
Dow Jones Industrial Average: 809

Down the belly of the state rides the governor of California, tight in fiscal policy, extravagant in charm.
—*Los Angeles Times*, 1970

In early 1970 a lawyer named Bayard Berman sat down for a breakfast with a *Los Angeles Times* columnist.[1] Berman was celebrating a court victory. More than half a decade before, the families of two high school girls, Mary Ellen Crawford and Inita Watkins, had joined the American Civil Liberties Union in a case against the Los Angeles Board of Education. The ACLU had started with an argument that sounded like *Brown v. Board of Education*, the 1954 Supreme Court case. The girls attended a local high school, Jordan High in Watts, where the students were nearly all black. The girls should be able to attend South Gate, an all-white high school. *Crawford v. Board of Education* had made only halting progress until recently. Then Berman had stepped in. Litigating for the ACLU, Berman had argued not only that the girls had a right to attend South Gate, but also that for Los Angeles to run a school system that wasn't integrated everywhere represented illegal segregation. Berman won in Los Angeles County Superior Court. The judge, Alfred Gitelson, sanctioned Berman's claim: a school district or city where blacks and whites were not integrated in schools was as guilty of segregation as any Jim Crow school board in Alabama. Gitelson ruled that school authorities must integrate all of Los Angeles County, 730,000 students in six hundred schools, by September 1971.

The columnist, whose name was Art Seidenbaum, didn't focus on the implications of the judge's finding. Seidenbaum didn't detail the specific facts of *Crawford*, either. He did not say anything in his article about Elnora Crowder, the African-American schoolteacher who had originally made the effort to patrol minority neighborhoods bravely, "like an Avon lady," as someone said, hunting for plaintiffs for the desegregation case.[2] Nor did the columnist write about Jordan High, whose students the year before had scored an average of eight, compared with a nationwide norm of fifty, on a national reading test.[3]

The subject of Seidenbaum's column was the lawyer. Seidenbaum reported what Berman had for breakfast (eggs and whole wheat toast), what Berman thought about the political popularity of the consequences of the *Crawford* victory (Berman recognized that busing, the likeliest method for integrating Los Angeles schools, was controversial), even what Berman thought about the zeitgeist. In the interview, Berman expounded the failings of politicians—they had "abdicated," Berman thought, when it came to civil rights of school pupils. That was why Berman, Gitelson, and the ACLU had had to step in. Berman was no stranger to celebrity. An entertainment industry lawyer, he had represented Trish Hilton, the wife of the heir to the hotel dynasty. Berman had appeared in court for the actress Rita Hayworth in her fifth divorce. The difference was that this time the celebrity was not a Berman client but Berman himself.

Nor was Berman the only new celebrity lawyer. All over the country lawyers, and indeed judges, were becoming stars. Not the old stodgy corporate lawyers or bankruptcy judges, but rather jurists involved in flashy civil rights cases. The name of William Kunstler, the lawyer for eight protesters at the Democratic National Convention, had made a deep impression on American youth, who honored Kunstler for risking a conviction for contempt and jail to do battle with the judge on the case, Julius Hoffman. Every spectacle needs a villain, and Judge Hoffman had become that villain, guaranteeing the blockbuster success of Kunstler's show by making the unwise decision to order the binding and gagging of one of the defendants, Black Panther Bobby Seale. If Hoffman was a villain, Judge Gitelson, who ruled in *Crawford*, was a hero. Now Gitelson was becoming the subject of praiseful profiles, with the *Los Angeles Times* noting respectfully that Gitelson was so busy with the law that he never read a mystery novel, though for context he once in a while would pick up an account of an episode from legal history, such as the trial and beheading of England's Charles I.[4]

Some of the new legal stars shone from law offices or the bench, but some lodged at universities. The greatest such academic star was Charles Reich of Yale Law School, the one who had begun his career as a clerk for Supreme Court justice Hugo Black. Reich was already well known for the law review article he had written contending that welfare benefits were, like dollars, patents, or houses, the property of those who received them. From California to New York, public interest lawyers now referred to Reich's "new property" when they drafted their cases. But this year, Reich's fame would increase to another magnitude when he would publish a book titled *The Greening of America*."[5] *The Greening* was not about the rise of the environmental movement, but rather about social change led by "greens"—America's young shoots, youth. Reich argued that America had a while back transcended the old culture of self-reliance, the culture of his former boss, Hugo Black, which Reich categorized as Consciousness I. Next the nation had moved through an intermediate culture of organization (Henry Ford's assembly line, the technocratic 1950s, even Roosevelt's New Deal). This was Consciousness II. America was now arriving at what Reich called Consciousness III, an era of compassion, creativity, blue jeans, recreational sex, and recreational drugs. (The government's position on marijuana, Reich offered, "offers the most clear-cut and self-defeating example of the rigidity-repression syndrome.")[6] Consciousness III rejected the old socialist order, but it resembled Hayden's socialism in that "it was always in a state of becoming." Consciousness III might also include the creative society of Robert Noyce, the one Reagan had described on the campaign trail in 1966. The capaciousness of

the new category appealed to college students, as the Port Huron Statement had appealed to them. Younger readers also liked that Reich made
them the stars along with himself. By the second half of 1970, *The Greening* would be a bestseller. Reich was alive, indeed still a young man, but
his reputation was rising so fast that he appeared to be approaching a
state of beatitude. The *Washington Post* that year called him "the Saint
of New Haven."

There was one figure who was not pleased to see lawyers and judges
under the lights. That figure was a former celebrity himself, Ronald Reagan, governor of California. From his own years as an actor, Reagan could
see how Berman's and Gitelson's showboating distracted from the radical
nature of their work. Reagan saw that only busing kids could integrate
Los Angeles schools to the extent Berman and Gitelson demanded. The
busing would "seriously damage the education of Los Angeles youngsters," Reagan told the press. When the rubber of bus wheels met the
road, families and teachers would see the formidable waste that busing
caused: waste in hours on buses, waste in outlays, waste in friendships
ended when kids and parents lost neighborhood connections. Busing
would transform Los Angeles, one of the nation's largest school districts,
and set a precedent other show-off lawyers and judges in other states
would follow. Reagan had won his first gubernatorial election in 1966
by a margin of a million votes. Voters would again give their opinion of
him when they decided whether to reelect him at the end of 1970. Superior court judge was in California an elected post. Voters that fall would
therefore have a chance to rehire, or throw out, Judge Gitelson. But the
lawyers—when was their election?

THREE YEARS before, when he arrived in Sacramento, Reagan had not
intended to focus on lawyers or judges. As a freshman governor he had to
pick his battles. Reagan, or, more specifically, Reagan's Republican advisors, had decided that as a rookie he should not follow to the letter every
principle in the "Time for Choosing" speech at the Republican National
Convention that had launched his career. To take all the pure positions

of Barry Goldwater was to fail, as Goldwater had failed. A new governor had to pick his battles.

The battle that Reagan had picked first, in his early days, was the Golden State's budget deficit. That law said the state must balance the budget. It had been difficult for Ronald Reagan, the same Reagan who at GE had railed against statists, to raise taxes. But to narrow the deficit, in his first years as governor Reagan had signed laws that had done so. The deficit disappeared; by 1969, California, whose total budget was $6.2 billion, suddenly enjoyed a surplus of half a billion dollars. But now, in 1970, California seemed to be moving into a recession, the kind that would reduce state tax revenues and widen deficits again. The state's aerospace industry was shedding tens of thousands of jobs. Companies that had boomed now busted. Even the electronics industry, a true star of the creative society, was encountering trouble. Intel had recently introduced the 1101, a new chip, the first to use high-volume metal-oxide semiconductor memory and silicon gates. The engineers had worked on the chip while listening to the 1969 moon landing on the radio. But the chip wasn't selling.[7] In June, 1970, Intel laid off 10 percent of its employees. An internal memo carried a line that read, "Management Near Panic."[8] Les Vadász, one of the big names at Intel, thought of Simon and Garfunkel's song "Fakin' It," as did Andy Grove, another big name. "I've just been fakin' it. Not really makin' it." Years later Grove would recall how the Simon and Garfunkel song haunted him. "We have to prove something," Vadász wrote, "or else are we faking it?" The Golden State suffered an additional blemish: unemployment was worse than the national average. California law set jobless benefits at one of the highest levels in the nation. Cash was now short in Sacramento. Reagan didn't like the idea of raising taxes in an election year, but both municipal and state costs in California kept rising. And the lawyers had something to do with that.

A good example was the effect on city and state budgets of the courts' integration rulings. Setting aside whether integration by busing children to schools was necessary, or benefited blacks and whites, busing was costly. The school district of Los Angeles already had a deficit of

$40 million a year. Achieving full integration in Los Angeles would be difficult. Some children would have to ride many miles from home. The busing would widen that school district deficit to $60 million. The book-keepers estimated that applying Judge Gitelson's ruling statewide would cost the state $40 million in the first year, and $180 million over ten. Yet no one could even be sure if Gitelson's idea would work. Though Gitelson had ordained integration throughout Los Angeles, he could not stop white families from putting For Sale signs on the lawn and leaving, thereby rendering schools all the tougher to integrate. There was an irony for Reagan and Mayor Yorty to savor: in one way, Los Angeles was lucky. Because half the pupils there were black, Mexican-American, or Asian, mixing them in even numbers would be a statistically straightforward chore. Finding enough "white" schools to integrate according to a judge's order in Washington, DC, for example, would be difficult, since 80 per-cent of the pupils in Washington were black. As was true of the OEO's old community action projects, the mayors and school boards were in any event not in charge. In integration cases like Crawford, judges such as Gitelson supervised and made the calls.

Another example of fiscal damage from new litigation was welfare, the area where Moynihan and Nixon were flailing. Not only Washington but also the states paid for welfare. Thanks in part to the expansion of welfare eligibility by Johnson, Nixon, and Congress, some forty thou-sand new recipients joined the California's welfare rolls each month. That meant the state's caseload was growing at a rate of 20 percent a year.[9] And even more Americans were likely to claim welfare in the future. Reagan put it bluntly, as he had during his first campaign: he wanted the authority to send "the welfare bums back to work."[10] State governments should, to Reagan's mind, have the ability to make deci-sions about who received welfare and when to halt payments. Ten years ago California officials would have had that authority. Then, the Su-preme Court had handed down *Flemming v. Nestor*, holding that just because a worker paid Social Security taxes while working did not mean he was entitled to receive his pension later. Social Security, the Supreme Court had said then, was not a contract like an insurance policy. But now

Charles Reich's "new property" gave welfare recipients a powerful tool against bureaucrats.

A third law-driven challenge to California's growth involved changes in the agricultural sector. Farmworkers in five California counties were threatening to strike. The workers might need—or deserve—higher pay, but such strikes cost growers profits, too.[11] Legal action by farmworkers had long been encouraged by unions—Reuther had itched to capture California—but the new force was a public interest law firm funded by Washington called California Rural Legal Assistance. CRLA brought in lawyers from the East Coast to manage suits against employers and the counties or states. CRLA's suits, which it often won, had political implications, as well as economic ones; the nonprofit was also suing to invalidate California's constitutional English literacy requirement for voters. The CRLA took on Reagan so often the agency was a thorn in Reagan's side. In California, the governor had the authority to strike out individual items in the state budget—the line-item veto. That was vital for constitutional reasons, the constitution in this instance being the state of California's, which required that the governor submit balanced budgets or find new sources to zero out deficits. Yet CRLA attorneys and their colleagues convinced a court to reverse a budget cut of $220 million the governor had made to Medi-Cal, California's Medicaid program.[12] They also forced Reagan to expand the number of food stamp beneficiaries. CRLA forced the establishment of a minimum wage for farmworkers, and in so doing forced Reagan to violate his own constitution. When California's farmworkers went on strike, growers hired Mexican guest workers, *braceros.* Reagan, business oriented, sided with the growers. CRLA sued and, setting a precedent, blocked the hiring of Mexicans as strikebreakers. These were not mere thorns in the governor's side. They were body blows.

The year before, hitting back, Reagan and U.S. senator George Murphy, also a former actor, had sought to push an amendment through the U.S. Senate giving governors a say over such federally funded legal services nonprofits.[13] The amendment had not survived, in part because of lawyers, again: a few law school deans and the director of the NAACP Legal Defense Fund had scared off supporters by warning that "if CRLA is destroyed, the message will be clear to programs that might contemplate challenging, innovative litigation: Do not invite displeasure of public officials."[14] Congress in the Johnson years had reduced governors' power by passing a law that said OEO could override a gubernatorial veto of an OEO project in the governor's state. A governor could still make a show of vetoing, but this—as Reagan, or any governor, knew—was a high-stakes action: humiliation of the governor by overriding OEO might be the only outcome.

There were two other areas where Reagan came head-to-head with lawyers. One involved the state universities, where civil rights lawyers and the professors themselves challenged the state's authority to set the curriculum, manage the campus, or hire and fire professionals. In 1969, Reagan had such trouble enforcing the law in Berkeley that he had called in the National Guard, and unapologetically watched as the Guard and police used tear gas to clear demonstrations.[15] With great effort, and serious challenges from the Democratic leader in the California assembly, Jesse Unruh, Reagan had recently seen to it that a communist associate professor, Angela Davis, was fired by UCLA. Reagan believed in free speech, but he also believed that the state, as chaperone of the universities, was there to school students in Western Civ, not communism.

The final field of contest with the lawyers was the public space, the state legislature, say, or the courtroom. In 1967, early in Reagan's first term, a group of Black Panthers had walked into the California state building armed with rifles and shotguns and occupied the capitol. Police ordered them to leave the premises. Bobby Seale, the same Bobby Seale in Judge Hoffman's courtroom in Chicago, had argued that the Panthers had as much right to guns as whites did, and made a statement that "City Hall turns a deaf ear to the pleas of black people."[16] The armed protesters had garnered more support than Reagan rated warranted. In 1969, the maniac Charles Manson instructed a group of followers to break into a home in Los Angeles and murder a group of people, the pregnant actress Sharon Tate included. The Manson trial had become something like a horror show version of the trial of the rioters in Chicago, with Manson representing himself and the case dragging out. To Reagan's mind, the courts were too solicitous of Manson and the others. Reagan believed courtrooms were like universities: places that enjoyed not only the right to free expression but also the obligation to operate within the bounds of common sense. But mutiny in the courtroom was the 1970 fashion. That summer a California lawyer, Michael Tigar, spoke out at a legal conference in St. Louis during a session titled "The Spirited Lawyers Representing Political Defendants." Tigar—an acting professor of law on the payroll at Reagan's own UCLA—argued that if courtrooms were "instruments of intolerable repression, then they may well turn into instruments of revolution." To a man like Reagan, or for that matter Justice Black, such a statement was anathema. To condone or even tolerate violence was to beget violence.

The very same day Michael Tigar spoke, August 7, brought a tragic confirmation of Reagan's point. In Marin County an armed seventeen-year-old named Jonathan Jackson took superior court judge Harold Haley, a prosecutor, and three jurors hostage. Jackson, joined by three convicts, taped a gun to the judge's neck and then encouraged a terrified press photographer to capture the image. "Be sure to get a picture of the judge . . . we want the story out," one of the gunmen said. Later, one of the convicts or Jackson—it was not clear which—added, "You take all the pictures you want. We are revolutionaries." In the ensuing battle with police, Jackson, Judge Haley, and two inmates were killed. The prosecutor was shot in the back, paralyzed for life. In the investigation, police found that two of the guns—a Browning automatic pistol and a carbine rifle—were registered to Angela Davis, the former UCLA professor. Davis disappeared, a fugitive from justice.

The murder of Judge Haley changed the mood in California. The frontier era of unguarded courtrooms was clearly coming to an end. A few days after the courtroom shootings, civic leaders and thirty cars of law enforcement officials, along with San Francisco mayor Joseph Alioto and Archbishop Joseph McGucken, gathered in San Rafael to lay Judge Haley to rest. The same day, Reagan told reporters that California needed to prevent future Marin County scenes.[17] Reagan had recently signed what Californians called the "Law and Order Bill," which allowed local agencies to remove unruly guests—including the press—from meetings. A law passed after the Black Panthers occupied the Sacramento state-house had proscribed only loaded guns in public spaces, not unloaded guns. Perhaps that ban ought to be extended to all guns, Reagan said. "The type of thing we have seen, to disrupt the court with this kind of violence" was untenable. The legislature had to make sure it wouldn't happen again. That September, Reagan continued to push back the new legal culture where he could. A Republican assemblyman from South Gate, the site of one of the high schools in the Crawford case, offered a bill banning busing without parental consent in the state. The state assembly backed him, and on September 14, the governor signed that, too. To launch such whole-scale busing as *Crawford* seemed to warrant, Reagan said, would "shatter the concept of the neighborhood school."

If California was reconsidering its own situation, the rest of the nation was reconsidering California. California was the future, famous for Hollywood, famous for its population and economy, both now surpassing even that of New York. But now the California of kooky universities and outrageous violence was not a future the rest of the country necessarily wanted. Around the same time, Reagan found the suitable venue to express his thoughts about the state of the law: a meeting of the California Bar Association. Reagan, the first governor of California in decades not to hold a law degree, did not hesitate to speak soberly and frankly. That year, the governor noted, fifteen officers of the law had been killed in the line of duty, some killed execution-style because they were cops. Reagan also raised the topic of the trial of Charles Manson, and complained about the delays extraditing one of the accused in the Manson gang from Texas. Legal proceduralists were favoring the rights of the defendant, but not the rights of the prosecution or the people of California. "The public is frustrated and fed up," Reagan told the attorneys. The governor assigned a good share of the blame to legal professionals. Judges had the authority to restore order in their courtrooms. "Why," Reagan asked, "does a criminal defendant with a clever lawyer seem able to run circles around some of our finest prosecutors with a seemingly bottomless barrel of time-consuming gimmicks?" Courts nowadays tolerated behavior "that would not be tolerated in any kindergarten." Lawyers themselves should see to it that "lawyers who deliberately disrupt the courtroom can and will be disciplined, and swiftly and effectively." The emphasis of the speech was halting violence and courtroom theater, but Reagan was also taking aim at lawyers' vanity, their interest in making law rather than enforcing it. At his inauguration in 1967, Reagan had defined his job: to put California's "fiscal house in order." Reagan had done that, balancing the budget with tax increases. Now Reagan asked the legal profession to do the same: "put your own house in order." Leaving the lawyers to absorb his scolding, the governor flew off to a barbecue with one thousand visitors at the Santa Cruz County Fair. A few days later, at a Republican picnic in Yuba City, the governor was after the lawyers again, assailing California Rural Legal Assistance. The nonprofit should have stuck to individual legal aid cases for rural indigents, Reagan said, but instead had "converted itself into a vehicle for class action lawsuits against various government agencies." Reagan told the crowd that his staff had reckoned that if the CRLA won all its suits in California, the cost of welfare there would increase by $1 billion—the same amount Johnson and Shriver had first set as the budget for the entire War on Poverty.

In the California gubernatorial election, endorsements mattered, including endorsements from traditional stars, the Hollywood kind. As November approached, Jesse Unruh, Reagan's opponent, won the backing of Bill Cosby, Diahann Carroll, and Trini Lopez. Frank Sinatra had opposed Reagan in 1966 and didn't particularly like him: "He's such a bore," Sinatra had once said of Reagan. "Every time you get near the bastard he makes a speech and he never knows what he's talking about."[18] But Sinatra couldn't agree more with Reagan's stance on the universities, and was making sure the papers knew he was switching to RR. Hollywood was not Cambridge. But the reaction among actors who fancied themselves serious intellects resembled that of Moynihan's colleagues at news Moynihan was joining Nixon: horror. "[E]ven Frankie, despite his monomania," Richard Burton wrote in his diary, "should be able to see that Reagan is patched cardboard and dangerously stupid." Unruh taunted Sinatra by recalling that Sinatra had supported Adlai Stevenson and Hubert Humphrey—both losers. But Sinatra was not alone. Dean Martin and Jack Benny, like Sinatra former opponents of Reagan, also switched sides, endorsing the Republican. The columnist Art Seidenbaum, the same writer who had profiled the attorney Bayard Berman earlier that year, now suggested there was a kind of inevitability to Reagan's reelection: "Down the belly of the state rides the governor of California, tight in fiscal policy, extravagant in personal charm." It was obvious to all that Reagan was already looking past November to his second term and future battles with lawyers.

THE FACT that one trade, the law, became the single most important topic of the nation's most important gubernatorial contest was an example of how a small program, near unnoticed at its inception, could come to alter American life within half a decade. When Johnson, Shriver, Moynihan, and the team of the Office of Economic Opportunity had laid out their programs in 1964, they had focused on VISTA, a kind of domestic Peace Corps or community action and Head Start, the program for preschoolers. In the kit, but unnoticed by many, had been funding for Legal Services for the poor, which most Americans understood as federal funding to support individual people in individual cases. Legal Services might ensure the poor defendant had a genuine ally in the courtroom, not just an overtaxed pro bono lawyer from a private law firm or a locally assigned public defender, who might also be best friends with the judge. The Legal Services component of the Economic Opportunity Act appeared simply to augment the activity of existing legal aid societies across the nation, which at the time employed only four hundred full-time lawyers on a budget of some $4 million, much of that from private charities.[19]

One figure on the scene, however, had wanted more, and that figure was influential: Attorney General Robert Kennedy. When he spoke at the University of Chicago Law School back in 1964, Kennedy had been as frank as Ronald Reagan, but with the opposite message. Lawyers' obligations weren't discharged when you wrote a check for $100 or $1,000 to the legal aid society, or the NAACP and ACLU, the two great national public interest firms. The obligations weren't discharged when one lawyer protected one beleaguered defendant in one criminal trial. Lawyers, so cautious, were neglecting their duty to the new progressive era. Attorneys, Kennedy said, needed to "practice preventive law on behalf of the poor," helping citizens avoid the courtroom in the first place. In addition, Kennedy said, the law itself had to be changed: "we need to begin to develop new kinds of legal rights in situations that are not now perceived as involving legal issues."[20] It was time for lawyers to understand "fundamental changes" and to effect fundamental change, Kennedy said. Lawyers needed to "pledge to donate not once or twice but continuously the resources of our profession and our legal system." In other words, this kind of justice was a full-time job.

Shriver's Legal Services appropriation had provided the budget to fund such full-time jobs—indeed, entire firms—across the nation. The number of lawyers had started out small, but increased every year. Shriver had now been in Paris for two years. This kind of work behind him. But in Shriver's absence his little legal program had expanded wildly, into a kind of second national bar association. Legal Services brethren—they were nearly all men—sustained and taught one another. The election of Richard Nixon had seemed likely to put a halt to OEO's Legal Services: in his campaign, Nixon had seemed likely to abolish the OEO outright. But as in so many areas, Nixon once in office had softened, merely moving the pieces within the agency around, moving the Legal Services program out of community action to be independent within the agency and assigning Donald Rumsfeld, a former congressman from Illinois, to serve as OEO director and watchdog.[21] By 1970, the budget of Legal Services reached $58 million. The chain of lawyers in the OEO stretched across the country, two thousand of them, located in every state but North Dakota.[22]

Network was also safety net. When the attorneys in the small towns found themselves marooned, they merely had to dial 202. Legal Services blew the wind back into their sails, encouraging them and funding them so that they powered forward again. Legal Services staff in Washington stood ready to travel to states and tangle with local authorities or

judges who dared to question how Washington's poverty lawyers operated. The success and authority of Legal Services inspired older, national
nonprofits—the American Civil Liberties Union, the attorneys at the
NAACP—to expand their own lawyering. Public interest law continued
to lure lawyers fresh out of school. But it even lured successful middle-
aged attorneys, including an entertainment lawyer like Berman. These
oldsters viewed the civil rights cases as a chance to give back. But the
heart of the enterprise remained the Legal Services offices at the Office
of Economic Opportunity.

California Rural Legal Assistance was typical, both of OEO and of the
change in the legal culture. James Lorenz, Harvard Law '64, had founded
CRLA after a disappointing few months at a traditional firm, O'Melveny
and Myers in Los Angeles. On the surface, Lorenz's CRLA team, based
in San Francisco, did not look daunting; beardless young men in jackets
or cardigans with the same hair (short) they had sported in law school or
at corporate offices. A drunk who one day found himself in the CRLA offices in rural El Centro commented that "there aren't any lawyers in this
place, just a bunch of high school students." Californians were accustomed to the country lawyer model: a childhood playground buddy who
had left town briefly for in-state college and law school and then returned
to spend years earning local esteem as a storefront professional. These
strange new lawyers had never before set foot in California. They represented famous, faraway institutions. When they arrived, the foreigners
recruited the local lawyers. One such lawyer was Cruz Reynoso, who had
graduated from UC Berkeley's distinguished law school the same year,
1958, as Governor Reagan's chief of staff, Edwin Meese. Reynoso, who
had spent his childhood picking oranges, had his own practice in the Imperial Valley.[23] Taken together, the outsiders and the locals like Reynoso
constituted a kind of "best and brightest." Again, the fact that they were
in California was no accident. Ambitious as they were, the lawyers were
determined to lead reform in that showcase of America's future, the most
populous state, the state with the economy as big as Canada's, California.
Lorenz even recruited union leader Cesar Chavez to his board, a coup in
the culture of radical chic.

From the start, OEO had smiled on Lorenz's California project: though Lorenz had originally applied for a grant of $750,000, budgeting only $100 for long-distance calls, the OEO had come back with $1.3 million. Now CRLA fielded forty lawyers in the Golden State. A review of CRLA's caseload suggested the vast majority of its cases were the old-fashioned service kind, representing individuals. But the few class-action cases CRLA took up were significant ones, such as the one forcing California to restore $210 million in the state's Medi-Cal program.[24] CRLA's goal was to pick up where union leaders like Reuther and Chavez left off. Lorenz's CRLA won 80 percent of the cases it pursued; it continued to help limit migration into California by opposing a federal government decision to allow 8,100 Mexican nationals into California to harvest tomatoes.

By 1970, young lawyers everywhere aspired to work at places like CRLA. College students were heading to law school, even though President Johnson had ended deferments for graduate students back in 1967.[25] The following year, the law schools told Congress that they estimated applications were up 45 percent over the year earlier. Georgetown University Law Center told Congress that for the class entering in 1971 it might even receive six thousand applications, nearly double the number of the year before. The dean of Georgetown Law, Adrian S. Fisher, stated the obvious: "Many young people have come to believe that the law is where the action is."

One reason joining such a firm had become popular was that the courts that heard the cases were themselves changing, shifting from conservative to outright progressive. In 1963, Chief Justice Earl Warren, one of Reagan's predecessors as governor of California, led the court in *Gideon v. Wainwright*, where the justices underscored the need for adequate attorneys to represent even the poorest or guiltiest of defendants. Subtler but even more important than his position on defendants' rights was Justice Warren's emphasis on what was called incorporation, the principle that the Bill of Rights applies to state and local governments. Warren's successor, Warren Burger, could be just as liberal. In 1969, when Burger was still new on the bench, the Supreme Court had taken up a case regarding entitlement to welfare, one of the issues that challenged Reagan.

In New York, a disabled man on welfare, John Kelly, left the hotel to which welfare authorities had assigned him. The welfare office cut Kelly off without giving him an opportunity for a hearing. When the case, *Goldberg v. Kelly*, got to the Supreme Court, it had, as such cases do, withered down to the constitutional questions alone. Was a welfare recipient cut off by a welfare office being denied due process? Was welfare something an eligible recipient was entitled to? Kelly, the welfare recipient, went near forgotten in all the ceremony. The emphasis now was all law, all lawyers. When Chief Justice Burger called for the oral arguments, he even committed a telling slip of the tongue, referring to the case as "Loflin against Albert," Loflin and Albert being the attorneys arguing it.[26]

In *Goldberg v. Kelly*, Justice Hugo Black focused on the second question, arguing that no one was entitled to welfare. Welfare was charity, to be disbursed at the will of the donor, even if that donor was the federal government. "It somewhat strains credulity," Black wrote, "to say that the government's promise of charity to an individual is property belonging to that individual." Of course, the country might operate a welfare state, "a new experiment for our nation," Justice Black said. But to treat welfare as a right would ensure that welfare was "frozen into our constitutional structure." To define the recipient of a payment as "entitled" was to alter American law, indeed fundamentally. Lawyers and judges were presuming that by virtue of their trade, they could mete out the law more justly than a layman. Still, as Black wrote, "judges are as human as anyone, and as likely as others to see the world through their own eyes."[27] Almost as if he were rebutting the late Robert Kennedy's Chicago speech, not to mention his old clerk Charles Reich, Black took up the goal of public interest lawyers, "fundamental fairness." The National Welfare Rights Organization and the chairman of the John Birch Society could never agree on what was fundamentally fair.[28] In a companion case involving California welfare recipients, Justice Burger backed up Justice Black. The Supreme Court was "'legislating' via constitutional fiat."

Still, in March 1970, weeks after the *Crawford* finding in California, the majority of Supreme Court justices affirmed that welfare was a right. Justice William Brennan, leading the majority, said that to give Kelly's case a review was to honor the due process clause in the Fourteenth Amendment. No one contested that a party in an insurance contract was entitled to what the contract said he was owed. That was his property, or, to use the new term, his "entitlement." By the same token, welfare benefits were the property of welfare beneficiaries. In a footnote that apparently irritated dissenting Justice Black, Justice Brennan cited Black's clerk, Reich, and argued, just as Reich had, that "it may be realistic today to regard welfare entitlements as more like 'property' than a 'gratuity.'" That was all it took to enshrine—seemingly for all time—Professor Reich's quirky theory.[29] After March 1970, American welfare recipients and their attorneys, including those in California, could claim that welfare was their property.

Another case making its way up to the Supreme Court would also expand the power of judges and lawyers. That was *Swann v. Charlotte-Mecklenburg Board of Education*. In Charlotte, North Carolina, a federal district judge, James McMillan, a Johnson appointee, presided. McMillan ordered "two-way" busing of white and black children, drawing the line of the area for the busing to include the suburbs, a broad expanse, like Gitelson's. The lead attorney for the plaintiffs in the case was Julius L. Chambers, a local lawyer who had endured danger to fight such cases: in 1965, his home and car had been bombed. But the school board defendants were irritated at the heavy-handedness of the NAACP. As one of the school board's attorneys said, "the thing you've got to keep in mind is that this case was handled out of Columbus Circle," i.e., the New York headquarters of the NAACP's Legal Defense Fund. It was true that James Nabrit III joined the case, and Nabrit was the son of Howard University president and distinguished civil rights lawyer James Nabrit Jr. That meant the plaintiffs were represented by a kind of civil rights royalty. The Supreme Court heard *Swann* that fall, a few weeks before California's state elections. The Supreme Court's findings could affect Los Angeles, potentially vindicating busing not only within the city but also to and from the suburbs.

There were other explanations for the rise of the legal celebrities in the late 1960s and the power of the courts. One was disappointment in previous government reforms. Since John Kennedy had moved into the White House and Robert Kennedy set up shop at the Justice Department, Americans had watched as community activists, unions, mayors, federal lawmakers, and presidents of both parties had in their turn tried to deliver a better society—never mind "great." Even academics like Moynihan had had their moment. Yet that better society had not materialized. Now the lawyers and judges were up on the stage. A deeper factor also drove the legal boom. As Moynihan's saga demonstrated, Congress now lacked both the will and the funds for big legislative projects. If a politician wanted to claim he was promulgating reform, change, or action, regulations were the easiest route. Adding rules to a program did not mean the federal department that added them had to pay for any additional costs accompanying the change. The same held for changes in national law written by judges. The judges, like Lyndon Johnson, or for that matter John Maynard Keynes, simply assumed a government could afford what they ordered. The price of the courts' changes was real, and showed up in federal or state budgets regardless of what lawmakers had to say. Chief Justice Burger and Justice Hugo Black were correct. In 1970, the courts were supplanting the legislative bodies, with judges themselves "'legislating' via constitutional fiat."

COME ELECTION Day in 1970 in California, voters there chose as state superintendent of public instruction Wilson Riles, a black man who criticized the conservative incumbent, an ally of Reagan's. Californians voted out George Murphy, another Reagan ally, this time in the fight against CRLA. However, after thirteen years on the bench Judge Gitelson lost to an opponent of busing, William Kennedy. Reagan himself easily won reelection, though by a smaller majority than his 1966 landslide. Now the governor was ready to do battle, to show California and the nation what ought to be done. Reagan took on two projects: welfare reform and stopping the CRLA.

The budget had been Reagan's focus in the last term. This term, he started with welfare. Moynihan was back at Harvard, but Nixon, still, on some days, loyal to his Pat, appeared to want to make Family Assistance law. Moynihan's legislation threw money at the states, making it hard for governors of either party to resist it. The FAP traded that money for more federal authority over individual determinations in welfare cases. To Reagan, this was not a good trade, just a repeat of the community action bribe. In December, Reagan told the press that he opposed family assistance: "I believe the government is supposed to promote the general welfare," Reagan said. "I don't believe it is supposed to provide it."[30] For California, Reagan had his own welfare plan, which included its own pilot program that required the able-bodied to work for their welfare checks. Reagan's plan also included strict eligibility tests, harder to enforce in the period after *Goldberg*, but still worth trying. Those candidates who did meet the tough criteria got higher payments than before. Nixon hosted Reagan at San Clemente, the Nixons' home. He asked Reagan to lay off Family Assistance in exchange for HEW's support for Reagan's own California effort at reform. To Reagan this did seem an acceptable deal. If Reagan's plan succeeded, it would be a national model.

But when it came to CRLA or OEO, Reagan was not so easy to buy off. The agency was still seeking to increase CRLA's budget, and announced on December 1 that CRLA would receive $1.8 million the next year, a hefty increase. Don Rumsfeld might be a Republican, but like his predecessors at OEO, he could override Reagan's veto. And Rumsfeld liked Legal Services, which, as a staffer, Terry Lenzner, remembered Rumsfeld saying, "allowed people to settle problems through lawyers in courtrooms instead of with mob violence."[31] Reagan determined to craft a veto case so strong that the OEO would not dare to override it. Reagan's own director at the California Office of Economic Opportunity was Lew Uhler—a Boalt Hall classmate of both Cruz Reynoso and Meese. Reagan and Uhler decided to investigate what CRLA was doing. Uhler sent out a letter to three thousand lawyers in the state asking about CRLA's performance. Many of the attorneys complained that CRLA bullied both citizens and officials. On December 11, Reagan threatened to veto the CRLA grant. After Christmas, Reagan did veto it. Rumsfeld, who was moving over to the White House as Nixon's advisor, blasted Reagan's move: "the poor must have effective legal representation." The *Los Angeles Times* instantly criticized Reagan's veto in an editorial: unless Uhler found truly substantial flaws, OEO should override the governor. And the *New York Times* piled on with its own editorial, backing up the OEO and criticizing Reagan.

Before departing, Rumsfeld brought a former diplomat, Frank Carlucci, over to the OEO from the State Department. Now the Administration tapped Carlucci to succeed Rumsfeld, whom Nixon wanted at the White House. Alan Cranston, the senior California senator, had tried to stop Nixon from closing Job Corps centers across the nation—and failed. Now Cranston had a fight he might win—blocking Carlucci's confirmation. Cranston called Carlucci and told him: "Unless you override that veto, you're not going to get confirmed." But Reagan was not letting up, and even called Nixon to ask him to stop the OEO from overriding the veto. By some reports, Reagan even threatened to deprive Nixon of the backing of the mighty California delegation in 1972 if Nixon did not weaken.

It was a measure of the heat of the quarrel between Reagan and the OEO that Senator Cranston went ahead and blocked Carlucci's confirmation—unusually for the time. Senators Edward Kennedy and Walter Mondale supported Cranston in the rebellion. Kennedy even made an additional demand: Carlucci must not personally campaign against incumbent Democratic senators. Carlucci promised that the OEO would not become a subsidiary of the Republican National Committee, but also allowed that as an officer in the executive branch he couldn't promise not to speak on behalf of his president. The columnist David Broder noted that this was rich. In his day Sargent Shriver had showed no hesitation about campaigning for fellow Democrats, and had even, at his Maryland estate, hosted a $1,000-a-head function for major Democratic donors. Rumsfeld himself recalled a moment during one of his own campaigns, when the *Chicago American* had reported on Shriver's support for a Democrat in Chicago: "Shriver Boosts Williams' Drive Against Rumsfeld." It was wrong to single out Carlucci in this way.

Through January and February 1971 the Administration and the governor sparred over public-assistance lawyers and their cases. The media jumped in. A *Los Angeles Times* reporter found a disabled relation of the president, Philip Milhous of Grass Valley, California. The Milhouses had seen their welfare payments cut back and had sought legal assistance from the CRLA.[32] Nixon's own family needed public-assistance lawyers, the implication was, so Nixon had to support the lawyers. Reagan's veto inspired other governors, including Mississippi's John Bell Williams, who vetoed a $200,000 Legal Services grant in his own state.

And Reagan's attorneys now did their own highlighting of additional flaws of CRLA. Union work was outside the scope of OEO's brief. Yet the CRLA worked with Cesar Chavez in cases like that of the *braceros*. The CRLA had been sold in Washington, as Reagan often noted, as a project to help the man "who might be cheated of his wages or pushed around in some way, and it recognized that he might feel overwhelmed by the prospect of taking his case to court himself." But the class actions component was taking over. The CRLA was neglecting humdrum individual suits— divorce cases, for example. In fact, Reagan's men maintained, CRLA lawyers turned up their noses at such cases.[33]

The OEO, Reagan's team contended, was also a hopeless jurisdictional mess. The chief of the Model Cities Liaison Group needed approval for his work not only from the OEO in Washington but also from the Model Cities Administration and Romney's Department of Housing and Urban Development. And the requisite replies of course did not come promptly. Uhler had a typical letter from a frustrated staffer in his files: "I have held conversations with you about the desirability and feasibility of a pilot project designed to develop and test concepts of merging Community Action Programs with the Model Cities program in selected localities," wrote the staffer. "We have agreed, I believe, that this idea, which we called 'Project V,' should be pursued. . . . Project V is apparently about to begin. In order to give it a firm foundation I'm asking that you concur on the facts."[34]

Relations between government offices had so deteriorated that those different departments could not agree on basics. Uhler flew to Washington to make the case for Reagan's veto of Legal Services. He thought he might find some friends in the Administration. Nixon hailed from Uhler's own district in California, and Nixon was supposed to be a conservative, Uhler recalled thinking later.[35] But Uhler found surprises in Washington. The White House reaction to the request that the Administration respect Reagan's veto was instantly hostile. This was not about ideas, Uhler later recalled discovering. A governor was attacking a part of Nixon's budget. Nixon was defending himself. For the Nixon Administration, CRLA was a simple turf war.

At OEO, Carlucci, Uhler's putative opponent, was coming to the same conclusion. Adding to Carlucci's trouble was the fact that the Nixon Administration redefined its own turf so often. The White House wasn't really sending clear guidance on the future of the OEO, Carlucci later recalled. "[J]ust survival was guidance." Carlucci was getting calls from the White House—every day, he noted. "Stop that circus in California. Don't override the veto," Ehrlichman said. Others in the Administration also liked Reagan's mutiny. "I had no support [for an override] inside the Nixon Administration other than Len Garment and Don Rumsfeld—Bob Finch, [HEW secretary, and a Californian] to some degree," remembered Carlucci later. "But everybody else was on the side of sustaining Reagan's veto."[36]

Carlucci decided the best step was to get Reagan to amend his veto of CRLA funding. Carlucci and his attorney traveled to California to strong-arm Reagan and Meese. The meetings lasted for days. Carlucci's lawyer played tough with Ed Meese, Reagan's proxy. Reagan should cease and desist on the veto business, Carlucci's man said. In exchange Carlucci would defend Reagan in Washington. "There are two movies here," the attorney with Carlucci said, perhaps seeking to provoke Reagan by suggesting that he was so dense he required analogies from his former trade to understand a complex problem. "The 'A' movie is that you accept Frank's offer and things go ahead smoothly. The 'B' movie is that you reject and we, in Washington, level Sacramento." The tough talk of his own lawyer shocked Carlucci, who was well aware that many in Washington sided with Reagan, not Nixon, on the crusading lawyers. "I thought, 'What is he talking about?'" Still, Meese went into a side room of the hotel where they were meeting, called Reagan, and came back. "We accept the 'A' movie," Meese said.

Carlucci, after all a former diplomat, went back to Washington and worked the compromise. The Reagan veto would not be overridden. But CRLA would be funded for a six-month provisional period. Carlucci was confirmed in March—then indeed an egregious delay. Speaking at the time of confirmation, Carlucci assured the press that he personally favored freedom for attorneys, even in class-action cases. Reagan, softening for the moment, called Carlucci to congratulate him and sent him a bottle of brandy. Many in the Republican Party still expected Nixon to abolish OEO. Nixon surprised them all again, again asking Congress for a flat two-year extension of current programs.

While Reagan and his staff went back and forth with Washington, the governor monitored other projects, especially welfare reform. In March 1971, soon after the implementation of Reagan's reform, a small miracle happened. The number of families on California welfare rolls began to fall—even though unemployment was high. By the following year that figure would be down by 161,000. Reagan wanted to undertake more such experiments. In his years as governor of California, he had tested his free-market theories, sometimes, to be sure, gingerly. The theories had performed. Now, Reagan was confident. The press and the university crowds dismissed the revival of free-market philosophy in the early part of the decade as a temporary fad, now past. That was especially true of the followers of Charles Reich's *The Greening of America*. The true fad, Reagan saw now, was *The Greening*. Free-market values were eternal, and eternally strong. The federal government's Great Society had failed, Reagan concluded. Maybe it was time the government pulled back all around and let American society try to make itself great.

In May 1971, Reagan returned to California lawyers to deliver a second speech, as blunt as his first. Addressing the Los Angeles County Bar Association, which had endorsed Gitelson, Reagan allowed he was tiring of revolutionaries. The governor also disapproved of "their legal champions" who denounced the American system but got away with it because they could "wrap themselves in the Constitution." The governor deplored the "growing tendency for the client himself to become the boss in the courtroom, to stage manage his own defense with disrespectful and contemptuous conduct toward the court." The governor told the lawyers he needed help from legislatures to impede the legal onslaught. But, he added, almost as an aside, the California legislature did not seem inclined to provide that help. The change in legal culture had come so fast: "If Moses himself stood on Nob Hill and solemnly intoned the Ten Commandments, he would probably be denounced as a reactionary," Reagan said.[37] Later in this second term, Reagan would underscore his lack of regard for the trade of law by signing a bill that created a fund to pay back clients who were rooked by lawyers. He would demonstrate his disregard for the legal mandarins by nominating to the California supreme court an appellate justice, William P. Clark, who had never received a law degree. Clark could practice because he had passed the state bar examination on his second try. Yet more controversial was that Clark had not always corrected documents indicating he had graduated from law school. When reporters uncovered details of Clark's failures and omissions—fatal for their guild—Ed Meese had his retort ready: Clark was being appointed "on the basis of his outstanding legal and judicial record."

Reagan knew that he would not necessarily achieve much in 1971. Indeed, there were many setbacks. In April, the U.S. Supreme Court ruled for busing in the case of *Swann*, an outcome that gave the federal seal of approval to Gitelson's plan, still on the books. Integration everywhere was necessary. Even de facto separation of blacks and whites in schools in the North, the court said, must end. "If school authorities fail in their affirmative obligations under these holdings, judicial authority may be invoked," wrote Chief Justice Burger for the Court. The lawyers' show looked likely to continue for years.

Literally. Warner Bros. and Robert Redford, wildly popular after *Butch Cassidy and the Sundance Kid*, were making a feature film about a fictional civil rights lawyer who decided to run for the U.S. Senate in California to correct all that was wrong in politics. Redford was working in partnership with a talented filmmaker named Michael Ritchie. Ritchie, who directed *The Candidate*, actually came from California. His father was Benbow Ritchie, a psychology professor at Berkeley. Ritchie added California touches. Redford played the upstart environmentalist attorney named William McKay. The screenplay styled McKay after John Tunney, the junior senator who had just defeated George Murphy. For good measure the screenwriters threw in a touch of Jerry Brown, Governor Edmund Brown's son; and Robert Kennedy. In the plot, the crusading attorney McKay challenged a stentorian, silver-haired Republican incumbent, a hybrid of George Murphy and Reagan himself. The casting department weighted the film in favor of McKay by picking for the role of the incumbent senator not Paul Newman or another superstar but rather a classic B-movie actor, Don Porter. At the time Porter was known best for a light television role, that of the father in the situation comedy *Gidget*. *Redford v. Porter* was scarcely an even match.

Like Jerry Brown, the fictional McKay campaigned and litigated for environmental causes. And like Tunney, McKay premised his whole campaign on rejecting "machine-type politics" and the old conservatives who practiced those politics. Asked about busing after he declared his run, for example, McKay answered as bluntly as Gitelson himself: "I'm for it." The movie maverick campaigned successfully, wooing construction men, police, and hippies—and the actress Natalie Wood, who played herself. But the process of campaigning gradually corrupted the hero. The Redford character hid behind phrases worthy of Charles Reich—"Our lives are more and more determined by forces that overwhelm the individual." The hero jettisoned principle after principle to climb in the polls. He met with a red-haired union leader, the screenplay author's nostalgic nod to the late Reuther, and perhaps Jimmy Hoffa, and agreed to work with unions he had avoided at the idealistic start of the campaign.[38] The unions' support pushed him toward victory. By the end of the campaign and the movie, Redford's McKay no longer defended busing directly, but said, sounding more like Hugo Black and Ronald Reagan than like Gitelson: "We must try to preserve the idea of the neighborhood schools."

Warner Bros. liked the film so well it spent $750,000 on promotion, half of the production costs. The studio went so far as to stage, as a publicity gimmick, a mini-fantasy campaign for Redford in the real-life streets of California. The studio even hired Nelson Rising, Tunney's strategist, to make the fake campaign feel genuine. "He is an excellent communicator," Rising told the press, of Redford. A few years back an older film, starring a Marilyn Monroe alternate, Mamie van Doren, had been titled *The Candidate*. The producers of the older film had also used *Party Girls for the Candidate* as a title. Now the van Doren film's producers wanted to use "The Candidate" as title again, in a new distribution of the film. Warner Bros. hired Bayard Berman, the lawyer in the Los Angeles desegregation case, to represent it. The California superior court ruled that Redford's film owned exclusive rights to the *The Candidate*, another victory for Berman.

When *The Candidate* reached theaters in 1972, viewers could see that it was one long brag for the new legal culture. The poverty lawyers liked seeing themselves played by Redford on the screen. Another of the insider jokes in *The Candidate* was that real politicians and journalists had jumped in along with Natalie Wood to play themselves: Senator Alan Cranston, Reagan's opponent on CRLA, took a cameo, as did Mayor Yorty, and even Reagan's principal sparring partner in his welfare reform battle, state assemblyman Robert Moretti. Hubert Humphrey and George McGovern, already real-life presidential possibles for 1972, could be spotted in the footage as well. The former senator George Murphy, who had throat cancer and could not speak above a whisper, did not appear in the film. Neither did Ronald Reagan. Appearing in this show or any other now mattered little to Reagan. Reagan was through with screens and entertainment. Soon enough, he thought, he would take his policies to the nation for real.

12

Scarcity: Burns Agonistes

1971

Guns: 7% of GDP
Butter: 7.1% of GDP
Dow Jones Industrial Average: 898

Faced with a choice between introducing economic ratio-nality and the maintenance of their political power, the Russian rulers chose power.
—Federal Reserve chairman Arthur Burns
on the Soviet Union, 1970[1]

In the decade since Ronald Reagan had wrested a commitment from studios to pay the actors in a movie every time it appeared on television, the word for such royalty payments, "residuals," had become holy to actors. Residuals funded children's college. Residuals gave even the most unstable actor a retirement as good as a school principal's. So when in 1971 film studios demanded cuts in residual rates, members of Reagan's old union, the Screen Actors Guild, went on strike.[2] Yet the actors couldn't marshal the kind of hope for victory they might have five years before: by 1971 the old movie studios were finding costs high, and their coffers precariously short of cash. Even mighty television networks were finding they might not have the resources to ensure actors' future. Rising prices were eating away at the value of future dollars.

When it came to residuals from television, the luckiest were clearly the stars of *Bonanza*. *Bonanza* was popular not just at home but worldwide. Every week, the show aired in eighty-nine countries, with payments from foreign television making their way back to NBC. *Bonanza* could provide wealth to Lorne Greene, Michael Landon, and their families for generations. Yet recently the *Bonanza* stars had done something unexpected. They sold the rights to their residuals back to NBC in exchange for immediate cash payments.[3] Each actor, word had it, received at least $1 million. Nonetheless the sale looked panicky. *Bonanza* actors did not have confidence that the show would provide them with bonanzas in the future.

The actors weren't the only ones suddenly concerned about their financial future. At the United Auto Workers one day that March, Leonard Woodcock, Walter Reuther's successor, walked out of Solidarity House to find a surprise: a group of pickets, women, picketing *him.* "On Strike," read their posters. The picket line fell back politely so that Woodcock could get to his car. Reporters were present, and photographers snapped pictures of the union leader. The strikers, Woodcock's own employees, were finding they had trouble paying their own bills, and so were seeking $100 bonuses and a pay increase. Woodcock's UAW would have trouble coming up with either. The women couldn't resist the chance to hassle Woodcock: "Smile pretty, Leonard," yelled one of them after him.[4] But Woodcock did not smile. There was something odd, and certainly nothing funny, about a union picketing itself.

Prices and costs were punishing the poor, especially those on fixed incomes that could not be adjusted for inflation. For the first time since Mollie Orshansky devised her poverty line, the number of Americans under the line was growing, by one million in 1970 alone.[5] Higher costs were also dogging public housing offices, especially the St. Louis Housing Authority, the managers of Pruitt-Igoe. The cost of fuel for the authority's vehicles had gone up 20 percent since 1965. Utility bills were now rising so fast they ate up the budget. Vandalism had long been a problem at Pruitt-Igoe. Thieves even stole the copper flashing installed to protect the roofs. To keep up with the vandalism, the caretakers had to refit constantly. But prices for the copper equipment the authority needed after the vandalism had almost doubled in just a few years. The daily costs for the repairs had once run around $1,000. Now the vandalism bill was $1,700 a day.[6] The new challenge to Pruitt-Igoe, and indeed to public housing in every city, was price rises. "It just costs more today . . ." a housing official in Detroit had told the papers recently. "We get deeper and deeper in the hole each year." The question was no longer what might be done for housing, since HUD itself had moved into austerity mode. "Down in the dogboned-shape building that is home for the Department of Housing and Urban Development," wrote one reporter in an inglorious description of Marcel Breuer's HUD masterpiece, "it is as if the hardworking clean-up crew had come along to tidy up after those improvident impractical academic types had had their binge and gone away." The president had ordered all departments to restrain their spending, and that spending included wages. It would not do for government officials to get big raises when the president was asking for austerity. Yet prices were so high that Nixon's own Office of Management and Budget, after consulting with officials in all parts of the executive branch, found itself recommending stiff pay raises for government employees. The salary recommended for the post of Federal Reserve chairman, for example, experts decided, had to be $62,500, not the current $42,500.[7]

Prices were moving up so fast that they affected every corner of business as well. They even changed the language of business itself. Accountants at companies had long used FIFO, a system under which profits and taxes were calculated on "first in," the oldest items in inventory, and "first out" prices. But the prices so distorted the automakers' books that, as Chrysler would carefully explain to reporters later that year, some companies were shifting to a new kind of accounting that could accommodate such rapid increases, "last in, first out" or LIFO.[8] You could joke about the costs. A Bonanza Sirloin Pit in Arkansas, part of a chain that Dan Blocker of the television show had started, did. "If you're teed off, Bonanza has the answer," read the steak house advertisement. The answer was a Tuesday special: rib eye steak, tossed salad, Texas toast, and baked potato for $1.29. But what, citizens could ask, about the rest of the week?[9] The price increases touched citizens every day, and in the most mundane aspects of life. The Post Office was planning to issue two new stamps for first class letters to mark U.S. achievements in space. The space achievements were cause for celebration. But the amount on the stamp, 8 cents, was not. To send a letter now cost double what it had when John Glenn first orbited in *Friendship Seven* back in 1962.

SUPERSTARS WHO didn't trust the value of their own residuals. A union that struck against itself. A housing project that couldn't make repairs even when it had the equipment. Numbers so strange they altered the very system of accounting. A federal government so desperate to pay its employees adequately that it would risk scandal. What to make of these price puzzles? In the 1960s, authorities had warned so often about inflation that the term became one of those half-meaningless words you heard on the evening news. Nothing terribly alarming had ever happened, beyond Johnson's ridiculous and short-lived travel ban. Besides, as the newscasters told their audiences, there was always that trade-off: the country had to pick its poison, inflation or unemployment. So inflation might be worthwhile if it accompanied the arrival of new jobs. Now, though, the strange events of 1971 were making inflation real to Americans. When you defined inflation, you didn't have to talk about money supply, or discount rates, or sterling, or trade deficits. Inflation was simple to explain. Inflation was when you didn't have enough money, even when you were making more money than you ever dreamed you would.[10]

Or maybe, even, when you weren't. For in 1970 and early 1971 a second problem was making itself felt: joblessness. Unemployment was rising to levels higher than the country had seen in a decade. Imports were continuing to punish Detroit, with imported trucks making inroads similar to cars, now 15 percent of the market.[11] Many new companies were struggling. Both poisons at once: this wasn't supposed to happen, either. A new word to describe the double trouble, "stagflation," was entering the American vocabulary. Perhaps Americans, like the *Bonanza* stars, ought not to assume the America bonanza would always be theirs, after all. Perhaps the bonanza was finished. Paul Ehrlich, the Stanford scholar, had already declared defeat: "the battle to feed all of humanity is over," Ehrlich wrote—even, eventually in America. Millions, Ehrlich said, would starve to death. Readers were making Ehrlich's new book,

The Population Bomb, a bestseller, and Ehrlich appeared frequently on *The Tonight Show Starring Johnny Carson.*[12]

The Air Force and the Army cut or canceled contracts, and now Lockheed, the number one defense contractor in the nation, the magisterial maker of the Starlifters that had transported the gold to England, was struggling. The slowdown in defense spending was the hidden cost of the Vietnam retreat. Lockheed's troubles came on top of those of Seattle-based Boeing. Boeing had laid off so many people that, the year before, two men had bought a billboard to post a poignant joke: "Will the last person leaving Seattle—turn out the lights."

Such pessimism felt almost un-American. "Politics first," or "Great Society first," or "Vietnam first," had been the rule in the Johnson years, when the economic bounty had seemed endless and crises like Britain's, far away. It was all too clear now that Fed chairman William McChesney Martin, who had seemed so independent, had given in too often when Johnson pushed him to lower interest rates. A new consensus was forming: the Administration needed a professional to lead an economic revival. Someone who could not be moved by politics, as Martin had been in the end. Someone who understood markets, a statesman capitalist. With a serious economic mind at the helm, the government might indeed make everything right again.

───────────

NO MAN in the United States seemed more suited to the task of economic rescue than the new Federal Reserve chairman, Arthur Burns. Burns was no dreamer like Moynihan, and had emerged the solid victor in their battle over Moynihan's guaranteed income program. Burns was also no William McChesney Martin, for Martin had been, at least originally, a banker. Burns, who moved into the Fed job in 1970, was, by contrast, a pure economist. It appeared a form of national luck that the new Fed chairman was the most highly-reputed economist in the land, the forecasting genius of the General Motors sales rooms.[13] Markets, especially international markets, trusted Burns. Burns regularly traveled overseas to lecture foreign leaders on the merits of capitalism. The trick, he told the foreigners, was to conduct your work with integrity. In a speech he gave in Seoul, Korea, that year, Burns went out of his way to point out that the Soviet leaders' lust for power doomed the Soviet economy. "Unless and until they [the Russians] are willing to change their approach, it seems likely that their own economy and that of the satellites will lag," Burns intoned. Burns's profession respected him even more now that he had done battle against Moynihan on the costly guaranteed income bill. Few in Washington had the guts to fight someone as popular with the president as Moynihan had been in 1969. The economists had a phrase they used to capture Burns's authority: wherever he sat became the head of the table.[14] Burns understood the arguments of others, including, of course, the argument of the famous Phillips curve, the trade-off between the poisons of inflation and unemployment. But he also maintained his own medicine cabinet of cures, and believed there could be moments when the vaunted curve didn't hold. His colleagues worried aloud that the Soviet Union and China, whose economies grew rapidly, might one day overtake the United States. Not Burns, whose eagle eye discerned that Soviet and Chinese growth numbers were exaggerated, an insight that would, decades later, prove him a geopolitical prophet.

If the fact that Burns was America's top inflation hawk had sounded valuable at the time of Nixon's inauguration, now that qualification seemed crucial. "There can be no danger of a galloping or runaway inflation in the reckonable future unless our monetary and fiscal policies become utterly reckless," Burns had preached in his early monograph, *Prosperity Without Inflation*. To economists, especially, the independence of the Federal Reserve also seemed crucial, because it gave markets at home and abroad confidence that U.S. monetary policy was honest. Many Americans had watched in discomfort as Johnson bullied William McChesney Martin, wondering if Johnson would put forward legislation to end the Fed's independence. Nixon, too, might be tempted to weaken the Fed, and bring it into the executive branch. Burns considered the Federal Reserve a fourth branch of government, as unassailable and holy as the other three. Burns, observers reckoned, would fight Nixon to the death to protect the Fed's independence.

But the charm was that he probably wouldn't have to. More important to a successful Washington reformer than even the respect of fellow economists, markets, or foreign governments was the respect of one individual: the president. And Burns had always had Nixon's ear. As only a few in the White House knew, Nixon had sent a message to Burns during the Family Assistance Plan fight: Burns didn't have to worry about the FAP, because it would never become law. Preparing to turn out the sitting treasury secretary, David Kennedy, Nixon had actually asked Burns himself to serve as treasury secretary. Burns had demurred, but receiving the offer was another feather in his cap. Observers confident in Burns took comfort in another key factor: Burns appeared to care, even desperately, about his own legacy. Elections, or presidential favor, might matter to Burns, but doing the right thing would matter more. Burns was approaching age sixty-seven, around the age at which Lemuel Boulware had retired. People knew, and Burns knew, that the inflation battle of 1971 was Burns's last shot.

Even before he had moved over to the Fed from the Old Executive Office Building, therefore, Burns had begun to compound his own inflation cure, a cure that would be uniquely Burns. The monetarist economists, relatively new on the scene, were blaming the inflation on increases in the money supply. The gold standard fans blamed the current trouble on Johnson's actions to weaken the gold standard, such as ending the old gold cover. Yet other scholars held that the government should spend more, and could stimulate enough growth to render inflation irrelevant. These mono-causal explanations irked Burns. To him, inflations were like sick patients, each different, and each requiring its own prescription. What mattered more than models was clinical evidence and the quality of the doctor. "I wish the world were as simple as the Friedmanites and the Keynesians wish to make it," Burns said, "but it never has been, and, I dare say, never will be."[15]

In Burns's prescription, there would be no return to the gold cover—that was simply retrograde. The Federal Reserve chairman might even allow that devaluation of the dollar was possible: the price of $35 an ounce had stood since the 1930s, and sliding the figure up to, say, $38 would do much to reduce trade imbalances. Raising the discount rate was the Fed's key tool for adjusting credit and money, but Burns was reluctant to use it too often, for the rate already stood at 5.5 percent, far above the 2–3 percent rates of the 1950s, when Burns had warned about inflation as a young star.[16] On the growth side he advocated tax cuts, for those would help business and at least reduce joblessness. Congress, for its part, Burns said, had to show restraint and stop spending. As Burns had pointed out at the time of his confirmation hearings, the budget had grown more in the past nine years than it grew in the two centuries before.[17] The trouble now wasn't merely inflation; it was that, as his colleague and student Milton Friedman said, people were now building inflation into their expectations. If unions and businesses demonstrated restraint, then Americans would see less inflation and move out of panic mode. Wage and price restraint, or even, conceivably, outright government controls on wages and prices, might therefore be warranted, Burns argued. Burns didn't recommend mandatory controls, at least not at first. But mandatory controls could conceivably work as a shock treatment to jolt people out of an inflationary mind-set that Friedman described. This was the kind of paradox the pipe-puffing Burns longed to set in action: using socialist-style pressure to successfully revive capitalism.

Others—Friedman himself, for example—found that last Burns idea too clever by half. People weren't lab rats. You couldn't trick them out of recognizing inflationary habits in a government. Wage and price control, which was where the government was likely to end up, was like a seal on a boiling kettle. Unless you turned down the heat—reduced the money supply, or raised interest rates—the kettle eventually exploded. And besides, compulsory price-setting just wasn't compatible with markets: compulsion was the hallmark of a socialist regime. Such criticisms were why government economists like Burns referred to centrally managed wages and prices with a euphemism, "incomes policy."

To win Nixon over to some of these ideas might be difficult, Burns knew. Nixon had no coherent economic view; Nixon policy was a jumble of impulses. Nixon might concede the existence of inflation. But he nonetheless wanted Burns to lower interest rates, the politics trumping the economics in that instance. And Nixon rejected the use of another anti-inflation tool, wage and price rules. That was where the free-market Nixon popped up. Like Johnson, Nixon was in denial over the fact that the United States was sliding toward European social democracy. Everyone at the White House recalled the cabinet meeting the year before, when Romney of HUD had dared to argue that wage and price controls had worked in England. Nixon had growled his contempt.[18] But Burns liked a challenge. If in other years Burns had talked Nixon around to new ideas—and he had—in 1971 Burns could talk him around to wage and price controls, too.

With his prescription in hand, Burns found only one challenge: actually getting the busy president's ear. And to his surprise, the new Fed chairman was finding that he was having trouble doing so. The chief executive spent hours closeted with foreign policy advisors, and continued to give afternoons, even whole days, to Henry Kissinger. When Burns did see Nixon, the president seemed difficult, secretive. Burns still had trouble reconciling himself to the fact that he must deal with the president's two yes-men, John Ehrlichman and Bob Haldeman, when it was RN he really needed. To Burns these political men, glorified advance men, really, were underqualified "boys in the basement." Yet, as Burns observed to his chagrin, Nixon was continuing to rearrange protocol in ways that made access to the president yet tougher to obtain. If Burns did have to make compromises to get to Nixon, he told himself, weakening a bit, the compromises might after all be worth it, as long as Nixon applied Burns's prescription. After all, as Burns wrote in his diary, he, Burns, was Nixon's best friend.[19]

Lately, Nixon had imposed a new and unexpected blocker. When Burns had turned down the Treasury post, he had recommended some respectable names. But Nixon had instead installed a figure at Treasury so unlikely that the move left Burns speechless: John Connally of Texas. Connally, until recently governor of Texas, wasn't just a Democrat, he was a second, larger, Lyndon Johnson, a swaggerer of the kind who showed up to challenge the Cartwrights on *Bonanza* on Sunday night. That Connally had quarreled with Johnson from time to time mattered far less than the fact that he had served as Johnson's right-hand man in campaigns. It seemed ridiculous to statesmen to consider physical stature, but Connally's height, six foot four, mattered, and Burns was of only medium height. Moynihan had been tall as well, but had not used his own size to intimidate others: Moynihan was too much of a gentleman. Connally however used his height to tower over Burns, just as Johnson had towered over William McChesney Martin. That Connally had been shot with John Kennedy in Dallas placed over all his height a kind of halo, which made him yet harder to challenge. Connally scared not only Burns, but the other men in Nixon's circle, even that master operator, Henry Kissinger, who was himself also well under six feet. Kissinger would never forget Connally's analysis of Washington—"You will be measured in this town by the enemies you destroy. The bigger they are, the bigger you will be."[20] Even Lyndon Johnson found Connally rough, telling George Ball, who served Johnson in the State Department, that Connally could "leave more dead bodies in the field than any politician I ever knew."[21]

Though Burns fancied himself apolitical, he well understood Nixon's reason for luring Connally to Treasury. Nixon thought working with Democrats would make some Democrats vote for him, whether on the Hill or in the voting booth. Hence Nixon's hire of Moynihan, and his invitation to Sargent Shriver to take the job of UN ambassador. ("That lacquered fellow," as Burns referred to Shriver in his diary, had turned Nixon down.) The papers were already speculating that in 1972 Nixon might even drop Spiro Agnew and make Connally his vice-presidential candidate, creating an irresistible Republican-Democratic fusion ticket. Just as Nixon had showcased a Democratic intellectual, Moynihan, to woo Democrats in Congress, now he was showcasing a star Democratic politician, this time to win voters. It also distressed Burns that Nixon had selected a governor and a lawyer for the Treasury spot, a non-expert, a man who knew so little about international finance that his sole credential in that department was serving as a director on the boards of two banks. Economics was just a tool for politics to Connally. Just as disturbing, at least to Burns, was the fact that Connally had started the Treasury job by taking a crash course in economics not from

Burns but from Burns's predecessor, Martin. It was Martin who taught Connally the basic principles that all central bankers and the Treasury staff shared, such as the rule that devaluing the dollar against gold was a smaller sin than ending the gold standard altogether. It was Martin who explained the symbolic importance of U.S. gold holdings, and that America risked losing its very status as an international superstar if gold holdings went below the symbolic $10 billion line.

The reality was that Connally wasn't the only new obstacle between Burns and his president. Nixon was growing ambivalent about several of his advisors, but none more than Burns. The president's respect for Burns was so deep he had trouble disagreeing with the Fed chairman directly. But Nixon was finding he was having trouble tolerating Burns day to day. Nixon believed, with all the reason in the world, that where *he*, Nixon, chose to sit was the head of the table. "Four minutes with Pat," Nixon said once, referring to Moynihan, was "worth four hours with Burns." Burns's sanctimony bugged Nixon. When Burns was on a roll, he had, as one White House staffer put it, "an avuncular style that drove Nixon bats." Burns didn't understand the value of presidential time.

What Burns also did not entirely grasp was that the Nixon of late 1970 or early 1971 was already a different man from the Nixon of the euphoric transition meetings at the Pierre in New York in 1968, or even the Nixon who had promised welfare reform to Moynihan in 1969. The man in the Oval Office was impatient and preparing for the next election. Nixon, like Johnson, and indeed Truman before him, had come over the course of his presidency to resent the Federal Reserve, this fourth branch. Like Johnson and Truman, Nixon dismissed talk of Fed independence as mere grandstanding, not merely irritating but downright counterproductive. The president wanted his economic team, including "his" man at the Fed, to speak with one voice. And ironically for Burns, Nixon seemed to recall Burns's lesson of the 1960 election all too well. This election cycle, Nixon would do anything to forestall the kind of recession America had endured in 1960, the one that had lost Nixon the election. Burns told Nixon that he was doing all he could to loosen money, citing expansions of the money supply. Nixon told others he suspected that Burns was exaggerating the money supply numbers to get the Fed off the hook.[22] Yet Nixon still had trouble telling Burns all these things to his face.

The tension between the Fed chairman and the president had first become overt when, just before the New Year, in December 1970, Burns did get a meeting at the White House. Burns warned the president that sooner or later, the United States would have to figure out a way to devalue the dollar against other currencies. He told Nixon that France and Germany were bringing dollars in and collecting gold at the "gold window."[23] Collecting their ounces for dollars was those countries' gold-standard right, technically speaking, but in practice the foreign nations required the United States' okay. Nixon approved France, but put a delay on the German request. Then the president became frank. "Domestically, we should err on the side of a too liberal monetary policy, Arthur," he told Burns. Inflation was awful, but it was better for politics than unemployment. "We should risk some inflation," the president said—drop the discount rate. Burns's own priority, of course, was still the reverse. He did not want to drop interest rates. "Arthur wants high interest rates," Nixon told the others. "He fears investment money will all flow to the Swiss otherwise"—not an unreasonable surmise. At the rate they were withdrawing, France, Japan, and Germany could indeed drain the United States of more billions remaining in America vaults. But Nixon, resembling Johnson more and more, didn't care about gold. He wanted Burns to give him an economy that would sail forward past November 1972. If Burns didn't go along, Nixon told the others, "I'll unload on him like he's never seen before."

Burns got the message, directly or indirectly. The Fed chairman led his board in dropping the interest rate twice, to 5.25 percent and then to 5 percent. He also, however, rallied his colleagues on the imperative of wage and price constraints. Some duly joined the cheerleading. The vice chairman of the Fed, James L. Robertson, warned that the Administration was perpetuating economic problems by rejecting wage and price constraints: the economy had troubles and, "in the absence of help from the Administration in the form of an incomes policy, it is going to take longer to resolve them."[24] To Burns's chagrin, however, Nixon began plugging his own policy mix, more political than logical. In his budget message of late January 1971, for example, the president pointedly mentioned the need for "increased restraint in wage and price decisions," a warning to business that if labor and unions did not restrain themselves, Nixon might consider Burns's recommendation of government-led restraint. In the same message, however, the president also proposed "full employment," which meant greater spending, the opposite of what Burns hoped for. The president proudly noted that spending on "human resources"— entitlements—was finally surpassing military spending, hardly a good sign from Burns's point of view. Burns was the economist who had warned that the United States couldn't even afford butter. Finally, the president also needled Burns by echoing the title of Burns's old book *Prosperity Without Inflation*, to suggest Burns wasn't doing his duty now when it came to interest rates. "Our objective of prosperity without inflation," Nixon said, "cannot be achieved by budget policy alone. It also requires the monetary policy adopted by the independent Federal Reserve system to provide fully for the growing needs of the economy."

Such jabs put Burns into a state. He couldn't keep lowering interest rates with the cost of living rising as it had been in December, by 0.5 percent for the month. But he might have to, to win Nixon's attention. In February, the anxious Fed chairman risked his own reputation and led the Fed in cutting the discount rate once more, this time from 5 percent to 4.75 percent. After that move Burns discerned glints of hope for his income plan in the Administration's behavior. Nixon actually followed one of Burns's recommendations and used emergency powers to suspend a set of rules that drove up wages for federal contractors. Even more important, Nixon signed an extension of an existing law that allowed the president to impose wage and price controls: as far as Burns's wage and price idea was concerned, another positive portent. Nixon applied pressure on wages to federal contractors. The president's actions suggested Nixon was getting ready to order up what Burns wanted, broad restraints on wages and prices.

Still, when the president got word that Burns might argue for wage and price controls when he testified before Congress in March, Nixon was not pleased. "He's still pushing this goddamned wage-price board. He knows the President opposed it," said Nixon, referring to himself in the ominous third person. Nixon ordered his aide Bob Haldeman to pour cold water over Burns and his testimony plans. "Tell him that the President is furious," Nixon said. "Say I'm hurt and distressed, and when he asks for a meeting, say 'The President is unavailable.'" Sunday religious services at the White House were not the moment to bring up business matters. But they were events to which senior members of the Administration and important outsiders were invited, and at which they enjoyed that rarest of commodities, presidential access.[25] Nixon sometimes disinvited Burns at the last hour, and even wrote to Haldeman in February ordering him to keep Burns "off the Church [list] etc."[26]

Burns nonetheless somehow managed to attend the March 7 services, and exploited the occasion to request a private meeting with Nixon. "Why does Arthur need to see me?" Nixon asked his men pointedly. "He says we don't understand him," George Shultz of the Office and Management and Budget replied. "He feels the White House is pushing him too hard."[27] Nixon allowed he would give Burns an audience *after* Burns's upcoming testimony. But Burns did not believe he could loosen money any more. So even with the plum of a meeting dangling before him, Burns on March 11 misbehaved again before Congress, playing more to his colleagues in the economics guild than to Nixon's expectations. The Fed chairman suggested to Congress that the White House notion that you could force prosperity by forcing up the growth of the money supply was "attractively simple but misleading."[28] Burns asserted that he was "very skeptical" of mandatory controls for wages and prices, not exactly the reality. But he added that the idea of such controls had to be considered. In any case, Burns said, it was "terribly important" to create a wage and price review board—an insult to Nixon, at that point.

Nixon's new action figure, Connally, sprang up, making it more than clear to reporters that his own power center, Treasury, didn't share Burns's ideas. Connally told the press that any consideration of a wage-price review board would have to wait. "I'd like to look at at least six months of the year before I make a judgment of this kind"—"I," as if policy were up to Connally alone. Connally took his own jab at Burns. Americans had to display a bit of "statesmanship," Connally said, "if we're going to get by in this country with the free play of market forces instead of the imposition of mandatory wage and price controls." Nixon now badly wanted Burns to cut rates further, but found he was not ready to deploy the terrifying Texan to bully his old advisor. Instead Nixon sent Ehrlichman. Approached, Burns vowed fealty to Nixon. "The idea that I would ever let a conflict arise between what I think is right and my loyalty to Dick Nixon is outrageous," Burns told Ehrlichman, a statement even more ambiguous than it sounded.

Church services or no, Burns could see that he was not the only high official frustrated at lack of access to the chief executive. This new campaigning Nixon was no longer interested in meritorious advisors or intellectuals. The same March, Housing Secretary Romney, irrepressible, also felt the need to speak up about his own challenges at HUD. After all, even though lower than before, interest rates were still well above the usual postwar level. The high rates combined with the high prices were making the arithmetic of public housing projects impossible, and they were sabotaging all the loan programs his HUD developed for working-class homebuyers. The housing secretary invited both Burns and part of the cabinet to his own morning shadow meeting. As speaker Romney invited the chairman of the Council of Economic Advisers, Paul McCracken, who would talk about wage rules for government contractors that Nixon had tightened in February. When Nixon got wind of the meeting, he again deputized Ehrlichman to represent him. "You go to that meeting of that damn rump committee," Nixon said. "You just walk in and sit down. It's an end run of the system!" Nixon already had little faith in Romney, who might, after all, again compete with him in the next presidential race. But he couldn't believe Burns would be in on such a betrayal.[29]

On March 19, nonetheless, Burns managed to snag another meeting with Nixon. To defend his position, Burns combined pleas for pity with threats. Burns had to do what was right, which was not to lower interest rates all the time. It was a matter of patriotic duty. Burns had been born Burnseig, at the eastern end of the Austro-Hungarian Empire. "I came here as an immigrant boy," he reminded Nixon—as did someone Nixon appeared to favor more at the moment, Henry Kissinger. Burns was here in government service in the first place because he owed a debt to America. Nixon had to let Burns do the job he had hired him for.[30] Burns reminded the president that in the private sector, "I could command higher fees than any economist."

Nixon, too, turned histrionic: this Administration might be the last conservative government if they all didn't do something about the economy, he told Burns. Then the president fell back to his old habit of trying to soothe the Fed chairman. Burns, Nixon said, should really consider loosening money through the money supply, a less public change than moving interest rates down by notches. Burns replied that money expansion was proceeding at 6 percent, more than the 5 percent Nixon demanded earlier. Nixon, turning teacher, played back what he'd learned from economists, pointing out that there was "a hell of a lag" between loosening by the Fed and any spurt in the economy, the kind of spurt you would need to affect the election. The general economy had grown smartly until recently, but the Dow Jones Industrial Average had never risen above the key 1,000 line. You just had to get the Dow past that landmark, Nixon told Burns. You could ask, "Is it going to be 1,065 or 1,050?" Nixon allowed, and concluded: "I just hope that it's up." Therefore, when it came to the money supply, "we've really got to think of goosing it"—"we," not Burns—and probably that year. "Yes," said Burns thoughtfully. Henceforward Burns, Nixon said, should try to work with the treasury secretary: "Because you know—you understand politics, Arthur. You know the effect of what is said and done, fortunately." Nixon was reminding Burns that he recalled that Burns was the one who had warned about the election of 1960. "And Connally is a genius at the thing. He's really probably as good as Johnson." Burns had to understand how important teamwork was. Burns for his part assured Nixon that the choice of Connally for Treasury was proving "brilliant."

With each day that passed, however, it was clear the Administration, divided or no, would have to do something about money, something big. Foreign governments were still collecting gold from American coffers for their dollars, indeed bringing the United States "perilously close," as the *Washington Post* put it, to the psychologically crucial $10 billion line. At Treasury and the Fed, the experts kept tabs on the international numbers. Markets were concluding that a dollar devaluation was inevitable. By the end of April the price on the London market, where gold was traded privately, was at an eighteen-month high. In early May, Germany's central bank, the Bundesbank, drowning in dollars, acted. The Bundesbank simply stopped allowing other governments to buy marks for dollars at the set exchange rate. And Germany stopped buying dollars. Allowed to "float," the German mark bobbed up like a rubber duck.

Though knowledge of it would have done little to assuage Burns, Nixon actually did have a monetary plan. That plan, too, was the opposite of economic coherence. Nixon was going to spend the spring bluffing his way through economic trouble; hope the inflation would abate; and stun the world, over the summer, with statesmanlike foreign policy work—not even on Vietnam but, more dramatically, via a rapprochement with his old communist foe China. Such a show would strengthen America's reputation on all fronts, including when it came to the dollar. Perhaps, Nixon told himself, he did have enough time to pull off the bluff. The increase in the Consumer Price Index was down to an annualized rate of 3.6 percent, better than at the end of the last year. And on April 28, the Dow hit 951, within spitting distance of the record of 995.15 in 1966. Nixon was gleeful over that. Burns, a data hound to the core, could sniff out some good news in the Federal Reserve's reports. Reporting in the "Beige Book," the collation of updates on regional conditions from the Federal Reserve Districts, the San Francisco Fed wrote in April that "the general opinion of businessmen and bankers in the twelfth district is that the economy is beginning a period of gradual expansion."[31] But a stronger economy was, in 1971, an argument for tighter money, not looser.

One thing on which Nixon and Burns did concur was that cutting back federal spending, or at least the appearance of doing so, would restore some confidence in the economy. The Democrat-dominated Hill wouldn't go along with the kind of cuts Burns or Nixon envisioned. So Nixon used authority he did have, presidential impoundment, to restrain government spending, holding back some $12 billion in construction money for federal projects. George Meany of the AFL-CIO, whose construction men worked on those federal projects, complained publicly. "We're getting fed up with this rosy rhetoric and Madison Avenue gimmickry," Meany told four thousand delegates from the construction trades at a convention in Washington on April 19. Nixon invited the union leaders over to the White House afterward to schmooze them, but a "meet and greet" did not satisfy the union men. They wanted to complain about the $12 billion, as well as the high unemployment and the high joblessness. "As far as I'm concerned nothing happened," Edward Carlough, president of the Sheet Metal Workers International Association, said.[32] Nixon had eagerly pursued the hard hats when running for office in 1968, yet now, the union leaders argued, he was ignoring the substance of their complaints. The union leaders also leveled criticism at the Democrats. To the unions, there was not enough difference between Johnson and Nixon, and neither seemed to understand the inflation situation. Leonard Woodcock warned that union men had tired of Congress, as well, and "the social snobbery of the Democratic Party." The worker, Woodcock said, was "always pictured as a stupid clod . . . not only a stupid clod but a racist clod." The government funded "everyone except the working man."

As spring moved toward summer Burns saw to his dismay that Nixon was turning increasingly to Big John the Texan for advice and action on economic matters. It was evident to the White House staff that Nixon really did hope to deepen his relationship with Connally, and take that relationship, in whatever form, into the next administration. Lockheed was still flailing. The company that made the engine for Lockheed's new TriStar Airbus, Rolls-Royce of Britain, had already gone belly-up in February. Without the engine, Lockheed was a goner. Nixon thought the Treasury ideal for handling the matter. The new treasury secretary concluded—with Nixon's guidance—that a federal rescue of Lockheed, or Rolls-Royce, or both, was necessary. Burns disapproved of that. Rescues of individual companies were exactly the kind of economic favoritism that slowed growth. But who was listening?

At the end of May, Connally and Shultz made a foray to a bankers' conference in Munich to argue foreign nations into understanding that their strong exports were hurting their partner, the United States. If the pair still held back sometimes with Burns, they could at least vent their anger on Germany or Japan.[33] The Europeans imposed more trade barriers than the United States did. So did Japan. Toyota thought its own rise was due to both cheap prices and the fact that Toyota factories were winning the productivity race against the UAW's Detroit. But Connally depicted Japanese automakers and the Japanese government as mercenary, as not playing fair, and as exploiting an exchange rate they enjoyed only courtesy of American magnanimity to destroy the U.S. auto industry. The United States didn't slap huge tariffs on Japanese autos, yet Japan imposed heavy tariffs on U.S. cars. Japan especially infuriated Connally, and later that year he would go to the trouble to spell out the numbers: because of tariffs and other Japanese rules, a Ford Pinto cost $5,000 in Japan. Thanks to U.S. free-market magnanimity, a Datsun sold for less than $2,000 here.[34]

In Munich, Connally and Shultz let their audience know America could also play the protectionist. And that's what the United States would do if Europe and Japan did not lower their barriers. Europe had to understand, Shultz said, that the United States was ready to "refurbish and revitalize our tradition of being fair, hard-bargaining Yankee traders." If European nations didn't fall into line, both by opening to trade and by permitting their currency to weaken, Connally said, then America had "to get tough with those countries."[35]

The United States continued, however, to assure other nations that it would not support a change in the gold price from $35 an ounce. The differential between official gold at $35 an ounce and private gold was like a meter that measured the world market's lack of trust in that promise. The price for private gold in London dropped below $40 an ounce after Connally's grandstanding. But the effect lasted about as long as Nixon's scoldings of Arthur Burns.

Fresh from Munich, Connally returned to the States and a congressional hearing on Lockheed. He assured Congress that a bankruptcy of Lockheed, its TriStar program, or government-sponsored loans wouldn't hurt the economy. Burns, who had also been invited to testify, seized the chance to engage his new foe, easily puncturing Big John's logic. If "the effect on the economy would not be serious," Burns said, "the loan should not be guaranteed."[36] Senator William Proxmire of Wisconsin also piled on. "If the TriStar program is as sound . . . as you think it is," Proxmire asked Connally, "wouldn't the banks have a natural incentive to loan Lockheed the additional $250 million to protect their investment?" Well, replied Connally, he wasn't a banker. "I don't know how a banker thinks. I have always been a borrower, not a banker." Proxmire wondered aloud why a mega-bailout was really necessary. The senator noted that the United States had recently turned down another behemoth, Penn Central, when it got into trouble. Was it really federal business to rescue big companies? Arranging a loan for Lockheed was well and good, but where was the guarantee that Lockheed management would perform with all the money it got, and deliver its plane? When you rescued a company, you spared the company "the very direct painful price that business has to pay if it does fail. Once that is out of the picture, an important part of the discipline of the American economic system disappears." Connally, Proxmire was suggesting, was creating a welfare program for larger businesses. In this instance it was Connally's turn to drop the shocking rebuttal. The treasury secretary said the numbers on the company's books didn't matter. "What do we care whether they perform?" What mattered was the visual—the jobs. Those jobs should win the support of any workers who had lost their confidence in the president.

Burns and Proxmire abhorred this kind of political management of companies. If this confusing era was teaching anything about the U.S. economy, it was that if Lockheed and Boeing went, something else would eventually take their place in Maryland, Georgia, and the now desolate Seattle. Some of the platforms for funding the new companies that would repopulate old industrial centers were already emerging. That February the National Association of Securities Dealers had opened something new, an electronic ticker for over-the-counter stocks, so that the average investor could get better information about smaller companies that might have a big future. The Nasdaq, as it was called, was not a trading platform yet, but clearly it could become one. Even as a glorified ticker, the Nasdaq could show the investor a menu that was broader than the usual names, most on the big exchanges, like Penn Central, Lockheed, or Boeing. The first company to list on the computerized Nasdaq, suitably enough, was in the computer business: Robert Noyce's Intel.[37] Intel's revenues, like the microchips, appeared to be following Moore's Law: the growth of Intel's business was exponential. The flop of its new chip had been only temporary. In 1970, revenues of the company had been $4.2 million. In 1971 they were $9.4 million, and in 1972 they would be $23.4 million. Intel was creating jobs not only on the West Coast, but elsewhere, too. A microprocessor Intel had developed for the Japanese company Busicom clearly would also have applications in the United States.[38]

One reason Connally was mounting such drama on the economic stage was to distract attention from Nixon's challenges on the stage of foreign policy. In June, the *New York Times* and the *Washington Post* published an old Pentagon report revealing that years ago, even in the time of Mc-Namara, the Defense Department had covered up the failure of the U.S. war in Vietnam. Though the Pentagon Papers, as the report would be known, dealt largely with Johnson's era, Nixon saw that the content discredited not only Johnson but any Administration—his own—still in Vietnam. Nixon sicced his Justice Department on the *Times* and the *Post* newspapers, trying to halt publication. While the president waited to see if he could humiliate the newspapers, the gold price on the private market in London again bounced past $40 an ounce. Nixon called together Shultz and Connally. Perhaps theirs was still a messaging problem, the president suggested: if the Administration (and, the president hoped, the Fed) spoke with one voice, it would sound strong. Perhaps Connally needed more authority. Connally dared to point out Nixon's inconsistency. "Well," said Connally, "if you want me to be the spokesman, Mr. President, you are going to have to order those other fellows to shut up."

Nixon did. With Ehrlichman as witness and scribe, Nixon formalized what had heretofore been informal. Every economic policy hand would report to Connally. Even Burns, regardless of his and Nixon's old friendship or Fed independence. "You know I think Connally is anti-Semitic,"

Nixon confessed before Shultz and Ehrlichman. "It probably troubles him to deal with Herbert Stein and Arthur Burns and Henry Kissinger and [speechwriter William] Safire. Too bad." He called the economic point men of the executive branch into the Cabinet Room—the secretaries of Treasury, Commerce, and Labor; Shultz of OMB; and others. The cabinet members were told to get in line—"Or else," Ehrlichman later recalled Nixon saying, "you can quit." As for Burns, Nixon had a special line: "Just tell Arthur to report to Connally. The President won't see him."[39]

Connally advertised his new power by appearing before the White House press corps to lay out the federal government's unified position on the economy once and for all. In Munich, Connally had already assured the press that the United States would not devalue, and that it would not change the price of gold, either. On this day Connally added "four nos" to the Nixon Administration list. Nixon was not going to institute a wage-price board (as Burns sought). Nixon was not going to impose mandatory wage and price controls. He was not going to ask for a tax reduction. He was not going to engage in further spending.

In mid-June, the Supreme Court ruled that the *Post* and the *Times* could publish the Pentagon Papers—another humiliation for the White House. Each news hour that the Administration could fill with reports of economic initiatives was a news hour that did not discuss the Pentagon Papers. A panel of experts convened earlier by the White House now published "inflation alerts," tagging regulators, companies, or industries that were allowing prices to rise egregiously. There would be, as Shultz sheepishly allowed in July, "no whacking" of individual companies. The idea was to give the market and the government economic information. Shultz was a University of Chicago man, after all. But to the companies or agencies named, the move certainly felt like whacking. One of the first "inflation alerts" hit the Interstate Commerce Commission for permitting a rise in freight fees on mobile and prefabricated homes of up to 58 percent.[40] Now the experts reprised the Kennedy Administration attack on U.S. Steel and placed an "inflation alert" on the company, which had dared to raise prices 8 percent. To add to the sting the White House deputy press spokesman even berated U.S. Steel on its business judgment: the company had taken an action, the White House asserted, that would render it uncompetitive. When it came to harassment of U.S. Steel, it was not the Johnson Administration that the Nixon Administration resembled. It was the Kennedy Administration.

By early July, there was another good number for Nixon: June unemployment was 5.6 percent, down from 6.2 percent the month before. The Consumer Price Index had increased at an annualized rate of 6 percent, down from an almost incomprehensibly high rate of 7.2 percent for May. An *Evening Star* article, however, carried a line saying that the "Labor Department warned that the dip might have been caused by a statistical quirk." Nixon had been informed there truly was a quirk: unemployment went down in the summer when young people in school temporarily joined the workforce. Nonetheless Nixon went ballistic at the Labor Department staff for marring his good news. The president ordered Charles Colson, the White House counsel, to find out who had said "quirk" and see to it that he was fired. "I've had it. I don't want any crap about this. You understand?"[41]

Instead of relenting now that he might have a tolerable economy for the election, Nixon was becoming obsessed with Burns's habit of going his own way. Why wasn't Burns getting the message about unity? Nixon asked his men. Ehrlichman, in his memoirs, would later call moments like these part of the "get-Burns-under-control cycle." In these cycles, Ehrlichman would religiously transcribe Nixon's points before he took Burns to the woodshed. Ehrlichman's memoirs repeat the lines for one such script: "The President made you chairman of the Fed, Arthur. You are deeply in his debt. He expects you to be loyal." Even as he dispatched deputies to work his mischief, Nixon rambled on to those who would listen. The president thought Jews were a problem. "The government is full of Jews," Nixon told Haldeman. Jews were disloyal. He could trust Kissinger and Safire. But as for the rest, they were "a Jewish cabal." They worked with people like Burns. "And they all only talk to Jews." In Burns's case, this was hardly so. The person Burns *wanted* to talk to was Nixon.

On July 15 the president was finally ready to unveil his great foreign policy coup: he would visit Red China the following February.[42] It was a daring move. The United States had denied China diplomatic relations since the communist revolution, two decades before. The FBI's J. Edgar Hoover regarded any effort by citizens to make contact with China as worse than sinister—Tom Hayden's, for example. Tough anticommunists, Nixon's old allies, felt that it was scarcely better for a sitting president to make such a rash move. Nixon luxuriated in his own boldness, and believed this was the moment for triumph. China would certainly keep the economy off the front page. By now Burns, who believed the inflation battle was far from over, was becoming desperate. Gold continued to leave the United States. The United States looked on track to record a trade deficit for the entire year, something far worse than occasional monthly dips. Inflation might dip from 7 percent to 5 percent, but that was still only the difference between terrible and awful. The Fed chair had already compromised on interest rates, risking his reputation. Public criticism of the Fed's easy-money policy was already mounting. Burns's student Milton Friedman was openly mocking the Fed, saying that the money supply was "exploding."[43] These Burns policies would "fan" the fire of inflation, Friedman said. Just as humiliatingly, Friedman was delineating a time frame for the monetary mismanagement—"In the last six months." That period was entirely within Burns's tenure at the Fed. Another jab came from the labor secretary, who slapped down Burns's hoped-for wage rules, saying, "Controls merely make an already difficult process even more difficult." Whom should Burns appease this time, Nixon or his own guild?

Burns chose the guild. In the same week when Nixon proudly made his announcement about China, Burns dissed the Supreme Statesman. The Federal Reserve, led by Burns, reversed its policy of the past half year and nudged the discount rate back up to 5 percent. The Dow, which had already begun dropping back from a near-1,000 high, dropped some more, and mortgage rates rose to over 7.5 percent, an embarrassment for an administration whose Treasury had predicted more than a year before that the mortgage rate would soon head down to 6 percent. On Air Force One, Nixon told Kissinger he really had to do something, the economy was "bleeding to death slowly."[44] On July 23, Burns, now operating on sheer impulse and fumes, offered a kind of mea culpa and warning in testimony to Congress. "I wish I could report that we are making substantial progress in dampening the inflationary spiral," Burns said mournfully to lawmakers at a hearing. "I cannot do so."[45] And then Burns confessed. "The rules of economics are not working in quite the way they used to," he said, referring to the venerable trade-off between unemployment and inflation. "Despite extensive unemployment in our country, wage rate increases have not moderated. Despite much idle industrial capacity, commodity prices continue to rise rapidly." The suggestion was that Burns would have to raise rates some more. For all his show of melancholy, Burns was well aware that the current situation supplied evidence for one of his older theses, that inflation and growth could operate independently. Burns had, after all, titled that early monograph *Prosperity Without Inflation*. Now, he was noting, there was inflation without prosperity. Keynesian economic planning by Washington had for decades now been the planning that enabled all other planning, the government management to end all managements by government. Yet now Keynesian planning was failing, too.

Economists always debate their models among themselves—the White House knew that. But for the Nixon White House of 1971, Burns's public expression of uncertainty amounted to a new scale of sin. Uncertainty was the opposite of speaking in "one voice." Burns knew he could expect another dressing-down from Ehrlichman or even Connally for that. Burns also sensed he was in for the long-delayed larger fight, the fight about Fed independence. The same month Burns wrote in his diary about the changes he observed in his president. "I had often noticed RN's love of the imperial manner and its trappings but now I knew that I would be accepted in the future only if I suppressed my will and yielded completely—even though it was wrong at law and morally—to his authority."[46]

If Nixon was an emperor now, he was a vindictive emperor. Fiery with rage at the Fed chairman, Nixon permitted, and sometimes ordered, the men around him to undermine Burns. Burns wanted to select the nominee for a seat on the Federal Reserve board; he learned from George Shultz that the president was going to pick the nominee himself. Nixon and Connally prepared a trick on the Fed chairman. They would ask Charles Colson to give reporters word that again Nixon was angry with Burns. The leaker would start rumors that strengthened arguments for subordinating the mighty Fed. The leak would also include an assertion that was patently untrue: that Burns had personally asked for a raise for himself. In reality the only suggestion of a raise for the Fed chairman was the one recommended as part of the broader series of raises in a recent government report. On July 29, the story duly appeared in the *Wall Street Journal.* "President Called 'Furious,'" read the caption below the headline. The *Journal* reported that an anonymous presidential aide had told the reporters that the president "has under serious consideration legislative recommendations, in which many of his principal advisors concur, that specifically would bring the Federal Reserve into the executive branch." The same story reported gossip about top federal officials' salaries. The sanctimonious housing secretary, Romney, had the year before suggested that the president and his senior appointees accept a 25 percent cut in their salaries to model austerity. This story reported that Burns, by contrast, was "trying to get his own salary raised to $62,500, from $42,500."

Nixon and Connally chortled together when Burns in his turn went ballistic. Nixon told Connally, "Your little tactic you suggested got home to our friends across the street."[47] In Congress, the populist Wright Patman, Connally's fellow Texan, reacted with satisfying predictability, assailing the Fed. Patman, Nixon noted, had "stepped up to it right nice." Connally vowed he'd tell no one of their ruse: "I'll play it dumb."[48]

But the markets did not chortle. Overwhelmed at the idea of so brash a White House consolidation of power, the Dow fell a total of 27 points within days. Peter Flanigan, another Nixon advisor, warned Nixon that to play up a fight between the Fed and the White House undermined "essential stability." Burns complained loud and hard to fellow insiders that he had never sought a raise for himself. Burns could accept it when Nixon was tough on him. He lived with the fact that Nixon was—another insult—refusing to allow him to guide the selection of a candidate for the spot opening on the Federal Reserve Board, which Burns regarded as the chairman's prerogative. But the proposal to emasculate the Fed and the public salary smear Burns rated just untenable.

Now it was the Nixon team's turn to panic. What if Burns complained to the press about this trick? While Nixon didn't mind shaming Burns in the papers, he didn't want to be shamed back. In a press conference on August 4, the president offered the closest thing to an apology he was willing to give. He allowed to the press that he was taking "the chance to set the record straight with regard to some blown up differences that I am supposed to have with my very good friend Arthur Burns." Nixon went on to let it be known that Burns had endured an unfair shot on the salary question—he had never asked for a raise for himself personally. And the president praised Burns for having "followed a course that I think is the most responsible and statesmanlike of any chairman of the Federal Reserve in my memory," citing as an example Burns's general willingness to pursue an expansionary monetary policy despite inflation.[49]

To all observers, not just Burns, it was obvious that this president was now thinking not partially but almost entirely in terms of 1972. If Nixon had to permit a devaluation of the dollar, he was more likely to do it in a preelection year than an election year. Congress was going along, sometimes enthusiastically. In a report, a Joint Economic Committee led by Representative Henry Reuss, a Democrat, called the need for devaluing the dollar "inescapable." The world was simply ready for gold to be worth more than $35 an ounce. Years later it would come out that the president was also thinking about the makeup of the 1972 ticket. It was in this period that Nixon, almost like a beau, sprang the question on Connally. Would Connally join him on the ticket? Nixon dropped the idea one day for Connally to contemplate, then took it up the next. It was necessary, again, to think in "very bold terms," Nixon told him.[50] A Republican-Democratic ticket *was* bold, Connally conceded. He wasn't sure the idea was wise for Nixon, or that he himself would be more useful there: as vice president Connally would have less "freedom of action than the least of your cabinet people."

Connally knew all about the vice presidency. He had grown up in the Texas of John Nance Garner, Roosevelt's vice president, who had said that the office "was not worth a bucket of warm spit." Connally had served Johnson, indeed had been present at the 1960 convention at the very moment when Johnson had to make the choice to accept Kennedy's offer of the second spot, and recalled very well the purgatory Johnson had endured as vice president. Well, Nixon said, he understood Connally's hesitation. Nixon had been vice president himself—and vice president to a president who hadn't particularly liked him. This time would be different. "You in the job would be the president's stand in, and basically everybody would know it." Warming, Nixon said, "You would have a prestige and a backing that's just unbelievable." Connally didn't bite. Nixon turned to Ehrlichman: "You woo him."[51]

The economic news now conspired to aid Nixon in his suit. The inflation was becoming not just a problem but a true crisis—Shultz and Burns actually made the cover of *Time*, struggling in what the magazine termed a "Battle of the Economy." In early August, shaming by inflation alert or no, the steel industry announced it would raise wages by 30 percent over thirty-six months, and raise prices by 8 percent to cover some of the cost. On August 7, the public got word that the U.S. gold supply would indeed fall "perilously close" to the $10 billion mark. France was cashing in $191 million for gold at the gold window. And the price of gold in London, on the private market, now stood at $44 an ounce. The gap between $44 and the official price of $35 was the widest since the two-tier system, another one of those favors from the Europeans, under Johnson in 1968, had been patched together.

The world pricked up its ears. Even *Pravda*, the communist organ, got the story: there were more "gray green papers" (dollars) than the United States could redeem for gold. "This leads to the inevitable drop in the dollar's exchange rate," *Pravda* helpfully noted, "the increasing menace of its devaluation and new shocks for capitalism's monetary system."

On August 12, a day when the *Wall Street Journal* carried a report of the dollar sinking to a record low against the German mark, Nixon discussed with his colleagues the idea of a plan to end the dollar and inflation problem. Now Nixon could demonstrate to Connally that he really did trust him by handing over to him a genuine crisis to manage, not just a mundane matter like Lockheed. Together, Nixon, the suitor; and Connally, the pursued, made moves that would change the future of the international finance system. Connally, taking Nixon at his word, wanted to push through his own action plan, an entire economic program to jumpstart the economy. Wage and price controls, dollar devaluation, tariffs, closing the gold window, and busting the whole international monetary system—all were on Connally's list. As far as Connally was concerned, the more action items, the better.

Observing it all, mostly from afar, Burns analyzed the documents and rumors. It appeared Nixon wanted to act any day now. If you imposed wage and price controls, you held back inflation and allowed the economy to cool—at least in Burns's view. That was a good stopgap, as Burns had told Nixon all along. Burns was however still so stunned over the nasty salary trick that he could scarcely marshal joy at word that Nixon would now consider his favorite idea, wage and price restraints. You might not need to do much else. To plop an import tax on top of a devaluation was to do twice as much work as you needed to, and to insult U.S. allies twice instead of once.

Burns worried about Connally's bold gold talk. It was one thing to reset the dollar price in gold, devaluation. It was another to suspend the gold standard totally, even temporarily, possibly Nixon's current plan. Burns's name would be forever linked to this U.S. abdication. Why close the gold window when the other measures would stave off a panic? And why do it suddenly, instead of through the orderly process of a monetary treaty? Burns thought over all the times he had advised against ending the gold standard. He had tried with Connally, he had tried with a junior official at Treasury named Paul Volcker, and he had tried with OMB. "My efforts to prevent the closing of the gold window—working through Connally, Volcker and Shultz—do not seem to have succeeded," Burns wrote in his diary. "The gold window may have to be closed tomorrow because we now have a government that seems incapable, not only of constructive leadership, but of any action at all. What a tragedy for mankind!" Burns was desperate to share his wisdom in the key discussions.

Yet those discussions were now proceeding without him. Shultz and

Connally worked well together, almost like a pair of stand-up comics, with Shultz playing the straight man. The OMB director reminded Nixon tactfully that Nixon himself understood that "as you [Nixon] pointed out, a tax is a form of a devaluation."[52] Maybe, asked Shultz, as Burns might have, the package did not need to include both import tax and devaluation? Perhaps, Shultz suggested, it might be wise to "let the border tax come a little later." Shultz offered that any material that went to the public ought to include background tables and data, to show that the dollar crisis was not Nixon's alone. This was Connally's hour. Congress had just voted to support Connally on the Lockheed rescue. Nixon was courting him. Connally was now more confident than ever. Forget caution, Connally said. Stage the news politically, Connally told Nixon. Place the blame where it belongs, on past presidents. The same taping system that collected Nixon's reactions to the Pentagon Papers recorded the exchange between Nixon and Connally on economic policy.

CONNALLY: The reason you want this background, in detail along
    these lines, is to show that we've been deteriorating for 25
    years—
NIXON: Right.
CONNALLY: —and that you're the first president that's had the guts—
NIXON: Yeah.
CONNALLY: —to take this comprehensive—
NIXON: Great.
CONNALLY: —action.[53]

Soon afterward, Connally received what he needed to move, which was the report of another gold withdrawal. The United Kingdom, word had it, was going to pull $3 billion in gold from the United States vaults.[54]As it happened, this was later proved inaccurate.[55] But the news was a convenient last straw. Such a move would take U.S. gold holdings far below $10 billion, their envelope arithmetic showed clearly. Nixon and Connally would now present a policy package containing most of or all their ideas, a package so sudden and revolutionary, like Nixon's decision to go to China, that it outclassed either the New Frontier or the Great Society for sheer drama. Shultz and Connally got in the spirit. "I think it's the biggest thing in economic policy since World War II," Shultz concluded, accurately enough. Nixon had always known he could out-Kennedy Kennedy and out-Johnson Johnson, and now he was going to do it.

There remained only one problem: getting the sanction of the top economics guru in Washington—in other words, Arthur Burns. The best way to do that, Nixon said, was for Nixon to "whip up" to Camp David and take all his economists, Burns of course included, for an economic summit to blueprint the package over the weekend. By the end of the weekend Nixon would have socialized not only Burns but all his economic advisors, whether Paul McCracken of the Council of Economic Advisers or Connally's staff, to his proposal. That big economists backed the White House would impress markets.

The collection of minds invited to travel to Camp David that Friday was indeed one of the most impressive in the history of economic policy. There was Burns, of course. George Shultz had served as dean of arguably the best business school in the country. The group included Shultz's deputy, Caspar Weinberger, who boasted a cost-cutting ability so fine that his nickname was "Cap the Knife." Pete Peterson, the new presidential assistant for economic affairs, was a former head of Bell and Howell. Martin Anderson of the Council of Economic Advisers had written the best book on urban renewal around. Paul McCracken, who had also served in the Eisenhower Administration, specialized in studying the social trade-offs of anti-inflationary policy. McCracken could diagnose every twinge and grimace on the face of the UAW's Leonard Woodcock, and tell you what *would* make Woodcock smile. Then there was Paul Volcker of the Treasury, who knew more than almost any other American about international financial markets. (In the height department, Volcker, at six foot seven inches, dwarfed even Big John Connally.) Herbert Stein, one of McCracken's deputies, was perhaps the single greatest economic communicator in the country, and William Safire, also along, the best speechwriter. Not included, however, were other figures who would have to clean up the consequences of the new Nixon program: the usually omnipresent Henry Kissinger; the secretary of state, William Rogers; the commerce secretary, Maurice Stans; or HUD's Romney. When Kissinger did see the package, he would recognize it for what it was: an unnecessary declaration of economic war on our allies. What would happen to Toyota or Datsun? What would Japan, still reeling from being displaced by China as America's Asian favorite, make of this?[56]

The president had guessed right about Burns. Burns's great pride, that he was an outsider, an independent thinker at an independent institution, melted at the pleasure of the president's company on such a trip. The exclusivity felt delicious. As the men lifted off in the helicopters, they sensed themselves moving to a new political level, the closest the United States comes to royalty, presidential royalty. At Camp David, Navy personnel waited on them hand and foot; at Camp David, they might eat anything they liked, or ride, or shoot skeet, or swim. They all received gifts: blue Camp David jackets, embroidered with their names. (As Arnold Weber, one of the attendees, later recalled, the jackets were the right brand for what was after all a protectionists' summit: bona fide American "Mr. Wrangler" from Sears.)[57] The fact that the attendees were sworn to secrecy, told to keep the details from even their wives, made the moment unusual as well. Best of all, once they arrived, Nixon, for whose attention Burns had vied vainly over the course of the spring, now made himself available to the Fed chairman. Burns, assuaged, noted that the malign Nixon was gone. This weekend Nixon moved close to Burns, took notes on one of his yellow legal pads, and was "particularly deferential" to Burns's views.

The other hands at Camp David, especially Haldeman and Ehrlichman, were impatient. They had long since wearied of fearmongering central bankers like Burns and Paul Volcker, who, though at Treasury, specialized in central banking. Men like Volcker issued dire warnings even as they sanctimoniously suggested that the basis of those warnings was too complex for the average man to comprehend. When Volcker reiterated that what happened at Camp David that weekend must be secret, for "fortunes could be made with this information," Haldeman leaned forward and, half-challenging, asked: "Exactly how?" The rest broke out in laughter. Volcker struck back. How much is your deficit? Volcker asked Shultz, the budget man. The federal deficit was $23 billion or so, Shultz allowed. Well, said Volcker, looking at the ceiling, "Give me a billion and a free hand Monday, and I could make up that deficit in the money markets."

At Camp David, Burns posed the obvious question again. Why did they have to close the gold window at all? A price freeze, a border tax on imports, and government spending cuts would achieve the same effect. Connally, though, still liked the idea of a tax on imports, 10 to 15 percent, "primarily a negotiating weapon," as McCracken later remembered. Connally didn't care that this would be the first general tariff since Herbert Hoover. Connally's modus operandi was to terrify other nations, then negotiate. The other party wouldn't like you. But who cared? You got more out of that party in the ultimate compromise. Tokyo, Bonn, and the others would be scared, Connally said, and they would give the United States a "fair deal." Pete Peterson, the president's international advisor, concurred that a tax on imports would be the stick; the tax's removal, the carrot. Peterson insisted, though, that the federal government levy the surtax temporarily—until the Europeans gave in and raised the values of their currencies.

Burns watched it all unwind. Instead of asking for voluntary commitments from companies and labor, the president was going all the way, further than even Burns had suggested, and planning for actual controls, a "freeze." Others argued for a tax cut for business—Burns had argued for such a cut. Now that went in, another item that pleased Burns. One could trim personal income taxes. As if an import tax and a devaluation wouldn't do enough for automakers, the men threw in the tax cuts.

In reality Burns was ready to go along with the entire package, with one exception: closing the gold window. The others told Burns that the window would be closed only temporarily, until the industrial nations agreed on new exchange rates. Burns kept reiterating the point that once you took all the other measures, closing the gold window, even temporarily, wasn't needed. All you had to do was raise the gold price. Nations would buy gold at $35 an ounce, but would they demand gold at the gold window when it cost $40, $50, or $70 an ounce? Less likely. Connally told Burns and the others they had to make the bold move of closing the window: if you waited to close the window, then you were, as Connally put it, "in the hands of the money changers." Burns fought back—bravely, considering that "money changers" was a New Testament barb everyone knew referred to people of the Old Testament, such as himself. When the rest retired at one point, Burns dared to stay with Nixon, Haldeman later remembered, to make a final, personal pitch against closing the gold window. The others knew it was bound to be a doozy. Paul McCracken, Nixon's economic advisor, later noted that some of them already knew that if Burns "wants to give a performance worthy of Sophocles, he can do it."

And Burns indeed sang his heart out. Nixon, Burns said, didn't seem to understand that many Americans still believed in the dollar, as John Kennedy had believed when he promised a dollar that was "good as gold." No matter how you analyzed the value of the gold system, to change it unilaterally was to change a commitment that one party, the government, had made with another party, the American people, many decades ago. If Nixon closed the gold window, the stock market could go down by 500 points.

To give up gold, especially so suddenly, was also to betray all foreign governments within the gold-exchange system, governments that, just weeks before, Connally with his "four nos" had assured no change was coming. Reducing the value of the dollar broke the old promise between the United States, Germany, France, and Japan: they would support us as allies, and we would give them favorable terms of trade. With a weaker dollar, the Germans or Japanese would lose their export advantage. Employees of companies in foreign countries would lose their jobs because of what happened at Camp David, no doubt about it. Even calling those foreign governments that traded gold "money changers," as Connally called them, only partially disguised such a betrayal. If you closed the gold window, the balance of payments would improve. But to do so was to suggest that the United States didn't mind being insolvent. *Pravda* would write that this was a sign of the collapse of capitalism, Burns lectured Nixon.[58]

Still, it was clear to them all, Burns included, that Nixon was leaning toward closing the window. Nixon woke well before dawn on Saturday to draft the speech and make the final choices. By 4:30 a.m. the president was calling Haldeman, telling Haldeman he might, which meant "would," close the gold window. What really mattered, Nixon said, was the same thing that had mattered in Roosevelt's time: "we need to raise the spirit of the country." Safire and Nixon worked further on the language, including not just one or the other of the proposals, but all of them. The plan was set, though at midnight Saturday, Burns, in his Camp David windbreaker, would tap on the screen door of Safire, who was running a draft through his typewriter, and ask that the laden phrase "international money changers" be deleted from the speech. Safire complied.

Burns would later tell himself he had to surrender on gold—he had no choice. What mattered to him coming out of Camp David were two things. One was that Nixon was making some of Burns's policies his own: "incomes policy," wage and price controls, and tax cuts for business. Burns had done well with that, and he was already rewriting the rest of his positions in his mind to conform to the Connally plan. Seated next to Safire at dinner in Laurel Cabin, Burns told the speechwriter, "You know, I argued pretty strenuously against the gold move—that's the only difference I have with the whole policy. But even on that I don't feel so cocky. Nobody can be sure. When it was decided, I told the president he would have my wholehearted support."

The second thing that mattered to Burns was the relationship. Nixon had showed that he respected Burns, and would show that respect when they got back to Washington. Nixon would shortly even throw Burns an extra gift: the news that Burns could choose the nominee for the spot opening on the Federal Reserve Board. After a long winter and spring in the cold, Burns was back in Nixon's good graces. Burns could write future reforms. He had prevailed after all.

———

BUT OF course Burns was not the only professional economist at Camp David. And while the chairman was throwing in the gold towel, some of the others had second thoughts about the Nixon package. It was one thing to hear about proposals or pose clever hypotheticals, another to watch those proposals become reality. It was ironic for the others to see Burns, the inflation hawk, go along with what would surely reduce the purchasing power of the dollar. It was ironic, too, that Nixon assigned the job of handling the details of creating a wage and price freeze to Shultz and Herbert Stein, two big free marketeers. The White House staff would joke that "the plan was certain to work because it had been designed by people who did not believe in controls."[59] Nixon, Shultz said defensively, wouldn't even have the burden of choosing when to end his wage and price freeze—the unions, by striking militantly, would do that for the president.

Pete Peterson, a junior staffer, couldn't believe his ears. No matter how Nixon, Connally, and Burns spun the plan for wage and price controls, "it was about as non–market oriented, non-Republican an idea as I could imagine," Peterson later remembered. Peterson thought the whole package weird. Months later, he would express the perversities he saw. Between the Camp David devaluation of the dollar, so painful for Germany and Japan, and Nixon's approach to China, Nixon was proceeding "to burn bridges to our best friends while you build them up to our erstwhile enemies."[60] Volcker was appalled at the amount of foreign goodwill that Nixon had jettisoned with the sudden move. Perhaps recognizing that he himself, as chairman of the Federal Reserve, would one day have to put down the inflation that this move generated, Volcker also expressed reservations about the way the gold action had been handled. The men saw not only that the package was political, but that the rest of the world would recognize it for what it was, the opening of Nixon's election campaign. The number that mattered to Nixon was clearly not ten, for the $10 billion gold reserve line. It was twenty-five, the number of votes that Texas, Connally's state, had in the Electoral College. The entire history of price controls suggested they would do the opposite of what Burns hoped: citizens, aware that the controls were only temporary, would expect even more inflation, and demand higher wages, or set higher prices, accordingly.

Also dogging the Camp David economists was the question of whether a president really had the legal authority to act as Nixon wanted to. Americans were already deeply distressed at the overreaching by the executive branch in Vietnam. Johnson's Gulf of Tonkin trick no longer appeared cute. Many, like the mayors and the governors, were also distressed at the executive overreach in the towns, states, and courts. Now, again, an administration—this time, Nixon's—would overreach, this time, on currency. The plan hardening at Camp David was not only a grab bag but also a power grab. A few days later, the *Wall Street Journal* would publish an editorial on the policy planned this weekend. The paper would punt on its analysis of the economic merits of the plan, and pointedly raise the question of whether Nixon had the right to do all he was trying: "If Congress agrees . . ." the paper carefully inserted. "If Congress goes along . . ." "If Congress approves . . ." Foreign governments would later lodge complaints that the import surcharge violated an international treaty, the General Agreement on Tariffs and Trade.

A deeper problem troubled them all. The story of the 1960s was public reform upon reform: first community action, then housing, then the random tinkering with the currency system, then guaranteed income and the assault of the lawyers. Like the Vietnam record, the record of the "Best and the Brightest" at home suggested that planning was far tougher than authorities pretended. Indeed, the only reason they all had to make these momentous choices at Camp David at this time was that the earlier reforms proved so costly that foreign governments were losing faith in the United States. Might not this effort at managing the economy, the most extravagant planning hubris of all, fail as well?

Nixon admitted they were not all sure on the economics. "Nobody knows what the public reaction will be to the gold window," Nixon had said before Camp David, "because, frankly, good God, the people that are the experts don't know what the hell it ought to be." At Camp David, Nixon reminded the others that the great planner in the Great Depression, Franklin Roosevelt, had failed with his New Deal. "After eight years of the New Deal, in 1940, there were nine million unemployed." Recovery, Nixon said, came only at the time of the military ramp-up for

World War II. Nixon took from that Depression experience a lesson: giant stimuli were sometimes the only answer. But some of the economists at Camp David drew the opposite lesson from the 1930s: there had been too much intervention and too much arbitrariness, especially in the monetary field. John Connally was not the first enfant terrible. Roosevelt had been as arbitrary about gold as Nixon and Connally, and when FDR took the United States off the gold standard, the stock market recovery of 1933 had halted. The real question about the Great Depression was not whether the war spending had ended it, but why the Depression had lasted all the way to the war.

A professor who had spent time at George Shultz's and Milton Friedman's school, the University of Chicago, was especially skeptical of the kind of planning now happening at Camp David. The professor, Friedrich von Hayek, noted that in the private world anyone who was planning—making business decisions—was subject to a constant barrage of facts, which came in the form of prices. That barrage might make life tough—keeping up with a competitor like Toyota or Intel was a constant struggle. Just as Senator Proxmire had told Secretary Connally with regard to aerospace companies, a business that made the wrong step had to pay the "direct painful price" of failing. Enduring the barrage did force businesses to be flexible, and sometimes they made better decisions. If a government planner possessed "all the relevant information," Hayek said, then the planner, too, could make decisions and succeed. The planner need merely to work out the logic of the problem.

But public planners did not possess all the information. Their very jobs insulated them from the real-time price barrage that would test their hypotheses in a timely fashion. Unions, for example, negotiated their "prices," wages, on a three-year cycle. Presidencies, of course, operated on a four-year cycle. So did the Fed chairmanship. These cycles permitted institutions to plan for long periods without instant price feedback. The planners made errors, and the errors made it harder for the private businesses to make their own plans. A few months later, George Meany, the AFL-CIO head, would complain loudly when a Nixon price control prohibited his workers from collecting money due them. "They have abrogated our contract," Meany complained.[61] The political price of an action—a benefit, or a cost—was by contrast clear to officials instantly, and soon enough became to those in public office more real than anything having to do with genuine currency-denominated prices. This problem, sometimes called the "knowledge problem," affected all government officials and their allies, whether executive branch economic advisors, unions, or even central bankers.[62] Hayek had written his idea up back in the 1940s, but he was describing, all too precisely, the capture of Burns.

No one at Camp David would ever go as far as the libertarian Murray Rothbard, who several days later would put his opinion bluntly: "On August 15, 1971, fascism came to America." But all the economists saw that, with the Camp David measures, they were moving the economy farther away from traditional capitalism. As the *Spectator* of London, reviewing Nixon policy a year later, would conclude, "President Nixon, like Mr. Wilson, is turning socialist." The provisional name the White House team had given to the package was the New Economic Policy. Later, however, "NEP" would be quickly dropped when the Administration realized that it was Lenin's old name for a program in communist Russia.

Much later, many of the attendees would wince at the memory of their participation in the weekend. A number of them wrote explanations, or even apologies, in their memoirs. Volcker later recalled that he had not been able to stop it all because he had been so junior, and "Connally and Treasury were rather dominant in policymaking at the moment." George Shultz for his part would remind others that he had never backed wage and price freezes, just gone along with them. "Almost everyone associated with the sweeping interventions begun on August 15, 1971, has recanted or admitted error," Arnold Weber, the junior staffer, would later say. The very fact that the men went along was evidence of "the profound innocence that sometimes afflicts economic policy making." During the freeze, Weber would point out, the authorities would issue a rule regarding the futures market that so went against logic and precedent that "the markets simply shut down." Pete Peterson had supported the temporary income tax, but when, later, Connally and Nixon advocated keeping the tax in place through the 1972 election year, Peterson was, by his own description, "aghast." Doubly infuriating was that Nixon broke a promise, by making something he'd labeled "temporary" seemingly permanent.

Herb Stein, the most reflective in the group, wrote several essays about Camp David. "Even now, I am amazed to think of how little we looked ahead during that exciting weekend at Camp David when we (the president, really) made those big decisions," he wrote in 1996. "We were going to freeze wages and prices for ninety days. What would happen after the ninety days? I don't remember any discussion of that."[63] As it turned out, Stein noted, some of the freezes lasted more like a thousand days. But even during the weekend Stein felt queasy. As he thought through the wage and price moves, *Macbeth* popped into his head.

I am in blood
Stept in so far that, should I wade no more
Returning were as tedious as go o'er.

Stein was saying aloud what they all knew. Prettifying a political grab by dressing it as an economic rescue was precisely the kind of action against which eminences like Burns warned foreign governments when they made grand speeches abroad. Nixon was indeed now preparing to do what Harold Wilson had done in 1967: disingenuously pretend that devaluing a currency would not affect the consumer. Stimulating the economy in this way might win Nixon the election, but inflation would eventually explode, as Friedman sometimes said, like a closed pot over high heat. Wage and price controls and taxes on imports could make the kind of growth America was accustomed to, the old bonanza, disappear for years, even a decade. True scarcity of key goods might suddenly become the rule. And that was true no matter how many times that cowboy Connally went around bragging about tariffs and telling others that America was "the strongest economy on earth."

———

BUT FOR the moment, the Olympians at Camp David in the end silenced all doubts. Like Burns, the men stopped pointing out which policy con-

tradicted the others, or which represented the kind of federal intrusion
against which Nixon had so long spoken out, or even quibbling about language. The environment, both cozy and formal, moved them to set aside
what they had taught at their companies or learned in graduate school
as selfish detail, and join in crafting the great package. The only thing
one could do now was forge ahead, do as Nixon said, and throw yourself
selflessly into service. It was hard not to feel like a statesman anyhow at
Camp David: Nixon pointed out to Burns during one of their conversations that Burns was sitting in the very chair where Nikita Khrushchev
had sat during a late-1950s meeting with President Eisenhower. Stein
noted of his colleagues that they stepped away from reality and "acquired
the attitudes of a group of scriptwriters preparing a TV special to be
broadcast." In a decade of planning, they were doing more planning than
any president had done before. The responsibility of the group was sobering, Safire recalled later, and "it was also more fun than any of the men
there had ever had in their lives."[64] They had all received their personal-
ized Camp David jackets, and Burns noticed that he himself got something extra: Camp David drinking glasses. Memorializing the endeavor,
photographers posed the summiteers in a group shot before they flew off.

The plan Nixon carried back was Connally's, so extensive it awed them
all. A wage and price freeze to halt inflation temporarily. A cut in federal
outlays and even in federal employment. A postponement in pay raises
for government employees. Closing the gold window, at least temporarily.
Reduction in foreign aid. A broad 10 percent tax on imports—Americans
wanted to buy American anyhow, didn't they? An end to the auto excise
tax for car buyers at home—the equivalent of $200 for each car buyer—
and retroactive, to boot. The way Nixon wrote it, the speech was more
than just an announcement. It was a challenge to Americans' patriotism
and foreign governments' good character. "When the unfair treatment is
ended the import tax will end as well," the president had written. The
president would tell his audience that he was closing the gold window to
stop "the speculators"—not "money changers"—"from waging an all-out
war on the American dollar." Get behind the plan, Nixon was going to
say, if you believed America's best days lay ahead. Get behind the plan,

or show yourself to be un-American. Though Nixon, like Johnson, nursed contempt for the British economic policy, his speech was a replay of Harold Wilson's 1967 speech devaluing sterling, all bravado, daring citizens to disagree. Connally would back up Nixon all fall, daring foreign nations and markets to comply. And the Administration would promise that the Nixon plan would return America to prosperity.

Struck at the grandeur of Nixon's planned remarks, Stein penned a mock version of the Ten Commandments, with Nixon playing the role of Moses:

> On the 15th day of the Eighth Month the president came down from the mountain and spoke to the people on all networks, saying:
>
> I bring you a Comprehensive Eight-Point Program, as follows:
>
> First, thou shall raise no price, neither any wage, rent, interest, fee, or dividend.
>
> Second, thou shall pay out no gold, neither metallic nor paper
>
> Third, thou shall drive no Japanese car, wear no Italian shoe, nor drink any French wine, neither red nor white . . . [65]

All that remained was to schedule Nixon's speech. The group returned on Sunday. Perhaps Nixon should speak on Monday? To minimize disruption of markets, Volcker warned, the best time to announce the shock would actually be Sunday evening, so that Europe had overnight to digest the news. The men thought about how the public would react if they replaced the usual, popular, Sunday evening lineup. Nixon, again like Johnson before him, recognized that interrupting prime programming irritated viewers. Nonetheless, Nixon felt, as Johnson had, that a key speech had to air in prime time to make a splash. There was no way around it, the president and his men saw. Nixon would have to preempt *Bonanza*.

Coda:
Demolition in St. Louis

MARCH 1972

The crowd that assembled at Pruitt-Igoe that day in March 1972 was large, hundreds, standing around, sitting on folding chairs, senior citizens with their hands in their pockets, mothers, photographers from the press, schoolchildren. The people of Pruitt-Igoe had gathered to see what the assistant to the mayor of St. Louis advertised as "the best show in town."[1] The spectators arrived early or on time, at 1:30. Still, by 2:15 nothing had happened. Even with the temperature in the low fifties, the crowd chose to wait. The people kept their eyes on one structure, 2207 O'Fallon Street. They had come to see something that as far as they knew, no one had ever seen: men use dynamite to slice away half of an eleven-story building.

Of course the papers didn't call the event a "slicing," they called it "revising." No matter. In the past week and that morning, the people from the neighborhood had watched as the engineer on the project led the men from Local 53 of the construction union in drilling holes for his dynamite at 2207 O'Fallon Street. This would not be the usual "headache ball" demolition job St. Louis knew so well. Controlled Demolition, the company managing the job, was renowned for innovative precision work. Its engineers would fire off dynamite at intervals calibrated to fractions of a second. The goal was for the second half of the building to remain not only standing, but habitable. The lead engineer, a young man named Mark Loizeaux, was the son of the founder. Loizeaux described his approach to the papers. "I think of a building as a person," he said. "I have to find out all I can about it, searching in every corner for any secrets it might have, and then prepare my plan of attack. That building is fighting me and I've got to bring her to her knees." He also reminded everyone that an effort to cut away half a building was an experiment. "Write it in capitals," he told the reporters, E-X-P-E-R-I-M-E-N-T. "I don't know whether we can do it, really," he said.

They could do it. Once a missing blasting machine was delivered, the final wires were connected and someone pushed the plunger. Before the spectators' eyes, within seven seconds, the western half of 2207 O'Fallon Street indeed sank to her knees. "At first dust shot out from the bottom of the building," a reporter carefully noted, "then the crumbling action moved from the bottom to the top until only rubble was left." It was, as Loizeaux later said, "a perfect vertical severance." The children from Pruitt Elementary School cheered.

Not all the adults joined them. To the adults, Pruitt-Igoe wasn't an experiment. It was their home. Or the home of someone they knew. Or their former home, a place they had once wanted to build up, not knock down. A rent strike a few years back had not achieved much. To this crowd, whoever ran Pruitt-Igoe was anonymous, just a collective "they" who always let the residents down. Still, the fact that you are giving up your own hopes doesn't mean you are not interested in someone else's. The crowd was curious. Surgery on a building such as this cost a lot. Who was paying for the it? The city of St. Louis? The St. Louis Housing Authority? HUD and Secretary Romney, in Washington? It seemed the tens of thousands of dollars being spent on these pyrotechnics were a signal that someone else, someone important, still believed in Pruitt-Igoe.

This was a shift. The year before, Mayor Alfonso Cervantes had announced that to raze the project entirely was the only answer to the Pruitt-Igoe problem. The mayor and the St. Louis Civic Alliance for Housing, another mysterious entity, had put forward a redevelopment plan to build four new villages, each with its own convenience shops, at the Pruitt-Igoe site. A major shopping center was also in the plan, as were parks for the old people and the kids. The new development would be less dense, housing twelve families per acre instead of the forty-four per acre that Pruitt-Igoe could house now. The Civic Alliance blueprint included garden apartments and townhouses that "make much nicer communities than high-rise buildings," Mayor Cervantes said. This new site plan would cost an additional $50 million, a good share of it the tab for retiring all the debt on Pruitt-Igoe. That was one of the ironies. Though Pruitt-Igoe was public housing, it carried a heavy mortgage.

Several federal officials had loudly backed complete demolition as well. "We have this War on Poverty," one of Secretary Romney's staffers at HUD told the Associated Press, "and we got our ships out and we got one that's lost. It's sunk, let's face it."[2] The only question had seemed to be who would do the demolition and the cleanup. At one point HUD staffers had informed the mayor in writing that when it came to Pruitt-Igoe, St. Louis was on its own. Saint Louis in turn let HUD know it didn't have the money. The St. Louis tax base was narrowing. Once proud St. Louis could afford little of its infrastructure, not even the Children's Zoo. Father Shocklee of St. Bridget's Church had long since begun helping Pruitt-Igoe families move out and buy their own homes through the Bicentennial Civic Improvement Corp. Over time, Shocklee had become even more convinced that finding the new homes, and helping people pay for them, was the answer for Pruitt-Igoe. "I can't really improve this place," Shocklee told a visiting writer, of Pruitt-Igoe. "My job is to help people get out."

But then had come a change. Secretary Romney had approved a bid by St. Louis to make it one of eight pilot cities in his own housing drive, Operation Breakthrough. Operation Breakthrough came on top of various pilots being run or contemplated for the older programs: Model Cities, Johnson's other housing projects, the original urban renewal. Among Operation Breakthrough, Model Cities, and other programs, observers speculated, there might be funding to improve Pruitt-Igoe after all—if someone mustered the will. Perhaps Romney was a miracle worker. He acted like one.

Mayor Cervantes had therefore felt his spirits rise as he watched Romney's Learjet touch down at Lambert Field the prior May. Romney lunched with the mayor and, together with Congresswoman Leonor Sullivan, who knew so much about Pruitt-Igoe, toured the buildings. But when Cervantes asked for funding to raze Pruitt-Igoe, Romney had snapped, "Nonsense!" The secretary strode around Pruitt-Igoe and told people he met that it seemed to be making progress, and that to tear down something like this would be "quite an investment." The project would have to be rehabilitated, not razed. HUD didn't want to set a precedent, a staffer explained to the papers. If you tore down Pruitt-Igoe, "everyone with a sleazy housing project would want us to tear it down," the staffer said. HUD now seemed ready to help out St. Louis, one way or another. Romney talked over ideas with his hosts. The elderly were among the few in public housing who seemed to like to live together in tall buildings, social scientists had found. Leonor Sullivan, ever practical, played to Romney's rehab cue. The congresswoman suggested that Pruitt-Igoe, rehabbed, might make a good home for pensioners.

Romney ordered the mayor to try finding financing from the private sector in St. Louis, as if that were a new idea. That seemed another joke to Cervantes, given that he and every one of his predecessors had long worked closely with businesspeople such as the brewing family Busch, which owned the Cardinals. Saint Louis had once been known for its mighty community chest. But Cervantes tried to find a bright side. He could see that Romney liked to tinker. Romney tinkered with Operation Breakthrough as he had once tinkered at American Motors with the Rambler. This time his pet innovation was using modular homes to reduce the cost of new housing for working-class people. Romney knew Pruitt-Igoe fairly well: he had also paid a visit back in 1967, when he was considering running in the 1968 presidential election. Romney's leanings were Cervantes's opening. If Cervantes could come up with another tinkering project for Romney, one where he tinkered with building models as if with houses made of Lego on a table, then HUD would be likely to fund the project.

That the federal government do something about Pruitt-Igoe, whether replacing it or fixing it, was important to Cervantes. The mayor viewed Pruitt-Igoe as a moral issue. Cervantes remembered, correctly enough, that it was the federal government that caused Pruitt-Igoe to be built in the first place, positing that St. Louis would grow and Pruitt-Igoe would pay for itself. The growth hadn't happened. You could argue that the great deterioration of public housing Romney always spoke about was caused by his own departments, the housing authorities, and members of Congress. The people in Washington were the ones whose rules and

laws forced down public housing rent levels. The levels Washington required bankrupted Pruitt-Igoe. The project simply needed more tenants
or higher rents to pay its maintenance bills. For the federal government to
avoid helping out now would be "shirking," Cervantes said. The federal
government owed St. Louis.

That Washington owed St. Louis was also the view of Father Shocklee.
In the summer of 1971, a brutal murder at Pruitt-Igoe made national
news. The body of a nine-year-old girl had been found on the ninth-floor
stairway at 2420 Cass Street. Someone had suffocated her. Where was
the government then? Father Shocklee asked. Washington could spend
$1 million every twenty minutes on Vietnam. But "they don't seem to
have enough funds to do what is needed here, where people are getting
killed." Elmer Hammond, chairman of the Pruitt-Igoe District Community Corporation, felt the same way. "They do not care. Believe me, they
do not care."

Nonetheless, this time it might be that "they," somewhere, did care.
The mayor and his colleagues managed to get Romney to approve the
outlay of $60,000 for a new blue-ribbon panel to draft new and differ-
ent rehab plans. In the fall of 1971, the remaining tenants of Pruitt-Igoe
had watched as a fresh team of economists and housing professionals,
that blue-ribbon panel, moved into the Pruitt-Igoe Community Building.[3] Among the experts was an eminent senior architect named Walter
Netsch. Netsch came to St. Louis from one of the top firms in the world,
the mighty Skidmore, Owings and Merrill of Chicago. The professionals in the Community Building had come up with not one but a menu
of plans, all prepared to lure Romney into funding the entire redevelopment of Pruitt-Igoe. Just about all the plans the panel produced contained
low-rise buildings. Some citizens in St. Louis recognized this as another
one of those Pruitt-Igoe ironies, because Pruitt-Igoe's original architect,
Minoru Yamasaki, had included walk-ups in his original drawings. It was
Washington's housers who had stricken those low-rise structures from the
Yamasaki blueprints. One of the new plans called for six villages, not
three. These plans color-coded Pruitt-Igoe. Buildings scheduled for "To-

tal Demolition" were black, those for "Partial Demolition" were marked with lines, and "Buildings to Remain"—just a few, sometimes fractions of buildings—were white.

The architects in the Community Building were the ones who came up with the idea of demolishing part of a building and leaving the rest standing. They had considered not only splitting the buildings, as they would try doing at 2207 O'Fallon Street, but also lopping the tops off. If you knocked the top off a high-rise, you might indeed use the lower floors for a low-rise or townhouse. Before they had settled on precision dynamiting, the consultants at the Community Building scrutinized the possible methods for such surgery. They might use thermal torches exuding a heat of 1500 degrees Fahrenheit, the idea being to cut sideways through the towers' concrete floors so that the part to be destroyed would be easily knocked out by traditional jackhammers, dynamite, and high-speed saws. Or one could hire dynamite geniuses, like the Loizeaux family at Controlled Demolition. All too aware that budgets were tight, the blue-ribbon panelists sought to include economies in their plan. To spare HUD the price of hauling away the mountains of rubble that would result from demolition, one could coat the rubble with grass or dirt and fashion berms, artificial hills. City planners liked berms. The planners seemed to be making progress; in January 1972, Romney okayed the experimental demolition as a pilot.[4]

Teachers and students at the Pruitt School, not far from the Pruitt-Igoe Community Building, created their own plan for the Pruitt-Igoe of the future in their classrooms. What if the jobs came back to St. Louis as well?

———

BUT IT was hard for cities like St. Louis to find their way to believing in this 1972 fix-up. Like so many Americans whom the Great Society had aimed to serve, the citizens of St. Louis had hoped many times before. They had hoped when the War on Poverty commenced, but poverty, or at least dependence, was still here. They had hoped when civil rights laws were passed, but the jobs that would have made them able to enjoy those rights had moved away. They had hoped when Johnson's giant housing law funded rehab at Pruitt-Igoe, but the housing complex was now a shambles again.

What had caused these flops, local and national? The first factor was the authorities' conviction that St. Louis would grow and sustain its citizens. Instead, in part because of other interventions by authorities, the city shrank. Economies, it turned out, were like humans. They made choices. The U.S. economy was choosing to stay away from high-cost cities like St. Louis.

The second reason for the failures at Pruitt-Igoe was simple arrogance. The government authorities had assumed that when there was enough money—and there was, sometimes—they knew better. The authorities had assumed that a project that fell into several jurisdictions—the jurisdiction of the federal government, of the St. Louis Housing Authority, of the state of Missouri, and of the city—would be all the better for having so many shepherds. Yet because Pruitt-Igoe had many overseers, it had none. As it turned out, the authorities did not always know better. And more government offices were not better than fewer.

There was hypocrisy in the different treatment of the middle class and poor. For the middle class, the government had aimed to re-create and sustain the world of Alexis de Tocqueville, subsidizing home purchasers for suburban settlers. For the poor, however, the government had operated in the world of Karl Marx: government-sponsored housing blocks with tenants, not owners. Black citizens—Pruitt-Igoe was now all black—had been ripped from their roots when they moved North, uprooted again when they were moved for urban renewal, and then placed in high-rise rentals where putting down new roots was impossible.

Few in St. Louis knew of Garrett Hardin, the professor who argued that the absence of a government shepherd created a Tragedy of the Commons. But St. Louis did see that the Tragedy of the Commons that was Pruitt-Igoe resulted from a second lack: the lack of property rights for inhabitants, whether individuals or local community institutions. Pruitt-Igoe's playgrounds and halls became wrecks because no one local was responsible for this commons. People did not accept communities handed to them by faraway offices such as Sargent Shriver's OEO. They needed to build their communities, and their homes, themselves.

How might neighborhoods like this one have turned out if local companies, local authorities, and local individuals had led in the 1950s and 1960s, building their own Great Society? How might St. Louis have looked if the jobs had stayed? No one knew.[5] But here in the shadow of Pruitt-Igoe, Father Shocklee and Pruitt-Igoe tenants had discovered one possibility. With his small housing program, Father Shocklee had shown that "the poor" were more like the middle class than people supposed. They gained from something only when they had a chance to own it.

———————

AS 1972 got under way, Mayor Cervantes, his aides, and the eminent Walter Netsch began to see that Romney might not pick up one of the projects they had laid before him, however much tinkering appealed to him. Romney, St. Louis could see, was struggling in his job at HUD. Pruitt-Igoe stole hours he wanted to dedicate to what he considered more important work. His new passion was integrating the suburbs, and to do so he was willing to take measures at which even Sargent Shriver would blanch. Romney made HUD water and sewer grants to heretofore white suburban towns conditional on the towns' agreement to accept subsidized multifamily housing—housing that would include blacks. President Nixon wasn't wild about such bold blackmail.

The continued existence of Pruitt-Igoe helped Romney's opponents in the suburban integration battle. Federal pressure for suburban integration was the subject of a test case on fair housing that had commenced right in the St. Louis area. The case involved a newly incorporated suburb just beyond Ferguson and Florissant, northward from St. Louis. The town of Black Jack, all white, had passed an ordinance banning multifamily homes, a clear effort to keep out the poor and blacks, again relegated to rentals. Now the Justice Department was fighting Black Jack in the courts, with Romney backing Justice all the way. The town fathers of Black Jack wheeled out the Pruitt-Igoe scare whenever they wanted to bolster their case against multifamily housing. "This is not a Pruitt-Igoe type thing," said Black Jack's Francis Huss of the multifamily housing, "but it is an experiment, and so was Pruitt-Igoe. We don't want anything experimental out here."

Nixon's price freezes were putting a chill on Romney's existing projects as well. The freezes affected many areas of the economy, not just a few prices on a list. One way to slow spending was to impound appropriations money, and Nixon did that—he impounded $105 million for Model Cities, for example, rendering the work of Romney and all other housing officials more difficult. Romney had to show Nixon he was a loyal member of the austerity team. A simple way to lower a single year's budget was for HUD simply to postpone decisions on expensive projects, such as the one the experts were planning in the Pruitt-Igoe Community Building. As long as a decision on a proposal wasn't made, the money for that proposal could not flow. Washington did seem to be delaying any decisions on Pruitt-Igoe. Saint Louis was not alone in grant limbo. In 1970 a housing project nearly as notorious as Pruitt-Igoe, Cabrini-Green of Chicago, had proposed that HUD back a $32 million plan for security, new playgrounds, and sports. But Romney was not ruling on that, either.

There were other troubles that distracted not only Romney, but the whole federal housing bureaucracy. With great fanfare Romney, to his credit picking up on the need for ownership, had promised to enable more poor people to buy homes, and backed what he called a "massive federal leap into the field of subsidized home ownership."[6] The Federal Housing Authority had encouraged such purchases by insuring loans by private companies to low earners. Now it was emerging that FHA officials and the private lenders had colluded to overprice the homes, and to hide the fact that borrowers lacked the income to sustain the mortgages. Many of the borrowers were indeed not able to make their payments, and the private mortgage companies were simply foreclosing, keeping deposits, and then selling the homes again. The investigations that ensued did further damage, slowing lending to the poor to an icy trickle. The tight budgets, the inflation, and Romney's impotence all meant trouble for smaller projects.[7]

As 1972 moved forward, the consultants who had been hired to write the latest plan for Pruitt-Igoe lost courage. Fresh economic data revealed that the number of jobs in the metropolitan area of St. Louis had dropped by forty-two thousand just since 1969, when Romney had been settling in as housing secretary. "Every time I look," one of the blue-ribbon men in the Community Building told an architecture magazine, "employment has slipped a little more." The consultants could see that, engineering feats with explosives notwithstanding, the federal government was losing interest in Pruitt-Igoe. Tenants continued to move out. Mark Loizeaux's blast experiments were experiments for a rehab project that was already doomed.

That summer of 1972, and in the months and years following, there would be fresh proposals for the use of the Pruitt-Igoe site. At one point, city officials envisioned Pruitt-Igoe's second life as part of plans for a new convention center. At another point, a Republican candidate for the House of Representatives proposed that the site be made over into a horse track.[8] In the mid-1970s, Washington University's seismologists won a $219,000 National Science Foundation grant to take their turn with Pruitt-Igoe, trying out a new earthquake machine on the empty buildings. The scientists wanted to see how much vibration it took to make one of the buildings tremble.[9]

But meantime, in the spring of 1972, the pilot demolition continued. The second structure on the wreckers' list was Building C-15 on Dickson Street, a thoroughfare that divided Pruitt from Igoe. Building C-15 was large, 360 feet wide, and had once housed 200 families. This second time, as it turned out, there was to be no fancy splitting, just a series of explosions to bring down the entire building. In April, a crew came to drill sixteen-inch holes in C-15's concrete pillars, preparing the pillars for seventy-two explosive charges on the ground floor, seventy-two above, and eight in the basement. On demolition day, the press again arrived to photograph the explosions. The crowd from the neighborhood was smaller. Most people in St. Louis already sensed the truth. After so many years of effort, there was really nothing left that anyone could do for Pruitt-Igoe. The wreckers came, and inspected the dynamite, and checked the wires trailing from C-15. Then they blew it all to bits.

Acknowledgments

A great society of advisors and supporters surrounded this book from the beginning. The author would like to thank the students of King's College in Manhattan, who debated the merits and demerits of the Great Society for several years in my classes. So did King's professor Josiah Peterson, who thought through the book with me over years. I thank Provost Mark Hijleh, a scholar of music himself and a gracious host at King's. Thank you to Gregory Thornbury, who while president of the college invited me to teach at King's in the first place; and to Kimberly Thornbury, who made much at King's possible and stuck with me through thick and thin. The late Lee Hanley showed great interest in the book; Allie Hanley continues to provide encouragement. I owe a great debt to Tom Patrick, who made this work possible. Kim Dennis and the Searle Freedom Trust supported the research and the work on images so crucial to this book. Alexandra Salavitch helped out multiple times, as did Jen Buxton, Madeline Crook, Rushad Thomas, and C. C. Borzilleri.

At the Calvin Coolidge Presidential Foundation, President Matt Denhart and my fellow trustees supported the project. Especial thanks to Governor Jim Douglas, Roby Harrington, Boyden Gray, and Professor Thomas F. Cooley. Additional friends include Christopher DeMuth of the Hudson Institute. Ravenel Curry and Jim Piereson have been especially helpful. Thomas and Diane Smith deserve thanks for their support and wonderful, useful memories of the late Daniel Patrick Moynihan. William Beach gave support. So did John Cogan and Daniel Heil of the Hoover Institution, who generously provided time and enlightening charts. Ira Stoll, author of *JFK Conservative*, offered key guidance. Thomas F. Cooley, my former boss at New York University's Stern School, caught some bloopers.

Thank you to Barry Hirsch of Georgia Tech, who talked over labor data. All errors are my own.

Researchers, readers, and editors who made this book possible include Roger Labrie, Charles Knittle, Alexandra Hoopes, Brett Greene, Charis Gibson, Peter Collier, Ed Weintrob, Celia Weintrob, and John Fund. Larry Lindsey supplied key advice. I thank Beatrice Barran and my children: Eli, Theo, Helen, and Flora. Seth Lipsky inspired this book and continues to do so.

A heartfelt thank-you goes to Jin Auh, Sarah Chalfant, and Andrew Wylie, with whom this is my fourth book. Much gratitude is due to the book's excellent editor, Jonathan Jao of HarperCollins, a man who sees through detail to the structure and necessity of a narrative. I also thank Brian Murray and Jonathan Burnham. HarperCollins's support has been—no other adjective will do—great.

Amity Shlaes,
New York, 2019

Appendix of Graphic Data

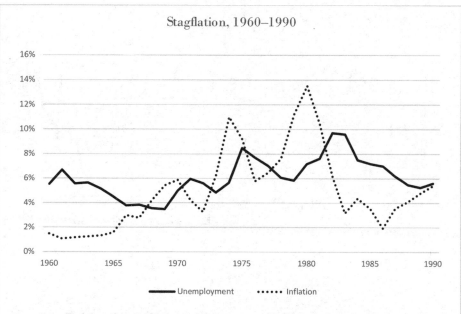

Stagflation, 1960–1990

Notes: The fathers of the Great Society argued the country could suffer from inflation or unemployment. But not both at the same time. 1960s policies, however, delivered simultaneous inflation and unemployment in the 1970s. A term described the perversity: "stagflation."

Source: Bureau of Labor Statistics

A Stock Market on Strike

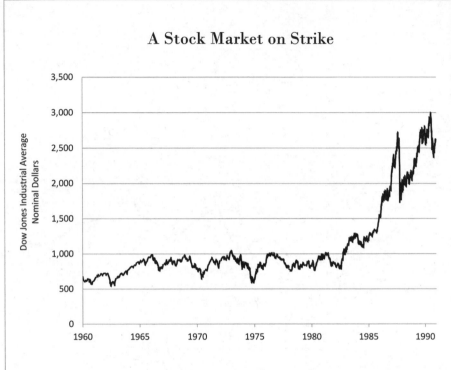

Note: The Dow Jones Industrial Average, America's historic index, is a meter of markets' view on the nation's progress. In the mid-1960s, as Johnson's Great Society was launched, the Dow Jones Industrial Average seemed likely to pass the "1000 landmark." But the Dow did not pass that level definitively until the presidency of Ronald Reagan.

Source: Dow Jones & Co.

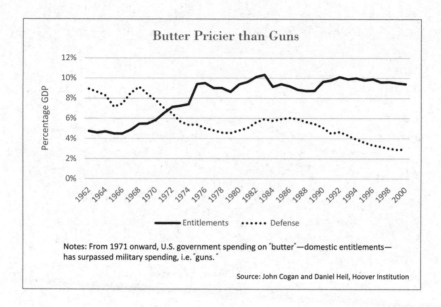

Butter Pricier than Guns

Notes: From 1971 onward, U.S. government spending on "butter"—domestic entitlements—has surpassed military spending, i.e. "guns."

Source: John Cogan and Daniel Heil, Hoover Institution

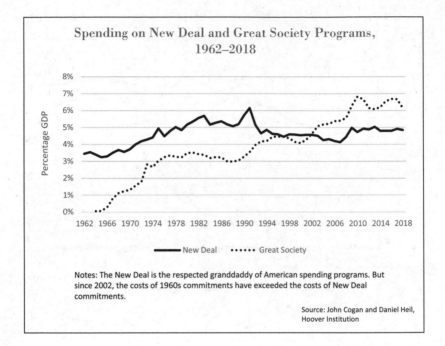

Spending on New Deal and Great Society Programs, 1962–2018

Notes: The New Deal is the respected granddaddy of American spending programs. But since 2002, the costs of 1960s commitments have exceeded the costs of New Deal commitments.

Source: John Cogan and Daniel Heil, Hoover Institution

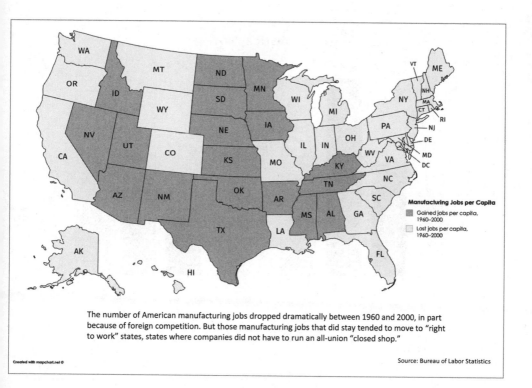

The number of American manufacturing jobs dropped dramatically between 1960 and 2000, in part because of foreign competition. But those manufacturing jobs that did stay tended to move to "right to work" states, states where companies did not have to run an all-union "closed shop."

Created with mapchart.net ©

Source: Bureau of Labor Statistics

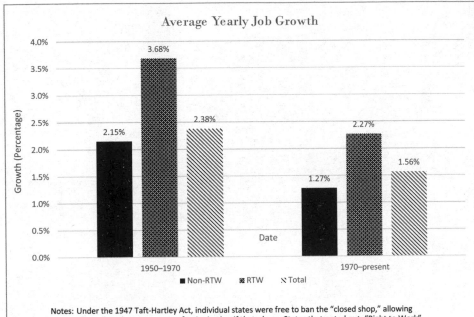

Notes: Under the 1947 Taft-Hartley Act, individual states were free to ban the "closed shop," allowing companies and workers to opt out of unionization if they chose. States that opted out, "Right to Work" states, saw faster job growth.

Source: Bureau of Labor Statistics

Union Membership

Percentage of Nonfarm Wage and Salary Workers in Unions

35 — 30 — 25 — 20 — 15 — 10 — 5 — 0

1964   1970   1976   1982   1988   1994   2000

Notes: In the early 1960s, unions ran America, not only economically but politically. Unions seemed only likely to strengthen after President John F. Kennedy signed an executive order sanctioning government worker union membership. But Americans themselves became disenchanted with organized labor, and the share of Americans in unions shrank over time.

Source: Barry T. Hirsch, David A. Macpherson, and Wayne G. Vroman, "Estimates of Union Density by State," *Monthly Labor Review* 124, no. 7 (July 2001): 54, https://www.bls.gov/opub/mlr/2001/07/ressum2.pdf. Chart reflects both public-sector and private-sector membership.

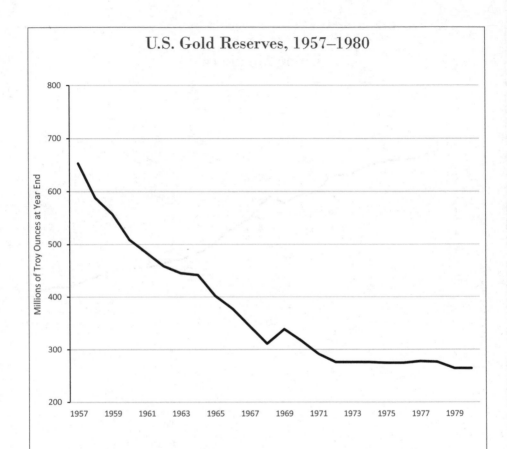

U.S. Gold Reserves, 1957–1980

Millions of Troy Ounces at Year End

Notes: As guns and butter spending rose, America's official gold stock dropped. When the level reached the equivalent of $10 billion, America closed "the gold window, " preferring to block redemptions of gold rather than acknowledge foreigners were shorting the U.S. economy.

Source: Alan Greenspan and Jeffrey Young

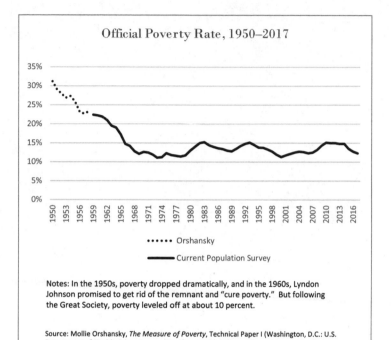

Official Poverty Rate, 1950–2017

•••••• Orshansky

——— Current Population Survey

Notes: In the 1950s, poverty dropped dramatically, and in the 1960s, Lyndon Johnson promised to get rid of the remnant and "cure poverty." But following the Great Society, poverty leveled off at about 10 percent.

Source: Mollie Orshansky, *The Measure of Poverty*, Technical Paper I (Washington, D.C.: U.S. Department of Health, Education, and Welfare, 1977), 349; and Current Population Survey.

Notes

Introduction: The Clash

1. Arthur Krock, "Blocking the Rent Subsidy," *Austin American*, October 27, 1965.
2. Maurice Isserman, *The Other American: The Life of Michael Harrington* (New York: Public Affairs, 2000), 211. This insightful biography captures the man and the decade.
3. Isserman, *The Other American*, 212.
4. Isserman, *The Other American*, 210.
5. Alan Greenspan and Adrian Wooldridge, *Capitalism in America: A History* (New York: Penguin, 2018), 365.
6. Letter from Daniel Patrick Moynihan to William Buckley, published in *National Review*, September 29, 1978, 1196.
7. Michael A. Cusumano, *The Japanese Automobile Industry: Technology and Management at Nissan and Toyota* (Cambridge, MA: Harvard University Press, 1984), 201; Bob Thomas, "What Can Detroit Do About Imports? Sweat!" *Los Angeles Times*, June 30, 1968, H1; Greenspan and Wooldridge, *Capitalism in America*, 315; Peter Lindert, "U.S. Foreign Trade and Trade Policy in the Twentieth Century," in *The Cambridge Economic History of the United States*, eds. Stanley L. Engerman and Robert E. Gallman (Cambridge: Cambridge University Press, 2000), 3: 432–35.
8. Samuel Brittan, "Thatcher Was Right—There Is No 'Society,'" *Financial Times*, April 18, 2013, https://www.ft.com/content/d1387b70-a5d5-11e2-9b77-00144feabdc0.

1: The Bonanza

1. John F. Cogan, *The High Cost of Good Intentions* (Stanford, CA: Stanford University Press, 2017); and John F. Cogan and Daniel Heil, "America Off Balance: Charting the Federal Government's Fiscal Path," Hoover Institution, Stanford University, 2019. The data heading these chapters were compiled by Cogan and Heil. For entitlements, Cogan and Heil used the Office of Management and Budget definition, "a program in which the Federal Government is legally obligated to make payments or provide services to any person, state or local government

that meets the legal criteria for eligibility." Under entitlements, therefore, Cogan and Heil include major social insurance programs ranging from Social Security to publicly required pensions, major means-tested programs such as Medicaid, the Earned Income Tax Credit, Temporary Assistance for Needy Families, and federal student loans. Veterans' programs and programs for federal employees are also included. Such entitlements fall under the label "Butter" in the chapter headings. "Guns" are defense spending.

2. January 4, 1960, DJIA. Dow Jones Industrial Average, nominal, 1895–2010, Dow Jones and Co. This data set appears throughout the book.

3. *Bonanza*, season 1, episode 16, "El Toro Grande," directed by Christian Nyby, written by John Tucker Battle, aired January 2, 1960, on NBC.

4. James L. Clayton, "Defense Spending: Key to California's Growth," *Western Political Quarterly* 15, no. 2 (June 1962): 281, http://journals.sagepub.com/doi/abs/10.1177/106591296201500206.

5. Clayton, "Defense Spending: Key to California's Growth," 280.

6. "General Dynamics Had Largest Defense Work Volume," *Wall Street Journal*, January 14, 1960, 18.

7. Kim McQuaid, "Young, Swope and General Electric's 'New Capitalism': A Study in Corporate Liberalism, 1920–33," *American Journal of Economics and Sociology* 36, no. 3 (July 1977): 323–34.

8. "Report of Advisory Council on Social Security for Broadening Coverage of Act," *New York Times*, December 19, 1938, 16–17.

9. Ida A. Tarbell, *Owen D Young: A New Type of Industrial Leader* (New York: Macmillan, 1932), 107.

10. Anecdote told to the author by a member of the Coffin family, March 2019.

11. McQuaid, "Young, Swope and General Electric's 'New Capitalism,'" 323–34.

12. Kim Phillips-Fein, "American Counterrevolutionary: Lemuel Ricketts Boulware and General Electric, 1950–60," in *American Capitalism: Social Thought and Political Economy in the Twentieth Century*, ed. Nelson Lichtenstein (Philadelphia: University of Pennsylvania Press, 2006), 251.

13. Thomas W. Evans, *The Education of Ronald Reagan: The General Electric Years and the Untold Story of His Conversion to Conservatism* (New York: Columbia University Press, 2006). Evans traces Reagan's entire career at GE.

14. Bernard Gorowitz, *The General Electric Story: A Heritage of Innovation, 1876–1999* (Schenectady, NY: Schenectady Museum, 1999), 229.

15. George Snively, "Anecdotes: General Electric Enters the Computer Business," *Annals of the History of Computing* 10, no. 1 (1988): 75, https://ieeexplore.ieee.org/stamp/stamp.jsp?tp=&arnumber=4640535; and J. A. N. Lee, "The Rise and Fall of the General Electric Corporation Computer Department," *Annals of the History of Computing* 17, no. 4 (1995): 24–45, https://ban.ai/multics/doc/The%20Rise%20and%20Fall%20of%20GE.pdf.

16. "GE's Edsel?" *Forbes*, April 1, 1967, 21.

17. Lee, "The Rise and Fall of the General Electric Corporation Computer Department," 27.

18. John Herling, *The Great Price Conspiracy* (Washington, DC: Robert Luce, 1962), 3; "Eisenhower Points to the T. V. A. as 'Creeping Socialism,'" *New York Times*, June 18, 1953; and *Public Papers of the Presidents of the United States: Dwight D. Eisenhower, 1953* (Washington, DC: Office of the Federal Register, 1960), 433.

19. Evans, *The Education of Ronald Reagan*, 100.

20. Earl Dunckel, "Ronald Reagan and the General Electric Theater, 1954–1955," interview conducted in 1982 by Gabrielle Morris, Government History Documentation Project, University of California, Berkeley, 3, https://archive.org/stream/reagangetheatre00duncrich.

21. Herbert R. Northrup, *Boulwarism: The Labor Relations Policies of the General Electric Company, Their Implications for Public Policy and Management Action* (Ann Arbor: The University of Michigan, 1965), 2–3.

22. Ira Stoll, *JFK: Conservative* (Boston: Houghton Mifflin Harcourt, 2013), 94; and John F. Kennedy, "Convention Acceptance Speech," July 15, 1960, John F. Kennedy Presidential Library and Museum, transcript, 6, https://www.jfklibrary.org/asset-viewer/archives/JFKPOF/137/JFKPOF-137-003.

23. Clayton Knowles, "Kennedy Charges Urban 'Neglect' by Republicans," *New York Times*, October 11, 1960.

24. GE pamphlet, *Your Mayor Is Murdering Pittsfield*, Lemuel Boulware Papers, University of Pennsylvania.

25. Boulware to Edward Reilly, December 16, 1960, Lemuel R. Boulware Papers, University of Pennsylvania Libraries.

26. "Federal Reserve Reports," *Wall Street Journal*, November 28, 1960, 21.

27. H. J. Aibel, "Corporate Counsel and Business Ethics: A Personal Review," *Missouri Law Review* 59, no. 2 (Spring 1994): 427–40, https://scholarship.law.missouri.edu/mlr/vol59/iss2/4. General Electric also found itself mired in the Justice Department antitrust suit.

28. Anthony Lewis, "7 Electrical Officials Get Jail Terms in Trust Case," *New York Times*, February 7, 1961.

29. Thomas F. O'Boyle, *At Any Cost: Jack Welch, General Electric, and the Pursuit of Profit* (New York: Vintage Books, 1999), 307.

30. O'Boyle, *At Any Cost*, 307.

31. Peter Braestrup, "Goldberg Finds Labor Peace Gain," *New York Times*, January 22, 1962.

32. James Hoopes, *Corporate Dreams: Big Business in American Democracy from the Great Depression to the Great Recession* (Newark, NJ: Rutgers University Press, 2011), 106–10.

33. Roger M. Blough, *The Washington Embrace of Business* (New York: Columbia University Press, 1975), 79.

34. Associated Press, "FBI Rouses Reporter at 3 a.m. to Check Steel Pricing Remark Laid to Bethlehem," *Wall Street Journal*, April 13, 1962.

35. "Text of President Kennedy's Address to Senior Citizens' Rally at Garden," *New York Times*, May 21, 1962, 20.

36. John Brooks, *Business Adventures: Twelve Classic Tales from the World of Wall Street* (New York: Open Road Integrated Media, 2014), 24.

37. John D. Pomfret, "Labor Leaders Aim for Bigger Raises," *New York Times*, November 18, 1963.

38. Bob Spitz, *Reagan: An American Journey* (New York: Penguin, 2018), 362.

2: Port Huron

1. Thomas W. Evans, *The Education of Ronald Reagan: The General Electric Years and the Untold Story of His Conversion to Conservatism* (New York: Columbia University Press, 2006), 224.

2. "Port Huron: Thomas Edison," *Michigan History*, http://michiganhistory.leadr .msu.edu/port-huron-thomas-edison.

3. Students for a Democratic Society, "Port Huron Statement," 1962, https://web.ar chive.org/web/20090123114146/http://coursesa.matrix.msu.edu/~hst306/docu ments/huron.html; and Richard Flacks and Nelson Lichtenstein, eds., *The Port Huron Statement: Sources and Legacies of the New Left's Founding Manifesto* (Philadelphia: University of Pennsylvania Press, 2015), 237.

4. Tom Hayden, *Rebel: A Personal History of the 1960s* (Los Angeles: Red Hen Press, 2003), 62.

5. Jim Bloch, "Author of Port Huron Statement Tom Hayden Dead at 76," *Voice*, November 4, 2016, http://www.voicenews.com/news/author-of-port-huron-state ment-tom-hayden-dead-at/article_0c033122-c6a6-5584-893f-ef89db84de41 .html.

6. Tom Hayden, "The Port Huron Statement at 50" (lecture, Madison, WI, May 2012), 11:40, https://www.youtube.com/watch?v=oBwla6MjIqc.

7. Jim Bloch, "Port Huron Statement Could Have Been Finalized Elsewhere," *Voice*, September 12, 2012, http://www.voicenews.com/news/port-huron-state ment-could-have-been-finalized-elsewhere/article_26df063a-7396-5c2c-82eb -bda358775137.html.

8. Kevin Boyle, *The UAW and the Heyday of American Liberalism 1945–1968* (Ithaca, NY: Cornell University Press, 1998), 159.

9. Nelson Lichtenstein, *The Most Dangerous Man in Detroit: Walter Reuther and the Fate of American Labor* (New York: Basic Books, 1995), 391, an excellent biography with many insights.

10. Boyle, *The UAW and the Heyday of American Liberalism*, 159. See also UAW correspondence, Wayne State University.

11. Hayden, "The Port Huron Statement at 50," 12:00.

12. *Martin Luther King, Jr. Encyclopedia* (2008), s.v. "Reuther, Walter Philip," https://kinginstitute.stanford.edu/encyclopedia/reuther-walter-philip.

13. David Maraniss, *Once in a Great City: A Detroit Story* (New York: Simon and Schuster, 2015), 139.

14. Elisabeth Reuther Dickmeyer, *Putting the World Together: My Father Walter Reuther, the Liberal Warrior* (Lake Orion, MI: Living Force Publishing, 2004), 19.

15. John Barnard, *Walter Reuther and the Rise of the Auto Workers* (Boston: Little, Brown, 1983), 9; and William Doyle, *Inside the Oval Office: The White House Tapes from FDR to Clinton* (New York: Kodansha America Inc., 1999), 19.

16. Victor G. Reuther, *The Brothers Reuther and the Story of the UAW: A Memoir* (Boston: Houghton Mifflin, 1976), 121. Victor Reuther supplies a detailed account of the brothers' trip abroad in this memoir.

17. Daniel Horowitz, *Betty Friedan and the Making of "The Feminine Mystique"* (Amherst: University of Massachusetts Press, 1998), 118.

18. Both Lemuel Boulware's Harvard speech and Walter Reuther's Howard speech are published in Evans, *The Education of Ronald Reagan*, 224–37. This book, along with Kevin Boyle's *UAW*, contains many insights.

19. Robert Kennedy, *The Enemy Within* (New York: Harper and Row, 1960), 277.

20. Barnard, *Walter Reuther*, 179.

21. "AMC Profit Sharing Criticized in Detroit," *Washington Post*, December 28, 1961, D6.

22. David Stebenne, *Arthur J. Goldberg: New Deal Liberal* (Oxford, UK: Oxford University Press, 1996), 152.

23. Anthony Carew, *Lives of the Left: Walter Reuther* (Manchester, UK: Manchester University Press, 1993), 98.

24. Reuther spoke at the May Day Freedom Rally in West Berlin on May 1, 1959.

25. Jean Gould and Lorena Hickok, *Walter Reuther: Labor's Rugged Individualist* (New York: Dodd, Mead and Company, 1972), 338.

26. Reuther, *The Brothers Reuther*, 428.

27. "U.M. Professor Predicts Vast Changes Ahead." *Ironwood Daily Globe*, August 16, 1960, 10.

28. Howard Brick and Gregory Parker, eds., *A New Insurgency: The Port Huron Statement and Its Times* (Ann Arbor: Maize Books, Michigan Publishing Services, 2015), 111.

29. Theodore Lowi, *The End of Liberalism: Ideology, Policy and the Crisis of Public Authority* (New York, W.W. Norton, 1969), 264. For a broader discussion, see Martin Anderson, *The Federal Bulldozer* (New York: McGraw-Hill, 1967).

30. Michael Harrington, *The Other America: Poverty in the United States* (Middlesex, UK: Penguin Specials, 1963), 139.

31. Robert A. Gorman, *Michael Harrington: Speaking American* (New York: Routledge, 1995), 53.

32. Brick and Parker, *A New Insurgency*, 37

33. Todd Gitlin, *The Sixties: Years of Hope, Days of Rage* (New York: Bantam Books, 1993), 112.

34. James Miller, *Democracy Is in the Streets: From Port Huron to the Siege of Chicago* (New York: Simon and Schuster Inc., 1987), 114.

35. Tom Hayden, *Inspiring Participatory Democracy, Student Movements from Port Huron to Today* (Boulder, CO: Paradigm Publishing, 2013), 64.

36. Hayden, "The Port Huron Statement at 50," 12:45, https://www.youtube.com/watch?v=oBw1a6MjIqc.

37. Casey Hayden, "Fields of Blue," in *Deep in Our Hearts: Nine White Women in the Freedom Movement*, ed. Constance Curry (Athens: University of Georgia Press, 2000), 348.

38. Brick and Parker, *A New Insurgency*, 51.

39. Michael Harrington, *Fragments of the Century* (New York: Saturday Review Press, 1973), 148. Harrington's account of the tensions between the old guard socialists on the one hand and the Port Huron activists on the other contains many insights.

40. Harrington, *Fragments of the Century*, 148.

41. Thomas D. Snyder, ed., *120 Years of American Education: A Statistical Portrait*, National Center for Education Statistics, U.S. Department of Education, January 1993, 75, https://nces.ed.gov/pubs93/93442.pdf.

42. Arthur M. Schlesinger Jr., *Journals: 1952–2000* (London: Atlantic Books, 2007), 188.

43. Jennifer Frost, *An Interracial Movement of the Poor: Community Organizing and the New Left in the 1960s* (New York: New York University Press, 2001), 17; and Peter B. Levy, *The New Left and Labor in the 1960s* (Champaign: University of Illinois Press, 1994) 30. Frost and Levy cover the establishment of ERAP and the unions' role in it in detail.

44. Levy, *The New Left*, 54.

45. Hayden, *Rebel*, 114.

46. Lichtenstein, *Walter Reuther*, 381.

47. *Brothers on the Line*, directed by Sasha Reuther (Richmond, VA, Porter Street Pictures, 2012).

48. Lichtenstein, *Walter Reuther*, 387. Lichtenstein captures the moment, and Kennedy's fatigue.

49. Lawson Bowling, *Shapers of the Great Debate on the Great Society: A Biographical Dictionary* (Westport, CT: Greenwood Press, 2005), 12.

50. Reuther, *The Brothers Reuther*, 446.

51. Johnson, daily diary entries, November 23, 1963, President's Daily Diary Collection, Lyndon B. Johnson Presidential Library. The first days of the Johnson presidency are well captured here. https://discoverlbj.org/item/pdd-19631123.

52. Johnson and David McDonald, sound recording, November 23, 1963, 4:15 p.m., #22, Recordings and Transcripts of Telephone Conversations and Meetings, Lyndon B. Johnson Presidential Library, https://www.discoverlbj.org/item/tel -00022.

53. Johnson and Walter Reuther, sound recording, November 23, 1963, 4:20 p.m., #23, Recordings and Transcripts of Telephone Conversations and Meetings, Lyndon B. Johnson Presidential Library, https://www.discoverlbj.org/item/tel -00023.

54. Joseph L. Rauh, transcript of interview by Paige E. Mulhollan, August 8, 1969, Interview 3, Oral Histories, Lyndon B. Johnson Presidential Library, https://dis coverlbj.org/item/oh-rauhj-19690808-3-77-30-c.

55. Victor Riesel, "Labor's White House Stock Rises," *Los Angeles Times*, November 29, 1963, A5.

56. Johnson and Kermit Gordon, sound recording, December 10, 1963, 5:12 p.m., #400, Recordings and Transcripts of Telephone Conversations and Meetings, Lyndon B. Johnson Presidential Library, http://www.discoverlbj.org/item/tel-0400.

57. Jeff Shesol, *Mutual Contempt: Lyndon Johnson, Robert Kennedy, and the Feud That Defined a Decade* (New York: W.W. Norton and Company, 1998), 161.

58. Michael R. Beschloss, *Taking Charge: The Johnson White House Tapes, 1963–1964* (New York: Touchstone, 1998), 204. Also at: Johnson and Sargent Shriver, sound recording, February 1, 1964, 1:02 p.m., #1804, Recordings and Transcripts of Telephone Conversations and Meetings, Lyndon B. Johnson Presidential Library, https://www.discoverlbj.org/item/tel-01804; and Johnson and Sargent Shriver, sound recording, February 1, 1964, 2:25 p.m., #1807, Recordings and Transcripts of Telephone Conversations and Meetings, Lyndon B. Johnson Presidential Library, https://www.discoverlbj.org/item/tel-01807.

59. The 1961 Social Security Amendments in Public-Law 87-64, approved June 30, 1961, provided increased or new benefits to 4.4 million citizens, costing some $800 million in the first year. Source: John F. Kennedy Library, Legislative Summary: Social Security. The growth of Social Security commitments under presidents from Roosevelt on is detailed in John F. Cogan, *The High Cost of Good Intentions* (Stanford, CA: Stanford University Press, 2017).

60. Patrick Foster, *George Romney: An American Life* (Grapevine, TX: Waldorf Publishing, 2017), 212.

61. Schlesinger, *Journals*, 191.

62. M. S. Handler, "Author of Book on Poverty Hails President's 'War' to Help Needy," *New York Times*, February 15, 1964, 8.

3: Great Society

1. Brian A. Williams, "The Great Society and Michigan," Bentley Historical Library, University of Michigan, https://bentley.umich.edu/features/the-great-society-and-michigan/.

2. Johnson, daily diary entry, May 22, 1964, President's Daily Diary Collection, Lyndon B. Johnson Presidential Library, https://discoverlbj.org/item/pdd-19640522.

3. Robert M. Warner, "Anatomy of a Speech: Lyndon Johnson's Great Society Address," *Michigan Historical Collections*, no. 28 (December 1978): 2.

4. Robert Young, "'Great Cities,' Johnson Abundance Key," *Chicago Tribune*, May 23, 1964, 3.

5. John Lewis and Archie E. Allen, "Black Voter Registration Efforts in the South," *Notre Dame Law Review* 48, no. 1 (1972): 112, https://scholarship.law.nd.edu/cgi/viewcontent.cgi?article=2861&context=ndlr.

6. Robert Dallek, *Flawed Giant* (New York: Oxford University Press, 1998), 81.

7. Robert Schlesinger, *White House Ghosts: Presidents and Their Speechwriters* (New York: Simon and Schuster, 2008), 152.

8. Hubert H. Humphrey, *The Education of a Public Man* (New York: Doubleday, 1976), 42.

9. Robert Caro, *The Path to Power* (New York: Knopf, 1982), 258. Caro also describes the mules.

10. "Cotton Plow-Up Brings Texas Farmers $22,078,043," *Bonham Daily Favorite*, November 28, 1934.

11. "Experience a Dramatic Story of Texas at the LBJ Library and Museum," Lyndon B. Johnson Presidential Library, September 2, 2006, http://www.lbjlibrary.org/press/experience-a-dramatic-story-of-texas-at-the-lbj-library.

12. Caro, *Path to Power*, 259–60.

13. Drew Pearson and Robert S. Allen, "Lyndon Johnson Saves Democratic Solons From Rout," *Minneapolis Star*, November 16, 1940, 4.

14. National Bureau of Economic Research, *Unemployment Rate for the United States*, FRED, Federal Reserve Bank of St. Louis, https://fred.stlouisfed.org/series/M0892AUSM156SNBR.

15. Walter Lippmann, *The Good Society* (New York: Routledge, 2017), xxi.

16. International Monetary Fund, *Interest Rates, Discount Rate for the United States*, FRED, Federal Reserve Bank of St. Louis, https://fred.stlouisfed.org/series/INTDSRUSM193N.

17. Louis Harris, "40% of California GOP Lean Toward Johnson," *Washington Post*, June 8, 1964, A1.

18. Johnson and Jesse Unruh, sound recording, 3 June 1964, 6:50 p.m., #3615, Recordings and Transcripts of Telephone Conversations and Meetings, Lyn-

don B. Johnson Presidential Library, https://www.discoverlbj.org/item/tel -03615.

19. Byron Hulsey, *Everett Dirksen and His Presidents: How a Senate Giant Shaped American Politics* (Lawrence: University Press of Kansas, 2000), 189.

20. William J. Bennett, *America: The Last Best Hope* (Nashville, TN: Thomas Nelson, 2006), 1:387.

21. Robert C. Wood, *Whatever Possessed the President? Academic Experts and Presidential Policy, 1960–1988* (Amherst: University of Massachusetts Press, 1993), 68.

22. Daniel Moynihan, "The Professionalization of Reform," *Public Interest* 1 (Fall 1965): 6.

23. Lewis and Allen, "Black Voter Registration Efforts," 112.

24. Joseph Dorman and Toby Perl Freilich, dirs., *Moynihan*, New York: First Run Features, 2018.

25. James M. McGeever, *The Decline of Standardized Test Scores in the United States from 1965 to the Present* (Charleston, WV: Appalachia Educational Laboratory, 1983), i, https://files.eric.ed.gov/fulltext/ED252565.pdf.

26. Gordon M. Fisher, "The Development of the Orshansky Poverty Thresholds and Their Subsequent History as the Official U.S. Poverty Measure" (unpublished manuscript, 1992), 6. https://www.census.gov/content/dam/Census/library/work ing-papers/1997/demo/orshansky.pdf.

27. *Economic Report of the President* (Washington, DC: U.S. Government Printing Office, 1963), 142, https://fraser.stlouisfed.org/files/docs/publications/ERP /1963/ERP_1963.pdf.

28. Scott Stossel, *Sarge: The Life and Times of Sargent Shriver* (Washington, DC: Smithsonian Books, 2004), 36.

29. Sargent Shriver, Georgetown University commencement address (Washington, DC, June 8, 1964), http://www.sargentshriver.org/speech-article/georgetown -university-commencement.

30. "The Peace Corps in Washington—The Early '60s," Peace Corps Worldwide, October 24, 2017, https://peacecorpsworldwide.org/the-peace-corps-in-washington -the-60s.

31. James F. Cogan, *The High Cost of Good Intentions* (Stanford, CA: Stanford University Press, 2017), 191.

32. Kennedy, speech at University of Chicago Law School (Chicago, IL, May 1, 1964), https://www.justice.gov/sites/default/files/ag/legacy/2011/01/20/05-01-1964 .pdf; Eve Edstrom, "Poor to Receive U.S. Aid In Asserting Their Rights," *Washington Post*, November 26, 1964, A8; Edgar S. Cahn, interview by Alan Houseman, July 3, 2002, National Equal Justice Library Oral History Collection, Georgetown Law Library, https://repository.library.georgetown.edu/bitstream /handle/10822/709336/nejl009_edgar_cahn.pdf.

33. Lyndon Baines Johnson, *The Vantage Point: Perspectives of the Presidency 1963–1969* (New York: Holt, Rinehart and Winston, 1971), 76.

34. Bennett Schiff and Stephen Goodell, *The Office of Economic Opportunity During the Administration of President Lyndon B. Johnson*, vol. 1, part 1 (unpublished manuscript), 17, 52, http://www.cencomfut.com/OEO%20and%20CSA%20Instructions/OEO%20Administrative%20History%20Nov%201963%20--%20Jan%201969.pdf.

35. Stossel, *Sarge*, 379.

36. Daniel P. Moynihan, *Maximum Feasible Misunderstanding: Community Action in the War on Poverty* (New York: Arkville Press, 1969), 98.

37. New York Times Service, "Don't Start Spiral, UAW Advised," *Louisville Courier-Journal*, March 24, 1964, 3.

38. Laura Visser-Maessen, *Robert Parris Moses: A Life in Civil Rights and Leadership at the Grassroots* (Chapel Hill: University of North Carolina Press, 2016), 246.

39. Visser-Maessen, *Robert Parris Moses*, 233.

40. Joseph Rauh, interview conducted for *Eyes on the Prize*, 1985, video, 40:20, Washington University in St. Louis, October 2016, http://repository.wustl.edu/concern/videos/rj430634r.

41. Robert P. Moses and Charles E. Cobb, *Radical Equations: Civil Rights from Mississippi to the Algebra Project* (Boston: Beacon Press, 2001), 82.

42. Mary King, *Freedom Song: A Personal Story of the 1960s Civil Rights Movement* (New York: William Morrow, 1987), 348.

43. George Gallup, "Johnson Ticket Holds 2-to-1 Lead in Midwest," *Washington Post*, October 21, 1964, A2.

44. Johnson and Reuther, sound recording, January 14, 1965, 10:40 a.m., #6730, Recordings and Transcripts of Telephone Conversations and Meetings, Lyndon B. Johnson Presidential Library, https://www.discoverlbj.org/item/tel-06730.

45. Nelson Lichtenstein, *Walter Reuther: The Most Dangerous Man in Detroit* (New York: Basic Books, 1995), 401.

4: Revolt of the Mayors

1. "Cities: Magnet in the West," *Time*, September 2, 1966, http://content.time.com/time/subscriber/article/0,33009,842728,00.html.

2. Michael K. Honey, *To the Promised Land: Martin Luther King and the Fight for Economic Justice* (New York: W.W. Norton, 2018), 103.

3. Josh Sides, *L.A. City Limits: African American Los Angeles from the Great Depression to the Present* (Berkeley: University of California Press, 2006), 124. Here Sides describes the destructive penalties of rent control and highway construction.

4. California Department of Industrial Relations, Division of Fair Employment Prac-

tices, *Negroes and Mexican Americans in South and East Los Angeles, Changes Between 1960 and 1965 in Population, Employment, Income, and Family Status* (San Francisco, 1966), 17, https://files.eric.ed.gov/fulltext/ED022589.pdf.

5. Gladwin Hill, "Los Angeles Vote Elects Three Negroes," *New York Times*, May 30, 1963, 14.

6. Sides, *L.A. City Limits*, 155.

7. Judith Michaelson and Myrna Oliver, "Three Term L.A. Mayor Sam Yorty Dies at 88," *Los Angeles Times*, June 6, 1998, http://www.latimes.com/local/obituaries/archives/la-me-sam-yorty-19980660-story.html.

8. Bessie Smith, "Conference Work Paper" (unpublished manuscript, n.d.), 1, PDF file, http://riseupnewark.com/wp-content/uploads/2017/06/Conference-Work-Paper-by-Bessie-Smith.pdf.

9. Fred Powledge, *Free at Last? The Civil Rights Movement and the People Who Made It* (New York: Perennial, 1992), 34.

10. Samuel W. Yorty, *I Cannot Take Kennedy* (pamphlet, 1960), 20.

11. Samuel Yorty, transcript of interview by Joe B. Frantz, February 7, 1970, Interview 1, Oral Histories, Lyndon B. Johnson Presidential Library, https://www.discoverlbj.org/item/oh-yortys-19700207-1-75-9.

12. U.S. Department of Labor, "Wage and Hour Division (WHD): History of Federal Minimum Wage Rates Under the Fair Labor Standards Act, 1938–2009," table, https://www.dol.gov/whd/minwage/chart.htm; and California Department of Industrial Relations, "History of California Minimum Wage," table, https://www.dir.ca.gov/iwc/minimumwagehistory.htm.

13. Stephen Schryer, *Maximum Feasible Participation: American Literature and the War on Poverty* (Stanford, CA: Stanford University Press, 2018), 189.

14. Mary King, *Freedom Song: A Personal Story of the 1960s Civil Rights Movement* (New York: William Morrow, 1987), 523.

15. Dionne Danns, Michelle A. Purdy, and Christopher M. Span, eds., *Using Past as Prologue: Contemporary Perspectives on African American Educational History* (Charlotte, NC: Information Age Publishing, 2015), 197.

16. Rebecca Miller Davis, "The Three R's—'Reading, 'Riting, and Race: The Evolution of Race in Mississippi History Textbooks, 1900–1995," *Journal of Mississippi History* 72, no. 1 (2010): 7, https://www.mdah.ms.gov/new/wp-content/uploads/2013/07/davis_race-in-textbooks.pdf.

17. Valora Washington and Ura Jean Oyemade Bailey, *Project Head Start: Models and Strategies for the Twenty-First Century* (New York: Garland Publishing, 1995), 23.

18. Walter Reuther, speech at Citizens Crusade Against Poverty (Washington, DC, February 10, 1965), http://www2.mnhs.org/library/findaids/00442/pdfa/00442-01506.pdf.

19. Community Action Program, *Workbook: Community Action Program* (Washing-

ton, DC: Office of Economic Opportunity, 1965), https://files.eric.ed.gov/fulltext
/ED103502.pdf.

20. Nicholas Lemann, *The Promised Land: The Great Black Migration and How It
Changed America* (New York: Vintage Books, 1992), 167.

21. Adam Cohen and Elizabeth Taylor, *American Pharaoh: Mayor Richard J.
Daley—His Battle for Chicago and the Nation* (Boston: Little, Brown and Company, 2000), 344.

22. Matthew Algeo, "Grover Cleveland's Hurricane," editorial, *New York Times*,
October 31, 2012, https://www.nytimes.com/2012/11/01/opinion/grover-cleve
lands-hurricane.html; and Calvin Coolidge, "Dedication of the Arizona State
Stone in the Washington Monument," speech, April 15, 1924, Washington, DC,
Calvin Coolidge Presidential Foundation, https://www.coolidgefoundation.org
/resources/speeches-as-president-1923-1928-3.

23. Alexis de Tocqueville, *Democracy in America*, Henry Reeve, translator (New
York: Alfred Knopf, 1945), Vol. I, 45.

24. "Cities: Magnet in the West," *Time*, September 2, 1966, cover story, http://con
tent.time.com/time/subscriber/article/0,33009,842728,00.html.

25. Samuel Yorty, transcript of interview by Joe B. Frantz, February 7, 1970.

26. Lee Rainwater and William L. Yancey, *The Moynihan Report and the Politics of
Controversy* (Cambridge, MA: MIT Press, 1967), 27.

27. James Reston, *The Lone Star: The Life of John Connally* (New York: Harper and
Row, 1989), 301.

28. William S. Clayson, *Freedom Is Not Enough: The War on Poverty and the Civil
Rights Movement in Texas* (Austin: University of Texas Press, 2010), 40.

29. Clayson, *Freedom Is Not Enough*, 40.

30. Richard N. Goodwin, *Remembering America: A Voice from the Sixties* (New York:
Open Road, 2014), 342.

31. Lemann, *Promised Land*, 170.

32. James L. Sundquist, ed., *On Fighting Poverty: Perspectives from Experience*,
Vol. 2 of *Perspectives on Poverty* (New York: Basic Books, 1969), 81.

33. Murray Kaufman, *Murray the K Tells It Like It Is, Baby* (New York: Holt, Rinehart and Winston, 1966), 101.

34. Joseph A. Califano Jr., *The Triumph and Tragedy of Lyndon Johnson* (New York:
Touchstone, 2015), 176.

35. Robert P. Bremner, *Chairman of the Fed: William McChesney Martin Jr., and
the Creation of the Modern American Financial System* (New Haven, CT, Yale
University Press, 2004), 203.

36. Paul Weeks, "Poverty War—More Shouting Than Shooting," *Los Angeles Times*,
June 13, 1965, F1.

37. Ethan Rarick, *California Rising: The Life and Times of Pat Brown* (Berkeley:
University of California Press, 2005), 314.

38. Califano, *The Triumph and Tragedy of Lyndon Johnson*, 48, 49. Califano's portrait captures Johnson at this moment of crisis.

5: Creative Society

1. Leslie Berlin, *The Man Behind the Microchip: Robert Noyce and the Invention of Silicon Valley* (Oxford, UK: Oxford University Press, 2005), 149. Berlin's perspicacious work illuminates the entire story of Noyce, Gordon Moore, and Intel.

2. Governor's Commission on the Los Angeles Riots, *Violence in the City: An End or a Beginning?* (Los Angeles: State of California, 1965), 19.

3. Allen J. Matusow, *The Unraveling of America: A History of Liberalism in the 1960s* (New York: Harper and Row, 1984), 250.

4. P. W. Malik and G. A. Souris, *Project Gemini: A Technical Summary* (Washington, DC: NASA, 1968); James M. Grimwood, Barton C. Hacker, and Peter J. Vorzimmer, *Project Gemini: Technology and Operations* (Washington, DC: NASA, 1969), 285, https://archive.org/details/NASA_NTRS_Archive_19690027123.

5. John Brooks, *Business Adventures: Twelve Classic Tales from the World of Wall Street* (New York: Open Road Integrated Media, 2014), 338.

6. Arnold Thackray, David Brock, and Rachel Jones, *Moore's Law: The Life of Gordon Moore, Silicon Valley's Quiet Revolutionary* (New York: Basic Books, 2015), 133.

7. Berlin, *The Man Behind the Microchip*, 113.

8. Robert N. Noyce, Semiconductor Device and Lead Structure, U.S. Patent 2,981,877, filed July 30, 1959, and issued April 25, 1961.

9. Leslie R. Berlin, "Robert Noyce and Fairchild Semiconductor, 1957–1968," *Business History Review* 75, no. 1 (2001): 89.

10. Berlin, *Man Behind the Microchip*, 62.

11. Chong-Moon Lee, William F. Miller, Marguerite Gong Hancock, and Henry S. Rowen, eds., *The Silicon Valley Edge: A Habit for Innovation and Entrepreneurship* (Stanford, CA: Stanford University Press, 2000), 61.

12. *LeadWire* (newsletter of Fairchild Semiconductor Corp.), November 1959, reproduced in Christophe Lécuyer and David C. Brock, *Makers of the Microchip: A Documentary History of the Fairchild Semiconductor* (Cambridge, MA: MIT Press, 2010), 181. According to the U.S. Census, the median price of a California home in 1960 was $15,100. Historical Census of Housing Tables, Median Home Values: Unadjusted, https://www.census.gov/hhes/www/housing/census/historic/values.html.

13. Lee et al., *Silicon Valley Edge*, 60.

14. Fairchild Camera and Instrument Corporation, *Annual Report 1961*, https://archive.computerhistory.org/resources/access/text/2017/01/102770279-05-01-acc.pdf.

15. Bo Lojek, *History of Semiconductor Engineering* (Berlin: Springer, 2007), 282.

16. Gordon E. Moore, "Cramming More Components onto Integrated Circuits," *Electronics* 38, no. 8 (April 1965): 114–17, http://www.monolithic3d.com/up loads/6/0/5/5/6055488/gordon_moore_1965_article.pdf.

17. Lisa Nakamura, "Indigenous Circuits," *@CHM* (blog), Computer History Museum, January 2, 2014, https://www.computerhistory.org/atchm/indigenous-circuits.

18. Charles A. Reich, "The New Property," *Yale Law Journal* 73, no. 5 (April 1964): 768.

19. John Johnson, *Succeeding Against the Odds* (New York: Warner Books, 1989), 288.

20. Johnson and Everett Dirksen, sound recording, August 21, 1965, 5:00 p.m., #8589, Recordings and Transcripts of Telephone Conversations and Meetings, Lyndon B. Johnson Presidential Library, https://www.discoverlbj.org/item/tel -08589.

21. Byron Hulsey, *Everett Dirksen and His Presidents: How a Senate Giant Shaped American Politics* (Lawrence: University Press of Kansas, 2000), 219.

22. Theodore N. Pappas, "The President's Gallbladder: A Historical Account of the Cholecystectomy of Lyndon Baines Johnson," *Surgery* 147, no. 1 (January 2010): 165.

23. Robert P. Bremner, *Chairman of the Fed: William McChesney Martin Jr. and the Creation of the American Financial System* (New Haven, CT: Yale University Press, 2004), 206.

24. Kevin Granville, "A President at War with His Fed Chief, 5 Decades Before Trump," *New York Times*, June 15, 2017, https://www.nytimes.com/2017/06/13 /business/economy/a-president-at-war-with-his-fed-chief-5-decades-before -trump.html. An illuminating account with audio of President Johnson.

25. International Monetary Fund, *Interest Rates, Discount Rate for the United States*. FRED, Federal Reserve Bank of St. Louis, https://fred.stlouisfed.org/series/IN TDSRUSM193N.

26. William McChesney Martin, "Reminiscences and Reflections" (speech, The Business Council, Hot Springs, VA, October 17, 1969), 7, https://fraser.stlouis fed.org/scribd/?item_id=7946&filepath=/files/docs/historical/martin/martin 69_1017.pdf.

27. Governor's Commission on the Los Angeles Riots, *Violence in the City*, 72.

28. Governor's Commission on the Los Angeles Riots, *Violence in the City*, 38.

29. Ronald Reagan to Lemuel Boulware, January 13, 1966, Lemuel Boulware Papers.

30. Alan Costy, "Somebody Out There Hates the Mayor," *New Republic*, September 4, 1965, 9.

6: Interlude: Looking for Socialism

1. Staughton Lynd and Thomas Hayden, *The Other Side* (New York: New American Library), 63. This chapter draws principally from three accounts of a 1965 trip to North Vietnam: *Reunion*, by Tom Hayden; *The Other Side*; and Herbert Aptheker's *Mission to Hanoi* (New York: International Publishers), 1966.

2. Norman Fruchter and Robert Machover, *Troublemakers* (New York: Film-Makers' Cooperative, 1966).

3. State of New Jersey, *Results of the General Election Held November 5th, 1963* (Trenton: New Jersey Department of State, 1963), https://www.njelections.org/1920 -1970-results/1963-general-election.pdf; State of New Jersey, *Results of the General Election Held November 2, 1965* (Trenton: New Jersey Department of State, 1965), https://www.njelections.org/1920-1970-results/1965-general-election.pdf; and Walter Waggoner, "Republican Rule Ended in Jersey: Democrats Carry Bergen in Taking Over Legislature," *New York Times*, November 3, 1965.

4. Jennifer Frost, *An Interracial Movement of the Poor: Community Organizing and the New Left in the 1960s* (New York: New York University Press, 2001), 158.

5. Carol Stevens, "SDS Re-Examined at Dec. Conference," *New Left Notes*, January 21, 1966, https://www.sds-1960s.org/NewLeftNotes-vol1-no01.pdf.

6. Casey Hayden, "Fields of Blue," in *Deep in Our Hearts: Nine White Women in the Freedom Movement*, ed. Constance Curry (Athens: University of Georgia Press, 2000), 350.

7. Mary Hershberger, *Traveling to Vietnam: American Peace Activists and the War* (Syracuse, NY: Syracuse University Press, 1998), 37.

8. Carl Mirra, *The Admirable Radical: Staughton Lynd and Cold War Dissent, 1945–1970* (Kent, OH: Kent State University Press, 2010), 124.

9. Staughton Lynd, *From Here to There: The Staughton Lynd Reader*, ed. Andrej Grubacic (Oakland, CA: PM Press, 2010), 116.

10. Hershberger, *Traveling to Vietnam*, 36.

11. Carl Oglesby, *Ravens in the Storm: A Personal History of the 1960s Anti-War Movement* (New York: Scribner, 2008), 105.

12. Though Michael Harrington could not know the precise number of those killed in the consolidation of communism in Vietnam, later historians put the figure at twelve thousand or more.

13. Maurice Isserman, *The Other American: The Life of Michael Harrington* (New York: Public Affairs, 2000), 261.

14. Stuart Chase, "How Russia Charts Her Economic Course," *New York Times*, December 11, 1927; and Amity Shlaes, *The Forgotten Man: A New History of the Great Depression* (New York: HarperCollins, 2007), 73.

15. Irving Louis Horowitz, *C. Wright Mills: An American Utopian* (New York: Free Press, 1983), 142.

16. C. Wright Mills, *Listen, Yankee: The Revolution in Cuba* (New York: Ballantine, 1960), 115.

17. Associated Press, "Cuba Mourns Professor Mills," *New York Times*, March 24, 1962.

18. Todd Gitlin, *The Sixties: Years of Hope, Days of Rage* (New York: Bantam Books, 1993), 266.

19. Mills, *Listen Yankee*, 115.

20. Lynd and Hayden, *The Other Side*, 31.

21. Guenter Lewy, *America in Vietnam* (New York: Oxford University Press, 1978), 381.

22. Lynd and Hayden, *The Other Side*, 55–56.

23. Aptheker, *Mission to Hanoi*, 52.

24. Associated Press, "Pentagon Absolves 2 Freed by Vietcong of Helping Enemy," *New York Times*, April 16, 1966.

25. It is not clear that even early on it was true there was no torture. Jeremiah Denton, also downed in 1965, would seek to alert the United States to torture there in a filmed 1966 interview, when he blinked the letters T-O-R-T-U-R-E in Morse code.

26. Lynd and Hayden, *The Other Side*, 200.

27. David Freed, "The Missile Men of North Vietnam," *Air and Space*, December 2014, https://www.airspacemag.com/military-aviation/missile-men-north-vietnam-180953375.

28. Harvey Henry Smith, *Area Handbook for North Vietnam, 1967* (Washington, DC: U.S. Government Printing Office, 1967), 125.

29. John Colvin, *Twice Around the World: Some Memoirs of Diplomatic Life in North Vietnam and Outer Mongolia* (London: Leo Cooper, 1991), 66.

30. New York Times/Chicago Tribune news service, "U.S. to Lift Passports of 3 Viet Visitors," *Chicago Tribune*, February 3, 1966.

31. Hayden gave this comb to Peter Collier, a fellow activist.

32. Oglesby, *Ravens in the Storm*, 104.

7: Housing Society

1. Kevin Boyle, *The UAW and the Heyday of American Liberalism 1945–1968* (Ithaca, NY: Cornell University Press, 1998), 246.

2. Ben Schnall, *HUD Office Building, Washington, D.C., Not Before 1968*, photograph, Marcel Breuer Papers, 1920–1986, Archives of American Art, Smithsonian Institute, Washington, DC, https://www.aaa.si.edu/collections/items/detail/hud-office-building-washington-dc-1012.

3. Ada Louise Huxtable, "The House That HUD Built," *New York Times*, September 22, 1968.

4. "History of FBI Headquarters," History, Federal Bureau of Investigation, https://www.fbi.gov/history/history-of-fbi-headquarters.

5. Daniel Patrick Moynihan, *Guiding Principles for Federal Architecture*, Ad Hoc Committee on Federal Office Space, Report to the President, June 1, 1962, https://www.gsa.gov/real-estate/design-construction/design-excellence/design-excellence-program/guiding-principles-for-federal-architecture.

6. "Headquarters for HUD by Breuer and Beckhard," *Architectural Record*, December 1968, 106, https://www.architecturalrecord.com/ext/resources/archives/backissues/1968-12.pdf?-34196400.

7. James Glanz and Eric Lipton, *City in the Sky: The Rise and Fall of the World Trade Center* (New York: Times Books, 2003), 93. Walter Reuther, Ludwig Mies van der Rohe, and Minoru Yamasaki all attended the ground-breaking for Lafayette Park in 1956.

8. Associated Press, "Jobs Are Lagging for Negro Youth," *New York Times*, March 3, 1968.

9. Boyle, *The UAW*, 246. Boyle's history of the UAW and its interactions with the Democratic Party offer many insights on the period.

10. Betty Boyd Caroli, *Lady Bird and Lyndon: The Hidden Story of a Marriage That Made a President* (New York: Simon and Schuster, 2015), 377.

11. Benjamin Hufbauer, *Presidential Temples: How Memorials and Libraries Shape Public Memory* (Lawrence: University of Kansas Press, 2005), 78.

12. Victor G. Reuther, *The Brothers Reuther and the Story of the UAW: A Memoir* (Boston: Houghton Mifflin, 1976), 460.

13. Jane Jacobs, *The Death and Life of Great American Cities* (New York: Vintage Books, 1992), 360.

14. Dr. Kenneth Clark and James Baldwin, interview, May 24, 1963, WGBH Media Library and Archives, http://openvault.wgbh.org/catalog/V_C03ED1927DCF46B5A8C82275DF4239F9; and Jack Gould, "TV: Challenge on Racism," *New York Times*, May 30, 1963.

15. Francesca Russello Ammon, *Southwest Washington Urban Renewal Area*, Historic American Buildings Survey, No. DC-856 (Washington, DC: National Park Service, 2004), 2. Ammon details the size and scale of urban activity before urban renewal. https://www.swdc.org/wp-content/uploads/2015/08/HABS-Southwest-Washington-Urban-Renewal-Area.pdf.

16. Ammon, *Southwest Washington Urban Renewal Area*, 22; and Berman v. Parker, 348 U.S. 26, 31 (1954). Details of the story of Max Morris and Goldie Schneider are found in Barak Atiram, "The Wretched of Eminent Domain: Holdouts, Free-Riding, and the Overshadowed Problem of Blinded-Riders," *Berkeley Journal of African-American Law and Policy* 52, no. 60 (2016).

17. More detail on Morris and Schneider in Amy Lavine, "Urban Renewal and the Story of *Berman v. Parker*," *Urban Lawyer* 42, no. 2, 453n142.

18. Lavine, "Urban Renewal," 456.

19. *Berman*, 348 U.S. at 33.

20. "Beauty and the Police Power," *Chicago Tribune*, November 29, 1954, 16.

21. Martin Anderson, *The Federal Bulldozer* (New York: McGraw Hill, 1967), 8.

22. Lavine, "Urban Renewal," 462.

23. Lavine, "Urban Renewal," 469.

24. Ammon, *Southwest Washington Urban Renewal Area*, 135. As Ammon writes, the disappointed community "largely disappeared."

25. Howard Husock, "The Myths of *The Pruitt-Igoe Myth*," *City Journal*, February 17, 2012, https://www.city-journal.org/html/myths-pruitt-igoe-myth-9698.html.

26. Chad Freidrichs, dir., *The Pruitt-Igoe Myth*, First Run Features, 2011.

27. Freidrichs, *Pruitt-Igoe Myth*, 44:00.

28. "The Case History of a Failure," *Architectural Forum*, December 1965, 23, http://www.usmodernist.org/AF/AF-1965-12.pdf.

29. Robert Adams, "Unbreakable Items Designed for Pruitt-Igoe," *St. Louis Post-Dispatch*, October 30, 1966.

30. Harry E. Berndt, *Only a Priest: A Biography of Monsignor John Alexander Shocklee* (self-pub., 2010), 87–89, https://archive.org/details/OnlyAPriestABiog raphyOfMonsignorJohnAlexanderShocklee/page/n93.

31. John McClaughry, interview with the author, Rangeley, ME, August 2019.

32. Eve Edstrom, "Housing Plan Inspires Hope," *Washington Post*, May 16, 1968, G1; and Olivia Skinner, "Neighborhood Leaders Bringing New Hope," *St. Louis Post-Dispatch*, March 2, 1967, 3H.

33. "Historical Census of Housing Tables," Census of Housing, U.S. Census Bureau, last modified October 31, 2011, https://www.census.gov/hhes/www/housing/cen sus/historic/owner.html.

34. Nicholas Lemann, *The Promised Land: The Great Black Migration and How It Changed America* (New York: Vintage Books, 1992), 102.

35. "Dr. King Twice Denied Rental in Chicago Slum," *Los Angeles Times*, January 21, 1966, 16.

36. David Bernstein, "The Longest March," *Chicago*, July 25, 2016, https://www .chicagomag.com/Chicago-Magazine/August-2016/Martin-Luther-King-Chicago -Freedom-Movement.

37. "The Biggest Landlord in Chicago," *Chicago Tribune*, April 10, 1966, 16; Lawrence M. Friedman, "Public Housing and the Poor: An Overview," *California Law Review* 54, no. 2 (May 1966): 643, https://scholarship.law.berkeley.edu/cgi /viewcontent.cgi?article=2930&context=californialawreview.

38. Oscar Newman, *Defensible Space: Crime Prevention Through Urban Design* (New York: Collier Books, 1973), 135.

39. Jacobs, *Death and Life of Great American Cities*, 224. Jacobs develops the concept of "unslumming" throughout the book.

40. "Detroit '67," *Detroit Free Press*, 2017, https://www.freep.com/pages/inter actives/1967-detroit-riot/.

41. Patrick Foster, *George Romney: An American Life* (Grapevine, TX: Waldorf Publishing, 2017), 219.

42. Johnson, daily diary entry, July 24, 1967, President's Daily Diary Collection, Lyndon B. Johnson Presidential Library, https://discoverlbj.org/item/pdd-19670724.

8: Guns, Butter, and Gold

1. James Ledbetter, *One Nation Under Gold: How One Precious Metal Has Dominated the American Imagination for Four Centuries* (New York: Liveright Publishing Corporation, 2017), 180–93. Ledbetter covers the gold exploration and the 1967 gold crisis in wonderful detail.

2. The gold cover and gold stock figures can be found in the *Wall Street Journal*'s weekly "Federal Reserve Report."

3. Ledbetter, *One Nation Under Gold*, 181.

4. Don Cook, "The Rise and Fall of Harold Wilson," *Los Angeles Times*, April 28, 1968.

5. Jonathan Colman, *A "Special Relationship"? Harold Wilson, Lyndon B Johnson and Anglo-American Relations "at the Summit," 1964–68* (Manchester, UK: Manchester University Press, 2004), 153.

6. Robert B. Semple Jr., "Rise in Mail Rate and Federal Pay Voted by House," *New York Times*, October 12, 1967.

7. Clark Clifford, with Richard Holbrooke, *Counsel to the President: A Memoir* (New York: Random House, 1991), 457–58.

8. Robert Kennedy, *To Seek a Newer World* (New York: Ishi Press, 2017), 182.

9. Deborah Shapley, *Promise and Power: The Life and Times of Robert McNamara* (Boston: Little, Brown and Company, 1993), 410.

10. Gerald Mayer, *Union Membership Trends in the United States* (Washington, DC: Congressional Research Service, 2004), 22, https://digitalcommons.ilr.cornell .edu/cgi/viewcontent.cgi?article=1176&context=key_workplace.

11. Johnson to Reuther, telegram, January 10, 1968, box 369, Walter P. Reuther Collection, Wayne State University Library.

12. William M. Blair, "Gold and Silver Found in Remains of Waste Burned in Washington's Dumps," *New York Times*, January 7, 1968, 31.

13. Walter Bilitz, "New Half-Dollars Scarce: Only 355 Million Around," *Chicago Tribune*, September 26, 1967, E5.

14. Paul Sabin, *The Bet: Paul Ehrlich, Julian Simon, and Our Gamble over Earth's Future* (New Haven, CT: Yale University Press, 2013), 22.

15. Alfred L. Malabre, "Boom for Whom?," *Wall Street Journal*, February 28, 1968, 1.

16. Ayn Rand, *Capitalism: The Unknown Ideal* (New York: New American Library, 1966), 93–95.

17. James Sikes, "Economist Warns of Spending Peril," *New York Times*, March 5, 1967.

18. Leslie Berlin, *The Man Behind the Microchip: Robert Noyce and the Invention of Silicon Valley* (Oxford, UK: Oxford University Press, 2005), 168.

19. Johnson, daily diary entry, January 17, 1968, President's Daily Diary Collection, Lyndon B. Johnson Presidential Library, https://discoverlbj.org/item/pdd -19680117.

20. DeNeen L. Brown, "'Sex Kitten' vs. Lady Bird: The Day Eartha Kitt Attacked the Vietnam War at the White House," *Washington Post*, January 19, 2018; and Califano, *The Triumph and Tragedy of Lyndon Johnson*, 258; *The Smothers Brothers Comedy Hour*, season 2, on CBS.

21. Lyndon and Lady Bird Johnson, daily diary entry, January 27 1968, President's Daily Diary Collection, Lyndon B. Johnson Presidential Library, https://discover lbj.org/item/pdd-19680127.

22. Johnson, daily diary entry, January 28, 1968, President's Daily Diary Collection, Lyndon B. Johnson Presidential Library, https://discoverlbj.org/item/pdd -19680128.

23. Clifford, *Counsel to the President*, 472.

24. Clayton Fritchey, "Johnson on Shaky Ground," *Los Angeles Times*, November 10, 1966.

25. Charles Peters, *Lyndon Johnson* (New York: Henry Holt, 2010), 141; Stanley Karnow, "Giap Remembers," *New York Times*, June 24, 1990, 22.

26. John G. Morris, *Get the Picture: A Personal History of Photojournalism* (New York: Random House, 1998), 240–41.

27. "Federal Reserve Report," *Wall Street Journal*, February 9, 1968, 19.

28. Johnson, daily diary entry, February 8, 1968, President's Daily Diary Collection, Lyndon B. Johnson Presidential Library, https://discoverlbj.org/item/pdd -19680208.

29. John F. Cogan, *The High Cost of Good Intentions* (Stanford, CA: Stanford University Press, 2017), 201.

30. Kay Collett Goss, *Mr. Chairman: The Life and Legacy of Wilbur D. Mills* (Chicago: Parkhurst Brothers Inc., 2012), 134.

31. Joseph J. Thorndike, "Historical Perspective: Sacrifice and Surcharge," December 5, 2005. http://www.taxhistory.org/thp/readings.nsf/cf7c9c870b600b958525 6df80075b9dd/6b24abb33fe1996c852570d200756a5d?OpenDocument. Thorndike, a tax historian, offers an excellent account of the Mills-Johnson standoff.

32. Joseph A. Califano, Jr., *The Triumph and Tragedy of Lyndon Johnson* (New York: Touchstone, 2015), 261.

33. Goss, *Mr. Chairman*, 135.

34. Wilbur Mills, transcript of interview by Michael L. Gillette, March 25, 1987, Interview 2, p. 15, Oral Histories, Lyndon B. Johnson Presidential Library, https:// discoverlbj.org/item/oh-millsw-19870325-2-94-18.

35. Robert P. Bremner, *Chairman of the Fed: William McChesney Martin Jr. and the Creation of the American Financial System* (New Haven, CT: Yale University Press, 2004), 242.

36. Johnson and Everett Dirksen, sound recording, March 12, 1968, 5:36 p.m., #12807, Recordings and Transcripts of Telephone Conversations and Meetings, Lyndon B. Johnson Presidential Library, https://www.discoverlbj.org/item/tel -12807.

37. Ray Vicker, "The Gold Hustlers," *Wall Street Journal*, February 26, 1968, 1.

38. Bremner, *Chairman of the Fed*, 242.

39. William McChesney Martin, "Good Money Is Coined Freedom" (speech and question and answer, 50th anniversary of the Detroit Branch of the Federal Reserve Bank, Economic Club of Detroit, MI, March 18, 1968), 50, https://fraser .stlouisfed.org/title/448/item/7929.

40. The discussion about Walter Reuther took place March 23. Johnson and Everett Dirksen, sound recording, March 23, 1968, 10:41 a.m. #12837, Recordings and Transcripts of Telephone Conversations and Meetings, Lyndon B. Johnson Presidential Library, https://www.discoverlbj.org/item/tel-12837.

41. Jan Jarboe Russell, *Lady Bird: A Biography of Mrs. Johnson* (New York: Scribner, 1999), 300.

42. Jarboe Russell, *Lady Bird*, 300.

9: Reuther and the Intruder

1. "Corolla, New Economy Car, Is Shown Here by Toyota," *New York Times*, August 28, 1968, 94.

2. Charles B. Camp, "Volkswagen Raises Prices Average of 2.8%," *Wall Street Journal*, September 6, 1968.

3. Max Frankel, "Delegate Fights Transform Party," *New York Times*, August 28, 1968, 1.

4. Carl Solberg, *Hubert Humphrey: A Biography* (Ontario, Canada: Borealis Books, 2003), 283.

5. Nelson Lichtenstein, *Walter Reuther: The Most Dangerous Man in Detroit* (New York: Basic Books, 1995), 396.

6. Elisabeth Reuther Dickmeyer, *Putting the World Together: My Father Walter Reuther, the Liberal Warrior* (Lake Orion, MI: Living Force Publishing, 2004), 323.

7. Max Lerner, "Ending a Revolution," *Los Angeles Times*, June 17, 1968, 5.

8. "Speeches and Street Action," Democratic National Convention, Chicago, 1968, video, 9:34, https://www.youtube.com/watch?v=a4O6Tat4yYw. This tape covers

Jean Genet's and Allen Ginsberg's appearances at the Democratic National Convention.

9. Elaine Woo, "Tom Hayden, Preeminent 1960s Political Radical and Antiwar Protester, Dies at 76," *Washington Post*, October 24, 2016.

10. James Alan McPherson, "Chicago's Blackstone Rangers (Part I)," *Atlantic*, May 1969, https://www.theatlantic.com/magazine/archive/1969/05/chicagos-black stone-rangers-i/305741. In this remarkable article, McPherson profiles the Blackstone Rangers of the late 1960s.

11. Johnson and Richard Daley, sound recording, August 29, 1968, 7:31 p.m., #13344, Recordings and Transcripts of Telephone Conversations and Meetings, Lyndon B. Johnson Presidential Library, https://www.discoverlbj.org/item/tel -13344.

12. Peter B. Levy, *The New Left and Labor in the 1960s* (Champaign: University of Illinois Press, 1994), 100–1.

13. Adam Cohen and Elizabeth Taylor, *American Pharaoh: Mayor Richard J. Daley—His Battle for Chicago and the Nation* (Boston: Little, Brown and Company, 2000), 468.

14. Thomas A. Crumm, *What Is Good for General Motors? Solving America's Industrial Conundrum* (New York: Algora Publishing, 2010), 99.

15. Dan T. Carter, *The Politics of Rage: George Wallace, the Origins of the New Conservatism, and the Transformation of American Politics* (Baton Rouge: Louisiana State University Press, 2000), 233.

16. Kevin Boyle, *The UAW and the Heyday of American Liberalism 1945–1968* (Ithaca, NY: Cornell University Press, 1998), 252.

17. The documentary *Brothers on the Line*, directed by Sasha Reuther (Richmond, VA: Porter Street Pictures, 2012), captures Reuther's struggles in detail and perspicaciously.

18. The story of Sakichi Toyoda's innovations can be found in many places, including Toyota Industries' own website. "The Story of Sakichi Toyoda," Company History, Toyota Industries Corporation, https://www.toyota-industries.com/company /history/toyoda_sakichi.

19. "Corolla, New Economy Car, Is Shown Here by Toyota," *New York Times*, August 28, 1968, 94; and Hirohisa Kohama, *Industrial Development in Postwar Japan* (London: Routledge, 2007), 144.

20. Kohama, *Industrial Development*, 143.

21. One of the best guides to the Japanese productivity miracle is Michael A. Cusumano's *The Japanese Automobile Industry: Technology and Management at Nissan and Toyota* (Cambridge, MA: Harvard University Press, 1984).

22. Kenneth G. Dau-Schmidt and Benjamin C. Ellis, "The Relative Bargaining Power of Employers and Unions in the Global Information Age: A Comparative Analysis of the United States and Japan," *Indiana International and Compara-*

tive Law Review 20, no. 1 (2010): 11, http://journals.iupui.edu/index.php/iiclr /article/view/17618.

23. Reuther visited Japan in 1962 and argued against communism during that trip. United Press International, "Spurn Reds, Reuther Tells Japan Labor," *Washington Post*, November 25, 1962, A9.

24. Cusumano, *The Japanese Automobile Industry*, 201.

25. Gertrude Samuels, "Help Wanted: The Hard-Core Unemployed," *New York Times Magazine*, January 28, 1968, 26.

26. Johnson and Robert Kennedy, sound recording, February 25, 1964, 11:10 a.m., #2187, Recordings and Transcripts of Telephone Conversations and Meetings, Lyndon B. Johnson Presidential Library, https://www.discoverlbj.org/item/tel -02187.

27. Johnson and Kennedy, sound recording.

28. Walter Hayes, *Henry: A Life of Henry Ford II* (New York: Grove Weidenfeld, 1990), 83.

29. Thomas J. Sugrue, *The Origins of the Urban Crisis: Race and Inequality in Postwar Detroit* (Princeton, NJ: Princeton University Press, 1996), 151.

30. Johnson and George Ball, sound recording, September 30, 1968, 8:15 p.m., #13436, Recordings and Transcripts of Telephone Conversations and Meetings, Lyndon B. Johnson Presidential Library, https://www.discoverlbj.org/item/tel -13436.

31. Humphrey telephoned to alert Johnson to the broadcast of his pretaped television statement. Johnson and Hubert Humphrey, sound recording, September 30, 1968, 7:30 p.m., #13435, Recordings and Transcripts of Telephone Conversations and Meetings, Lyndon B. Johnson Presidential Library, https://www.discov erlbj.org/item/tel-13435.

32. Associated Press, "Reuther to Aid Nixon," *New York Times*, November 16, 1968, 17.

33. Victor G. Reuther, *The Brothers Reuther and the Story of the UAW: A Memoir* (Boston: Houghton Mifflin, 1976), 462.

10: Moynihan Agonistes

1. "Nixon Says He'd Balance Economy, Not the Budget," *Wall Street Journal*, October 24, 1968.

2. Godfrey Hodgson, *The Gentleman from New York* (New York: Houghton Mifflin, 2000), 144.

3. Daniel P. Moynihan, *Daniel Patrick Moynihan: A Portrait in Letters of an American Visionary*, ed. Steven R. Weisman (New York: Public Affairs, 2010), 155. Many of the figures in this chapter kept diaries at the time or later wrote memoirs. In some cases, such as Moynihan's, much of what happened was captured

in correspondence. This chapter relies heavily on Moynihan's letters, as well as Nixon's memoirs and the diaries of Bob Haldeman, John Ehrlichman, and Arthur Burns.

4. "Lindsay, Reuther, Rockefeller, Udall Receive Honorary Degrees," *Harvard Crimson*, June 12, 1969, https://www.thecrimson.com/article/1969/6/12/lind say-reuther-rockefeller-udall-receive-honorary.

5. Joseph Dorman and Toby Perl Freilich, dirs., *Moynihan* (New York: First Run Features, 2018).

6. For Moynihan's commonalities with the great statesman Edmund Burke, see Greg Weiner's excellent, perspicacious *American Burke* (Lawrence: University Press of Kansas, 2015).

7. Steve Estes, *I Am a Man! Race, Manhood, and the Civil Rights Movement* (Chapel Hill: University of North Carolina Press, 2006), 120.

8. Daniel Geary, *Beyond Civil Rights: The Moynihan Report and Its Legacy* (Philadelphia: University of Pennsylvania Press, 2015), 110.

9. Peter Schuck, *One Nation Undecided* (Princeton, NJ: Princeton University Press, 2019), 67.

10. John F. Cogan, *The High Cost of Good Intentions* (Stanford, CA: Stanford University Press, 2017), 231.

11. James Buchanan, "Inaugural Address," March 4, 1857, Miller Center, University of Virginia, transcript, https://millercenter.org/the-presidency/presidential -speeches/march-4-1857-inaugural-address.

12. H. R. Haldeman, *The Haldeman Diaries: Inside the Nixon White House* (New York: G.P. Putnam's Sons, 1994), 36. Haldeman, who accompanied Nixon to Paris, wrote in his diary that it was "interesting to watch Eunice Shriver last night and tonight, she obviously hates seeing Nixon as president."

13. William Safire, *Before the Fall: An Inside View of the Pre-Watergate White House* (New Brunswick, NJ: Transaction Publishers, 2005), 108.

14. Robert H. Ferrell, ed., *Inside the Nixon Administration: The Secret Diary of Arthur Burns, 1969–1974* (Lawrence: University of Kansas Press, 2010), 23.

15. Leonard Garment, *Crazy Rhythm: From Brooklyn and Jazz to Nixon's White House, Watergate, and Beyond* (Boston: Da Capo Press, 2001), loc. 1853 Kindle edition.

16. Safire, *Before the Fall*, 115.

17. Nathan Wright Jr., *Let's Work Together* (New York: Hawthorne Books, 1968), 54.

18. James Alan McPherson, "Chicago's Blackstone Rangers (II)," *Atlantic*, June 1969, https://www.theatlantic.com/magazine/archive/1969/06/chicagos-blackstone -rangers-ii/305742.

19. Stephen Hess, *The Professor and the President: Daniel Patrick Moynihan in the Nixon White House* (Washington, DC: Brookings Institution Press, 2015), 144.

20. Christopher DeMuth, interview with the author, Rangeley, ME, August 2019.

21. Richard Nixon, *RN: The Memoirs of Richard Nixon* (New York: Simon and Schuster, 1990), 426.

22. Hess, *Professor and the President*, 73.

23. "Despair Seen in Universities by Moynihan," *Los Angeles Times*, June 2, 1969, A10.

24. Richard Homan, "McNamara Warns on Population," *Washington Post*, May 2, 1969, A1.

25. Ferrell, *Inside the Nixon Administration*, 15.

26. Haldeman, *Haldeman Diaries*, 43.

27. Haldeman, *Haldeman Diaries*, 53.

28. "New Weapon Against Poverty," *New York Times*, November 16, 1969, E12.

29. Cogan, *High Cost of Good Intentions*, 241.

30. Friedrich Engels, *The Condition of the Working Class in England* (Oxford: Oxford University Press, 1993).

31. Martin Anderson, *Welfare: The Political Economy of Welfare Reform in the United States* (Stanford: Hoover Institution Press, 1978), 92–98.

32. Appendix A to the *Report from His Majesty's Commissioners for Inquiring into the Administration and Practical Operation of the Poor Laws* (London, 1834), 342, https://parlipapers.proquest.com/parlipapers/docview/t70.d75.1834-014987.

33. Marvin Olasky, *The Tragedy of American Compassion* (Wheaton, IL: Crossway Books, 1992), 118.

34. Roger Kimball, "The Death of Socialism," *New Criterion*, April 2002, https://www.newcriterion.com/issues/2002/4/the-death-of-socialism.

35. Frances Perkins, *The Roosevelt I Knew* (New York: Penguin, 2011), 294.

36. Philip Ziegler, *Wilson: The Authorised Life* (London: Weidenfeld and Nicolson, 1993), 25.

37. 702 Parl. Deb. H.C. (5th ser.) (1964) col. 1320.

38. Ben A. Franklin, "Welfare Parley Cautious on Nixon: He Is Hailed for Initiative but Plan Is Criticized," *New York Times*, August 24, 1969, 34.

39. Cogan, *High Cost of Good Intentions*, 244.

40. Cogan, *High Cost of Good Intentions*, 244, 432.

41. Robert P. Bremner, *Chairman of the Fed: William McChesney Martin Jr. and the Creation of the American Financial System* (New Haven, CT: Yale University Press, 2004), 276.

42. Haldeman, *Haldeman Diaries*, 128.

43. Hess, *The Professor and the President*, 99.

44. Moynihan, *Daniel Patrick Moynihan*, 203.

45. Leslie Berlin, *The Man Behind the Microchip: Robert Noyce and the Invention of Silicon Valley* (Oxford, UK: Oxford University Press, 2005), 194.

46. Haldeman, *Haldeman Diaries*, 163.

47. "Reuther Hits Extremists of the Ultra-Left," *Washington Post*, April 23, 1970, A2.

48. Moynihan, *Daniel Patrick Moynihan*, 225.

11: The Governor of California

1. Art Seidenbaum, "Policy vs. Politics," *Los Angeles Times*, March 6, 1970, SF7.

2. Herbert R. Rosa, "Fragmented Diversity: School Desegregation, Student Activism, and Busing in Los Angeles, 1963–1982" (PhD diss., University of Michigan, 2013), 45, https://deepblue.lib.umich.edu/handle/2027.42/97911.

3. Jack McCurdy, "Most L.A. Schools Score Below U.S. Average in Reading Tests," *Los Angeles Times*, September 30, 1969, 1.

4. Rudy Villasenor, "Judge Gitelson—His Only Hobby Is the Law," *Los Angeles Times*, February 21, 1970.

5. Charles A. Reich, *The Greening of America* (New York: Random House, 1970).

6. Reich, *The Greening*, 209.

7. Warren E. George, "Development of the Legal Services Corporation," *Cornell Law Review* 61, no. 5 (1976): http://scholarship.law.cornell.edu/clr/vol61/iss5/3.

8. Richard S. Tedlow, *Andy Grove: The Life and Times of an American Business Icon* (New York: Penguin, 2006), 137.

9. Martin Anderson, *Welfare: The Political Economy of Welfare Reform in the United States* (Stanford: Hoover Institution Press, 1978), 154.

10. Jeffery Kahn, "Ronald Reagan Launched Political Career Using the Berkeley Campus as a Target," UC Berkeley News, https://www.berkeley.edu/news/media/releases/2004/06/08_reagan.shtml.

11. "Ten Thousand Farm Workers on Strike in California," *El Malcriado*, September 1, 1970, 3, https://libraries.ucsd.edu/farmworkermovement/ufwarchives/elmalcriado/1970/September%201,%201970%20%20No%206_PDF.pdf.

12. Terry Lenzner, *The Investigator: Fifty Years of Uncovering the Truth* (New York: Blue Rider Press, 2013), 71.

13. Lenzner, *The Investigator*, 71.

14. Jerome B. Falk Jr. and Stuart R. Pollak, "Political Interference with Publicly Funded Lawyers: The CRLA Controversy and the Future of Legal Services," *Hastings Law Journal* 24, no. 4 (1973): 609, https://repository.uchastings.edu/hastings_law_journal/vol24/iss4/1.

15. Lou Cannon, *Governor Reagan: His Rise to Power* (New York: Public Affairs, 2009), 292.

16. Bobby Seale, *Seize the Time: The Story of the Black Panther Party and Huey P. Newton* (Baltimore: Black Classic Press, 1991), 162.

17. "Press Conference of Governor Ronald Reagan," August 11, 1970, box P03, Press

Unit, Gubernatorial Papers, 1966–74, Ronald Reagan Presidential Library, https://www.reaganlibrary.gov/sites/default/files/digitallibrary/gubernatorial /pressunit/p03/40-840-7408622-p03-005-2017.pdf.

18. Spencer Leigh, *Frank Sinatra: An Extraordinary Life* (Carmarthen, UK: McNidder and Grace, 2015), 297.

19. Mark Neal Aaronson, *Representing the Poor: Legal Advocacy and Welfare Reform During Reagan's Gubernatorial Years* (New Orleans: Quid Pro Books, 2014), n27.

20. Kennedy, speech at the University of Chicago Law School (Chicago, IL, May 1, 1964), https://www.justice.gov/sites/default/files/ag/legacy/2011/01/20/05-01 -1964.pdf.

21. George, "Development of the Legal Services Corporation," 689.

22. Lenzner, *The Investigator*, 67; Aaronson, *Representing the Poor*, note 27.

23. Cruz Reynoso, interview by Alan Houseman, August 12, 2002, National Equal Justice Library Oral History Collection, Georgetown Law Library, https://reposi tory.library.georgetown.edu/handle/10822/1042295.

24. George, "Development of the Legal Services Corporation," 684.

25. For a typical college response to the news of graduate school deferment, see Robert J. Samuelson, "LBJ Signs Draft Law Cutting Graduate 2-S," *Harvard Crimson*, July 3, 1967, https://www.thecrimson.com/article/1967/7/3/lbj-signs -draft-law-cutting-graduate.

26. Transcript of oral argument, Goldberg v. Kelly, 397 U.S. 254 (1970), https:// www.oyez.org/cases/1969/62?page=15.

27. *Goldberg*, 397 U.S. at 276 n.6.

28. Aaronson, *Representing the Poor*, 11n7.

29. *Goldberg*, 397 U.S. at 262 n.8.

30. Cannon, *Governor Reagan*, 352; and H. W. Brands, *Reagan: The Life* (New York: Anchor Books, 2016), 180.

31. Lenzner, *The Investigator*, 67.

32. Harry Bernstein, "Disabled Cousin, Wife: Nixon Relatives on Welfare Assisted in Suit by CRLA," *Los Angeles Times*, February 12, 1971, C1.

33. Jeffrey Hart, "An Interview with Ronald Reagan," *Anaheim Bulletin*, May 14, 1971, https://www.reaganlibrary.gov/sites/default/files/digitallibrary/gubernatorial /pressunit/p29/40-840-7408627-p29-011-2017.pdf.

34. Memorandum by Thomas N. Duffy, February 3, 1971, box P27, Press Unit, Gubernatorial Papers, 1966–74, Ronald Reagan Presidential Library, https:// www.reaganlibrary.gov/sites/default/files/digitallibrary/gubernatorial/pressunit /p27/40-840-7408627-p27-007-2017.pdf.

35. Uhler, interview with the author, May 2018.

36. Frank Carlucci tells the story of his negotiations with Ed Meese in an oral history archived at the Richard Nixon Presidential Library. Carlucci, transcript

of interview by Timothy Naftali, June 25, 2007, 5-6, Oral Histories, Richard Nixon Presidential Library, https://www.nixonlibrary.gov/sites/default/files/for researchers/find/histories/carlucci-2007-06-25.pdf.

37. Carl Greenberg, "Gimmickry Makes Shambles of Justice, Reagan Charges," *Los Angeles Times*, May 27, 1971, D1.

38. Michael Ritchie, dir., *The Candidate* (Burbank, CA: Warner Bros., 1972), 1:24.

12: Scarcity: Burns Agonistes

1. Arthur F. Burns, "The Economic Contest Between Freedom and Authoritarianism" (speech, Chung-Ang University, Seoul, South Korea, June 26, 1970), 9, https://fraser.stlouisfed.org/title/449/item/7955.

2. "Strike Authorized by Screen Actors," *Los Angeles Times*, June 23, 1971, 3.

3. Lawrence Laurent, "Lorne Greene Has Heard All Those Jokes About 'Bonanza' and He Doesn't Mind a Bit," *Washington Post*, June 27, 1971, 9.

4. Ralph Orr, "Office Workers Strike, Shut UAW Headquarters," *Detroit Free Press*, March 13, 1971, 7; and Seth Lipsky, "UAW Strike Begins: Office Workers Picket Union's Headquarters," *Wall Street Journal*, March 15, 1971, 4.

5. Jack Rosenthal, "Poor in Nation Rise by Five Percent, Reversing Trend," *New York Times*, May 8, 1971, 1.

6. Ken Hartnett, "St. Louis Slum Epitomizes Housing Problem," *Sedalia Democrat*, April 27, 1970, 14.

7. Richard F. Janssen and Albert R. Hunt, "War of Nerves Quickens: White House Hints It Plans Attack on Reserve Board's Independence," *Wall Street Journal*, July 29, 1971, 26.

8. "Chrysler's Rise in Profit Slowed by Price Freeze," *Wall Street Journal*, October 26, 1971, 3.

9. "If You're Teed Off at Inflation, Bonanza Has the Answer to the High Cost of Eating!" advertisement, *Northwest Arkansas Times*, January 19, 1971, 10.

10. Much of the detail of the monetary crisis of 1971 is covered in James Ledbetter's magisterial *One Nation Under Gold* (New York: Liveright Publishing Corporation, 2017).

11. Lawrence B. Krause, "How Much of Current Unemployment Did We Import?" *Brookings Papers on Economic Activity* 1971, no. 2 (1971): 417–28, https://www.brookings.edu/wp-content/uploads/1971/06/1971b_bpea_krause_mathieson.pdf.

12. Paul Sabin, *The Bet: Paul Ehrlich, Julian Simon, and Our Gamble over Earth's Future* (New Haven, CT: Yale University Press, 2013), 2; and Norman Pearlstine, "Shifting into High," *Wall Street Journal*, April 9, 1971.

13. Robert L. Hetzel, "Arthur Burns and Inflation," *Federal Reserve Bank of Rich-*

mond Economic Quarterly 84, no. 1 (Winter 1998): 31, https://www.richmondfed .org/-/media/richmondfedorg/publications/research/economic_quarterly/1998 /winter/pdf/hetzel.pdf.

14. Robert H. Ferrell, ed., *Inside the Nixon Administration: The Secret Diary of Arthur Burns, 1969–1974* (Lawrence: University of Kansas Press, 2010). This chapter relies on multiple narratives from the period, especially Arthur Burns's own diary. The Connally-Nixon story is told well and in great detail by James Ledbetter.

15. Wyatt Wells, *Economist in an Uncertain World: Arthur F. Burns and the Federal Reserve, 1970–1978* (New York: Columbia University Press, 1994), 25.

16. International Monetary Fund, *Interest Rates, Discount Rate for the United States*; and Michael D. Bordo and Mark A. Wynne, eds., *The Federal Reserve's Role in the Global Economy: A Historical Perspective* (New York: Cambridge University Press, 2016).

17. 115 Cong. Rec. 40,181 (1969).

18. H. R. Haldeman, *The Haldeman Diaries: Inside the Nixon White House* (New York: G.P. Putnam's Sons, 1994), 128.

19. Ferrell, *Inside the Nixon Administration.*

20. James Reston, *The Lone Star: The Life of John Connally* (New York: Harper and Row, 1989), 417.

21. Reston, *The Lone Star*, 471.

22. Burton A. Abrams, "How Richard Nixon Pressured Arthur Burns: Evidence from the Nixon Tapes," *Journal of Economic Perspectives* 20, no. 4 (Fall 2006): 186, https://pubs.aeaweb.org/doi/pdfplus/10.1257/jep.20.4.177.

23. John Ehrlichman, *Witness to Power: The Nixon Years* (New York: Simon and Schuster, 1982), 254.

24. Federal Open Market Committee, Memorandum of Discussion (Federal Reserve Board of Governors, Washington, DC, January 12, 1971), 63, https://www.federal reserve.gov/monetarypolicy/files/fomcmod19710112.pdf.

25. Bob Woodward, *The Last of the President's Men* (New York: Simon and Schuster, 2015), 219.

26. Woodward, *The Last of the President's Men*, 75.

27. Ehrlichman, *Witness to Power*, 255.

28. "Burns Says Reserve Board Should Resist Pressure for an Easier Monetary Policy," *Wall Street Journal*, March 11, 1971, 3.

29. Ehrlichman, *Witness to Power*, 107.

30. Nixon and Arthur F. Burns, transcript of conversation, March 19, 1971, 1:30 p.m., Presidential Recordings Digital Edition, Miller Center, University of Virginia, https://prde.upress.virginia.edu/conversations/4006733.

31. Federal Reserve Board of Governors, "Beige Book Report: San Francisco," *Beige*

Book, April 16, 1971, https://www.minneapolisfed.org/news-and-events/beige
-book-archive/1971-04-sf.

32. Frank C. Porter, "Building Union Chiefs Grimly Meet President," *Washington Post*, April 20, 1971, 2.

33. Hobart Rowen, "U.S. Going Protectionist Following Monetary Crisis," *Washington Post*, June 7, 1971, 22.

34. "Connally Stands by Foreign Trade Policy: Says 'Misconceptions' Imperil Its Success," *Wall Street Journal*, November 17, 1971, 3.

35. Rowen, "U.S. Going Protectionist Following Monetary Crisis," 2.

36. Reston, *Lone Star*, 401.

37. Ciaran Driver and Grahame Thompson, *Corporate Governance in Contention* (Oxford: Oxford University Press, 2018), 135.

38. Leslie Berlin, *The Man Behind the Microchip: Robert Noyce and the Invention of Silicon Valley* (Oxford, UK: Oxford University Press, 2005), 183–88.

39. Ehrlichman, *Witness to Power*, 260.

40. Hobart Rowen, "White House Blocked ICC on Rate Rise," *Washington Post*, February 9, 1971.

41. Nixon and Charles Colson, transcript of conversation, July 2, 1971, 7:05 p.m., Presidential Recordings Digital Edition, Miller Center, University of Virginia, https://prde.upress.virginia.edu/conversations/4002171.

42. Allen J. Matusow, *Nixon's Economy: Booms, Busts, Dollars, and Votes* (Lawrence: University Press of Kansas, 1998), 112.

43. Milton Friedman, "Money Explodes," *Newsweek*, May 3, 1971, 81, https://milton friedman.hoover.org/friedman_images/Collections/2016c21/NW_05_03_1971 .pdf.

44. Matusow, *Nixon's Economy*, 112.

45. 117 Cong. Rec. 27,002–05 (1971).

46. Ferrell, *Inside the Nixon Administration*, 47–48.

47. Nixon and John B. Connally, transcript of conversation, July 28, 1971, 5:41 p.m., Presidential Recordings Digital Edition, Miller Center, University of Virginia, https://prde.upress.virginia.edu/conversations/4006552.xml.

48. Nixon and Connally conversation.

49. Richard Nixon, transcript of press conference, August 4, 1971, American Presidency Project, UC Santa Barbara, https://www.presidency.ucsb.edu/node /240508.

50. Jules Witcover, *Very Strange Bedfellows: The Short and Unhappy Marriage of Richard Nixon and Spiro Agnew* (New York: Public Affairs, 2007), 193.

51. Ehrlichman, *Witness to Power*, 261.

52. Douglas Brinkley and Luke Nichter, eds., *The Nixon Tapes, 1971–1972* (Boston: Mariner Books, 2015), 244.

53. Brinkley and Nichter, *The Nixon Tapes*, 243.

54. Douglas A. Irwin, "The Nixon Shock After Forty Years: The Import Surcharge Revisited," *World Trade Review* 12, no. 1 (2013): 35–36, https://doi.org/10.1017/S1474745612000444.

55. Irwin, "The Nixon Shock," 35–36.

56. Henry Kissinger, *White House Years* (New York: Little, Brown and Company 1975), 955.

57. Arnold Weber, "Wincing Now at Wage-Price Controls," *New York Times*, August 16, 1981.

58. John H. Wood, *A History of Central Banking in Great Britain and the United States* (Cambridge, UK: Cambridge University Press. 2005), 368.

59. Reston, *The Lone Star*, 240.

60. Peter G. Peterson, *The Education of an American Dreamer: How a Son of Greek Immigrants Learned His Way from a Nebraska Diner to Washington, Wall Street, and Beyond* (New York: Twelve, 2009), 162.

61. Paul Greenberg, "Regulation and the Rule of Law," *Minneapolis Star*, November 15, 1971, 5.

62. Friedrich von Hayek, "The Use of Knowledge in Society," *American Economic Review*, September 1945.

63. Herbert Stein, *What I Think: Essays on Economics, Politics, and Life* (Washington, DC: AEI Press, 1998), 122.

64. William Safire, B*efore the Fall: An Inside View of the Pre-Watergate White House* (New Brunswick, NJ: Transaction Publishers, 2005), 522.

65. Safire, *Before the Fall*, 522.

Coda: Demolition in St. Louis

1. Bob Hansman, *Pruitt-Igoe (Images of America)* (Charleston, SC: Arcadia Publishing, 2017), 102. Many of the details of the Pruitt-Igoe demolition were reported by the *St. Louis Post Dispatch*. Further details, and much insight, are to be found in Bob Hansman's *Pruitt-Igoe*.

2. Associated Press, "US May Tear Down $36M Housing Project," *Boston Globe*, February 6, 1971.

3. George McCue, "$57,000,000 Later: An Interdisciplinary Effort Is Made to Put Pruitt Igoe Together Again," *Architectural Forum*, May 1973, 44, http://usmodernist.org/AF/AF-1973-05.pdf.

4. Marguerite Shepard, "Demolition May Fix Goof of $41 Million," *Press and Sun Bulletin*, January 26, 1972, 41.

5. Darryl R. Francis, "St. Louis in the Seventies," Fraser, https://fraser.stlouisfed.org/title/481/item/18592.

6. "Coddling Housing," Editorial, *Wall Street Journal*, January 12, 1971, 14.

7. John McClaughry, "The Troubled Dream: The Life and Times of Section 235 of the National Housing Act," *Loyola University Law Journal* 6, no. 1 (Winter 1975): 24, http://lawecommons.luc.edu/luclj/vol6/iss1/2.

8. Dana L. Spitzer, "Badaracco for Racing, Lottery," *St. Louis Post-Dispatch*, October 31, 1976, 14A.

9. United Press International, "Earthquake Tester Gives Buildings Shakes," *Hartford Courant*, October 10, 1976, 50A.

Bibliography

Archival Sources

Dictabelts. Audio Collections. Richard Nixon Presidential Library, Yorba Linda, CA.

Lemuel R. Boulware Papers. University of Pennsylvania Libraries.

Mildred Jeffrey Papers. Walter P. Reuther Library. Wayne State University, Detroit, MI.

Oral Histories. Lyndon B. Johnson Presidential Library, Austin, TX.

Presidential Daily Diary. Presidential (General) Collection. Richard Nixon Presidential Library, Yorba Linda, CA.

President's Daily Diary. Special Files, Presidential Papers. Lyndon B. Johnson Presidential Library, Austin, TX.

President's Office Files. Presidential Papers. John F. Kennedy Presidential Library, Boston.

Rauh, Joseph. Interview conducted for *Eyes on the Prize*. 1985, video, 40:20. Washington University in St. Louis, October 2016. http://repository.wustl.edu/concern/videos/rj430634r.

Telephone Conversations. Lyndon B. Johnson Presidential Library, Austin, TX.

United Auto Workers' President's Office. Walter P. Reuther Records. Walter P. Reuther Library. Wayne State University, Detroit MI.

White House Tapes. Richard Nixon Presidential Library, Yorba Linda, CA.

Books

Ainsworth, Ed. *Maverick Mayor: A Biography of Sam Yorty, Mayor of Los Angeles.* Garden City, NY: Doubleday and Company, 1966.

Allen, Joe. *Vietnam: The (Last) War the U.S. Lost.* Chicago: Haymarket Books, 2008.

Anderson, Martin. *The Federal Bulldozer.* New York: McGraw Hill, 1967.

Andrew, John A. *Lyndon Johnson and the Great Society.* Chicago: Ivan R. Dee, 1999.

Ashman, Charles. *Connally: The Adventures of Big Bad John.* New York: William Morrow and Company, 1974.

Banfield, Edward C. *Political Influence.* New York: Free Press, 1962.

———. *The Unheavenly City Revisited.* Boston: Little, Brown and Company, 1974.

Barnard, John. *Walter Reuther and the Rise of the Auto Workers.* Boston: Little, Brown, 1983.

Beaufort Wijnholds, Onno de. *Gold, the Dollar and Watergate: How a Political and Economic Meltdown Was Narrowly Avoided.* New York: Palgrave Macmillan, 2015.

Berlin, Leslie. *The Man Behind the Microchip: Robert Noyce and the Invention of Silicon Valley.* Oxford, UK: Oxford University Press, 2005.

Beschloss, Michael R. *Taking Charge: The Johnson White House Tapes, 1963–1964.* New York: Touchstone, 1998.

Bishop, Jim. *A Day in the Life of President Kennedy.* New York: Random House, 1964.

Blough, Roger M. *The Washington Embrace of Business.* New York: Columbia University Press, 1975.

Bordo, Michael D., and Mark A. Wynne. *The Federal Reserve's Role in the Global Economy: A Historical Perspective.* New York: Cambridge University Press, 2016.

Boulware, Lemuel R. *The Truth About Boulwarism: Trying to Do the Right Thing Voluntarily.* Washington, DC: Bureau of National Affairs Inc., 1969.

Bowling, Lawson. *Shapers of the Great Debate on the Great Society: A Biographical Dictionary.* Westport, CT: Greenwood Press, 2005.

Boyle, Kevin. *Organized Labor and American Politics, 1894–1994: The Labor-Liberal Alliance.* Albany, NY: SUNY Press, 1998.

———. *The UAW and the Heyday of American Liberalism 1945–1968.* Ithaca, NY: Cornell University Press, 1998.

Bremner, Robert P. *Chairman of the Fed: William McChesney Martin Jr. and the Creation of the Modern American Financial System.* New Haven, CT, Yale University Press, 2004.

Brick, Howard, and Gregory Parker, eds. *A New Insurgency: The Port Huron Statement and Its Times.* Ann Arbor: Maize Books, Michigan Publishing Services, 2015.

Brinkley, Douglas, and Luke Nichter. *The Nixon Tapes: 1971–1972.* Boston: Mariner Books, 2015.

Brooks, John. *Business Adventures: Twelve Classic Tales from the World of Wall Street.* New York: Open Road Integrated Media, 2014.

Browder, Earl. *The Road Ahead to Victory and Lasting Peace.* Whitefish, MT: Literary Licensing, 2013.

Browne, Blaine T., and Robert C. Cottrell. *Modern American Lives: Individuals and Issues in American History Since 1945.* New York: Routledge, 2007.

Bundy, McGeorge. *The Strength of Government.* Cambridge, MA: Harvard University Press, 1968.

Burns, Arthur F. *Prosperity Without Inflation.* New York: Fordham University Press, 1958.

Butzner, Jane. *Constitutional Chaff—Rejected Suggestions of the Constitutional*

Convention of 1787 with Explanatory Argument. New York: Columbia University Press, 1941.

Califano, Joseph A., Jr. *The Triumph and Tragedy of Lyndon Johnson*. New York: Touchstone, 2015.

Carew, Anthony. *Lives of the Left: Walter Reuther*. Manchester, UK: Manchester University Press, 1993.

Caroli, Betty Boyd. *Lady Bird and Lyndon: The Hidden Story of a Marriage That Made a President*. New York: Simon and Schuster, 2015.

Carter, Dan T. *The Politics of Rage: George Wallace, the Origins of the New Conservatism, and the Transformation of American Politics*. Baton Rouge: Louisiana State University Press, 2000.

Cervantes, Alfonso J., with Lawrence G. Blochman. *Mr. Mayor*. Los Angeles: Nash Publishing, 1974.

Checkoway, Barry, and Carl V. Patton. *The Metropolitan Midwest: Policy Problems and Prospects for Change*. Champaign: University of Illinois Press, 1985.

Clayson, William. *Freedom Is Not Enough: The War on Poverty and the Civil Rights Movement in Texas*. Austin: University of Texas Press, 2010.

Clifford, Clark, and Richard Holbrooke. *Counsel to the President: A Memoir*. New York: Random House, 1991.

Cogan, John F. *The High Cost of Good Intentions: A History of U.S. Federal Entitlement Programs*. Stanford, CA: Stanford University Press, 2017.

Cohen, Adam, and Elizabeth Taylor. *American Pharaoh: Mayor Richard J. Daley— His Battle for Chicago and the Nation*. Boston: Little, Brown and Company, 2000.

Colman, Jonathan. *A "Special Relationship"? Harold Wilson, Lyndon B. Johnson and Anglo-American Relations "at the Summit," 1964–8*. New York: Manchester University Press, 2004.

Coombs, C. A. *The Arena of International Finance*. New York: John Wiley and Sons, 1976.

Cormier, Frank, and William J. Eaton. *Reuther*. Englewood Cliffs: Prentice-Hall, 1970.

Crumm, Thomas A. *What Is Good for General Motors? Solving America's Industrial Conundrum*. New York: Algora Publishing, 2010.

Curry, Constance. *Deep in Our Hearts: Nine White Women in the Freedom Movement*. Athens: University of Georgia Press, 2000.

Dallek, Robert. *Flawed Giant*. New York: Oxford University Press, 1998.

Dayton, Eldorous L. *Walter Reuther: The Autocrat of the Bargaining Table*. New York: Devin-Adair Company, 1958.

Doyle, William. *Inside the Oval Office: The White House Tapes from FDR to Clinton*. New York: Kodansha America Inc., 1999.

Driver, Ciaran, and Grahame Thompson. *Corporate Governance in Contention*. Oxford, UK: Oxford University Press, 2018.

Dunckel, Earl B. *Ronald Reagan and the General Electric Theater, 1954–1955: Oral History Transcript / and Related Material, 1982.* Berkeley, CA: Andesite Press, 2015.

Ehrlichman, John. *Witness to Power: The Nixon Years.* New York: Simon and Schuster, 1982.

Epstein, Lee J., and Thomas G. Walker. *Constitutional Law for a Changing America: Institutional Powers and Constraints.* Thousand Oaks, CA: CQ Press, 2017.

Evans, Thomas W. *The Education of Ronald Reagan: The General Electric Years and the Untold Story of His Conversion to Conservatism.* New York: Columbia University Press, 2006.

Ferrell, Robert H. *Inside the Nixon Administration: The Secret Diary of Arthur Burns, 1969–1974.* Lawrence: University of Kansas Press, 2010.

Fisse, Brent, and John Braithwaite. *The Impact of Publicity on Corporate Offenders.* Albany, NY: SUNY Press, 1984.

Flacks, Richard, and Nelson Lichtenstein. *The Port Huron Statement: Sources and Legacies of the New Left's Founding Manifesto.* Philadelphia: University of Pennsylvania Press, 2015.

Foster, Patrick. *George Romney: An American Life.* Grapevine, TX: Waldorf Publishing, 2017.

Frost, Jennifer. *An Interracial Movement of the Poor: Community Organizing and the New Left in the 1960s.* New York: New York University Press, 2001.

Galbraith, John Kenneth. *Letters to Kennedy.* Edited by James Goodman. Cambridge, MA: Harvard University Press, 1998.

Garnett, Nicole Stelle. *Ordering the City: Land Use, Policing, and the Restoration of Urban America.* New Haven, CT: Yale University Press, 2010.

Gitlin, Todd. *The Sixties: Years of Hope, Days of Rage.* New York: Bantam Books, 1993.

Goetz, Edward. *The One-Way Street of Integration.* Ithaca, NY: Cornell University, 2018.

Goldberg, Robert Alan. *Barry Goldwater.* New Haven, CT: Yale University Press, 1995.

Goldman, Eric F. *The Tragedy of Lyndon Johnson.* New York: Alfred A. Knopf, 1969.

Goodwin, Doris Kearns. *Lyndon Johnson and the American Dream.* New York: St. Martin's Press, 1991.

Goodwin, Richard N. *Remembering America: A Voice from the Sixties.* New York: Open Road, 2014.

Gorman, Robert A. *Michael Harrington: Speaking American.* New York: Routledge, 1995.

Gorowitz, Bernard. *A Century of Progress: The General Electric Story, 1876–1978.* Schenectady, NY: Hall of History, 1981.

Goss, Kay Collett. *Mr. Chairman: The Life and Legacy of Wilbur D. Mills*. Chicago: Parkhurst Brothers Inc., 2012.

Gould, Jean, and Lorena Hickok. *Walter Reuther: Labor's Rugged Individualist*. New York: Dodd, Mead and Company, 1972.

Greenspan, Alan, and Adrian Wooldridge. *Capitalism in America: A History*. New York: Penguin, 2018.

Haldeman, H. R. *The Haldeman Diaries: Inside the Nixon White House*. New York: G.P. Putnam's Sons, 1994.

Hansman, Bob. *Pruitt-Igoe (Images of America)*. Charleston, SC: Arcadia Publishing, 2017.

Hargrove, Edwin C., and Samuel A. Morley. *The President and the Council of Economic Advisers: Interviews with CEA Chairmen*. Boulder, CO: Westview Press, 1984.

Harrington, Michael. *The Accidental Century*. New York: Macmillan Company, 1965.

———. *Fragments of the Century*. New York: Saturday Review Press, 1973.

———. *The Long-Distance Runner: An Autobiography*. New York: Henry Holt and Company, 1988.

———. *The Other America: Poverty in the United States*. Middlesex, UK: Penguin Specials, 1963.

———. *The Other America: Poverty in the United States*. New York: Macmillan Company, 1964.

———. *The Other America: Poverty in the United States*. New York: Macmillan Publishing Co. Inc., 1974.

Hayden, Casey. "Fields of Blue." In *Deep in Our Hearts: Nine White Women in the Freedom Movement*. Edited by Constance Curry. Athens: University of Georgia Press, 2000, 333–76.

Hayden, Tom. *Inspiring Participatory Democracy: Student Movements from Port Huron to Today*. Boulder, CO: Paradigm Publishers, 2013.

———. *The Long Sixties: From 1960 to Barack Obama*. New York: Paradigm Publishers, 2009.

———. *Rebel: A Personal History of the 1960s*. Los Angeles: Red Hen Press, 2003.

Hayes, Walter. *Henry: A Life of Henry Ford II*. New York: Grove Weidenfeld, 1990.

Hazlitt, Henry. *Economics in One Lesson: The Shortest and Surest Way to Understand Basic Economics*. New York: Random House, 1988.

Herbert, Bob. *Losing Our Way: An Intimate Portrait of a Troubled America*. New York: Anchor Books, 2015.

Herling, John. *The Great Price Conspiracy*. Washington, DC: Robert B. Luce Inc. 1962.

Hickam, Homer H., Jr. *Rocket Boys*. New York: Delacorte Press, 1998.

Hodgson, Godfrey. *The Gentleman from New York: Daniel Patrick Moynihan*. New York: Houghton Mifflin, 2000.

Honey, Michael K. *To the Promised Land: Martin Luther King and the Fight for Economic Justice*. New York: W.W. Norton, 2018.

Horne, Gerald. *Fire This Time: The Watts Uprising and the 1960s*. Charlottesville: University Press of Virginia, 1995.

Horowitz, Daniel. *Betty Friedan and the Making of "The Feminine Mystique": The American Left, the Cold War, and Modern Feminism*. Amherst: University of Massachusetts Press, 1998.

Hufbauer, Benjamin. *Presidential Temples: How Memorials and Libraries Shape Public Memory*. Lawrence: University of Kansas Press, 2005.

Hulsey, Byron. *Everett Dirksen and His Presidents: How a Senate Giant Shaped American Politics*. Lawrence: University Press of Kansas, 2000.

Humphrey, Hubert H. *The Education of a Public Man*. New York: Doubleday, 1976.

Isserman, Maurice. *The Other American: The Life of Michael Harrington*. New York: Public Affairs, 2000.

Jacobs, Jane. *The Death and Life of Great American Cities*. New York: Vintage Books, 1992.

———. *The Death and Life of Great American Cities*. New York: Modern Library, 2011.

———. *Ideas That Matter: The Worlds of Jane Jacobs*. Edited by Max Allen. Ontario, Canada: Ginger Press, 1997.

———. *Vital Little Plans: The Short Works of Jane Jacobs*. Edited by Samuel Zipp and Nathan Strorring. New York: Random House, 2016.

Jarboe Russell, Jan. *Lady Bird: A Biography of Mrs. Johnson*. New York: Scribner, 1999.

Johnson, Lyndon Baines. *The Vantage Point: Perspectives of the Presidency 1963–1969*. New York: Holt, Rinehart, and Winston, 1971.

Johnson, Sam, and Jan Winebrenner. *Captive Warriors: A Vietnam POW's Story*. College Station: Texas A&M University, 2006.

Kaufman, Murray. *Murray the K Tells It Like It Is, Baby*. New York: Holt, Rinehart and Winston, 1966.

Kennedy, Robert F. *The Enemy Within*. New York: Harper and Row, 1960.

———. *To Seek a Newer World*. New York: Ishi Press, 2017.

King, Mary. *Freedom Song: A Personal Story of the 1960s Civil Rights Movement*. New York: William Morrow, 1987.

Kudlow, Lawrence, and Brian Domintrovic. *JFK and the Reagan Revolution*. New York: Portfolio, 2016.

Laurence, Peter L. *Becoming Jane Jacobs*. Philadelphia: University of Pennsylvania Press, 2016.

Ledbetter, James. *One Nation Under Gold: How One Precious Metal Has Dominated the American Imagination for Four Centuries*. New York: Liveright Publishing Corporation, 2017.

Lee, Chong-Moon, William F. Miller, Marguerite Gong Hancock, and Henry S. Rowen, eds. *The Silicon Valley Edge: A Habit for Innovation and Entrepreneurship.* Stanford, CA: Stanford University Press, 2000.

Leiby, Bruce R., and Linda F. Leiby. *A Reference Guide to Television's "Bonanza": Episodes, Personnel and Broadcast History.* Jefferson, NC: McFarland and Co., 2001.

Lemann, Nicholas. *The Promised Land: The Great Black Migration and How It Changed America.* New York: Vintage Books, 1992.

Levy, Peter B. *The New Left and Labor in the 1960s.* Champaign: University of Illinois Press, 1994.

Lichtenstein, Nelson. *Walter Reuther: The Most Dangerous Man in Detroit.* New York: Basic Books, 1995.

Lippmann, Walter. *The Good Society.* New York: Routledge, 1938.

Lowi, Theodore J. *The End of Liberalism: Ideology, Policy, and the Crisis of Public Authority.* New York: W.W. Norton, 1969.

Lynd, Staughton. *From Here to There: The Staughton Lynd Reader.* Edited by Andrej Grubacic. Oakland, CA: PM Press, 2010.

Lynd, Staughton, and Thomas Hayden. *The Other Side.* New York: New American Library, 1966.

Mann, Robert. *Daisy Petals and Mushroom Clouds: LBJ, Barry Goldwater and the Ad That Changed American Politics.* Baton Rouge: Louisiana State University Press, 2011.

Maraniss, David. *Once in a Great City: A Detroit Story.* New York: Simon and Schuster, 2015.

Matusow, Allen J. *Nixon's Economy: Booms, Busts, Dollars, and Votes.* Lawrence: University Press of Kansas, 1998.

———. *The Unraveling of America: A History of Liberalism in the 1960s.* New York: Harper and Row, 1984.

Meehan, Eugene J. *The Quality of Federal Policymaking: Programmed Failure in Public Housing.* Columbia: University of Missouri Press, 1979.

Miller, James. *Democracy Is in the Streets: From Port Huron to the Siege of Chicago.* New York: Simon and Schuster, 1987.

Morris, John G. *Get the Picture: A Personal History of Photojournalism.* New York: Random House, 1998.

Moses, Robert P., and Charles E. Cobb. *Radical Equations: Civil Rights from Mississippi to the Algebra Project.* Boston: Beacon Press, 2001.

Moynihan, Daniel P. *Daniel Patrick Moynihan: A Portrait in Letters of an American Visionary.* Edited by Steven R. Weisman. New York: Public Affairs, 2010.

———. *Maximum Feasible Misunderstanding: Community Action in the War on Poverty.* New York: Arkville Press, 1969.

———. *The Negro Family: The Case for National Action.* Milwaukee: Office of Policy Planning and Research, United States Department of Labor, 1965.

————. *The Politics of a Guaranteed Income: The Nixon Administration and the Family Assistance Plan*. New York: Random House, 1973.

Mumford, Kevin. *Newark: A History of Race, Rights, and Riots in America*. New York: New York University Press, 2007.

Newman, Oscar. *Defensible Space: Crime Prevention Through Urban Design*. New York: Collier Books, 1973.

Nixon, Richard. *RN: The Memoirs of Richard Nixon*. New York: Simon and Schuster, 1990.

Northrup, Herbert R. *Boulwarism: The Labor Relations Policies of the General Electric Company, Their Implications for Public Policy and Management Action*. Ann Arbor: University of Michigan, 1965.

O'Boyle, Thomas F. *At Any Cost: Jack Welch, General Electric, and the Pursuit of Profit*. New York: Vintage Books, 1999.

Olasky, Marvin. *The Tragedy of American Compassion*. Wheaton, IL: Crossway Books, 1992.

Oldfield, Homer R. *King of the Seven Dwarfs: General Electric's Ambiguous Challenge to the Computer Industry*. Los Alamitos, CA: IEEE Press, 1966.

Olson, Lynne. *Freedom's Daughters: The Unsung Heroines of the Civil Rights Movement from 1830 to 1970*. New York: Touchstone, 2002.

Perlstein, Rick. *Before the Storm: Barry Goldwater and the Unmaking of the American Consensus*. New York: Hill and Wang, 2009.

Peterson, Peter G. *The Education of an American Dreamer: How a Son of Greek Immigrants Learned His Way from a Nebraska Diner to Washington, Wall Street, and Beyond*. New York: Twelve, 2009.

Phillips-Fein, Kimberly. *Invisible Hands: The Businessmen's Crusade Against the New Deal*. New York: W.W. Norton and Company, 2010.

Phillips-Fein, Kimberly. "American Counterrevolutionary: Lemuel Ricketts Boulware and General Electric, 1950–60." In *American Capitalism: Social Thought and Political Economy in the Twentieth Century*. Edited by Nelson Lichtenstein, 249–70. Philadelphia: University of Pennsylvania Press, 2006.

Piereson, James. *Camelot and the Cultural Revolution: How the Assassination of John F. Kennedy Shattered American Liberalism*. New York: Encounter Books, 2007.

Polletta, Francesca. *Freedom Is an Endless Meeting: Democracy in American Social Movements*. Chicago: University of Chicago Press, 2002.

Powledge, Fred. *Free at Last? The Civil Rights Movement and the People Who Made It*. New York: Perennial, 1992.

Qualter, Terence H. *Graham Wallas and the Great Society*. New York: St. Martin's Press, 1979.

Rainwater, Lee, and William L. Yancey. *The Moynihan Report and the Politics of Controversy*. Cambridge, MA: MIT Press, 1967.

Rand, Ayn. *Capitalism: The Unknown Ideal*. New York: New American Library Inc., 1966.

Rarick, Ethan. *California Rising: The Life and Times of Pat Brown*. Berkeley: University of California Press, 2005.

Reston, James. *The Lone Star: The Life of John Connally*. New York: Harper and Row, 1989.

Reuther Dickmeyer, Elisabeth. *Putting the World Together: My Father Walter Reuther, the Liberal Warrior*. Lake Orion, MI: Living Force Publishing, 2004.

Reuther, Victor G. *The Brothers Reuther and the Story of the UAW: A Memoir*. Boston: Houghton Mifflin Company, 1976.

Sabin, Paul. *The Bet: Paul Ehrlich, Julian Simon, and Our Gamble over Earth's Future*. New Haven, CT: Yale University Press, 2013.

Safire, William. *Before the Fall: An Inside View of the Pre-Watergate White House*. New Brunswick, NJ: Transaction Publishers, 2005.

Schlesinger, Arthur M., Jr. *Journals: 1952–2000*. London: Atlantic Books, 2007.

———. *A Thousand Days: John F. Kennedy in the White House*. New York: Mariner Books, 2002.

Schlesinger, Robert. *White House Ghosts: Presidents and Their Speechwriters*. New York: Simon and Schuster, 2008.

Schryer, Stephen. *Maximum Feasible Participation: American Literature and the War on Poverty*. Stanford, CA: Stanford University Press, 2018.

Shapley, Deborah. *Promise and Power: The Life and Times of Robert McNamara*. Boston: Little, Brown and Company, 1993.

Sharma, Patrick Allan. *Robert McNamara's Other War: The World Bank and International Development*. Philadelphia: University of Pennsylvania Press, 2017.

Shesol, Jeff. *Mutual Contempt: Lyndon Johnson, Robert Kennedy, and the Feud That Defined a Decade*. New York: W.W. Norton and Company, 1998.

Sides, Josh. *L.A. City Limits: African American Los Angeles from the Great Depression to the Present*. Berkeley: University of California Press, 2006.

Silber, William L. *Volcker: The Triumph of Persistence*. New York: Bloomsbury Press, 2012.

Smith, Harvey Henry. *Area Handbook for North Vietnam, 1967*. Washington, DC: U.S. Government Printing Office, 1967.

Solberg, Carl. *Hubert Humphrey: A Biography*. Ontario, Canada: Borealis Books, 2003.

Sowell, Thomas. *A Personal Odyssey*. New York: Free Press, 2000.

Spitz, Bob. *Reagan: An American Journey*. New York: Penguin, 2018.

Stebenne, David. *Arthur J. Goldberg: New Deal Liberal*. Oxford, UK: Oxford University Press, 1996.

Stein, Herbert. *The Fiscal Revolution in America*. Washington, DC: AEI Press, 1996.

————. *Presidential Economics: The Making of Economic Policy from Roosevelt to Clinton*. Washington, DC: American Enterprise Institute, 1994.

————. *What I Think: Essays on Economics, Politics, and Life*. Washington, DC: AEI Press, 1998.

Stoll, Ira. *JFK: Conservative*. Boston: Houghton Mifflin Harcourt, 2013.

Stossel, Scott. *Sarge: The Life and Times of Sargent Shriver*. Washington, DC: Smithsonian Books, 2004.

Sugrue, Thomas J. *The Origins of the Urban Crisis: Race and Inequality in Postwar Detroit*. Princeton, NJ: Princeton University Press, 1996.

Sundquist, James L., ed. *On Fighting Poverty: Perspectives from Experience*. Vol. 2 of *Perspectives on Poverty*. New York: Basic Books Inc., 1969.

Swedin, Eric G., and David L. Ferro. *Computers: The Life Story of a Technology*. Baltimore: Johns Hopkins University Press, 2007.

Tarbell, Ida A. *Owen D. Young: A New Type of Industrial Leader*. New York: Macmillan Company, 1932.

Tedlow, Richard S. *Andy Grove: The Life and Times of an American*. New York: Penguin Group, 2006.

Thackray, Arnold, David Brock, and Rachel Jones. *Moore's Law: The Life of Gordon Moore, Silicon Valley's Quiet Revolutionary*. New York: Basic Books, 2015.

Tocqueville, Alexis de. *Democracy in America*. Henry Reeve, translator (New York: Alfred Knopf, 1945), Vol. I, 45.

Visser-Maessen, Laura. *Robert Parris Moses: A Life in Civil Rights and Leadership at the Grassroots*. Chapel Hill: University of North Carolina Press, 2016.

Volcker, Paul A. *Keeping at It: The Quest for Sound Money and Good Government*. New York: Public Affairs, 2018.

Volcker, Paul A., and Toyoo Gyohten. *Changing Fortunes: The World's Money and the Threat to American Leadership*. New York: Times Books, 1992.

Wallas, Graham. *The Great Society: A Psychological Analysis*. New York: Macmillan Company, 1914.

Ward, Barbara. *The Rich Nations and the Poor Nations*. New York: W.W. Norton and Company, 1962.

Washington, Valora, and Ura Jean Oyemade Bailey. *Project Head Start: Models and Strategies for the Twenty-First Century*. New York: Garland Publishing, 1995.

Weiner, Greg. *American Burke: The Uncommon Liberalism of Daniel Patrick Moynihan*. Lawrence: University Press of Kansas, 2015.

Wells, Wyett. *Economist in an Uncertain World: Arthur F. Burns and the Federal Reserve, 1970–1978*. New York: Columbia University Press, 1994.

White, Theodore H. *The Making of the President 1968*. New York: Harper Perennial, 2010.

Widick, B. J. *Detroit: City of Race and Class Violence*. Detroit: Wayne State University Press, 1989.

Wilson, Sir Harold. *The Labour Government, 1964–70: A Personal Record.* London: Weidenfeld and Nicolson, 1971.

Witcover, Jules. *Very Strange Bedfellows: The Short and Unhappy Marriage of Richard Nixon and Spiro Agnew.* New York: Public Affairs, 2007.

Wood, Robert C. *Whatever Possessed the President? Academic Experts and Presidential Policy, 1960–1988.* Amherst: University of Massachusetts Press, 1993.

Woods, Randall B. *Prisoners of Hope: Lyndon B. Johnson, the Great Society, and the Limits of Liberalism.* New York: Basic Books, 2016.

Woodward, Bob. *The Last of the President's Men.* New York: Simon and Schuster, 2015.

Wright, Nathan, Jr. *Black Power and Urban Unrest.* New York: Hawthorn Books Inc., 1968.

———. *Ready to Riot.* New York: Holt, Rinehart and Winston, 1968.

Zeitz, Joshua. *Building the Great Society: Inside Lyndon Johnson's White House.* New York: Penguin Random House, 2018.

Economic Databases

International Monetary Fund. *Interest Rates, Discount Rate for the United States.* FRED. Federal Reserve Bank of St. Louis. https://fred.stlouisfed.org/series/INTDSRUSM193N.

National Bureau of Economic Research. *Unemployment Rate for the United States.* FRED. Federal Reserve Bank of St. Louis. https://fred.stlouisfed.org/series/M0892AUSM156SNBR.

Films and Television

Dorman, Joseph, and Toby Perl Freilich, dirs. *Moynihan.* New York: First Run Features, 2018.

Freidrichs, Chad, dir. *The Pruitt-Igoe Myth.* New York: First Run Features, 2011. https://vimeo.com/ondemand/thepruittigoemyth.

Nyby, Christian, dir. *Bonanza.* Season 1, episode 16, "El Toro Grande." Written by John Tucker Battle. Aired January 2, 1960, on NBC.

Reuther, Sasha, dir. *Brothers on the Line.* Richmond, VA: Porter Street Pictures, 2012.

Journal Articles

Cogan, John F., and Daniel Heil. "America Off Balance: Charting the Federal Government's Fiscal Path." Hoover Institution. Stanford University. Forthcoming.

McClaughry, John. "The Troubled Dream: The Life and Times of Section 235 of the

National Housing Act." *Loyola University Law Journal* 6, no. 1 (Winter 1975): 1–45. http://lawecommons.luc.edu/luclj/vol6/iss1/2.

Reder, Melvin W. "The Rise and Fall of Unions: The Public Sector and the Private." *Journal of Economic Perspectives* 2, no. 2 (Spring 1988): 89–110.

Reich, Charles A. "The New Property." *Yale Law Journal* 73, no. 5 (April 1964): 733–87.

Reports

Economic Report of the President. Washington, DC: U.S. Government Printing Office, 1963. https://fraser.stlouisfed.org/files/docs/publications/ERP/1963/ERP_1963 .pdf.

Economic Report of the President. Washington, DC: U.S. Government Printing Office, 1964. https://fraser.stlouisfed.org/title/45/item/8135.

Fleenor, Patrick. *Facts and Figures on Government Finance.* 32nd ed. Washington, DC: Tax Foundation, 1998.

Governor's Commission on the Los Angeles Riots. *Violence in the City: An End or a Beginning?* Los Angeles: State of California, 1965.

Hoffman, David. *Facts and Figures on Government Finance.* 37th ed. Washington, DC: Tax Foundation, 2003.

Office of Economic Opportunity. *The Office of Economic Opportunity During the Administration of President Lyndon B. Johnson, November 1963–January 1969.* Vol. I. Washington, DC: Office of Economic Opportunity, 1969.

———. *Workbook: Community Action Program.* Washington, DC: Office of Economic Opportunity, 1965.

Snyder, Thomas, ed. *120 Years of American Education: A Statistical Portrait.* Washington, DC: National Center for Education Statistics, 1993. https://nces.ed.gov /pubs93/93442.pdf.

Index

About the Author

AMITY SHLAES is the author of four *New York Times* best-sellers: *The Forgotten Man: A New History of the Great Depression*, *The Forgotten Man* graphic edition, *Coolidge*, and *The Greedy Hand: How Taxes Drive Americans Crazy*. Shlaes chairs the board of the Calvin Coolidge Presidential Foundation and the Manhattan Institute's Hayek Book Prize, and serves as a scholar at the King's College. A former member of the *Wall Street Journal*'s editorial board, Shlaes published a weekly syndicated column for more than a decade, appearing first in the *Financial Times* and then in *Bloomberg*.